1998

Fourth Edition

ETHICAL ISSUES IN BUSINESS

A Philosophical Approach

 Edited by

Thomas Donaldson
Patricia H. Werhane

Loyola University of Chicago

Prentice Hall, Englewood Cliffs, New Jersey 07632

Library of Congress Cataloging-in-Publication Data

Ethical issues in business: a philosophical approach/edited by
 Thomas Donaldson, Patricia H. Werhane.—4th ed.
    p.   cm.
  Includes bibliographical references and index.
  ISBN 0-13-282716-6
    1. Business ethics—Case studies. 2. Social responsibility of
business—Case studies. I. Donaldson, Thomas
II. Werhane, Patricia Hogue.
HF5387.E8   1993
174'.4—dc20   92-20811
                                                    CIP

Acquisitions editor: Ted Bolen
Editorial/production supervision and
  interior design: John Rousselle and Jenny Moss
Cover design: Ben Santora
Prepress buyer: Herb Klein
Manufacturing buyer: Robert Anderson
Editorial assistant: Nicole Gray
Cover illustration: Daniel Kirk/The Image Bank

Printed in the United States of America

10 9 8 7 6 5 4 3 2

ISBN 0-13-282716-6

Prentice-Hall International (UK) Limited, *London*
Prentice-Hall of Australia Pty. Limited, *Sydney*
Prentice-Hall Canada Inc., *Toronto*
Prentice-Hall Hispanoamericana, S.A., *Mexico*
Prentice-Hall of India Private Limited, *New Delhi*
Prentice-Hall of Japan, Inc., *Tokyo*
Simon & Schuster Asia Pte. Ltd., *Singapore*
Editora Prentice-Hall do Brasil, Ltda., *Rio de Janeiro*

Contents

iii

🌿

PART TWO: MORALITY AND CORPORATIONS

⁂

PART FOUR: EMPLOYER–EMPLOYEE
RELATIONSHIPS

PART FIVE: CONTEMPORARY BUSINESS ISSUES

Preface

The fourth edition of *Ethical Issues in Business* brings great satisfaction to its originators—for surely no one can predict continued success for one's efforts. In this instance the satisfaction is linked not only to past success but also to present demands. The demands arise from the field of business as well as business ethics, fields which are tied to the changing economic and ethical relationships in our society and in multicultural contexts. It is this context that demands that the published discussions remain relevant.

Some theoretical perspectives do maintain relevance throughout the historical flux. The insights of Adam Smith or the challenges of Karl Marx are no less relevant today than in the eighteenth or nineteenth centuries. Yet others are clearly time-bound. When the first edition of this book appeared, Three Mile Island and Chernobyl had not darkened our knowledge of the atom, computers were clever gadgets with few ethical implications, and Ivan Boesky had not yet discovered insider trading. New issues have appeared since the third edition. Consequently, the present volume contains many new case studies including ones dealing with mergers, women in the workplace, AIDS, Bhopal, the Exxon Valdez incident, plant relocation, and manufacturing in the third world.

Happily, challenging problems in business have been accompanied by a rapidly growing business ethics literature. Upon the appearance of the first edition in 1979, *Ethical Issues in Business* was only one of three texts in business ethics; by 1983, upon the appearance of the second edition, the selection had grown to ten or fifteen, and today there are at least fifty textbooks. Along with the growth of college teaching materials has been an explosion in the production of articles, cases, and commentaries. The present edition takes advantage of this abundance and contains many new articles including ones on relativism, moral agency, stakeholder theory, rational choice and economic efficiency, employment at will, environmental ethics, and women as managers.

The present edition, as the earlier ones, has not been simply the product of its editors, but owes greatly to those whose suggestions, criticisms, and editorial assistance made it a better book. These include Thomas Carson, Kendall D'Andrade, A. R. Gini, Mark Schneider, and a number of blind reviewers for Prentice Hall. We also want to thank Cynthia Rudolph for her excellent organizational and secretarial skills without which there would not have been a fourth edition, and we are indebted to the patience of the editors at Prentice Hall.

THOMAS DONALDSON

PATRICIA H. WERHANE

General Introduction

There is one and only one social responsibility of business . . . to i..crease its profits. . . .

Milton Friedman

Business executives and the companies they serve have a personal and vested interest in the resolution of ethical and social responsibility dilemmas.

Steven Brenner and Earl Molander

It has often been suggested—though perhaps in jest—that the idea of business ethics constitutes a contradiction in terms. "Business is business," it has been said, "and ethics is not business." Yet each day we hear of the controversies about discrimination in hiring, consumer rights, deceptive advertising, bribery and payoffs, and pollution problems of such magnitude that we cannot remain unaffected.

Ethical problems in business are as old as business itself. Just as we are acutely aware of the problems surrounding the Ivan Boesky case or the Bhopal tragedy, earlier generations were aware of other ethical problems in business. Names such as the "Teapot Dome scandal" or the "Mississippi bubble" are not familiar today, but they were once as well known as "Boesky" and "Bhopal" are now. The issues about which there has been public concern include trusts and monopolies, child labor, working hours and conditions, meat packing standards, the distribution of salaries, and the liability of producers for dangerous products. Not only complaints but attempts at reform have a long and interesting history. The Code of Hammurabi, written nearly two thousand years before Christ, records the fact that Mesopotamian rulers attempted to legislate honest prices from local merchants by instituting wage and price controls.

To explain the special relationship between business and ethics, it is necessary to see how focusing merely on problems of business efficiency and profit making may overlook important moral issues. For example, when the manufacture of a certain product can eventually be linked to human disease or a decrease in the quality of human life, then the issues surrounding it are

1

no longer simply traditional "business" issues. No amount of expertise in marketing, accounting, or management can deal adequately with such problems, and yet they are clearly connected to the activities of the business world. Nor can situations like these be reduced simply to legal problems, understandable only to the lawyer. When Ralph Nader claimed in the late 1960s that General Motors was producing automobiles which, despite their many consumer advantages, were contributing to thousands of highway deaths each year, he was not arguing that GM's practices were against the law—because at that time they were not illegal at all. Rather, Nader was arguing that General Motors had special obligations to its consumers, which were not simply of a traditional business nature, and that the company was not living up to them. Those obligations were *ethical* or *moral* ones.

It appears, then, that confronting questions like those implied by the Nader case—such as, Does business have an obligation to its consumers (or to others) which extends beyond its obligation to make a profit and satisfy its investors?—means confronting ethical and moral issues. The words *ethical* and *moral* in this book are not simply used as they might be by a modern newspaper, for example, "That movie is thoroughly immoral" (meaning, "That movie is pornographic"). Instead, they are used as philosophers have traditionally used them, as words that arise from the study of what is good or right. Although there is dispute even among philosophers over how to define the subject matter of ethics, most would agree that it includes the study of what people ought to pursue, that is, what the *good* is for people, or alternatively, the determination of which actions are the *right* actions for people to perform. Such general definitions may leave one with the feeling that studying ethics must be a hopelessly vague task; yet interestingly, ethical philosophers have succeeded in presenting a great many detailed ethical theses and in conducting a number of successful investigations into specific ethical topics.

The word *ethics*, then, refers generally to the study of whatever is right and good for humans. The study of *business* ethics seeks to understand business practices, institutions, and actions in light of some concept of human value. Traditional business ends—e.g., profit making, growth, or technical advance—are certainly relevant to the subject of business ethics insofar as they can be related to the achievement of some more human good. In other words, business ethics looks at corporate profits not for their own sake but with respect to the achievement of some basic human good, perhaps increased investor satisfaction, higher levels of employment, or increased capacity to improve working conditions.

Because business ethics involves relating business activities to some concept of human good, it is a study which has as one of its aspects the *evaluation* of business practices. Indeed, most of the fundamental criticisms and commendations of contemporary business practices are cast in terms of how modern business either contributes or fails to contribute to the general human good. For example, when modern corporations are criticized for their failure to respond to environmental needs by limiting the amount of pollutants they discharge, they are being evaluated on ethical grounds; the charge is that they are neglecting the public good. Alternatively, when businesses are praised for achieving high levels of efficiency and satisfying consumer needs, it is implied that efficiency and consumer satisfaction contribute directly to the sum total of human good. Even traditional conservative economic theory justifies economic practices in the light of their contribution to human good.

Another aspect of the evaluative dimension in business ethics—or any ethical study—is seen in the contrast between evaluation and simple description. There is special difference between answering a moral question and answering a question in the areas of, say, marketing and economics. In the latter, it is often sufficient to establish the immediate facts which pertain to the subject. For example, if one hopes to determine the best advertising strategy for the introduction of a new product, one would only need to determine that a certain advertising strategy will have, as a matter of fact, the desired effect, i.e., that it *will* sell the product. It is usually possible in such cases to utilize indicators which more or less establish whether or not a given strategy will be effective: consumer polls, trends in sales, etc. These indicators are then used as factual information upon which one's strategy is based.

However, answering an ethical question may demand very different methods. Determining the immediate and specific facts may only be the first step in a long process which, in the end, may take one far beyond immediate facts. For example, if one wants to determine whether discriminatory hiring practices by corporations *ought* to be corrected by instituting affirmative action programs that favor women and minorities, there may be no question at all about the immediate facts. Two people could thoroughly agree that discrimination of a certain type has taken place and that blacks and women need equal job opportunities to reach relevant levels of social equality. Yet, after agreeing on all these facts the two people may still disagree—and disagree vehemently—over whether affirmative action programs *ought* to be imposed in the wake of past discriminatory practices. Thus, solving an ethical problem may require making *evaluative* judgments about issues which seem far removed from the facts at hand.

Even though business ethics focuses primarily on evaluative issues, its scope is surprisingly large. Insofar as it is concerned with relating business practices to some concept of human good, almost any business issue that relates to human values may become part of its subject matter. Thus the scope of business ethics includes such issues as

1. advertising practices, for example, false or misleading advertising;
2. product safety;
3. monopolistic price schemes and their effects on the consumer;
4. the pursuit of profits;
5. employee rights, including rights to free speech and due process;

6. the treatment of workers, including wages, working conditions, worker participation, and access to pension plans and benefits;
7. economic and environmental effects of pollution;
8. uses of natural resources;
9. multinational operations, including manufacturing and sales of products in other countries;
10. "sensitive payments" to foreign governments, foreign agents, or local politicians;
11. stakeholder concerns;
12. the proper roles of shareholders, management, government, and the public in determining corporate policy;
13. discriminatory hiring policies, conditions, and policies of advancement;
14. drugs and AIDS in the workplace;
15. plant relocation;
16. consumer liability, customer rights and responsibilities;
17. mergers and acquisitions;
18. insider trading;
19. the limits of free enterprise and regulation.

The analysis of such issues requires a systematic investigation of both general ethical theory and specific business practices. To accomplish this goal the editors of this anthology have selected a series of writings which includes not only theoretical and philosophical material relevant to business practices but actual case descriptions of ethical problems found in the business world. Much of the philosophical material has gained wide support in traditional ethical philosophy, and the cases include ones that have had a dramatic impact upon our society.

The advantage of investigating ethical problems from a philosophical point of view should be apparent. One cannot successfully examine a case involving payments made by U.S. corporations to foreign governments, for example, until one has considered the more general issue of whether differing ethical attitudes in the United States and in foreign countries affect the morality of such actions. Thus studying the contributions of philosophers can be of great help in sorting out the issues and solving ethical dilemmas.

However, this book has not attempted to provide a list of ethical codes of conduct. Such codes have sometimes proven unsuccessful in achieving their presumed purpose. More importantly, their existence can imply something false about the field of business ethics: that the work needed to understand ethical issues can be unnecessary, and that serious issues can be resolved simply by writing and studying lists of ethical rules and codes. The essays and cases in this book, then, are intended to stimulate discussion of ethical issues and provide grounds for justifying ethical decisions in business. But the actual solution of ethical dilemmas is left to the reader.

Introduction
to Ethical Reasoning

THOMAS DONALDSON AND PATRICIA H. WERHANE

What is the basis for making ethical decisions? Should Joan challenge Fred the next time he cracks a chauvinist joke? Should John refrain from lying on his job application despite his temptation to do so? What, if anything, should make Hillary decide that eating meat is corrupting, whereas vegetarianism is uplifting? It is obvious that the kind of evidence required for an ethical decision is different from that needed to make a nonethical one; but what is the nature of the difference? These questions give rise to a search for a *method* of ethical justification and decision making, a method that will specify the conditions that any good ethical decision should meet.

To see how such questions arise concretely, consider the following case.[1]

Some years ago, a large German chemical firm, BASF, decided to follow the lead of many other European firms and build a factory in the United States. BASF needed land, lots of it (1,800 acres), an inexpensive labor pool, almost 5 million gallons of fresh water every day, a surrounding area free of import taxes, and a nearby railroad and ocean port. Obviously, only a handful of locations could meet all these requirements. The spot the company finally picked seemed perfect, an area near the coast of South Carolina called Beaufort County. It purchased 1,800 acres.

South Carolina and Beaufort County were pleased with BASF's decision. The surrounding area, from which the company would pick its workers, was economically depressed and per capita income stood well below the national average. Jobs of any kind were desperately needed. Even the Governor of South Carolina and his staff were eager for BASF to build in South Carolina, and although BASF had not yet finalized its exact production plans, the State Pollution Central Authority saw no problems with meeting the State pollution laws. BASF itself said that although it would dump chemical byproducts into the local Colleton River, it planned not to lower the river's quality.

But trouble started immediately. To see why, one needs to know that Beaufort County is the home of the internationally famous resort area called "Hilton Head." Hilton Head attracts thousands of vacationers every year—most of them with plenty of money—and its developers worried that the scenic splendor of the area might be marred by the air and water pollution. Especially concerned about water pollution, resort developers charged that the proposed chemical plant would pollute the Colleton River. They argued that BASF plants in Germany had polluted the Rhine and, in Belgium, the Schelde River. Further, they noted that on BASF's list of proposed expenditures, pollution control was allocated only one million dollars.

The citizens of Beaufort County, in contrast to the Hilton Head Developers, welcomed BASF. They presented the company with a petition bearing over

7,000 signatures endorsing the new plant. As one local businessman commented, "I would say 80 percent of the people in Beaufort County are in favor of BASF. Those who aren't rich." (William D. McDonald, "Youth Corps Looking for Jobs," *The State*, February 23, 1970.)

The manager of BASF's U.S. operations was clearly confronted by an economic and moral dilemma. He knew that preventing massive pollution was virtually impossible and, in any case, outrageously expensive. The eagerness of South Carolina officials for new industry suggested that pollution standards might be "relaxed" for BASF. If it decided to go ahead and build, was the company to push for the minimum pollution control it could get away with under the law? Such a policy might maximize corporate profits and the financial interests of the shareholders, while at the same time it would lower the aesthetic quality of the environment. It might make jobs available to Beaufort County while ignoring the resort industry and the enjoyment of vacationers. Moreover, the long-term effects of dumping chemicals was hard to predict, but past experience did not give the manager a feeling of optimism. Pollution seemed to be not only a business issue, but a *moral* one. But how should the manager sort out, and eventually decide upon, such a moral issue?

To solve his moral problem, BASF's manager might try a variety of strategies. He might, for example, begin by assuming that he has three basic options: (1) Build with minimal pollution control; (2) build with maximal pollution control; or (3) do not build.

Then, he might reason

The consequences of option 1 will be significant but tolerable water pollution, hostility from the Hilton Head Developers, high short-term corporate profits, and satisfied shareholders.

The consequences of option 2 will be unnoticeable pollution, no complaints from the Hilton Head Developers, high pollution-control costs, low profits and unsatisfied stockholders.

The consequences of 3 will be approval from the Hilton Head Developers, low short-term profits (while a search for a new location is underway), strong disapproval from the local townspeople.

My job from a *moral* perspective is to weigh these consequences and consider which of the alternatives constitutes a maximization of good. Who will benefit from each decision? How many people will be adversely affected and in what ways?

Or the manager might reason

Both BASF Corporation and I are confronted with a variety of *duties, rights,* and *obligations.* First there is the company's obligation to its stockholders, and my duty as manager is to protect the economic interests and rights of our stockholders. Next there are the rights of those Beaufort residents and visitors in the area to clean air and water. Finally there are the rights of other property owners in the area, including the Hilton Head Developers, not to be harmed unreasonably by other industries. There is an implied obligation to future generations to protect the river. And finally, there are broader considerations: Is this an act I would want others to do? What kind of moral example will I be setting?

My job from a *moral* perspective is to balance and assess these duties, rights, and obligations, and determine which have priority.

Finally, the manager might reason

I cannot confront a moral problem from either the abstract perspective of "consequences," or of "duties, rights, and obligations." Instead, I must use a concrete concept of *human nature* to guide my deliberations. Acts that aid persons to develop their potential human nature are morally good; ones that do the opposite are bad.

I believe that the crucial potentialities of human nature include such things as health, knowledge, moral maturity, meaningful employment, political freedom, and self-respect.

My job from a *moral* perspective is to assess the situation in terms of its harmony or disharmony with these basic concepts of human potential.

Notice how different each of these approaches is. The first focuses on the concept of *consequences*; the second on *duties, rights and obligations*; and the third on *human nature*. Of course, the three methods may overlap; for example, applying the concept of "human nature" in the third approach may necessitate referring to concepts drawn from the first and second, such as "consequences" and "rights," and vice versa. Even so, the approaches reflect three classical types of ethical theory in the history of philosophy. Each has been championed by a well-known traditional philosopher, and most ethical theories can be catagorized under one of the three headings. The first may be called *consequentialism*, the second, *deontology*, and the third, *human nature ethics*.

CONSEQUENTIALISM

As its name implies, a consequentialist theory of ethical reasoning concentrates on the consequences of human actions, and all actions are evaluated in terms of the extent to which they achieve desirable results. Such theories are also frequently labeled *teleological*, a term derived from the Greek work *telos*, which means "end" or "purpose." According to consequentialist theories, the concepts of right, wrong, and duty are subordinated to the concept of the end or purpose of an action.

There are at least two types of consequentialist theory. The first— advocated by only a few consequentialists—is a version of what philosophers call ethical egoism. It construes right action as action whose consequences, considered among all the alternatives, maximizes *my* good—that is, action that benefits *me* the most or harms *me* the least. The second type—advocated by most consequentialists—denies that right action concerns only *me*. Rather, right action must maximize *overall* good; that is, it must maximize good (or minimize bad) from the standpoint of the entire human community. The best-accepted label for this type of consequentialism is *utilitarianism*. This term was coined by the eighteenth-century philosopher Jeremy Bentham, although its best-known proponent was the nineteenth-century English philosopher John Stuart Mill. As Bentham formulated it, the principle of utility states that an action is right if it produces the greatest balance of pleasure or happiness and unhappiness in light of alternative actions. Mill supported a similar principle, using what he called the "proof" of the principle of utility—namely, the recognition that the only proof for something's being desirable is that someone actually desires it. Since everybody desires pleasure or happiness, it follows, according to Mill, that happiness is the most desirable thing. The purpose of moral action is to achieve greatest overall happiness, and actions are evaluated in terms of the extent to which they contribute to this end. The most desirable state of affairs, the greatest good and the goal of morality, said Mill, is the "greatest happiness for the greatest number."

While later utilitarians accept the general framework of Mill's argument, not all utilitarians are hedonists. That is, not all utilitarians equate "the good" with pleasure or happiness. Some utilitarians have argued that in maximizing the "good," one must be concerned not only with maximizing pleasure, but with maximizing other things, such as knowledge, moral maturity, and friendship. Although it could be claimed that such goods also bring pleasure and happiness to their possessor, it is arguable whether their goodness is ultimately *reducible* to whatever pleasure they bring. These philosophers are sometimes call pluralistic utilitarians. Still other philosophers have adapted utilitarianism to modern methods of economic theory by championing what is known as preference utilitarianism. Instead of referring to the maximization of specific goods, such as pleasure or knowledge, preference utilitarians understand the ultimate foundation of goodness to be the set of preferences people actually possess. One person prefers oysters to strawberries; another prefers rock music to Mozart. Each person has a set of preferences, and so long as the set is internally consistent, it makes no sense to label one set morally superior to another. Preference utilitarianism thus interprets right action as that which is optimal among alternatives in terms of everyone's preferences. Disputes, however, rage among preference utilitarians and their critics over how to specify the meaning of *optimal*.

Bentham and Mill thought that utilitarianism was a revolutionary theory, both because it accurately reflected human motivation and because it had clear application to the political and social problems of their day. If one could measure the benefit or harm of any action, rule or law, they believed, one could sort out good and bad social and political legislation as well as good and bad individual actions.

But how, specifically, does one apply the traditional principle of utility? To begin with, one's race, religion, intelligence, or condition of birth is acknowledged to be irrelevant in calculating one's ultimate worth. Each person counts for "one," and no more than "one." Second, in evaluating happiness, one must take into account not only present generations, but ones in the future. In calculating the effects of pollution, for instance, one must measure the possible effects pollution might have on health, genetics, and the supply of natural resources for future generations. Third, pleasure or happiness is measured *en toto* so that the thesis does not reduce to the idea that "one ought to do what makes the most persons happy." Utilitarianism does not reduce to a dictatorship of majority interests. One person's considerable unhappiness might outweigh the minor pleasures of many other persons added together. Utilitarians also consider the long-term consequences for single individuals. For instance, it might be pleasureable to drink a full bottle of wine every evening, but the long-term drawbacks of such a habit might well outweigh its temporary pleasures.

Finally, according to many utilitarians (such as Mill), some pleasures are *qualitatively* better than others. Intellectual pleasure, for example, is said to be higher than physical pleasure. "Better to be Socrates unsatisfied," writes Mill, "than a pig satisfied." The reasons that drove Mill to formulate this qualitative distinction among pleasures are worth noting. Since Mill believed that the optimal situation was one of "greatest happiness for the greatest number," than what was he to say about a world of people living at the zenith of merely *physical* happiness? If science could invent a wonder drug, like the "soma" in Aldous Huxley's *Brave New World*, that provided a permanent state of drugged happiness (without even a hangover), would the consequence be a perfect world? Mill believed not, and to remedy this difficulty in his theory, he introduced *qualitative levels* of happiness. For example, he said that the happiness of understanding Plato is "higher" than that of drinking three martinis. But how was Mill to say *which* pleasures were higher? Here he retreated to an ingenious proposal: When deciding which of two pleasures is higher, one should poll the group of persons who are experienced—that is, who know *both* pleasures. Their decision will indicate which is the higher pleasure. Ah, but might the majority decision not be wrong? Here Mill provides no clear answer.

Modern-day utilitarians divide themselves roughly into two groups: *act utilitarians* and *rule utilitarians*. An *act* utilitarian believes that the principle of utility should be applied to individual acts. Thus one measures the consequences of each *individual action* according to whether it maximizes good. For example, suppose a certain community were offered the opportunity to receive a great deal of wealth in the form of a gift. The only stipulation was that the community force some of its citizens with ugly, deteriorated homes to repair and beautify them. Next, suppose the community held an election to decide whether to accept the gift. An act utilitarian would analyze the problem of whether to vote for or against the proposal from the standpoint of the *individual voter*. Would an individual's vote to accept the gift be more likely to maximize the community's overall good than would a vote to the contrary?

A *rule* utilitarian, on the other hand, believes that instead of considering the results of specific actions, one must weigh the consequences of adopting a *general rule* exemplified by that action. According to the rule utilitarian, one should act according to a general rule which, if adopted, would maximize good. For example, in the hypothetical case of the community deciding whether to accept a gift, a rule utilitarian might adopt the rule "Never vote in a way that lowers the self-respect of a given class of citizens." She might accept this rule because of the general unhappiness that would ensue if society systematically treated some persons as second-class citizens. Here the focus is on the general rule and not on the individual act.

Critics raise objections to utilitarianism. Perhaps the most serious objection is that it is unable to account for justice. Because the utilitarian concentrates on the consequences of an action for a majority, the employment of the principle of utility can be argued to allow injustice for a small minority. For example, if overall goodness were maximized in the long run by making slaves of 2 percent of the population, utilitarianism seemingly is forced to condone slavery. But clearly this is unjust. Utilitarianism's obvious response is that such slavery will not, as a matter of empirical fact, maximize goodness. Rule utilitarians, as we have seen, can argue that society should embrace the rule "Never enslave others," because following such a principle will, in the long run, maximize goodness. Even so, the battle continues between utilitarians and their critics. Can utilitarianism account for the widely held moral conviction that injustice to a minority is wrong *regardless* of the consequences? The answer is hotly contested.

Another criticism concerns the determination of the good to be maximized. Any consequentialist has the problem of identifying and ranking whatever is to be maximized. For a utilitarian such as Mill, as we have seen, the problem involves distinguishing between higher and lower pleasures. But for pluralistic utilitarians, a similar problem exists: What is the basis for selecting, for example, friendship and happiness as goods to be maximized and not, say, aesthetic sensitivity? And even granted that this problem can be solved, there is the future problem of arbitrating trade-offs between goods such as happiness and friendship when they *conflict*. When one is forced to choose between enhancing happiness and enhancing friendship, which gets priority? And under what conditions?

An interesting fact about consequentialist reasoning is that most of us employ it to some degree in ordinary decisions. We weigh the consequences of alternatives in choosing colleges, in deciding on a career, in hiring and promoting others, and in many other judgments. We frequently weigh good consequences over bad ones and predict the long-and short-term effects of our choices. We often even cite consequentialist-style principles—for example, "No one should choose a college where he or she will be unhappy," or, "No one should pollute the environment when his or her action harms others."

However, for a variety of reasons including the objections to utilitarianism mentioned earlier, some philosophers refuse to acknowledge consequentialism as an adequate theory of ethics. They argue that the proper focus for ethical judgments should not be consequences, but moral *precepts*—that is, the rules, norms, and principles we use to guide our actions. Such philosophers are known as deontologists, and the next section will examine their views.

DEONTOLOGY

The term *deontological* comes from the Greek word for "duty," and what is crucial according to the deontologist are the rules and principles that guide actions. We shall discuss here two approaches to deontological ethical reasoning that have profoundly influenced ethics. The first is that of the eighteenth-century philosopher Immanuel Kant and his followers. This approach focuses on duty and universal rules to determine right actions. The second—actually a subspecies of deontological reasoning—is known as the "social contract" approach. It focuses not on individual decision making, but on the general social principles that rational persons in certain ideal situations would agree upon and adopt.

Kantian Deontology

Kant believed that ethical reasoning should concern activities that are rationally motivated and should utilize precepts that apply universally to all human actions. To this end, he opens his treatise on ethics by declaring

> It is impossible to conceive anything at all in the world, . . . which can be taken as good without qualification except a *good* will.[2]

This statement sums up much of what Kant wants to say about ethics and is worth unraveling. What Kant means is that the only thing that can be good or worthwhile without any provisos or stipulations is an action of the will freely motivated for the right reasons. Other goods such as wealth, beauty, and intelligence are certainly valuable, but they are not good *without qualification* because they have the potential to create both good and bad effects. Wealth, beauty, and intelligence can be bad when they are used for purely selfish ends. Even human happiness—which Mill held as the highest good—can, according to Kant, create complacency, disinterest, and excessive self-assurance under certain conditions.

According to Kant, reason is the faculty that can aid in the discovery of correct moral principles; thus it is *reason*, not *inclination*, that should guide the will. When reason guides the will, Kant calls the resulting actions ones done from "duty." Kant's use of the term *duty* turns out to be less formidable than it first appears. Kant is simply saying that a purely good and free act of the will is one done not merely because you have an *inclination* to do it, but because you have the right reasons for doing it. For example, suppose you discover a wallet belonging to a stranger. Kant would say that despite one's inclination to keep the money (which the stranger may not even need), one should return it. This is an act you know is right despite your inclinations. Kant also believes you should return the wallet even when you believe the *consequences* of not returning it are better. Here his views are at sharp odds with consequentialism. Suppose that the stranger is known for her stinginess, and you plan to donate the money to a children's hospital. No matter. For Kant, you must return the wallet. Thus the moral worth lies in the act itself and not in either your happiness or the consequences brought about by the act. Acts are good because they are done for the sake of what is right and not because of the consequences they might produce.

But how do I know what my duty is? While it may be clear that one should return a wallet, there are other circumstances in which one's duty is less evident. Suppose you are in a six-person lifeboat at sea with five others and a seventh person swims up? What is one's duty here? And how does one even know that what one *thinks* is right *is* right? To settle such problems, Kant claims that duty is more than doing merely what you "feel" is right. Duty is acting with *respect for other rational beings*. It almost goes without saying, then, that "acting from duty" is not to be interpreted as action done in obedience to local, state, or national laws, since these can be good or bad. Instead, "duty" is linked to the idea of universal principles that should govern all our actions.

But is there any principle that can govern *all* human beings? Kant believes the answer is yes, and he calls the highest such principle the "categorical imperative." He formulates the categorical imperative in three ways (although we shall only consider two formulations here). The first formulation, roughly translated, is

> One ought only to act such that the principle of one's act could become a universal law of human action in a world in which one would hope to live.

For example, one would want to live in a world where people followed the principle "Return property that belongs to others." Therefore one should return the stranger's wallet. We do not, however, want to live in a world where everyone lies. Therefore, one should not adopt the principle "Lie whenever it seems helpful."

The second formulation of the categorical imperative is

One ought to treat others as having intrinsic value in themselves, and *not* merely as means to achieve one's ends.

In other words, one should respect every person as a rational and free being. Hitler treated one group of persons as nonpersons in order to achieve his own ends, and thus he acted contrary to the categorical imperative. Another instance of treating persons as means would occur if a teacher looked up the grade records of new students to determine how to assign grades in her own class. She would be treating students as if they had no control over their destinies. Such actions are immoral according to Kant because they fail to respect the inherent dignity of rational beings.

Ethical reasoning for Kant implies adopting principles of action and evaluating one's actions in terms of those principles. Even Kant grants that the evaluation is sometimes difficult. For example, there is the problem of striking the proper level of generality in choosing a principle. A principle that read, "If one is named John Doe and attends Big State University and has two sisters, then he should borrow fifty dollars without intending to repay it," is far too specific. On the other hand, the principle "You should always pay your debts" might be too general, since it would require that a starving man repay the only money he possesses to buy a loaf of bread. Because of the problem of striking the proper degree of generality, many modern deontologists have reformulated Kant's basic question to read: "Could I wish that everyone in the world would follow this principle *under relevantly similar conditions?*"

As with utilitarianism, critics challenge deontological reasoning. Some assert that fanatics such as Hitler could at least *believe* that the rule "Persecute Jews whenever possible" is one that the world should live by. Similarly, a thief might universalize the principle "Steal whenever you have a good opportunity." Moreover, a strict interpretation of deontological ethical reasoning is said to allow no exceptions to a universal principle. Such strict adherence to universal principles might encourage moral rigidity and might fail to reflect the diversity of responses required by complex moral situations. Finally, critics argue that, in a given case, two principles may conflict without there being a clear way to decide which principle or rule should take precedence. Jean-Paul Sartre tells of his dilemma during World War II when he was forced to choose between staying to comfort his ill and aging mother, and fighting for the freedom of France. Two principles seemed valid: "Give aid to your father and mother," and "Contribute to the cause of freedom." But with conflicting principles, how is one to choose? Nevertheless, deontological ethical reasoning represents a well-respected and fundamentally distinctive mode of ethical reasoning, one which, like consequentialism, appears in the deliberations of ordinary persons as well as philosophers. We have all heard actions condemned by the comment, "what would it be like if everyone did that?"

The Contractarian Alternative

Kant assumes that the categorical imperative is something all rational individuals can discover and agree upon. A different version of deontology is offered by many philosophers who focus less on the actions of individuals, and more on the principles that govern society at large. These include two philosophers whose writings appear in our book: the seventeenth-century political philosopher John Locke and the twentieth-century American philosopher John Rawls. They and others try to establish universal principles of a just society through what might be called "social contract thought experiments." They ask us to imagine what it would be like to live in a situation where there are no laws, no social conventions, and no political state. In this so-called state of nature, we imagine that rational persons gather to formulate principles or rules to govern political and social communities. Such rules would resemble principles derived through the categorical imperative in that they are presumably principles to which every rational person would agree and which would hold universally.

Locke and Rawls differ in their approach to establishing rules or principles of justice, and the difference illustrates two distinct forms of contractarian reasoning. Locke argues from a "natural rights" position, while Rawls argues from a "reasonable person" position. Locke claims that every person is born with, and possesses, certain basic rights that are "natural." These rights are inherent to a person's nature, and they are possessed by every one equally. Like other inherent traits, they cannot be taken away. They are, in the words of the Declaration of Independence, "inalienable." When rational persons meet to formulate principles to govern the formation of social and political communities, they construct a social contract that is the basis for an agreement between themselves and their government, and whose rules protect natural rights. Rights, then, become deontological precepts by which one forms and evaluates rules, constitutions, government, and socioeconomic systems. While many philosophers disagree with Locke's view that each of us has inherent or *natural* rights, many do utilize a theory of human rights as the basis for justifying and evaluating political institutions.

Rawls adopts a different perspective. He does not begin from a natural rights position. Instead, he asks which principles of justice rational persons would formulate if they were behind a "veil of ignorance—that is, if each person knew nothing about who he or she was. That is, one would not know whether one were old or young, male or female, rich or poor, highly motivated or lazy, or anything about one's personal status in society. Unable to predict which principles, if picked, will favor them personally, Rawls argues, persons will be forced to choose principles that are fair to all.

Rawls and Locke are not in perfect agreement about which principles would be adopted in such hypothetical situations, and more will be said about their views later in the book. For now it is important to remember that the social contract approach maintains a deontological character. It is used to formulate principles of justice that apply universally. Some philosophers note, however, that from an original position in a "state of nature" or behind a "veil of ignorance," rational persons *could* adopt consequentialist principles as rules for a just society. Thus, while the social contract approach is deontological in style, the principles it generates are not necessarily ones that are incompatible with consequentialism.

In the moral evaluations of business, all deontologists—contractarians included—would ask questions such as the following:

1. Are the rules fair to everyone?
2. Do the rules hold universally even with the passage of time?
3. Is every person treated with equal respect?

What may be missing from a deontological approach to ethical reasoning is a satisfactory means of coping with valid exceptions to general rules. Under what circumstances, if any, are exceptions allowed? Deontologists believe that they can answer this question, but their solutions vary. Suffice it to say that deontologists, just as utilitarians, have not convinced everyone.

HUMAN NATURE ETHICS

According to some contemporary philosophers, the preceding two modes of ethical reasoning exhaust all possible modes. That is to say, all theories can be classified as either teleological or deontological. Whether this is true cannot be settled here, but it will be helpful to introduce briefly what some philosophers consider to be a third category, namely the *human nature* approach.

A *human nature* approach assumes that all humans have inherent capacities that constitute the ultimate basis for all ethical claims. Actions are evaluated in terms of whether they promote or hinder, coincide with, or conflict with these capacities. One of the most famous proponents of this theory was the Greek philosopher Aristotle. In Aristotle's opinion, human beings have inherent *potentialities*, and thus human development turns out to be the struggle for self-actualization, or in other words, the perfection of inherent human nature. Consider the acorn. It has the natural potential to become a sturdy oak tree. Its natural drive is not to become an elm or a cedar or even a stunted oak, but to become the most robust oak tree possible. Diseased or stunted oak trees are simply deficient; they are instances of things in nature whose potential has not been fully developed. Similarly, according to Aristotle, persons are born with inherent potentialities. Persons, like acorns, naturally are oriented to actualize their potentialities, and for them this means more than merely developing their physical potential. It also means developing their mental, moral, and social potential. Thus, human beings in this view are seen as basically good; evil is understood as a deficiency that occurs when one is unable to fulfill one's natural capacities.

It is important to understand that the concept of human nature need not be an individualistic one. According to Aristotle, persons are "social" by nature and cannot be understood apart from the larger community in which they participate. "Man," Aristotle wrote, is a "social animal." For Aristotle, then, fulfilling one's natural constitution implies developing wisdom, generosity, and self-restraint, all of which help to make one a good member of the community.

The criterion for judging the goodness of any action is whether or not the action is compatible with one's inherent human capacities. Actions that enhance human capacities are good; those that deter them are bad unless they are the best among generally negative alternatives. For example, eating nothing but starches is unhealthy, but it is clearly preferable to starving.

This theory puts great emphasis on the nature of persons and obviously, how one understands that "nature" will be the key to determining both what counts as a right action and how one defines the proper end of human action in general. Aristotle argued that intelligence and wisdom are uniquely human potentialities and consequently that intellectual virtue is the highest virtue. The life of contemplation, he believed, is the best sort of life, in part because it represents the highest fulfillment of human nature. Moral virtue, also crucial in Aristotle's theory, involves the rational control of one's desires. In action where a choice is possible, one exercises moral virtue by restraining harmful desires and cultivating beneficial ones. The development of virtue requires the cultivation of good habits, and this in turn leads Aristotle to emphasize the importance of good upbringing and education.

One problem said to affect human nature theories is that they have difficulty justifying the supposition that human beings *do* have specific inherent capacities and that these capacities are the same for all humans. Further, critics claim that it is difficult to warrant the assumption that humans are basically good. Perhaps the famous psychoanalyst Sigmund Freud is correct in his assertion that at bottom we are all naturally aggressive and selfish. Third, critics complain that it is difficult to employ this theory in ethical reasoning, since it appears to lack clear-cut rules and principles for use in moral decision making. Obviously, any well-argued human nature ethic will take pains to spell out the aspects of human nature which, when actualized, constitute the ultimate ground for moral judgments.

CONCLUSION

The three approaches to ethical reasoning we have discussed—consequentialism, deontology, and human nature ethics—all present theories of ethical reasoning distinguished in terms of their basic methodological elements. Each represents a type or model of moral reasoning that is applicable to practical decisions in concrete situations. Consider, for example, the case study with which we began our discussion, involving BASF and its proposed new plant. As it happened, BASF chose option 3 and decided to build elsewhere. In making his decision, did the BASF manager actually use any or all of the methods described above? Although we cannot know the answer to this question, it is clear, as we saw earlier, that each method was applicable to his problem. Indeed, the three methods of moral reasoning are sufficiently broad that each is applicable to the full range of problems confronting human moral experience. The question of which method, if any, is superior to the others must be left for another time. The intention of this essay is not to substitute for a thorough study of traditional ethical theories—something for which there is no substitute—but to introduce the reader to basic modes of ethical reasoning that will help to analyze the ethical problems in business that arise in the remainder of the book.

NOTES

1. "BASF Corporation vs. The Hilton Head Island Developers," in *Business and Society*, Robert D. Hay, et al., eds. (Cincinnati: South-Western Publishing Co., 1984). pp. 100–12.
2. Immanuel Kant, *Groundwork of the Metaphysic of Morals*, trans. H. J. Paton (New York: Harper & Row, 1948, 1956), p. 61.

•Part One•

GENERAL ISSUES IN ETHICS
Introduction

At a time when the reputation of business in general is low . . . one would expect corporate executives to be especially sensitive even to appearances of conflict of interest. . . . Yet this seems not, on the whole, to be the case. . . .

IRVING KRISTOL

If you were a manager of a large corporation doing business in a country where bribery was an accepted practice in getting business contracts would you participate in this activity?

Suppose as manager of a foreign division of a multinational corporation you discover that an allegedly benign product you manufacture is being used as a drug by a substantial population of children in that culture. Would you withdraw your product from that market or close your plant in that country?

If you were operating a branch of a U.S. company in a foreign country, would you follow that country's tax procedures if they conflicted with procedures in the United States and even required falsifying earnings reports?

As an account executive, you feel that one of the advertisements for which you are responsible presents misleading information about the product. Would you request a change in the advertisement?

Each of these vignettes is drawn from an actual business situation illustrated in this section, and, in fact, such incidents occur more frequently than one might expect. Understanding their ethical implications requires not only an awareness of concrete situations but also the ability to subsume business problems under categories of more general ethical concern. The philosophical material in Part I introduces two traditional ethical concerns:

ethical relativism and truth telling. Stated as questions these concerns are as follows:

Ethical relativism: Are values simply relative to the groups of people who espouse them such that value differences between cultures cannot be resolved? Or is it possible to identify universal values which resolve ethical differences and apply to all people? How *does* one resolve conflicts of values between cultures, between individuals and organizations, or even between individuals?

Truth telling: What obligations, if any, exist for individuals and organizations to communicate honestly? When, if ever, is not telling the truth justified?

ETHICAL RELATIVISM

The issue of honesty is difficult in practice because it must be faced every day. The issue of the relativity of value judgments is less obviously commonplace but no less difficult. It asks whether some moral principles apply universally to all persons or whether, instead, all values and ethical judgments are relative to particular contexts. This question is particularly acute in contemporary business because most major corporations today are "transnational" or "multinational" corporations that conduct business in many countries. How should businesses operate in foreign countries? For example, should an American multinational company adopt the practices of the host country even when those practices conflict with an American way of doing business and are morally questionable at least according to United States standards? In general, should one lie, bribe, or submit to extortion in a foreign country if that activity is common practice in that culture? According to some views of ethical relativism, one cannot say that bribery, for example, is wrong in a particular culture if it is an acceptable practice in the value system of that culture. According to the ethical relativist, there are no universal standards or objective values by which one can judge the moral principles of all cultures. Nor are there any general standards by which one can adjudicate between two clashing principles.

Ethical relativism frequently uses evidence provided by another, but closely related, point of view known as *cultural* relativism. Cultural relativism emphasizes how the ways in which people reason about morality vary in different cultures because of different customs, religious traditions, and methods of education. Citing the fact of moral diversity, ethical relativism holds that no ethical assertion or set of assertions has any greater claim to objectivity or universality than any other. From the obvious empirical evidence of differences between cultures, an ethical relativist may go further to argue that there are no ultimate, universal ethical principles and that all value judgments are relative to particular contexts. Therefore, the truth of an ethical statement such as "Bribery is wrong" is determined solely by the beliefs of the culture espousing that claim. Although Americans typically think bribery is wrong, in some other cultures it seems to be an accepted part of business and political practice; and according to a relativist, this value conflict cannot be resolved. Value conflicts within a particular society, too, may for the same reason not be resolvable. For at least some ethical disagreements, there is no single correct view to which even an ideal rational observer can appeal in solving conflicts of values, particularly those of a more serious nature.

The relativity of value judgments can be an issue within a culture as well. One can argue that values are not merely relative to particular cultures but also relative to particular spheres of activity. For example, although tackling in football is part of that game, it is not an accepted practice in other social interactions. If business itself is a game, as Albert Carr argues, then that sphere of activity has certain conventions and values that might not be acceptable in other spheres.

According to this line of argument, the values of the medical community might differ from, say, those of certain religious groups, or the values espoused by corporations might differ from, and sometimes even conflict with, ideals espoused by individuals. Because values affect expectations, what is expected of a person as an employee, for example, might be different from the values she espouses away from the workplace.

An obvious way to challenge ethical relativism is to argue that there are some values that are universal, that is, which apply without exception. For example, one might argue that skinning live babies for sport is not acceptable anywhere, despite anyone's belief. Carl Wellman defends just such a point of view. He recognizes that there are practical difficulties in specifying particular ethical principles that apply universally, but these difficulties do not imply that ethical relativism is correct. Although it may be the case that certain value conflicts are never resolved, this does not imply that they are not in principle resolvable. In an intricate set of arguments, Wellman points out that what appear to be differences in value are often based on agreements concerning very basic ethical principles. Moreover, the claim that moral reasoning is relative cannot by itself be justified. So the alleged fact that moral reasoning is culturally relative may rest on some ultimate justification for which there is no further appeal.

If Wellman's arguments are correct, they might be used to show that justifications for making sensitive payments abroad are questionable and that other justifications are inconsistent with claims of relativism. For when some corporations defend their activities by referring to the economic advantages for the foreign countries in which they operate, are they not assuming that economic growth is a universal value and should be espoused by every country?

The conduct of multinational corporations has been under severe scrutiny in recent years. As a result of incidents involving sensitive payments, in 1977 the U.S. Congress passed the Foreign Corrupt Practices Act (FCPA). The FCPA is an attempt to legislate standards of conduct for multinational corporations by making it a crime for U.S.-based multinationals to offer or to acquiesce to sensitive payments to officials of foreign governments. The Act implies that what we in this country think is morally right should apply to our dealings in other countries. This position would be criticized by ethical relativists, since according to them, value differences between cultures preclude the justification of exporting the laws or moral principles of one country to another.

The FCPA raises the issue of whether one can justify sensitive payments—that is, bribery and extortion—in any context, and also that of whether one can legislate moral behavior. Mark Pastin and Michael Hooker consider this question in their article "Ethics and the Foreign Corrupt Practices Act." They argue that the moral rule prohibiting bribery is a *prima facie* rule that can be overridden to prevent a greater harm—the greater harm in this instance being the loss of American business and the accompanying loss of jobs by American multinational corporations which cannot compete in the international market. In response, Kenneth Alpern suggests that one cannot justify overriding a moral rule such as that prohibiting bribery except in dire circumstances, a condition which hardly describes the state of American business. Abolishing the FCPA, according to Alpern, is tantamount to endorsing a general policy of bribery.

In his article "Moral Minimums for Multinationals," Thomas Donaldson considers the vexing problems that arise when moral and legal standards vary between countries, especially between a multinational corporation's home and host countries. How, he asks, should highly placed multinational managers, typically schooled in home-country moral traditions, reconcile conflicts between their values and the practices of the host country? If host-country standards appear lower than home-country ones, should the multinational manager always take the "high road" and implement home-country standards? Or does the "high road" sometimes signal a failure to respect cultural diversity and national integrity? The answer may be fairly obvious in the instance of South Africa (where acquiescing to racism and discrimination would surely be immoral), but how about other instances—ones involving differences in wage rates, pollution standards, or "sensitive payments"?

To deal with these complex issues, Donaldson appeals to the notion of a human right to establish minimum requirements for morally acceptable behavior in multinational settings. Respecting very basic rights, it turns out, entails a number of duties, duties not merely not to harm others, but positive duties to assist in protecting workers, customers, and the public from harm. Donaldson carries his arguments further. In order to settle conflicts of norms without resolving all cultural disputes in terms of one's own cultural norms, or acquiescing to practices one ordinarily finds morally questionable, Donaldson develops what he calls a two-step moral algorithm that takes into account basic rights, economic development of the country in which one is operating, and an analysis of the norms of the host and home countries. Such an algorithm brings into question ethical relativism in multinational decision-making while respecting cultural and national differences.

The case study "H. B. Fuller" raises a complex set of issues. Fuller is a well-managed company with the highest ethical standards. But when what they thought was an innocent product, glue, is sniffed as a drug by Honduran children, they are faced with a number of ethical dilemmas. Should one continue to manufacture a product in a country where children have easy access to the product and misuse it? Do multinationals have social responsibilities to the country in which they operate, responsibilities that go beyond merely manufacturing safe products and include such matters as alleviating poverty, improving educational standards, and the like?

TRUTH TELLING

The concept of truth telling can be used to investigate a wide variety of issues, including those relating to nondeceptive advertising, the accuracy of consumer information, and the responsibilities a business has to communicate honestly with its employees and stockholders. A philosopher well known for his vigorous defense of truth telling is the eighteenth-century German philosopher Immanuel Kant. In this section, selections from his *Lectures on Ethics* are presented in which Kant claims that truth telling is an essential feature of morally right communication. Kant equates honesty both with frankness and reserve, and supports the principle of never telling a lie on three grounds. First, the principle of truth telling is one which each of us would like everyone else to follow. In other words, it is a principle that philosophers call "universalizable," meaning that each of us would like to see it universally followed by all human beings. Second, truth telling is a necessary element for society because all societies depend upon mutual bonds of honesty and truthfulness to enforce their unity and orderly continuation. Finally, lying destroys the major source of human development—that is, knowledge—since it thwarts the discovery of new truths.

In contrast with Kant, Albert Carr, in a lively article, "Is Business Bluffing Ethical?" suggests that the moral requirement of truth telling depends on the context in which the activity takes place. For example, in advertising, although few advertisers actually lie about their products, many advertisements "puff" their products or make unfair comparisons between their product and the competition. This is all right, according to Carr, because everyone understands the "game" of advertising and no one is really fooled by the puffery.

Because perfect market information, or in Kant's terms, the "whole truth," is never obtainable, it is usually impossible to determine whether an advertiser or person is bluffing or lying. So it is not always to the economic advantage of business to reveal the "whole truth" about a product or service, nor is it unprofitable to engage in competitive bluffing when other businesses are doing so. Despite Carr's persuasive arguments, many advertisers as well as other business persons and philosophers are worried about the impact of the "game" of advertising on the public. Is bluffing or puffery justified when some persons affected by them do not understand the game and are deceived or misled?

If Carr's game analogy is questionable in advertising, the reader might want to consider its application to other aspects of business. Does the analogy ever justify making an exception to Kant's dictum that one should never lie? The case study "Italian Tax Mores" presents a situation in which truth telling, as well as relativism, are major issues. The case concerns an American executive managing a branch of a U.S. bank in Italy, who finds that typical Italian practices encourage actions that he believes constitute both bribery and lying. Is it morally acceptable to misrepresent the bank's income tax figures if it appears that most other companies in Italy do the same thing, and if truth telling will do harm to the bank? As a matter of self-defense, should the executive "play the game" and adopt the practices of the Italian tax system when those practices involve outright lying? Or can the manager justify providing the truth to the Italian tax authorities even when this might threaten the well-being of his bank?

Ethical Relativism and International Business

Case Study

H. B. Fuller in Honduras: Street Children and Substance Abuse

NORMAN BOWIE AND STEFANIE ANN LENWAY

In the summer of 1985 the following news story was brought to the attention of an official of the H. B. Fuller Company in St. Paul Minnesota.

Glue Sniffing Among Honduran Street Children in Honduras: Children Sniffing Their Lives Away

AN INTER PRESS SERVICE FEATURE
BY PETER FORD

Tegucigalpa July 16, 1985 (IPS)—They lie senseless on doorsteps and pavements, grimy and loose limbed, like discarded rag dolls.

Some are just five or six years old. Others are already young adults, and all are addicted to sniffing a commonly sold glue that is doing them irreversible brain damage.

Roger, 21, has been sniffing "Resistol" for eight years. Today, even when he is not high, Roger walks with a stagger, his motor control wrecked. His scarred face puckers with concentration, his right foot taps nervously, incessantly, as he talks.

Since he was 11, when he ran away from the aunt who raised him, Roger's home has been the streets of the capital of Honduras, the second poorest nation in the western hemisphere after Haiti.

Roger spends his time begging, shining shoes, washing car windows, scratching together a few pesos a day, and sleeping in doorways at night.

Sniffing glue, he says, "makes me feel happy, makes me feel big. What do I care if my family does not love me? I know it's doing me damage, but it's a habit I have got, and a habit's a habit. I can not give it up, even though I want to."

No one knows how many of Teg-

Norman Bowie and Stefanie Ann Lenway, University of Minnesota. All rights reserved by Graduate School of Business, Columbia University. The authors express their deep appreciation to the H. B. Fuller Company for providing access to company documents and personnel relevant to this case.

ucigalpa's street urchins seek escape from the squalor and misery of their daily existence through the hallucinogenic fumes of "Resistol." No one has spent the time and money needed to study the question.

But one thing is clear, according to Dr. Rosalio Zavala, Head of the Health Ministry's Mental Health Department, "these children come from the poorest slums of the big cities. They have grown up as illegal squatters in very disturbed states of mental health, tense, depressed, aggressive."

"Some turn that aggression on society, and start stealing. Others turn it on themselves, and adopt self destructive behavior . . ."

But, he understands the attraction of the glue, whose solvent, toluene, produces feelings of elation. "It gives you delusions of grandeur, you feel powerful, and that compensates these kids for reality, where they feel completely worthless, like nobodies."

From the sketchy research he has conducted, Dr. Zavala believes that most boys discover Resistol for the first time when they are about 11, though some children as young as five are on their way to becoming addicts.

Of a small sample group of children interviewed in reform schools here, 56 percent told Zavala that friends introduced them to the glue, but it is easy to find on the streets for oneself.

Resistol is a contact cement glue, widely used by shoe repairers, and available at household goods stores everywhere . . .

In some states of the United States, glue containing addictive narcotics such as toluene must also contain oil of mustard—the chemical used to produce poisonous mustard gas—which makes sniffing the glue so painful it is impossible to tolerate. There is no federal U.S. law on the use of oil of mustard, however . . .

But even for Dr. Zavala, change is far more than a matter of just including a chemical compound, such as oil of mustard, in a contact cement.

"This is a social problem," he acknowledges. "What we need is a change in philosophy, a change in social organization."

Resistol is manufactured by H. B. Fuller S. A., a subsidiary of Kativo Chemical Industries, S. A. which in turn is a wholly owned subsidiary of the H. B. Fuller Company of St. Paul, Minnesota.[1] Kativo sells more than a dozen different adhesives under the Resistol brand name in several countries in Latin America for a variety of industrial and commercial applications. In Honduras the Resistol products have a strong market position.

Three of the Resistol products are solvent-based adhesives designed with certain properties that are not possible to attain with a water-based formula. These properties include rapid set, strong adhesion, and water resistance. These products are similar to airplane glue or rubber cement and are primarily intended for use in shoe manufacturing and repair, leatherwork, and carpentry.

Even though the street children of each Central American country may have a different choice of a drug for substance abuse, and even though Resistol is not the only glue that Honduran street children use as an inhalant, the term "Resistolero" stuck and has become synonymous with all street children, whether they use inhalants or not. In Honduras Resistol is identified as the abused substance.

Edward Sheehan writes in the *Agony in the Garden.*

Resistol. I had heard about Resistol, It was a glue, the angel dust of Honduran orphans. . . . In Tegucigalpa, their addiction had become so common they were known as los Resistoleros. (p. 32)

HONDURAS[2]

The social problems that contribute to widespread inhalant abuse among street children can be attributed to the depth of poverty in Honduras. In 1989, 65 percent of all households and 40 percent of urban households in Honduras were living in poverty, making it one of the poorest countries in Latin America. Between 1950 and 1988, the increase in the Honduran gross domestic product (GDP) was 3.8 percent, only slightly greater than the average yearly increase in population growth. In 1986, the Honduran GDP was about U.S. $740 per capita and has only grown slightly since. Infant and child mortality rates are high, life expectancy for adults is 64 years, and the adult literacy rate is estimated to be about 60 percent.

Honduras has faced several economic obstacles in its efforts to industrialize. First, it lacks abundant natural resources. The mountainous terrain has restricted agricultural productivity and growth. In addition, the small domestic market and competition from more industrially advanced countries has prevented the manufacturing sector from progressing much beyond textiles, food processing, and assembly operations.

The key to the growth of the Honduran economy has been the production and export of two commodities—bananas and coffee. Both the vagaries in the weather and the volatility of commodity markets had made the foreign exchange earned from these products very unstable. Without consistently strong export sales, Honduras has not been able to buy sufficient fuel and other productive input to allow the growth of its manufacturing sector. It also had to import basic grains (corn and rice) because the country's traditional staples are produced inefficiently by small farmers using traditional technologies with poor soil.

In the 1970s the Honduran government relied on external financing to invest in physical and social infrastructures and to implement development programs intended to diversify the economy. Government spending increased 10.4 percent a year from 1973. By 1981, the failure of many of these development projects led the government to stop financing state-owned industrial projects. The public sector failures were attributed to wasteful administration, mismanagement, and corruption. Left with little increase in productivity to show for these investments, Honduras continues to face massive budgetry deficits and unprecedented levels of external borrowing.

The government deficit was further exacerbated in the early 1980s by increasing levels of unemployment. By 1983, unemployment reached 20–30 percent of the economically active population, with an additional 40 percent of the population underemployed, primarily in agriculture. The rising unemployment, falling real wages, and low level of existing social infrastructure in education and health care contributed to the low level of labor productivity. Unemployment benefits were very limited and only about 7.3 percent of the population was covered by social security.

Rural-to-urban migration has been a major contributor to urban growth in Honduras. In the 1970s the urban population grew at more than twice as fast a rate as the rural population. This migration has increased in part as a result of a high birth rate among the rural population, along with a move by large landholders to convert forest and fallow land, driving off subsistence farmers to use the land for big-scale cotton and beef farming. As more and more land was enclosed, an increasing number of landless sought the cities for a better life.

Tegucigalpa, the capital, has had one of the fastest population increases among Central American cities, growing by 178,000 between 1970 and 1980, with a projected population of 975,000 by the year 2000. Honduras' second largest city, San Pedro Sula, is projected to have a population of 650,000 by 2000.

The slow growth in the industrial and commercial sectors has not been adequate to provide jobs for those moving to the city. The migrants to the urban areas typically move first to cuarterias (rows) of connected rooms. The rooms are generally constructed of wood with dirt floors, and they are usually windowless. The average household contains about seven persons, who live together in a single room. For those living in the rooms facing an alley, the narrow passageway between buildings serves both as sewage and waste disposal area and as a courtyard for as many as 150 persons.

Although more than 70 percent of the families living in these cuarterias had one member with a permanent salaried job, few could survive on that income alone. For stable extended families, salaried income is supplemented by entrepreneurial activities, such as selling tortillas. Given migratory labor, high unemployment, and income insecurity many family relationships are unstable. Often the support of children is left to mothers. Children are frequently forced to leave school helping support the family through shining shoes, selling newspapers, or guarding cars, such help often is essential income. If a lone mother has become sick or dies, her children may be abandoned to the streets.

KATIVO CHEMICAL INDUSTRIES S.A.[3]

Kativo celebrated its 40th anniversary in 1989. It is now one of the 500 largest private corporations in Latin America. In 1989, improved sales in most of Central American were partially offset by a reduction of its sales in Honduras.

Walter Kissling, chairman of Kativo's board and senior vice president for H. B. Fuller's international operations Fuller has the reputation of giving the company's local managers a high degree of autonomy. Local managers often have to respond quickly because of unexpected currency fluctuations. He comments that, "In Latin America, if you know what you are doing, you can make more money managing your balance sheet than by selling products." The emphasis on managing the balance sheet in countries with high rates of inflation has led Kativo managers to develop a distinctive competence in finance.

In spite of the competitive challenge of operating under unstable political and economic conditions Kativo managers emphasized in the annual report the importance of going beyond the bottom line:

> Kativo is an organization with a profound philosophy and ethical conduct, worthy of the most advanced firms. It carries out business with the utmost respect for ethical and legal principles and its orientation is not solely directed to the customer, who has the highest priority, but also to the shareholders, and communities where it operates.

In the early 1980s the managers of Kativo, which was primarily a paint company, decided to enter the adhesive market in Latin America. Their strategy was to combine their marketing experience with H. B. Fuller's products. Kativo found the adhesive market potentially profitable in Latin America because it lacked strong competitors. Kativo's initial concern was to win market share. Resistol was the brand name for all adhesive products including the water-based school glue.

KATIVO AND THE STREET CHILDREN

In 1983, Honduran newspapers carried articles about police arrests of "Resistoleros"—street children drugging themselves by sniffing glue. In response to these newspaper articles, Kativo's Honduras advertising agency, Calderon Publicidad, informed the newspapers that Resistol was not the only substance abused by street children and that the image of the manufacturer was being damaged by using a prestigious trademark as a synonym for drug abusers. Moreover glue sniffing was not caused by something inherent in the product but was a social problem. For example, on one occasion the company complained to the editor, requesting that he "make the necessary effort to recommend to the editorial staff that they abstain from using the brand name Resistol as a synonym for the drug, and the adjective Resistolero, as a synonym for the drug addict."

The man on the spot was Kativo's Vice President, Humberto Larach ("Beto"), a Honduran, who headed Kativo's North Adhesives Division. Managers in nine countries including all of Central America, Mexico, the Caribbean and two South American countries, Ecuador and Columbia, reported to him. He had became manager of the adhesive division after demonstrating his entrepreneurial talents managing Kativo's paint business in Honduras.

Beto had proven his courage and his business creativity when he was among 105 taken hostage in the Chamber of Commerce building in downtown San Pedro Sula by guerrillas from the Communist Popular Liberation Front. Despite fire fights between the guerrillas and government troops, threats of execution, and being used as a human shield, Beto had sold his product to two clients (fellow hostages) who had previously been buying products from Kativo's chief competitor! Beto also has a reputation for emphasizing the importance of "Making the bottom line," as a part of Kativo corporate culture.

By summer 1985, more than corporate image was at stake. As a solution to the glue sniffing problem social activists working with street children suggested that oil of mustard, allyl isothiocyanate, could be added to the product to prevent its abuse. They argued that a person attempting to sniff glue with oil of mustard added would find it too powerful to tolerate. Sniffing it has been described like getting an "overdose of horseradish." An attempt to legislate the addition of oil of mustard received a boost when Honduran Peace Corps volunteer, Timothy Bicknell, convinced a local group called the "Committee for the Prevention of Drugs at the National Level," of the necessity of adding oil of mustard to Resistol. All members of the committee were prominent members of Honduran society.

Beto, in response to the growing publicity about the "Resistoleros," requested staff members of H. B. Fuller's U.S. headquarters to look into the viability of oil of mustard as a solution with special attention to side effects and whether it was required or used in the U.S.. H. B. Fuller's corporate industrial hygiene staff found 1983 toxicology reports that oil of mustard was a cancer-causing agent in tests run with rats. A 1986 toxicology report from the Aldrich Chemical Company described the health hazard data of allyl isothiocyanate as:

Acute Effects

May be fatal if inhaled, swallowed, or absorbed through skin.
Carcinogen.
Causes burns.
Material is extremely destructive to tissue of the mucous membranes and upper respiratory tract, eyes and skin.

Prolonged Contact Can Cause:

Nausea, dizziness and headache.
Severe irritation or burns.
Lung irritation, chest pain and edema which may be fatal.
Repeated exposure may cause asthma.

In addition the product had a maximum shelf-life of six months.

To the best of our knowledge, the chemical, physical and toxicological properties have not been thoroughly investigated.

In 1986, Beto contacted Hugh Young, president of Solvent Abuse Foundation for Education (SAFE), and gathered information on programs SAFE had developed in Mexico. Young who believed that there was no effective deterrent took the position that the only viable approach to substance abuse was education, not product modification. He argued that reformulating the product was an exercise in futility because "nothing is available in the solvent area that is not abusable." With these reports in hand, Beto attempted to persuade Resistol's critics, relief agencies, and government officials that adding oil of mustard to Resistol was not the solution to the glue sniffing problem.

During the summer of 1986 Beto had his first success in changing the mind of one journalist. Earlier in the year Mary Kawas, an independent writer, wrote an article sympathetic to the position of Timothy Bicknell and the Committee for the Prevention of Drugs in Honduras. In June, Beto met with her and explained how both SAFE and Kativo sought a solution that was not product-oriented but that was directed at changing human behavior. She was also informed of the research on the dangers of oil of mustard (about which additional information had been obtained). Kawas then wrote an article:

Education Is The Solution For Drug Addiction

LA CEIBA. (BY MARIE J. KAWAS).

A lot of people have been interested in combating drug addiction among youths and children, but few have sought solutions, and almost no one looks in to the feasibility of the alternatives that are so desperately proposed . . .

Oil of mustard (allyl isothiocyanate) may well have been an irresponsible solution in the United States of America during the sixties and seventies, and the Hondurans want to adopt this as a panacea without realizing that their information sources are out of date. Through scientific progress, it has been found that the inclusion of oil of mustard in products which contain solvents, in order to prevent their perversion into use as an addictive drug, only causes greater harm to the consumers and workers involved in their manufacture . . .

Education is a primordial instrument for destroying a social cancer. An effort of this magnitude requires the cooperation of different individuals and organizations . . .

Future generations of Hondurans will be in danger of turning into human parasites, without a clear awareness of what is harmful to them. But if drugs and ignorance are to blame, it is even more harmful to sin by indifference before those very beings who are growing up in an environment without the basic advantages for a healthy physical and mental existence. Who will be the standard bearer in the philanthropic activities which will provide Honduras with the education necessary to combat drug addiction? Who will be remiss in their duty in the face of the nation's altruism?

At first, Beto did not have much success at the governmental level. In September 1986, Dr. Rosalio Zavala, Head of the Mental Health Division of the Honduran Ministry of Health, wrote an article attacking the improper use of Resistol by youth. Beto was unsuccessful in his attempt to contact Dr. Zavala. He had better luck with Mrs. Norma Castro, Governor of the State of Cortes, who after a conversation with Beto became convinced that oil of mustard had serious dangers and the glue sniffing was a social problem.

Beto's efforts continued into the new year. Early in 1987, Kativo began to establish Community Affairs Councils, as a planned expansion of the worldwide company's philosophy of community involvement. These employee committees had already been in place in the U.S. since 1978.

A company document gave the purpose of Community Affairs Councils:

> To educate employees about community issues.
>
> To develop understanding of, and be responsive to the communities near our facilities.
>
> To contribute to Kativo/H. B. Fuller's corporate presence in the neighborhoods and communities we are a part of.
>
> To encourage and support employee involvement in the community.
>
> To spark a true interest in the concerns of the communities in which we live and work.

The document goes on to state, "We want to be more than just bricks, mortar, machines and people. We want to be a company with recognized values, demonstrating involvement, and commitment to the betterment of the communities we are a part of." Later that year, the Honduran community affairs committees went on to make contributions to several organizations working with street children.

In March 1987, Beto visited Jose Oqueli, Vice-Minister of Public Health to explain the philosophy behind H. B. Fuller's Community Affairs program. He also informed him of the health hazards with oil of mustard; they discussed the cultural, family and economic roots of the problem of glue-sniffing among street children.

In June 1987, Parents Resource Institute for Drug Education (PRIDE) set up an office in San Pedro Sula. PRIDE's philosophy was that through adequate *parental* education on the drug problem, it would be possible to deal with the problems of inhalant use. PRIDE was a North American organization that had taken international Nancy Reagan's "just say no" approach to inhalant abuse. Like SAFE, PRIDE took the position that oil of mustard was not the solution to glue-sniffing.

Through PRIDE, Beto was introduced to Wilfredo Alvarado, the new Head of the Mental Health Division in the Ministry of Health. Dr. Alvarado, an advisor to the Congressional Committee on Health, was in charge of preparing draft legislation and evaluating legislation received by Congress.

Together with Dr. Alvarado, the Kativo staff worked to prepare draft legislation addressing the problem of inhalant addicted children. At the same time, five Congressmen drafted a proposed law that required the use of oil of mustard in locally produced or imported solvent based adhesives.

In June 1988, Dr. Alvarado asked the Congressional Committee on Health to reject the legislation proposed by the five congressmen. Alvarado was given 60 days to present a complete draft of legislation. In August 1988, however, he retired from his position and Kativo lost its primary communication channel with the Committee. This was critical because Beto was relying on Alvarado to help insure that the legislation reflected the technical information that he had collected.

The company did not have an active lobbying or government monitoring function in Tegucigalpa, the capital, which tends to be isolated from the rest of the country. (In fact, the company's philosophy has generally been not to lobby on behalf of its own narrow self-interest.) Beto, located in San Pedro Sula, had no staff support to help him monitor political developments. Monitoring, unfortunately, was an addition to his regularly, daily responsibilities. His ability to keep track of political developments were made more difficult by the fact that he traveled about 45 percent of the time outside of Honduras. It took over two months for Beto to learn of Alvarado's departure from government. When the legislation was passed in March, he was completely absorbed in reviewing strategic plans for the nine-country divisions which report to him.

On March 30, 1989, the Honduran Congress approved the legislation drafted by the five congressmen.

After the law's passage Beto spoke to the press about the problems with the legislation. He argued:

> This type of cement is utilized in industry, in crafts, in the home, schools, and other places where it has become indispensable; thus by altering the product, he said, not only will the drug addiction problem not be solved, but rather, the country's development would be slowed.

> In order to put an end to the inhalation of Resistol by dozens of people, various products which are daily necessities would have to be eliminated from the marketplace. This is impossible, he added, since it would mean a serious setback to industry at several levels . . .

> There are studies that show that the problem is not the glue itself, but rather the individual. The mere removal of this substance would immediately be substituted by some other, to play the same hallucinogenic trip for the person who was sniffing it.

H. B. FULLER: THE CORPORATE RESPONSE

In late April 1986, Elmer Andersen, H. B. Fuller Chairman of the Board, received the following letter:

4/21/86

Elmer L. Andersen
H. B. Fuller Co.

Dear Mr. Andersen

I heard part of your talk on public radio recently, and was favorably impressed with your philosophy that business should not be primarily for profit. This was consistent with my previous impression of H. B. Fuller Co. since I am a public health nurse and have been aware of your benevolence to the nursing profession.

However, on a recent trip to Honduras, I spent some time at a new home for chemically dependent "street boys" who are addicted to glue sniffing. It was estimated that there are 600 of these children still on the streets in San Pedro Sula alone. The glue is sold for repairing *tennis shoes* and I am told it is made by H. B. Fuller in *Costa Rica.* These children also suffer toxic effects of liver and brain damage from the glue . . .

Hearing you on the radio, I immediately wondered how this condemnation of H. B. Fuller Company could be consistent with the company as I knew it before and with your business philosophy.

Are you aware of this problem in Honduras, and, if so, how are you dealing with it?

That a stockholder should write the 76 year old Chairman of the Board directly is significant. Elmer Andersen is a legendary figure in Minnesota. He is responsible for the financial success of H. B. Fuller from 1941–1971 and his values reflected in his actions as CEO are embodied in H. B. Fuller's mission statement.

H. B. FULLER MISSION STATEMENT

The H. B. Fuller corporate mission is to be a leading and profitable worldwide formulator, manufacturer, and marketer of quality specialty chemicals, emphasizing service to customers and managed in accordance with a strategic plan.

H. B. Fuller Company is committed to its responsibilities, in order of priority, to its customers, employees and shareholders. H. B. Fuller will conduct business legally and ethically, support the activities of its employees in their communities, and be a responsible corporate citizen.

It was also Elmer Andersen, who as President and CEO, made the decision that foreign acquisitions should be managed by locals. Concerning the 1967 acquisition of Kativo Chemical Industries Ltd. Elmer Andersen said:

> We had two objectives in mind. One was directly business related and one was altruistic. Just as we had expanded in America, our international business strategy was to pursue markets where our competitors were not active. We were convinced that we had something to offer Latin America that the region did not have locally. In our own small way, we also wanted to be of help to that part of the world. We believed that by producing adhesives in Latin America and by employing only local people, we would create new jobs and help elevate the standard of living. We were convinced that the way to aid world peace was to help Latin America become more prosperous.

Three years later a stockholder dramatically raised the Resistol issue for a second time directly by a stockholder. On June 7, 1989, Vice President for Corporate Relations, Dick Johnson, received a call from a stockholder whose daughter was in the Peace Corps in Honduras. She asked, "How can a company like H. B. Fuller claim to have a social conscience and continue to sell Resistol which is 'literally burning out the brains' of children in Latin America?"

Johnson was galvanized into action. This complaint was of special concern because he was about to meet with a national group of socially responsible investors who were considering including H. B. Fuller's stock in their portfolio. Fortunately Karen Muller, Director of Community Affairs, had been keeping a file on the glue sniffing problem. Within 24 hours of receiving the call, Dick had written a memo to CEO Tony Andersen.

In that memo he set forth the basic values to be considered as H. B. Fuller wrestled with the problem. Among them were the following:

1. H. B. Fuller's explicitly stated public concern about substance abuse.
2. H. B. Fuller's "Concern for Youth" focus in its community affairs projects.
3. H. B. Fuller's reputation as a socially responsible company.
4. H. B. Fuller's history of ethical conduct.
5. H. B. Fuller's commitment to the intrinsic value of each individual.

Whatever "solution" was ultimately adopted would have to be consistent with these values. In addition, Dick suggested a number of options including the company's withdrawal from the market or perhaps altering the formula to make Resistol a water-based product, eliminating sniffing as an issue.

Tony responded by suggesting that Dick create a task force to find a solution and a plan to implement it. Dick decided to accept Beto's invitation to travel to Honduras to view the situation first hand. He understood that the problem crossed functional and divisional responsibilities. Given H. B.

Fuller's high visibility as a socially responsible corporation, the glue sniffing problem had the potential for becoming a public relations nightmare. The brand name of one of H. B. Fuller's products had become synonymous with a serious social problem. Additionally, Dick understood that there was an issue larger than product misuse involved, and it had social and community ramifications. The issue was substance abuse by children, whether the substance is a H. B. Fuller product or not. As a part of the solution, a community relations response was required. Therefore, he invited Karen to join him on his trip to Honduras.

Karen recalled a memo she had written about a year earlier directed to Beto. In it she had suggested a community relations approach rather than Beto's government relations approach. In that memo Karen wrote:

> This community relations process involves developing a community-wide coalition from all those with a vested interest in solving the community issue— those providing services in dealing with the street children and drug users, other businesses, and the government. It does require leadership over the long-term both with a clear set of objectives and a commitment on the part of each group represented to share in the solution . . .

In support of the community relations approach Karen argued that:

1. It takes the focus and pressure off H. B. Fuller as one individual company.
2. It can educate the broader community and focus on the best solution, not just the easiest ones.
3. It holds everyone responsible, the government, educators, H. B. Fuller's customers, legitimate consumers of our product, social service workers and agencies.
4. It provides H. B. Fuller with an expanded good image as a company that cares and will stay with the problem—that we are willing to go the second mile.
5. It can de-politicize the issue.
6. It offers the opportunity to counterbalance the negative impact of the use of our product name Resistol by re-identifying the problem.

Karen and Dick left on a four day trip to Honduras September 18. Upon arriving they were joined by Beto, Oscar Sahuri, General Manager for Kativo's adhesives business in Honduras, and Jorge Walter Bolanos, Vice-President Director of Finance, Kativo. Karen had also asked Mark Connelly, a health consultant from an international agency working with street children, to join the group. They began the process of looking at all aspects of the situation. Visits to two different small shoe manufacturing shops and a shoe supply distributor helped to clarify the issues around pricing, sales, distribution, and the packaging of the product.

A visit to a well-run shelter for street children provided them with some insight into the dynamics of substance abuse among this vulnerable population in the streets of Tegucigalpa and San Pedro Sula. At a meeting with the officials at the Ministry of Health, they reviewed the issue if implementing the oil-of-mustard law, and the Kativo managers offered to assist the committee as it reviewed the details of the law. In both Tegucigalpa and San Pedro Sula, the National Commission for Technical Assistance to Children in Irregular Situations (CONATNSI), a county-wide association of private and public agencies working with street children, organized meetings of its members at which the Kativo managers offered an explanation of the company's philosophy and the hazards involved in the use of oil of mustard.

As they returned from their trip to Honduras, Karen and Dick had the opportunity to reflect on what they had learned. They agreed that removing Resistol from the market would not resolve the problem. However, the problem was extremely complex. The use of inhalants by street children was a symptom of Honduras' underlying economic problems—problems with social, cultural, and political aspects as well as economic dimensions.

Honduran street children come from many different circumstances. Some are true orphans while others are abandoned. Some are runaways, while others are working the streets to help support their parents. Children working at street jobs or begging usually earn more than the minimum wage. Nevertheless, they are often punished if they bring home too little. This creates a vicious circle; they would rather be on the street than take punishment at home—a situation that increases the likelihood they will fall victim to drug addiction. The street children's problems are exacerbated by the general lack of opportunities and a lack of enforcement of school attendance laws. In addition, the police sometimes abuse street children.

Karen and Dick realized that Resistol appeared to be the drug of choice for young street children, and were able to obtain it in a number of different ways. There was no clear pattern, and hence the solution could not be found in simply changing some features of the distribution system. Children might obtain the glue from legitimate customers, small shoe repair stalls, by theft, from "illegal" dealers or from third parties who purchased it from legitimate stores and then sold it to children. For some sellers the sale of Resistol to children could be profitable. The glue was available in small packages which made it more affordable, but the economic circumstances of the typical legitimate customer made packaging in small packages economically sensible.

The government had long been unstable. As a result there was a tendency for people working with the government to hope that new policy initiatives would fade away within a few months. Moreover there was a large continuing turnover of government, so that any knowledge of H. B. Fuller and its corporate philosophy soon disappeared. Government officials usually had to settle for a quick fix, for they were seldom around long enough to manage any other kind of policy. Although it was on the books for six months by the time of their trip, the oil-of-mustard law had not yet been implemented, and national elections were to be held in three months. During meetings with government officials, it appeared to Karen and Dick that no further actions would be taken as current officials waited for the election outcome.

Kativo company officers, Jorge Walter Bolanos and Humberto Larach, discussed continuing the government relations strategy hoping that the law might be repealed or modified. They were also concerned with the damage done to H. B. Fuller's image. Karen and Dick thought the focus should be on community relations. From their perspective, efforts directed toward changing the law seemed important but would do nothing to help with the long term solution to the problems of the street children who abused glue.

Much of the concern for street children was found in private agencies. The chief coordinating association was CONATNSI, created as a result of a seminar sponsored by UNICEF in 1987. CONATNSI was under the direction of a general assembly and a Board of Directors elected by the General Assembly. It began its work in 1988; its objectives included a) improving the quality of services, b) promoting interchange of experiences, c) coordinating human and material resources, d) offering technical support, and e) promoting research. Karen and others believe that CONATNSI had a shortage of both financial and human resources, but it appeared to be well-organized and was a potential intermediary for the company.

As a result of their trip, they knew that a community relations strategy would be complex and risky. H. B. Fuller was committed to a community relations approach, but what would a community relations solution look like in Honduras? The mission statement did not provide a complete answer. It indicated the company had responsibilities to its Honduran customers and employees, but exactly what kind? Were there other responsibilities beyond that directly involving its product? What effect can a single company have in solving an intractable social problem? How should the differing emphases in perspective of Kativo and its parent, H. B. Fuller, be handled? What does corporate citizenship require in situations like this?

NOTES

1. The Subsidiaries of the North Adhesives Division of Kativo Chemical Industries, S.A. go by the name "H. B. Fuller (Country of Operation)," e.g., H. B. Fuller S. A. Honduras. To prevent confusion with the parent company we will refer to H. B. Fuller S. A. Honduras by the name of its parent, "Kativo."
2. The following discussion is based on *Honduras: A Country Study*, 2nd ed., James D. Rudolph, ed. (Washington, D.C.: Department of the Army, 1984).
3. Unless otherwise indicated all references and quotations regarding H. B. Fuller and its subsidiary Kativo Chemical Industries S. A. are from company documents.

SOURCES

Acker, Alison, *The Making of a Banana Republic* (Boston: South End Press, 1988).
Rudolph James D., ed., *Honduras: A Country Study*, 2nd ed. (Washington, D.C.:
Department of the Army, 1984).
H. B. Fuller Company, *A Fuller Life: The Story of H. B. Fuller Company: 1887–1987*
(St. Paul: H. B. Fuller Company, 1986).
Schine, Eric, "Preparing for Banana Republic U.S.," *Corporate Finance* (December,
1987).
Sheehan, Edward, *Agony in the Garden: A Stranger in Central America* (Boston:
Houghton Mifflin, 1989).

A Critique
of Cultural Relativism

CARL WELLMAN

It is often thought that the discoveries of anthropology have revolutionary
implications for ethics. Readers of Sumner, Benedict, and Herskovits are apt
to come away with the impression that the only moral obligation is to conform to one's society, that polygamy is as good as monogamy, or that no
ethical judgment can be rationally justified. While these anthropologists
might complain that they are being misinterpreted, they would not deny that
their real intent is to challenge the traditional view of morals. Even the
anthropologist whose scientific training has made him skeptical of sweeping
generalities and wary of philosophical entanglements is inclined to believe
that the scientific study of cultures has undermined the belief in ethical
absolutes of any kind.

Just what has been discovered that forces us to revise our ethics?
Science has shown that certain things that were once thought to be absolute
are actually relative to culture. Something is relative to culture when it varies
with and is causally determined by culture. Clearly, nothing can be both

From Carl Wellman, "The Ethical Implications of Cultural Relativity," *Journal of Philosophy* LX, No. 7 (1963), 169–84. With omissions. Copyright 1963 by *Journal of Philosophy*.
Reprinted by permission of the Journal of Philosophy and Carl Wellman.

relative to culture and absolute, for to be absolute is to be fixed and invariable, independent of man and the same for all men.

Exactly which things are relative and in what degree is a question still being debated by cultural anthropologists. Important as this question is, I do not propose to discuss it. It is the empirical scientist who must tell us which things vary from culture to culture and to what extent each is causally determined by its culture. It is not for me to question the findings of the anthropologists in this area. Instead, let me turn to the philosophical problem of the implications of cultural relativity. Assuming for the moment that cultural relativity is a fact, what follows for ethics?

What follows depends in part upon just what turns out to be relative. Anthropologists are apt to use the word "values" to refer indiscriminately to the things which have value, the characteristics which give these things their value, the attitudes of the persons who value these things, and the judgments of those people that these things have value. Similarly, one finds it hard to be sure whether "morals" refers to the mores of a people, the set of principles an observer might formulate after observing their conduct, the practical beliefs the people themselves entertain, or the way they feel about certain kinds of conduct. Until such ambiguities are cleared up, one hardly knows what is being asserted when it is claimed that "values" or "morals" are relative.

It seems to me there are . . . different things of interest to the ethicist that the anthropologist might discover to be relative to culture: mores, . . . human nature, acts, goals, . . . moral judgments, and moral reasoning. Since I can hardly discuss all the ethical conclusions that various writers have tried to draw from these different facts of cultural relativity, what I propose to do is to examine critically the reasoning by which one ethical conclusion might be derived from each of them.

MORES

It has long been recognized that mores are relative to culture. Mores are those customs which are enforced by social pressure. They are established patterns of action to which the individual is expected to conform and from which he deviates only at the risk of disapproval and punishment. It seems clear that mores vary from society to society and that the mores of any given society depend upon its culture. What does this imply for ethics?

The conclusion most frequently drawn is that what is right in one society may be wrong in another. For example, although it would be wrong for one of us to kill his aged parents, this very act is right for an Eskimo. This is because our mores are different from those of Eskimo society, and it is the mores that make an act right or wrong.

Let us grant, for the sake of discussion, that different societies do have different mores. Why should we grant that the mores make an act right or wrong? It has been claimed that this is true by definition. "Right" simply means according to the mores, and "wrong" means in violation of the mores. There is something to be said for this analysis of our concepts of right and wrong. It seems to explain both the imperativeness and the impersonality of obligation. The "ought" seems to tell one what to do and yet to be more than the command of any individual; perhaps its bindingness lies in the demands of society. Attractive as this interpretation appears at first glance, I cannot accept it. It can be shown that no naturalistic analysis of the meaning of ethical words is adequate. In addition, this particular analysis is objectionable in that it makes it self-contradictory to say that any customary way of acting is wrong. No doubt social reformers are often confused, but they are not always inconsistent.

If the view that the mores make an act right or wrong is not true by definition, it amounts to the moral principle that one ought always to con- form to the mores of his society. None of the ways in which this principle is usually supported is adequate. (a) Any society unconsciously develops those mores which are conducive to survival and well-being under its special circumstances. Each individual ought to obey the mores of his society be- cause this is the best way to promote the good life for the members of that society. I admit that there is a tendency for any society to develop those mores which fit its special circumstances, but I doubt that this is more than a tendency. There is room for reform in most societies, and this is particularly true when conditions are changing for one reason or another. (b) One ought to obey the mores of his society because disobedience would tend to destroy those mores. Without mores any society would lapse into a state of anarchy that would be intolerable for its members. It seems to me that this argument deserves to be taken seriously, but it does not prove that one ought always to obey the mores of his society. What it does show is that one ought generally to obey the mores of his society and that whenever he considers disobedience he should give due weight to the effects of his example upon social stability. (c) One ought to obey the mores of his society because disobedience tends to undermine their existence. It is important to preserve the mores, not simply to avoid anarchy, but because it is their mores which give shape and meaning to the life of any people. I grant that the individual does tend to think of his life in terms of the mores of his group and that anything which disrupts those mores tends to rob his life of significance. But once again, all this shows is that one should conform to the mores of his society on the whole. Although there is some obligation to conformity, this is not the only nor the most important obligation on the member of any society.

Therefore, it does not seem to me that one can properly say that the mores make an act right or wrong. One cannot define the meaning of these ethical words in terms of the mores, nor can one maintain the ethical principle that one ought always to obey the mores of his society. If the mores do not make acts right or wrong, the fact that different societies have different mores does not imply that the same kind of act can be right in one society and wrong in another. . . .

HUMAN NATURE

Another thing which may be relative to culture is human nature. As soon as one ponders the differences between the Chinese aristocrat and the Australian bushman, the American tycoon and the Indian yogi, one finds it hard to believe that there is anything basic to human nature which is shared by all men. And reflection upon the profound effects of enculturation easily leads one to the conclusion that what a man is depends upon the society in which he has been brought up. Therefore, let us assume that human nature is culturally relative and see what this implies.

This seems to imply that no kind of action, moral character, or social institution is made inevitable by human nature. This conclusion is important because it cuts the ground out from under one popular type of justification in ethics. For example, capitalism is sometimes defended as an ideal on the grounds that this is the only economic system that is possible in the light of man's greedy and competitive nature. Or it might be claimed that adultery is permissible because the ideal of marital fidelity runs counter to man's innate drives or instincts. If there is no fixed human nature, such arguments are left without any basis.

One may wonder, however, whether the only alternatives are entirely fixed and an entirely plastic human nature. It might be the enculturation could mold a human being but only within certain limits. These limits might exist either because certain parts of human nature are not at all plastic or because all parts are only moderately plastic. For example, it might turn out that the need for food and the tendency to grow in a certain way cannot be modified at all by enculturation, or it might turn out that every element in human nature can be modified in some ways but not in others. In either case, what a man becomes would depend partly upon enculturation and partly upon the nature of the organism being enculturated.

Thus cultural relativity may be a matter of degree. Before we can decide just what follows from the fact that human nature is relative to culture we must know how far and in what ways it is relative. If there are certain limits to the plasticity of human nature, these do rule out some kinds of action, character, or institution. But anthropology indicates that within any such limits a great many alternatives remain. Human nature may make eating inevitable, but what we eat and when we eat and how we eat is up to us. At least we can say that to the degree that human nature is relative to culture no kind of action, moral character, or social institution is made impossible by human nature.

ACTS

It has been claimed that acts are also relative to culture. This is to say that the same general type of action may take on specific differences when performed in different societies because those societies have different cultures. For example, it is one thing for one of us to kill his aged parent; it is quite a different thing for an Eskimo to do such an act. One difference lies in the consequences of these two acts. In our society disposing of old and useless parents merely allows one to live in greater luxury; to an Eskimo this act may mean the difference between barely adequate subsistence and malnutrition for himself and his family. What are we to make of this fact that the nature of an act is culturally relative?

One possible conclusion is that the same kind of act may be right in one society and wrong in another. This presupposes that the rightness of an act depends upon its consequences and that its consequences may vary from society to society. Since I accept these presuppositions, I agree that the rightness or wrongness of an act is relative to its social context.

It is important, however, to distinguish this conclusion from two others with which it is often confused. To say that the rightness of an act is relative to the society in which it is performed is not to say that exactly the same sort of act can be both right and wrong. It is because the social context makes the acts different in kind that one can be right while the other is wrong. Compare an act of infanticide in our society with an act of infanticide in some South Seas society. Are these two acts the same or different? They are of the same kind inasmuch as both are acts of killing an infant. On the other hand, they are different in that such an act may be necessary to preserve the balance between family size and food resources in the South Seas while this is not the case in our society. These two acts are generically similar but specifically different; that is, they belong to different species of the same genus. Therefore, the conclusion that the same kind of act may be right in one society and wrong in another does not amount to saying that two acts which are precisely the same in every respect may differ in rightness or wrongness.

Neither is this conclusion to be confused with the view that acts are made right or wrong by the mores of society. No doubt our society disapproves of infanticide and some South Seas societies approve of it, but it is not this which makes infanticide wrong for us and right for them. If infanticide is wrong for us and right for them, it is because acts of infanticide have very different consequences in our society and in theirs, not because the practice is discouraged here and customary there.

GOALS

The goals that individuals or groups aim for also seem relative to culture. What objects people select as goals vary from society to society depending upon the cultures of those societies. One group may strive for social prestige and the accumulation of great wealth, another may aim at easy comfort and the avoidance of any danger, a third may seek military glory and the conquest of other peoples. What follows from this fact of cultural relativity?

This fact is often taken as a basis for arguing that it is impossible to compare the value of acts, institutions, or total ways of life belonging to different societies. The argument rests on the assumptions that acts, institutions, and ways of life are means directed at certain ends, that means can be evaluated only in terms of their ends, and that ends are incommensurable with respect to value.

Granted these assumptions, the argument seems a good one, but I doubt that ends are really incommensurable. It seems to me that we can recognize that certain ends are more worthwhile than others, for example that pleasure is intrinsically better than pain. I may be mistaken, but until this has been shown, the conclusion that it is impossible to compare the value of acts, institutions, or ways of life belonging to different societies has not been established. . . .

MORAL JUDGMENTS

The aspect of cultural relativity most often emphasized is that pertaining to moral judgments. Objects that the members of one society think to be good are considered bad by another group; acts considered wrong in one society are thought of as right in another. Moreover, these differences in judgments of value and obligation seem to reflect cultural differences between the respective societies. There is a great deal of evidence to suggest that ethical judgments are relative to culture.

To many anthropologists and philosophers it is a corollary of this fact that one of a set of contrary ethical judgments is no more valid than another, or, put positively, that all ethical judgments are equally valid. Unfortunately, there is a crucial ambiguity lurking in this epistemological thicket. Ethical judgments might have equal validity either because all are valid or because none are: similarly one ethical judgment might be no more valid than another either because both are equally valid or because both are equally lacking in validity. Since these two interpretations are quite different, let us consider them separately.

On the first interpretation, the conclusion to be drawn from the fact that ethical judgments are relative to culture is that every moral judgment is valid for the society in which it is made. Instead of denying the objective validity of ethical judgments, this view affirms it, but in a qualified form which will allow for the variations in ethical belief.

There seem to be three main ways of defending this position. (a) Ethical judgments have objective validity because it is possible to justify them rationally. However, this validity is limited to a given society because the premises used in such justification are those which are agreed upon in that society. Since there are no universally accepted premises, no universal validity is possible. I would wish to deny that justification is real if it is limited in this way. If all our reasoning really does rest on certain premises which can be rejected by others without error, then we must give up the claim to objective validity. When I claim validity for ethical judgments, I intend to claim more than that it is possible to support them with logical arguments; I also claim that it is incorrect to deny the premises of such arguments. (b) Any ethical judgment is an expression of a total pattern of culture. Hence it is possible to justify any single judgment in terms of its coherence with the total cultural configuration of the judger. But one cannot justify the culture as a whole, for it is not part of a more inclusive pattern. Therefore, ethical judgments have objective validity, but only in terms of a given cultural pattern. I would make the same objection to this view as to the preceding one. Since it allows justification to rest upon an arbitrary foundation, it is inadequate to support any significant claim to objective validity. (c) Any ethical judgment has objective validity because it is an expression of a moral code. The validity of a moral code rests on the fact that without conformity to a common code social cohesion breaks down, leading to disastrous results. Since any given moral code provides cohesion for one and only one society, each ethical judgment has validity for a single society. There are at least two difficulties with this defense of objectivity. Surely one could deny some ethical judgments without destroying the entire moral code they reflect; not every judgment could be shown to be essential to social stability. Moreover, the argument seems to rest on the ethical judgment that one ought not to contribute to the breakdown of social stability. How is this judgment to be shown to be valid? One must either appeal to some other basis of validity or argue in a circle. None of these arguments to show that every moral judgment is valid for the society in which it is made is adequate.

On the second interpretation, the conclusion to be drawn from the fact that moral judgments are relative to culture is that moral judgments have no objective validity. This amounts to saying that the distinction between true and false, correct and incorrect, does not apply to such judgments. This conclusion obviously does not follow simply from the fact that people disagree about ethical questions. We do not deny the objective validity of scientific judgments either on the grounds that different scientists propose alternative theories or on the grounds that the members of some societies hold fast to many unscientific beliefs.

Why, then, does the fact that moral judgments are relative to culture imply that they have no objective validity? (a) Individuals make different ethical judgments because they judge in terms of different frames of reference, and they adopt these frames of reference uncritically from their cultures. Since ethical judgments are the product of enculturation rather than reasoning, they cannot claim rational justification. I do not find this argument convincing, for it seems to confuse the origin of a judgment with its justification. The causes of a judgment are one thing; the reasons for or against it are another. It remains to be shown that any information about what causes us to judge as we do has any bearing on the question of whether or not our judgments are correct. (b) It is impossible to settle ethical questions by using the scientific method. Therefore, there is no objective way to show that one ethical judgment is any more correct than another, and, in the absence of any method of establishing the claim to objective validity, it makes no sense to continue to make the claim. I will concede that, if there is no rational method of establishing ethical judgments, then we might as well give up the claim to objective validity. And if the scientific method is restricted to the testing of hypotheses by checking the predictions they imply against the results of observation and experiment, it does seem to be inapplicable to ethical questions. What I will not concede is the tacit assumption that the scientific method is the only method of establishing the truth. Observation and experimentation do not figure prominently in the method used by mathematicians. I even wonder whether the person who concludes that ethical judgments have no objective validity can establish this conclusion by using the scientific method. The fact that ethical judgments cannot be established scientifically does not by itself prove that they cannot be established by any method of reasoning. (c) There might be some method of settling ethical disputes, but it could not be a method of reasoning. Any possible reasoning would have to rest upon certain premises. Since the members of different societies start from different premises, there is no basis for argument that does not beg the question. I suspect, however, that we have been looking for our premises in the wrong place. The model of deduction tempts us to search for very general premises from which all our more specific judgments can be deduced. Unfortunately, it is just in this area of universal moral principles that disagreement seems most frequent and irremedial. But suppose that these ethical generalizations are themselves inductions based upon particular moral judgments. Then we could argue for or against them in terms of relatively specific ethical judgments and the factual judgments that are in turn relevant to these. Until this possibility is explored further, we need not admit that there is no adequate basis for ethical reasoning. Thus it appears that none of these refutations of the objective validity of ethical judgments is really conclusive.

The fact that ethical judgments are relative to culture is often taken to prove that no ethical judgment can claim to be any more valid than any of its contraries. I have tried to show that, on neither of the two possible interpretations of this conclusion, does the conclusion necessarily follow from the fact of cultural relativity.

MORAL REASONING

Finally, moral reasoning might turn out to be relative to culture. When some ethical statement is denied or even questioned, the person who made the statement is apt to leap to its defense. He attempts to justify his statement by producing reasons to support it. But speakers from different societies tend to justify their statements in different ways. The difference in their reasoning may be of two kinds. Either their reasoning may rest on different assumptions or they may draw inferences in a different manner. That is, the arguments they advance may either start from different premises or obey different logics. We can ignore the former case here; for it boils down to a difference in their judgments, and we have discussed that at length in the preceding section. Instead let us assume that people who belong to different societies tend to draw their moral conclusions according to different logics depending upon their respective cultures. What difference would it make if moral reasoning were thus culturally relative?

The most interesting conclusion that might be drawn from the fact that moral reasoning is relative to culture is that it has no objective validity. The claim to objective validity is empty where it cannot be substantiated. But how could one justify the claim that any given kind of moral reasoning is valid? To appeal to the same kind of reasoning would be circular. To appeal to some other kind of reasoning would not be sufficient to justify this kind; for each kind of reasoning involves principles of inference which go beyond, and therefore cannot be justified by appealing to, any other kind.

I find this line of argument inconclusive for several reasons. First, it is not clear that a given kind of reasoning cannot be justified by appealing to a different kind of reasoning. In fact, this seems to be a fairly common practice in logic. Various forms of syllogistic argument can be shown to be valid by reducing them to arguments of the form Barbara. Again, a logician will sometimes justify certain rules for natural deduction by an involved logical argument which does not itself use these same rules. Second, in what sense is it impossible to show another person that my moral arguments are valid? I can show him that the various moral arguments I advance conform to the principles of my logic. If he does not accept these principles, he will remain unconvinced. This may show that I cannot persuade him that my arguments are valid, but does it show that I have not proved that they are? It is not obvious that persuading a person and proving a point are identical. Third, is the claim to objective validity always empty in the absence of any justification for it? Perhaps some reasoning is ultimate in that it requires no further justification. To assume the opposite seems to lead to an infinite regress. If every valid justification stands in need of further justification, no amount of justification would ever be sufficient.

I do not claim to have established the objective validity of moral reasoning. I am not even sure how that validity might be established or even whether it needs to be established. All I have been trying to do is to suggest that such validity is not ruled out by the fact, if it is a fact, that moral reasoning is relative to culture. . . .

Ethics and the Foreign Corrupt Practices Act

MARK PASTIN AND MICHAEL HOOKER

Not long ago it was feared that as a fallout of Watergate, government officials would be hamstrung by artificially inflated moral standards. Recent events, however, suggest that the scapegoat of post-Watergate morality may have become American business rather than government officials.

One aspect of the recent attention paid to corporate morality is the controversy surrounding payments made by American corporations to foreign officials for the purpose of securing business abroad. Like any law or system of laws, the Foreign Corrupt Practices Act (FCPA), designed to control or eliminate such payments, should be grounded in morality, and should therefore be judged from an ethical perspective. Unfortunately, neither the law nor the question of its repeal has been adequately addressed from that perspective.

On December 20, 1977, President Carter signed into law S.305, the Foreign Corrupt Practices Act (FCPA), which makes it a crime for American corporations to offer or provide payments to officials of foreign governments for the purpose of obtaining or retaining business. The FCPA also established record keeping requirements for publicly held corporations to make it difficult to conceal political payments proscribed by the Act. Violators of the FCPA, both corporations and managers, face severe penalties. A company may be fined up to $1 million, while its officers who directly participated in violations of the Act or had reason to know of such violations face up to five years in prison and/or $10,000 in fines. The Act also prohibits corporations from indemnifying fines imposed on their directors, officers, employees, or agents. The Act does not prohibit "grease" payments to foreign government employees whose duties are primarily ministerial or clerical, since such payments are sometimes required to persuade the recipients to perform their normal duties.

At the time of this writing, the precise consequences of the FCPA for American business are unclear, mainly because of confusion surrounding

Mark Pastin and Michael Hooker, "Ethics and the Foreign Corrupt Practices Act," *Business Horizons*, December 1980, pp. 43–47. Copyright, 1980 by the Foundation for the School of Business at Indiana University. Reprinted by permission.

the government's enforcement intentions. Vigorous objections have been raised against the Act by corporate attorneys and recently by a few government officials. Among the latter is Frank A. Weil, former Assistant Secretary of Commerce, who has stated, "The questionable payments problem may turn out to be one of the most serious impediments to doing business in the rest of the world.[1]

The potentially severe economic impact of the FCPA was highlighted by the fall 1978 report of the Export Disincentives Task Force, which was created by the White House to recommend ways of improving our balance of trade. The Task Force identified the FCPA as contributing significantly to economic and political losses in the United States. Economic losses come from constricting the ability of American corporations to do business abroad, and political losses come from the creation of a holier-than-thou image.

The Task Force made three recommendations in regard to the FCPA:

> The Justice Department should issue guidelines on its enforcement policies and establish procedures by which corporations could get advance government reaction to anticipated payments to foreign officials.
>
> The FCPA should be amended to remove enforcement from the SEC, which now shares enforcement responsibility with the Department of Justice.
>
> The administration should periodically report to Congress and the public on export losses caused by the FCPA.

In response to the Task Force's report, the Justice Department, over SEC objections, drew up guidelines to enable corporations to check any proposed action possibly in violation of the FCPA. In response to such an inquiry, the Justice Department would inform the corporation of its enforcement intentions. The purpose of such an arrangement is in part to circumvent the intent of the law. As of this writing, the SEC appears to have been successful in blocking publication of the guidelines. Being more responsive to political winds, Justice may be less inclined than the SEC to rigidly enforce the Act.

Particular concern has been expressed about the way in which bookkeeping requirements of the Act will be enforced by the SEC. The act requires that company records will "accurately and fairly reflect the transactions and dispositions of the assets of the issuer." What is at question is the interpretation of the Sec will give to the requirement and the degree of accuracy and detail it will demand. The SEC's post-Watergate behavior suggests that it will be rigid in requiring the disclosure of all information that bears on financial relationships between the company and any foreign or domestic public official. This level of accountability in record keeping, to which auditors and corporate attorneys have strongly objected, goes far beyond previous SEC requirements that records display only facts material to the financial position of the company.

Since the potential consequences of the FCPA for American businesses and business managers are very serious, it is important that the Act have a rationale capable of bearing close scrutiny. In looking at the foundation of the FCPA, it should be noted that its passage followed in the wake of intense newspaper coverage of the financial dealings of corporations. Such media attention was engendered by the dramatic disclosure of corporate slush funds during the Watergate hearings and by a voluntary disclosure program established shortly thereafter by the SEC. As a result of the SEC program, more than 400 corporations, including 117 of the Fortune 500, admitted to making more than $300 million in foreign political payments in less than ten years.

Throughout the period of media coverage leading up to passage of the FCPA, and especially during the hearings on the Act, there was in all public discussions of the issue a tone of righteous moral indignation at the idea of American companies making foreign political payments. Such payments were ubiquitously termed "bribes," although many of these could more accurately be called extortions, while others were more akin to brokers' fees or sales commissions.

American business can be faulted for its reluctance during this period to bring to public attention the fact that in a very large number of countries, payments to foreign officials are virtually required for doing business. Part of that reluctance, no doubt, comes from the awkwardly difficult position of attempting to excuse bribery or something closely resembling it. There is a popular abhorrence in this country of bribery directed at domestic government officials, and that abhorrence transfers itself to payments directed toward foreign officials as well.

Since its passage, the FCPA has been subjected to considerable critical analysis, and many practical arguments have been advanced in favor of its repeal.[2] However, there is always lurking in back of such analyses the uneasy feeling that no matter how strong considerations of practicality and economics may count against this law, the fact remains that the law protects morality in forbidding bribery. For example, Gerald McLaughlin, professor of law at Fordham, has shown persuasively that where the legal system of a foreign country affords inadequate protection against the arbitrary exercise of power to the disadvantage of American corporations, payments to foreign officials may be required to provide a compensating mechanism against the use of such arbitrary power. McLaughlin observes, however, that "this does not mean that taking advantage of the compensating mechanism would necessarily make the payment moral."[3]

The FCPA, and questions regarding its enforcement or repeal, will not be addressed adequately until an effort has been made to come to terms with the Act's foundation on morality. While it may be very difficult, or even impossible, to legislate morality (that is, to change the moral character and sentiments of people by passing laws that regulate their behavior), the existing laws undoubtedly still reflect the moral beliefs we hold. Passage of the

FCPA in Congress was eased by the simple connection most Congressmen made between bribery, seen as morally repugnant, and the Act, which is designed to prevent bribery.

Given the importance of the FCPA to American business and labor, it is imperative that attention be given to the question of whether there is adequate moral justification for law. The question we will address is not whether each payment prohibited by the FCPA is moral or immoral, but rather, whether the FCPA, given all its consequences and ramifications, is itself moral. It is well known that morally sound laws and institutions may tolerate some immoral acts. The First Amendment's guarantee of freedom of speech allows individuals to utter racial slurs. And immoral laws and institutions may have some beneficial consequences, for example, segregationist legislation bringing deep-seated racism into the national limelight. But our concern is with the overall morality of the FCPA.

The ethical tradition has two distinct ways of assessing social institutions, including laws: *End-Point Assessment and Rule Assessment.* Since there is no consensus as to which approach is correct, we will apply both types of assessment to the FCPA.

The End-Point approach assesses a law in terms of its contribution to general social well-being. The ethical theory underlying End-Point Assessment is utilitarianism. According to utilitarianism, a law is morally sound if and only if the law promotes the well-being of those affected by the law to the greatest extent practically achievable. To satisfy the utilitarian principle, a law must promote the well-being of those affected by it at least as well as any alternative law that we might propose, and better than no law at all. A conclusive End-Point Assessment of a law requires specification of what constitutes the welfare of those affected by the law, which the liberal tradition generally sidesteps by identifying an individual's welfare with what he takes to be in his interests.

Considerations raised earlier in the paper suggested that the FCPA does not pass the End-Point test. The argument is not the too facile one that we could propose a better law. (Amendments to the FCPA are now being considered.[4]) The argument is that it may be better to have *no* such law than to have the FCPA. The main domestic consequences of the FCPA seem to include an adverse effect on the balance of payments, a loss of business and jobs, and another opportunity for the SEC and the Justice Department to compete. These negative effects must be weighed against possible gains in the conduct of American business within the United States. From the perspective of foreign countries in which American firms do business, the main consequence of the FCPA seems to be that certain officials now accept bribes and influence from non-American businesses. It is hard to see that who pays bribes makes much difference to these nations.

Rule Assessment of the morality of laws is often favored by those who find that End-Point Assessment is too lax in supporting their moral codes.

According to the Rule Assessment approach: A law is morally sound if and only if the law accords with a code embodying correct ethical rules. This approach has no content until the rules are stated, and different rules will lead to different ethical assessments. Fortunately, what we have to say about Rule Assessment of the FCPA does not depend on the details of a particular ethical code.

Those who regard the FCPA as a worthwhile expression of morality, despite the adverse effects on American business and labor, clearly subscribe to a rule stating that it is unethical to bribe. Even if it is conceded that the payments proscribed by the FCPA warrant classifications as bribes, citing a rule prohibiting bribery does not suffice to justify the FCPA.

Most of the rules in an ethical code are not *categorical* rules; they are *prima facie* rules. A categorical rule does not allow exceptions, whereas a prima facie rule does. The ethical rule that a person ought to keep promises is an example of a prima facie rule. If I promise to loan you a book on nuclear energy and later find out that you are a terrorist building a private atomic bomb, I am ethically obligated not to keep my promise. The rule that one ought to keep promises is "overridden" by the rule that one ought to prevent harm to others.

A rule prohibiting bribery is a prima facie rule. There are cases in which morality requires that a bribe be paid. If the only way to get essential medical care for a dying child is to bribe a doctor, morality requires one to bribe the doctor. So adopting an ethical code which includes a rule prohibiting the payment of bribes does not guarantee that a Rule Assessment of the FCPA will be favorable to it.

The fact that the FCPA imposes a cost on American business and labor weighs against the prima facie obligation not to bribe. If we suppose that American corporations have obligations, tantamount to promises, to promote the job security of their employees and the investments of shareholders, these obligations will also weigh against the obligation not to bribe. Again, if government legislative and enforcement bodies have an obligation to secure the welfare of American business and workers, the FCPA may force them to violate their public obligations.

The FCPA's moral status appears even more dubious if we note that many of the payments prohibited by the Act are neither bribes nor share features that make bribes morally reprehensible. Bribes are generally held to be malefic if they persuade one to act against his good judgment, and consequently purchase an inferior product. But the payments at issue in the FCPA are usually extorted *from the seller*. Further it is arguable that not paying the bribe is more likely to lead to purchase of an inferior product than paying the bribe. Finally, bribes paid to foreign officials may not involve deception when they accord with recognized local practices.

In conclusion, neither End-Point nor Rule Assessment uncovers a sound moral basis for the FCPA. It is shocking to find that a law prohibiting bribery has no clear moral basis, and may even be an immoral law. However, this is precisely what examination of the FCPA from a moral perspective reveals. This is symptomatic of the fact that moral conceptions which were appropriate to a simpler world are not adequate to the complex world in which contemporary business functions. Failure to appreciate this point often leads to righteous condemnation of business, when it should lead to careful reflection on one's own moral preconceptions.

ADDENDUM TO "ETHICS AND THE FOREIGN CORRUPT PRACTICES ACT," AUGUST 1981

There has been an increasing outcry against the FCPA since this article originally appeared. The Reagan administration has called for weakening of the law, especially the burdensome accounting provisions. While we view such weakening of the law as commendable, on the ground that it decreases the cost of the law to business and the American public, the key issue has not been joined. That issue is whether the payments proscribed by the law, heavy-handedly or otherwise, are in fact unethical. There is no doubt that many executives and government officials hold the view that these payments are not unethical. But it is unacceptable to publicly argue that bribes to foreign officials are ethical. Thus it will take considerable audacity to argue for total repeal of the FCPA. Only an increasing appreciation of the barriers to international trade attributable to the law, and of the ethical pointlessness of the law, can be effective.

MARK PASTIN

NOTES

1. *National Journal*, June 3, 1978: 880.
2. David C. Gustman, "The Foreign Corrupt Practices Act of 1977," *The Journal of International Law and Economics*, Vol. 13, 1979:367–401; and Walter S. Surrey, "The Foreign Corrupt Practices Act: Let the Punishment Fit the Crime," *Harvard International Law Journal*, Spring 1979: 203–303.
3. Gerald T. McLaughlin, "The Criminalization of Questionable Foreign Payments by Corporations," *Fordham Law Review*, Vol. 46: 1095.
4. "Foreign Bribery Law Amendments Drafted," *American Bar Association Journal*, February 1980: 135.

Moral Dimensions of the Foreign Corrupt Practices Act: Comments on Pastin and Hooker

KENNETH D. ALPERN

Michael Hooker and Mark Pastin[1] claim that the Foreign Corrupt Practices Act (FCPA) is not supported by either utilitarian or deontological ("rule-based") moral considerations. I will argue that deontological moral considerations do in fact support the FCPA and that much utilitarian criticism of it is not conceptually well-founded.[2]

Hooker and Pastin offer two argument sketches intended to show that the Act does not receive support from deontological considerations. Spelling out the first gives roughly this:

1. The FCPA is essentially a prohibition of bribery. (Allow for the sake of argument.)
2. Bribery is morally wrong in the sense that there is a *prima facie* moral obligation not to engage in bribery.
3. Corporations have (*prima facie*) moral obligations to protect the investments of their shareholders and the jobs of their employees. The federal government may also have a *prima facie* moral obligation to secure the welfare of American business and workers.
4. There are situations governed by the FCPA in which the *prima facie* moral obligations of corporations and government override the *prima facie* moral obligations not to bribe.[3]
5. Situations in which the FCPA requires actions that are thus contrary to morality are numerous or of great moral moment.
6. Therefore, the FCPA does not have the support of morality from a deontological perspective.

There is much to agree with in this argument. Its pattern of reasoning is good—the premises do license the conclusion. It is certainly the case that any moral rule prohibiting bribery cannot be absolute. And it is surely true that corporations have some sort of obligation to pursue profit. It could even be allowed that situations are conceivable in which the prohibition of bribery is overridden by other moral obligations of corporations. Nonetheless, the conclusion of the argument is still false.

Kenneth D. Alpern, "Moral Dimensions of the Foreign Corrupt Practices Act: Comments on Hooker and Pastin." Reprinted with permission of the author.

Much of the argument's appeal derives from its apparent discovery of a second moral principle, the principle that promises should be kept. In situations covered by the FCPA, the principle of promise-keeping is supposed to weigh against and outweigh the moral principle prohibiting bribery, though Hooker and Pastin do not go far enough into the argument to indicate which sorts of considerations are supposed to tip the scales in favor of promise-keeping.

Against this position I will argue that the supposed conflict is only apparent and that the introduction of the rule of promise-keeping at this place in the argument is misleading and largely irrelevant. Furthermore, I will argue that the moral considerations which do properly stand in the place thought to be held by the obligation to keep promises are insufficient on conceptual grounds to justify bribery. In order to make my case, it is necessary to look more closely at the way obligations to keep promises enter the picture.

Hooker and Pastin mention three specific obligations deriving from the principle of promise-keeping: (1) an obligation of corporations to promote the investments of their shareholders; (2) an obligation of corporations to protect the security of their employees' jobs; and (3) an obligation which the federal government may possibly be under to protect the welfare of American business and workers. I will focus on the first obligation, which I take to be most important, and comment only briefly on the other two obligations.

The obligation of corporations to their investors seems to come about in this way: corporations are *agents* for their investors. In effect a corporation says: "If you allow us the use of your capital, we promise to return to work to increase the value of your investment.[4] Having made the promise to act as agents, corporations are morally obligated, by virtue of the moral rule that promises be kept, to promote the financial interests of their principals.

What difference does this promise make to the morality of international corporate bribery? The answer is: none. The promise merely *transfers* the responsibility for looking after the investors' interests. It does nothing to affect the type or weight of claim that can be made on behalf of those interests against other moral considerations. In the situations with which we are concerned, who the guardian is and how that guardianship comes about makes no difference outside the relationship between the agent and the principal. If this were not the case, then one could indefinitely increase the moral righteousness of one's causes merely by enlisting a series of agents each promising the other to pursue one's ends.[5]

Talk of the solemn promises or sacred trusts of corporations, while it may refer to actual obligations, is irrelevant to the issue of the weight of investor interests against moral rules. There is no conflict here between a moral principle requiring that promises be kept and a moral principle prohibiting bribery. What stands in opposition to the moral rule prohibiting bribery is not a moral principle at all, but is, at best, merely the *self-interest* of the investors.

Now it must be recognized that unadorned self-interest may carry moral weight. However, it is quite unlikely that this weight will often be great enough to render international corporate bribery moral. For, first of all, within the deontological perspective (which we are being asked to take), moral rules are just the sort of things that override claims of self-interest. As long as we view morality from this perspective, there is a strong *a priori* reason to hold that the rule prohibiting bribery controls. Second, though the rule prohibiting bribery may have exceptions—e.g., Hooker and Pastin's case of bribing a doctor as the only means by which to secure essential medical treatment for a dying child—the relevant exceptions appear to exhibit two characteristic features: (1) the personal interest at issue is not a mere desire, but a dire need, and (2) the rule is broken on a special occasion, not as a continuing general policy.[6] In contrast, when we are asked to reject the FCPA, we are asked to endorse a *policy* of bribery, and this for the promotion of interests that are not literally matters of life and death. Finally, to the objection that the moral claim of corporate investors' interests is considerable and thus outweighs the bribery rule, it should be pointed out that not all interests are of equal moral weight. Classical utilitarianism is mistaken in holding that equal additions to the sum total happiness or well-being are morally indifferent. For example, an increase in happiness which satisfies a need is of greater moral moment than the same increment added to the total happiness by way of providing someone with adventitious pleasure. It is morally better to raise a person from poverty to security than to add an equal amount to the total happiness in effecting a person's rise from ease to opulence. So, when it comes to comparing personal interests against moral rules, interests based on mere desires, and not needs, have comparatively little moral weight. This point applies to the FCPA in two ways. First, although American investors include pension plans, philanthropic organizations, and people of modest income, "the average American investor" is nonetheless quite comfortable by world standards and return on investment is not a matter of survival. Secondly, even if return on investment were a matter of survival, corporations can and in fact do derive substantial profits from activities not calling for bribery; most American corporations have dealt successfully in international trade without resorting to payments made unlawful by the FCPA.

One misunderstanding of the preceding argument must be forestalled. At issue is not the comparative need of American investors and need of citizens of the country in which the bribery takes place. Rather, the point is that because American investors are, on the whole, not in dire need, the moral weight of their financial interests is small compared to the moral weight of moral *principles.*

It remains to say something, necessarily very brief, about the obligation of corporations to their employees and the obligation of the federal government to American business and workers. First, corporations are not morally obligated to secure profits "by whatever means it takes" in order to fulfill their responsibilities to their employees. There are restrictions, such as those imposed by law. If a corporation fails to meet its obligations due to the costs and effects of adhering to the law, then, other things being equal, the employees can have no *moral* complaint against the corporation.

In addition to restrictions imposed on profit-seeking activities through the law, I submit that there are also moral restrictions. For example, corporations are not morally culpable for reduced profits incurred by a failure to be ruthless, even when ruthlessness is within the limits set by the law. Employees (and other interested parties) cannot complain on *moral* grounds that they have suffered because the corporation failed to cheat, lie, deceive, bribe, or pay extortion.

The situation with respect to the moral obligations of the federal government is similar to that of corporations. Roughly, a government can have no *moral* (contrasted with legal or political) obligation to promote the welfare of its citizens by means which are themselves immoral. Bribery, we have been allowing, is immoral. So the government cannot be morally obligated to promote the welfare of American businesses or workers by allowing bribery.

In their second argument against the FCPA, Hooker and Pastin marshal three distinct considerations behind the idea that "many of the payments prohibited by the Act are neither bribes nor share features that make bribes morally reprehensible": (1) payments often are not bribes, but rather are *extorted* from corporations;[7] (2) failure to make payments may lead to the purchase of what are in fact *inferior* products; and (3) such payments may be in accordance with local practices and so lack the deceptiveness of bribery.

Against these considerations it may be pointed out that a payment needn't be bribery to be morally objectionable. Caving in to extortion demands contributes to corruption and fosters its expansion in the country in which payments are made; it leads to unfair competition if the payments are concealed, and even more immediately to the disintegration of free bargaining and a return to a Hobbesian state of nature—in which anything goes—if they are not. These morally objectionable results will generally outweigh harm resulting from the purchase of inferior products. Engaging in such practices *openly* hardly does much to excuse them.

Some business people may feel that international corporate competition *is* in fact a Hobbesian state of nature. However, this is surely hyperbole: murder is still fairly rare in negotiating contracts; not everyone in the business community behaves like the Mafia. But even if they did, that would not make it *moral* to do so. It is also worth pointing out that the state of nature is not a condition that we *want* to be in—few of us *want* to deal with a government like Amin's Uganda or live in a world in which that was the norm.

Hooker and Pastin's third point, that it would be wrong for us to try to impose our standards in countries in which bribery and extortion are commonly practiced, raises important conceptual issues about intercultural social, legal, and moral standards which are too complex to be treated adequately here. However, I can offer a few comments which I think considerably reduce the problems about how one ought to act. First, it is absolutely essential to distinguish between practices that are engaged in, recognized, even tolerated, and those that are condoned and held to be moral. To say simply that in many countries bribery is the norm disguises the fact that what is regularly done may not be what is held to be proper or moral even in the countries where that is the practice. A rough indicator of international moral judgment is the illegality of bribery in every part of the world.[8] Second, requiring American corporations to adhere to "our" moral standards with respect to bribery and extortion is hardly to *impose* our standards on the rest of the world: for a Muslim to refrain from eating pork in England is not for him to impose Muslim standards on the British. Finally, there is some reason for us to refrain from a practice that *we* judge to be wrong and harmful to others even if we do not receive agreement: that settlers in the upper Amazon hunt native Indians for sport does not give us good reason to conform to that practice when in their company. Obviously, more needs to be said on these issues, but I hope that it has been made clear that a passing reference to moral relativism establishes nothing and that there are a number of lines of defense which can be taken against more serious relativistic criticism.

In closing, I want to add a few short remarks. First, in asserting that the FCPA is supported by moral considerations, I am not claiming that the Act defines the morally best behavior in every single case. All laws can be improved; an imperfect law can still be moral and just. Second, it should be noted that if Hooker and Pastin were correct, their arguments would go a long way toward justifying bribery and extortion *within* the United States by both foreign and domestic companies—unless we are to believe that a return to the state of nature is morally acceptable in one place (someone else's country) but not in another. Finally, I think that I have shown that the FCPA is supported by considerations of morality. This should count heavily in favor of retaining the law. However, I do not claim to have necessarily provided *motivation* for suporting this law or adhering to its stipulations. Morality may require sacrifice, in this case at least sacrifice of financial gain. For those who care more for financial gain and for the ruthlessness through which it can be obtained than for the moral values of justice and integrity, I cannot claim to have provided motivation.

NOTES

1. See this volume, pages 47–52.
2. The arguments sketched in this paper are more fully defended in my forthcoming "International Corporate Bribery." The present paper is a considerably shortened version of a paper read at the Conference on Business and Professional Ethics, in Chicago, May 1981.

3. That is, in some cases, considered individually and other things being equal, corporations *morally ought to bribe* and the government *morally ought not to punish* corporations for bribing. Thus, as the law now stands, some actions are legally required that are contrary to morality.

4. This promise must be understood as a promise to endeavor to a reasonable extent to increase investment value, not to maximize it at all costs.

5. The general moral principle here is, very roughly, that a promise to pursue the interests of another cannot increase the moral weight of those interests against moral considerations external to the relationship of promiser and promisee.

6. For continuing treatment of the child or in situations in which there is continuing and widespread corruption among doctors, it would be necessary to endorse bribery as a policy. However, then one's obligation would not be merely to engage in bribery, but rather to engage in bribery while doing what one can to rectify the situation. Regardless of the precise way this is to be worked out, a simple endorsement of bribery is not what is justified in such cases.

7. In practice it may be difficult to distinguish between bribery and extortion on the one hand, and goodwill gestures (e.g., gifts) and facilitating payments (so-called "grease") on the other. However, the conceptual issue of the wrongness of extortion does not turn on how the practical problem is solved.

8. Judson J. Wambold, "Prohibiting Foreign Bribes: Criminal Sanctions for Corporate Payments Abroad," *Cornell International Law Journal* 10 (1977), pp. 235–237. Wambold also found that though bribery is generally illegal, corporate contributions to political parties are acceptable in many countries. This complicates the moral evaluation of the FCPA. The next two points in my text suggest directions in which to go to defend the Act in this connection.

Moral Minimums for Multinationals[1]

THOMAS DONALDSON

When exploring issues of international ethics, researchers frequently neglect multinational corporations. They are prone to forget that these commercial leviathans often rival nation-states in power and organizational skill, and that their remarkable powers imply nonlegal responsibilities. Critics and defenders agree on the enormity of corporate multinational power. Richard Barnet and Ronald Muller, well-known critics of multinationals, remark that the global corporation is the "most powerful human organization yet devised for colonizing the future."[2] The business analyst, P. P. Gabriel, writing in the

"Moral Minimums for Multinationals," by Thomas Donaldson, *Ethics and International Affairs* (1989). Reprinted with permission of the publisher and author.

Harvard Business Review, characterizes the multinational as the "dominant institution" in a new era of world trade.[3] Indeed, with the exception of a handful of nation-states, multinationals are alone in possessing the size, technology, and economic reach necessary to influence human affairs on a global basis.

Ethical issues stemming from multinational corporate activities often derive from a clash between the cultural attitudes in home and host countries. When standards for pollution, discrimination, and salary schedules appear lower in a multinational's host country than in the home country, should multinational managers always insist on home-country standards? Or does using home standards imply a failure to respect cultural diversity and national integrity? Is a factory worker in Mexico justified in complaining about being paid three dollars an hour for the same work a U.S. factory worker, employed by the same company, is paid ten dollars?[4] Is an asbestos worker in India justified in criticizing the lower standards for regulating in-plant asbestos pollution maintained by a British multinational relative to standards in Britain, when the standards in question fall within Indian government guidelines and, indeed, are stricter than the standards maintained by other Indian asbestos manufacturers? Furthermore, what obligations, if any, do multinationals have to the people they affect indirectly? If a company buys land from wealthy landowners and turns it to the production of a cash crop, should it ensure that displaced farmers will avoid malnutrition?

I

It is well to remember that multinational power is not a wholly new phenomenon. Hundreds of years ago, the East India Company deployed over 40 warships, possessed the largest standing army in the world, was lord and master of an entire subcontinent, had dominion over 250 million people, and even hired its own church bishops.[5] The modern multinational is a product of the post-World War II era, and its dramatic success has stemmed from, among other factors, spiraling labor costs in developed countries, increasing importance of economies of scale in manufacturing, better communication systems, improved transportation, and increasing worldwide consumer demand for new products.[6] Never far from the evolution of the multinational has been a host of ethical issues, including bribery and corrupt payments, employment and personnel issues, marketing practices, impact on the economy and development of host countries, effects on the natural environment, cultural impacts of multinational operations, relations with host governments, and relations with the home countries.[7]

The formal responsibilities of multinationals as defined in domestic and international law, as well as in codes of conduct, are expanding dramatically. While many codes are nonbinding in the sense that noncompliance will fail to trigger sanctions, these principles, taken as a group, are coming to exert

significant influence on multinational conduct. A number of specific reasons
lie behind the present surge in international codes and regulations. To begin
with, some of the same forces propelling domestic attempts to bring difficult-
to-control activities under stricter supervision are influencing multinationals.[8] Consider, for example, hazardous technology, a threat which by
its nature recognizes no national boundaries yet must be regulated in both
domestic and foreign contexts. The pesticide industry, which relies on such
hazardous technology (of which Union Carbide's Bhopal plant is one instance), in 1987 grossed over $13 billion a year and has been experiencing
mushrooming growth, especially in the developing countries.[9] It is little
surprise that the rapid spread of hazardous technology has prompted the
emergence of international codes on hazardous technology, such as the
various U.N. resolutions on the transfer of technology and the use of pesticides.

Furthermore, just as a multiplicity of state regulations and laws generates confusion and inefficiency, and stimulates federal attempts to manage
conduct, a multiplicity of national regulations stimulates international attempts at control. Precisely this push for uniformity lies behind, for example,
many of the international codes of ethics, such as the WHO Code of Marketing Breast Milk Substitutes. Another well-known instance illustrating the
need for uniformity involved the collision of French and U.S. law in the sale
of equipment by Dresser Industries to the Soviets for the planned European
pipeline. U.S. law forbade the sale of such technology to the Soviets for
reasons of national security while French law (which affected a Dresser
subsidiary) encouraged it in order to stimulate commercial growth. It was
neither to the advantage of Dresser Industries nor to the advantage of the
French and U.S. governments to be forced to operate in an arena of conflict
and inconsistency. For months the two governments engaged in a public
standoff while Dresser, and Dresser's public image, were caught in the
middle.

National laws, heretofore unchallenged in authority, are now being
eclipsed by regulatory efforts falling into four categories: namely, inter-firm,
inter-government, cooperative, and world-organizational efforts.[10] The first
category of "inter-firm" standards is one which reflects initiatives from industries, firms, and consumer groups, and it includes the numerous inter-
industry codes of conduct that are operative for international business, such
as the World Health Organization's Code on Pharmaceuticals and Tobacco,
and the World Intellectual Property Organization's Revision of the Paris
Convention for the Protection of Industrial Patents and Trademarks. The
second category of "inter-government" efforts includes specific-purpose arrangements between and among nation-states, such as the General Agreement on Tariffs and Trade (GATT), the International Monetary Fund
(IMF), and the World Bank.[11] "Cooperative" efforts, which comprise the

third category, involve governments and industries coordinating skills in mutual arrangements that regulate international commerce. The European Community (EC) and the Andean Common Market (ANCOM) are two notable examples of such cooperative efforts.[12]

Finally, the fourth or "world-organizational" category includes efforts from broad-based global institutions such as the World Court, the International Labor Organization (ILO), the Organization for Economic Cooperation and Development (OECD), and the various sub-entities of the United Nations.

II

The growing tradition of international business codes and policies suggests that the investigation of ethical issues in international business is pressing and proper. But what issues deserve attention?

One key set of issues relates to business practices that clearly conflict with the moral attitudes of most multinational's home countries. Consider, for example, the practice of child labor, which continues to plague developing countries. While not the worst example, Central America offers a sobering lesson. In dozens of interviews with workers throughout Central America conducted in the fall of 1987, most respondents said they started working between the ages of 12 and 14.[13] The work week lasts six days, and the median salary (for all workers including adults) is scarcely over a dollar a day. The area is largely non-unionized, and strikes are almost always declared illegal. There is strong similarity between the pressures compelling child labor in Central America and those in early nineteenth-century England during the Industrial Revolution. With unemployment ranging from a low of 24 percent in Costa Rica to a high of 50 percent in Guatemala, and with families malnourished and older breadwinners unable to work, children are often forced to make growth-stunting sacrifices.[14]

Then, too, there are issues about which our moral intuitions seem confused, issues which pose difficult questions for researchers. Consider an unusual case involving the sale of banned goods abroad—one in which a developing country argued that being able to buy a banned product was important to meeting its needs. Banned pharmaceuticals, in contrast to other banned goods, have been subject to export restrictions for over 40 years. Yet, in defense of a recent Reagan initiative, drug manufacturers in the United States argued by appealing to differing cultural variables. For example, a spokesman for the American division of Ciba-Geigy Pharmaceuticals justified relaxing restrictions on the sale of its Entero-Vioform, a drug he agrees has been associated with blindness and paralysis, on the basis of culture-specific, cost-benefit analysis. "The government of India," he pointed out, "has requested Ciba-Geigy to continue producing the drug because it treats a dysentery problem that can be life threatening."[15]

III

The task for the international ethicist is to develop or discover concepts capable of specifying the obligations of multinational corporations in cases such as these. One such important concept is that of a human right.

Rights establish minimum levels of morally acceptable behavior. One well-known definition of a right construes it as a "trump" over a collective good, which is to say that the assertion of one's right to something, such as free speech, takes precedence over all but the most compelling collective goals, and overrides, for example, the state's interest in civil harmony or moral consensus.[16] Rights are at the rock bottom of modern moral deliberation. Maurice Cranston writes that the litmus test for whether something is a right or not is whether it protects something of "paramount importance."[17] Hence, it may help to define what minimal responsibilities should be assigned to multinational corporations by asking, "What specific rights ought multinationals to respect?"

The flip side of a right typically is a duty.[18] This, in part, is what gives aptness to Joel Feinberg's well-known definition of a right as a "justified entitlement *to* something *from* someone."[19] It is the "from someone" part of the definition which reflects the assumption of a duty, for without a correlative obligation that attaches to some moral agent or group of agents, a right is weakened—if not beyond the status of a right entirely, then significantly. If we cannot say that a multinational corporation has a duty to keep the levels of arsenic low in the work place, then the worker's right not to be poisoned means little.

Often, duties associated with rights fall upon more than one class of moral agent. Consider, for example, the furor over the dumping of toxic waste in West Africa by multinational corporations. During 1988, virtually every country from Morocco to the Congo on Africa's west coast received offers from companies seeking cheap sites for dumping waste.[20] In the years prior, dumping in the U.S. and Europe had become enormously expensive, in large part because of the costly safety measures mandated by U.S. and European governments. In February of 1988, officials in Guinea-Bissau, one of the world's poorest nations, agreed to bury 15 million tons of toxic wastes from European tanneries and pharmaceutical companies. The companies agreed to pay about $120 million, which is only slightly less than the country's entire gross national product. In Nigeria in 1987, five European ships unloaded toxic waste in Nigeria containing dangerous poisons such as polychlorinated biphenyls, or PCBs. Workers wearing thongs and shorts unloaded the barrels for $2.50 a day, and placed them in a dirt lot in a residential area in the town of Kiko.[21] They were not told about the contents of the barrels.[22]

Who bears responsibility for protecting the workers' and inhabitants' rights to safety in such instances? It would be wrong to place it entirely upon a single agent such as the government of a West African nation. As it happens, the toxic waste dumped in Nigeria entered under an import permit for "non-explosive, nonradioactive and non-self-combusting chemicals." But the permit turned out to be a loophole; Nigeria had not meant to accept the waste and demanded its removal once word about its presence filtered into official channels. The example reveals the difficulty many developing countries have in creating the sophisticated language and regulatory procedures necessary to control high-technology hazards. It seems reasonable in such instances, then, to place the responsibility not upon a single class of agents, but upon a broad collection of them, including governments, corporate executives, host-country companies and officials, and international organizations.

One list receiving significant international attention is the Universal Declaration of Human Rights.[23] However, it and the subsequent International Covenant on Social, Economic and Cultural Rights have spawned controversy, despite the fact that the Declaration was endorsed by virtually all of the important post-World War II nations in 1948 as part of the affirmation of the U.N. Charter. What distinguishes these lists from their predecessors, and what serves also as the focus of controversy, is their inclusion of rights that have come to be called, alternatively, "social," "economic," "positive," or "welfare" rights.

Many have balked at such rights, arguing that no one can have a right to a specific supply of an economic good. Can anyone be said to have a "right," for example, to 128 hours of sleep and leisure each week? And, in the same spirit, some international documents have simply refused to adopt the welfare-affirming blueprint established in the Universal Declaration. For example, the European Convention of Human Rights omits mention of welfare rights, preferring instead to create an auxiliary document (The European Social Charter of 1961) which references many of what earlier had been treated as "rights," as "goals." Similar objections underlie the bifurcated covenants drawn up in an attempt to implement the Universal Declaration: one such covenant, entitled the Covenant on Civil and Political Rights, was drawn up for all signers, including those who objected to welfare rights, while a companion covenant, entitled the Covenant on Social, Economic, and Cultural Rights, was drawn up for welfare rights defenders. Of course, many countries signed both; but some signed only the former.[24]

Many who criticize welfare rights utilize a traditional philosophical distinction between so-called negative and positive rights. A positive right is said to be one that requires persons to act positively to *do* something, while a negative one requires only that people not directly deprive others. Hence, the right to liberty is said to be a negative right, whereas the right to enough food is said to be a positive one. With this distinction in hand, the point is commonly made that no one can be bound to improve the welfare of another (unless, say, that person has entered into an agreement to do so); rather, they can be bound at most to *refrain* from damaging the welfare of another.

Nonetheless, Henry Shue has argued persuasively against the very distinction between negative and positive rights. Consider the most celebrated and best accepted example of a negative right: namely, the right to freedom. The meaningful preservation of the right to freedom requires a variety of positive actions: for example, on the part of the government it requires the establishment and maintenance of a police force, courts, and the military, and on the part of the citizenry it requires ongoing cooperation and diligent (not merely passive) forbearance. The protection of another so-called negative right, the right to physical security, necessitates "police forces; criminal rights; penitentiaries; schools for training police, lawyers, and guards; and taxes to support an enormous system for the prevention, detention, and punishment of violations of personal security."[25]

This is compelling. The maintenance and preservation of many non-welfare rights (where, again, such maintenance and preservation is the key to a right's status as basic) require the support of certain basic welfare rights. Certain liberties depend upon the enjoyment of subsistence, just as subsistence sometimes depends upon the enjoyment of some liberties. One's freedom to speak freely is meaningless if one is weakened by hunger to the point of silence.

What list of rights, then, ought to be endorsed on the international level? Elsewhere I have argued that the rights appearing on such a list should pass the following three conditions:[26] 1) the right must protect something of very great importance; 2) the right must be subject to substantial and recurrent threats; and 3) the obligations or burdens imposed by the right must satisfy a fairness-affordability test.[27]

In turn, I have argued that the list of fundamental international rights generated from these conditions include: 1) the right to freedom of physical movement; 2) the right to ownership of property; 3) the right to freedom from torture; 4) the right to a fair trial; 5) the right to nondiscriminatory treatment (e.g., freedom from discrimination on the basis of such characteristics as race or sex); 6) the right to physical security; 7) the right to freedom of speech and association; 8) the right to minimal education; 9) the right to political participation; and 10) the right to subsistence.

This seems a minimal list. Some will wish to add entries such as the right to employment, to social security, or to a certain standard of living (say, as might be prescribed by Rawls's well-known "difference" principle). The list as presented aims to suggest, albeit incompletely, a description of a *minimal* set of rights and to serve as a point of beginning and consensus for evaluating international conduct. If I am correct, many would wish to add entries, but few would wish to subtract them.

As we look over the list, it is noteworthy that, except for a few isolated instances, multinational corporations have probably succeeded in fulfilling their duty not to actively deprive persons of their enjoyment of the rights at issue. But correlative duties involve more than failing to actively deprive people of the enjoyment of their rights. Shue, for example, notes that three types of correlative duties (i.e., duties corresponding to a particular right) are possible: 1) to avoid depriving, 2) to help protect from deprivation; and 3) to aid the deprived.[28]

While it is obvious that the honoring of rights clearly imposes duties of the first kind, i.e., to avoid depriving directly, it is less obvious, but frequently true, that honoring them involves acts or omissions that help prevent the deprivation of rights. If I receive a note from Murder, Incorporated, and it looks like business, my right to security is clearly threatened. Let's say that a third party (X) has relevant information which, if revealed to the police, would help protect my right to security. In this case, there is no excuse for X to remain silent, claiming that it is Murder, Incorporated, and not X, who wishes to murder me.

Similarly, the duties associated with rights often include ones from the third category, i.e., that of aiding the deprived, as when a government is bound to honor the right of its citizens to adequate nutrition by distributing food in the wake of famine or natural disaster, or when the same government, in the defense of political liberty, is required to demand that an employer reinstate or compensate an employee fired for voting for a particular candidate in a government election.

Which of these duties apply to corporations, and which apply only to governments? It would be unfair, not to mention unreasonable, to hold corporations to the same standards for enhancing and protecting social welfare to which we hold civil governments—since frequently governments are formally dedicated to enhancing the welfare of, and actively preserving the liberties of, their citizens. The profit-making corporation, in contrast, is designed to achieve an economic mission and as a moral actor possesses an exceedingly narrow personality. It is an undemocratic institution, furthermore, which is ill-suited to the broader task of distributing society's goods in accordance with a conception of general welfare. The corporation is an economic animal; although its responsibilities extend beyond maximizing return on investment for shareholders, they are informed directly by its economic mission. Hence, while it would be strikingly generous for multinationals to sacrifice some of their profits to buy milk, grain, and shelter for persons in poor countries, it seems difficult to consider this one of their minimal moral requirements. If anyone has such minimal obligations, it is the peoples' respective governments or, perhaps, better-off individuals.

The same, however, is not true of the second class of duties, i.e., to protect from deprivation. While these duties, like those in the third class, are also usually the province of government, it sometimes happens that the rights to which they correlate are ones whose protection is a direct outcome of ordinary corporate activities. For example, the duties associated with protecting a worker from the physical threats of other workers may fall not only upon the local police but also upon the employer. These duties, in turn, are properly viewed as correlative duties of the right—in this instance, the worker's right—to personal security. This will become clearer in a moment when we discuss the correlative duties of specific rights.

The following list of correlative duties reflects a second-stage application of the fairness-affordability condition to the earlier list of fundamental international rights, and indicates which rights do, and which do not, impose correlative duties upon multinational corporations of the three various kinds.[29]

MINIMAL CORRELATIVE DUTIES OF MULTINATIONAL CORPORATIONS

FUNDAMENTAL RIGHTS	TO AVOID DEPRIVING	TO HELP PROTECT FROM DEPRIVATION	TO AID THE DEPRIVED
Freedom of physical movement	X		
Ownership of property	X		
Freedom from torture	X		
Fair trial	X		
Nondiscriminatory treatment	X	X	
Physical security	X	X	
Freedom of speech and association	X	X	
Minimal education	X	X	
Political Participation	X	X	
Subsistence	X	X	

Let us illustrate the duty to protect from deprivation with specific examples. The right to physical security entails duties of protection. If a Japanese multinational corporation operating in Nigeria hires shop workers to run metal lathes in an assembly factory, but fails to provide them with protective goggles, then the corporation has failed to honor the workers' moral right to physical security (no matter what the local law might decree). Injuries from such a failure would be the moral responsibility of the Japanese multinational despite the fact that the company could not be said to have inflicted the injuries directly.

Another correlative duty, to protect the right of education, may be illustrated through the example mentioned earlier: namely, the prevalence of child labor in developing countries. A multinational in Central America is not entitled to hire an eight-year-old for full-time, ongoing work because, among other reasons, doing so blocks the child's ability to receive a minimally sufficient education. While what counts as a "minimally sufficient" education may be debated, and while it seems likely, moreover, that the specification of the right to a certain level of education will depend at least in part upon the level of economic resources available in a given country, it is reasonable to assume that any action by a corporation which has the effect of blocking the development of a child's ability to read or write will be proscribed on the basis of rights.

In some instances, corporations have failed to honor the correlative duty of protecting the right to political participation from deprivation. The most blatant examples of direct deprivation are fortunately becoming so rare as to be nonexistent, namely, cases in which companies directly aid in overthrowing democratic regimes, as when United Fruit, Inc., allegedly contributed to overthrowing a democratically elected regime in Guatemala during the 1950s. But a few corporations have continued indirectly to threaten this right by failing to protect it from deprivation. A few have persisted, for example, in supporting military dictatorships in countries with growing democratic sentiment, and others have blatantly bribed publicly elected officials with large sums of money. Perhaps the most celebrated example of the latter occurred when the prime minister of Japan was bribed with $7 million by the Lockheed Corporation to secure a lucrative Tri-Star Jet contract. The complaint from the perspective of this right is not against bribes or "sensitive payments" in general, but against bribes in contexts where they serve to undermine a democratic system in which publicly elected officials are in a position of public trust.

Even the buying and owning of major segments of a foreign country's land and industry have been criticized in this regard. As Brian Barry has remarked, "The paranoia created in Britain and the United States by land purchases by foreigners (especially the Arabs and the Japanese, it seems) should serve to make it understandable that the citizenry of a country might be unhappy with a state of affairs in which the most important natural resources are in foreign ownership."[30] At what point would Americans regard their democratic control threatened by foreign ownership of U.S. industry and resources? At 20 percent ownership? At 40 percent? At 60 percent? At 80 percent? The answer is debatable, yet there seems to be some point beyond which the right to national self-determination, and in turn national democratic control, is violated by foreign ownership of property.[31]

Corporations also have duties to protect the right to subsistence from deprivation. Consider the following scenario. A number of square miles of land in an underdeveloped country has been used for years to grow black beans. The bulk of the land is owned, as it has been for centuries, by two wealthy landowners. Poorer members of the community work the land and receive a portion of the crop, a portion barely sufficient to satisfy nutritional needs. Next, imagine that a multinational corporation offers the two wealthy owners a handsome sum for the land, and does so because it plans to grow coffee for export. Now if—and this, admittedly, is a crucial "if"—the corporation has reason to *know* that a significant number of people in the community will suffer malnutrition as a result—that is, if it has convincing reasons to believe either those persons will fail to be hired by the company and paid sufficiently or, if forced to migrate to the city, will receive wages insufficient to provide adequate food and shelter—then the multinational may be said to have failed in its correlative duty to protect persons from the deprivation of the right to subsistence. This despite the fact that the corporation would never have stooped to take food from workers' mouths, and despite the fact that the malnourished will, in Coleridge's words, "die so slowly that none call it murder."

In addition to articulating a list of rights and the correlative duties imposed upon multinational corporations, there is also a need to articulate a practical stratagem for use in applying the home-country norms of the multinational manager to the vexing problems arising in developing countries. In particular, how should highly-placed multinational managers, typically schooled in home-country moral traditions, reconcile conflicts between those traditions and ones of the host country? When host-country standards for pollution, discrimination, and salary schedules appear substandard from the perspective of the home country, should the manager take the high road and implement home-country standards? Or does the high road imply a failure to respect cultural diversity and national integrity?

What distinguishes these issues from standard ones about corporate practices is that they involve reference to a conflict of norms, either moral or legal, between home and host country. Consider two actual instances of the problem at issue.

Case #1: A new American bank in Italy was advised by its Italian attorneys to file a tax return that misstated income and expenses and consequently grossly underestimated actual taxes due. The bank learned, however, that most other Italian companies regarded the practice as standard operating procedure and merely the first move in a complex negotiating process with the Italian internal revenue service. The bank initially refused to file a fallacious return on moral grounds and submitted an "American-style" return instead. But because the resulting tax bill was many times higher than what comparable Italian companies were asked to pay, the bank changed policy in later years to agree with the "Italian style."[32]

Case #2: In 1966 Charles Pettis, employee of an American multinational, became resident engineer for one of the company's projects in Peru: a 146-mile, $46 million project to build a highway across the Andes. Pettis soon discovered that Peruvian safety standards were far below those in the United States. The highway design called for cutting through mountains in areas where rock formations were unstable. Unless special precautions were taken, slides could occur. Pettis blew the whistle, complaining first to Peruvian government officials and later to U.S. officials. No special precautions were taken, with the result that 31 men were killed by landslides during the construction of the road. Pettis was fired and had difficulty finding a job with another company.[33]

One may well decide that enforcing home-country standards was necessary in one of the above cases, but not in the other. One may decide that host-country precautions in Peru were unacceptable, while at the same time acknowledging that, however inequitable and inefficient Italian tax mores may be, a decision to file "Italian style" is permissible.

Thus, despite claims to the contrary, one must reject the simple dictum that whenever the practice violates a moral standard of the home country, it is impermissible for the multinational company. Arnold Berleant has argued that the principle of equal treatment endorsed by most U.S. citizens requires that U.S. corporations pay workers in less developed countries exactly the same wages paid to U.S. workers in comparable jobs (after appropriate adjustments are made for cost of living levels in the relevant areas).[34] But most observers, including those from the less developed countries, believe this stretches the doctrine of equality too far in a way that is detrimental to host countries. By arbitrarily establishing U.S. wage levels as the benchmark for fairness, one eliminates the role of the international market in establishing salary levels, and this in turn eliminates the incentive U.S. corporations have to hire foreign workers. Perhaps U.S. firms should exceed market rate for foreign labor as a matter of moral principle, but to pay strictly equal rates would freeze less developed countries out of the international labor market.[35] Lacking a simple formula such as "the practice is wrong when it violates the home country's norms," one seems driven to undertake a more complex analysis of the types and degrees of responsibilities multinationals possess.

What is needed is a more comprehensive test than a simple appeal to rights. Of course the earlier rights-based approach clarifies a moral bottom line regarding, say, extreme threats to workers' safety. But it leaves obscure not only the issue of less extreme threats, but of harms other than physical injury. Granted, the celebrated dangers of asbestos call for recognizing the right to workers' safety no matter how broadly the language of rights is framed. But what are we to say of a less toxic pollutant? Is the level of sulphur-dioxide air pollution we should tolerate in a struggling nation, one with only a few fertilizer plants working overtime to help feed its malnourished population, the same we should demand in Portland, Oregon?

In the end, nothing less than a general moral theory working in tandem with an analysis of the foundations of corporate existence is needed. But at the practical level a need exists for an interpretive mechanism or algorithm that multinational managers could use in determining the implications of their own moral views.

The first step in generating such an ethical algorithm is to isolate the distinct sense in which the norms of the home and host country conflict. If the practice is morally and/or legally permitted in the host country, but not in the home country, then either: 1) the moral reasons underlying the host country's view that the practice is permissible refer to the host country's relative level of economic development; or 2) the moral reasons underlying the host country's view that the practice is permissible are independent of the host country's relative level of economic development.

Let us call the conflict of norms described in (1) a type 1 conflict. In such a conflict, an African country that permits slightly higher levels of thermal pollution from electric power generating plants, or a lower minimum wage than that prescribed in European countries, would do so not because higher standards would be undesirable per se, but because its level of economic development requires an ordering of priorities. In the future, when it succeeds in matching European economic achievements, it may well implement the higher standards.

Let us call the conflict of norms described in (2) a type 2 conflict. In such cases, levels of economic development play no role. For example, low-level institutional nepotism, common in many developing countries, is justified not on economic grounds, but on the basis of clan and family loyalty. Presumably the same loyalties will be operative even after the country has risen to economic success—as the nepotism prevalent in Saudi Arabia would indicate. The Italian tax case also reflects an Italian cultural style with a penchant for personal negotiation and an unwillingness to formalize transactions, more than a strategy based on level of economical development.

The difference in norms between the home and host country, i.e., whether the conflict is of type 1 or 2, does not determine the correctness, or truth value, of the host country's claim that the practice is permissible. The practice may or may not be permissible, whether the conflict is of type 1 or 2. This is not to say that the truth value of the host country's claim is independent of the nature of the conflict. A different test will be required to determine whether the practice is permissible when the conflict is of type 1 as opposed to type 2. In a type 1 dispute, the following formula is appropriate:

> The practice is permissible if and only if the members of the home country would, under conditions of economic development similar to those of the host country, regard the practice as permissible.

Under this test, excessive levels of asbestos pollution would almost certainly not be tolerated by the members of the home country under similar economic conditions, whereas higher levels of thermal pollution would be tolerated. The test, happily, explains and confirms our initial moral intuitions.

Since in type 2 conflicts the dispute between the home and host country depends upon a fundamental difference of perspective, a different test is needed. In type 2 conflicts, the opposing evils of ethnocentricism and ethical relativism must be avoided. A multinational must forego the temptation to remake all societies in the image of its home society, while at the same time rejecting a relativism that conveniently forgets ethics when the payoff is sufficient. Thus, the ethical task is to tolerate cultural diversity while drawing the line at moral recklessness.

Since in type 2 cases the practice is in conflict with an embedded norm of the home country, one should first ask whether the practice is necessary to do business in the host country, for if it is not, the solution clearly is to adopt some other practice that is permissible from the standpoint of the home country. If petty bribery of public officials is unnecessary for the business of the Cummins Engine Company in India, then the company is obliged to abandon such bribery. If, on the other hand, the practice proves necessary for business, one must next ask whether the practice constitutes a direct violation of a basic human right. Here the notion of a fundamental international right outlined earlier, specifying a minimum below which corporate conduct should not fall, has special application. If Toyota, a Japanese company, confronts South African laws that mandate systematic discrimination against non-whites, then Toyota must refuse to comply with the laws. In type

2 cases, the evaluator must ask the following questions: 1) Is it possible to conduct business successfully in the host country without undertaking the practice? and 2) Is the practice a clear violation of a fundamental international right? The practice would be permissible if and only if the answer to both questions is "no."

What sorts of practice might satisfy both criteria? Consider the practice of low-level bribery of public officials in some developing nations. In some South American countries, for example, it is impossible for any company, foreign or national, to move goods through customs without paying low-level officials a few dollars. Indeed, the salaries of such officials are sufficiently low that one suspects they are set with the prevalence of the practice in mind. The payments are relatively small, uniformly assessed, and accepted as standard practice by the surrounding culture. Here, the practice of petty bribery would pass the type 2 test and, barring other moral factors, would be permissible.

The algorithm does not obviate the need for multinational managers to appeal to moral concepts both more general and specific than the algorithm itself. It is not intended as a substitute for a general theory of morality or even an interpretation of the basic responsibilities of multinationals. Its power lies in its ability to tease out implications of the moral presuppositions of a manager's acceptance of "home" morality, and in this sense to serve as a clarifying device for multinational decision-making. The algorithm makes no appeal to a universal concept of morality (as the appeal to fundamental rights does in type 2 cases), save for the purported universality of the ethics endorsed by the home-country culture. When the home country's morality is wrong or confused, the algorithm can reflect this ethnocentricity, leading either to a mild paternalism or to the imposition of parochial standards. For example, the home country's oversensitivity to aesthetic features of the environment may lead it to reject a certain level of thermal pollution, even under strained economic circumstances. This results in a paternalistic refusal to allow such levels in the host country, despite the host country's acceptance of the higher levels and its belief that tolerating such levels is necessary for stimulating economic development. It would be a mistake, however, to exaggerate this weakness of the algorithm; coming up with actual cases in which the force of the algorithm would be relativized is extremely difficult. Indeed, I have been unable to discover a single, non-hypothetical set of facts fitting this description.

IV

How might multinational corporations improve their moral performance and come to embody the normative concepts advanced in this article? Two classes of remedies suggest themselves: external remedies, i.e., those that rely on international associations or agreements on the one hand; and internal remedies, i.e., those that rely on internal, corporate initiative on the other.

Earlier we discussed the dramatic expansion of external remedies in the form of international laws, agreements, and codes of conduct. Again, while many of these are nonbinding in the sense that noncompliance will fail to trigger sanctions, they are as a group coming to exert significant influence on multinational conduct. One of the principal advantages of such global and industry-wide initiatives is that they distribute costs more fairly than initiatives undertaken by individual corporations. When, in line with the WHO Code of Marketing Breast Milk Substitutes, Nestle curtails questionable marketing practices for the sale of infant formula, it does so with the confidence that the other signers of the WHO Code will not be taking unfair advantage by undertaking the same questionable practices, for they must adhere to its provisions. Still another advantage of external remedies stems from the fact that many nation-states, especially developing ones, are unable to gather sufficient information about, much less control, the multinational corporations that operate within their borders. Thus, the use of supranational entities, whether of an international or inter-industry form, will sometimes augment, or supplement, the power and information-gathering abilities of developing nations. It seems difficult to deny that the growth and maturation of such entities can enhance the ethical conduct of multinational corporations.

The most important change of an internal nature likely to enhance the ethical behavior of multinationals is for multinationals themselves to introduce ethical deliberation, i.e., to introduce factors of ethics into their decision-making mechanisms. That they should do so is a clear implication of the preceding discussion, yet it is a conclusion some will resist. Those who place great confidence in the efficacy of the market may, for example, believe that a corporate policy of moral disinterest and profit maximization will—*pace* Adam Smith's invisible hand—maximize overall global welfare.

This kind of ideological confidence in the international market may have been understandable decades ago. But persisting in the belief that market mechanisms will automatically ensure adequate moral conduct today seems recklessly idealistic. Forces such as Islamic fundamentalism, the global debt bomb, and massive unemployment in developing countries have drastically distorted the operation of the free market in international commerce, and even though a further selective freeing of market forces may enhance global productivity, it cannot solve automatically questions of fair treatment, hazardous technology, or discrimination.

Even adopting the minimal guidelines for corporate conduct advanced here would involve dramatic changes in the decision-making mechanisms of multinational corporations. Such firms would need to alter established patterns of information flow and collection in order to accommodate new forms of morally relevant information. The already complex parameters of corporate decision-making would become more so. Even scholarly research about international business would need to change. At present, research choices tend to be dictated by the goals of increased profits, long-term access to basic commodities needed for manufactured items, and increased global market share; but clearly these goals sometimes conflict with broader moral ends, such as refraining from violating human rights. Revised goals call for a revised program of research. And although we have rejected the view that multinational corporations must shoulder the world's problems of poverty, discrimination, and political injustice because, as economic entities, they have limited social missions, their goals nonetheless must include the aim of not impeding solutions to such problems.

Are such changes in the decision-making of multinational corporations likely or even possible? Resistance will be intense; clearly, there should be no delusions on this score. Yet, without minimizing the difficulties, I do not think the task impossible. At a minimum, corporations are capable of choosing the more ethical alternative in instances where alternative courses of action yield equal profits—and I believe they are capable of even more. Corporations are run by human beings, not beasts. As multinationals continue to mature in the context of an ever-expanding, more sophisticated global economy, we have reason to hope that they are capable of looking beyond their national borders and recognizing the same minimal claims made in the name of our shared humanity, that they accept at home.

NOTES

1. Much of this article is extracted from Thomas Donaldson's book, *The Ethics of International Business* (Oxford: Oxford University Press, 1989). The book provides a framework for interpreting the ethics of global business. Excerpts reprinted by permission of Oxford University Press.
2. Richard Barnet and Ronald Muller, *Global Reach: The Power of Multinational Corporations* (New York: Simon and Schuster, 1974) p. 363.
3. P. P. Gabriel, "MNCs in the Third World: Is Conflict Unavoidable?" *Harvard Business Review*, Vol. 56 (March–April 1978) pp. 83–93.
4. An example of disparity in wages between Mexican and U.S. workers is documented in the case study by John H. Haddox, "Twin-Plants and Corporate Responsibilities," in *Profits and Responsibility*, eds. Patricia Werhane and Kendall D'Andrade (New York: Random House, 1985).
5. Barnet and Muller, *Global Reach*, p. 72.
6. J. R. Simpson, "Ethics and Multinational Corporations vis-à-vis Developing Nations," *Journal of Business Ethics*, Vol. 1 (1982) pp. 227–37.
7. I have borrowed this eight-fold scheme of categories from researchers Farr and Stening in Lisa Farr and Bruce W. Stening, "Ethics and the Multinational Corporation" (an unpublished paper) p. 4.
8. An analysis of such reasons, one which also contains many observations on the evolution of international public policy, is Lee E. Preston's "The Evolution of Multinational Public Policy Toward Business: Codes of Conduct," a paper read at the annual meeting of the American Academy of Management, New Orleans, August 1987.
9. Jon R. Luoma, "A Disaster That Didn't Wait," *The New York Times Book Review*, November 29, 1987, p. 16.

10. While I personally have coined the terms, "inter-industry," "inter-government," etc., the basic four-fold division of international initiatives is drawn from Preston, *op. cit.*
11. See, for example, Raymond J. Waldman, *Regulating International Business through Codes of Conduct* (Washington, D.C.: American Enterprise Institute, 1980).
12. See, for example, P. S. Tharp, Jr., "Transnational Enterprises and International Regulation: A Survey of Various Approaches to International Organizations," *International Organization*, Vol. 30 (Winter 1976) pp. 47–73.
13. James LeMoyne. "In Central America, the Workers Suffer Most," *The New York Times*, October 26, 1987. pp. 1 and 4.
14. *Ibid.*
15. Quoted in "Products Unsafe at Home are Still Unloaded Abroad," *The New York Times*, August 22, 1982, p. 22.
16. Ronald Dworkin, *Taking Rights Seriously* (Cambridge: Harvard University Press, 1977). For other standard definitions of rights, see: James W. Nickel, *Making Sense of Human Rights: Philosophical Reflections on the Universal Declaration of Human Rights* (Berkeley: University of California Press, 1987) especially chapter 2; Joel Feinberg, "Duties, Rights and Claims," *American Philosophical Quarterly*, Vol. 3 (1966) pp. 137–44. See also Feinberg, "The Nature and Value of Rights," *Journal of Value Inquiry*, Vol. 4 (1970) pp. 243–57; Wesley N. Hohfeld, *Fundamental Legal Conceptions* (New Haven: Yale University Press, 1964); and H. J. McCloskey, "Rights—Some Conceptual Issues," *Australasian Journal of Philosophy*, Vol. 54 (1976) pp. 99–115.
17. Maurice Cranston, *What Are Human Rights?* (New York: Taplinger, 1973) p. 67.
18. H. J. McCloskey, for example, understands a right as a positive entitlement that need not specify who bears the responsibility for satisfying that entitlement. H. J. McCloskey, "Rights—Some Conceptual Issues," p. 99.
19. Joel Feinberg, "Duties, Rights and Claims," *American Philosophical Quarterly*, Vol. 3 (1966) pp. 137–44. See also Feinberg, "The Nature and Value of Rights," pp. 243–57.
20. James Brooke, "Waste Dumpers Turning to West Africa," *The New York Times*, July 17, 1988, pp. 1 and 7.
21. *Ibid.*
22. *Ibid.*, p. 7. Nigeria and other countries have struck back, often by imposing strict rules against the acceptance of toxic waste. For example, in Nigeria officials now warn that anyone caught importing toxic waste will face the firing squad.
23. See Ian Brownlie, *Basic Documents on Human Rights* (Oxford: Oxford University Press, 1975).
24. James W. Nickel, "The Feasibility of Welfare Rights in Less Developed Countries," in *Economic Justice: Private Rights and Public Responsibilities*, eds. Kenneth Kipnis and Diana T. Meyers (Totowa, N. J.: Rowman and Allenheld, 1985) pp. 217–26.
25. Henry Shue, *Basic Rights: Subsistence, Affluence, and U. S. Foreign Policy* (Princeton: Princeton University Press, 1980) pp. 37–38.
26. Donaldson, *The Ethics of International Business*, see especially chapter 5. My formulation of these three conditions is an adaptation from four conditions presented and defended by James Nickel in James W. Nickel, *Making Sense of Human Rights: Philosophical Reflections on the Universal Declaration of Human Rights* (Berkeley: University of California Press, 1987).
27. The fairness-affordability test implies that in order for a proposed right to qualify as a genuine right, all moral agents (including nation-states, individuals, and corporations) must be able under ordinary circumstances, both economically and otherwise, to assume the various burdens and duties that fall fairly upon them in

honoring the right. "Affordable" here means literally capable of paying for; it does not mean "affordable" in the vernacular sense that something is not affordable because it would constitute an inefficient luxury, or would necessitate trading off other more valuable economic goods. This definition implies that—at least under unusual circumstances—honoring a right may be mandatory for a given multi-national corporation, even when the result is bankrupting the firm. For example, it would be "affordable" under ordinary circumstances for multinational corporations to employ older workers and refuse to hire eight-year-old children for full-time, ongoing labor, and hence doing so would be mandatory even in the unusual situation where a particular firm's paying the higher salaries necessary to hire older laborers would probably bankrupt the firm. By the same logic, it would probably not be "affordable" for either multinational corporations or nation-states around the world to guarantee kidney dialysis for all citizens who need it. The definition also implies that any act of forbearance (of a kind involved in not violating a right directly) is "affordable" for all moral agents.

28. Shue, *Basic Rights*, p. 57.
29. It is possible to understand even the first four rights as imposing correlative duties to protect from deprivation under highly unusual or hypothetical circumstances.
30. Brian Barry, "The Case for a New International Economic Order," in *Ethics, Economics, and the Law: Nomos XXIV*, eds. J. Roland Pennock and John W. Chapman (New York: New York University Press, 1982).
31. Companies are also charged with undermining local governments, and hence infringing on basic rights, by sophisticated tax evasion schemes. Especially when companies buy from their own subsidiaries, they can establish prices that have little connection to existing market values. This, in turn, means that profits can be shifted from high-tax to low-tax countries, with the result that poor nations can be deprived of their rightful share.
32. Arthur Kelly, "Italian Tax Mores," in this volume, pp. 81–83.
33. Charles Peters and Taylor Branch, *Blowing the Whistle: Dissent in the Public Interest* (New York: Praeger, 1974) pp. 182–85.
34. Arnold Berleant, "Multinationals and the Problem of Ethical Consistency," *Journal of Business Ethics*, Vol. 3 (August 1982) pp. 182–95.
35. Some have argued that insulating the economies of the less developed countries would be advantageous to the less developed countries in the long run. But whether correct or not, such an argument is independent of the present issue, for it is independent of the claim that if a practice violates the norms of the home country, then it is impermissible.

The United Nations Declaration of Human Rights

Now, Therefore, The General Assembly proclaims

This universal declaration of human rights as a common standard of achievement for all peoples and all nations, to the end that every individual and every organ of society, keeping this Declaration constantly in mind, shall strive by teaching and education to promote respect for these rights and freedoms and by progressive measures, national and international, to secure their universal and effective recognition and observance, both among the peoples of Member States themselves and among the peoples of territories under their jurisdiction.

ARTICLE 1
All human beings are born free and equal in dignity and rights. They are endowed with reason and conscience and should act towards one another in a spirit of brotherhood.

ARTICLE 2
Everyone is entitled to all the rights and freedoms set forth in this Declaration without distinction of any kind, such as race, colour, sex, language, religion, political or other opinion, national or social origin, property, birth or other status.

Furthermore, no distinction shall be made on the basis of the political jurisdictional or international status of the country or territory to which a person belongs, whether it be independent, trust, non-self-governing or under any other limitation of sovereignty.

ARTICLE 3
Everyone has the right to life, liberty and security of person.

ARTICLE 4
No one shall be held in slavery or servitude; slavery and the slave trade shall be prohibited in all their forms.

ARTICLE 5
No one shall be subjected to torture or to cruel, inhuman or degrading treatment or punishment.

ARTICLE 6
Everyone has the right to recognition everywhere as a person before the law.

ARTICLE 7

All are equal before the law and are entitled without any discrimination to equal protection of the law. All are entitled to equal protection against any discrimination in violation of this Declaration and against any incitement to such discrimination.

ARTICLE 8

Everyone has the right to an effective remedy by the competent national tribunals for acts violating the fundamental rights granted him by the constitution or by law.

ARTICLE 9

No one shall be subjected to arbitrary arrest, detention or exile.

ARTICLE 10

Everyone is entitled in full equality to a fair and public hearing by an independent and impartial tribunal, in the determination of his rights and obligations and of any criminal charge against him.

ARTICLE 11

1. Everyone charged with a penal offence has the right to be presumed innocent until proved guilty according to law in a public trial at which he has had all the guarantees necessary for his defense.
2. No one shall be held guilty of any penal offence on account of any act or omission which did not constitute a penal offence, under national or international law, at the time when it was committed. Nor shall a heavier penalty be imposed than the one that was applicable at the time the penal offence was committed.

ARTICLE 12

No one shall be subjected to arbitrary interference with his privacy, family, home or correspondence, nor to attacks upon his honour and reputation. Everyone has the right to the protection of the law against such interference or attacks.

ARTICLE 13

1. Everyone has the right to freedom of movement and residence within the borders of each state.
2. Everyone has the right to leave any country, including his own, and to return to his country.

ARTICLE 14

1. Everyone has the right to seek and to enjoy in other countries asylum from persecution.
2. This right may not be invoked in the case of prosecutions genuinely arising from non-political crimes or from acts contrary to the purposes and principles of the United Nations.

ARTICLE 15

1. Everyone has the right to a nationality.
2. No one shall be arbitrarily deprived of his nationality nor denied the right to change his nationality.

ARTICLE 16

1. Men and women of full age, without any limitation due to race, nationality or religion, have the right to marry and to found a family. They are entitled to equal rights as to marriage, during marriage and at its dissolution.
2. Marriage shall be entered into only with the free and full consent of the intending spouses.
3. The family is the natural and fundamental group unit of society and is entitled to protection by society and the State.

ARTICLE 17

1. Everyone has the right to own property alone as well as in association with others.
2. No one shall be arbitrarily deprived of his property.

ARTICLE 18

Everyone has the right to freedom of thought, conscience and religion; this right includes freedom to change his religion or belief, and freedom, either alone or in community with others and in public or private, to manifest his religion or belief in teaching, practice, worship and observance.

ARTICLE 19

Everyone has the right to freedom of opinion and expression; this right includes freedom to hold opinions without interference and to seek, receive and impart information and ideas through any media and regardless of frontiers.

ARTICLE 20

1. Everyone has the right to freedom of peaceful assembly and association.
2. No one may be compelled to belong to an association.

ARTICLE 21

1. Everyone has the right to take part in the government of his country, directly or through freely chosen representatives.
2. Everyone has the right of equal access to public service in his country.
3. The will of the people shall be the basis of the authority of government; this will shall be expressed in periodic and genuine elections which shall be by universal and equal suffrage and shall be held by secret vote or by equivalent free voting procedures.

ARTICLE 22

Everyone, as a member of society, has the right to social security and is entitled to realization, through national effort and international co-operation and in accordance with the organization and resources of each State, of the economic, social and cultural rights indispensable for his dignity and the free development of his personality.

ARTICLE 23

1. Everyone has the right to work, to free choice of employment, to just and favourable conditions of work and to protection against unemployment.
2. Everyone without any discrimination, has the right to equal pay for equal work.
3. Everyone who works has the right to just and favourable remuneration ensuring for himself and his family an existence worthy of human dignity, and supplemented, if necessary, by other means of social protection.
4. Everyone has the right to form and to join trade unions for the protection of his interests.

ARTICLE 24

Everyone has the right to rest and leisure, including reasonable limitation of working hours and periodic holidays with pay.

ARTICLE 25

1. Everyone has the right to a standard of living adequate for the health and well-being of himself and of his family, including food, clothing, housing and medical care and necessary social services, and the right to security in the event of unemployment, sickness, disability, widowhood, old age or other lack of livelihood in circumstances beyond his control.
2. Motherhood and childhood are entitled to special care and assistance. All children, whether born in or out of wedlock, shall enjoy the same social protection.

ARTICLE 26

1. Everyone has the right to education. Education shall be free, at least in the elementary and fundamental stages. Elementary education shall be compulsory. Technical and professional education shall be made generally available and higher education shall be equally accessible to all on the basis of merit.
2. Education shall be directed to the full development of the human personality and to the strengthening of respect for human rights and fundamental freedoms. It shall promote understanding, tolerance and friendship among all nations, racial or religious groups, and shall further the activities of the United Nations for the maintenance of peace.
3. Parents have a prior right to choose the kind of education that shall be given to their children.

ARTICLE 27

1. Everyone has the right freely to participate in the cultural life of the community, to enjoy the arts and to share in scientific advancement and its benefits.
2. Everyone has the right to the protection of the moral and material interests resulting from any scientific, literary or artistic production of which he is the author.

ARTICLE 28

Everyone is entitled to a social and international order in which the rights and freedoms set forth in this Declaration can be fully realized.

ARTICLE 29

1. Everyone has duties to the community in which alone the free and full development of his personality is possible.
2. In the exercise of his rights and freedoms, everyone shall be subject only to such limitations as are determined by law solely for the purpose of securing due recognition and respect for the rights and freedoms of others and of meeting the just requirements of morality, public order and the general welfare in a democratic society.
3. These rights and freedoms may in no case be exercised contrary to the purposes and principles of the United Nations.

ARTICLE 30

Nothing in this Declaration may be interpreted as implying for any State, group or person any right to engage in any activity or to perform any act aimed at the destruction of any of the rights and freedoms set forth herein.

Truth Telling

Case Study

Italian Tax Mores

ARTHUR L. KELLY

The Italian federal corporate tax system has an official, legal tax structure and tax rates just as the U.S. system does. However, all similarity between the two systems ends there.

The Italian tax authorities assume that no Italian corporation would ever submit a tax return which shows its true profits but rather would submit a return which understates actual profits by anywhere between 30 percent and 70 percent; their assumption is essentially correct. Therefore, about six months after the annual deadline for filing corporate tax returns, the tax authorities issue to each corporation an "invitation to discuss" its tax return. The purpose of this notice is to arrange a personal meeting between them and representatives of the corporation. At this meeting, the Italian revenue service states the amount of corporate income tax which it believes is due. Its position is developed from both prior years' taxes actually paid and the current year's return; the amount which the tax authorities claim is due is generally several times that shown on the corporation's return for the current year. In short, the corporation's tax return and the revenue service's stated position are the opening offers for the several rounds of bargaining which will follow.

The Italian corporation is typically represented in such negotiations by its *commercialista*, a function which exists in Italian society for the primary purpose of negotiating corporate (and individual) tax payments with the Italian tax authorities; thus, the management of an Italian corporation seldom, if ever, has to meet directly with the Italian revenue service and probably has a minimum awareness of the details of the negotiation other than the final settlement.

Both the final settlement and the negotiation are extremely important to the corporation, the tax authorities, and the *commercialista*. Since the tax

This case—prepared by Arthur L. Kelly (Managing Partner, KEL Enterprises Ltd.; formerly vice-president—International of A. T. Kearney, Inc.)—was presented at Loyola University of Chicago at a Mellon Foundation symposium entitled "Foundations of Corporate Responsibility to Society," April 1977. Printed with the permission of Arthur L. Kelly.

authorities assume that a corporation *always* earned more money this year than last year and *never* has a loss, the amount of the final settlement, i.e., corporate taxes which will actually be paid, becomes, for all practical purposes, the floor for the start of next year's negotiations. The final settlement also represents the amount of revenue the Italian government will collect in taxes to help finance the cost of running the country. However, since large amounts of money are involved and two individuals having vested personal interests are conducting the negotiations, the amount of *bustarella*—typically a substantial cash payment "requested" by the Italian revenue agent from the *commercialista*—usually determines whether the final settlement is closer to the corporation's original tax return or to the fiscal authority's original negotiating position.

Whatever *bustarella* is paid during the negotiation is usually included by the *commercialista* in his lump-sum fee "for services rendered" to his corporate client. If the final settlement is favorable to the corporation, and it is the *commercialista's* job to see that it is, then the corporation is not likely to complain about the amount of its *commercialista's* fee, nor will it ever know how much of that fee was represented by *bustarella* and how much remained for the *commercialista* as payment for his negotiating services. In any case, the tax authorities will recognize the full amount of the fee as a tax deductible expense on the corporation's tax return for the following year.

About ten years ago, a leading American bank opened a banking subsidiary in a major Italian city. At the end of its first year of operation, the bank was advised by its local lawyers and tax accountants, both from branches of U.S. companies, to file its tax return "Italian-style," i.e., to understate its actual profits by a significant amount. The American general manager of the bank, who was on his first overseas assignment, refused to do so both because he considered it dishonest and because it was inconsistent with the practices of his parent company in the United States.

About six months after filing its "American-style" tax return, the bank received an "invitation to discuss" notice from the Italian tax authorities. The bank's general manager consulted with his laywers and tax accountants who suggested he hire a *commercialista*. He rejected this advice and instead wrote a letter to the Italian revenue service not only stating that his firm's corporate return was correct as filed but also requesting that they inform him of any specific items about which they had questions. His letter was never answered.

About sixty days after receiving the initial "invitation to discuss" notice, the bank received a formal tax assessment notice calling for a tax of approximately three times that shown on the bank's corporate tax return; the tax authorities simply assumed the bank's original return had been based on generally accepted Italian practices, and they reacted accordingly. The bank's general manager again consulted with his lawyers and tax accountants who again suggested he hire a *commercialista* who knew how to handle these matters. Upon learning that the *commercialista* would probably have to pay *bustarella* to his revenue service counterpart in order to reach a settlement, the general manager again chose to ignore his advisors. Instead, he responded by sending the Italian revenue service a check for the full amount of taxes due according to the bank's American-style tax return even though the due date for the payment was almost six months hence; he made no reference to the amount of corporate taxes shown on the formal tax assessment notice.

Ninety days after paying its taxes, the bank received a third notice from the fiscal authorities. This one contained the statement, "We have reviewed your corporate tax return for 19__ and have determined that [the lira equivalent of] $6,000,000 of interest paid on deposits is not an allowable expense for federal tax purposes. Accordingly, the total tax due for 19__ is lira _____ ." Since interest paid on deposits is any bank's largest single expense item, the new tax assessment was for an amount many times larger than that shown in the initial tax assessment notice and almost fifteen times larger than the taxes which the bank had actually paid.

The bank's general manger was understandably very upset. He immediately arranged an appointment to meet personally with the manager of the Italian revenue service's local office. Shortly after the start of their meeting, the conversation went something like this:

General Manager:	"You can't really be serious about disallowing interest paid on deposits as a tax deductible expense."
Italian Revenue Service:	"Perhaps. However, we thought it would get your attention. Now that you're here, shall we begin our negotiations?"[1]

QUESTIONS

1. Would you, as the general manager of the Italian subsidiary of an American corporation, "when in Rome" do as other Italian corporations do or adhere strictly to U.S. tax reporting practices?

2. Would you, as chief executive officer of a publicly traded corporation (subject to Securities Exchange Commission rules, regulations, and scrutiny), advise the general manager of your Italian subsidiary to follow common Italian tax reporting practices or to adhere to U.S. standards?

NOTE

1. For readers interested in what happened subsequently, the bank was forced to pay the taxes shown in the initial tax assessment, and the American manager was recalled to the United States and replaced.

Ethical Duties Towards Others: "Truthfulness"

IMMANUEL KANT

The exchange of our sentiments is the principal factor in social intercourse, and truth must be the guiding principle herein. Without truth social intercourse and conversation become valueless. We can only know what a man thinks if he tells us his thoughts, and when he undertakes to express them he must really do so, or else there can be no society of men. Fellowship is only the second condition of society, and a liar destroys fellowship. Lying makes it impossible to derive any benefit from conversation. Liars are, therefore, held in general contempt. Man is inclined to be reserved and to pretend. . . . Man is reserved in order to conceal faults and shortcomings which he has; he pretends in order to make others attribute to him merits and virtues which he has not. Our proclivity to reserve and concealment is due to the will of Providence that the defects of which we are full should not be too obvious. Many of our propensities and peculiarities are objectionable to others, and if they became patent we should be foolish and hateful in their eyes. Moreover, the parading of these objectionable characteristics would so familiarize men with them that they would themselves acquire them. Therefore we arrange our conduct either to conceal our faults or to appear other than we are. We possess the art of simulation. In consequence, our inner weakness and error is revealed to the eyes of men only as an appearance of well-being, while we ourselves develop the habit of dispositions which are conducive to good conduct. No man in his true senses, therefore, is candid. Were man candid, were the request of Momus[1] to be complied with that Jupiter should place a mirror in each man's heart so that his disposition might be visible to all, man would have to be better constituted and possess good principles. If all men were good there would be no need for any of us to be reserved; but since they are not, we have to keep the shutters closed. Every house keeps its dustbin in a place of its own. We do not press our friends to come into our water-closet, although they know that we have one just like themselves. Familiarity in such things is the ruin of good taste. In the same way we make no exhibition of our defects, but try to conceal them. We try to conceal our mistrust by affecting a courteous demeanour and so accustom ourselves to courtesy that at last it becomes a reality and we set a good example by it. If that were not so, if there were none who were better than we, we should become neglectful. Accordingly, the endeavour to appear good ultimately makes us really good. If all men were good, they could be candid, but as things are they cannot be.

From *Lectures on Ethics*, trans. Louis Infield (London: Methuen, 1930; rpt. New York: Harper & Row, 1963), pp 224–35. Reprinted by permission of the publishers.

To be reserved is to be restrained in expressing one's mind. We can, of course, keep absolute silence. This is the readiest and most absolute method of reserve, but it is unsociable, and a silent man is not only unwanted in social circles but is also suspected; every one thinks him deep and disparaging, for if when asked for his opinion he remains silent people think that he must be taking the worst view or he would not be averse from expressing it. Silence, in fact, is always a treacherous ally, and therefore it is not even prudent to be completely reserved. Yet there is such a thing as prudent reserve, which requires not silence but careful deliberation; a man who is wisely reserved weighs his words carefully and speaks his mind about everything excepting only those things in regard to which he deems it wise to be reserved.

We must distinguish between reserve and secretiveness, which is something entirely different. There are matters about which one has no desire to speak and in regard to which reserve is easy. We are, for instance, not naturally tempted to speak about and to betray our own misdemeanours. Everyone finds it easy to keep a reserve about some of his private affairs, but there are things about which it requires an effort to be silent. Secrets have a way of coming out, and strength is required to prevent ourselves betraying them. Secrets are always matters deposited with us by other people and they ought not to be placed at the disposal of third parties. But man has a great liking for conversation, and the telling of secrets adds much to the interest of conversation; a secret told is like a present given; how then are we to keep secrets? Men who are not very talkative as a rule keep secrets well, but good conversationalists, who are at the same time clever, keep them better. The former might be induced to betray something, but the latter's gift of repartee invariably enables them to invent on the spur of the moment something non-committal.

The person who is as silent as a mute goes to one extreme; the person who is loquacious goes to the opposite. Both tendencies are weaknesses. Men are liable to the first, women to the second. Someone has said that women are talkative because the training of infants is their special charge, and their talkativeness soon teaches a child to speak, because they can chatter to it all day long. If men had the care of the child, they would take much longer to learn to talk. However that may be, we dislike anyone who will not speak: he annoys us; his silence betrays his pride. On the other hand, loquaciousness in men is contemptible and contrary to the strength of the male. All this by the way; we shall now pass to more weighty matters.

If I announce my intention to tell what is in my mind, ought I knowingly to tell everything, or can I keep anything back? If I indicate that I mean to speak my mind, and instead of doing so make a false declaration, what I say is an untruth, a *falsiloquium*. But there can be *falsiloquium* even when people have no right to assume that we are expressing our thoughts. It is possible to deceive without making any statement whatever. I can make believe, make a demonstration from which others will draw the conclusion I want, though they have no right to expect that my action will express my real mind. In that case I have not lied to them, because I had not undertaken to express my mind. I may, for instance, wish people to think that I am off on a journey, and so I pack my luggage; people draw the conclusion I want them to draw; but others have no right to demand a declaration of my will from me.

. . . Again, I may make a false statement (*falsiloquium*), when my purpose is to hide from another what is in my mind and when the latter can assume that such is my purpose, his own purpose being to make a wrong use of the truth. Thus, for instance, if my enemy takes me by the throat and asks where I keep my money, I need not tell him the truth, because he will abuse it; and my untruth is not a lie (*mendacium*) because the thief knows full well that I will not, if I can help it, tell him the truth and that he has no right to demand it of me. But let us assume that I really say to the fellow, who is fully aware that he has no right to demand it, because he is a swindler, that I will tell him the truth, and I do not, am I then a liar? He has deceived me and I deceive him in return; to him, as an individual, I have done no injustice and he cannot complain; but I am none the less a liar in that my conduct is an infringement of the rights of humanity. It follows that a *falsiloquium* can be a *mendacium*—a lie—especially when it contravenes the right of an individual. Although I do a man no injustice by lying to him when he has lied to me, yet I act against the right of mankind, since I set myself in opposition to the condition and means through which any human society is possible. If one country breaks the peace this does not justify the other in doing likewise in revenge, for if it did no peace would ever be secure. Even though a statement does not contravene any particular human right it is nevertheless a lie if it is contrary to the general right of mankind. If a man spreads false news, though he does no wrong to anyone in particular, he offends against mankind, because if such a practice were universal man's desire for knowledge would be frustrated. For, apart from speculation, there are only two ways in which I can increase my fund of knowledge, by experience or by what others tell me. My own experience must necessarily be limited, and if what others told me was false, I could not satisfy my craving for knowledge.

. . . Not every untruth is a lie; it is a lie only if I have expressly given the other to understand that I am willing to acquaint him with my thought. Every lie is objectionable and contemptible in that we purposely let people think that we are telling them our thoughts and do not do so. We have broken our pact and violated the right of mankind. But if we were to be at all times punctiliously truthful we might often become victims of the wickedness of others who were ready to abuse our truthfulness. If all men were well-intentioned it would not only be a duty not to lie, but no one would do so because there would be no point in it. But as men are malicious, it cannot be denied that to be punctiliously truthful is often dangerous. This has given rise to the conception of a white lie, the lie enforced upon us by necessity—a difficult point for moral philosophers. For if necessity is urged as an excuse it might be urged to justify stealing, cheating and killing, and the whole basis of morality goes by the board. Then, again, what is a case of necessity? Everyone will interpret it in his own way. And, as there is then no definite standard to judge by, the application of moral rules becomes uncertain. Consider, for example, the following case. A man who knows that I have money asks me: "Have you any money on you?" If I fail to reply, he will conclude that I have; if I reply in the affirmative he will take it from me; if I reply in the negative, I tell a lie. What am I to do? If force is used to extort a confession from me, if any confession is improperly used against me, and if I cannot save myself by maintaining silence, then my lie is a weapon of defence. The misuse of a declaration extorted by force justifies me in defending myself. For whether it is my money or a confession that is extorted makes no difference. The forcing of a statement from me under conditions which convince me that improper use would be made of it is the only case in which I can be justified in telling a white lie. But if a lie does no harm to anyone and no one's interests are affected by it, is it a lie? Certainly, I undertake to express my mind, and if I do not really do so, though my statement may not be to the prejudice of the particular individual to whom it is made, it is none the less in *praejudicium humanitatis*. Then, again, there are lies which cheat. To cheat is to make a lying promise, while a breach of faith is a true promise which is not kept. A lying promise is an insult to the person to whom it is made, and even if this is not always so, yet there is always something mean about it. If, for instance, I promise to send some one a bottle of wine, and afterwards make a joke of it, I really swindle him. It is true that he has no right to demand the present of me, but in Idea it is already a part of his own property.

. . . . If a man tries to extort the truth from us and we cannot tell it [to] him and at the same time do not wish to lie, we are justified in resorting to equivocation in order to reduce him to silence and put a stop to his questionings. If he is wise, he will leave it at that. But if we let it be understood that we are expressing our sentiments and we proceed to equivocate we are in a different case; for our listeners might then draw wrong conclusions from our statements and we should have deceived them. . . . . But a lie is a lie, and is in itself intrinsically base whether it be told with good or bad intent. For formally a lie is always evil; though if it is evil materially as well, it is a much meaner thing. There are no lies which may not be the source of evil. A liar is a coward; he is a man who has recourse to lying because he is unable to help himself and gain his ends by any other means. But a stout-hearted man will love truth and will not recognize a *casus necessitatis*. All expedients which take us off our guard are thoroughly mean. Such are lying, assassination, and poisoning. To attack a man on the highway is less vile than to attempt to poison him. In the former case he can at least defend himself, but, as he must eat, he is defenceless against the poisoner. A flatterer is not always a liar; he is merely lacking in self-esteem; he has no scruple in reducing his own worth and raising that of another in order to gain something by it. But there exists a form of flattery which springs from kindness of heart. Some kind souls flatter people whom they hold in high esteem. There are thus two kinds of flattery, kindly and treacherous; the first is weak, while the second is mean. People who are not given to flattery are apt to be fault-finders.

If a man is often the subject of conversation, he becomes a subject of criticism. If he is our friend, we ought not invariably to speak well of him or else we arouse jealousy and grudge against him; for people, knowing that he is only human, will not believe that he has only good qualities. We must, therefore, concede a little to the adverse criticism of our listeners and point out some of our friend's faults; if we allow him faults which are common and unessential, while extolling his merits, our friend cannot take it in ill part. Toadies are people who praise others in company in hope of gain. Men are meant to form opinions regarding their fellows and to judge them. Nature has made us judges of our neighbors so that things which are false but are outside the scope of the established legal authority should be arraigned before the court of social opinion. Thus, if a man dishonours some one, the authorities do not punish him, but his fellows judge and punish him, though only so far as it is within their right to punish him and without doing violence to him. People shun him, and that is punishment enough. If that were not so, conduct not punished by the authorities would go altogether unpunished. What then is meant by the enjoinder that we ought not to judge others? As we are ignorant of their dispositions we cannot tell whether they are punishable before God or not, and we cannot, therefore, pass an adequate moral judgment upon them. The moral dispositions of others are for God to judge, but we are competent judges of our own. We cannot judge the inner core of morality: no man can do that; but we are competent to judge its outer manifestations. In matters of morality we are not judges of our fellows, but nature has given us the right to form judgments about others and she also has ordained that we should judge ourselves in accordance with judgments that others form about us. The man who turns a deaf ear to other people's opinion of him is base and reprehensible. There is nothing that happens in this world about which we ought not to form an opinion, and we show considerable subtlety in judging conduct. Those who judge our conduct with exactness are our best friends. Only friends can be quite candid and open with each other. But in judging a man a further question arises. In what terms are we to judge him? Must we pronounce him either good or evil? We must proceed from the assumption that humanity is lovable, and, particularly in regard to wickedness, we ought never to pronounce a verdict either of condemnation or of acquittal. We pronounce such a verdict whenever we judge from his conduct that a man deserves to be condemned or acquitted. But though we are entitled to form opinions about our fellows, we have no right to spy upon them. Everyone has a right to prevent others from watching and scrutinizing his actions. The spy arrogates to himself the right to watch the doings of strangers; no one ought to presume to do such a thing. If I see two people whispering to each other so as not to be heard, my inclination ought to be to get farther away so that no sound may reach my ears. Or if I am left alone in a room and I see a letter lying open on the table, it would be contemptible to try to read it; a right-thinking man would not do so; in fact, in order to avoid suspicion and distrust he will endeavour not to be left alone in a room where money is left lying about, and he will be averse from learning other people's secrets in order to avoid the risk of the suspicion that he has betrayed them; other people's secrets trouble him, for even between the most intimate of friends suspicion might arise. A man who will let his inclination or appetite drive him to deprive his friend of anything, of his fiancée, for instance, is contemptible beyond a doubt. If he can cherish a passion for my sweetheart, he can equally well cherish a passion for my purse. It is very mean to lie in wait and spy upon a friend, or on anyone else, and to elicit information about him from menials by lowering ourselves to the level of our inferiors, who will thereafter not forget to regard themselves as our equals. Whatever militates against frankness lowers the dignity of man. Insidious, underhand conduct uses means which strike at the roots of society because they make frankness impossible; it is far viler than violence; for against violence we can defend ourselves, and a violent man who spurns meanness can be tamed to goodness, but the mean rogue, who has not the courage to come out into the open with his roguery, is devoid of every vestige of nobility of character. For that reason a wife who attempts to poison her husband in England is burnt at the stake, for if such conduct spread, no man would be safe from his wife.

As I am not entitled to spy upon my neighbour, I am equally not entitled to point out his faults to him; and even if he should ask me to do so he would feel hurt if I complied. He knows his faults better than I, he knows that he has them, but he likes to believe that I have not noticed them, and if I tell him of them he realizes that I have. To say, therefore, that friends ought to point out each other's faults, is not sound advice. My friend may know better than I whether my gait or deportment is proper or not, but if I will only examine myself, who can know me better than I can know myself? To point out his faults to a friend is sheer impertinence; and once fault finding begins between friends their friendship will not last long. We must turn a blind eye to the faults of others, lest they conclude that they have lost our respect and we lose theirs. Only if placed in positions of authority over others should we point out to them their defects. Thus a husband is entitled to teach and correct his wife, but his corrections must be well-intentioned and kindly and must be dominated by respect, for if they be prompted only by displeasure they result in mere blame and bitterness. If we must blame, we must temper the blame with a sweetening of love, good-will, and respect. Nothing else will avail to bring about improvement.

NOTE

1. CF. *Babrii fabulae Aesopeae*, ed. O. Cousins, 1897, Fable 59, p. 54.

Is Business Bluffing Ethical?

ALBERT CARR

A respected businessman with whom I discussed the theme of this article remarked with some heat, "You mean to say you're going to encourage men to bluff? Why, bluffing is nothing more than a form of lying! You're advising them to lie!"

I agreed that the basis of private morality is a respect for truth and that the closer a businessman comes to the truth, the more he deserves respect. At the same time, I suggested that most bluffing in business might be regarded simply as game strategy—much like bluffing in poker, which does not reflect on the morality of the bluffer.

I quoted Henry Taylor, the British statesman who pointed out that "falsehood ceases to be falsehood when it is understood on all sides that the truth is not expected to be spoken"—an exact description of bluffing in poker, diplomacy, and business. I cited the analogy of the criminal court, where the criminal is not expected to tell the truth when he pleads "not guilty." Everyone from the judge down takes it for granted that the job of the defendant's attorney is to get his client off, not to reveal the truth; and this is considered ethical practice. I mentioned Representative Omar Burleson, the Democrat from Texas, who was quoted as saying, in regard to the ethics of Congress, "Ethics is a barrel of worms"[1]—a pungent summing up of the problem of deciding who is ethical in politics.

I reminded my friend that millions of businessmen feel constrained every day to say *yes* to their bosses when they secretly believe *no* and that this is generally accepted as permissible strategy when the alternative might be the loss of a job. The essential point, I said, is that the ethics of business are game ethics, different from the ethics of religion.

He remained unconvinced. Referring to the company of which he is president, he declared: "Maybe that's good enough for some businessmen, but I can tell you that we pride ourselves on our ethics. In 30 years not one customer has ever questioned my word or asked to check our figures. We're loyal to our customers and fair to our suppliers. I regard my handshake on a deal as a contract. I've never entered into price-fixing schemes with my competitors. I've never allowed my salesmen to spread injurious rumors about other companies. Our union contract is the best in our industry. And, if I do say so myself, our ethical standards are of the highest!"

He really was saying, without realizing it, that he was living up to the ethical standards of the business game—which are a far cry from those of private life. Like a gentlemanly poker player, he did not play in cahoots with others at the table, try to smear their reputations, or hold back chips he owed them.

But this same fine man, at that very time, was allowing one of his products to be advertised in a way that made it sound a great deal better than it actually was. Another item in his product line was notorious among dealers for its "built-in-obsolescence." He was holding back from the market a much-improved product because he did not want to interfere with sales of the inferior item it would have replaced. He had joined with certain of his competitors in hiring a lobbyist to push a state legislature, by methods that he preferred not to know too much about, into amending a bill then being enacted.

In his view these things had nothing to do with ethics; they were merely normal business practice. He himself undoubtedly avoided outright falsehoods—never lied in so many words. But the entire organization that he ruled was deeply involved in numerous strategies of deception.

PRESSURE TO DECEIVE

Most executives from time to time are almost compelled, in the interests of their companies or themselves, to practice some form of deception when negotiating with customers, dealers, labor unions, government officials, or even other departments of their companies. By conscious misstatements, concealment of pertinent facts, or exaggeration—in short, by bluffing—they seek to persuade others to agree with them. I think it is fair to say that if the individual executive refuses to bluff from time to time—if he feels obligated to tell the truth, the whole truth, and nothing but the truth—he is ignoring opportunities permitted under the rules and is at a heavy disadvantage in his business dealings.

But here and there a businessman is unable to reconcile himself to the bluff in which he plays a part. His conscience, perhaps spurred by religious idealism, troubles him. He feels guilty; he may develop an ulcer or a nervous tic. Before any executive can make profitable use of the strategy of the bluff, he needs to make sure that in bluffing he will not lose self-respect or become emotionally disturbed. If he is to reconcile personal integrity and high standards of honesty with the practical requirements of business, he must feel that his bluffs are ethically justified. The justification rests on the fact that business, as practiced by individuals as well as by corporations, has the impersonal character of a game—a game that demands both special strategy and an understanding of its special ethics.

The game is played at all levels of corporate life, from the highest to the lowest. At the very instant that a man decides to enter business, he may be forced into a game situation, as is shown by the recent experience of a Cornell honor graduate who applied for a job with a large company:

• This applicant was given a psychological test which included the statement, "Of the following magazines, check any that you have read either regularly or from time to time, and double-check those which interest you most. *Reader's Digest, Time, Fortune, Saturday Evening Post, The New Republic, Life, Look, Ramparts, Newsweek, Business Week, U.S. News & World Report, The Nation, Playboy, Esquire, Harper's, Sports Illustrated.*

His tastes in reading were broad, and at one time or another he had read almost all of these magazines. He was a subscriber to the *The New Republic*, an enthusiast for *Ramparts*, and an avid student of the pictures in *Playboy*. He was not sure whether his interest in *Playboy* would be held against him, but he had a shrewd suspicion that if he confessed to an interest in *Ramparts* and *The New Republic*, he would be thought a liberal, a radical, or at least an intellectual, and his chances of getting the job, which he needed, would greatly diminish. He therefore checked five of the more conservative magazines. Apparently it was a sound decision, for he got the job.

He had made a game player's decision, consistent with business ethics.

A similar case is that of a magazine space salesman who, owing to a merger, suddenly found himself out of a job:

• This man was 58, and, in spite of a good record, his chances of getting a job elsewhere in a business where youth is favored in hiring practice was not good. He was a vigorous, healthy man, and only a considerable amount of gray in his hair suggested his age. Before beginning his job search he touched up his hair with a black dye to confine the gray to his temples. He knew that the truth about his age might well come out in time, but he calculated that he could deal with that situation when it arose. He and his wife decided that he could easily pass for 45, and he so stated his age on his résumé.

This was a lie; yet within the accepted rules of the business game, no moral culpability attaches to it.

THE POKER ANALOGY

We can learn a good deal about the nature of business by comparing it with poker. While both have a large element of chance, in the long run the winner is the man who plays with steady skill. In both games ultimate victory requires intimate knowledge of the rules, insight into the psychology of the other players, a bold front, a considerable amount of self-discipline and the ability to respond swiftly and effectively to opportunities provided by chance.

No one expects poker to be played on the ethical principles preached in churches. In poker it is right and proper to bluff a friend out of the rewards of being dealt a good hand. A player feels no more than a slight twinge of sympathy, if that, when—with nothing better than a single ace in his hand—he strips a heavy loser, who holds a pair, of the rest of his chips. It was up to the other fellow to protect himself. In the words of an excellent poker player, former President Harry Truman, "If you can't stand the heat, stay out of the kitchen." If one shows mercy to a loser in poker, it is a personal gesture, divorced from the rules of the game.

Poker has its special ethics, and here I am not referring to rules against cheating. The man who keeps an ace up his sleeve or who marks the cards is more than unethical; he is a crook, and can be punished as such—kicked out of the game or, in the Old West, shot.

In contrast to the cheat, the unethical poker player is one who, while abiding by the letter of the rules, finds ways to put the other players at an unfair disadvantage. Perhaps he unnerves them with loud talk. Or he tries to get them drunk. Or he plays in cahoots with someone else at the table. Ethical poker players frown on such tactics.

Poker's own brand of ethics is different from the ethical ideals of civilized human relationships. The game calls for distrust of the other fellow. It ignores the claim of friendship. Cunning deception and concealment of one's strength and intentions, not kindness and openheartedness, are vital in poker. No one thinks any the worse of poker on that account. And no one should think any the worse of the game of business because its standards of right and wrong differ from the prevailing traditions of morality in our society. . . .

WE DON'T MAKE THE LAWS

Wherever we turn in business, we can perceive the sharp distinction between its ethical standards and those of the churches. Newspapers abound with sensational stories growing out of this distinction:

- We read one day that Senator Philip A. Hart of Michigan has attacked food processors for deceptive packaging of numerous products.[2]
- The next day there is a Congressional to-do over Ralph Nader's book, *Unsafe At Any Speed*, which demonstrates that automobile companies for years have neglected the safety of car-owning families.[3]
- Then another Senator, Lee Metcalf of Montana, and journalist Vic Reinemer show in their book, *Overcharge*, the methods by which utility companies elude regulating government bodies to extract unduly large payments from users of electricity.[4]

These are merely dramatic instances of a prevailing condition; there is hardly a major industry at which a similar attack could not be aimed. Critics of business regard such behavior as unethical, but the companies concerned know that they are merely playing the business game.

Among the most respected of our business institutions are the insurance companies. A group of insurance executives meeting recently in New England was started when their guest speaker, social critic Daniel Patrick Moynihan, roundly berated them for "unethical" practices. They had been guilty, Moynihan alleged, of using outdated actuarial tables to obtain unfairly high premiums. They habitually delayed the hearings of lawsuits against them in order to tire out the plaintiffs and win cheap settlements. In their employment policies they used ingenious devices to discriminate against certain minority groups.[5]

It was difficult for the audience to deny the validity of these charges. But these men were business game players. Their reaction to Moynihan's attack was much the same as that of the automobile manufacturers to Nader, of the utilities to Senator Metcalf, and of the food processors to Senator Hart. If the laws governing their business change, or if public opinion becomes clamorous, they will make the necessary adjustments. But morally they have in their view done nothing wrong. As long as they comply with the letter of the law, they are within their rights to operate their businesses as they see fit.

The small business is in the same position as the great corporation in this respect. For example:

• In 1967 a key manufacturer was accused of providing master keys for automobiles to mail-order customers, although it was obvious that some of the purchasers might be automobile thieves. His defense was plain and straightforward. If there was nothing in the law to prevent him from selling his keys to anyone who ordered them, it was not up to him to inquire as to his customers' motives. Why was it any worse, he insisted, for him to sell car keys by mail, than for mail-order houses to sell guns that might be used for murder? Until the law was changed, the key manufacturer could regard himself as being just as ethical as any other businessman by the rules of the business game.[6]

Violations of the ethical ideals of society are common in business, but they are not necessarily violations of business practices. Each year the Federal Trade Commission orders hundreds of companies, many of them of the first magnitude, to "cease and desist" from practices which, judged by ordinary standards, are of questionable morality but which are stoutly defended by the companies concerned.

In one case, a firm manufacturing a well-known mouthwash was accused of using a cheap form of alcohol possibly deleterious to health. The company's chief executive, after testifying in Washington, made this comment privately:

> We broke no law. We're in a highly competitive industry. If we're going to stay in business, we have to look for profit wherever the law permits. We don't make up the laws. We obey them. Then why do we have to put up with this 'holier

than thou' talk about ethics? It's sheer hypocrisy. We're not in business to promote ethics. Look at the cigarette companies, for God's sake! If the ethics aren't embodied in the laws by the men who made them, you can't expect businessmen to fill the lack. Why, a sudden submission to Christian ethics by businessmen would bring about the greatest economic upheaval in history!

It may be noted that the government failed to prove its case against him.

CAST ILLUSIONS ASIDE

Talk about ethics by businessmen is often a thin decorative coating over the hard realities of the game:

• Once I listened to a speech by a young executive who pointed to a new industry code as proof that his company and its competitors were deeply aware of their responsibilities to society. It was a code of ethics, he said. The industry was going to police itself, to dissuade constituent companies from wrongdoing. His eyes shone with conviction and enthusiasm.

The same day there was a meeting in a hotel room where the industry's top executives met with the "czar" who was to administer the new code, a man of high repute. No one who was present could doubt their common attitude. In their eyes the code was designed primarily to forestall a move by the federal government to impose stern restrictions on the industry. They felt that the code would hamper them a good deal less than new federal laws would. It was, in other words, conceived as a protection for the industry, not for the public.

The young executive accepted the surface explanation of the code; these leaders, all experienced game players, did not deceive themselves for a moment about its purpose.

The illusion that business can afford to be guided by ethics as conceived in private life is often fostered by speeches and articles containing such phrases as, "It pays to be ethical," or, "Sound ethics is good business." Actually this is not an ethical question at all; it is a self-serving calculation in disguise. The speaker is really saying that in the long run a company can make more money if it does not antagonize competitors, suppliers, employees, and customers by squeezing them too hard. He is saying that oversharp policies reduce ultimate gains. That is true, but it has nothing to do with ethics. The underlying attitude is much like that in the familiar story of the shopkeeper who finds an extra $20 bill in the cash register, debates with himself the ethical problem—should he tell his partner?—and finally decides to share the money because the gesture will give him an edge over the s.o.b. the next time they quarrel.

I think it is fair to sum up the prevailing attitude of businessmen on ethics as follows:

We live in what is probably the most competitive of the world's civilized societies. Our customs encourage a high degree of aggression in the individual's striving for success. Business is our main area of competition, and it has been ritualized into a game of strategy. The basic rules of the game have been set by the government, which attempts to detect and punish business frauds. But as long as a company does not transgress the rules of the game set by law, it has the legal right to shape its strategy without reference to anything but its profits. If it takes a long-term view of its profits, it will preserve amicable relations, so far as possible, with those with whom it deals. A wise businessman will not seek advantage to the point where he generates dangerous hostility among employees, competitors, customers, government, or the public at large. But decisions in this area are, in the final test, decisions of strategy, not of ethics.

PLAYING TO WIN

. . . If a man plans to make a seat in the business game, he owes it to himself to master the principles by which the game is played, including its special ethical outlook. He can then hardly fail to recognize that an occasional bluff may well be justified in terms of the game's ethics and warranted in terms of economic necessity. Once he clears his mind on this point, he is in a good position to match his strategy against that of the other players. He can then determine objectively whether a bluff in a given situation has a good chance of succeeding and can decide when and how to bluff, without a feeling of ethical transgression.

To be a winner, a man must play to win. This does not mean that he must be ruthless, cruel, harsh, or treacherous. On the contrary, the better his reputation for integrity, honesty, and decency, the better his chances of victory will be in the long run. But from time to time every businessman, like every poker player, is offered a choice between certain loss or bluffing within the legal rules of the game. If he is not resigned to losing, if he wants to rise in his company and industry, then in such a crisis he will bluff—and bluff hard.

Every now and then one meets a successful businessman who has conveniently forgotten the small or large deceptions that he practiced on his way to fortune. "God gave me my money," old John D. Rockefeller once piously told a Sunday school class. It would be a rare tycoon in our time who would risk the horse laugh with which such a remark would be greeted.

In the last third of the twentieth century even children are aware that if a man has become prosperous in business, he has sometimes departed from the strict truth in order to overcome obstacles or has practiced the more subtle deceptions of the half-truth or the misleading omission. Whatever the form of the bluff, it is an integral part of the game, and the executive who does not master its techniques is not likely to accumulate much money or power.

NOTES
1. *The New York Times*, March 9, 1967.
2. *The New York Times*, November 21, 1966.
3. New York, Grossman Publishers, Inc., 1965.
4. New York, David McKay Company, Inc., 1967.
5. *The New York Times*, January 17, 1967.
6. Cited by Ralph Nader in "Business Crime," *The New Republic*, July 1, 1967, p. 7.

•Part Two•

MORALITY
AND CORPORATIONS
Introduction

People eat, sleep, vote, love, hate, and suffer guilt. Corporations do none of these. Yet corporations are considered "persons" under the law and have many of the same rights as humans: to sue, to own property, to conduct business and conclude contracts, and to enjoy freedom of speech, of the press, and freedom from unreasonable searches and seizures. Corporations are legal citizens of the state in which they are chartered. They even possess two rights not held by humans: unlimited longevity and limited liability. This means that corporations have unlimited charters—they never "die"—and their shareholders are liable for corporate debts only up to the extent of their personal investment.

One of the most stubborn ethical issues surrounding the corporation is not what it should do, but how it should be understood. *What* is a corporation? Is it a distinct individual in its own right, or merely an aggregate of individuals, for example, stockholders, managers, and employees? The answer to this question is crucial for understanding corporations and their activities. We must know, morally speaking, whether a corporation has responsibilities and rights in addition to the rights and responsibilities of the aggregate of individuals that make it up. We already know that individual members of a corporation can be held morally responsible. For example, if a chemical engineer intentionally puts a dangerous chemical in a new cosmetic product, he is morally blameworthy. But can we hold the corporation, considered as something distinct from its individual members, morally blameworthy too?

On the one hand, the very concept of a corporation seems to involve more than the individual actions of specific persons. The corporation is understood to exist even after all its original members are deceased; it is said to hire employees or fire them when only a handful of the corporate members are involved in the decision, and it is said to have obligations through its charter that override the desires of its individual members. Let us grant that the corporation is a distinct entity such that its actions are not reducible—at least in a straightforward way—to the actions of individuals. Does it follow that the corporation has moral characteristics that are not reducible to the moral characteristics of its members? Philosophers have addressed this issue by asking whether the corporation is a "moral agent." Rocks, trees, and machines are clearly not moral agents. People clearly are. What are we to say about corporations?

Whatever the answer to this question, a second immediately follows, namely, What should society expect from corporations? The two questions are closely connected. For if we answer the first by concluding that the corporation is a moral agent, then we will formulate the second by asking, What is the nature of a corporation's rights and obligations? If, on the other hand, we answer the first question by denying that the corporation is a moral agent, and hence refuse to ascribe to it any rights or obligations, we will formulate the second question by asking, What behavior should society expect from the individual persons that make up the corporation, that is, those who hold its offices, perform its tasks, and construct its rules? By phrasing the second question this way, we do not attribute moral agency to the corporation but treat it as a powerful nonmoral entity.

Both the first and second questions have enormous practical and philosophical significance, for if corporations are true moral agents, we should expect them to develop and manifest a sense of right and wrong, and to possess certain rights, privileges, and responsibilities. But if they are not moral agents, we must proceed to determine what sorts of entities they really are in order to discover how best to treat them and what to expect from them. For example, if it is determined that corporations are similar to large machines, they must be externally controlled like any large machine with the capacity to harm society. According to this view, we must abandon hope of a corporation exercising genuine moral responsibility. But then we are forced to regulate those corporate activities which are socially unacceptable, a move which may not be altogether palatable to the business community.

THE MORAL STATUS OF CORPORATIONS

When discussing whether corporations are moral agents, a good place to begin is with corporate legal history, that is, with the series of legislative acts and court decisions that have defined the corporation's existence. From its beginning in the Middle Ages, the corporation has been subject to differing legal interpretations. In the Middle Ages the law did not recognize any profit-making organizations as corporations; instead, it granted corporate status only to guilds, boroughs, and the church. In some instances the law decreed that corporations follow strict guidelines; for example, in 1279 the French Statute of Mortmain declared that a corporation's property could not exceed a specified amount. Even hundreds of years after its beginning, the corporation remained subject to strict legal sanctions on the conditions of its charter. As late as the nineteenth century, some U.S. corporations were granted charters only on the condition that they restrict land purchases to a certain geographic location and to a maximum number of acres. Thus corporations were viewed merely as artificial beings, created by the state and owing their very existence to a decree by the government.

But in the latter part of the nineteenth century and in the twentieth century, especially in the United States, this view suffered a dramatic change. Instead of treating corporations as mere creations of the state, the courts began to see them as natural outcomes of the habits of business persons. It saw them as the predictable results of the actions of business persons who, exercising their inalienable right to associate freely with others, gathered together to conduct business and pursue a profit. As such, incorporation came to be seen less as a privilege granted by the state and more as a right to be protected by the state. Chartering a corporation became easier, and government restrictions less severe. Even so, the traditional view of a corporation continues to influence the law. The most accepted legal definition of a corporation remains the one offered by Chief Justice Marshall in 1819: "A corporation," he wrote, "is an artificial being, invisible, intangible, and existing only in the contemplation of law. Being the mere creation of law, it possesses only those properties which the charter of its creation confers upon it . . . "

Throughout the evolution of corporate law, the problem of whether and how to ascribe responsibility to the corporation persisted. In the sixteenth century the large trading corporations were not themselves held responsible when one ship collided with another; instead, the individual boat owners, who participated in the corporation only to secure special trading rights, were held individually responsible. By the seventeenth century, the notion of "corporate" responsibility was thoroughly established in the law, but some sticky issues remained. Could a corporation be criminally liable? What rights, if any, did corporations share with ordinary persons? In the early twentieth century and again in recent years, U.S. corporations have been charged with homicide—one such case involved the Ford Pinto's exploding gas tank—but in every instance so far, although the court has been willing to impose stiff fines, it has stopped short of entering a verdict of homicide.

In 1978 the U.S. Supreme Court delivered a landmark verdict in the case of *First National Bank of Boston v. Bellotti*. The fundamental issue was whether a corporation should be allowed the right to free speech even when exercising that right by spending corporate money to promote political causes not directly related to corporate profits. Should corporations have full-fledged first amendment rights to free speech even when that means that they can use their vast financial reserves to support partisan political ends? In a split decision the Supreme Court decided in favor of recognizing such a right, although the decision itself remains controversial.

Whatever the courts eventually decide about the legal status of a corporation, questions about its moral status will remain. Two distinct and dramatically opposed moral views on this topic are presented in this section. The first, represented in an article by the contemporary philosopher Peter French, holds that corporations are moral agents in the sense that they can have moral responsibility attributed to them more or less on a par with persons. The second, represented by John Ladd, takes a reverse stand. Ladd argues that corporations are not "persons" at all—even of the fictional kind —and hence cannot truly be said to possess rights and responsibilities.

Professor French, in his article "The Corporation as a Moral Person," constructs an argument for corporate moral agency by relying on the nature of a corporation's "internal decision-making structure." Corporations have policies, rules, and decision-making procedures, all of which, when considered together, qualify them for the status of a moral agent. They can be praised or blamed for such decisions; this decision-making capacity requires that they be "intentional beings" and have essentially the same responsibilities and rights as ordinary persons.

John Ladd, in his well-known article "Morality and the Ideal of Rationality in Formal Organizations," argues that a corporation is structured to achieve certain goals. In contrast with French, Ladd challenges the claim that a corporation is an autonomous, independent, formal organization which has its own self-determined goals. Because of its very structure, it can try to achieve only its formal ends, which cannot, by definition, be moral ones. Consequently a corporation is not a moral agent at all, but more like a complicated machine; and like a machine, a corporation cannot be said to have genuine moral and social responsibilities.

The debate between French and Ladd is of more than abstract philosophical interest, as the Union Carbide case illustrates. On December 2, 1984 the disaster in Bhopal, India left more than two thousand dead and two hundred thousand injured. One of the striking facts about the disaster was the paucity of regulatory control in Bhopal. Regulations were in place, but they were inadequately constructed and enforced. Almost anyone familiar with the details of the case grants that the Union Carbide corporation is *financially liable* to compensate the victims of the disaster, that is, they grant that Union Carbide should pay damages to the victims and their families. But as we have noted, Ladd and others would deny that it is *morally responsible*. And, more important, if one agrees with Ladd on this point, it appears we can never expect Union Carbide or any other company to develop a moral conscience that would prevent similar mistakes. At least companies could never develop a conscience sufficiently sophisticated to go beyond wanting to avoid paying fines and damages. From this perspective, Union Carbide, by virtue of its very nature as a corporation, may be doomed to repeat mistakes that have tragic human consequences, especially in environments where laws are lax.

The Union Carbide case also raises the earlier question about how responsibility can be realized in complex organizations. The company formally took responsibility for managing an operation that existed halfway around the world, in a country with a technological infrastructure very different from its home country, the United States. Was its "internal decision-making structure," to use French's phrase, adequate for such a responsibility?

One of the implications of Ladd's approach is that the moral agency of the employee is swallowed by the amoral agency of the corporation for which she works. In other words, the demands upon the employee imposed by the profit-seeking character of the corporation tend to drive out that individual's moral decision-making power. This very issue is the subject of R. M. Hare's article, "Can I be Blamed for Obeying Orders?," which asserts that a point exists beyond which we cannot escape our own moral responsibilities by laying them on the shoulders of a corporate officer, priest, or politician. If Hare is correct, whatever pressures Ladd has identified that push employees to abandon their own conscience, must—and can—be resisted.

THE MORAL RESPONSIBILITIES OF CORPORATIONS

The second section deals with a more difficult issue: What should we hope for in terms of corporate behavior? Whether a corporation is a moral agent or not, it must adhere to certain norms of behavior. For example, at a minimum a corporation must not deliberately murder or systematically harm others. But beyond specifying a bare minimum, what can one say? How can one *evaluate* corporate behavior from a moral perspective?

In the *Harvard Business Review* article, "Uncommon Decency: Pacific Bell Responds to AIDS," we find after a great deal of foot dragging, a California corporation moving to develop one of the most respected AIDS programs in the country. At one point the company even decided to enter the political fray, taking a stand to oppose a measure that would have eliminated anonymous AIDS testing throughout the state.

How are we to understand the moral responsibility of a corporation? Does it extend, as Pacific Bell seems to believe, to creating exemplary programs to deal with broad problems of public interest? Does it extend to fighting proposed laws that the corporation opposes? In this section we find three articles that help answer such questions. In Evan and Freeman's "Article on Stakeholder Theory," we encounter an increasingly popular concept in business ethics literature, namely, that of the corporate "stakeholder." Defined as any group or individual who can affect or is affected by a business, the "stakeholder" can be a shareholder, an employee, a supplier, a customer, or other individuals or groups. Notice that the stakeholder concept, if accepted, conflicts with the assumption that the moral responsibility of business is nothing other than profit maximization (a view associated with Milton Friedman that we will examine in the next section). It assumes, rather, that the job of the manager is to weigh and balance the interests of a variety of stakeholders including, but not limited to, those of the investors.

The sociologist James Coleman provides a starkly different view of the corporation, one that relies heavily on modern economic interpretations of the firm. His concept of the firm as emerging, at least in part, in response to the costs of individuals attempting to do business for themselves (without benefit of firms) offers an economic explanation for why markets tolerate corporations, and raises interesting ethical questions. Is one form of control in the corporation precisely *moral* in character? Coleman answers this question with a "yes," and speaks of the arrangement of rights in a firm as one of the key instruments of *control to hold* largely self-interested individuals in harmony. Does it follow that the moral character of a corporation can and should vary from corporation to corporation? In the concluding sections of the article, Coleman offers his personal views about the key failing of the modern corporation: its inability to accommodate the needs of the family and, in particular, those of children.

If, as Coleman suggests, corporations are capable of assigning rights to employees and other organizational participants in different ways, then the next question is whether they are capable of shaping the overall corporate moral character. In retelling a dramatic true-to-life episode in which he played a role, a Wall Street financier, Bowen McCoy, attempts to establish an analogy between personal and corporate ethics. When mountain climbing in the Himalaya Mountains, McCoy and his climbing party left an Indian Holy man behind in the snow in order to achieve their goal of reaching the summit. What similarities, he asks, are there between this episode and decisions facing corporate managers? And, equally important, what lessons from the behavior of McCoy's climbing party extend to the corporate organization?

The Moral Status
of Corporations

Case Study

Union Carbide:
Chemical Dangers

ROGENE A. BUCHHOLZ

During the evening of Sunday, December 2, 1984, an incident happened in
Bhopal, India, that has been called the worst industrial accident in history.
The first sign that something was wrong came shortly before midnight when
a worker at the Union Carbide pesticide plant on the outskirts of Bhopal
(pop. 672,000) noticed that pressure was building up in a tank that contained
45 tons of methyl isocyanate (MIC), a deadly chemical used to make pesticides. Pressure in the tank continued to build until sometime after midnight
when the highly volatile and highly toxic MIC began to escape from the tank
into the surrounding atmosphere. The escaping gas overwhelmed inadequate and reportedly out-of-commission safety backup systems and spread in
a foglike cloud over a large and highly populated area close to the plant.

The cloud first passed over the shantytowns of Jaiparakash and Chola,
just outside the walls of the plant, and then quickly enveloped the city's
railway station. From there the cloud spread noiselessly and lethally across a
25-square-mile area of the city. Apparently the night air at that time was fairly
cool, the wind was calm, and a heavy mist clung to the ground. These
conditions prevented the gas from dissipating as it would have done during
the day. Thus the cloud continued to move across the city (Figure 1) spread-
ing death and injury in its wake.[1]

Early reports indicated that twenty-five hundred people had died and at
least another one thousand were expected to die within a two-week period.
Some one hundred fifty thousand people were said to have been treated at
hospitals and clinics in Bhopal and surrounding communities. Most of the
deaths were caused by the lungs filling up with fluid, causing the equivalent
of death by drowning. Other people suffered heart attacks. Some of the

Reprinted by permission of the author.

Figure 1. Escaping Gas Blanketed Much of Bhopal

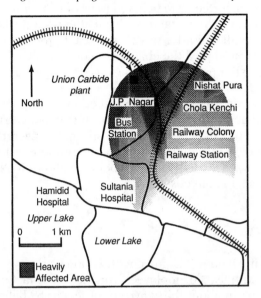

Source: Reprinted with permission from Wil Lepkowski, "People of India Struggle Toward Appropriate Response to Tragedy." *Chemical and Engineering News* 63, no. 6 (February 11, 1985), p. 16. Copyright 1985 American Chemical Society.

survivors were permanently blinded; others suffered serious lesions in their nasal and bronchial passages. Doctors also noticed concussions, paralysis, and signs of epilepsy. Six days after the accident it was reported that patients were still arriving at Hamidia Hospital in Bhopal at the rate of one per minute, many of them doubling over with racking coughs, gasping for breath, or convulsing with violent spasms.[2]

Almost four months later there was still a great deal of dispute about the exact number of victims that were killed and injured by the cloud. The chief lawyer for Union Carbide said that the number of victims had been significantly exaggerated by the Indian government and by American lawyers. The Indian government said that the recorded death toll was approximately one thousand seven hundred persons with as many as two hundred thousand persons physically injured. A number of public interest and medical groups in India estimated the death toll to be between ten thousand and thirty thousand people, contending that many of the victims were cremated or dumped into mass graves without any record ever being made.[3]

An accurate estimate of the number of victims was complicated by the large numbers of impoverished beggars and nomadic gypsies who were living in Bhopal at the time and for whom no records existed. Nonetheless the company only accepted the 1,408 deaths that were actually recorded at Bhopal hospitals and believed that the true number of injuries was a small fraction of the 200,000 figure used by the government of India. Many of the injuries that were reported were believed to be only minor ailments, such as temporary nausea and eye irritations.[4] No matter what the final figures turn out to be, however, the disaster was of significant proportions.

The disaster prompted the chairperson of Union Carbide, Warren M. Anderson, to fly to Bhopal soon after the tragedy happened. When he arrived in India, he along with two officials of the company's Indian subsidiary were arrested and charged with "negligence and criminal corporate liability" and "criminal conspiracy." These charges under Indian law carried a maximum penalty of death. Instead of being taken to prison, however, the three executives were detained at the company's Bhopal guesthouse. After more than six hours Anderson was released on $2,500 bond and flown to New Delhi while his colleagues remained in custody.[5]

THE COMPANY

Headquartered in Danbury, Connecticut, Union Carbide is a multinational corporate giant with 99,000 employees working in 700 factories, mills, labs, and other facilities in about thirty-five countries. Its $9 billion sales in 1983 were down from a peak of $10.17 billion in 1981 and came from a diversity of industrial and consumer products. Many of Union Carbide's products are familiar names such as Prestone antifreeze, Glad bags, and Eveready batteries. But the company's best customers are other businesses. Such industrial products include polyethylene, industrial gases such as argon and acetylene, and other products that bear unmemorable technical labels of which methyl isocyanate has become a historic exception.[6] These industrial products accounted for 79 percent of sales in 1983.[7]

Many observers believed the company took environmental concerns very seriously. In 1977 Russell Train, the highly visible and respected former administrator of the Environmental Protection Agency (EPA), was elected a director of Union Carbide. Even before he joined the board, Union Carbide had commissioned a study on how to respond to environmental problems and had established the corporate Department of Health, Safety, and Environmental Affairs. A study by the Council on Economic Priorities rated the company first among the nation's eight largest chemical companies in terms of its compliance with Occupational Safety and Health Administration (OSHA) standards between 1972 and 1979.[8]

Union Carbide was first incorporated in India some fifty years ago when the company began manufacturing batteries. The Indian subsidiary was allowed to stay on after India won independence from Britain and was one of the few firms in India in which the parent company was permitted to hold a majority interest. Union Carbide owns 50.9 percent of the Bhopal facility. The Indian government has long favored Union Carbide because of its interests in developing sophisticated industry and in promoting the Green

Revolution in agriculture. Pesticides are an important ingredient in this revolution, which is important to India because of its huge population, much of which is very poor by U.S. standards.[9]

The Bhopal plant was built in 1969 with approval from the local authorities and the blessing of the national government. The firm was exempted from a number of local taxes and even provided with water and electricity at concessional prices. When the plant was first built, it was located just outside the city limits in an open area, but by the time an expansion program got underway six years later, the area between the town and the plant was settled by squatters. Many of them were attracted by the roads and water lines that accompanied the plant. In 1975 the administrator of the municipal corporation asked that the plant be removed because of potential dangers to the people living nearby. Instead the administrator was removed from office and the plant remained.[10]

In July of 1984 the Department of the Environment in India announced strict guidelines banning the location of plants that produced such hazardous substances as gases, poisons, and explosives in areas where population growth was expected. But whether this ruling was supposed to apply to facilities already constructed was unclear. In any event the ruling ran counter to the desire of many local governments to attract industry.[11] As far as Union Carbide was concerned, the Bhopal plant was at best a marginal operation because of slumping demand for pesticides. Sales of products from the plant dropped 23 percent in 1983 to $17 million, and the plant was operating at less than one-third of its capacity at the time of the accident.[12]

THE LEGAL ISSUES

The deadly cloud had hardly dissipated before lawyers became involved. Five American attorneys, including Melvin M. Belli, filed a class-action suit against Union Carbide on behalf of the victims that asked $15 billion in damages. The suit sought to represent all those who were injured or who lost relatives as a result of the disaster. The suit claimed that the corporation was negligent in designing the Bhopal plant and that the company failed to warn the area's residents about the dangers presented by the stored chemical. The suit charged that Union Carbide acted "willfully and wantonly" with utter disregard for the safety of Bhopal residents. This charge was partly based on the allegation that the Bhopal plant lacked a computerized early warning system that had been installed in the company's plant in Institute, West Virginia, which was supposedly identical to the Bhopal facility.[13]

The $15 billion in damages sought in this first suit was greater than the net worth of the company. With assets of $10 billion and 1983 sales of $9 billion, the company was the thirty-seventh largest U.S. industrial corporation and the third largest chemical manufacturer, after DuPont and Dow Chemical. One of the most critical problems faced by the company was whether the courts would conclude that it was negligent and therefore assess punitive as well as compensatory damages. Insurance policies do not normally cover punitive damages, which in the case of Union Carbide could amount to staggering sums of money that would overwhelm Carbide's ability to pay and perhaps force it to file for bankruptcy in order to protect itself against further lawsuits.[14]

One of the major issues to be settled in regard to this lawsuit (as well as others) was whether a U.S. court would be the proper place to hear the suit or whether the trial should take place in India. The company was expected to argue that the trial should take place where the accident happened and where the victims lived and worked. Because most of the witnesses and evidence would have to be moved from India to the United States for a trial, an Indian forum would be better. Critics were quick to point out that a settlement in India would be much better for the company. Courts in both countries would probably calculate compensation in much the same way by focusing on the value of lost earnings from death or injury. But given that an Indian foreman, for example, may earn less than $100 a month, the total value of such awards in India would be something the company could handle with its existing resources.[15]

The plaintiff's attorneys, on the other hand, argued that the case should be handled in U.S. courts. Their clients would have a better chance of quick and substantial relief in the United States than in the Indian courts, which were extremely slow in settling liability cases. U.S. courts also would operate according to the theory of strict liability under which it would have to be proved only that the company made or used the chemical involved in the disaster. Juries were also considered to be more favorable to plaintiffs in the United States and likely to award greater amounts of money in both compensatory and punitive damages. (Juries in this country have awarded verdicts as high as $40 million for a single wrongful death, although such awards were usually reduced on appeal.) Finally the process of discovery or gathering of evidence tended to be more extensive in U.S. courts.[16]

Legal precedent was not clear in terms of where the trial should be held. In the 1982 case *Piper Aircraft v. Reyno* (495 U.S., 928, 1982), the U.S. Supreme Court ruled that the case, which involved the crash of a Piper-built airplane carrying Scottish citizens in Scotland, could not be moved to the United States but had to be tried in Scotland. However in another case involving Boeing and Lear Siegler, the federal district court for the western district of Washington agreed to hear the case, which concerned a 1978 air crash near Bombay.[17]

Another issue concerned the question of the extent to which the parent company actually ran its subsidiary in Bhopal. If the parent company played a major role in the operation of the Bhopal facility, this could be taken as a reason for a U.S. forum and would also increase the responsibility of the company for the disaster. The managers of the Bhopal facility reported to Union Carbide India Ltd. (UCIL) headquarters in Bombay, which reported to Union Carbide Eastern in Hong Kong, which reported to corporate headquarters in the United States. One of the six corporate executive vice-presidents of the parent company sat on the board of directors of UCIL, as did four Union Carbide Eastern executives.[18]

Just how closely linked UCIL was to corporate headquarters of the American plant at Institute, West Virginia, where MIC was also produced, will probably come out in the legal discovery process. In the meantime an affidavit filed by a man named Edward A. Munoz, former managing director of UCIL, reported a dispute between the parent company and the subsidiary in the early 1970s about the amount and method of storage of MIC at the Bhopal plant. According to the affidavit Union Carbide directed UCIL to install large storage tanks rather than smaller ones, which were believed to be safer.[19]

The number of personal injury suits against Union Carbide continued to rise, and eventually these suits were consolidated in one court, a step that would facilitate attempts to engineer a settlement. A judicial panel in New Orleans that dealt with multidistrict litigation decided to consolidate for pretrial purposes all Bhopal-related personal injury and death suits in the U.S. District Court for the Southern District in Manhattan. Eventually more than fifty lawsuits were involved in this consolidation. The pretrial conference began on April 16, 1985, with Judge John Keenan presiding. One of his first acts was to suggest that Union Carbide provide a "substantial amount" of money—in the range of $5 million to $10 million—toward "systematic emergency relief." Such payments, the judge said, would not entail an admission of guilt or liability on the company's part and could be credited against any future settlement or judgment.[20] Two days later Union Carbide agreed to finance a $5 million emergency aid program for victims of the Bhopal disaster. This $5 million was in addition to the $1 million the company had already donated to the Indian government.[21]

Meanwhile the Indian government got into the legal picture and further complicated matters. Union Carbide had been trying to work out a settlement with the government and according to some sources had offered the government an immediate $60 million and a further $180 million during the next thirty years as compensation for the victims of the disaster.[22] Whatever the amount was, it was rejected by the Indian government when it filed suit on April 8, 1985, in New York on its own behalf. The suit was filed for the Indian government by the Minneapolis law firm Robins, Zelle, Larson, and Kaplan, which had handled other large disasters, such as the MGM Grand Hotel fire in Las Vegas and the collapsed skywalk at the Kansas City Hyatt Regency Hotel.[23]

The suit charged that Union Carbide was liable for any and all damages arising from the poison gas leak, but because of the enormity of the disaster the government was not able to allege with particularity the amount of compensatory damages being sought. The suit also sought punitive damages "in an amount sufficient to deter Union Carbide and any other multinational corporation from the willful, malicious and wanton disregard of the rights and safety of the citizens of those countries in which they do business." The suit said that Union Carbide should be accountable for all damages because the company was a "monolithic multinational" corporation. "In reality, there is but one entity . . . which is responsible for the design, development and dissemination of information and technology worldwide," the suit alleged.[24]

The suit claimed that Union Carbide was negligent in designing and maintaining the Bhopal plant and that the company made false representations to the government about the plant's safety. According to the suit the company encouraged the storing of MIC in "dangerously large quantities"; failed to equip the storage tanks with alarm devices and temperature indicators; and did not provide "even basic information" about appropriate medical treatment for exposure to the chemical.[25]

The basis for the suit was the government's claim to represent all Bhopal victims under the legal doctrine of *parens patriae*, which held that a government could act on behalf of all its citizens much as a parent would act for a child. Another basis for the suit was an ordinance enacted by the Indian government that reserved for the government the right to oversee representation of the Bhopal victims and to distribute compensation. Some U.S. lawyers joined in a challenge to India regarding the constitutionality of the ordinance. Their petition to the Indian Supreme Court contended that the law deprived Bhopal victims of the right to choose their own counsel and also involved a conflict of interest because the Indian government itself could become a defendant in suits related to the Bhopal disaster.[26]

In March 1986 Union Carbide offered to pay $350 million to settle damage claims stemming from the Bhopal disaster. This agreement was made between the company and the court-appointed U.S. attorneys representing the victims. The $350 million would be paid out during a period of time and would eventually produce a fund of $500 to $600 million. The Minneapolis law firm representing the Indian government was not involved in the settlement.[27] This settlement plan was agreed to by plaintiffs' attorneys because they would be left empty-handed should Judge Keenan send the case to India. Nonetheless the Indian government opposed the plan and insisted that it would only agree to an amount that would fully and fairly compensate all the victims, thus casting doubt on whether the plan would ever be adopted.[28]

After failing in several efforts to settle the litigation, Judge Keenan finally did decide to send the case back to India where the accident happened. For the victims this decision seemed likely to mean more delay as the decision would undoubtedly be appealed. Although the company initially was pleased with this decision, several conditions imposed by the judge made the decision less than satisfactory for the company. As part of the decision Union Carbide had to agree to liberal American discovery rules in the trial and had to accept the Indian courts' jurisdiction over the corporation. The company also had to pay any judgment the Indian courts might render, thus removing an important layer of insulation between the parent company and its majority-owned subsidiary.[29]

After this question of jurisdiction was settled, the Indian government said it would seek at least $3 billion from the company, a move that appeared part of a strategy to force Union Carbide to raise its settlement offer. This figure was said to represent the amount the government would seek in damages if the case went to trial. An Indian court also barred the company from selling assets, paying dividends, or buying back some of its debt until the court reviewed government claims that such moves would impair victims' recovery rights. The government raised the death toll from the disaster to 2,347, an increase of 593 from previous estimates. The government also claimed that between thirty thousand and forty thousand people suffered serious injuries in this accident.[30] In response to this action, the company agreed to maintain at least $3 billion in unencumbered assets to be used as collateral against any claims. The Indian government agreed to this proposal, and the injunction against the company was lifted.[31]

Thus the legal problems for Union Carbide mounted, and the company faced a great deal of uncertainty regarding the eventual outcome of the situation. The greatest uncertainty, of course, involved the amount of eventual compensation awarded to the victims of the tragedy. With a reported $200 million in insurance coverage, Carbide could probably weather a settlement in the range of $250 to $300 million, but anything near $500 million would hurt the company's performance. If the final settlement were to be paid out during a period of time, this would substantially reduce the immediate burden for the company.[32]

COMPANY RESPONSE

John Tollefson, dean of the School of Business at the University of Kansas, stated that three things were crucial for the successful management of a crisis situation such as the tragedy at Bhopal: (1) executives had to give long-range considerations priority over short-term costs and benefits; (2) action had to be taken immediately; and (3) truthful information had to be provided to the public from the beginning. The worst thing that could happen in a situation like Bhopal, added John D. Aram, professor of management at Case Western Reserve University, "is that (executives) get into a bunker mentality where assumptions get frozen and alternatives get closed down instead of opened up."[33]

The trip made by Anderson to India was the key element in the company's early response to the Bhopal tragedy. It was the kind of swift, decisive action that was necessary to manage such a crisis situation successfully. Even though the trip did not turn out as expected, the fact that the chairperson himself went to India was an important step in dealing with the situation.

Other elements of the company's strategy to deal with the crisis included the following:

> The company halted production of MIC at its Institute, West Virginia, plant until an investigation of the Bhopal incident was completed. This was the only other facility where the company made the highly toxic gas, and production was halted to ensure the safety of nearby residents.
>
> Union Carbide said that it would not reopen the Bhopal plant if Indian officials wanted it closed permanently, although it temporarily resumed operations to use up the remaining MIC stored there.
>
> The president and chief operating officer, Alec Flamm, went on closed circuit television at the company's headquarters to assure employees that the company was financially sound and was doing everything possible to address the needs of the victims. The presentation was taped and duplicated and sent to each of the company's 500 locations around the world. Other communications to the concern's employees went out by mail, telex, and computer.
>
> Employees were asked to observe a moment of silence for the victims. Flags were also flown at half mast through December 12, 1984, at most U.S. locations.
>
> The company prepared a letter to stockholders to express confidence that the company's financial structure was not threatened by the disaster. There had been some speculation in news articles that the company could face staggering damage claims beyond its insurance coverage if severe punitive damages were awarded in any of the liability suits resulting from the accident.
>
> The company scheduled a press tour of the West Virginia facility to explain publicly the manufacturing process for the chemical. The company was certain to be asked to explain its original position that the plants were essentially the same, given that the company later admitted that a computerized early warning system at the West Virginia plant to detect any buildup of temperature or pressure in the storage tanks was not installed at the Bhopal.[34]

This latter problem was particularly embarrassing for the company. The company later stated that the plants were designed according to the same "process safety standards" but that the two plants were not identical. Carbide insisted that the equipment at Bhopal offered an equivalent measure of safety.[35] Later the company confirmed that tank problems were found at the Bhopal plant in a May 1982 inspection but that it was not clear that the problems were corrected before the December 3, 1984, disaster. The report apparently found several deficiencies in the MIC tanks; raised a question "about the adequacy of the tank relief valve to relieve a runaway reaction"; and expressed concern about the lack of backup equipment that might be needed to prevent accidental overfilling of a tank.[36]

The tank relief valve was checked and "found to be adequate," but the purchase of equipment to prevent overfilling depended on the availability of money. It was not immediately known whether this equipment had ever been installed or whether any of the problems contributed to the accident.[37] While

Union Carbide was conducting its own investigation of the incident, an inquiry was conducted by the government of India that identified a number of design flaws, operating errors, and management mistakes that helped cause the accident. Sources close to the investigation disclosed the following findings:

> Plant safety procedures were inadequate to deal with a large-scale leak of the deadly MIC, despite the fact that the dangers such a leak would pose were well known. Nor had any precautions been taken to protect people living near the plant. No procedures were developed for alerting or evacuating the population that would be affected by an accident.
>
> Leaky valves were a constant problem at the plant. Six serious accidents occurred at the Bhopal installation between 1978 and 1982, and three, one of which was fatal, involved gas leaks.
>
> Some important safety systems were not working at the time of the accident. Refrigeration units designed to keep MIC cool so that it could not vaporize had been shut down before the accident. Other equipment, including devices designed to vent and burn off excess gases, was so inadequate that it would have been ineffective even if it had been operating at the time of the accident.
>
> Plant workers failed to grasp the gravity of the situation as it developed, allowing the leak to go unattended for about an hour. Brief and frantic efforts to check the leak failed. As the situation deteriorated, the workers panicked and fled the plant.[38]

Finally the company issued its own report about what caused the disaster. The company report stated that it believed that the accident resulted from a large amount of water entering a storage tank and triggering a chemical chain reaction. The report stated that the water was put in the tank either "inadvertently or deliberately," but the chairperson of the company could not say that it was an act of sabotage. One possible source of the water was a utility station where a pipe marked water was located next to one marked nitrogen, which was used to pressurize the tank. Quite possibly someone connected the wrong pipe to the tank and allowed as much as 240 gallons of water to mix with the MIC in the tank. The report covered an investigation of nearly three months by a team of company scientists and engineers who conducted about five hundred experiments to determine the technical aspects of the accident.[39]

The report also showed that the Bhopal plant was ill run, violated a number of standard operating procedures, and failed to maintain safety devices. Conditions were so poor at the time of the disaster that the plant "shouldn't have been operated," according to Warren M. Anderson. The report confirmed that the scrubber unit intended to neutralize the escaping gas was not operating prior to the accident and that another safety device, a flare tower, also was not operating because it had been shut down for maintenance.[40]

After this report was issued, the company made plans to resume producing MIC at its West Virginia plant. The company replaced its salt-water cooling system with one that used chloroform, which was nonreactant with MIC. The company also made other revisions, such as more frequent sampling of tanks and destruction of stocks if they became contaminated with even small amounts of water.[41] The company also announced that it would triple the number of safety inspections at all of its plants. The company disclosed that its plant at West Virginia had seventy-one MIC leaks since 1980 but that the leaks were small and thus not reportable to federal authorities.[42]

Then in August 1985 another incident happened to plague the company. A noxious cloud of methylene chloride and aldicarb oxime escaped from its West Virginia plant and hospitalized 135 people. This leakage did not involve MIC, but this was no comfort to the victims who experienced shortness of breath, a burning in the eyes and throat, and vomiting. Aldicarb oxime was mixed with MIC to form the active ingredient for Temik, a pesticide widely used on citrus crops. Apparently steam accidentally entered a metal jacket surrounding a tank where the chemical was stored, which caused the pressure to increase and eventually ruptured three gaskets, thereby allowing 500 gallons of the solution to escape.[43]

Union Carbide eventually disclosed that the aldicarb oxime facility was not equipped with the safety devices installed in the MIC facility after the Bhopal incident, including a computerized monitoring system to detect leaks. A computer system designed to predict the dispersion of poison-gas clouds was also not programmed to track the substances that leaked in this instance.[44] Union Carbide was sued for $88.2 million by thirty people seeking both compensatory and punitive damages who claimed they were injured by the leak. The suits charged that the company was negligent in failing to warn citizens of the dangers of leaks and in failing to maintain effective warning or monitoring systems.[45] Meanwhile OSHA fined the company $1.37 million for 221 alleged safety violations at the West Virginia plant and gave its files to the Justice Department for possible criminal prosecution.[46]

As if all this were not enough to keep management busy, the company also faced a takeover bid from GAF Corporation. The bid was successfully repelled by a major restructuring that involved cutting the domestic work force by 4,000 people, raising $500 million by selling assets, taking $500 million from the overfunded pension plan, and offering to buy back 10 million of the company's 70.4 billion shares. This offer was later revised to include 55 percent of the stock at a cost of $3.3 billion. The company also started a drastic reorganization of its eighty or so business operations. Union Carbide claimed that many of these moves had started long before the GAF bid and were not part of a takeover defense.[47] Nonetheless the company took on a $2.53 billion debt to successfully preserve its autonomy, which it later offered to repurchase.[48]

IMPLICATIONS

The United States is estimated to have some six thousand chemical plants; the worldwide total is about twice that number. Add to these totals nuclear power plants and related facilities, equipment for handling liquefied natural gas and other explosive fuels, laboratories for studying new biological organisms, and the transportation of these and similar substances and we are dealing with potential calamities numbering in the tens of thousands. Even if the probability of a major disaster like Bhopal is extremely low, one is bound to occur every few years somewhere in the world. The poison cloud at Bhopal, incidentally, came just two weeks after tanks of liquefied gas exploded and killed 452 people in Mexico City.[49]

The problem is one of controlling and reducing the risks inherent in modern technology to an acceptable level. Nearly 1 billion tons of pesticides and herbicides, comprising 225 different chemicals, were produced in the United States in 1983, with an additional 79 million pounds imported.[50] Every day about 275 million gallons of gasoline are produced by the chemical and petroleum industries, 723,000 tons of dangerous wastes are generated, and 250,000 loads of hazardous materials are shipped across the country.[51] Given this potential for calamity the chemical industry has one of the best safety records of all the industries in the United States. In 1983 the industry had only 5.2 injury cases for every 100 full-time workers, compared with 9.7 for all manufacturing industries. Chemical companies are reported to regularly drill their employees in emergency procedures and can help rush experts to the site of an accident.[52] The Chemical Manufacturers Association maintains a hotline to help local authorities identify what kind of chemical they are dealing with in a spill.[53]

Even with all these precautions, however, accidents still happen. Earlier in the same year as the Bhopal tragedy, a small amount of MIC was released from which FMC pesticide plant in Middleport, New York, which caused eye injuries to nine children in a nearby school. In October 1984 an American Cyanamid plant in Linden, New Jersey, spewed pesticide chemicals into the air that hospitalized 160 people in New Jersey and New York.[54] Can these kinds of incidents be prevented by stricter enforcement of existing regulations, new regulations to impose more controls on business, or more legislation that would plug supposed loopholes in existing laws and regulations? Several important questions were considered by Congress after the Bhopal disaster.

What percentage of the U.S. public lives in close proximity to facilities that produce or use hazardous materials?

Is it known what these materials are and what hazards they present to adjacent communities?

How adequate are the emergency procedures established by the federal and state governments to respond to environmental disasters?

Does the national emergency response team set up under the Superfund law have the capability to provide or coordinate essential services in the event of a disaster?

How would victims of exposure be compensated?[55]

The Bhopal tragedy gave a boost to efforts involving chemical disclosure laws. OSHA had issued a communication standard in November 1983 that required companies to provide information to their employees on hazards in the workplace by means of labels, material safety data sheets, and training programs. But there was much criticism of this standard in that it preempted stronger state laws that had already been passed. Such a situation occurred in New Jersey where a U.S. district court ruled that the state could not enforce its right-to-know law as it applied to manufacturing establishments because the law was stricter than the federal standard.[56]

The OSHA standard also did not address the issue of community or public access to information about hazardous substances. This was a serious issue for many communities, including the city of Akron, Ohio, which passed such a right-to-know law just a week after the Bhopal accident. Many other cities and communities were considering similar measures.[57] The Senate Environment and Public Works Committee scheduled hearings to examine the question of whether communities were adequately prepared to deal with chemical emergencies.[58] Meanwhile, in an effort to stave off a new wave of legislation and regulation dealing with this issue, Monsanto Company announced a voluntary right-to-know program designed to distribute information about possible hazards and precautions to residents near its fifty-three plants around the country. One executive at the company said, "It's clear that we need to be more open than in the past."[59]

The Bhopal incident also had an impact on the insurance industry. In 1982 the EPA ordered hazardous waste facilities to get liability insurance against chemical accidents—both sudden accidents such as explosions, and nonsudden occurrences such as leaks that might slowly poison residents. But after Bhopal and similar incidents the pollution liability insurance industry virtually collapsed. Rates climbed 50 to 200 percent and even higher in some cases, and coverage was sharply curtailed with maximums generally reduced to $10 million or less. All but three or four of the fourteen companies and pools that issued this kind of insurance pulled out of the market entirely. These companies appreciated the magnitude and complexity of chemical risks and decided that pollution liability insurance was not worth the effort.[60]

Finally, the Bhopal tragedy raised the issue of technology transfer to countries that were not technologically sophisticated and did not have extensive safety and health regulations. Are we thrusting twentieth-century technology into countries that are not ready to deal with it adequately? Although countries like India may want such plants as Bhopal because of the employment opportunities and because of a need for their products, the inherent dangers of such a plant and the potential for harm to the public may not be understood or overlooked. The mayor of Bhopal, for example, had no idea of the potential dangers posed by the Union Carbide plant.[61] The state government, which was responsible for worker safety, had only fifteen factory inspectors who were supposed to monitor more than eight thousand plants located in the state of Madhya Pradesh, of which Bhopal was the capital.[62] The Environmental Department of India had a staff of 150 persons compared with the U.S. EPA's staff of 4,400 persons at its headquarters, to say nothing of regional offices. Yet India did more to enforce safety than did most Third World nations, partly because of the British legacy of laws and inspection procedures.[63]

Monte Throdahl, a former Monsanto vice-president who was at one time the company's general manager for international operations, stated that "the leaders of [developing] countries are more interested in economic development than in a clean environment or safe workplace." An analyst with the Conservation Foundation said that India was mired in an early stage of industrialization with environment and health and safety standards geared to the smokestack industries of that era. At the same time the country was eagerly accepting the innovations and hazards of the organic chemical revolution that occurred after World War II.[64]

> It is all too easy to transfer hardware from industrialized to developing nations, but just about impossible—and unethical—to impose the political-economic structures, the regulatory apparatus, and western-scientific world view that are necessary for the hardware to work efficiently and safely. That is the lesson of Bhopal.[65]

High turnover rates are a serious problem in foreign nations. In its 1982 report about the Bhopal plant, Union Carbide expressed a concern that "personnel were being released for independent operation without having gained sufficient understanding of safe operating procedures." The report also expressed concern about training by "rote memorization" without "a basic understanding of the reasoning behind procedures."[66]

In an emergency situation the primitive transportation and communications systems of Third World countries pose a problem. The organization of an orderly evacuation of a community, a most difficult task under the best of circumstances, becomes a near impossibility when a slum has grown up around the plant, as was the situation at Bhopal. The problem of moving so many people so quickly is almost beyond comprehension.[67]

Bhopal has become the catalyst for some companies to reexamine their policies and practices abroad. At DuPont, officials say a major safety audit of each foreign operation is conducted every twelve to twenty-two months. Monsanto in St. Louis says it inspects foreign plants annually, except for Far Eastern operations, where audits take place every two years. After Bhopal the company said these plants would also get annual inspections.[68] One reason for this stepped-up activity is because the suit by the government of India against Union Carbide could strip many multinational corporations of the insulation they now have from the liabilities of their foreign subsidiaries. The suit argues that multinationals engaged in hazardous activities are not entitled to the standard legal shields that protect parent corporations. Andreas F. Lowenfeld, professor of international law at New York University, stated that "in some circumstances, the concept that separate incorporation [of subsidiaries and parent companies] makes companies separate legal entities ought to be rethought."[69]

NOTES

1. "India's Night of Death," *Time*, December 17, 1984, p. 22.
2. Ibid., pp. 22–23.
3. "Carbide Lawyer Says Number of Bhopal Victims Overstated," *Dallas Times Herald*, April 18, 1985, p. 28-A.
4. Ibid.
5. "India's Night of Death," p. 23.
6. Barry Meier and Ron Winslow, "Struggling Giant: Union Carbide Faces a Difficult Challenge Even Without Bhopal," *Wall Street Journal*, December 27, 1984, p. 1.
7. "A Calamity for Union Carbide," *Time*, December 17, 1984, p. 38.
8. Meier and Winslow, "Struggling Giant," p. 1.
9. "India's Night of Death," p. 26.
10. Ibid.
11. Ibid.
12. "A Calamity for Union Carbide," p. 38.
13. "Union Carbide Fights for Its Life," *Business Week*, December 24, 1984, pp. 53–56.
14. "A Calamity for Union Carbide," p. 38.
15. Union Carbide Fights for Its Life," p. 55.
16. David Webber, "Settlement or Litigation? For Union Carbide, That is the Question," *Chemical and Engineering News* 63, no. 6 (February 11, 1985): 50.
17. Ibid.
18. Ibid., p. 51.
19. Ibid.
20. Robert Friedman, "Carbide Should Make Interim Payments to Bhopal Disaster Victims, Judge Says," *Wall Street Journal*, April 17, 1985, p. 6.
21. "Carbide Donates $5 Million to Victims," *Dallas Times Herald*, April 19, 1985, p. A-3.
22. "India's Bhopal Suit Could Change All the Rules," *Business Week*, April 22, 1985, p. 38.
23. "Kings of Catastrophe," *Time*, April 22, 1985, p. 80.
24. Roger Friedman and Matt Miller, "Union Carbide Is Sued by India in U.S. Court," *Wall Street Journal*, April 9, 1985, p. 14.
25. Ibid.
26. "Legal Tangle: Parties in Bhopal Case Want Fast Settlement, but Hurdles Are High," *Wall Street Journal*, April 12, 1985, p. 1.
27. "Carbide to Settle Bhopal Claims for $350 Million," *Wall Street Journal*, March 24, 1986, p. 3.

28. Barry Meier, "India Opposes Carbide's Offer in Bhopal Case," *Wall Street Journal*, March 25, 1986, p. 2.
29. "Nobody Wins in the Carbide Ruling," *Business Week*, May 26, 1986, pp. 41–42.
30. Barry Meier and Matt Miller, "India Plans to Seek at Least $3 Billion from Union Carbide for Bhopal Claims," *Wall Street Journal*, November 24, 1986, p. 3.
31. Matt Miller, "India Lifts Ban on Carbide Plan for Asset Sales," *Wall Street Journal*, December 1, 1986, p. 2.
32. Ibid.
33. Ron Winslow, "Union Carbide Mobilizes Resources to Control Damage from Gas Leak," *Wall Street Journal*, December 10, 1984, p. 29.
34. Ibid.
35. Ron Winslow, "Union Carbide Moved to Bar Accident at U.S. Plant Before Bhopal Tragedy," *Wall Street Journal*, January 28, 1985, p. 6.
36. Ron Winslow, "Union Carbide Confirms that Problems with Tanks in India Were Found in '82," *Wall Street Journal*, December 11, 1984, p. 3.
37. Ibid.
38. "Frightening Findings at Bhopal," *Time*, February 18, 1985, p. 78. Copyright 1985 Time Inc. All rights reserved. Reprinted by permission from *Time*.
39. Barry Meier, "Union Carbide Says Facility Should Have Been Shut Before Accident," *Wall Street Journal*, March 21, 1985, p. 3. Union Carbide raised the possibility of sabotage again later in an apparent effort to lower expectations about the size of a final settlement. See Barry Meier, "Carbide's Bhopal Sabotage Claim Seen by Some as Effort to Shape Settlement," *Wall Street Journal*, August 15, 1986, p. 5.
40. Ibid.
41. Robert E. Taylor, "Carbide Bolstering Methyl Isocyanata Precautions in U.S." *Wall Street Journal*, March 25, 1985, p. 25.
42. Barry Meier, "Union Carbide Says Institute Plant Had 71 Toxic Gas Leaks," *Wall Street Journal*, January 31, 1985, p. 12.
43. "Under a Noxious Cloud of Fear," *Time*, August 26, 1985, p. 13.
44. Barry Meier and Terrence Roth, "Union Carbide Says Site Lacked New Safety Gear," *Wall Street Journal*, August 13, 1985, p. 3; Robert E. Taylor, "Union Carbide Gas-Leak Tank Is Cited by EPA," *Wall Street Journal*, August 16, 1985, p. 4.
45. Terrence Roth and Robert Friedman, "Carbide Is Sued for $88.2 Million on Toxic-Gas Leak," *Wall Street Journal*, August 21, 1985, p. 18.
46. "Union Carbide Is Fined," *Dallas Times Herald*, April 2, 1986, p. A-2; Cathy Trost, "OSHA Plans to Fine Carbide $1.4 Million, Alleges Violations at West Virginia Plant," *Wall Street Journal*, April 2, 1986, p. 2.
47. The Threat That's Stirring Carbide's Survival Instincts," *Business Week*, September 16, 1985, p. 29. See also James B. Stewart and Daniel Hertzberg, "Landmark Victory: Outside Directors Led the Carbide Defense that Fended Off GAF," *Wall Street Journal*, January 13, 1986, p. 1.
48. Barry Meier, "India Court Bars Carbide Debt Buyback, Asset Sales and Payout Pending Hearing," *Wall Street Journal*, November 18, 1986, p. 4.
49. "A Backlash Is Threatening Chemical Makers," *Business Week*, December 24, 1984, p. 61.
50. "Hazards of a Toxic Wasteland," *Time*, December 17, 1984, p. 33.
51. "An Unending Search for Safety," *Time*, December 17, 1984, p. 35.
52. "A Backlash Is Threatening Chemical Makers," p. 60.
53. "An Unending Search for Safety," p. 35.
54. "A Backlash Is Threatening Chemical Makers," p. 60.
55. Reprinted in part with permission from Janice R. Long and David J. Hanson, "Bhopal Triggers Massive Response from Congress, the Administration,"

Chemical and Engineering News 63, no. 6 (February 11, 1985): 53. Copyright 1985 American Chemical Society.

56. Long and Hanson, "Bhopal Triggers Massive Response," p. 57.
57. Bhopal Has Americans Demanding the 'Right to Know,' " *Business Week*, February 18, 1985, p. 36.
58. Long and Hanson, "Bhopal Triggers Massive Response," p. 58.
59. "Bhopal Has Americans Demanding," p. 36.
60. Mary Williams Walsh, "Risky Business: Insurers Are Shunning Coverage of Chemical and Other Pollution," *Wall Street Journal*, March 19, 1985, p. 1.
61. Long and Hanson, "Bhopal Triggers Massive Response," p. 60.
62. Lois R. Ember, "Technology in India: An Uneasy Balance of Progress and Tradition," *Chemical and Engineering News* 63, no. 6 (February 11, 1985): 62.
63. Cathy Trost, "Danger Zone: Chemical-Plant Safety Is Still Just Developing in Developing Nations," *Wall Street Journal*, December 13, 1984, p. 1.
64. Ember, "Technology in India," p. 64.
65. Ibid., p. 65.
66. Trost, "Danger Zone," p. 1.
67. Ibid.
68. Barry Meier, "Carbide Suits May Affect Industry Norms," *Wall Street Journal*, April 5, 1985, p. 6.
69. "India's Bhopal Suit Could Change All the Rules," *Business Week*, April 22, 1985, p. 38.

The Corporation as a Moral Person

PETER A. FRENCH

In one of his *New York Times* columns of not too long ago Tom Wicker's ire was aroused by a Gulf Oil Corporation advertisement that "pointed the finger of blame" for the energy crisis at all elements of our society (and supposedly away from the oil company). Wicker attacked Gulf Oil as the major, if not the sole perpetrator of that crisis and virtually every other social ill, with the possible exception of venereal disease. It does not matter whether Wicker was serious or sarcastic in making his charges (I suspect he was in deadly earnest). I am interested in the sense ascriptions of moral responsibility make when their subjects are corporations. I hope to provide the foundation of a theory that allows treatment of corporations as members of the moral community, of equal standing with the traditionally acknowledged residents: biological human beings, and hence treats Wicker-type responsibility ascriptions as

Peter A. French, "The Corporation as a Moral Person," *American Philosophical Quarterly*, 3(1979), pp. 207–15. Reprinted with permission.

unexceptionable instances of a perfectly proper sort without having to para-phrase them. In short, corporations can be full-fledged moral persons and have whatever privileges, rights and duties as are, in the normal course of affairs, accorded to moral persons.

It is important to distinguish three quite different notions of what constitutes personhood that are entangled in our tradition: the metaphysical, moral and legal concepts. The entanglement is clearly evident in Locke's account of personal identity. He writes that the term "person" is "a *forensic* term, appropriating actions and their merit; and so belongs only to *intelligent agents*, capable of law, and happiness, and misery."[1] He goes on to say that by consciousness and memory persons are capable of extending themselves into the past and thereby become "concerned and *accountable*."[2] Locke is histori-cally correct in citing the law as a primary origin of the term "person." But he is incorrect in maintaining that its legal usage somehow entails its metaphysi-cal sense, agency; and whether or not either sense, but especially the meta-physical, is interdependent on the moral sense, accountability, is surely controversial. Regarding the relationship between metaphysical and moral persons there are two distinct schools of thought. According to one, to be a metaphysical person is to be a moral one; to understand what it is to be accountable one must understand what it is to be an intelligent or a rational agent and vice versa; while according to the other, being an agent is a necessary but not sufficient condition of being a moral person. Locke holds the interdependence view with which I agree, but he roots both moral and metaphysical persons in the juristic person, which is, I think, wrongheaded. The preponderance of current thinking tends to some version of the neces-sary pre-condition view, but it does have the virtue of treating the legal person as something apart.

It is of note that many contemporary moral philosophers and econo-mists both take a pre-condition view of the relationship between the meta-physical and moral person and also adopt a particular view of the legal personhood of corporations that effectually excludes corporations *per se* from the class of moral persons. Such philosophers and economists cham-pion the least defensible of a number of possible interpretations of the juristic personhood of corporations, but their doing so allows them to systematically sidestep the question of whether corporations can meet the conditions of metaphysical personhood.[3]

🔱

Many philosophers, including, I think, Rawls, have rather uncritically relied upon what they incorrectly perceive to be the most defensible juristic treatment of collectivities such as corporations as a paradigm for the treat-ment of corporations in their moral theories. The concept of corporate legal personhood under any of its popular interpretations is, I want to argue, virtually useless for moral purposes.

Following many writers on jurisprudence, a juristic person may be defined as any entity that is a subject of a right. There are good etymological grounds for such an inclusive neutral definition. The Latin *"persona"* originally referred to *dramatis personae,* and in Roman law the term was adopted to refer to anything that could act on either side of a legal dispute. [It was not until Boethius' definition of a person: *"Persona est naturae rationabilis individua substantia* (a person is the individual subsistence of a rational nature)"* that metaphysical traits were ascribed to persons.] In effect, in Roman legal tradition persons are creations, artifacts, of the law itself, i.e., of the legislature that enacts the law, and are not considered to have, or only have incidentally, existence of any kind outside of the legal sphere. The law, on the Roman interpretation, is systematically ignorant of the biological status of its subjects.

The Roman notion applied to corporations is popularly known as the Fiction Theory. . . .

⚜

The Fiction Theory's major rival in American jurisprudence and the view that does seem to inform Rawls' account is what I shall call "the Legal Aggregate theory of the Corporation." It holds that the names of corporate bodies are only umbrellas that cover (but do not shield) certain biological persons. The Aggregate Theory treats biological status as having legal priority and corporate existence as a contrivance for purposes of summary reference. (Generally, it may be worth mention, Aggregate Theorists tend to ignore employees and identify corporations with directors, executives and stockholders. The model on which they stake their claim is no doubt that of the primitive partnership.) I have shown elsewhere[4] that to treat a corporation as an aggregate for any purposes is to fail to recognize the key logical differences between corporations and mobs. The Aggregate Theory, then, despite the fact that it has been quite popular in legislatures, courtrooms, and on street corners, simply ignores key logical, socio-economic and historical facts of corporate existence. It might prove of some value in clarifying the dispute between Fiction and Aggregate theorists to mention a rather famous case in the English law. (The case is cited by Hallis.) It is that of *Continental Tyre and Rubber Co., Ltd.* vs. *Daimler Co., Ltd.* Very sketchily, the Continental Tyre Company was incorporated in England and carried on its business there. Its business was the selling of tires made in Germany, and all of its directors were German subjects in residence in Germany, and all but one of its shares were held by German subjects. The case arose during the First World War, and it turned on the issue of whether the company was an English subject by virtue of its being incorporated under the English law and independent of its directors and stockholders, and could hence bring suit in an English court against an English subject while a state of war existed. The majority opinion of The Court of Appeals (5–1) was that the corporation was an entity created by statute and hence was "a different person altogether from the subscribers to the memorandum or the shareholders on the register."[5]

🌿

Underlying all of these interpretations of corporate legal personhood is a distinction, embedded in the law itself, that renders them unhelpful for our purposes. Being a subject of rights is often contrasted in the law with being an "administrator of rights." Any number of entities and associations can and have been the subjects of legal rights. Legislatures have given rights to unborn human beings, they have reserved rights for human beings long after their death, and in some recent cases they have invested rights in generations of the future.[6] Of course such subjects of rights, though they are legal persons, cannot dispose of their rights, cannot administer them, because to administer a right one must be an agent, i.e., able to act in certain ways. It may be only an historical accident that most legal cases are cases in which "the subject of right X" and "the administrator of right X" are co-referential. It is nowhere required by law, under any of the three above theories or elsewhere, that it be so. Yet, it is possession of the attributes of an administrator of rights and not those of a subject of rights that are among the generally regarded conditions of moral personhood. It is a fundamental mistake to regard the fact of juristic corporate personhood as having settled the question of the moral personhood of a corporation one way or the other.

Two helpful lessons however, are learned from an investigation of the legal personhood of corporations: (1) biological existence is not essentially associated with the concept of a person (only the fallacious Aggregate Theory depends upon reduction to biological referents) and (2) a paradigm for the form of an inclusive neutral definition of a moral person is provided: "a subject of a right." I shall define a moral person as the referent of any proper name or description that can be a non-eliminatable subject of what I shall call (and presently discuss) a responsibility ascription of the second type. The non-eliminatable nature of the subject should be stressed because responsibility and other moral predicates are neutral as regards person and *personum* prediction.[7] Though we might say that the Ox-Bow mob should be held responsible for the death of three men, a mob is an example of what I have elsewhere called an aggregate collectivity with no identity over and above that of the sum of the identities of its component membership, and hence to use "the Ox-Bow mob" as the subject of such ascriptions is to make summary reference to each member of the mob. For that reason mobs do not qualify as metaphysical or moral persons.

There are at least two significantly different types of responsibility ascriptions that should be distinguished in ordinary usage (not counting the laudatory recommendations, "He is a responsible lad.") The first type pins responsibility on someone or something, the who-dun-it or what-dun-it sense. Austin has pointed out that it is usually used when an event or action is thought by the speaker to be untoward. (Perhaps we are most interested in the failures rather than the successes that punctuate our lives.)

The second type of responsibility ascription, parasitic upon the first, involves the notion of accountability. "Having a responsibility" is interwoven with the notion "Having a liability to answer," and having such a liability or obligation seems to imply (as Anscombe has noted[8]) the existence of some sort of authority relationship either between people or between people and a deity or in some weaker versions between people and social norms. The kernel of insight that I find intuitively compelling, is that for someone to legitimately hold someone else responsible for some event there must exist or have existed a responsibility relationship between them such that in regard to the event in question the latter was answerable to the former. In other words, "X is responsible for *y*," as a second-type ascription, is properly uttered by someone Z if X in respect to *y* is or was accountable to Z. Responsibility relationships are created in a multitude of ways, e.g., through promises, contracts, compacts, hirings, assignments, appointments, by agreeing to enter a Rawlsian original position, etc. The right to hold responsible is often delegatable to third parties; though in the case of moral responsibility no delegation occurs because no person is excluded from the relationship; moral responsibility relationships hold reciprocally and without prior agreements among all moral persons. No special arrangement needs to be established between parties for anyone to hold someone morally responsible for his acts, or, what amounts to the same thing, every person is a party to a responsibility relationship with all other persons as regards the doing or refraining from doing of certain acts: those that take descriptions that use moral notions.

Because our interest is in the criteria of moral personhood and not the content of morality we need not pursue this idea further. What I have maintained is that moral responsibility, although it is neither contractual nor optional, is not a class apart but an extension of ordinary, garden-variety, responsibility. What is needed in regard to the present subject then is an account of the requirements for entry into any responsibility relationship, and we have already seen that the notion of the juristic person does not provide a sufficient account. For example, the deceased in a probate case cannot be held responsible in the relevant way by anyone, even though the deceased is a juristic person, a subject of rights.

A responsibility ascription of the second type amounts to the assertion of a conjunctive proposition, the first conjunct of which identifies the subject's actions with or as the cause of an event (usually an untoward one) and the second conjunct asserts that the action in question was intended by the subject or that the event was the direct result of an intentional act of the subject. In addition to what it asserts it implies that the subject is accountable to the speaker (in the case at hand) because of the subject's relationship to the speaker (who the speaker is or what the speaker is, a member of the "moral community," a surrogate for that aggregate). The primary focus of responsibility ascriptions of the second type is on the subject's intentions rather than, though not to the exclusion of, occasions. Austin wrote: "In considering responsibility, few things are considered more important than to establish whether a man *intended* to do A, or whether he did A intentionally."[9] To be the subject of a responsibility ascription of the second type, to be a party in responsibility relationships, hence to be a moral person, the subject must be at minimum, what I shall call a Davidsonian agent.[10] If corporations are moral persons, they will be non-eliminatable Davidsonian agents.

For a corporation to be treated as a Davidsonian agent it must be the case that some things that happen, some events, are describable in a way that makes certain sentences true, sentences that say that some of the things a corporation does were intended by the corporation itself. That is not accomplished if attributing intentions to a corporation is only a shorthand way of attributing intentions to the biological persons who comprise, e.g., its board of directors. If that were to turn out to be the case then on metaphysical if not logical grounds there would be no way to distinguish between corporations and mobs. I shall argue, however, that a Corporation's Internal Decision Structure (its CID Structure) is the requisite redescription device that licenses the predication of corporate intentionality.

⚜

Certain events, that is, actions, are describable as simply the bodily movements of human beings and sometimes those same events are redescribable in terms of their upshots, as bringing about something, e.g., (from Austin[11]) feeding penguins *by* throwing them peanuts ("by" is the most common way we connect different descriptions of the same event[12]), and sometimes those events can be redescribed as the effects of some prior cause; then they are described as done for reasons, done in order to bring about something, e.g., feeding the penguins peanuts in order to kill them. Usually what we single out as that prior cause is some desire or felt need combined with the belief that the object of the desire will be achieved by the action undertaken. (This, I think, is what Aristotle meant when he maintained that acting requires desire.) Saying "someone (X) did y intentionally" is to describe an event (y) as the upshot of X's having had a reason for doing it which was the cause of his doing it.

It is obvious that a corporation's doing something involves or includes human beings doing things and that the human beings who occupy various positions in a corporation usually can be described as having reasons for *their* behavior. In virtue of those descriptions they may be properly held responsible for their behavior, *ceteris paribus*. What needs to be shown is that there is sense in saying that corporations and not just people who work in them, have reasons for doing what they do. Typically, we will be told that it is the directors, or the managers, etc., that really have the corporate reasons and desires, etc., and that although corporate actions may not be reducible without remainder, corporate intentions are always reducible to human intentions.

Every corporation has an internal decision structure. CID Structures have two elements of interest to us here: (1) an organizational or responsibility flow chart that delineates stations and levels within the corporate power structure and (2) corporate decision recognition rule(s) (usually embedded in something called "corporation policy"). The CID Structure is the personnel organization for the exercise of the corporation's power with respect to its ventures, and as such its primary function is to draw experience from various levels of the corporation into a decision-making and ratification process. When operative and properly activated, the CID Structure accomplishes a subordination and synthesis of the intentions and acts of various biological persons into a corporate decision. When viewed in another way, as already suggested, the CID Structure licenses the descriptive transformation of events, seen under another aspect as the acts of biological persons (those who occupy various stations on the organizational chart), to corporate acts by exposing the corporate character of those events. A functioning CID Structure *incorporates* acts of biological persons. For illustrative purposes, suppose we imagine that an event E has at least two aspects, that is, can be described in two non-identical ways. One of those aspects is "Executive X's doing y" and one is "Corporation C's doing z." The corporate act and the individual act may have different properties; indeed they have different causal ancestors though they are causally inseparable. (The causal inseparability of these acts I hope to show is a product of the CID Structure, X's doing y is not the cause of C's doing z nor is C's doing z the cause of X's doing y although if X's doing y causes event F then C's doing z causes F and vice versa.

Suppose, for illustrative purposes, we activate a CID Structure in a corporation, Wicker's favorite, the Gulf Oil Corporation. Imagine that three executives, X, Y and Z have the task of deciding whether or not Gulf Oil will join a world uranium cartel. X, Y, and Z have before them an Everest of papers that have been prepared by lower echelon executives. Some of the papers will be purely factual reports, some will be contingency plans, some will be formulations of positions developed by various departments, some will outline financial considerations, some will be legal opinions and so on. Insofar as these will all have been processed through Gulf's CID Structure system, the personal reasons, if any, individual executives may have had when writing their reports and recommendations in a specific way will have been diluted by the subordination of individual inputs to peer group input even before X, Y and Z review the matter. X, Y and Z take a vote. Their taking of a vote is authorized procedure in the Gulf CID Structure, which is to say that under these circumstances the vote of X, Y and Z can be redescribed as the corporation's making a decision: that is, the event "XYZ voting" may be redescribed to expose an aspect otherwise unrevealed that is quite different from its other aspects, e.g., from X's voting in the affirmative. Redescriptive exposure of a procedurally corporate aspect of an event, however, is not to be confused with a description of an event that makes true a sentence that says that the corporation did something intentionally. But the CID Structure, as already suggested, also provides the grounds in its other type of recognitor for such an attribution of corporate intentionality. Simply, when the corporate act is consistent with an instantiation or an implementation of established corporate policy, then it is proper to describe it as having been done for corporate reasons, as having been caused by a corporate desire coupled with a corporate belief and so, in other words, as corporate-intentional.

An event may, under one of its aspects, be described as the conjunctive act, "X did *a* (or as X intentionally did *a*) & Y did *a* (or as Y intentionally did *a*) & Z did *a* (or as Z intentionally did *a*)" (where *a* = voted in the affirmative on the question of Gulf Oil joining the cartel). Given the Gulf CID Structure, formulated in this instance as the conjunction of rules: when the occupants of positions *A*, *B* and *C* on the organizational chart unanimously vote to do something and if doing that something is consistent with an instantiation or an implementation of general corporate policy and *ceteris paribus*, then the corporation has decided to do it for corporate reasons, the event is redescribable as "the Gulf Oil Corporation did *j* for corporate reasons *f*" (where *j* is "decided to join the cartel" and *f* is any reason (desire + belief) consistent with basic policy of Gulf Oil, e.g., increasing profits) or simply as "Gulf Oil Corporation intentionally did *j*." This is a rather technical way of saying that in these circumstances the executives' voting is, given its CID Structure, also the corporation deciding to do something, and that regardless of the personal reasons the executives have for voting as they do and even if their reasons are inconsistent with established corporate policy or even if one of them has no reason at all for voting as he does, the corporation still has reasons for joining the cartel; that is, joining is consistent with the inviolate corporate general policies as encrusted in the precedent of previous corporate actions and its statements of purpose as recorded in its certificate of incorporation, annual reports, etc. The corporation's only method of achieving its desires or goals is the activation of the personnel who occupy its various positions. However, if X voted affirmatively purely for reasons of personal monetary gain (suppose he had been bribed to do so) that does not alter the fact that the corporate reason for joining the cartel was to minimize competition and hence pay higher dividends to its shareholders. Corporations have reasons because they have interest in doing those things that are likely to result in realization of their established corporate goals regardless of the transient self-interest of directors, managers, etc. If there is a difference between corporate goals and desires and those of human beings it is probably that the corporate ones are relatively stable and not very wide ranging, but that is only because corporations can do relatively fewer things than human beings, being confined in action predominately to a limited socio-economic sphere. The attribution of corporate intentionality is opaque with respect to other possible descriptions of the event in question. It is, of course, in a corporation's interest that its component membership view the corporate purposes as instrumental in the achievement of their own goals. (Financial reward is the most common way this is achieved.)

It will be objected that a corporation's policies reflect only the current goals of its directors. But that is certainly not logically necessary nor is it in practice true for most large corporations. Usually, of course, the original incorporators will have organized to further their individual interests and/or to meet goals which they shared. But even in infancy the melding of disparate interests and purposes gives rise to a corporate long-range point of view that is distinct from the intents and purposes of the collection of incorporators viewed individually. Also, corporate basic purposes and policies, as already mentioned, tend to be relatively stable when compared to those of individuals and not couched in the kind of language that would be appropriate to individual purposes. Furthermore, as histories of corporations will show, when policies are amended or altered it is usually only peripheral issues that are involved. Radical policy alteration constitutes a new corporation, a point that is captured in the incorporation laws of such states as Delaware. ("Any power which is not enumerated in the charter and the general law or which cannot be inferred from those two sources is *ultra vires* of the corporation.") Obviously underlying the objection is an uneasiness about the fact that corporate intent is dependent upon policy and purpose that is but an artifact of the socio-psychology of a group of biological persons. Corporate intent seems somehow to be a tarnished illegitimate offspring of human intent. But this objection is another form of the anthropocentric bias. By concentrating on possible descriptions of events and by acknowledging only that the possibility of describing something as an agent depends upon whether or not it can be properly described as having done something (the description of some aspect of an event) for a reason, we avoid the temptation to look for extensional criteria that would necessitate reduction to human referents.

The CID Structure licenses redescriptions of events as corporate and attributions of corporate intentionality while it does not obscure the private acts of executives, directors, etc. Although X voted to support the joining of the cartel because he was bribed to do so, X did not join the cartel, Gulf Oil Corporation joined the cartel. Consequently, we may say that X did something for which he should be held morally responsible, yet whether or not Gulf Oil Corporation should be held morally responsible for joining the cartel is a question that turns on issues that may be unrelated to X's having accepted a bribe.

Of course Gulf Oil Corporation cannot join the cartel unless X or somebody who occupies position A on the organizational chart votes in the affirmative. What that shows, however, is that corporations are collectivities. That should not, however, rule out the possibility of their having metaphysical status, as being Davidsonian agents, and being thereby full-fledged moral persons.

This much seems to me clear: we can describe many events in terms of certain physical movements of human beings and we also can sometimes describe those events as done for reasons by those human beings, but further we can sometimes describe those events as corporate and still further as done for corporate reasons that are qualitatively different from whatever personal reasons, if any, component members may have for doing what they do.

Corporate agency resides in the possibility of CID Structure licensed redescription of events as corporate-intentional. That may still appear to be downright mysterious, although I do not think it is, for human agency as I have suggested, resides in the possibility of description as well.

Although further elaboration is needed, I hope I have said enough to make plausible the view that we have good reasons to acknowledge the noneliminatable agency of corporations. I have maintained that David-sonian agency is a necessary and sufficient condition of moral personhood. I cannot further argue that position here (I have done so elsewhere). On the basis of the foregoing analysis, however, I think that grounds have been provided for holding corporations *per se* to account for what they do, for treating them as metaphysical persons *qua* moral persons.

NOTES

1. John Locke, *An Essay Concerning Human Understanding* (1960), Bk. II, Ch. XXVII.
2. Ibid.
3. For a particularly flagrant example see Michael Jensen and William Meckling, "Theory of the Firm: Managerial Behavior, Agency Costs and Ownership Structure," *Journal of Financial Economics*, vol. 3 (1976), pp. 305–60. On p. 311 they write, "The private corporation or firm is simply on form of legal fiction which serves as a nexus for contracting relationships. . . ."
4. "Types of Collectivities and Blame." *The Personalist*, vol. 56 (1975), pp. 160–69, and in the first chapter of my *Corporate and Collective Responsibility*, Columbia University Press, 1984.
5. "Continental Tyre and Rubber Co., Ltd. vs. Daimler Co., Ltd." (1915) K.B., p. 893.
6. And, of course, in earlier times animals have been given legal rights.
7. See Gerald Massey, "Tom, Dick, and Harry, and All The King's Men," *American Philosophical Quarterly*, vol. 13 (1976), pp. 89–108.
8. G. E. M. Anscombe, "Modern Moral Philosophy," *Philosophy*, vol. 33 (1958), pp. 1–9.
9. J. L. Austin, "Three Ways of Spilling Ink," in *Philosophical Papers* (Oxford, 1970), p. 273.
10. See, for example, Donald Davidson, "Agency," in *Agent, Action, and Reason*, ed. by Binkley, Bronaugh, and Marras (Toronto, 1971).
11. Austin, p. 275.
12. See Joel Feinberg, *Doing and Deserving* (Princeton, 1970), p. 134f.

Morality and the Ideal
of Rationality
in Formal Organizations

JOHN LADD

I. INTRODUCTION

The purpose of this paper is to explore some of the moral problems that arise out of the interrelationships between individuals and formal organizations (or bureaucracies) in our society. In particular, I shall be concerned with the moral implications of the so-called ideal of rationality of formal organizations with regard to, on the one hand, the obligations of individuals both inside and outside an organization to that organization and, on the other hand, the moral responsibilities of organizations to individuals and to the public at large. I shall argue that certain facets of the organizational ideal are incompatible with the ordinary principles of morality and that the dilemma created by this incompatibility is one source of alienation in our contemporary, industrial society. The very conception of a formal organization or bureaucracy presents us with an ideological challenge that desperately needs to be met in some way or other.

The term "formal organization" will be used in a more or less technical sense to cover all sorts of bureaucracies, private and public. A distinctive mark of such organizations is that they make a clear-cut distinction between the acts and relationships of individuals in their official capacity within the organization and in their private capacity. Decisions of individual decision-makers in an organization are attributed to the organization and not to the individual. In that sense, they are impersonal. Individual office-holders are in principle replaceable by other individuals without affecting the continuity or identity of the organization. In this sense, it has sometimes been said that an organization is "immortal."

This kind of impersonality, in particular, the substitutability of individuals, is one way in which formal organizations differ from other kinds of social systems, e.g. the family, the community or the nation, which are collectivities that are dependent for their existence on specific individuals or groups of specific individuals and that change when they change. . . .

Social critics, e.g., W. H. Whyte, use phrases like the "smothering of the individual" to describe the contemporary situation created by organizations. It is not my purpose here to decry once more the unhappy condition of

John Ladd, "Morality and the Ideal of Rationality in Formal Organizations," Copyright © 1970, *The Monist*, LaSalle, Illinois 61301. Reprinted with the permission of the author and the publisher.

man occasioned by his submergence as an individual in the vast social, economic and political processes created by formal organizations. Instead, I shall try to show that the kind of alienation that we all feel and complain about is, at least in part, a logical necessity flowing from the concept of formal organizations itself, that is, it is a logical consequence of the particular language-game one is playing in organizational decision-making. My analysis is intended to be a logical analysis, but one that also has important ethical implications. . . .

Here we may find the concept of a language-game, as advanced by Wittgenstein and others, a useful tool of analysis. The point about a language-game is that it emphasizes the way language and action are interwoven: "I shall call the whole, consisting of language and the actions into which it is woven, the language-game."[1] A language-game is thus more than simply an abstract set of propositions constituting, say, a formal system. The game not only determines what should and what should not be done, but also sets forth the goals and the moves by which they are to be attained. More important even than these, a particular language-game determines how the activities within it are to be conceptualized, prescribed, justified and evaluated. Take as an example what is meant by a "good" move in chess: we have to refer to the rules of chess to determine what a "move" is, how to make one, what its consequences will be, what its objective is and whether or not it is a good move in the light of this objective.[2] Finally, this system of rules performs the logical function of defining the game itself. . . .

If we pursue the game-analogy one step further, we find that there may be even more striking similarities between the language-game of formal organizations and the language-game of other types of games. For instance, the rules and rationale obtaining in most typical games like chess and baseball tend to make the activity logically autonomous, i.e. the moves, defenses and evaluations are made independently of external considerations. In this sense they are self-contained. Furthermore, while playing a game it is thought to be "unfair" to challenge the rules. Sometimes it is even maintained that any questioning of the rules is unintelligible. In any case, there is a kind of sanctity attached to the rules of a game that renders them immune to criticism on the part of those engaged in playing. The resemblance of the autonomy of the activity and the immunity of the rules governing the game to the operations of bureaucracies can hardly be coincidental.[3]

II. THE CONCEPTS OF SOCIAL DECISION AND SOCIAL ACTION

Let us take as our point of departure Herbert Simon's definition of a formal organization as a "decision-making structure."[4] The central concept with which we must deal is that of a decision (or action) that is attributable to the organization rather than to the individuals who are actually involved in the decisional process. The decision is regarded as the organization's decision even though it is made by certain individuals acting as its representatives. The latter make the decision only for and on behalf of the organization. Their role is, i.e. is supposed to be, impersonal. Such nonindividual decisions will be called *social decisions*, choices or actions. (I borrow the term "social choice" from Arrow, who uses it to refer to a choice made on behalf of a group as distinct from the aggregate of individual choices.)[5]

The officials of an organization are "envisaged as more or less ethically neutral . . . (and) the values to be taken as data are not those which would guide the individual if he were a private citizen. . . ."[6] When the official decides for the organization, his aim is (or should be) to implement the objectives of the organization *impersonally*, as it were. The decisions are made for the organization, with a view to its objectives and not on the basis of the personal interests or convictions of the individual official who makes the decision. This is the theory of organizational decision-making.

One might be tempted to call such organizational decisions "collective decisions," but that would be a misnomer if we take a collective decision to be a decision made by a collection of individuals. Social decisions are precisely decisions (or actions) that are to be *attributed* to the organizations themselves and not to collections of individuals. In practice, of course, the organizational decisions made by officials may actually be collective decisions. But in theory the two must be kept separate; for the "logic" of decisions attributed to organizations is critically different from the "logic" of collective decisions, i.e. those attributed to a collection of individuals.

Underlying the concept of social decisions (choices, actions) as outlined here is the notion that a person (or group of persons) can make decisions that are not his, i.e. are not attributable to him. He makes the decisions on behalf of someone else and with a view to the latter's interest, not his own. In such cases, we ordinarily consider the person (or group) that acts to be a representative or agent of the person or thing he is acting for. . . .

Accordingly, a social decision, as intended here, would be an action performed by an official as actor but owned by the organization as author. For all the consequences of the decision so made are imputed to the organization and not to the individual decision-maker. The individual decision-making official is not personally bound by the agreements he makes for the organization, nor is he personally responsible for the results of these decisions.

The theory of social decision-making that we are considering becomes even clearer if we examine the theory of organizational authority with which it is conjoined. Formal organizations are hierarchical in structure, that is, they are organized along the principle that superiors issue commands to those below them. The superior exercises authority over the subordinates. . . .

In summary, then, the organizational order requires that its social decisions be attributed to the organization rather than to the individual decision-maker, the "decision is to be made nonpersonally from the point of view of its organization effect and its relation to the organizational purpose,"[7] and the officials, as its agents, are required to abdicate their choice in obedience to the impersonal organizational order.

We now turn to another essential facet of the organizational language-game, namely, that every formal organization must have a goal, or a set of goals. In fact, organizations are differentiated and defined by reference to their aims or goals, e.g. the aim of the Internal Revenue Service is to collect taxes. The goal of most business ventures is to maximize profits, etc. We may find it useful to distinguish between the real and stated goals of an organization. Thus, as Galbraith has pointed out, although the stated goal of large industrial organizations is the maximization of profits, that is a pure myth; their actual, operative goals are the securing of their own survival, autonomy and economic growth.[8] There may, indeed, be a struggle over the goals of an organization, e.g. a power play between officials.[9]

For our present purposes, we may consider the real goal of an organization to be that objective (or set of objectives) that is used as a basis for decision-making, i.e. for prescribing and justifying the actions and decisions of the organization itself, as distinct from the actions and decisions of individual persons within the organization. As such, then, the goal is an essential element in the language-game of a formal organization's activities in somewhat the same way as the goal of checkmating the king is an essential element in the game of chess. Indeed, formal organizations are often differentiated from other kinds of social organizations in that they are "deliberately constructed and reconstructed to seek specific goals."[10]

The logical function of the goal in the organizational language-game is to supply the value premises to be used in making decisions, and justifying and evaluating them. "Decisions in private management, like decisions in public management, must take as their ethical premises the objectives that have been set for the organization."[11]

It follows that any considerations that are not related to the aims or goals of the organization are automatically excluded as irrelevant to the organizational decision-making process. This principle of the exclusion of the irrelevant is part of the language-game. It is a logical requirement of the process of prescribing, justifying and evaluating social decisions. Consequently, apart from purely legal considerations, decisions and actions of individual officers that are unrelated to the organization's aims or goals are construed, instead, as actions of those individuals rather than of the organization. If an individual official makes a mistake or does something that fails to satisfy this criterion of social decision, he will be said to have "exceeded his authority," and will probably be sacked or made a vice-president! Again, the point is a logical one, namely, that only those actions that are related to the goal of the organization are to be attributed to the organization; those actions that are inconsistent with it are attributed to the individual officers as individuals. The individual, rather than the organization, is then forced to take the blame for whatever evil results.

Thus, for example, a naval officer who runs his ship aground is court-martialed because what he did was inconsistent with the aims of the naval organization; the action is attributed to him rather than to the Navy. On the other hand, an officer who successfully bombards a village, killing all of its inhabitants, in accordance with the objectives of his organization, is performing a social action, an action that is attributable to the organization and not to him as an individual. Whether or not the organization should take responsibility in a particular case for the mistakes of its officials is a policy decision to be made in the light of the objectives of the organization.

In other words, the concept of a social decision or action is bound up logically with the notion of an organizational aim. The consequence of this co-implication of action and aim is that the notion of an action or decision taken by an organization that is not related to one of its aims makes no sense. It is an unintelligible notion within the language-game of formal organizations. Within that language-game such an action would be as difficult to understand as it would be to understand how a man's knocking over the pieces in a chess game can be part of playing chess.

We finally come to the concept of "rationality," the so-called "ideal of pure rationality."[12] From the preceding observations concerning the organizational language-game, it should be clear that the sole standard for the evaluation of an organization, its activities and its decisions, is its effectiveness in achieving its objectives—within the framework of existing conditions and available means. This kind of effectiveness is called "rationality." Thus rationality is defined in terms of the category of means and ends. . . .

"Rationality," so construed, is relative, that is, to be rational means to be efficient in pursuing a desired goal, whatever it might be. In the case of organizations, "a decision is 'organizationally' rational if it is oriented to the organization's goals."[13] Rationality is consequently neutral as to "what goals are to be attained."[14] Or to be more accurate, "rationality" is an incomplete term that requires reference to a goal before it is completely intelligible. . . .

Let us return to the organizational language-game. It was observed that within that game the sole standard of evaluation of, e.g. a decision, is the "rational" one, namely, that it be effective in achieving the organization's goal. Hence, any considerations that are taken into account in deliberation about these social decisions and in the evaluation of them are relevant only if they are related to the attainment of the organization's objectives. Let us suppose that there are certain factual conditions that must be considered in arriving at a decision, e.g. the available means, costs, and conditions of feasibility. The determination of such conditions is presumably a matter of empirical knowledge and a subject for empirical investigation. Among these empirical conditions there is a special class that I shall call *limiting operating conditions*. These are conditions that set the upper limits to an organization's

operations, e.g. the scarcity of resources, of equipment, of trained personnel, legal restrictions, factors involving employee morale. Such conditions
must be taken into account as *data*, so to speak, in organizational decision-
making and planning. In this respect information about them is on a par
logically with other information utilized in decision-making, e.g. cost-benefit
computations.

Now the only way that moral considerations could be relevant to the
operations of a formal organization in the language-game that I have been
describing is by becoming limiting operating conditions. Strictly speaking,
they could not even be introduced as such, because morality is itself not a
matter of empirical knowledge. Insofar as morality in the strict sense enters
into practical reasoning it must do so as an "ethical" premise, not as an
empirical one. Hence morality as such must be excluded as irrelevant in
organizational decision-making—by the rules of the language-game. The
situation is somewhat parallel to the language-game used in playing chess:
moral considerations are not relevant to the decisions about what move to
make there either.

Morality enters in only indirectly, namely, as moral opinion, what John
Austin calls "positive morality."[15] Obviously the positive morality, laws and
customs of the society in which the organization operates, must be taken into
account in decision-making and planning. The same thing goes for the
religious beliefs and practices of the community. A decision-maker cannot
ignore them, and it makes no difference whether he shares them or accepts
them himself personally. But the determination of whether or not there are
such limiting conditions set by positive morality, customs, law, and religion is
an empirical matter. Whether there are such limitations is simply a matter of
fact and their relevance to the decision-making is entirely dependent upon
how they affect the efficiency of the organization's operations.

Social decisions, then, are not and cannot be governed by the principles of morality, or, if one wishes, they are governed by a different set of
moral principles from those governing the conduct of individuals as individuals. For, as Simon says: "Decisions in private management, like decisions in
public management, must take as their ethical premises the objectives that
have been set for the organization."[16] By implication, they cannot take their
ethical premises from the principles of morality.

Thus, for logical reasons it is improper to expect organizational conduct to conform to the ordinary principles of morality. We cannot and must
not expect formal organizations, or their representatives acting in their
official capacities, to be honest, courageous, considerate, sympathetic, or to
have any kind of moral integrity. Such concepts are not in the vocabulary, so
to speak, of the organizational language-game. (We do not find them in the
vocabulary of chess either!) Actions that are wrong by ordinary moral standards are not so for organizations; indeed, they may often be required.
Secrecy, espionage and deception do not make organizational action wrong;
rather they are right, proper and, indeed, *rational*, if they serve the objectives

of the organization. They are no more or no less wrong than, say, bluffing is in poker. From the point of view of organizational decision-making they are "ethically neutral."

Of course, I do not want to deny that it may be in the best interests of a formal organization to pay lip service to popular morality (and religion). That is a matter of public relations. But public relations operations themselves are evaluated and justified on the same basis as the other operations of the organization. The official function of the public relations officer is to facilitate the operations of the organization, not to promote morality. . . .

The upshot of our discussion so far is that actions are subject to two entirely different and, at times, incompatible standards: social decisions are subject to the standard of rational efficiency (utility) whereas the actions of individuals as such are subject to the ordinary standards of morality. An action that is right from the point of view of one of these standards may be wrong from the point of view of the other. Indeed, it is safe to say that our own experience attests to the fact that our actual expectations and social approvals are to a large extent based on a tacit acceptance of a double-standard—one for the individual when he is in his office working for the company and another for him when he is at home among friends and neighbors. Take as an example the matter of lying: nobody would think of condemning Joe X, a movie star, for lying on a TV commercial about what brand of cigarettes he smokes, for it is part of his job. On the other hand, if he were to do the same thing when he is at home among friends, we should consider his action to be improper and immoral. Or again, an individual who, acting in his official capacity, refuses help to a needy suppliant, would be roundly condemned if he were to adopt the same course of action in his private life.

III. THE MORAL RELATIONSHIP OF INDIVIDUALS TO ORGANIZATIONS

It follows from what has already been said that the standard governing an individual's relationship to an organization is likely to be different from the one governing the converse relationship, i.e. of an organization to individuals. The individual, for his part, is supposed to conduct himself in his relationship to an organization according to the same standards that he would employ in his personal relationships, i.e. the standards of ordinary morality. Thus, he is expected to be honest, open, respectful, conscientious, and loyal towards the organization of which he is a member or with which he has dealings. The organization, represented by its officials, can, however, be none of these in return. "Officials are expected to assume an impersonal orientation. . . . Clients are to be treated as cases . . . and subordinates are to be treated in a similar fashion."[17]

The question I now want to explore is whether or not the individual is justified in applying the standard of individual morality to his relations with formal organizations. It will, of course, generally be in the interest of the formal organizations themselves to encourage him to do so, e.g. to be honest, although the organization as such cannot "reciprocate." But we must ask this question from the point of view of the individual or, if you wish, from the moral point of view: what good moral reasons can be given for an individual to assume a moral stance in his conduct and relations with formal organizations, in contradistinction, say, to his conduct and relations with individuals who happen to be employees of such an organization?

The problem, which may be regarded as a question of loyalty and fidelity, puts the age-old problem of authority and obedience in a new light. Authority has become diffused, as I have already pointed out, and the problem of obedience can no longer be treated in terms of the personal relationship of an individual to his sovereign lord. The problem today is not so easily focused on one relationship; for the demands of authority, as represented in modern organizations, are at once more extensive, more pervasive and less personal. The question we face today is, for example, why should I, as an individual, comply with the mass of regulations laid down by an impersonal order, a bureaucratic organization? Why, for example, should I comply with draft-registration procedures? with passport regulations? with income-tax requirements? with mortage, credit, licensing, fair-trade regulations or with anti-trust laws? Or, indeed, has the individual any moral obligation at all to comply with them?[18]

It might be thought that, before trying to answer such questions, we must be careful to distinguish between individuals within an organization, e.g. officials and employees, and those outside it who have dealings with it, e.g. clients and the general public: what each of these classes ought to do is different. Granting that the specific demands placed on individuals in these various categories may be quite different, they all involve the question of authority in one way or another. Hence, for our purposes, the distinction is unimportant. For example, the authority, or the claims to it, of governmental bureaucracies extends far beyond those who are actually in their employ, e.g. the Internal Revenue Service. For convenience, I shall call those who come under the authority of an organization in some capacity or other, directly or indirectly, the *subjects* of the organization. Thus, we are all subjects of the IRS.

Can any moral reasons by given why individual subjects should comply with the decisions of organizations? Or, what amounts to the same thing, what is the basis of the authority of organizations by virtue of which we have an obligation to accept and obey their directives? And why, if at all, do we owe them loyalty and fidelity?

The most obvious answer, although perhaps not the most satisfactory one ethically, is that it is generally expedient for the individual to go along with what is required by formal organizations. If I want a new automobile, I have to comply with the financing requirements. If I want to avoid being harassed by an internal revenue agent, I make out my income tax form properly. If I want to be legally married, I comply with the regulations of the Department of Public Health. In other words, I comply from practical necessity, that is, I act under a hypothetical imperative.

Still, this sort of answer is just as unsatisfactory from the point of view of moral philosophy as the same kind of answer always has been with regard to political obligation, namely, it fails to meet the challenge of the conscientious objector.

Furthermore, there are many occasions and even whole areas where self-interest is not immediately or obviously involved in which, nevertheless, it makes good sense to ask: why comply? The traditional Lockean argument that our acceptance of the benefits of part of the social and political order commits us morally to the acceptance and conformity with the rest of it rests on the dubious assumption that the social and political order is all of one piece, a seamless web. But when we apply the argument to formal organizations it becomes especially implausible, because there are so many competing claims and conflicting regulations, not to mention loyalties. Not only logically, but as a matter of practicality, it seems obvious that accepting the benefits of one bureaucratic procedure, e.g., mailing letters, does not, from the moral point of view, *eo ipso* bind us to accept and comply with all the other regulations and procedures laid down by the formal organization and much less, those laid down by formal organizations in general. . . .

In sum, we cannot make compacts with organizations because the standard of conduct which requires that promises be honored is that of individual conduct.[19] It does not and cannot apply to formal organizations. This follows from the fact of a double standard. . . .

I have been able to touch only on some very limited aspects of the relationship of individuals to organizations. I hope, however, that it is now abundantly clear that some sort of crisis is taking place in our moral relationships, and in particular in our conceptions of authority, and that this crisis is due not only to complex historical, psychological and sociological factors, but also to an inherent *logical* paradox in the foundations of our social relations.

IV. THE MORAL RELATIONSHIP OF ORGANIZATIONS TO INDIVIDUALS

For logical reasons that have already been mentioned, formal organizations cannot assume a genuine moral posture towards individuals. Although the language-game of social decision permits actions to be attributed to organizations as such, rather than to the officials that actually make them, it does not contain concepts like"moral obligation," "moral responsibility," or "moral integrity." For the only relevant principles in rational decision-making are those relating to the objectives of the organization. Hence individual officers who make the decisions for and in the name of the organization, as its representatives, must decide solely by reference to the objectives of the organization.

According to the theory, then, the individuals who are officers of an organization, i.e. those who run it, operate simply as vehicles or instruments of the organization. The organizational language-game requires that they be treated as such. That is why, in principle at least, any individual is dispensable and replaceable by another. An individual is selected for a position, retained in it, or fired from it solely on the grounds of efficiency, i.e. of what will best serve the interests of the organization. The interests and needs of the individuals concerned, as individuals, must be considered only insofar as they establish limiting operating conditions. Organizational rationality dictates that these interests and needs must not be considered in their own right or on their own merits. If we think of an organization as a machine, it is easy to see why we cannot reasonably expect it to have any moral obligations to people or for them to have any to it.

For precisely the same reason, the rights and interests of persons outside the organization and of the general public are *eo ipso* ruled out as logically irrelevant to rational organizational decision, except insofar as these rights and interests set limiting conditions to the effectiveness of the organization's operations or insofar as the promoting of such rights and interests constitutes part of the goal of the organization. Hence it is fatuous to expect an industrial organization to go out of its way to avoid polluting the atmosphere or to refrain from making napalm bombs or to desist from wiretapping on purely moral grounds. Such actions would be irrational.

It follows that the only way to make the rights and interests of individuals or of the people logically relevant to organizational decision-making is to convert them into pressures of one sort or another, e.g. to bring the pressure of the law or of public opinion to bear on the organizations. Such pressures would then be introduced into the rational decision-making as limiting operating conditions. . . .

Since, as I have argued in some detail, formal organizations are not moral persons, and have no moral responsibilities, they have no moral rights. In particular, they have no *moral* right to freedom or autonomy. There can be nothing morally wrong in exercising coercion against a formal organization as there would be in exercising it against an individual. Hence, the other side of the coin is that it would be irrational for us, as moral persons, to feel any moral scruples about what we do to organizations. (We should constantly bear in mind that the officials themselves, as individuals, must still be treated as moral persons with rights and responsibilities attached to them as individuals.). . .

V. UTILITARIANISM AND ALIENATION

It is abundantly evident that the use of a double standard for the evaluation of actions is not confined to the operations of formal organizations, as I have described them. The double standard for social morality is pervasive in our society. For almost all our social decisions, administrative, political and economic, are made and justified by reference to the "rational" standard, which amounts to the principle that the end justifies the means; and yet as individuals in our personal relations with one another, we are bound by the ordinary principles of morality, i.e. the principles of obligation, responsibility and integrity. . . .

A great deal more needs to be said about the effects of working from a double standard of morality. In our highly organized (and utilitarian) society, most of us, as individuals, are forced to live double lives, and in order to accommodate ourselves to two different and incompatible standards, we tend to compartmentalize our lives, as I have already pointed out. For the most part, however, the organizational (or utilitarian) standard tends to take over.

Accordingly, our actions as individuals are increasingly submerged into social actions, that is, we tend more and more to use the social standard as a basis for our decisions and to evaluate our actions. As a result, the individual's own decisions and actions become separated from himself as a person and become the decisions and actions of another, e.g. of an organization. They become social decisions, not decisions of the individual. And in becoming social decisions, they are, in Hobbes's terms, no longer "his," they are "owned" by another, e.g. an organization or society.

This is one way of rendering the Marxian concept of alienation. As his actions are turned into social decisions, the individual is alienated from them and is *eo ipso* alienated from other men and from morality. In adopting the administrator's point of view (or that of a utilitarian) and so losing his actions, the individual becomes dehumanized and demoralized. For morality is essentially a relation between men, as individuals, and in losing this relation, one loses morality itself.

VI.   CLOSING REMARKS ON THE SOURCE OF THE PARADOX

It is unnecessary to dwell on the intolerable character of the moral schizophrenia in which we find ourselves as the result of the double standard of conduct that has been pointed out. The question is: what can be done about it? The simplest and most obvious solution is to jettison one of the conflicting standards. But which one? The choice is difficult, if not impossible. If we give up the standard of "rationality," e.g. of organizational operations, then we surrender one of the chief conditions of civilized life and progress as well as the hope of ever solving mankind's perennial practical problems, e.g. the problems of hunger, disease, ignorance and overpopulation. On the other hand, if we give up the standard of ordinary moral conduct, then in effect we destroy ourselves as moral beings and reduce our relationships to each other to purely mechanical and materialistic ones. To find a third way out of the dilemma is not only a practical, political and sociological necessity, but a moral one as well. . . .

NOTES

1. Ludwig Wittgenstein, *Philosophical Investigations* (New York: Macmillan Company, 1953), p. 7.
2. These rules are called "constitutive rules" by John Searle. See his *Speech Acts* (Cambridge: The University Press, 1969), Ch. 2, Sec. 5.
3. For further discussion of the game-model and this aspect of rules see my "Moral and Legal Obligation," in J. Roland Pennock and John W. Chapman, editors, *Political and Legal Obligations, Nomos*, 12 (New York: Atherton Press, 1970).
4. Herbert A. Simon, *Administrative Behavior*, 2nd ed. (New York: Free Press, 1965), p. 9. Hereinafter cited as Simon, AB. For a useful survey of the subject of formal organizations see Peter M. Blau and W. Richard Scott, *Formal Organizations* (San Francisco: Chandler Publishing Company, 1962), p. 36. Hereinafter cited as Blau and Scott, FO.
5. See Kenneth Arrow, *Social Choice and Individual Values* (New York: John Wiley, 1951), *passim*.
6. Quoted from A. Bergson by Kenneth Arrow in "Public and Private Values," in *Human Values and Economic Policy*, ed. S. Hook (New York: New York University Press, 1967), p. 14.
7. Quoted from Chester I. Barnard in Simon, AB, p. 203.
8. See John Kenneth Galbraith, *The New Industrial State* (Boston: Houghton Mifflin, 1967), pp. 171–78. Hereinafter cited in NIS.
9. Amitai Etzioni, *Modern Organizations* (Englewood Cliffs, N.J.: Prentice-Hall, 1964), p. 4. Hereinafter cited as MO.
10. Etzioni MO, p. 3. See also Blau and Scott, FO, p. 5. In a forthcoming article on "Community," I try to show that communities, as distinct from formal organizations, do not have specific goals. Indeed, the having of a specific goal may be what differentiates a *Gesellschaft* from a *Gemeinschaft* in Tönnies's sense. See Ferdinand Tönnies, *Community and Society*, trans. Charles P. Loomis (New York: Harper and Row, 1957), *passim*.
11. Simon, AB, p. 52.
12. "The ideal of pure rationality is basic to operations research and the modern management sciences." Yehezkel Dror, *Public Policymaking Reexamined* (San Francisco: Chandler Publishing Company, 1968), p. 336. Dror gives a useful bibliography of this subject on pp. 336–40.
13. Simon, AB, p. 77.
14. Simon, AB, p. 14.
15. "The name *morality*, when standing unqualified or alone, may signify the human laws which I style positive morality, without regard to their goodness or badness. For example, such laws of the class as are peculiar to a given age, or such laws of the class as are peculiar to a given nation, we style the morality of that given age or nation, whether we think them good or bad, etc." John Austin, *Province of Jurisprudence Determined*, ed. H. L. A. Hart (New York: Noonday Press, 1954),

p. 125. The study of positive moralities belongs to what I call "descriptive ethics."
See my *Structure of a Moral Code* (Cambridge, Mass: Harvard University Press,
1957).
16. Simon, AB, p. 52.
17. Blau and Scott, FO, p. 34.
18. See my "Moral and Legal Obligation," referred to in note 3.
19. The fact that promising involves an extremely personal relation between individuals is almost universally overlooked by philosophers who discuss promises.

Can I Be Blamed
for Obeying Orders?[1]

R. M. Hare

Many people, if asked for the distinctive feature of present-day British philosophy, would say that it lies in the peculiar attention which we tend to pay to the study of language. Perhaps most British philosophers would agree that the study of language, in some sense, is a very potent philosophical tool; and many would say that it is *the* philosophical method—that any problem which is properly philosophical reduces in the end to an elucidation of our use of words. Criticisms of this approach to philosophy are frequently made by those who have not practised the sort of method we use, and therefore do not understand either what the method is, or how fruitful it can be. It is alleged that we are turning philosophy away from matters of substance to trivial verbal matters (as if it were a trivial matter to understand the words we use); and it is also sometimes said that we are to be contrasted unfavourably in this respect with the great philosophers of the past.

The purpose of these talks is to indicate, by means of two examples taken from political philosophy, that both these criticisms arise from misunderstandings of the nature of philosophy in general and of our kind of philosophy in particular. The point could have been made by means of a general discussion about philosophical method; or it could have been made by taking examples out of the works of famous philosophers, and showing how much kinship there is between their methods of argumentation and ours. But I thought it better to take two practical problems of political morality—problems which exercise us currently, or ought to—and to show how a great deal of light can be shed on these by an understanding of the words used in discussing them: an understanding of the sort which it is the

Applications of Moral Philosophy, R. M. Hare (London: Macmillan, 1972) pp. 1–8.

purpose of contemporary moral philosophy to achieve. None of the things I shall say will be original; indeed, it is part of the point of these talks that they are not original: I am merely translating into a new, and I think clearer, idiom things which have been said by great philosophers of the past, and thereby showing that the new idiom is a vehicle for philosophy as it has always been understood.

In the first of these talks I shall discuss a problem which arises frequently in wartime and in connexion with war-crimes trials. The thesis is sometimes maintained that a soldier's duty is always to obey orders; and this is often brought forward as a defence when someone is accused of having committed some atrocity. It is said that, since it is a soldier's duty to obey his orders, and he is liable to blame if he disobeys them, we cannot consistently also blame him if in a particular case he obeys them—even though the act which he has committed is of itself wrong. We may blame his superiors who gave the orders, but not the man who carried them out. Others, in opposition to this, maintain that the individual is always responsible for his own acts.

Can the study of moral language shed any light on this problem? I want to maintain that it can; and the way I shall do this is by exhibiting the formal features of the problem, as they arise out of the logical properties of the words used in discussing it. I wish to show that these formal features are common to a large range of questions which are not at first sight similar, and that the key to the whole matter is a purely linguistic and logical observation made a long time ago by Hume.

The formal features of this problem are brought out extremely clearly by Kant in a famous passage,[2] in which he is arguing that we have to make our own moral judgements, and cannot get them made for us, without any decision on our part, by God. Suppose that I am commanded by God to do something. The Bible is full of stories where this is said to have happened. Can I without further consideration conclude that I ought to do it? Kant argued (rightly) that I cannot—not without further consideration. For it does not follow automatically, as it were, from the fact that God wills me to do something, that I ought to do it. From the fact that God wills me to do something, I can only conclude that I ought to do it if I am given the additional premiss that God wills that and that only to be done, which ought to be done. This additional premiss is one which indeed Christians all accept, because they believe that God is good; and part of what we mean by saying that God is good is that he wills that and that only to be done which ought to be done. But we have to assume this, if we are to pass from the fact that God wills us to do something to the conclusion that we ought to do it. So we can indeed, as it were, get out of making the particular moral decision as to whether we ought to do this particular thing, by putting it on the shoulders of God; but only at the cost of having to make for ourselves a more general moral decision, that we ought always to do what God commands (the very fundamental, crucial decision that is made when anyone decides to become, or to remain, an adherent of the Christian or some other religion). This more general moral judgement obviously cannot, without arguing in a circle, be shuffled off our shoulders in the same way.

Yet, if we do not assume that God is good, the only conception we have left of him is one of power without goodness—one, as Kant picturesquely puts it, compounded of lust for glory and domination, together with frightful ideas of power and vengefulness; and to make our duty the obedience to the will of such a being would be to adopt a highly immoral morality. We might rather be inclined to approve of disobeying an evil God, as Shelley portrays Prometheus doing, however appalling the consequences.

I want you to notice that this argument does not depend on its being God's will in particular upon which it is sought to base morality. The same argument would apply were we to substitute for "God" the name of any other person whatever, divine or human. Kant is here making use of a principle in ethics which was, so far as I am aware, first stated by Hume. The actual passage is worth quoting, both because it is rightly held to be one of the two or three most important observations in moral philosophy, and because it illustrates very well my thesis that the subject-matter of philosophy is the use of words. Hume says:

> In every system of morality, which I have hitherto met with, I have always remark'd, that the author proceeds for some time in the ordinary way of reasoning, and establishes the being of a God, or makes observations concerning human affairs; when of a sudden I am surpriz'd to find, that instead of the usual copulations of propositions, *is*, and *is not*, I meet with no proposition that is not connected with an *ought*, or an *ought not*. This change is imperceptible; but is, however, of the last consequence. For as this *ought*, or *ought not*, expresses some new relation or affirmation, 'tis necessary that it shou'd be observ'd and explain'd; and at the same time that a reason should be given, for what seems altogether inconceivable, how this new relation can be a deduction from others, which are entirely different from it. But as authors do not commonly use this precaution, I shall presume to recommend it to the readers; and am persuaded that this small attention wou'd subvert all the vulgar systems of morality. . . .(*Treatise*, III I i)

It is easy to apply this canon of Hume's to our example. The proposition "X's will is, that I do A" (where X is any person whatever and A is any act whatever) is a proposition of fact, an 'is'-proposition. It does not matter who X is; in Kant's example it was God; but it might be some human ruler. From this 'is'-proposition the 'ought'-proposition "I ought to do A" cannot be derived. The first proposition states a mere fact, a fact about what someone wills that I do. From this fact no moral proposition follows. Only if we are given the *moral* premiss, "X wills that and that only to be done, which ought to be done" or "Everything which X wills to be done, ought to be done" can we, from this, in conjunction with the premiss "X's will is, that I do A," conclude that I ought to do A. This is all right, because we have added to our factual minor premiss a moral major premiss; and from the two together we can infer a moral conclusion; but not from the factual minor premiss alone.

In the example with which I started, X was God. But I wish to discuss the first and most celebrated example of a philosopher who thought that moral decisions could be made on his subjects' behalf by a ruler, namely Plato. Plato thought that, just as there are experts in riding and in other skills, so there ought to be experts in morals. All we had to do, in order to solve all moral problems, was to get such an expert, make him our philosopher-king, and leave him to decide for us what was right and what was wrong. He would make the laws, and we, by obeying them, could be absolutely certain of living morally blameless lives. This programme has an obvious and immediate appeal. For moral problems are difficult and tormenting; how fortunate it would be if we could leave them, like problems of engineering, to somebody who could solve them for us! To get rid of one's moral problems on to the shoulders of someone else—some political or military leader, some priest or commissar—is to be free of much worry; it is to exchange the tortured responsibility of the adult for the happy irresponsibility of the child; that is why so many have taken this course.

The flaw in this arrangement is that we could never know whether the philosopher-king really was a philosopher-king. Plato himself admits that his ideal republic might degenerate. The maintenance of the republic depended on the correct calculation of the famous Platonic Number,[3] which was used for determining the correct mating-season to produce the philosopher-kings of the next generation. If the Number were miscalculated, a person might be made ruler who did not really possess the required qualifications. Suppose that we are inhabitants of a Platonic republic, and are ordered by our so-called philosopher-king to do a certain act. And suppose that we are troubled about the morality of this act; suppose that it is the act of torturing some unfortunate person. It is perfectly true that if our ruler is a *true* philosopher-king, then, *ex hypothesi*, he knows infallibly what is right and what is wrong, and so we cannot do wrong to obey him. But the question is: Can we be sure that he is the genuine article? Can we be sure that they did not miscalculate the Number a generation ago, so that what we have at this moment is not a philosopher-king, but the most wicked of tyrants masquerading as one?

We can tell whether a man is a good man, or, specifically, whether a king is a good king, only by considering his acts. So that it is no use saying of *all* our ruler's acts, "He is the philosopher-king, and the philosopher-king can do no wrong; therefore each and every act of his must be right." For this would be to argue in a circle. It is only if we are satisfied that his acts are right that we can be satisfied that he is a good king. Therefore, if he commands us to perform what looks like an atrocity, the only thing we can do is look at the individual act and say, "What about this very thing that he is commanding me to do now? Could a good man command anyone to do this?" That is to say, we have to make up our own minds about the morality of the king's acts and orders.

Governing is different from engineering in an important respect. The engineer as such is concerned with means only; but government involves the choice both of means and of ends. If you know no engineering, you have to get the best engineer you can to build your bridge; but the engineer is not the man who decides that there shall be a bridge. Therefore, we can say to the engineer, "We want a bridge just here"; and leave him to build it. We judge him by his success in bringing about the end which we have set him. If his bridge falls into the river, we do not employ him again. Rulers also often have to find means to ends which are agreed upon. For example, it is recognised that it is a bad thing if large numbers of people starve through being unable to get employment; and we expect our rulers nowadays to see to it that this does not happen. The means to this end are very complicated, and only an economist can understand them; but we are content to leave our rulers to employ competent economists, understand their prescriptions as best they can, choose between them when, as often, they conflict, and generally do their best to realise the end of full employment without impairing any other of the ends which we also wish to realise. But in government someone has to decide on the ends of policy. In a democracy this is done by the voters. They do it in part explicitly and in advance, by choosing between parties with rival policies; but in the main they do it implicitly and by results, by turning out of office those parties who do not achieve the ends which the voters desire.

In Plato's republic it was different. The people were supposed to be entirely ignorant both about means and about ends; the rulers decided on both. And if the ruler decides both on the means and on the end, one cannot judge him as one judges the engineer. For one can say to the engineer, "You were told to produce a bridge that stood up to the weather, and your bridge has been blown into the river." But if we have not told our ruler to do anything—if we have just left it to him to decide on the ends of political action—then we cannot ever accuse him of not fulfilling the purposes which we intended him to fulfil. He can always say, "I did what I thought good, and I still think it good." This is the decisive point at which Plato's analogy between the ruler and the expert breaks down. The expert is an expert at getting something done, once it has been decided *what* is to be done. Plato's philosopher-king was supposed to do not merely this—he was supposed not merely to perform a task, but to decide what the task was to be. And this is a thing that cannot be left to experts; it is the responsibility of all of us.

If it is true that we cannot leave the moral problems about political ends to a Platonic philosopher-king, then it is still more obviously true that we cannot leave them to any ordinary human superior. As I said at the beginning, we often hear it said by someone who is accused of a war-crime—for example of killing some innocent people in cold blood—"I did it on the orders of my superior officers; I am not morally guilty." If the superior officers could likewise be found and charged they would say the same thing, until we got back, perhaps, to some high-up ruler who initiated in some very general terms some policy whose detailed execution involved the slaughtering of the innocents. But how can the orders of somebody else absolve *me* from moral responsibility? It may indeed absolve me from legal responsibility: that is a different matter, and depends on the law that is in force. But if we are speaking of a matter of morals, surely the man who is ordered to do such an act has to ask himself whether it is morally right for him to do it. It cannot follow, from the 'is'-proposition that X orders me to kill these people, that I ought to kill them. The people who order these crimes, and I who execute them, are accomplices, and share the responsibility.

In many cases, admittedly, a person in such a position can plead that he is acting under duress; he, or his family, will be shot if he does not obey orders. We do tend to excuse a man in such a position, or at any rate to blame him less. Why we do so is also a matter upon which the study of moral language can shed a good deal of light; but I have no time to discuss it now. Let us exclude duress from the argument by assuming that the subordinate knows that his superiors will not find out whether he has obeyed orders or not: let us suppose that he is the head of a mental home who has been ordered to poison all incurables, and that he himself does the classification into curables and incurables.

Up to a certain point, indeed, a person in this position can plead ignorance of fact; his superiors, no doubt, have access to more information than he has, and can foresee consequences of the omission to murder these people which might not be known to the person who has to perform the act. Up to a point a subordinate can say, "I cannot see the whole picture; I must be content to leave the formulation of policy to my superiors, whose job it is to know what the consequences would be of various alternative policies, and to make a choice between evils." But the point must in the end come when a subordinate has to say, "Any policy which involves my doing this sort of thing (for example, slaughtering all these people in cold blood) must be a wicked policy, and anyone who has conceived it must be a wicked man; it cannot therefore be my duty to obey him." To decide just when this point has been reached is one of the most difficult problems in morals. But we must never banish from our minds the thought that it might be reached. We must never lose sight of the distinction between what we are told to do and what we ought to do. There is a point beyond which we cannot get rid of our own moral responsibilites by laying them on the shoulders of a superior, whether he be general, priest or politician, human or divine. Anyone who thinks otherwise has not understood what a moral decision is.

NOTES

1. This was the first of two talks given in Germany, and later on the B.B.C. Third Programme, in 1955 under the title "Ethics and Politics." Both talks were published in *The Listener* for October 1955.
2. *Groundwork*, 2nd ed., p. 92 (tr. Paton, *The Moral Law*, p. 104).
3. *Republic*, 546 c.

The Moral
Responsibility of Corporations

Case Study

Uncommon Decency: Pacific
Bell Responds to AIDS

DAVID L. KIRP

Sitting nervously in the public health clinic that Friday before Labor Day in 1986, awaiting word on his AIDS test, Pacific Bell repairman Dave Goodenough already half knew what he would be told: he had AIDS. He'd suspected as much for seven months, ever since he first noticed the markings on his chest. His doctor dismissed them as bruises picked up at work, but when the purplish markings started showing up all over his body, Goodenough sought another opinion. It had taken the second doctor only moments to identify the symptoms as "KS"—Kaposi's sarcoma, a type of cancer frequently associated with AIDS—and the test results confirmed that diagnosis.

Suspicions of AIDS are one thing, certainty something very different. "I was wiped out," Goodenough recalls. As he began to sort out the implications of the news, one question kept recurring: Would he—could he—go back to work?

Goodenough had been with Pacific for a decade, and working meant a lot to him. He liked what he did and liked the crew he worked with; he appreciated the fact that he didn't have to hide his homosexuality. Back in Ohio, Goodenough had been sacked from a probation officer's job when word leaked out he was gay. But San Francisco was different. And even though the phone company had a reputation as a bastion of mid-America, operating with a rule book as thick as a phone directory, by the late 1970s Pacific had just begun learning how to cope with the reality that a sizable number of its employees were gay.

To Goodenough, confirmation of AIDS only reinforced how important it was to him to stay on the job. "If I left the job," he recalls thinking, "it would be like putting a limit on the amount of time I have to live." His friend, Tim

O'Hara, a long-time Communication Workers of America steward and a spokesman for gay concerns in the union, encouraged Goodenough not to quit—and to tell company officials that he had AIDS.

Initially, Goodenough resisted this last bit of advice. "I won't let anybody know," he insisted. But a few days later he changed his mind. "I can't hold something like this inside," he decided. "It'd be like being in the closet all over again."

On Goodenough's behalf, O'Hara went to Chuck Woodman, supervisor of the 750 people in Operations who keep the phone system in San Francisco up and running. Woodman's response was, "We'll do everything we need to do to keep Dave working," and he called Goodenough's immediate superior to enlist his support. Later that week, Goodenough phoned Woodman to thank him. "You could hear in his tone of voice how much Chuck cared," Goodenough remembers. "What he said kept me going. He told me, 'You've always got a job here.'"

Chuck Woodman hadn't always been so concerned about people with AIDS. To his subordinates Woodman had a reputation as a tough guy, a self-described redneck whose heroes included John Wayne and George Patton. A devout Mormon, father of 8, and grandfather of 20, Woodman's attitude about AIDS began to change in 1985 when he was transferred to San Francisco. He remembers how he was affected by a funeral for a worker who had died of AIDS.

"As I listened to that minister talking about how angry it made him that people with AIDS were shunned, I began to feel some of that anger," Woodman says. "The whole moral question of homosexuality got put aside."

To learn more, Woodman turned to Tim O'Hara, whom he knew and liked. With O'Hara's assistance, Woodman got a thorough education on AIDS. Information brought understanding, and understanding gradually eased the fear. After that first funeral, Woodman started asking questions. "What can we do for the people with AIDS on the job?" he wondered.

"They need to keep working," O'Hara answered. "It gives them a reason to stay alive."

Woodman began talking with supervisors and visiting workers with AIDS when they were too sick to work. Out of those talks with Woodman and Michael Eriksen, the company's director of preventative medicine and health education, came Pacific's first steps toward dealing with AIDS in the workplace: an AIDS Education Task Force, with company nurses and volunteering union members trained by the San Francisco AIDS Foundation giving presentations in offices and company garages all around the city. Woodman's bosses in the Pacific hierarchy were pleased with his AIDS initiatives. But peers who knew him from his earlier days were stunned. "I got maybe half a dozen calls from guys around the state. 'What are you doing, Woodman,' they'd say, 'do you love those gay guys?' I told them, 'Until you've walked in these tracks, you can't understand. You start buying in when it's someone you know.' And here's something. Each of those guys called me back later to say, 'I've got someone with AIDS. Now what do I do?' "

Chuck Woodman talks about AIDS as a managerial challenge, the toughest in his nearly 40 years at Pacific. "When I look at where I was and where I am now, AIDS has had a bigger impact on my thinking about people than anything I've come up against."

⚜

This comment about the impact of AIDS is no hyperbole; that isn't Woodman's style. And Woodman's remark applies not just to himself, not even just to Pacific, but to business generally. Just as AIDS has already changed American society, it will reshape American corporations.

That is not the conventional wisdom. To most managers, AIDS is a medical and social epidemic of still-unknown dimensions—the federal Centers for Disease Control conservatively estimate that 1.5 million Americans now carry the AIDS virus and that by 1991 every county in the United States will have at least one AIDS case. Much less common is a managerial awareness that American business must reckon with AIDS. Managers in general regard AIDS as a problem not for workers but for homosexuals and drug users and their promiscuous sexual partners, as a disease that attacks people outside the office and factory walls.

Such denial, however understandable, doesn't fit the facts. Among 273 companies responding to a 1987 American Society for Personnel Administration survey, one-third acknowledged having workers with AIDS. This was more than triple the percentage reported two years earlier and a figure that will steadily grow, if only because of AIDS's long incubation period (it can take seven years or more for symptoms to develop). Furthermore, those numbers represent only the most direct impact of AIDS, and this is not necessarily its most important dimension to the corporation.

AIDS molds behavior in many ways. In the worst, usually hushed-up incidents, employees afraid of AIDS-carrying coworkers have walked off the job. More common are dances of avoidance—workers refusing to share tools or even sit in the cafeteria with a stricken coworker. And then there is a very different reaction—grief at the loss of a friend and colleague. In a society where, for many, the workplace isn't merely the source of a paycheck but also a source of community, where fellow workers are also friends, there is simply no way for business to wall out AIDS.

How does a company respond to something as alien as AIDS? The best answer, as Pacific learned, is to recognize AIDS as a legitimate part of the corporate environment and to tailor a response, that is of a piece with all that the company stands for and is doing. Pacific's reaction to AIDS was affected by the fact that the utility is headquartered in San Francisco—with its large gay community—and that telecommunications is a highly regulated industry. Nevertheless, the remarkable turnaround of this unlikely innovator tells an instructive tale for every major U.S. corporation.

⚜

Three years after AIDS was first identified, in 1984, Pacific's preventative medicine and health education director, Michael Eriksen, began hearing stories about Pacific employees worried about getting AIDS on the job. There was the coin collector who refused to touch the phone booths in the predominantly gay Castro district of San Francisco. One Los Angeles crew balked at installing phones in the offices of the L.A. AIDS Foundation, and another San Francisco crew insisted on being issued head-to-toe covering before installing phones in General Hospital's AIDS ward. And there was the lineman who refused to use the truck of a fellow employee, rumored to have died of AIDS, until it was sterilized.

As the number of crisis phone calls mounted, Eriksen resolved to determine the dimensions of Pacific's AIDS problem, to conscript other activists in shaping a plan—and to act. Later, one colleague recalled, "Eriksen became our AIDS guru." Bearded, mid-thirties, casual, fresh out of a Johns Hopkins Ph.D. program, Eriksen had been hired several years earlier to move the company toward a "wellness" approach. Already he had developed an in-house program to help employees quit smoking and to enable women to spot the first signs of breast cancer. Eriksen brought an activist's impatience to Pacific. In a company where going by the book is the instinctive response of lifetime employees, he equated going through corporate channels with death by memo.

Eriksen's work on AIDS began with the facts. He reviewed the company's 1984 death certificates and turned up 20 employees who had died of the disease. This meant that, after cancer, AIDS was the most frequent cause of death among active Pacific employees. Pacific officials, who hadn't considered AIDS a workplace issue, were startled; but the data made sense, since the nearly 70,000 employees and 250,000 people in Pacific's larger "family" were concentrated in San Francisco and Los Angeles, two cities with a high incidence of AIDS cases.

Moreover, Eriksen knew that the figure of 20 was decidedly conservative since it excluded workers who had gone on the permanent disability rolls before dying and cases where the doctor had not specified AIDS on the death certificate as the cause of death. In the general population, the number of AIDS cases was doubling every year; this meant Pacific was seeing just the beginning of the epidemic. Add those deaths among the company's work force to the stories of Pacific workers' fears about encountering AIDS while serving customers, and something had to be done. But what, and by whom?

If AIDS had been a garden-variety disease, tracing the path of corporate response would be easy. Policy would have been designed by the company's human resources division, with the medical director, Ralph Alexander, having the final say. But because AIDS was new and frightening, it demanded the kind of cross-the-boundaries effort that is hard for a company to marshal on any issue, let alone on a subject so loaded with bias, contention, and misinformation.

The corporate medical group needed to sift prevailing medical wisdom— but that was just the start. The human resources division, drawing on corporate-safety and labor-relations experts, had to determine how AIDS would be treated in the workplace—whether prospective employees would be screened for the virus, whether workers with AIDS could continue on the job—and what benefits to offer people with AIDS. Potentially every manager in the company needed help in handling workplace fears, and not just in San Francisco and in Los Angeles. Phone operators in California's decidedly unswinging Central Valley had no personal fears about contracting AIDS, but expressed real concern for their children. And because the AIDS issue was so hot, whatever the company did was potentially news—that made the corporate communications division a player as well.

Urged on by Michael Eriksen, the lawyers and medics and corporate-safety staffers determined that workers with AIDS would be treated like anyone with a life-threatening illness. The culture of the phone company, with its strong emphasis on two-way commitment and loyalty, kept Pacific from seriously considering the option of revoking the medical coverage of employees with AIDS—a policy that some companies followed. Jim Henderson, the company's executive director of human resources policy and services, says bluntly, "People with AIDS are sick. We don't fire sick people."

This policy was not only humane but also affordable, a vital consideration for any business. Reviewing the company's 20 AIDS-related deaths, Michael Eriksen estimated that the lifetime cost of medical treatment for an AIDS patient ran about $30,000, about the same as costs for treating other life-threatening illnesses such as cancer. To Pacific, whose escalating health costs were subject to review by California's Public Utilities Commission, that news was reassuring.

In practice, AIDS forced the company to make much-needed reforms that went beyond this one disease. For example, Pacific was already searching for ways to reduce reliance on hospitalization. The company sought less expensive alternatives, and its sick workers considered less impersonal ones. Both preferred new options, like at-home or hospice care, which offered more personal settings and attention at reduced costs. These quickly became part of corporate health coverage. Pacific's capacity for individual case management also needed strengthening so it could better determine—on a case-by-case basis—which regimen of care made best sense. Moreover, since many drugs used to treat AIDS patients were most readily available by mail, the company extended its health plan to cover mail-order drugs.

None of these innovations applied to AIDS alone. Indeed, business organizations like the Washington Business Group on Health have preached for years that case management is the best way for a company to tame the costs of catastrophic diseases. But AIDS treatment demonstrated the efficacy of the approach. One Southeastern public utility, relying heavily on hospitalization for AIDS patients, reported that its first eight AIDS cases cost the company $1 million—almost four times Pacific's per-patient cost. At Pacific, AIDS was a catalyst for reshaping many employee health benefits. The resulting package offered better treatment at markedly lower costs.

🌿

Pacific was drawing from its own traditions in defining benefits for employees with AIDS. But in dealing with workers' fears about being exposed to AIDS through casual contact, Pacific had to determine entirely new responses.

The accounts that Eriksen and Jean Taylor, director of employee counseling, had collected—installers shunning customers, workers avoiding AIDS-stricken associates—hinted at a dangerous level of anxiety in the field. And those employees' misgivings mirrored feelings in the society. In 1984, when AIDS fears had first begun to surface at Pacific, far less was known about the disease than today, and uncertainty left ample room for fearfulness and misinformation.

Managers had to wrestle with difficult questions. How would Pacific allay its employees' worries and thereby ensure that an AIDS incident didn't escalate into a fiasco? How could it protect the confidentiality of disclosures about AIDS while attending to the concerns of employees with the disease? What changes were needed in Pacific's detailed rule book to help managers deal with the special needs of employees with AIDS?

The way Pacific handled the 1985 case of the phone installer who refused an assignment in San Francisco's Castro district suggests the delicacy of the issue and the need for new and nonpunitive approaches—educational approaches—to win over frightened workers. When the balking phone installer was suspended, he went to Shop Steward Tim O'Hara. But instead of lodging a grievance, O'Hara struck a deal. The worker would return to the job and a joint union-management AIDS education program would begin immediately at the site. The idea was feasible because Pacific and its union had developed an unusually cooperative and nonadversarial relationship during the last contract talks.

O'Hara's evenhanded approach respected the workers' fears and met the needs of the company's customers. Meanwhile, the shop steward put together a list of 30 volunteering workers, whose lifestyles ran the gamut from the most traditional heterosexual middle American to the openly gay. If other workers were ever unwilling to make an installation where there was an AIDS victim, this squad was ready to handle the job. Here again, preparation and education worked: no supervisor has ever had to turn to O'Hara's list.

But despite early agreement on nondiscrimination as the broad company policy, corporate AIDS education at Pacific did not advance beyond crisis intervention. Yes, several hundred employees did show up in April 1985 at the company's headquarters downtown for a question-and-answer session with Michael Eriksen and a San Francisco AIDS Foundation representative. But that was a one-time occasion. For all the other employees—the San

Francisco work crews who wouldn't dream of coming all the way downtown; the 7,200 back-room personnel working in "San Remote," a Pentagon-like fortress 35 miles outside the city in suburban San Ramon; the employees in Los Angeles and throughout California and Nevada—there was essentially no AIDS education.

Within Pacific's medical department, there was disagreement about the adequacy of the company's approach thus far. The dispute reflected deep differences in perspective between the classic medical approach and the newer views of wellness specialists.

For longtime medical director Ralph Alexander—a consistently conservative official who believed that, as an M.D., he should have the last say—what Pacific was doing sufficed. In discussions with other divisions, Alexander regularly stressed the need to keep a sense of proportion when responding to AIDS, which he viewed as a relatively minor health concern for the company. "There's danger of offending a hell of a lot of people," said Alexander. It was better, he argued, for the company to devote more attention to heart disease and cancer, far bigger killers and diseases that wouldn't "raise eyebrows."

Wellness specialist Michael Eriksen saw matters differently. AIDS, he believed, deserved special attention because it was new and unnerving. He began to hook up with other like-minded colleagues, most of them mid-level managers involved in communications both inside and outside the company. These middle-level policy entrepreneurs believed that acting decisively on AIDS was the right thing to do; moreover, such a stance would benefit the company. It was these middle managers who took the lead in shaping Pacific's response to AIDS, exercising leadership from below.

One opening salvo was an article on AIDS that slipped into Pacific's newspaper, *Update*, moving the issue higher on the corporate agenda. In early 1985, Eriksen had suggested to *Update* editor Diane Olberg that she run an AIDS story; coincidentally, the organizers of the company's blood drive made the same request. They were troubled by reports of workers refusing to donate blood for fear that they could get AIDS—reports that showed the workers' generally low level of knowledge about the disease. Higher-ups would balk at the idea of an article on AIDS, Olberg knew, insisting that this was really just a San Francisco issue. But sensing the importance of the topic, Olberg went ahead on her own.

That first article focused entirely on the facts about AIDS in the workplace, avoiding the sensitive matter of company policy. It appeared on July 22, 1985—the same day Rock Hudson went public with the fact that he had AIDS—and demand for that issue of *Update* was unprecedented. The newspaper had to run reprints. To corporate tea-leaf readers, the coverage said that AIDS was something Pacific cared about; the strong employee response showed that AIDS was something employees cared about, and that paved the way for other AIDS-related stories. This reaction and the increasing demand for AIDS education sessions in the field sent another message up the corporate ladder: informing those who were healthy but worried might be as important to Pacific as ministering to those with the disease.

⚓︎

On March 20, 1986, the conference room at Levi Strauss's downtown San Francisco headquarters was packed. Over 230 managers from 100 companies were there for the first-ever conference on "AIDS in the Workplace." The demand so exceeded the organizers' expectations that 100 would-be participants had to be turned away. Reporters from leading daily newspapers were in the audience and TV crews from as far away as France recorded the event.

It came as no surprise to California executives that Levi Strauss had a big part in organizing this conference. The company had a long history of social activism, and CEO Bob Haas had personally acquired a reputation for dealing forthrightly with AIDS. Back in 1982, when several Levi employees told him that they were nervous about distributing AIDS information leaflets on company property, Haas had responded by stationing himself in the headquarters lobby, handing out leaflets to passersby.

But sharing the spotlight with Levi Strauss was Pacific—and this *was* surprising, for here was a company that usually made itself invisible on provocative topics. The corporation's name was prominent among the conference sponsors because the Pacific Telesis Foundation (established by Pacific's parent) had underwritten—and in conjunction with the San Francisco AIDS Foundation, Pacific's corporate TV group had produced—the first AIDS video aimed at U.S. business.

First screened at a breakfast session attended by 20 CEOs and then shown at the conference, "An Epidemic of Fear" pulled no punches: in telling detail it presented the panic, the medical evidence, the emotional tugs. Present on camera was Todd Shuttlesworth, who had been fired from his job by Broward County, Florida when he was diagnosed with AIDS. Shuttlesworth's case served to remind managers how expensive a wrong-headed AIDS policy could be to a business; after his dismissal Shuttlesworth had taken his employer to court and secured a six-figure settlement.

Outsiders weren't the only ones surprised at Pacific's prominent visibility. Some high-ranking Pacific officials were amazed and decidedly uncomfortable about this unusual corporate position. It was appropriate for the company to treat its AIDS-stricken workers decently, they agreed. But to link AIDS with the corporation in the public mind was entirely different: that would associate Pacific with gays, drugs, and contagion, potentially driving away prospective employees, conceivably scaring creditors and customers who depended on the company's stability. There was every reason for the company to avoid sticking its neck out, said the advocates of a low corporate profile.

But Pacific did stick its neck out with AIDS-related decisions—decisions that in part reflected the company's determination to change its corporate culture to fit its new competitive realities. Gradually but steadily, Pacific went beyond the nondiscrimination policies that suited the old character of the company to real leadership that helped define the company Pacific was becoming.

☆

Pacific Telesis Group is a holding company for Pacific Bell, the regional phone company that accounts for over 90 percent of the entire business's revenue and PacTel Corporation, which manages the company's diversified businesses. When it was launched after the 1984 AT&T breakup, many viewed Pacific as the weakest of the Baby Bells. "Of all the Bell regional holding companies, Pacific Telephone holds the most risk for investors," declared the *New York Times*. "The company's record of poor earnings and its long-running feud with the California Public Utilities Commission make it a risky investment at best."

Like other AT&T offspring, Pacific had to learn how to respond to the discipline of the marketplace. And in California, the company found itself in the nation's most hotly contested, fiercely competitive telecommunications markets. Other Bell companies, including Nynex and Southwestern Bell, as well as a host of new entrants, were all clamoring for a piece of the action, advertising heavily to an urbanized population with a reputation for buying whatever is new.

To respond to these changed conditions, Pacific had to meet three challenges: to be financially successful where smart investors were betting against Pacific's likely financial performance; to create an innovative and forward-looking organization, where tradition dictated that long-standing employees had to mold themselves until they gradually developed "Bell-shaped heads"; and to adopt corporate positions responsive to new constituencies that were socially conscious, where the company had always been seen as socially and politically backward. Together these challenges called on Pacific to redefine itself. It was under these conditions that AIDS became a measure of the company's transformation—and a vehicle for it. And it did so at a time when the company's efforts at change consistently misfired, reminding managers just how difficult large-scale change really is.

In its enthusiasm to demonstrate its newfound competitive hustle, for example, Pacific launched aggressive marketing campaigns. But what came to light were dubious sales tactics, like selling unneeded phone services to non-English-speaking customers who didn't understand what they were buying. Morale suffered among employees who didn't expect the phone company to behave like a used car dealership.

Pacific's effort at organizational transformation also ran into problems. To become more innovative, top management realized, the company would need to shake up its rigidly hierarchical structure, a steep pyramid with 14 precisely delineated levels. The problem was, how to change?

Looking for direction, Pacific contracted with an outside consultant for

$40 million worth of leadership-development and personal-growth training. The system was called Kroning, after Charles Krone, the consultant who developed the training material. It backfired. Instead of opening up communication, it sharpened divisions between the "in" group, who claimed to fathom Kroning, and everyone else in the company. Instead of easing relations with the Public Utilities Commission, the controversial corporate expenditure triggered a "cease and desist" recommendation from the Commission's advocacy arm. Instead of improving Pacific's public image, the fiasco yielded a harvest of journalistic ridicule.

A big part of becoming competitive was learning about the state's shifting political environment—and that meant becoming more socially conscious. Historically, Pacific's idea of responsiveness was to join all the Rotary Clubs in California. While that approach might have worked in the 1950s, in the 1980s California's shifting coalitions of interest groups—blacks, Hispanics, consumer-oriented organizations—increasingly wielded political power. Pacific had long treated these groups as if they were the enemy. Now, however, these same groups were major purchasers of telecommunications services, and they had the ear of the most aggressive state Public Utilities Commission in the country. For the phone company to prosper on its own, it somehow had to co-opt these groups—to reach a mutually workable level of understanding and accommodation.

Steve Coulter, Pacific's director of consumer affairs, had the job of handling these troubling concerns. Coulter was a former Nevada legislator in his mid-thirties, a man who had made a political career out of enlisting constituencies to his cause. His collegial style and political savvy enabled him to get away with being a corporate guerrilla warrior. "A 'no' from above isn't necessarily the end of things," Coulter explains. "I'd ask 'Where's the block?' Then I'd go look for allies."

Working under Jim Moberg, then the vice president for corporate communications, Coulter had been devising company approaches to such new issues as minority procurement and multilingual services. Coulter was also involved in negotiations over minority hiring and procurement with the NAACP and HACER, a consortium of some of California's major Hispanic groups organized by Pacific. To Coulter, a visible Pacific presence on AIDS was appropriate: it was politically astute, operationally important, and morally right. In collaboration with Michael Eriksen and other allies, Coulter became a leading advocate for an AIDS policy inside Pacific.

The politics were particularly interesting. Pacific had long been in open warfare with San Francisco's affluent and influential gay community, and the company badly needed to mend its fences. In the early 1970s, Jim Henderson, now executive director of human resources policy and services, had helped draft the company's policy on homosexuals. Back then, Henderson recalls, "Some managers were afraid that gay activists would show up to work wearing dresses." In 1973, those fears prompted Pacific to adopt a policy against employing "manifest homosexuals." In practice, this rule meant that anyone who publicly acknowledged his or her homosexuality couldn't get a job with the phone company.

Although Pacific formally revoked its "manifest homosexuals" policy in 1976, it wasn't until 1986 that the then-defunct policy's earlier existence came to light. By then, Pacific had tangled with the City of San Francisco, refusing to subscribe to a city ordinance barring discrimination against homosexuals. In 1979, the company lost an employee-discrimination lawsuit in the California Supreme Court, which ruled that the state's human rights law prohibited public utilities from refusing to hire gays. Shortly before a trial for damages was scheduled to begin, Pacific lawyers produced a previously undisclosed 1973 job application that confirmed the company's former anti-homosexual policy. In December 1986, the company negotiated a $3 million settlement, the biggest ever in a gay discrimination case.

All this recent history—the disclosures of shoddy business practices, the troubles with Kroning, the acknowledged need to reach out to outsiders, the mishandling of the gay community—was artfully deployed by those within Pacific who pushed to make AIDS a visible corporate concern.

Eriksen provided the substantive information on AIDS, Coulter spoke mostly of politics and positioning. What Pacific needed, he argued to his bosses, was a winner, an issue on which the company could do well by doing good. AIDS could be the issue. Confronted with considerable internal opposition, it took all of Coulter's political experience and lots of help from other insiders to carry the day.

In March 1985, at a meeting of San Francisco's Business Leadership Task Force, Levi Strauss CEO Bob Haas raised the AIDS issue for the CEOs to discuss. The group's agenda already covered items like the role of the elderly worker and health-care cost containment. It was time, Haas said, to put AIDS on the list. Everyone else in the room, top officers from Wells Fargo, Chevron, Bank of America, and McKesson—and Pacific—said nothing, as if they could make something very embarrassing go away by being quiet.

Yet despite the CEOs' initial unease, AIDS did not disappear from the agenda. Haas continued to push the matter. So did Leslie Luttgens, organizer of the Leadership Task Force, who served on the boards of several important local foundations and blue-chip corporations, including Pacific. A one-time president of the United Way, Luttgens combined a strong commitment to social causes with a persuasive but diplomatic style. She had learned about AIDS as an overseer of the University of California-San Francisco Medical School; now she was convinced that trouble in the workplace was inevitable if businesses continued to deny the scary reality of the disease. After Haas made his proposal to the CEO group, Luttgens spent the next few months talking up the need to promote AIDS education, imparting a sense of urgency that kept the issue alive.

Making the rounds about this time was a request from the San Francisco AIDS Foundation asking for corporate financial support for an AIDS education video. Pacific Telesis Foundation officials expressed considerable interest in funding the video; the in-house filmmakers added their enthusiasm for actually producing it. But at the top of corporate communications, Jim Moberg was unpersuaded. For advice, Moberg turned to Pacific's medical director, Ralph Alexander—and what he heard was conservative medical and corporate policy. According to Alexander, Pacific's role on industrial health issues was as a "national weather vane—and that's why we need to be doubly cautious about having a public profile."

Steve Coulter, like Mike Eriksen, equated caution with timidity. An AIDS video was clearly needed by businesses. Moreover, as Coulter argued in a memo to Alexander, getting the phone company publicly involved in AIDS education might just bolster its position in the pending gay discrimination lawsuit. Such a stance might provide some sorely needed good publicity. It was responsive to the AIDS-related concerns of other stakeholder groups including the NAACP, which, as Coulter pointed out, identified AIDS as a top national health priority. It could also improve relations with California's Congressman Henry Waxman, a powerhouse in telecommunications policy who was historically no friend of Pacific's and the congressmember most knowledgeable about AIDS.

As a savvy corporate politician, Coulter knew that he could not realistically expect Moberg to reverse his decision against the video project. The idea had to be repackaged, and that meant reviving the notion of Leadership Task Force involvement. Perhaps if the AIDS video proposal appeared in a different guise from a different sponsor, the answer would be different. Working with Michael Eriksen and the AIDS Foundation, Coulter sharpened the video proposal, waiting for another chance to bring up the matter with Moberg.

The occasion came on the eve of a December 1985 meeting of the Leadership Task Force. Coulter had been designated to sit in for Moberg as Pacific's representative at the session. On the table was a plan put forth by Leslie Luttgens for an "AIDS in the Workplace" conference. Hoping that he could now deliver Pacific's support for the AIDS video, Coulter phoned Moberg in New York, where Pacific had just signed a statement of mutual cooperation with the NAACP. Coulter's pitch to his boss noted the internal support for the AIDS video—from Luttgens, corporate TV, and the Foundation—as well as the endorsement of enterprises like Bank of America, Chevron, and Levi Strauss. "I need to be able to say, 'We have $25,000 on the table,'" Coulter argued.

Jim Moberg, euphoric after his successful NAACP negotiation, gave his cautious go-ahead—"as long as we don't seek publicity and don't stand alone." Leslie Luttgens's quiet advocacy had reassured him that AIDS activism was not a far-out idea; after all, here was a Pacific board member offering encouragement and a degree of protection if things misfired.

Then Moberg took up the matter with his fellow VPs, who had questions of their own. "Anytime you do something different from what's normal in the business community," Moberg says, "questions will be raised: 'Why only us?'" Some of these officers wondered aloud whether AIDS wasn't just a passing phenomenon, but Moberg set them straight. "In the end, they accepted the proposal on faith . . . it was enough that someone they trusted advocated it." Now AIDS had become something "owned" by corporate Pacific—not just by some of its more enterprising staffers.

With that corporate approval, Coulter's group went to work. In less than three months, they prepared the video and an inch-thick managers' workbook on AIDS and organized and publicized the conference.

The reaction to the March 1986 gathering was more enthusiastic than even Steve Coulter could have hoped for. Pacific, a company that lately had seen little but media brickbats, was now getting raves; a company known for its habit of avoiding social issues had gone out front, to considerable applause. The thank-you letters and the press clips circulated inside the company. At the next meeting of the Pacific board, Leslie Luttgens made a point of noting that the AIDS video that Pacific had produced was being aired nationally on PBS, as well as in France and Japan.

There was one internal casualty of the struggle to promote AIDS education: Michael Eriksen was abruptly fired by Ralph Alexander immediately after the AIDS conference. "I no longer have any need for you," the medical director had told Eriksen. There had been continuing disagreements between the two men. For his part, Alexander says, "Some programs he was supposed to run didn't work out."

The loss of Eriksen was deeply troubling to his colleagues, who had relied on his expertise. But his loss at this point was sustainable. There was product and momentum. With the video in hand and the AIDS Education Task Force functioning, the internal education efforts began to pick up. Success led to success. Responding to a request from the union that Pacific require AIDS education, Operations Vice President Lee Cox sent a letter to all supervisors, not insisting but recommending that they show the video as part of an AIDS education session.

⚜

Producing the video pushed Pacific into the public arena on AIDS. What came next was even further removed from corporate tradition and even more dangerous: taking a public position on a statewide AIDS ballot proposition.

An organization led by political extremist Lyndon LaRouche, whose motto, "Spread panic, not AIDS," became the rallying cry for a cause, had garnered enough signatures to force a statewide vote on a measure— Proposition 64—that, if passed by the electorate in the November 1986 election, would turn panic into law. The implications of the badly drafted measure were that thousands of workers who had AIDS could be fired, hundreds of students who carried the virus could be removed from school and college; moreover, people with AIDS could be quarantined. It appealed to people's emotions and played on their fears—yet had the simple allure of seeming to offer voters their chance to do something to protect themselves from the dread AIDS virus.

Most of California's chief public figures—politicians, church leaders, educators—opposed the measure. Steve Coulter wanted Pacific to add its voice to the opposition. Yet the huge number of signatures—it took nearly half a million to qualify the measure for the ballot—testified to the proposition's popular appeal. And some of the state's leading political conservatives voiced their strong support for the measure.

Like most companies, Pacific seldom took a stand on any ballot measure that did not directly affect its business. This political principle gave the company an easy and clear dividing line and protected it from needlessly making enemies over extraneous issues. Instead, Pacific preferred to exert its political influence through quieter relationships between lobbyists and lawmakers in the state capital. On the ballot measure, Pacific's lobbyists in Sacramento adamantly urged the company to remain mute.

For months, the debate over Proposition 64 continued inside Pacific. The conservatives from government relations and human resources insisted that opposing the measure would only earn Pacific powerful political enemies. The corporate communications activists countered that silence would put Pacific in league with those who proposed quarantining AIDS carriers and would also offend key external stakeholders, who might then "find additional avenues to criticize the company."

The stalemate was finally broken at the officers' level. Art Latno and Gary McBee, the two top external-affairs officials, determined that the company would publicly urge the defeat of Proposition 64. McBee, who had come to know the human cost of AIDS when a member of his staff died from the disease, became a strong voice for taking on LaRouche. "Given our internal position on AIDS," he says, "it would have been unconscionable for us not to oppose Prop. 64." The officers authorized a $5,000 corporate contribution to the campaign, the biggest single donation from any California business.

The stance was different—a decided shift from business as usual. Yet it reflected a fact of life about the shifting relationship between business and politics. In California—and increasingly across the country—voters are deciding more and more significant policy questions, rather than leaving matters to the elected officials. If a company wants to have a say on those matters, it must go public.

In the November 1986 election, California's voters resoundingly rejected Proposition 64. Although some Sacramento lawmakers grumbled at Pacific's lobbyists, the feared retaliation never occurred; and when LaRouche put the same measure on the ballot in June 1988, Pacific officials opposed it without thinking twice.

But the real test of how far Pacific had come on the issue took place in November 1988, when Proposition 102 hit the ballot. This was no kooky extremists' handiwork but a proposal authored by GOP Congressman

William Dannemeyer that would essentially abolish anonymous AIDS testing. While leading public health figures opposed the measure, fearing that its reporting requirements would drive those at risk for AIDS underground, the proposition did not threaten quarantining. It had modest support among doctors—and, more important, an endorsement from the popular Republican governor, George Deukmejian, Pacific risked political wrath—facing down a barrage of appeals from Dannemeyer—by opposing the measure. McBee again championed that position. The proposition was defeated.

⚜

Now there were other constituencies enlisting Pacific in their efforts to combat AIDS. Prompted by Lynn Jiménez in corporate communications, Pacific spent nearly $100,000 in 1987 to promote a Spanish-language AIDS *videonovela*. This venture too had its risks, for the story line dealt candidly with homosexuality and drug use, two topics anathema to the conservative Hispanic community. But HACER, the coalition of Hispanic groups, urged the company to go ahead—despite the opposition of religious and political leaders in the community. The videonovela was yet another success story, with local TV stations reporting larger than usual audiences. Pacific Telesis Foundation proceeded with its plans to underwrite a dubbed-into-English version.

In 1988, Pacific and the Foundation received a presidential citation for their AIDS initiative. And there was more recognition: the *Wall Street Journal*, *Newsweek*, and *Business Week* lauded the company as enlightened; Sam Puckett and Alan Emery's book, *Managing AIDS in the Workplace*, called it a "role model for the rest of the nation" (along with other companies, including Dayton-Hudson, Bank of America, Digital Equipment Corporation, and Westinghouse). AIDS policy had become a winner inside Pacific. And more begat more, with new corporate enthusiasts for AIDS education emerging. "People love favorable recognition," points out Terry Mulready, Moberg's successor as corporate communications vice president. The company produced a video aimed at families, "Talking to Your Family About AIDS," and planned a video for the black community. The making of AIDS policy had taken on a life of its own.

⚜

On a sunny Wednesday afternoon in July 1988, 11 Pacific employees with the AIDS virus gather in the medical department's conference room for their weekly support group session. Three-piece suits sit amicably alongside flannel shirts. Janice Dragotta, a counselor who spends about a quarter of her company time on AIDS, encourages group members to check in.

As the talk moves around the table, members share information on drug treatments, describe their medical condition, offer advice, complain about a benefits nurse "who went to Auschwitz U," dish up tales of life in the gay bars, commiserate with those who tell how exhausted the preceding

Sunday's group-sponsored picnic left them. There is an edgy humor, gallows humor, in the talk. One man, off to visit his parents in Ohio, imagines the local headlines if he were to die—Gay Comes Home To Die—and his mother's reaction: "How can you do this to us—again?" The employees also talk about the strength they draw from the group, about how it helps to have a place to discuss questions that arise on the job, conflicts with colleagues, and guilt about not being able to work as hard as they once could.

Until recently, no one at Pacific would have imagined such a group on company premises and on company time. "When I first proposed it in 1985, there were no takers," says Dragotta. Employees with AIDS were afraid to come forward. "At the time I started doing AIDS education," counselor Jean Taylor recalls, "an embarrassed official buttonholed me and said, 'Do anything you want, Jean, just don't talk about condoms.'" Now everything related to AIDS is open to discussion. Union Steward Tim O'Hara, relying on a poll detailing workers' interests, is pushing the idea of a corporate-produced video on the correct use of condoms. The concern that some employees might be offended by frank talk about sex is receding.

In organizing discussions of safe sexual practices or running AIDS support groups, Pacific, like any company, has to walk a fine line. AIDS is still encased in moral debate, but discussions of private morality have no place in the business setting. What is relevant are sound business practices and sensible personal precautions. The AIDS support group is both a humane gesture and an appropriate business move. Taylor says, "We started seeing people with the AIDS virus, and those who were well but worried, going out on disability. These groups are a way to help people stay productive, a way for people to begin processing their own grief."

New evidence of Pacific's support for AIDS education is clear not only in these groups but also throughout the organization. At the second annual AIDS Walk, a citywide fund-raising event in July 1988, over 400 Pacific employees sporting company T-shirts walked together under the company's banner. Elsewhere in the company, AIDS-related causes have become almost as familar and noncontroversial as the United Way. At Pacific Telesis Foundation, the staff has made AIDS causes a top priority for charitable giving.

Still, there remain important and unresolved AIDS issues on Pacific's agenda. AIDS education is not a part of an overall corporatewide strategy. Whether employees ever see the AIDS video or get to talk through their concerns about AIDS depends entirely on whether a supervisor volunteers to organize such a session. This bottom-up approach means that, where such education is least needed—in San Francisco and Los Angeles, two cities where public knowledge about the disease is high—it is most likely to be provided. But elsewhere in California, in the fortress at San Ramon and the outposts beyond, where a majority of phone company workers are employed, many managers still treat AIDS as someone else's problem.

Those supervisors who phoned their colleague Chuck Woodman, asking how to handle an AIDS case on their work force, may still regard it as just a once-in-a-career concern; and their workers are still unwilling to talk openly about AIDS. "Whenever I get an AIDS call from Fresno," says counselor Jean Taylor at San Francisco headquarters, "it's always like Deep Throat, and it's always, 'Someone I know was wondering. . . .'"

For Pacific, an AIDS education effort pitched to the varying concerns of its employees is not only enlightened practice. It is sound business. Pacific may be among the companies with the most AIDS cases in the country. As those numbers continue to mount—and they will—the work force problem will become more critical. Already, Chuck Woodman has some 25 workers with AIDS, requiring regular shuffling of his 750-person roster. According to company sources, a 1987 estimate prepared by medical director Ralph Alexander—but never made public—indicated that as few as 200 and as many as 2,000 employees might be infected with the AIDS virus.

There is little that the company can do for these employees with AIDS that it isn't already doing—treating them just as it would treat anyone with a life-threatening illness—but it can do more to slow the spread of the disease. If Pacific can strengthen and expand the scope of its in-house AIDS education, intelligently implementing a program that will reach a quarter-of-a-million lives, then this unlikely corporate pioneer will continue to enlighten others coming to terms with AIDS.

Across the country, the corporate time clock of AIDS policy has run quickly if unevenly, with wide variations in responses reported. According to the 1987 American Society for Personnel Administration survey, some companies persist in punishing workers with AIDS, firing them or limiting their health benefits. A majority of companies offer no AIDS education and have no contingency plans for handling employees refusing to work with an AIDS victim. Barely one business in ten has a written AIDS policy. As discouraging as these data are, they probably exaggerate the degree of corporate responsiveness, since companies that deny the corporate reality of AIDS are unlikely to answer such a survey.

On the other side of the ledger, since the landmark 1986 Bay Area "AIDS in the Workplace" conference, there have been dozens of similar conferences across the country. In February 1988, 30 prominent corporations—among them, IBM, Warner-Lambert, Time Inc., Chemical Bank, Johnson & Johnson—endorsed an AIDS "bill of rights," ensuring that employees with AIDS would receive evenhanded treatment.

For the CEOs in Knoxville or Kansas City still wondering whether their companies should deal with AIDS, the answer should be plain: there is little choice. Nor can handling AIDS be just the province of corporate doctors or human resources specialists. Everyone has a stake in this boundary-crossing issue—that's one of the things that makes AIDS both so hard to manage and so important.

There is considerable help available to businesses. The groundbreaking experience at Pacific is instructive, AIDS educational materials are now widely marketed, and groups like the Red Cross and local AIDS organizations can assist. But to confront AIDS intelligently means having a new look at a wide range of business practices. It means rethinking a company's approach to medical benefits. Those issues Pacific found readily manageable several years ago have become tougher now because recent scientific advances have reshaped the equation. Medication like the antiviral drug AZT is now prolonging the productive lives of workers, but at a cost—one insurance company estimates that AIDS-related illnesses will make up between 2% and 5% of all group-health claims by 1991.

Devising an AIDS policy also means reexamining the company's approach to wellness education, its concern for prevention, and its willingness to talk about once-forbidden subjects like sex. It means rethinking relations between employer and employee, rethinking relations among units within the company, rethinking the boundaries between the company and the public domain.

The outcome of that reanalysis will likely reach far beyond AIDS education to produce a telling portrait of the corporation. For American business, as for Americans generally, AIDS is something like a mirror that, unwillingly and unexpectedly, we have come upon. The meaning of Chuck Woodman's, and Pacific's, odyssey is this: in our reactions to AIDS, something of significance about ourselves and about the character of our enterprises is revealed.

A Stakeholder Theory
of the Modern Corporation:
Kantian Capitalism

William M. Evan and R. Edward Freeman

*During the 1960s, the Stanford Research Institute coined the term
"stakeholders" to describe the various groups that provide critical
support to a business firm. The following article develops the
stakeholder theory as an alternative to the traditional legal viewpoint
that officers and directors must manage a corporation for the benefit of
shareholders. The authors base their theory on the ethical principle
articulated by Immanuel Kant that all human beings should be treated
as persons, not merely as means to ends. Although the stakeholder
theory has not supplanted the traditional principles of corporate law,
the basic concepts of the theory are used by many managers to analyze
issues of ethics and social responsibility.[1]*

🌱

[S]cholars and managers alike continue to hold sacred the view that managers bear a special relationship to the stockholders in the firm. Since stockholders own shares in the firm, they have certain rights and privileges, which
must be granted to them by management, as well as others. Since the greatest
good of all results from the self-interested pursuit of business, managers must
be free to respond quickly to market forces. Sanctions, in the form of "the law
of corporations," and other protective mechanisms in the form of social
custom, accepted management practice, myth, and ritual, serve to reinforce
the assumption of the primacy of the stockholder.

The purpose of this paper is to pose several challenges to this assumption, from within the framework of managerial capitalism, and to suggest the
bare bones of an alternative theory, *a stakeholder theory of the modern
corporation.* . . .

Our thesis is that we can revitalize the concept of managerial capitalism by replacing the notion that managers have a duty to stockholders with
the concept that managers bear a fiduciary relationship to stakeholders.
Stakeholders are those groups who have a stake in or claim on the firm.
Specifically, we include suppliers, customers, employees, stockholders, and

From *Ethical Theory and Business*, 3rd ed., T. Beauchamp and N. Bowie, eds. (Englewood Cliffs: Prentice Hall, 1988), pp. 97, 101–105. Reprinted by permission.

the local community, as well as management in its role as agent for these groups. We argue that the legal, economic, political, and moral challenges to the currently received theory of the firm, as a nexus of contracts among the owners of the factors of production and customers, require us to revise this concept along essentially Kantian lines. That is, each of these stakeholder groups has a right not to be treated as a means to some end, and therefore must participate in determining the future direction of the firm in which they have a stake. . . .

The crux of our argument is that we must reconceptualize the firm around the following question: For whose benefit and at whose expense should the firm be managed? We shall set forth such a reconceptualization in the form of a *stakeholder theory of the firm*. . . .

STAKEHOLDERS IN THE MODERN CORPORATION

Figure 1 depicts the stakeholders in a typical large corporation. The stakes of each are reciprocal, since each can affect the other in terms of harms and benefits as well as rights and duties. The stakes of each are not univocal and would vary by particular corporation. We merely set forth some general notions that seem to be common to many large firms.

Owners have some financial stake in the form of stocks, bonds, and so on, and expect some kind of financial return. Either they have given money directly to the firm, or they have some historical claim made through a series of morally justified exchanges. The firm affects their livelihood or, if a substantial portion of their retirement income is in stocks or bonds, their ability to care for themselves when they can no longer work. Of course, the stakes of owners will differ by type of owner, preferences for money, moral preferences, and so on, as well as by type of firm. The owners of AT&T are quite different from the owners of Ford Motor Company, with stock of the former company being widely dispersed among 3 million stockholders and that of the latter being held by a small family group, as well as a large group of public stockholders.

Employees have their jobs and usually their livelihood at stake; they

Figure 1. A Stakeholder Model of the Corporation

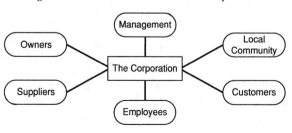

often have specialized skills for which there is usually no perfectly elastic market. In return for their labor, they expect some security, wages, and benefits, and meaningful work. Where they are used as means to an end, they must participate in decisions affecting such use. In return for their loyalty, the corporation is expected to provide for them and carry them through difficult times. Employees are expected to follow the instructions of management most of the time, to speak favorably about the company, and to be responsible citizens in the local communities in which the company operates. The evidence that such policies and values as described here lead to productive company-employee relationships is compelling. It is equally compelling to realize that the opportunities for "bad faith" on the part of both management and employees are enormous. "Mock participation" in quality circles, singing the company song, and wearing the company uniform solely to please management, as well as management by authoritarian supervisors, all lead to distrust and unproductive work.

Suppliers, interpreted in a stakeholder sense, are vital to the success of the firm, for raw materials will determine the final product quality and price. In turn the firm is a customer of the supplier and is therefore vital to the success and survival of the supplier. When the firm treats the supplier as a valued member of the stakeholder network, rather than simply as a source of materials, the supplier will respond when the firm is in need. Chrysler traditionally had very close ties to its suppliers, even to the extent that led some to suspect the transfer of illegal payments. And when Chrysler was on the brink of disaster, the suppliers responded with price cuts, accepting late payments, financing, and so on. Supplier and company can rise and fall together. Of course, again, the particular supplier relationships will depend on a number of variables such as the number of suppliers and whether the supplies are finished goods or raw materials.

Customers exchange resources for the products of the firm and in return receive the benefits of the products. Customers provide the lifeblood of the firm in the form of revenue. Given the level of reinvestment of earnings in large corporations, customers indirectly pay for the development of new products and services. . . . By paying attention to customers' needs, management automatically addresses the needs of suppliers and owners. Moreover, it seems that the ethic of customer service carries over to the community. . . .

The local community grants the firm the right to build facilities and benefits from the tax base and economic and social contributions of the firm. In return for the provision of local services, the firm is expected to be a good citizen, as is any person, either "natural or artificial." The firm cannot expose the community to unreasonable hazards in the form of pollution, toxic waste, and so on. If for some reason the firm must leave a community, it is expected to work with local leaders to make the transition as smooth as possible. Of course, the firm does not have perfect knowledge, but when it discovers some danger or runs afoul of new competition, it is expected to inform the local community and to work with the community to overcome any problem. When the firm mismanages its relationship with the local community, it is in the same position as a citizen who commits a crime. It has violated the implicit social contract with the community and should expect to be distrusted and ostracized. It should not be surprised when punitive measures are invoked.

We have not included "competitors" as stakeholders in the narrow sense, since strictly speaking they are not necessary for the survival and success of the firm; the stakeholders theory works equally well in monopoly contexts. However, competitors and government would be the first to be included in an extension of this basic theory. It is simply not true that the interests of competitors in an industry are always in conflict. There is no reason why trade associations and other multi-organizational groups cannot band together to solve common problems that have little to do with how to restrain trade. Implementation of stakeholder management principles, in the long run, mitigates the need for industrial policy and an increasing role for government intervention and regulation.

THE ROLE OF MANAGEMENT

Management plays a special role, for it too has a stake in the fiction that is the modern corporation. On the one hand, management's stake is like that of employees, with some kind of explicit or implicit employment contract. But, on the other hand, management has a duty of safeguarding the welfare of the abstract entity that is the corporation, which can override a stake as employee. In short, management, especially top management, must look after the health of the corporation, and this involves balancing the multiple claims of conflicting stakeholders. Owners want more financial returns, while customers want more money spent on research and development. Employees want higher wages and better benefits, while the local community wants better parks and day-care facilities.

The task of management in today's corporation is akin to that of King Solomon. The stakeholder theory does not give primacy to one stakeholder group over another, though there will surely be times when one group will benefit at the expense of others. In general, however, management must keep the relationships among stakeholders in balance. When these relationships become unbalanced, the survival of the firm is in jeopardy.

When wages are too high and product quality is too low, customers leave, suppliers suffer, and owners sell their stocks and bonds, depressing the stock price and making it difficult to raise new capital at favorable rates. Note, however, that the reason for paying returns to owners is not that they "own" the firm, but that their support is necessary for the survival of the firm, and that they have a legitimate claim on the firm. Similar reasoning applies in turn to each stakeholder group.

A stakeholder theory of the firm must redefine the purpose of the firm. The stockholder theory claims that the purpose of the firm is to maximize the welfare of the stockholders, perhaps subject to some moral or social constraints, either because such maximization leads to the greatest good or because of property rights. The purpose of the firm is quite different in our view. If a stakeholder theory is to be consistent with the principles of corporate effects and rights, then its purpose must take into account Kant's dictum of respect for persons. The very purpose of the firm is, in our view, to serve as a vehicle for coordinating stakeholder interests. It is through the firm that each stakeholder group makes itself better off through voluntary exchanges. The corporation serves at the pleasure of its stakeholders, and none may be used as a means to the ends of another without full rights of participation in that decision. . . . [Two] stakeholder management principles will serve as a foundation for articulating the theory. They are guiding ideals for the immortal corporation as it endures through generations of particular mortal stakeholders.

STAKEHOLDER MANAGEMENT PRINCIPLES

P1: The corporation should be managed for the benefit of its stakeholders: its customers, suppliers, owners, employees, and local communities. The rights of these groups must be ensured, and, further, the groups must participate, in some sense, in decisions that substantially affect their welfare.

P2: Management bears a fiduciary relationship to stakeholders and to the corporation as an abstract entity. It must act in the interests of the stakeholders as their agent, and it must act in the interests of the corporation to ensure the survival of the firm, safeguarding the long-term stakes of each group.

P1, which we might call The Principle of Corporate Legitimacy, redefines the purpose of the firm to be in line with the principles of corporate effects and rights. It implies the legitimacy of stakeholder claims on the firm. Any social contract that justifies the existence of the corporate form includes the notion that stakeholders are a party to that contract. Further, stakeholders have some inalienable rights to participate in decisions that substantially affect their welfare or involve their being used as a means to another's ends. We bring to bear our arguments for the incoherence of the stockholder view as justification for P1. If in fact there is no good reason for the stockholder theory, and if in fact there are harms, benefits, and rights of stakeholders involved in running the modern corporation, then we know of no other starting point, for a theory of the corporation than P1.

P2, which we might call The Stakeholder Fiduciary Principle, explicitly defines the duty of management to recognize these claims. It will not always be possible to meet all claims of all stakeholders all the time, since some of these claims will conflict. Here P2 recognizes the duty of management to act in the long-term best interests of the corporation, conceived as a forum of stakeholder interaction, when the interests of the group outweigh the interests of the individual parties to the collective contract. The duty described in P2 is a fiduciary duty, yet it does not suffer from the difficulties surrounding the fiduciary duty to stockholders, for the conflicts involved there are precisely those that P2 makes it mandatory for management to resolve. Of course, P2 gives no instructions for a magical resolution of the conflicts that arise from prima facie obligations to multiple parties. An analysis of such rules for decision making is a subject to be addressed on another occasion, but P2 does give these conflicts a legitimacy that they do not enjoy in the stockholder theory. It gives management a clear and distinct directive to pay attention to stakeholder claims.

P1 and P2 recognize the eventual need for changes in the law of corporations and other governance mechanisms if the stakeholder theory is to be put into practice. P1 and P2, if implemented as a major innovation in the structure of the corporation, will make manifest the eventual legal institutionalization of sanctions. . . .

The law of corporations needs to be redefined to recognize the legitimate purpose of the corporation as stated in P1. This has in fact developed in some areas of the law, such as products liability, where the claims of customers to safe products have emerged, and labor law, where the claims of employees have been safeguarded. . . . We envision that a body of case law will emerge to give meaning to "the proper claims of stakeholders," and in effect that the "wisdom of Solomon" necessary to make the stakeholder theory work will emerge naturally through the joint action of the courts, stakeholders, and management.

NOTE
1. Introduction by Beauchamp & Bowie, eds. *Ethical Theory in Business* 97, 101–105 (3d ed., 1988).

Social Organization
of the Corporation

James S. Coleman

The modern corporation can be seen as a new actor in society, endowed with rights by charter and by the common law's recognition of it as a "fictional person." This new conception of an actor as a legal entity abstracted from any physical person has come to be complemented by an idea of the actor's structure, composed of elements or "positions" equally as abstract. This is classical formal organization, a form that has attracted numerous theorists. Max Weber, writing in the late nineteenth century, developed the concept of "rational authority" as a structure of positions, filled according to merit, compensated with a money wage, and directed toward a purpose or goal determined by the ultimate authority in the organization.

This notion of an abstract actor containing within it abstract positions was a social invention of the first magnitude. The demographic explosion of this form—corporation—began in the second half of the nineteenth century; its emergence as a major locus of power has come about in the twentieth. It has, quite simply, transformed the structure of society.

Yet the theory of the functioning of formal organizations has a fundamental flaw: It recognizes only the single "goal of the corporation" as an actor, failing to include the interests and resources at each position in the corporation's structure. These interests and resources constitute a separate system of action within the corporation, not merely a set of agents dutifully implementing the central purpose of the corporation.

The theory of formal organizations has taken its cue from Max Weber, who contrasted rational authority with traditional forms based on custom, norms, and blood ties and with the transitory authority characteristic of charismatic leaders. This new, rational, explicitly purposive form of organization was sufficiently different from traditional organization that overlooking the purposes of the individuals who filled its positions was a natural error to make.

And it continues. Its legacy can be found in much organization theory, which takes the Weberian bureaucratic model as a starting point and looks for deviations from that model. It can also be found in the identification of the theory of formal organization with a theory of managerial decisionmaking.[1] This conception of the formal organization as one in which authoritative direction emanates from the top and is obeyed and transmitted downward at each successive level is difficult to overcome.

It should be clear, however, that as long as positions in the formal organization are filled by real persons, those persons will have interests or goals that may differ from the purposes of the organization and have resources (some that they bring with them and some that come with their positions in the organization) that can be used to further their interests.

All of this has not gone completely unrecognized, either in theory or in practice. One theoretical statement was that of an Italian sociologist writing in 1915:

> By a universally applicable social law, every organ of the collectivity, brought into existence through the need for the division of labor, creates for itself, as soon as it becomes consolidated, interests peculiar to itself. The existence of these special interests involves a necessary conflict with the interests of the collectivity.[2]

In general, however, the theory of organizational functioning has been led by practice as the modern corporation has evolved. Consequently, in this chapter, I will describe some of the variations in practice, emphasizing more recent developments to provide a sense of how this special system of action within the corporation functions. Toward the end of the chapter, I will attempt to characterize more generally the new conceptual basis for the organization implied by these changes in practice.

FORMAL ORGANIZATION AND MODES OF MAINTAINING VIABILITY

Oliver Williamson, among others, has compared the functioning of market organization and hierarchical organization of economic activities.[3] One aspect of the difference between markets and hierarchies is the modes of viability that they require.

As a system of action, a market requires "reciprocal viability." With money as a medium of exchange, the constraint of the "double coincidence of wants" in a barter market is removed; but for a market transaction to be carried out, there must be two positive accounts, one for each party.[4] Each exchange is a self-contained relation between a pair; any imbalances must be made up within that relation.

In modern authority structures, the corporation acts as a third party in relations between positions, eliminating the need for reciprocal viability between them. A secretary-clerk's obligations to a supervisor need not be balanced exactly by the supervisor's obligations to the secretary-clerk; the discrepancy is made up by the corporation. What is necessary is what I will call "independent viability." A structure in which both parties in each relation must benefit is transformed into a structure with a third party that balances debits and credits. In a structure of n persons in relation, an exchange system contains $n(n-1)/2$ potential relations, each of which must be reciprocally viable if a transaction is to take place. When the corporation serves as a third party, there need be only n viable relations, each being profitable to the firm and to the employee.

The difference between reciprocal and independent viability grows with the size of the structure. A complete network among four persons requires mutual benefit in 6 relations, or 12 positive accounts; in a formal organization of the same size, 4 mutually beneficial relations are required (between the organization and each of the 4), or 8 positive accounts. The difference between reciprocal and independent viability amounts to only 4 accounts. However, in a market of twenty-five persons, 300 ($25 \times 24/2$) mutually beneficial relations are necessary, 600 positive accounts altogether. In a formal organization, this is reduced to 25 relations, with a total of 50 positive accounts. This "balance of inducements and contributions" is exactly what Chester Barnard specified as necessary for the firm. Each employee must feel that the inducements are of greater value than what must be given up to stay at the firm, and, in turn, the firm must consider the employee's contributions to be of greater value than what it must give the employee as inducements.[5]

The number of accounts showing a positive balance may be decreased even further. Since the corporation is an actor in each relation, it can make up its losses in some relations with gains in others. Under "global viability," the employees' side of the equation remains the same, but the corporation need only show a profit on the total of all accounts to maintain viability. In an organization of twenty-five positions, only twenty-six positive balances are necessary, one for each employee and a global account for the corporation.

The Primary Danger of Global Viability

Global viability constitutes a danger to any organization, including corporations. If especially profitable relations (that is, especially valuable contributors) fail to provide excess value, then the whole system can become nonviable. If this excess value is produced by some employees because of their individual characteristics and if there is a market for the services of individuals who provide excess value, these individuals will receive better offers from other organizations and may leave their current employer, which will then become nonviable.[6]

The solution arrived at in economic theory is to reintroduce independent viability.[7] In such a case, the corporation is assumed to be capable of adjusting each employee's compensation to equal the value of that employee's marginal contribution. Each individual earns a market wage, ensuring that there will be no better offer from elsewhere, unless another employer can get more value from the employee's services. Furthermore, the market wage shows the employee's marginal contribution in the activity that can make the most valuable use of these services.

But this solution is seldom feasible in practice. Because of the interdependence of activities, it is often difficult to isolate the marginal contribution of each employee. And because of collective bargaining and other social constraints, the firm does not have the power to pay individual employees their marginal products.

A number of devices have evolved within the organizations to solve the problem of viability in other ways. A brief examination of three of these follows.

DIVISIONAL VIABILITY

In the 1930s General Motors and DuPont developed a management practice now widespread in large business firms: the creation of divisions that must each justify their products through "make or buy" decisions of the firm.[8] The central innovation was the partial introduction of the market into the firm by using the outside market to gauge the competitive viability of divisions within the firm. An extension of this has been the introduction of internal transfer pricing within the firm, with each division "selling" its services or products to other parts of the firm. If a way can be found to establish a market price for each product or service, this practice allows the firm to measure a division's contribution and compare it to that division's costs, providing the possibility of replacing global viability with "divisional viability," that is, global viability for each separate division.

Sometimes, transfer pricing is merely an accounting device to measure a division's performance; in other cases, divisions' budgets are determined in part by their shadow profits or losses. Obviously, only the latter constitutes a movement away from global to divisional viability.

Within a division, the same practice can be used to determine departmental contributions and thus departmental viability. In principle, internal pricing can be extended all the way to the level of the individual. For some jobs in some firms, this is done by paying a portion of wages in bonuses, the size of which depends on an evaluation of each individual's contribution. Carried far enough, this is equivalent to independent viability, realized through compensation equal to the employee's marginal contribution.

One serious weakness of divisional viability lies in the difficulty of setting appropriate transfer prices for goods and services for which there is no external market price to serve as a benchmark.[9] A second appears to be the lack of incentive, except in central management, which wants to measure the performance of various units of the firm, for establishing and maintaining an internal set of accounts. Unless the transfers are more than mere accounting devices and full divisional viability is realized through divisions receiving a share of the profit or loss they bring the firm as a whole, individual units will have little reason to embrace the system.

FORWARD POLICING

The classical means of attempting to ensure viability has been through the exercise of authority over the actions of employees. In such a system, the feedback loop through which viability is determined goes from the final product back to the starting point of the process, at the highest authority. Based on this feedback, modifications are introduced to increase viability, with authority continuing to be exercised downward.

I call this "forward policing" because actions at time t produce outputs for actions at time $t + 1$ throughout the sequence of the production process. Thus, policing follows a forward course.

BACKWARD POLICING

Around 1980 the general manager of the Pontiac Division of General Motors studied the production process at Honda to learn why the quality control on their automobiles was so high. He learned that Honda employed a form of backward policing: Each unit in the process of producing and shipping the automobiles had the right to reject its inputs and was held strictly accountable for its outputs by the unit next in line, which in turn had the right to reject out-of-specification inputs, even if this meant shutting down the line. The unit supplying the unacceptable parts would be held accountable for any downtime.

Each unit had an inspector, not at the end of its stage in the process, but at the beginning. Another property of the system, which appeared to be a consequence of this reallocation of rights, was that there was a much lower ratio of supervisors (forward policing) to operators. A third aspect of the system, again in apparent consequence of the reallocation of rights, was that operators themselves, who would be held accountable for the quality of the product, also acted as inspectors, of both inputs and outputs.

Each unit at each stage in the process had a set of rights similar to those held by the final customer for Honda's product. The policing thus operated backward, from the final product back to the first stages of the production process. The long feedback loop from the final customer was broken into a large number of very short loops. Most fundamentally, the shift from forward to backward policing involves nothing more—or less—than a reallocation of rights and accountability in the organization.

Further Consequences of Global Viability

If the transactions between each employee and the corporate actor are independently viable, as when wages and benefits equal marginal productivity, each of these internal transactions is self-policing. If the contribution declines, the wage declines; if it increases, so does the wage. If the wage is below the marginal contribution and competing employers will pay the marginal wage, the employee can move to the competitor.

With global viability, if the organization is to maintain viability, either or both of two devices is necessary: There must be detailed constitutional specification of the obligations of the occupant of each position; or there must be extensive policing to ensure that correct actions are taken. Even if the first of these devices is employed, only the second will guarantee that the proper actions are taken. And if only the second is employed, detailed prescriptions of what actions are correct must become part of the policing. But if a means can be found to move back to independent viability, the corporation is relieved of these two tasks. In the case of Honda, backward policing comes close to bringing about that move.

Although backward policing appears to be a satisfactory means of shifting from global to independent viability in some forms of productive activity, such as that found in the automobile industry, it is unclear how widely applicable it is. What does appear to be widely applicable, however, is the reallocation of rights found in backward policing. In the employment transaction, the employee-to-be gives up rights of control over actions in the realm covered by the employment contract. The reallocation of rights that allows backward policing returns a portion of those rights to their original owners, in exchange for the right of the corporation to make compensation contingent on productivity. Another portion of the rights, the right to reject the product of the employee's action, is given to the employee who must use this product.

CONSTITUTIONS IN CORPORATIONS, IMPLICIT AND EXPLICIT

The different allocation of rights and their reciprocal obligations in forward and backward policing forces recognition of the fact that, in every organization, there exists such an allocation, which may be called the "constitution" of the organization, whether explicitly stated or implicitly recognized as the legitimate order. Alongside any formal allocation of rights, the informal allocation that determines what is legitimate can be called the "informal constitution" of the organization.

Some rights and obligations are associated with relations between positions in the organization, as in the case of backward versus forward policing. Others concern relations between employees—occupants of the positions—and the corporation, such as rights of collective bargaining. But it is not possible to separate fully the two sets of rights. The conception of the corporation that allows this separation no longer holds. This evolution can be seen by reference to the classical legal concept of agency, where the agent's skills and services are employed in the principal's interest.

Because of the evolution of the corporation, this concept is now either inappropriate or, at least, subject to considerable revision. In it, the interests of the agent can be segregated from those of the principal by means of appropriate compensation (including compensation based on performance), and the functioning of the organization, like that of a machine, can be described in terms of the functions of each of the parts in relation to the others (the obligations and expectations associated with positions). But the evolution of corporations has come to intertwine and combine so fully the interests of the corporation and those of the persons who work in it that such a separation becomes increasingly difficult.

The modern corporation is less a machine with interdependent parts or agents than a system of action comparable to an unconstrained market. It is, however, a special sort of market, in which the organization defines rights, provides resources, and structures reward systems. Hierarchical authority remains as a last resort, but one that represents a failure in the structuring of incentives. Far from all organizational practice has evolved to this stage, just as much organizational theory continues to follow Max Weber's conception of bureaucratic authority. Yet it is clear that both the Weberian theory of bureaucracy and the practice that mirrors it are earlier, and less successful, stages in the evolution of purposive social organization. It is also clear that they are conceptually deficient in their failure to recognize formal organization as a system of action in which each actor has interests and attempts to implement them.

I will examine the character of constitution formation—formal and informal—in modern corporations by way of two examples, which illustrate, in differing ways, the evolution of organizational form beyond that of hierarchical authority and Weberian bureaucracy.

Quality of Work Life Programs

A number of American firms have initiated programs patterned after Japanese "quality circles." Sometimes termed "Quality of Work Life" (QWL) programs, they involve extensive restructuring of the organization of a manufacturing plant. The supervisor's activities are largely replaced by the collective decisions of a work team comprising about seven to fifteen persons engaged in interdependent activities (e.g., a section of an assembly line or a group of stamping machines). A team elects a chair, decides first how it will conduct its business, and then meets regularly, ordinarily once a week during work hours. Actions range from modifying the work structure to resolving interpersonal problems among members of the team.

A peculiar pattern characterizes QWL programs that are initiated when a plant first opens. For several months, a small group, made up of people from management (usually including the future plant manager), representatives from the production line (including union leaders in unionized plants), and a QWL advisor, meets full-time to work out the organization of the new plant. A major accomplishment of this group is the production of a statement expressing the "operating philosophy" of the plant, which is subsequently framed and hung on a wall. Surprisingly, the operating philosophies of different QWL plants are quite similar and appear to an outside observer to consist mostly of platitudes. One might question the purpose of this intensive preparation that produces nothing that could not have been borrowed directly from another plant.

The answer, I believe, is that this process leads to the creation of an informal constitution, a set of rights and obligations supported both by the core of production-line workers and the core of management. (Typically, the remaining managerial and work force is hired and trained by this group or a group drawn from it. A fundamental question posed to prospective employees is whether they agree with the operating philosophy and form of organization of the plant.) The nature of the informal constitution, that is, the structure of rights and obligations, derives largely from suggestions of the QWL advisor, who serves as a channel of information from other QWL programs. But the lengthy and intense collective effort that produces the operating philosophy represents a period during which members of the core group are building their own commitment to the constitution. Their commitment appears necessary to elicit the commitment of the rest of the work force, which, in turn, is essential to ensure that the allocation of rights provided by the constitution will be enforced by all members of the plant. The preproduction meetings by the core group, together with the elaborate procedures to induct new people into membership, are all systems that help bring about the legitimacy of the authority system under which all will work.

We may ask why such lengthy induction-and-commitment processes were not used (and possibly not useful) in earlier periods. The answer lies in the character of the two authority systems. In the classical hierarchical form of authority that has characterized industrial production, legitimacy of authority was intrinsic to the labor contract. Employees gave rights of control over their actions to the employer and received a money wage as compensation. Authority was either exercised directly or delegated by the employer to an intermediate agent.

When collective bargaining was introduced, the transaction took a different form, and its terms (such as the processing of grievances) changed, with some rights being reallocated to the collective body of workers made into a corporate actor through the formation of the union. The principal change, however, was that a smaller set of rights of control were transferred to the employer by the employee.

In QWL-organized plants, authority is diffused, with a large portion held and exercised collectively by the team. This implies that members must accept the collective authority of their peers and also exercise authority collectively. The allocation of rights in such an organization includes an allocation to the team as a corporate actor, and the members of the team must accept that allocation and exercise the rights. Thus, the allocation of rights that was accomplished in a single employment contract in the classical labor market is now much more complex. Acceptance of this allocation of rights presupposes an understanding of this more complex structure. Because the functioning of the system depends more on the acceptance and exercise of the rights by all workers, a period of indoctrination is valuable to increase commitment to the constitution.

Mitbestimmung in German Corporations

In 1976 the existing "Mitbestimmung" or codetermination law in Germany was extended to give new rights to workers.[10] An example of a general movement toward "industrial democracy" in Western societies, particularly in Western Europe, the law reflects a modified conception of the corporation, just as does the QWL movement.

The law makes extensive changes at both the level of the board and of the workplace. It fixes the size of the board of directors at twenty for large firms and specifies that ten must be representatives of stockholders and ten representatives of employees. It also details the procedure by which employees' representatives will be selected and defines the role of the board in the corporation, including the type of information to be made available to board members, the minimum frequency of meeting, and the kinds of decisions that must not be made without their approval.

At the level of the workplace, the law requires the creation of workers' councils with procedures for the election of representatives and with specific powers, such as those concerning grievances of workers. Workers' councils have some powers that previously had been prerogatives of management, exercised through supervision. The workers' councils, as well as the newly constituted board of directors, greatly increase workers' power in the organization.

RESTRUCTURING INCENTIVES
IN THE CORPORATION

The QWL programs in the United States, based on Japanese models, and European codetermination both constitute changes in the implicit constitution of the corporation and give additional rights to production workers. Codetermination, however, does not challenge the conception of the corporation as consisting of a managerial class and a class of workers; it establishes, in fact, a political structure emphasizing that division and the distinct interests on each side. It does not alter the structure of authority through which work is carried out but, instead, introduces a formal voice of labor within that authority structure. Codetermination is more compatible with a system of forward policing than with a system of backward policing.

QWL programs, on the other hand, and, even more, the Japanese patterns on which they are based, deemphasize the division between management and labor. More compatible with backward policing, they are founded on a conception of common interests throughout the corporation and utilize consensual decision-making for production decisions. Authority is exercised collectively, through group norms, rather than hierarchically.

These two different ways of redistributing rights appear to stem from the ways in which the corporation emerged from feudalism in Japan and in Europe. The Japanese corporation is derived more closely from the feudal estate, without the intervening history of enlightenment philosophy, with its emphasis on individualism, and revolutions that destroyed the vestiges of feudalism in eighteenth- and nineteenth-century Europe. Corporate paternalism in Japan is the residue of the feudal lord's responsibility for all in his demesne. For example, in Japan, the corporation is responsible for a number of the welfare activities that are state responsibilities in Europe.

In America, with no history of feudalism but an immigrant population of European descent, the corporation has inherited Europe's conceptual basis, though with muted class divisions. Potentially, the American corporation would seem to be hospitable to either of these reallocations of rights, although it may be revealing that neither had its origins in America. But another reallocation of rights that did begin in the United States appears to reflect its historical origins.

Ownership Rights to Innovations

In capitalist corporations, the standard employment agreement for persons engaged in activities that might result in patents includes the assignment of patent rights to the corporation. It also places restrictions on the employee's rights to employment or consultation by competing firms for a period following employment. The agreement for such employees of state-owned enterprises is similar, containing a provision that patent rights will be assigned to government.

The terms of faculty appointments at most universities in the United States are entirely different, probably because the origins of the university predate the modern corporation and the conception of the employment relation that is intrinsic to it. Ownership rights to ideas and innovations that originate in universities are vested in the person rather than the institution, except where a contract with a government, corporation, or other source of research funds specifies otherwise. This has led to what may be termed "professorial spin-offs," in which faculty members who have developed a set of ideas as part of their university research form a corporation to carry the ideas to commercial realization. Or university faculty members, working on their own time, may make use of a company's laboratories and facilities under a contractual arrangement in which the ownership of ideas is regarded as being shared by the person and the corporation. This has occurred not only in the physical sciences (where it is especially evident in electronics), but also extensively in the biological sciences (where firms for genetic engineering have been formed by groups of faculty members, sometimes in a joint venture with existing corporations) and even in the social sciences (especially in the development of data bases in law and economics and statistical software).[11]

In some corporations, the principle that ownership rights to ideas and innovations lie with the corporation has begun to erode. One corporation where this change came early was the 3M Company in Minneapolis. Donald Schon describes the development:

> They got Scotch tape out and it seemed to work and they sold a lot of it and then along came research with magnetic tape. They said, "We know how to make tape. We'll make magnetic tape."
>
> They had an invention along with this: the invention was that the man who developed the idea would go off and take a piece of the business and become in effect a semi-autonomous firm based around the product which he had developed. The company then kept profit and loss control over that division, but in no other way attempted to manage that man.
>
> And pretty soon what you had was a constellation of forty semi-autonomous firms surrounding a bank and a development facility. And if you asked what business MMM was in you could not say as long as you remained on the substantive product level. They are a company that makes money out of exploiting and comercializing entities that come from development. And the entities that come from development are organically related to one another and bear what Wittgenstein would call family resemblances to one another which reflects that organic process. But there's no Aristotelian basis for saying what the firm is, that is to say there is no set of characteristics which all and only products of that firm possess.[12]

The innovations in ownership rights to ideas and the potential variations in structure are especially great in the personal-computer software and hardware industry. In this industry, ideas are especially easily transportable. The production process itself requires little capital and few persons to implement an idea, so a person or a subgroup may resign from a firm and start a separate company without great difficulty. There are also many small firms in the industry, among which an extensive flow of persons (carrying ideas) can occur. Spin-offs of the sort described by Schon have been one response to this flow. Another has been to give partial ownership of the firm to an employee with an especially important idea.

Such organizational innovations are rarely found in certain industries, such as the automobile industry and other heavy industry. Their near absence, however, may have less to do with the nature of the product than with the traditions of these corporations, which were born before such ideas were widespread.

As in the case of the shift of rights to replace forward policing with backward policing, this change in ownership rights to innovations appears to have extensive consequences for the corporation as a system of action. Empirical observation suggests that a major effect is an increased rate of innovation. In the United States, university laboratories seem to be a much richer spawning ground for ideas than are corporation or government laboratories. Industries where there is extensive theft of ideas from firms by those who had the ideas (by resigning and forming a start-up firm or a new unit with special rights in another firm) have very high rates of innovation. For example, the rate of innovation in the computer industry has exploded since the invention of mini- and microcomputers (both of which began when innovators broke away from larger firms).

In another illustration, it is generally agreed that a major cause of IBM's extraordinary dominance of the infant microcomputer industry was that the IBM personal computer had an open architecture, that is, empty slots for hardware add-ons and an operating system developed by a third party. A small army of individuals and start-up firms began to construct and sell hardware and software that would fit the specifications of this open system. Within a very short time, the IBM specifications became the standard. In effect, the open architecture strategy expanded the set of persons working to enhance IBM's product far beyond the confines of the firm itself. (This was aided by the fact that Apple, a chief competitor, introduced a microcomputer that used closed architecture.)

The dangers of openness are apparent in this example, for the strategy facilitated the introduction of low-priced compatibles, designed to free ride on the specifications so firmly established by IBM's success. The matter is complex, as is determining the best strategy for a corporation to exploit innovations. It is clear, however, that neither the rate of innovation nor the corporation's best interests are maximized by closure that wholly prevents actors outside the corporation from exploiting the innovations.

Another observation suggests a more subtle inhibition to the exploitation of ideas. In many corporate research and development divisions, there exists the "NIH syndrome": a lack of motivation, interest, and effort applied to ideas "Not Invented Here" that originated either elsewhere in the firm or outside the firm. An investigation into an idea that originated elsewhere often seems to result in a catalog of the reasons why the idea will not be useful.

The prevalence of the NIH syndrome suggests another motivation that leads to a differential rate in innovation depending on the location of ownership rights. Persons have an interest in seeing an idea fail if it belongs to another and they cannot benefit from its exploitation. This appears to arise even in the absence of rights of ownership: By demonstrating the defects in another's idea, one justifies not having had the idea oneself; by demonstrating its potential, one is relatively worse off, because the other's status is elevated.

However, shared ownership rights between a corporation and the innovating person or group carry their own hazards. The potential divisiveness that such an allocation of rights can create is particularly deleterious to organizational functioning. If ideas become the partial property of their originator, they are less likely to be shared openly and worked on jointly. Disputes about ownership of ideas may arise within a unit of the organization, furthering the divisiveness. This problem can be reduced or eliminated, however, by appropriate allocation of ownership rights—for example, not in an individual, but in a group that works in a given area.

Altogether, we may describe the shift of ownership rights to the actor or group that innovates as a partial reuniting of the "split atom of private property," the separation of ownership and control that Berle and Means described as the major innovation of the modern joint-stock corporation.[13] But it reunites them in a different way than might have been envisaged by theorists of the corporation like Berle and Means, by vesting the rights to benefit from the action in the agents, rather than returning control to those who hold ownership rights (or, as Berle and Means proposed, giving control to "the community").

Modifying ownership rights affects motivation by changing interests. Changes in interests cannot be accounted for in rational choice theory; interests must be taken as given. However, interests may be changed easily, merely by altering the constraints on what is possible for an actor. Actors usually increase their satisfaction by gaining control of those goods or events in which they have an interest, often through exchange. Here, actors' satisfaction can be increased by giving them an interest in something over which they have control. Of course, this does not create an interest out of thin air; rather, interest arises because something in which actors already have an interest (money, prestige, or fame in this case) is made dependent on what they already control, that is, their ideas or innovations. The change in structure that gives an actor who has an idea interests in the innovation is achieved either by making money income (or something else in which the actor has an interest) directly contingent on the innovations or by making income contingent on the success of the product that results from the innovation.

Reward Structures Linking Interests to Actions

Ownership rights are only one means by which the interests of an actor may be made contingent on the initiation and development of innovations, and money is not the only thing of intrinsic interest on which these actions may be made to depend. Nor is a restructuring that creates this contingency always sufficient to bring about the actions that will lead to an improved corporate product. A change that gives the innovator some control over further development of the innovation may be important. In the organizational innovations described earlier, the innovator's partial control of the innovation's development appears to be important to success.

There are many successful examples of such organizational innovations, some of them striking because of the departure they represent for the corporation. An example shows some of the consequences when an organization fails to develop such a structure. An automobile manufacturer has an advanced product engineering division, responsible for innovations that, it is hoped, will come to be incorporated in new product designs by the divisions responsible for manufacturing and marketing the corporation's automobiles. In the 1970s this division had developed a cambering principle that was applicable to a range of vehicles including scooters, motorcycles, and small three-wheeled vehicles. The head of the advanced product engineering division was greatly taken with this principle and wanted to see it incorporated in products. The division developed the principle in a number of test vehicles, spending a great deal of attention, interest, and time on it. The division head attempted in vain to sell the idea of developing and marketing such vehicles to both the corporation and the automobile divisions. The decision not to do so may have been correct for the corporation and the divisions. But the failure to vest partial ownership rights in the developers and to create a spin-off outside the corporation resulted in the partial diversion of the division from other developments that would have been of interest to the automobile divisions as long as the division head was enraptured by the idea. More generally, this structure, in which new design ideas were developed in a unit that was not organizationally within a division that would carry the innovation through development, manufacture, and marketing, meant that design innovations seldom moved beyond the boundaries of the specialized division.

Breaking the Power of Norms

As in any system of action involving real persons, formal authority, consisting of regulations, laws, and explicit rules, is supplemented by informal norms. Peter Blau demonstrated this graphically for a government agency, and other well-known research, such as the Hawthorne experiments, show how informal norms affect production levels.[14] Some of these norms are beneficial to the overall purposes of the organization; others are not. How these norms can be made to serve the interests of the corporation is a difficult question, and I will not address it here. I will, instead, give one concrete illustration of a norm that was harmful to an organization and describe one organizational device that is sometimes used to break the power of a norm.

Some norms take the form of not questioning certain beliefs that are locally regarded as "facts." For example, the engineers in one American automobile company in the late 1970s "knew" that there were no significant advantages to overhead cam engines; but, for the engines the company was designing at the time, that was not a correct technical assessment. A pervasive technical culture prevented certain questions from being raised anew as conditions changed. All organizations are subject to such cultural norms; they are characteristic of every collectivity engaged in a common endeavor, arising from too-great pressures toward agreement.[15]

Certain organizational devices can prevent such norms from obscuring technically superior solutions. One is a procedure that may be termed "structured dissent," though variations of it are known by other names in different organizations. Structured dissent operates something like this: When a policy decision is to be made and there are several possibly viable alternatives, each alternative is assigned to a staff member, who must argue its merits in writing, orally, or both. The relevant official or committee then makes the decision after a presentation of these position papers, or briefs.

Structured dissent has been used by U.S. presidents confronted with policy decisions; NASA uses a similar procedure called "nonadvocacy policy review." The procedure, through the arbitrary assignments of alternatives, breaks the normative constraint against taking a position that is internally unpopular but may be the most viable. It reshapes the incentive structure to motivate staff members to show the best points of their assigned alternatives.

CHANGES IN THE CONCEPT OF THE CORPORATION

Max Weber's conception of rational authority, the legal conception of principal and agent, the economic work in principal-agent theory, and most organization theory in sociology have one element in common: They see the corporation as an extension of a single purpose, with an owner or set of owners (or principals) who bring together "factors of production" or "agents" or "office-holders" to implement this purpose. Employees, having no interest in the purpose of the owners, agree to fill the positions, become the agents, and constitute one of the factors of production, in exchange for compensation. They also acquire certain rights, mainly associated with the specific commodity—labor—that they bring to the marketplace.

The decline of shareholders' interest in the corporation except as a source of return on capital, QWL programs and the quality circles in the Japanese corporation on which they are patterned, the codetermination law of 1976 in Germany and the movement toward industrial democracy that it reflects, the trend toward vesting partial rights to innovations in their inventors, the use of company songs, company dress, and other symbolic actions to increase employees' identification with the firm—all of these developments challenge the traditional conception of the corporation. Whether the change is in the conception of rights or in the conception of interests, the distinction between owner as principal and employee as agent appears less sharp than in the past. Modes of governance are moving away from authority exercised by a superordinate toward discipline imposed by the structure of incentives.

As described earlier, the organization is best conceived as a system of action. The occupants of positions are the actors; their positions, the incentive structures, and their personal aims interact to determine their interests and to provide them with the resources to realize those interests. The difference between this and any other system of action is that the positions, rights, and incentive structures arise from the constitution of the organization, which is created, directly or indirectly, by those who bring the organization into being. This does not occur in the absence of constraints. Sometimes, as in the case of codetermination, these constraints even dictate specific elements of the constitution.

There is, however, the question of whether the rights to establish the organization's constitution are appropriately held. This is a step backward toward an infinite regress; but, in this case, the step lands squarely in the allocation of rights in civil law: It is the legal structure of the larger society that determines the allocation of rights in constructing the corporation's constitution.

We may ask, however, whether anything might be said more generally about appropriate allocations of rights in the constitutions of corporations. Two extreme cases may help to fix ideas in answering this. One is the start-up company created by one or two persons with an idea for an innovation and a source of venture capital, that is, a person or corporate actor with money to invest. Stock in the firm is divided between the persons with ideas and the venture capitalist. A number of persons are hired to aid in the implementation of the ideas. The company may or may not be successful, depending on a variety of factors, some internal to the company, some not under its control. The other extreme is a large, long-established corporation with many employees and stock widely dispersed among a set of stockholders who hold it because it offers a higher rate of return than other possible investments, or because it is safer than most, or for a variety of other reasons.

It seems unlikely that the same set of legal rights or the same conception of organization is appropriate in the two cases. If we consider only the criterion of survival (without attempting to settle the question of whether this is the only appropriate criterion), it is likely that organizational survival will be maximized by a different division of rights between owners and employees in each case. In the first, survival (which is in the interests of stockholders and employees alike) is much more contingent on the actions of the owners (the entrepreneurs pursuing the development of their idea and the venture capitalist providing additional capital at crucial points). In the second case, survival depends much more on the actions of employees.

Yet there is no single point marking where a partial reallocation of rights from owners to employees is natural, although much civil law affecting corporations recognizes some difference of this sort. Just as one cannot pinpoint when a tadpole becomes a frog, one cannot specify when a corporation's success depends less on the actions of its owners than on those of its employees or agents.

THE CORPORATION AND THE SOCIETY

This chapter has been confined thus far to an examination of the internal social organization of the corporation. But numerous additional questions concern the corporation as an element in the larger social system. I will examine only one of those questions here, an issue that is central to the functioning of society: the corporation's effect on child rearing.

Throughout history, the family has been the institution responsible for child rearing. Until this century, the family, or another social unit directly derived from it, was also the principal unit of economic production, which involved, in most cases, subsistence production of food and clothing within the family or labor in settings that had families as their basic units, such as the local community.

The modern corporation has changed all that, as a result of the different conceptual base from which it springs and the extraordinary prosperity that it has brought. First men, and now women, have been drawn away from the household to the corporation. In 1810, 87 percent of men were employed in agriculture, that is, in or near the household, and most of the remaining 13 percent were undoubtedly working in a setting socially proximate to the family. By 1900 the 87 percent had dropped to 42 percent; and by 1980 it was less than 5 percent. As for women, in 1810 almost none were in the employed labor force; nearly all were in the home. By 1900 the percentage in the home was 79 percent; by 1980 this had declined to 48 percent. Thus, the exodus of men from production in the household to production some distance beyond it began in the nineteenth century; women followed men out of the household into the corporation about a hundred years later.[16] These statistics indicate the movement of economically productive activity from the household to the corporation.

The raising of children has always been a coproduction with other activities; now, much of the time that adults once had to raise their children is spent in locations remote from them, behind the closed doors of a plant or office. Not only the family, but also the neighborhood, including the voluntary associations that sometimes thrive there, depend on the time and activity of these same adults.

If employment in the corporation is the primary means of distributing income in modern society, we see that the movement of productive activity from the family to the corporation has also redistributed income away from children. This redistribution occurs, not only because many children begin life without a connection to the corporation (e.g., children of welfare mothers), but also because of an increase in households termed "DINKS" (an acronym for "Double Income No Kids"), where income has no way to reach children. In confirmation of this, Samuel Preston reports that in 1970 persons over sixty-five made up the highest proportion of the population below the poverty line; by 1980 it was children under five who were highest.[17]

The corporation has replaced the family as the central institution around which modern society is constructed. But the substitution is not complete, for the corporation lacks one property necessary to the continuation of society: It has no place for the next generation. This might be remedied, either through modifications of the corporation or through the assumption by other institutions of some of the functions the family can no longer perform. But until such changes occur, it must be acknowledged that a society in which the corporation has replaced the family as the central institution is not naturally hospitable to children. Some legal changes and corporation-initiated actions have already altered this social structure to make it somewhat less inimical to children. One innovation, recognizing the centrality of the corporation, involves moving some of the social functions of child rearing into it. Company day-care centers are perhaps the most interesting development, because they bring children into the same corporate body as their parents. Company schools could constitute an equally interesting innovation, if the disincentive created by free public schools could be overcome.

Other accommodations adjust corporate demands to child-rearing demands. These include flextime, which is now widespread, the repartitioning of work to create more part-time jobs, and maternity leaves. Spatially distributed organizations, too, could allow much work to be done in the home, and, already, some unions have reduced their opposition to this alternative.

There are other changes that do nothing to increase the compatibility of the corporation with child rearing but merely take child-rearing activities out of the family. One is an increased comprehensiveness of the schools, which take responsibility for a wider range of child-rearing functions and a larger fraction of the child's time. Another is the existence of specialized child-care facilities. As with some of the accommodations by the corporation discussed above, changes in these directions have already occurred.

If the corporation remains the central institution of modern society and no comprehensive solutions are found to the problems described in this section we may find that we have lost the means to carry out one of the activities most crucial to survival: the process of getting from one generation to the next, through raising and socializing children.

NOTES

1. See, for example, R. M. Cyert and J. G. March, *A Behavioral Theory of the Firm* (Englewood Cliffs, N.J.: Prentice-Hall, 1963).
2. Robert Michels, *Political Parties* (1915; reprint, New York: The Free Press, 1949), p. 389.
3. Oliver E. Williamson, *Markets and Hierarchies* (New York: The Free Press, 1975).

4. F. Y. Edgeworth, *Mathematical Psychics; An Essay on the Application of Mathematics to the Moral Sciences* (1881; reprint, New York: A. M. Kelly, 1967).
5. Chester Barnard, *The Functions of the Executive* (Cambridge: Harvard University Press, 1938).
6. The family is subject to this as well. In the United States around 1970, when most households were supported by the husband-father, many families found themselves suddenly without an income as men were attracted away by a change in market conditions: a large influx of young unmarried women, a result of the baby boom of the late forties and early fifties.
7. John R. Hicks, *The Theory of Wages* (London: Macmillan, 1932).
8. Alfred D. Chandler, Jr., and Stephen Salsbury, *Pierre S. Du Pont and the Making of the Modern Corporation* (New York: Harper & Row, 1971).
9. For a discussion of the problem, see Robert Eccles and Harrison White, "Firm and Market Interfaces of Profit Center Control," in S. Lindenberg, J. Coleman, and S. Nowak, eds., *Approaches to Social Theory* (New York: Russell Sage, 1986), pp. 203–20.
10. See the Federal Minister of Labour and Social Affairs, *Codetermination in the Federal Republic of Germany* (Geneva: International Labour Organisation, 1976).
11. See James S. Coleman, "The University and Society's New Demands Upon It," in Carl Kaysen, ed., *Content and Context: Essays on College Education* (New York: McGraw-Hill, 1973), pp. 359–99.
12. Donald A. Schon, Reith Lectures (London: British Broadcasting Corporation, 1970).
13. Adolf A. Berle, Jr., and Gardiner C. Means. *The Modern Corporation and Private Property* (New York: Macmillan, 1934).
14. Peter Blau, *The Dynamics of Bureaucracy* (Chicago: University of Chicago Press, 1955); F. J. Roethlisberger and W. J. Dickson, *Management and the Worker* (Cambridge: Harvard University Press, 1959).
15. Group decisionmaking can also lead to inferior decisions in certain types of problems. Irving Janis discusses this phenomenon through examples such as the Kennedy decision to invade Cuba at the Bay of Pigs, which was arguably an incorrect policy decision given the information then available. See Irving Janis, *Victims of Groupthink: A Psychological Study of Foreign-Policy Decisions and Fiascos* (Boston: Houghton Mifflin, 1972).
16. Sources for these statistics may be found in J. Coleman, "Families and Schools," *Educational Researcher* 16, no. 5 (1987): 32–38.
17. Samuel Preston, "Children and the Elderly," *Scientific American* 251, no. 6 (1984): 44–49.

The Parable of the Sadhu

Bowen H. McCoy

It was early in the morning before the sun rose, which gave them time to climb the treacherous slope to the pass at 18,000 feet before the ice steps melted. They were also concerned about their stamina and altitude sickness, and felt the need to press on. Into this chance collection of climbers on that Himalayan slope an ethical dilemma arose in the guise of an unconscious, almost naked sadhu, an Indian holy man. Each climber gave the sadhu help but none made sure he would be safe. Should somebody have stopped to help the sadhu to safety? Would it have done any good? Was the group responsible? Since leaving the sadhu on the mountain slope, the author, who was one of the climbers, has pondered these issues. He sees many parallels for business people as they face ethical decisions at work.

🔱

Last year, as the first participant in the new six-month sabbatical program that Morgan Stanley has adopted, I enjoyed a rare opportunity to collect my thoughts as well as do some traveling. I spent the first three months in Nepal, walking 600 miles through 200 villages in the Himalayas and climbing some 120,000 vertical feet. On the trip my sole Western companion was an anthropologist who shed light on the cultural patterns of the villages we passed through.

During the Nepal hike, something occurred that has had a powerful impact on my thinking about corporate ethics. Although some might argue that the experience has no relevance to business, it was a situation in which a basic ethical dilemma suddenly intruded into the lives of a group of individuals. How the group responded I think holds a lesson for all organizations no matter how defined.

THE SADHU

The Nepal experience was more rugged and adventuresome than I had anticipated. Most commercial treks last two or three weeks and cover a quarter of the distance we traveled.

My friend Stephen, the anthropologist, and I were halfway through the 60-day Himalayan part of the trip when we reached the high point, an 18,000-foot pass over a crest that we'd have to traverse to reach to the village of Muklinath, an ancient holy place for pilgrims.

Six years earlier I had suffered pulmonary edema, an acute form of altitude sickness, at 16,500 feet in the vicinity of Everest base camp, so we were understandably concerned about what would happen at 18,000 feet. Moreover, the Himalayas were having their wettest spring in 20 years; hip-deep powder and ice had already driven us off one ridge. If we failed to cross the pass, I feared that the last half of our "once in a lifetime" trip would be ruined.

The night before we would try the pass, we camped at a hut at 14,500 feet. In the photos taken at that camp, my face appears wan. The last village we'd passed through was a sturdy two-day walk below us, and I was tired.

During the late afternoon, four backpackers from New Zealand joined us, and we spent most of the night awake, anticipating the climb. Below we could see the fires of two other parties, which turned out to be two Swiss couples and a Japanese hiking club.

To get over the steep part of the climb before the sun melted the steps cut in the ice, we departed at 3:30 A.M.. The New Zealanders left first, followed by Stephen and myself, our porters and Sherpas, and then the Swiss. The Japanese lingered in their camp. The sky was clear, and we were confident that no spring storm would erupt that day to close the pass.

At 15,500 feet, it looked to me as if Stephen were shuffling and staggering a bit, which are symptoms of altitude sickness. (The initial stage of altitude sickness brings a headache and nausea. As the condition worsens, a climber may encounter difficult breathing, disorientation, aphasia, and paralysis.) I felt strong, my adrenaline was flowing, but I was very concerned about my ultimate ability to get across. A couple of our porters were also suffering from the height, and Pasang, our Sherpa sirdar (leader), was worried.

Just after daybreak, while we rested at 15,500 feet, one of the New Zealanders, who had gone ahead, came staggering down toward us with a body slung across his shoulders. He dumped the almost naked, barefoot body of an Indian holy man—a sadhu—at my feet. He had found the pilgrim lying on the ice, shivering and suffering from hypothermia. I cradled the sadhu's head and laid him out on the rocks. The New Zealander was angry. He wanted to get across the pass before the bright sun melted the snow. He said, "Look, I've done what I can. You have porters and Sherpa guides. You care for him. We're going on!" He turned and went back up the mountain to join his friends.

I took a carotid pulse and found that the sadhu was still alive. We figured he had probably visited the holy shrines at Muklinath and was on his way home. It was fruitless to question why he had chosen this desperately high route instead of the safe, heavily traveled caravan route through the Kali Gandaki gorge. Or why he was almost naked and with no shoes, or how long he had been lying in the pass. The answers weren't going to solve our problem.

Stephen and the four Swiss began stripping off outer clothing and opening their packs. The sadhu was soon clothed from head to foot. He was not able to walk, but he was very much alive. I looked down the mountain and spotted below the Japanese climbers marching up with a horse.

Without a great deal of thought, I told Stephen and Pasang that I was concerned about withstanding the heights to come and wanted to get over the pass. I took off after several of our porters who had gone ahead.

On the steep part of the ascent where, if the ice steps had given way, I would have slid down about 3,000 feet, I felt vertigo. I stopped for a breather, allowing the Swiss to catch up with me. I inquired about the sadhu and Stephen. They said that the sadhu was fine and that Stephen was just behind. I set off again for the summit.

Stephen arrived at the summit an hour after I did. Still exhilarated by victory, I ran down the snow slope to congratulate him. He was suffering from altitude sickness, walking 15 steps, then stopping, walking 15 steps, then stopping. Pasang accompanied him all the way up. When I reached them, Stephen glared at me and said: "How do you feel about contributing to the death of a fellow man?"

I did not fully comprehend what he meant.

"Is the sadhu dead?" I inquired.

"No," replied Stephen, "but he surely will be!"

After I had gone, and the Swiss had departed not long after, Stephen had remained with the sadhu. When the Japanese had arrived, Stephen had asked to use their horse to transport the sadhu down to the hut. They had refused. He had then asked Pasang to have a group of our porters carry the sadhu. Pasang had resisted the idea, saying that the porters would have to exert all their energy to get themselves over the pass. He had thought they could not carry a man down 1,000 feet to the hut, reclimb the slope, and get across safely before the snow melted. Pasang had pressed Stephen not to delay any longer.

The Sherpas had carried the sadhu down to a rock in the sun at about 15,000 feet and had pointed out the hut another 500 feet below. The Japanese had given him food and drink. When they had last seen him he was listlessly throwing rocks at the Japanese party's dog, which had frightened him.

We do not know if the sadhu lived or died.

For many of the following days and evenings Stephen and I discussed and debated our behavior toward the sadhu. Stephen is a committed Quaker with deep moral vision. He said, "I feel that what happened with the sadhu is a good example of the breakdown between the individual ethic and the corporate ethic. No one person was willing to assume ultimate responsibility for the sadhu. Each was willing to do his bit just so long as it was not too inconvenient. When it got to be a bother, everyone just passed the buck to someone else and took off. Jesus was relevant to a more individualistic stage of society, but how do we interpret his teaching today in a world filled with large, impersonal organizations and groups?"

I defended the larger group, saying, "Look, we all cared. We all stopped and gave aid and comfort. Everyone did his bit. The New Zealander carried him down below the snow line. I took his pulse and suggested we treat him for hypothermia. You and the Swiss gave him clothing and got him warmed up. The Japanese gave him food and water. The Sherpas carried him down to the sun and pointed out the easy trail toward the hut. He was well enough to throw rocks at a dog. What more could we do?"

"You have just described the typical affluent Westerner's response to a problem. Throwing money—in this case food and sweaters—at it, but not solving the fundamentals!" Stephen retorted.

"What would satisfy you?" I said. "Here we are, a group of New Zealanders, Swiss, Americans, and Japanese who have never met before and who are at the apex of one of the most powerful experiences of our lives. Some years the pass is so bad no one gets over it. What right does an almost naked pilgrim who chooses the wrong trail have to disrupt our lives? Even the Sherpas had no interest in risking the trip to help him beyond a certain point."

Stephen calmly rebutted, "I wonder what the Sherpas would have done if the sadhu had been a well-dressed Nepali, or what the Japanese would have done if the sadhu had been a well-dressed Asian, or what you would have done, Buzz, if the sadhu had been a well-dressed Western woman?"

"Where, in your opinion," I asked instead, "is the limit of our responsibility in a situation like this? We had our own well-being to worry about. Our Sherpa guides were unwilling to jeopardize us or the porters for the sadhu. No one else on the mountain was willing to commit himself beyond certain self-imposed limits."

Stephen said, "As individual Christians or people with a Western ethical tradition, we can fulfill our obligations in such a situation only if (1) the sadhu dies in our care, (2) the sadhu demonstrates to us that he could undertake the two-day walk down to the village, or (3) we carry the sadhu for two days down to the village and convince someone there to care for him."

"Leaving the sadhu in the sun with food and clothing, while he demonstrated hand-eye coordination by throwing a rock at a dog, comes close to fulfilling items one and two," I answered. "And it wouldn't have made sense to take him to the village where the people appeared to be far less caring than the Sherpas, so the third condition is impractical. Are you really saying that, no matter what the implications, we should, at the drop of a hat, have changed our entire plan?"

THE INDIVIDUAL VS. THE GROUP ETHIC

Despite my arguments, I felt and continue to feel guilt about the sadhu. I had literally walked through a classic moral dilemma without fully thinking through the consequences. My excuses for my actions include a high adrenaline flow, a superordinate goal, and a once-in-a-lifetime opportunity—factors in the usual corporate situation, especially when one is under stress.

Real moral dilemmas are ambiguous, and many of us hike right through them, unaware that they exist. When, usually after the fact, someone makes an issue of them, we tend to resent his or her bringing it up. Often, when the full import of what we have done (or not done) falls on us, we dig into a defensive position from which it is very difficult to emerge. In rare circumstances we may contemplate what we have done from inside a prison.

Had we mountaineers been free of physical and mental stress caused by the effort and the high altitude, we might have treated the sadhu differently. Yet isn't stress the real test of personal and corporate values? The instant decisions executives make under pressure reveal the most about personal and corporate character.

Among the many questions that occur to me when pondering my experience are: What are the practical limits of moral imagination and vision? Is there a collective or institutional ethic beyond the ethics of the individual? At what level of effort or commitment can one discharge one's ethical responsibilities?

Not every ethical dilemma has a right solution. Reasonable people often disagree; otherwise there would be no dilemma. In a business context, however, it is essential that managers agree on a process for dealing with dilemmas.

The sadhu experience offers an interesting parallel to business situations. An immediate response was mandatory. Failure to act was a decision in itself. Up on the mountain we could not resign and submit our résumés to a headhunter. In contrast to philosophy, business involves action and implementation—getting things done. Managers must come up with answers to problems based on what they see and what they allow to influence their decision-making processes. On the mountain, none of us but Stephen realized the true dimensions of the situation we were facing.

One of our problems was that as a group we had no process for developing a consensus. We had no sense of purpose or plan. The difficulties of dealing with the sadhu were so complex that no one person could handle it. Because it did not have a set of preconditions that could guide its action to an acceptable resolution, the group reacted instinctively as individuals. The cross-cultural nature of the group added a further layer of complexity. We had no leader with whom we could all identify and in whose purpose we believed. Only Stephen was willing to take charge, but he could not gain adequate support to care for the sadhu.

Some organizations do have a value system that transcends the personal values of the managers. Such values, which go beyond profitability, are usually revealed when the organization is under stress. People throughout the organization generally accept its values, which, because they are not presented as a rigid list of commandments, may be somewhat ambiguous. The stories people tell, rather than printed materials, transmit these conceptions of what is proper behavior.

For 20 years I have been exposed at senior levels to a variety of corporations and organizations. It is amazing how quickly an outsider can sense the tone and style of an organization and the degree of tolerated openness and freedom to challenge management.

Organizations that do not have a heritage of mutually accepted, shared values tend to become unhinged during stress, with each individual bailing out for himself. In the great takeover battles we have witnessed during past years, companies that had strong cultures drew the wagons around them and fought it out, while other companies saw executives supported by their golden parachutes, bail out of the struggles.

Because corporations and their members are interdependent, for the corporation to be strong the members need to share a preconceived notion of what is correct behavior, a "business ethic," and think of it as a positive force, not a constraint.

As an investment banker I am continually warned by well-meaning lawyers, clients, and associates to be wary of conflicts of interest. Yet if I were to run away from every difficult situation, I wouldn't be an effective investment banker. I have to feel my way through conflicts. An effective manager can't run from risk either; he or she has to confront and deal with risk. To feel "safe" in doing this, managers need the guidelines of an agreed-on process and set of values within the organization.

After my three months in Nepal, I spent three months as an executive-in-residence at both Stanford Business School and the Center for Ethics and Social Policy at the Graduate Theological Union at Berkeley. These six months away from my job gave me time to assimilate 20 years of business experience. My thoughts turned often to the meaning of the leadership role in any large organization. Students at the seminary thought of themselves as antibusiness. But when I questioned them they agreed that they distrusted all large organizations, including the church. They perceived all large organizations as impersonal and opposed to individual values and needs. Yet we all know of organizations where peoples' values and beliefs are respected and their expressions encouraged. What makes the difference? Can we identify the difference and, as a result, manage more effectively?

The word "ethics" turns off many and confuses more. Yet the notions of shared values and an agreed-on process for dealing with adversity and change—what many people mean when they talk about corporate culture—seem to be at the heart of the ethical issue. People who are in touch with their own core beliefs and the beliefs of others and are sustained by them can be more comfortable living on the cutting edge. At times, taking a tough line or a decisive stand in a muddle of ambiguity is the only ethical thing to do. If a manager is indecisive and spends time trying to figure out the "good" thing to do, the enterprise may be lost.

Business ethics, then, has to do with the authenticity and integrity of the enterprise. To be ethical is to follow the business as well as the cultural goals of the corporation, its owners, its employees, and its customers. Those who cannot serve the corporate vision are not authentic business people and, therefore, are not ethical in the business sense.

At this stage of my own business experience I have a strong interest in organizational behavior. Sociologists are keenly studying what they call corporate stories, legends, and heroes as a way organizations have of transmitting the value system. Corporations such as Arco have even hired consultants to perform an audit of their corporate culture. In a company, the leader is the person who understands, interprets, and manages the corporate value system. Effective managers are then action-oriented people who resolve conflict, are tolerant of ambiguity, stress, and change, and have a strong sense of purpose for themselves and their organizations.

If all this is true, I wonder about the role of the professional manager who moves from company to company. How can he or she quickly absorb the values and culture of different organizations? Or is there, indeed, an art of management that is totally transportable? Assuming such fungible managers do exist, is it proper for them to manipulate the values of others?

What would have happened had Stephen and I carried the sadhu for two days back to the village and become involved with the villagers in his care? In four trips to Nepal my most interesting experiences occurred in 1975 when I lived in a Sherpa home in the Khumbu for five days recovering from altitude sickness. The high point of Stephen's trip was an invitation to participate in a family funeral ceremony in Manang. Neither experience had to do with climbing the high passes of the Himalayas. Why were we so reluctant to try the lower path, the ambiguous trail? Perhaps because we did not have a leader who could reveal the greater purpose of the trip to us.

Why didn't Stephen with his moral vision opt to take the sadhu under his personal care? The answer is because, in part, Stephen was hardstressed physically himself, and because, in part, without some support system that involved our involuntary and episodic community on the mountain, it was beyond his individual capacity to do so.

I see the current interest in corporate culture and corporate value systems as a positive response to Stephen's pessimism about the decline of the role of the individual in large organizations. Individuals who operate from a thoughtful set of personal values provide the foundation for a corporate culture. A corporate tradition that encourages freedom of inquiry, supports personal values, and reinforces a focused sense of direction can fulfill the need for individuality along with the prosperity and success of the group. Without such corporate support, the individual is lost.

That is the lesson of the sadhu. In a complex corporate situation, the individual requires and deserves the support of the group. If people cannot find such support from their organization, they don't know how to act. If such support is forthcoming, a person has a stake in the success of the group, and can add much to the process of establishing and maintaining a corporate culture. It is management's challenge to be sensitive to individual needs, to shape them, and to direct and focus them for the benefit of the group as a whole.

For each of us the sadhu lives. Should we stop what we are doing and comfort him; or should we keep trudging up toward the high pass? Should I pause to help the derelict I pass on the street each night as I walk by the Yale Club en route to Grand Central Station? Am I his brother? What is the nature of our responsibility if we consider ourselves to be ethical persons? Perhaps it is to change the values of the group so that it can, with all its resources, take the other road.

•Part Three•

PROPERTY, PROFIT, AND JUSTICE
Introduction

Issues about money and economics are often connected to those of ethics and values. If a friend borrows five dollars and later refuses to repay it, then the issue quickly becomes an ethical one: we say the friend really *should* repay the money. At all levels of economics, ethics plays an important role. For example, to decide how society should distribute wealth, one must know what ethical standards distinguish fair from unfair distributions. Thus it is not surprising that two well-known economists, Adam Smith and Karl Marx (both of whom are discussed in this section), began their careers as philosophers.

Two of the most volatile issues in economics have ethical implications: the importance of the profit motive, and whether restrictions should be placed on private ownership of property. The pursuit of profit and the existence of private property are said by some economists to be the foundation of a free society. The seventeenth-century philosopher John Locke argued that each person has a natural *right* to own property. However, others argue that the profit motive and private property are corrupting and result in labor abuses, unfair income distribution, monopolistic practices, and misuse of the environment.

A third issue involving both ethics and economics is the nature of justice. For example, is there such a thing as a just distribution of wealth, resources, and opportunities in society, and if so, what does that distribution look like? Is it fair that one person buys yachts and racehorses while another cannot even buy food? Or is it true, instead, that any time government attempts to insure "fairness" by interfering with the free accumulation of wealth, its attempt to redistribute wealth, resources, or opportunities commits a fundamental injustice by violating the liberty of those who have freely earned power, position, or property?

THE PROFIT MOTIVE

It is not uncommon today to hear a person or corporation condemned for being greedy. Such an attitude, which questions the morality of emphasizing profit, is not new. If anything, people today are more accepting of the profit motive than at any other time in history. Especially prior to the nineteenth century, pursuing wealth, and sometimes even lending money, were targets of intense criticism.

One of the great defenders of the profit motive was the eighteenth-century economist Adam Smith. Today, nearly two hundred years after Smith presented his ideas in *The Wealth of Nations* (excerpts of which are presented in this section), his name is almost synonymous with the defense of the free market or "laissez-faire" economic system. Smith asserted that the pursuit of profit, even for one's self-interest, is not always bad. In a famous quotation from *The Wealth of Nations* he writes

> It is not from the benevolence of the butcher, the brewer, or the baker that we expect our dinner, but from their regard of their own interest. We address ourselves not to their humanity, but to their self-love and never talk to them of our own necessities, but of their advantage.

However, Smith did not believe that economic gain was our most noble goal; rather he claimed that justice, not self-interest nor even benevolence, is the crowning virtue of humanity.

Smith emphasized the way in which pursuing one's own economic interests in the free marketplace could enhance public welfare so long as one acted with prudence, engaged in fair play, and respected the rights of others. Smith believed that an economic system could function such that people's pursuing their own economic ends could generate, in the absence of government intervention, great public economic good, so long as economic actors acted with restraint and respected basic principles of justice.

Criticisms of the Invisible Hand

By the time the Industrial Revolution was under way in the early nineteenth century, Smith's ideas dominated economic theory, and interestingly, many of the emerging social patterns of that era were justified by appealing to his philosophy. The increased specialization, the reduction of quotas and tariffs, and the decreased role of government in business were all justified by appealing to a reading of Smith's *Wealth of Nations*. Smith himself, however, did not live to see the changes, nor the human misery rampant during the Industrial Revolution, and his worries about the poor pay of workers give evidence that he would not have approved of the treatment of labor as a result of industrialization. In fact, labor was poorly paid, working conditions deplorable, and working hours long. One of the most depressing sights of all was children working in factories for sixteen hours a day, six days a week. For many children, such work was necessary to supplement their family's meager income.

Many witnesses to the Industrial Revolution were persuaded that the real villain was the economic system. The German philosopher and economist Karl Marx argued that the "free market" Smith championed was little more than a convenient fiction for capitalist property owners. Whereas Smith had praised the competitive market because of its ability to generate better products at lower prices, Marx argued that in the marketplace workers were mere commodities, available to the factory owners at the lowest possible wages. Indeed, he thought the pressures of the marketplace would force workers, who could not refuse to work without starving, to accept wages barely above a subsistence level. Meanwhile the owners of the means of production, the capitalists, could exploit workers by using their labor and then selling the resulting product at a profit. Marx identified the difference between the costs of production, including wages, and the selling price of products as "surplus value." For Marx, then, profits always meant exploitation of the worker by the capitalist. And he added that whenever technology develops, the economic gap between the capitalist and the worker must widen further, since technology allows products to be manufactured with less human labor and thus creates unemployment and lower wages.

In the selections taken from the *Economic and Philosophic Manuscripts of 1844*, Marx outlines his influential theory of alienation, in which he asserts that workers in capitalistic society are separated from, and deprived of, their own labor. When forced to work for the capitalist, workers are also forced to give the capitalist what most belongs to them: their own work. Factory employees toil away producing products that the factory owner will eventually sell, and they feel no connection to those products; rather, they have been alienated from the effects of their labor. Thus, through the concept of alienation, Marx offers a fundamental condemnation of the treatment of labor in early modern capitalism, a condemnation that was enormously influential in improving labor conditions, although less effective in its more revolutionary implications.

At the same time that Marx was developing his criticism of capitalism, there was another equally dramatic development occurring. In 1859 the English naturalist Charles Darwin published his monumental work on evolution, *The Origin of the Species*. Darwin argued, in short, that in the process of natural selection (1) organisms in the biological kingdom had evolved from simple to more complex species; and (2) during this process organisms less adaptable to the environment failed to survive, while the more adaptable ones flourished. This selection process maximizes benefits for individual organisms and species as well.

Darwin himself expressly stated that his ideas applied only to the biological kingdom, but many thinkers extended them to social and economic issues. The resulting theory of society, popularized by Herbert Spencer and industrialists such as Andrew Carnegie (whose article "Wealth" is reproduced in this section), was known as Social Darwinism.

Social Darwinism impacted issues dealt with by Adam Smith and Karl Marx, but in point of fact it agreed with neither. The Darwinists argued that the Industrial Revolution exemplified social evolution from simple to complex societies. In the evolution of a capitalistic industrial system, then, some individuals may suffer; but the system itself enhances human welfare, since it weeds out the unsuccessful, weak competitors while allowing the tougher ones to flourish. Thus, both marketplace and nature operate according to the same "natural" laws. Those who can, survive; those who cannot, perish. In this way the thesis of Social Darwinism came to view the profit motive in business as the essential motivating force in the struggle for economic survival. Unfortunately, Social Darwinism was also touted by a few wealthy tycoons in the nineteenth century as a justification for deplorable working conditions and massive economic inequalities.

The key issues of Part III—human motivation, human nature, and which economic system is preferable—are interrelated. For example, the ethical question of when, if at all, it is best for people to be motivated by profit is directly connected to the question of whether there is a common human nature. If, as some have argued, people must and will pursue their own self-interest because of their *very nature*, it is sometimes concluded that the pursuit of self-interest in the form of economic gain is often morally justified. In a similar fashion both issues are tied to that of discovering the best economic system. If people are naturally self-interested and will inevitably act on the basis of self-interest in the marketplace, perhaps society needs an economic system that proscribes such economic pursuits. On the other hand, if, self-interested people can regularly subordinate their interests to higher motives such as justice, then perhaps a free market can be morally viable economic framework.

Private Ownership

Another issue closely connected to that of profit is public versus private ownership. A common argument used by those who criticize private property asserts that the elimination of private property makes it impossible for people to strive to accumulate wealth, and thus discourages them from acting from a bad motive, that is, the profit motive. Defenders of the institution of private property disagree, citing the incentive for hard work and creativity that private property provides. But by far the most ingenious argument in favor of private property is the classical one offered by the seventeenth-century English philosopher John Locke.

Locke believed that human beings have a fundamental right to own private property, and the basic premises that establish this right can be found in the selection from his *Second Treatise on Government*. Even today his "social contract" argument is commonly used in defending the right to own property. Locke asserts what he claims is a truism: in the absence of any formally structured society—that is, in the "state of nature"—all people may be said to *own their own bodies*. It was upon this seemingly obvious premise that Locke rested his defense. If one admits that one has the right to own one's body, it follows that one owns the actions of that body, or in other words, one's own labor, and that one is free to do what one pleases with one's body, one's abilities, and one's labor. Finally, one may also be said to own, and to have a right to own, the things which one mixes and improves with one's labor. For example, if in the state of nature a person picks fruit from wild bushes, that person may be said to own the fruit. And if we grant that property may be freely traded, given, and accumulated, we have the beginning of the basis for justification of vast ownership of capital and land.

In sharp contrast with Locke's seemingly benign defense of private property, Marx argued that it is actually an institution that perpetuates the class struggle. He believed that it is likely that no such state of nature as Locke described ever existed, and he tried to give an accurate historical account of the evolution of the institution of property. He attempted to show how at every stage in the struggle for private property, one class succeeds in exploiting and alienating another. He argued that the institution of private property in a capitalistic economic system is nothing other than the means by which the privileged class—the capitalists—exploits the class of the less privileged, the workers.

We should remind ourselves that the immediate question confronting most people in the Western world is probably not whether to adopt a purely communistic or a purely free-market form of economy. Moreover, one should be reminded that Marx's ideal was a communal society, not the more totalitarian socialist systems that actually developed in his name. Of more immediate practical significance is the question of *how much* of society's goods and services should be placed in public ownership. How important is it, for example, that certain of society's economic institutions remain in the hands of private ownership? Can businesses that are privately owned contribute as much to the public welfare as those that are publicly owned? Is it possible for the latter, such as the post office or public utilities, to violate basic human rights and freedoms? In this context the case study "Plasma International" raises the question of the good or bad effects of allowing the market to distribute goods and services—especially when the good is a human necessity such as blood.

Profit and Property: Modern Discussions

One of the most outspoken critics of public ownership in the twentieth century is the economist Milton Friedman. Strongly opposing Marx, Friedman argues that the maintenance of the economic institution of private property is necessary to ensure basic political rights and freedoms. In his article "The Social Responsibility of Business Is to Increase Its Profits," Friedman denies the claim that businesses have obligations to society over and above their obligation to make a profit. In the spirit of Adam Smith, Friedman believes that the free market works best, and makes its greatest contribution, when companies compete for consumers' business and for the maximization of profits. Consequently, says Friedman, if a company were to make ethics or social responsibility a primary goal, it would be failing in its duty and hence, ironically, would not be fulfilling its real "social responsibility." Rather, the social responsibility of a corporate manager is simply to maximize profits on behalf of the corporation's owners, the shareholders.

Friedman strongly objects to placing society's major economic institutions in public ownership. Not only would the competitive marketplace be undermined, resulting in poorer products and services for the consumer, but a basic freedom would be denied insofar as the government would be interfering with the right to own property. In other of his writings, Friedman even argues that certain institutions that are now public, such as the post office and national parks, should be turned over to private investors.

How seriously one takes either Friedman's arguments or arguments asserting the opposite—that the railroads or oil industry, for example, should become publicly owned—will hinge on how seriously one takes the arguments of Locke and Marx. Is Locke correct in arguing that there is a natural right to private property? And how does his argument relate to Marx's claim that private property makes it possible for one class to exploit another?

Friedman's well-known edict that "the social responsibility of business is to increse its profits" is brought into question by another eminent Nobel Prize economist, Kenneth Arrow. While being a strong proponent of free markets, Arrow argues that profit maximization alone does not always create an efficient market and may in fact produce some other negative side-effects. Unequal competition and the imbalance of information between the corporation and other stakeholders such as employees or consumers, create inefficiencies that may be harmful to those stockholders. Moreover, even under perfect conditions or competition, profit maximization usually does not handle problems of poverty, pollution, and traffic congestion, and in fact a preoccupation with this goal appears to aggrandize selfish motives at the expense of altruistic ones.

These social and market injuries, Arrow argues, could be adjudicated with regulations, taxation, and enforcement of legal liability. But, interestingly, Arrow finds that the adoption, proliferation and enforcement of codes of ethics by corporations, codes analogous to those adopted by the medical profession, might do the work of regulation in a less intrusive and more flexible manner while preserving the benefits of an efficient competitive market.

In the case study "Dayton Hudson," issues of government regulation, competition, and free markets come together. The case describes the attempted takeover of Minnesota-based Dayton Hudson by the Dart Group.

By enacting legislation aimed at protecting Minnesota companies from take-overs, the intervention of the state of Minnesota was instrumental in preventing Dart's purchase, a takeover that in all likelihood would have changed the character and goals of a highly respected, profitable, and socially responsible company.

Justice

The subject of social justice, both for traditional and modern philosophers, is directly connected to economics and ethical theory. One important sub-category of justice dealt with in this section—namely, distributive justice—concerns the issue of how, and according to what principle(s), society's goods should be distributed. When thinking about justice it is important to remember that the concept of "justice" cannot include all ethical and political values. Thus, no matter how desirable it may be to have justice established in society, we must acknowledge other ideals such as benevolence and charity. Justice refers to a minimal condition that should exist in a good society, a condition that traditionally has been interpreted as "giving each individual his or her due."

The notion of distributive justice, i.e., what constitutes justice in distributing goods to persons, is an evasive concept, as is illustrated by the following story: Once a group of soldiers found themselves defending a fort against an enemy. The soldiers were in desperate need of water, and the only source was 200 yards from the fort in enemy territory. Courageously, a small group sneaked outside the fort, filled their canteens with water, and returned safely. After showing the water to their fellow soldiers, the successful adventurers proposed that it should be distributed in accordance with the principles of justice. Since justice requires distribution on the basis of *merit*, they said, they themselves should get the water because they risked their lives in obtaining it. There was considerable disagreement. Although agreeing that justice requires distribution on the basis of deserving characteristics, a different group of soldiers, which had been longest without water, claimed they deserved it more because they *needed* it more than the others. After all, they were the thirstiest. And still a different group, agreeing with the same general principle of justice, argued that *everyone* deserved *equal* amounts of water because all human beings, considered generally, have equal worth. The moral, obviously, is that interpretations of justice have difficulty specifying a particular characteristic or set of characteristics which, when possessed by human beings, will serve as the basis for "giving each person his or her due."

Although the subject of distributive justice is a popular topic among modern philosophers, some thinkers, such as Robert Nozick, claim that the mere idea is prejudicial and controversial. If society's goods are to be distributed, this implies the existence of a distributing agency such as the government to enforce certain principles of distribution, thus taking away from those who have acquired holdings through voluntary exchanges and desert and giving them to those who have and deserve less. In attacking any principles of distribution, Nozick is arguing that the very existence of such a process violates basic principles of individual liberty, because it denies individuals the opportunity to do as they please without interference, and thus to engage freely in exchanges of goods and property. In this way, Nozick maintains, distributive and redistributive practices necessitate the violation of basic liberties and therefore no willful distribution can itself be just.

Another modern writer presented in this section, John Rawls, also considers questions of justice and the social order. Rawls believes that the idea of distributive justice can be coordinated with principles of individual rights and liberties. He argues that a just society is one in which agreements are freely made, in which no one is left out, and in which deserving people are not shortchanged. Rawls argues that a just society is based on two principles: (1) ". . . each person engaged in an institution or affected by it has an equal right to the most extensive liberty compatible with a like liberty for all . . ." and (2) ". . . inequalities as defined by the institutional structure . . . are arbitrary unless it is reasonable to expect that they will work out to everyone's advantage and provided that the positions and offices to which they attach or from which they may be gained are open to all." Thus, Rawls is not arguing that in a just society things would be structured so as to give all people an equal number goods—for example, money, education, or status; and he allows that some people may have a great deal more than others. However, for a society to be just, such inequalities are only acceptable if their existence is to the advantage of the least fortunate as well as to everyone else. Rawls further specifies that no form of distribution in any society is just unless it satisfies the first condition of justice: freedom. Rawls's article "Distributive Justice," excerpts of which are presented in this section, first appeared in 1967 and is a precursor of his influential book *A Theory of Justice*[1], in which he more fully develops the views presented here.

The contemporary debate over the interpretation of justice begun by thinkers such as Rawls and Nozick in the 1970s was joined in the 1980s by a variety of voices, many of them critical of the very assumptions underlying the debate. Perhaps the modern political mind-set is preoccupied with individual liberty and fair procedures at the expense of a fuller and more positive concept of social-personal good.

NOTE

1. John Rawls, *A Theory of Justice* (Cambridge, Mass.: Harvard University Press, 1971).

Traditional Theories of Property and Profit

Case Study

Plasma International

T. W. ZIMMER AND P. L. PRESTON

The Sunday headline in the Tampa, Florida, newspaper read:

Blood Sales Result in Exorbitant Profits for Local Firm

The story went on to relate how the Plasma International Company, headquartered in Tampa, Florida, purchased blood in underdeveloped countries for as little as 45[1] cents a pint and resold the blood to hospitals in the United States and South America. A recent disaster in Nicaragua produced scores of injured persons and the need for fresh blood. Plasma International had 10,000 pints of blood flown to Nicaragua from West Africa and charged the hospitals $75 per pint, netting the firm nearly three quarters of a million dollars.

As a result of the newspaper story, a group of irate citizens, led by prominent civic leaders, demanded that the City of Tampa, and the State of Florida, revoke Plasma International's licenses to practice business. Others protested to their congressmen to seek enactment of legislation designed to halt the sale of blood for profit. The spokesperson was reported as saying, "What kind of people are these—selling life and death? These men prey on the needs of dying people, buying blood from poor, ignorant Africans for 45 cents worth of beads and junk, and selling it to injured people for $75 a pint. Well, this company will soon find out that the people of our community won't stand for their kind around here."

"I just don't understand it. We run a business just like any other business; we pay taxes and we try to make an honest profit," said Sol Levin as

"Plasma International," case prepared by T. W. Zimmer and P. L. Preston, reprinted from *Business and Society: Cases and Text*, by Robert D. Hay and Edmund R. Gray. Copyrighted 1976 by South-Western Publishing Co. Reprinted with permission from the publisher and authors.

he responded to reporters at the Tampa International Airport. He had just returned home from testifying before the House Subcommittee on Medical Standards. The recent publicity surrounding his firm's activities during the recent earthquakes had once again fanned the flames of public opinion. An election year was an unfortunate time for the publicity to occur. The politicians and the media were having a field day.

Levin was a successful stockbroker when he founded Plasma International Company three years ago. Recognizing the world's need for safe, uncontaminated, and reasonably priced whole blood and blood plasma, Levin and several of his colleagues pooled their resources and went into business. Initially, most of the blood and plasma they sold was purchased through store-front operations in the southeast United States. Most of the donors were, unfortunately, men and women who used the money obtained from the sale of their blood to purchase wine. While sales increased dramatically on the base of an innovative marketing approach, several cases of hepatitis were reported in recipients. The company wisely began a search for new sources.

Recognizing their own limitations in the medical-biological side of the business they recruited a highly qualified team of medical consultants. The consulting team, after extensive testing, and a worldwide search, recommended that the blood profiles and donor characteristics of several rural West African tribes made them ideal prospective donors. After extensive negotiations with the State Department and the government of the nation of Burami, the company was able to sign an agreement with several of the tribal chieftains.

As Levin reviewed these facts, and the many costs involved in the sale of a commodity as fragile as blood, he concluded that the publicity was grossly unfair. His thoughts were interrupted by the reporter's question: "Mr. Levin, is it necessary to sell a vitally needed medical supply, like blood, at such high prices especially to poor people in such a critical situation?" "Our prices are determined on the basis of a lot of costs that we incur that the public isn't even aware of," Levin responded. However, when reporters pressed him for details of these "relevant" costs, Levin refused any further comment. He noted that such information was proprietary in nature and not for public consumption.

NOTE

1. Prices have been adjusted in this article to allow for inflation occurring since the article was written (ed.).

Benefits of the Profit Motive

ADAM SMITH

BOOK I

OF THE CAUSES OF IMPROVEMENT IN THE PRODUCTIVE POWERS OF LABOR AND OF THE ORDER ACCORDING TO WHICH ITS PRODUCE IS NATURALLY DISTRIBUTED AMONG THE DIFFERENT RANKS OF THE PEOPLE

Chapter I
Of the Division of Labor

The greatest improvement in the productive powers of labor, and the greater part of the skill, dexterity, and judgment with which it is anywhere directed, or applied, seem to have been the effects of the division of labor. . . .

To take an example, therefore, from a very trifling manufacture; but one in which the division of labor has been very often taken notice of, the trade of the pin-maker; a workman not educated to this business (which the division of labor has rendered a distinct trade), nor acquainted with the use of the machinery employed in it (to the invention of which the same division of labor has probably given occasion), could scarce, perhaps, with his utmost industry, make one pin in a day, and certainly could not make twenty. But in the way in which this business is now carried on, not only the whole work is a peculiar trade, but it is divided into a number of branches, of which the greater part are likewise peculiar trades. One man draws out the wire, another straights it, a third cuts it, a fourth points it, a fifth grinds it at the top for receiving the head; to make the head requires two or three distinct operations; to put it on is a peculiar business, to whiten the pins is another; it is even a trade by itself to put them into the paper; and the important business of making a pin is, in this manner, divided into about eighteen distinct operations, which is some manufactories, are all performed by distinct hands, though in others the same man will sometimes perform two or three of them. I have seen a small manufactory of this kind where ten men only were employed, and where some of them consequently performed two or three distinct operations. But though they were very poor, and therefore but indifferently accommodated with the necessary machinery, they could,

From Adam Smith, *The Wealth of Nations*, Books I and IV (1776; rpt. Chicago: University of Chicago Press, 1976).

when they exerted themselves, make among them about twelve pounds of pins a day. There are in a pound upwards of four thousand pins of a middling size. Those ten persons, therefore, could make among them upwards of forty-eight thousand pins in a day. Each person, therefore, making a tenth part of forty-eight thousand pins, might be considered as making four thousand eight hundred pins in a day. But if they had all wrought separately and independently, and without any of them having been educated to this peculiar business, they certainly could not each of them have made twenty, perhaps not one pin in a day; that is, certainly, not the two hundred and fortieth, perhaps not the four thousand eight hundredth part, of what they are at present capable of performing in consequence of a proper division and combination of their different operations.

In every other art and manufacture, the effects of the division of labor are similar to what they are in this very trifling one; though in many of them, the labor can neither be so much subdivided, nor reduced to so great a simplicity of operation. The division of labor, however, so far as it can be introduced, occasions, in every art, a proportionate increase of the productive powers of labor. . . .

This great increase of the quantity of work, which in consequence of the division of labor, the same number of people are capable of performing, is owing to three different circumstances: first, to the increase of dexterity in every particular workman; secondly, to the saving of the time which is commonly lost in passing from one species of work to another; and lastly, to the invention of a great number of machines which facilitate and abridge labor, and enable one man to do the work of many.

First, the improvement of the dexterity of the workman necessarily increases the quantity of the work he can perform; and the division of labor, by reducing every man's business to some one simple operation and by making this operation the sole employment of his life, necessarily increases very much the dexterity of the workman. A common smith, who, though accustomed to handle the hammer, has never been used to make nails, if upon some particular occasion he is obliged to attempt it, will scarce, I am assured, be able to make about two or three hundred nails in a day, and those too very bad ones. A smith who has been accustomed to make nails, but whose sole or principal business has not been that of a nailer, can seldom with his utmost diligence make more than eight hundred or a thousand nails in a day. I have seen several boys under twenty years of age who had never exercised any other trade but that of making nails, and who, when they exerted themselves, could make, each of them, upwards of two thousand three hundred nails in a day. The making of a nail, however, is by no means one of the simplest operations. The same person blows the bellows, stirs or mends the fire as there is occasion, heats the iron, and forges every part of the nail: In forging the head too he is obliged to change his tools. The different operations into which the making of a pin or of a metal button is subdivided, are all of them much more simple; and the dexterity of the person, of whose life it has been the sole business to perform them, is usually much greater. The rapidity with which some of the operations of those manufacturers are performed exceeds what the human hand could, by those who had never seen them, be supposed capable of acquiring.

Secondly, the advantage which is gained by saving the time commonly lost in passing from one sort of work to another is much greater than we should at first view be apt to imagine it. It is impossible to pass very quickly from one kind of work to another, that is carried on in a different place, and with quite different tools. A country weaver who cultivates a small farm must lose a good deal of time in passing from his loom to the field, and from the field to his loom. When the two trades can be carried on in the same workhouse, the loss of time is no doubt much less. It is even in this case, however, very considerable. . . .

Thirdly, and lastly, every body must be sensible how much labor is facilitated and abridged by the application of proper machinery. . . .

. . . A great part of the machines made use of in those manufactures in which labor is most subdivided were originally the inventions of common workmen, who, being each of them employed in some very simple operation, naturally turned their thoughts toward finding out easier and readier methods of performing it. Whoever has been much accustomed to visit such manufacturers must frequently have been shown very pretty machines which were inventions of such workmen in order to facilitate and quicken their own particular part of the work. In the first fire-engines, a boy was constantly employed to open and shut alternately the communication between the boiler and the cylinder, according as the piston either ascended or descended. One of those boys, who loved to play with his companions, observed that, by tying a string from the handle of the valve which opened this communication to another part of the machine, the valve would open and shut without his assistance, and leave him at liberty to divert himself with his play-fellows. One of the greatest improvements that has been made upon this machine, since it was first invented, was in this manner the discovery of a boy who wanted to save his own labor. . . .

It is the great multiplication of the productions of all the different arts, in consequence of the division of labor, which occasions, in a well-governed society, that universal opulence which extends itself to the lowest ranks of the people. Every workman has a great quantity of his own work to dispose of beyond what he himself has occasion for; and every other workman being exactly in the same situation, he is enabled to exchange a great quantity of his own goods for a great quantity, or, what comes to the same thing, for the price of a great quantity of theirs. He supplies them abundantly with what they have occasion for, and they accommodate him as amply with what he has occasion for, and a general plenty diffuses itself through all the different ranks of the society. . . .

Chapter II
Of the Principle Which Gives Occasion to the Division of Labor

This division of labor, from which so many advantages are derived, is not originally the effect of any human wisdom which forsees and intends that general opulence to which it gives occasion. It is the necessary, though very slow and gradual, consequence of a certain propensity in human nature which has in view no such extensive utility: the propensity to truck, barter, and exchange one thing for another.

. . . In almost every other race of animals each individual, when it is grown up to maturity, is entirely independent, and in its natural state has occasion for the assistance of no other living creature. But man has almost constant occasion for the help of his brethren, and it is in vain for him to expect it from their benevolence only. He will be more likely to prevail if he can interest their self-love in his favor, and show them that it is for their own advantage to do for him what he requires of them. Whoever offers to another a bargain of any kind, proposes to do this. Give me that which I want, and you shall have this which you want, is the meaning of every such offer; and it is in the manner that we obtain from one another the far greater part of those good offices which we stand in need of. It is not from the benevolence of the butcher, the brewer, or the baker, that we expect our dinner, but from their regard to their own interest. We address ourselves, not to their humanity but to their self-love, and never talk to them of our own necessities but of their advantages. Nobody but a beggar chooses to depend chiefly upon the benevolence of his fellow-citizens. Even a beggar does not depend upon it entirely. The charity of well-disposed people, indeed, supplies him with the whole fund of his subsistence. But though this principle ultimately provides him with all the necessaries of life which he has occasion for, it neither does nor can provide him with them as he has occasion for them. The greater part of his occasional wants are supplied in the same manner as those of other people, by treaty, by barter, and by purchase. With the money which one man gives him he purchases food. The old clothes which another bestows upon him he exchanges for other old clothes which suit him better, or for lodging, or for food, or for money, with which he can buy either food, clothes, or lodging, as he has occasion.

As it is by treaty, by barter, and by purchase that we obtain from one another the greater part of those mutual good offices which we stand in need of, so it is this same trucking disposition which originally gives occasion to the division of labor. In a tribe of hunters or shepherds a particular person makes bows and arrows, for example, with more readiness and dexterity than any other. He frequently exchanges them for cattle or for venison with his companions; and he finds at last that he can in this manner get more cattle and venison than if he himself went to the field to catch them. From a regard to his own interest, therefore, the making of bows and arrows grows to be his chief business, and he becomes a sort of armorer. Another excels in making the frames and covers of their little huts or movable houses. He is accustomed to be of use in this way to his neighbors, who reward him in the same manner with cattle and with venison till at last he finds it his interest to dedicate himself entirely to this employment, and to become a sort of house carpenter. In the same manner a third becomes a smith or a brazier; a fourth a tanner or dresser of hides or skins, the principal part of the clothing of savages. And thus the certainty of being able to exchange all that surplus part of the produce of his own labor, which is over and above his own consumption, for such parts of the produce of other men's labor as he may have occasion for, encourages every man to apply himself to a particular occupation, and to cultivate and bring to perfection whatever talent or genius he may possess for that particular species of business.

The difference of natural talents in different men is, in reality, much less than we are aware of; and the very different genius which appears to distinguish men of different professions, when grown up to maturity, is not upon many occasions so much the cause as the effect of the division of labor. The difference between the most dissimilar characters, between a philosopher and a common street porter, for example, seems to arise not so much from nature as from habit, custom, and education. When they came into the world, and for the first six or eight years of their existence, they were, perhaps, very much alike, and neither their parents nor play-fellows could perceive any remarkable difference. About that age, or soon after, they come to be employed in very different occupations. The difference of talents comes then to be taken notice of, and widens by degrees, till at last the vanity of the philosopher is willing to acknowledge scarce any resemblance. But without the disposition to truck, barter, and exchange, every man must have procured to himself every necessary and conveniency of life which he wanted. All must have had the same duties to perform, and the same work to do, and there could have been no such difference of employment as could alone give occasion to any great difference of talents. . . .

BOOK IV

Chapter II

Every individual is continually exerting himself to find out the most advantageous employment for whatever capital he can command. It is his own advantage, indeed, and not that of the society, which he has in view. But the study of his own advantage, naturally, or rather necessarily, leads him to prefer that employment which is most advantageous to the society. . . .

As every individual, therefore, endeavours as much as he can both to employ his capital in the support of domestic industry, and so to direct that industry that its produce may be of the greatest value, every individual necessarily labors to render the annual revenue of the society as great as he can. He generally, indeed, neither intends to promote the public interest, nor knows how much he is promoting it. By preferring the support of domestic to that of foreign industry, he intends only his own security: and by directing that industry in such a manner as its produce may be of the greatest value, he intends only his own gain, and he is in this, as in many other cases, led by an invisible hand to promote an end which was no part of his intention. Nor is it always the worse for society that it was no part of it. By pursuing his own interest he frequently promotes that of the society more effectually than when he really intends to promote it. I have never known much good done by those who affected to trade for the public good. It is an affectation, indeed, not very common among merchants, and very few words need be employed in dissuading them from it.

The Justification of Private Property

JOHN LOCKE

. . . God, who hath given the world to men in common, hath also given them reason to make use of it to the best advantage of life and convenience. The earth and all that is therein is given to men for the support and comfort of their being. And though all the fruits it naturally produces, and beasts it feeds, belong to mankind in common, as they are produced by the spontaneous hand of nature; and nobody has originally a private dominion exclusive of the rest of mankind in any of them as they are thus in their natural state; yet being given for the use of men, there must of necessity be a means to appropriate them some way or other before they can be of any use or at all beneficial to any particular man. The fruit or venison which nourishes the wild Indian, who knows no enclosure, and is still a tenant in common, must be his, and so his, i.e., a part of him, that another can no longer have any right to it, before it can do any good for the support of his life.

   Though the earth and all inferior creatures be common to all men, yet every man has a property in his own person; this nobody has any right to but himself. The labor of his body and the work of his hands we may say are properly his. Whatsoever, then, he removes out of the state that nature hath provided and left it in, he hath mixed his labor with, and joined to it something that is his own, and thereby makes it his property. It being by him

From John Locke, *Second Treatise on Government* (1764; rpt. New York: MacMillan, 1956).

removed from the common state nature placed it in, it hath by this labor something annexed to it that excludes the common right of other men. For this labor being the unquestionable property of the laborer, no man but he can have a right to what that is once joined to, at least where there is enough, and as good left in common for others.

He that is nourished by the acorns he picked up under an oak, or the apples he gathered from the trees in the wood, has certainly appropriated them to himself. Nobody can deny but the nourishment is his. I ask, then, When did they begin to be his—when he digested, or when he ate, or when he boiled, or when he brought them home, or when he picked them up? And 'tis plain if the first gathering made them not his, nothing else could. That labor put a distinction between them and common; that added something to them more than nature, the common mother of all, had done, and so they became his private right. And will anyone say he had no right to those acorns or apples he thus appropriated, because he had not the consent of all mankind to make them his? Was it robbery thus to assume to himself what belonged to all in common? If such a consent as that was necessary, man had starved, notwithstanding the plenty God had given him. We see in commons which remains so by compact that 'tis the taking any part of what is common and removing it out of the state nature leaves it in, which begins the property; without which the common is of no use. And the taking of this or that does not depend on the express consent of all the commoners. Thus the grass my horse has bit, the turfs my servant has cut, and the ore I have dug in any place where I have a right to them in common with others, become my property without the assignation or consent of anybody. The labor that was mine removing them out of that common state they were in, hath fixed my property in them. . . .

It will perhaps be objected to this, that if gathering the acorns, or other fruits of the earth, etc., makes a right to them, then anyone may engross as much as he will. To which I answer, Not so. The same law of nature that does by this means give us property, does also bound that property too. "God has given us all things richly" (1 Tim. vi. 17), is the voice of reason confirmed by inspiration. But how far has He given it us? To enjoy. As much as anyone can make use of any advantage of life before it spoils, so much he may by his labor fix a property in; whatever is beyond this, is more than his share, and belongs to others. Nothing was made by God for man to spoil or destroy. And thus considering the plenty of natural provisions there was a long time in the world, and the few spenders, and to how small a part of that provision the industry of one man could extend itself, and engross it to the prejudice of others—especially keeping within the bounds, set by reason, of what might serve for his use—there could be then little room for quarrels or contentions about property so established.

But the chief matter of property being now not the fruits of the earth, and the beasts that subsist on it, but the earth itself, as that which takes in and carries with it all the rest, I think it is plain that property in that, too, is acquired as the former. As much land as a man tills, plants, improves, cultivates, and can use the product of, so much is his property. He by his labor does as it were enclose it from the common. Nor will it invalidate his right to say, everybody else has an equal title to it; and therefore he cannot appropriate, he cannot enclose, without the consent of all his fellow-commoners, all mankind. God, when He gave the world in common to all mankind, commanded man also to labor, and the penuary of his condition required it of him. God and his reason commanded him to subdue the earth, i.e., improve it for the benefit of life, and therein lay out something upon it that was his own, his labor. He that, in obedience to this command of God, subdued, tilled, and sowed any part of it, thereby annexed to it something that was his property, which another had no title to, nor could without injury take from him.

Nor was this appropriation of any parcel of land, by improving it, any prejudice to any other man, since there was still enough and as good left; and more than the yet unprovided could use. So that in effect, there was never the less left for others because of his enclosure for himself. For he that leaves as much as another can make use of, does as good as take nothing at all. Nobody could think himself injured by the drinking of another man, though he took a good draught, who had a whole river of the same water left him to quench his thirst; and the case of land and water, where there is enough of both, is perfectly the same.

God gave the world to men in common; but since He gave it them for their benefit, and the greatest conveniences of life they were capable to draw from it, it cannot be supposed He meant it should always remain common and uncultivated. He gave it to the use of the industrious and rational (and labor was to be his title to it), not to the fancy or coveteousness of the quarrelsome and contentious. He that had as good left for his improvement as was already taken up, needed not complain, ought not to meddle with what was already improved by another's labor; if he did, it is plain he desired the benefit of another's pains, which he had no right to, and not the ground which God had given him in common with others to labor on, and whereof there was as good left as that already possessed, and more than he knew what to do with, or his industry could reach to.

It is true, in land that is common in England, or any other country where there is plenty of people under Government, who have money and commerce, no one can enclose or appropriate any part without the consent of all his fellow-commoners: because this is left common by compact, i.e., by the law of the land, which is not to be violated. And though it be common in respect of some men, it is not so to all mankind; but is the joint property of this country, or this parish. Besides, the remainder, after such enclosure, would not be as good to the rest of the commoners as the whole was, when they could all make use of the whole, whereas in the beginning and first peopling of the great common of the world it was quite otherwise. The law man was under was rather for appropriating. God commanded, and his wants forced him, to labor. That was his property, which could not be taken from him wherever he had fixed it. And hence subduing or cultivating the earth, and having dominion, we see are joined together. The one gave title to the other. So that God, by commanding to subdue, gave authority so far to appropriate. And the condition of human life, which requires labor and materials to work on, necessarily introduces private possessions.

The measure of property nature has well set by the extent of men's labor and the conveniency of life. No man's labor could subdue or appropriate all, nor could his enjoyment consume more than a small part; so that it was impossible for any man, this way, to entrench upon the right of another or acquire to himself a property to the prejudice of his neighbor, who would still have room for as good and as large a possession (after the other had taken out his) as before it was appropriated. Which measure did confine every man's possession to a very moderate proportion, and such as he might appropriate to himself without injury to anybody in the first ages of the world, when men were more in danger to be lost, by wandering from their company, in the then vast wilderness of the earth than to be straitened for want of room to plant in. . . .

And thus, without supposing any private dominion and property in Adam over all the world, exclusive of all other men, which can no way be proved, nor any one's property be made out from it, but supposing the world, given as it was to the children of men in common, we see how labor could make men distinct titles to several parcels of it for their private uses, wherein there could be no doubt of right, no room for quarrel.

Nor is it so strange, as perhaps before consideration it may appear, that the property of labor should be able to overbalance the community of land. For it is labor indeed that puts the difference of value on everything; and let anyone consider what the difference is between an acre of land planted with tobacco or sugar, sown with wheat or barley, and an acre of the same land lying in common without any husbandry upon it, and he will find that the improvement of labor makes the far greater part of the value. I think it will be but a very modest computation to say that of the products of the earth useful to the life of man nine-tenths are the effects of labor; nay, if we will rightly estimate things as they come to our use, and cast up the several expenses about them—what in them is purely owing to nature, and what to labor—we shall find that in most of them ninety-nine hundredths are wholly to be put on the account of labor. . . .

From all which it is evident that, though the things of nature are given in common, yet man, by being master of himself and proprietor of his own person and the actions or labor of it, had still in himself the great foundation of property; and that which made up the great part of what he applied to the support or comfort of his being, when invention and arts had improved the conveniences of life, was perfectly his own, and did not belong in common to others.

Thus labor, in the beginning, gave a right of property, wherever anyone was pleased to employ it upon what was common, which remained a long while the far greater part, and is yet more than mankind makes use of. Men at first, for the most part, contented themselves with what unassisted nature offered to their necessities; and though afterwards, in some parts of the world (where the increase of people and stock, with the use of money, had made land scarce, and so of some value), the several communities settled the bounds of their distinct territories, and by laws within themselves, regulated the properties of the private men of their society, and so, by compact and agreement, settled the property which labor and industry began—and the leagues that have been made between several states and kingdoms, either expressly or tacitly disowning all claim and right to the land in the other's possession, have, by common consent, given up their pretenses to their natural common right, which originally they had to those countries; and so have, by positive agreement, settled a property amongst themselves in distant parts of the world—yet there are still great tracts of ground to be found which, the inhabitants thereof not having joined with the rest of mankind in the consent of the use of their common money, lie waste, and more than the people who dwell on it do or can make use of, and so still lie in common; though this can scarce happen amongst that part of mankind that have consented to the use of money.

The greatest part of things really useful to the life of man, and such as the necessity of subsisting made the first commoners of the world look after, as it doth the Americans now, are generally things of short duration, such as, if they are not consumed by use, will decay and perish of themselves: gold, silver, and diamonds are things that fancy or agreement have put the value on more than real use and the necessary support of life. Now of those good things which nature hath provided in common, everyone hath a right, as hath been said, to as much as he could use, and had a property in all he could effect with his labor—all that his industry could extend to, to alter from the state nature had put it in, was his. He that gathered a hundred bushels of acorns or apples had thereby a property in them; they were his goods as soon as gathered. He was only to look that he used them before they spoiled, else he took more than his share, and robbed others; and, indeed, it was a foolish thing, as well as dishonest, to hoard up more than he could make use of. If he gave away a part to anybody else, so that it perished not uselessly in his possession, these he also made use of; and if he also bartered away plums that would have rotted in a week, for nuts that would last good for his eating a whole year, he did no injury; he wasted not the common stock, destroyed no part of the portion of goods that belonged to others, so long as nothing perished uselessly in his hands. Again, if he would give his nuts for a piece of metal, pleased with its color, or exchange his sheep for shells, or wool for a sparkling pebble or a diamond, and keep those by him all his life, he invaded not the right of others; he might heap up as much as these durable things as he pleased, the exceeding of the bounds of his just property not lying in the largeness of his possessions, but the perishing of anything uselessly in it.

And thus came in the use of money—some lasting thing that men might keep without spoiling, and that, by mutual consent, men would take in exchange for the truly useful but perishable supports of life.

And as different degrees of industry were apt to give men possessions in different proportions, so this invention of money gave them the opportunity to continue and enlarge them; for supposing an island, separate from all possible commerce with the rest of the world, wherein there were but a hundred families—but there were sheep, horses, and cows, with other useful animals, wholesome fruits, and land enough for corn for a hundred thousand times as many, but nothing in the island, either because of its commonness or perishableness, fit to supply the place of money—what reason could anyone have there to enlarge his possessions beyond the use of his family and a plentiful supply to its consumption, either in what their own industry produced, or they could barter for like perishable useful commodities with others? Where there is not something both lasting and scarce, and so valuable to be hoarded up, there men will not be apt to enlarge their possessions of land, were it never so rich, never so free for them to take; for I ask, what would a man value ten thousand or a hundred thousand acres of excellent land, ready cultivated, and well stocked too with cattle, in the middle of the inland parts of America, where he had no hopes of commerce with other parts of the world, to draw money to him by the sale of the product? It would not be worth the enclosing, and we should see him give up again to the wild common of nature whatever was more than would supply the conveniences of life to be had there for him and his family.

Thus in the beginning all the world was America, and more so than that is now, for no such thing as money was anywhere known. Find out something that hath the use and value of money amongst his neighbors, you shall see the same man will begin presently to enlarge his possessions.

But since gold and silver, being little useful to the life of man in proportion to food, raiment, and carriage, has its value only from the consent of men, whereof labor yet makes, in great part, the measure, it is plain that the consent of men have agreed to a disproportionate and unequal possession of the earth—I mean out of the bounds of society and compact; for in governments the laws regulate it; they having, by consent, found out and agreed in a way how a man may rightfully and without injury possess more than he himself can make use of by receiving gold and silver, which may continue long in a man's possession, without decaying for the overplus, and agreeing those metals should have a value.

And thus, I think, it is very easy to conceive without any difficulty how labor could at first begin a title of property in the common things of nature, and how the spending it upon our uses bounded it; so that there could then be no reason of quarrelling about title, nor any doubt about the largeness of possession it gave. Right and conveniency went together; for as a man had a right to all he could employ his labor upon, so he had no temptation to labor for more than he could make use of. This left no room for controversy about the title, nor for encroachment on the right of others; what portion a man carved to himself was easily seen, and it was useless, as well as dishonest, to carve himself too much, or take more than he needed.

Alienated Labour

Karl Marx

We shall begin from a *contemporary* economic fact. The worker becomes poorer the more wealth he produces and the more his production increases in power and extent. The worker becomes an ever cheaper commodity the more goods he creates. The *devaluation* of the human world increases in direct relation with the *increase in value* of the world of things. Labour does not only create goods; it also produces itself and the worker as a *commodity*, and indeed in the same proportion as it produces goods. . . .

All these consequences follow from the fact that the worker is related to the *product of his labour* as to an *alien* object. For it is clear on this presupposition that the more the worker expends himself in work the more powerful becomes the world of objects which he creates in face of himself, the poorer he becomes in his inner life, and the less he belongs to himself. It is just the same as in religion. The more of himself man attributes to God the less he has left in himself. The worker puts his life into the object, and his life then belongs no longer to himself but to the object. The greater his activity, therefore, the less he possesses. What is embodied in the product of his labour is no longer his own. The greater this product is, therefore, the more he is diminished. The *alienation* of the worker in his product means not only that his labour becomes an object, assumes an *external* existence, but that it exists independently, *outside himself*, and alien to him, and that it stands opposed to him as an autonomous power. The life which he has given to the object sets itself against him as an alien and hostile force.

. . . The worker becomes a slave of the object; first, in that he receives an *object of work*, i.e. receives *work*, and secondly, in that he receives *means of subsistence*. Thus the object enables him to exist, first as a *worker* and secondly as a *physical subject*. The culmination of this enslavement is that he can only maintain himself as a *physical subject* so far as he is a *worker*, and that it is only as a *physical subject* that he is a worker. . . .

What constitutes the alienation of labour? First, that the work is *exter-*

nal to the worker, and that it is not part of his nature; and that, consequently, he does not fulfill himself in his work but denies himself, has a feeling of misery rather than well-being, does not develop freely his mental and physical energies but is physically exhausted and mentally debased. The worker, therefore, feels himself at home only during his leisure time, whereas at work he feels homeless. His work is not voluntary but imposed, *forced labour.* It is not the satisfaction of a need, but only a *means* for satisfying other needs. Its alien character is clearly shown by the fact that as soon as there is no physical or other compulsion it is avoided like the plague. External labour, labour in which man alienates himself, is a labour of self-sacrifice, of mortification. Finally, the external character of work for the worker is shown by the fact that it is not his own work but work for someone else, that in work he does not belong to himself but to another person. . . .

We arrive at the result that man (the worker) feels himself to be freely active only in his animal functions—eating, drinking, and procreating, or at most also in his dwelling and in personal adornment—while in his human functions he is reduced to an animal. The animal becomes human and the human becomes animal.

Eating, drinking, and procreating are of course also genuine human functions. But abstractly considered, apart from the environment of human activities, and turned into final and sole ends, they are animal functions.

We have now considered the act of alienation of practical human activity, labour, from two aspects: (1) the relationship of the worker to the *product of labour* as an alien object which dominates him. This relationship is at the same time the relationship to the sensuous external world, to natural objects, as an alien and hostile world; (2) the relationship of labour to the *act of production* within *labour.* This is the relationship of the worker to his own activity as something alien and not belonging to him, activity as suffering (passivity), strength as powerlessness, creation as emasculation, the *personal* physical and mental energy of the worker, his personal life (for what is life but activity?), as an activity which is directed against himself, independent of him and not belonging to him. This is *self-alienation* as against the above-mentioned alienation of the *thing.*

We have now to infer a third characteristic of *alienated labour* from the two we have considered.

Man is a species-being not only in the sense that he makes the community (his own as well as those of other things) his object both practically and theoretically, but also (and this is simply another expression for the same thing) in the sense that he treats himself as the present, living species, as a *universal* and consequently free being.[1]

Species-life, for man as for animals, has its physical basis in the fact that man (like animals) lives from inorganic nature, and since man is more universal than an animal so the range of inorganic nature from which he lives is more universal. . . . The universality of man appears in practice in the universality which makes the whole of nature into his inorganic body: (1) as a direct means of life; and equally (2) as the material object and instrument of his life activity. Nature is the inorganic body of man; that is to say nature, excluding the human body itself. To say that man *lives* from nature means that nature is his *body* with which he must remain in a continuous interchange in order not to die. The statement that the physical and mental life of man, and nature, are interdependent means simply that nature is interdependent with itself, for man is a part of nature.

Since alienated labour: (1)alienates nature from man; and (2) alienates man from himself, from his own active function, his life activity; so it alienates him from the species. It makes *species-life* into a means of individual life. In the first place it alienates species-life and individual life, and secondly, it turns the latter, as an abstraction, into the purpose of the former, also in its abstract and alienated form.

For labour, *life activity, productive life,* now appear to man only as *means* for the satisfaction of a need, the need to maintain his physical existence. Productive life is, however, species-life. It is life creating life. In the type of life activity resides the whole character of a species, its species-character; and free, conscious activity is the species-character of human beings. Life itself appears only as a *means of life.*

The animal is one with its life activity. It does not distinguish the activity from itself. It is *its activity.* But man makes his life activity itself an object of his will and consciousness. He has a conscious life activity. It is not a determination with which he is completely identified. Conscious life activity distinguishes man from the life activity of animals. Only for this reason is he a species-being. Or rather, he is only a self-conscious being, i.e. for his own life is an object for him, because he is a species-being. Only for this reason is his activity free activity. Alienated labour reverses the relationship, in that man because he is a self-conscious being makes his life activity, his *being,* only a means for his *existence.*

The practical construction of an *objective world,* the *manipulation* of inorganic nature, is the confirmation of man as a conscious species-being, i.e., a being who treats the species as his own being or himself as a species-being. . . .

It is just in his work upon the objective world that man really proves himself as a *species-being.* This production is his active species-life. By means of it nature appears as *his* work and his reality. The object of labour is, therefore, the *objectification of man's species-life:* for he no longer reproduces himself merely intellectually, as in consciousness, but actively and in a real sense, and he sees his own reflection in a world which he has constructed. While, therefore, alienated labour takes away the object of production from man, it also takes away his *species-life,* his real objectivity as a species-being, and changes his advantage over animals into a disadvantage in so far as his inorganic body, nature, is taken from him.

Just as alienated labour transforms free and self-directed activity into a means, so it transforms the species-life of man into a means of physical existence.

Consciousness, which man has from his species, is transformed through alienation so that species-life becomes only a means for him. (3) Thus alienated labour turns the *species-life of man*, and also nature as his mental species-property, into an *alien* being and into a *means* for his *individual existence*. It alienates from man his own body, external nature, his mental life and his *human* life. (4) A direct consequence of the alienation of man from the product of his labour, from his life activity and from his species-life, is that *man is alienated* from other *men*. When man confronts himself he also confronts *other* men. What is true of man's relationship to his work, to the product of his work and to himself, is also true of his relationship to other men, to their labour and to the objects of their labour.

In general, the statement that man is alienated from his species-life means that each man is alienated from others, and that each of the others is likewise alienated from human life.

Human alienation, and above all the relation of man to himself, is first realized and expressed in the relationship between each man and other men. Thus in the relationship of alienated labour every man regards other men according to the standards and relationships in which he finds himself placed as a worker.

We began with an economic fact, the alienation of the worker and his production. We have expressed this fact in conceptual terms as *alienated labour*, and in analysing the concept we have merely analysed an economic fact. . . .

The *alien* being to whom labour and the product of labour belong, to whose service labour is devoted, and to whose enjoyment the product of labour goes, can only be *man* himself. If the product of labour does not belong to the worker, but confronts him as an alien power, this can only be because it belongs to *a man other than the worker*. . . .

Thus, through alienated labour the worker creates the relation of another man, who does not work and is outside the work process, to this labour. The relation of the worker to work also produces the relation of the capitalist (or whatever one likes to call the lord of labour) to work. *Private property* is, therefore, the product, the necessary result, of *alienated labour*, of the external relation of the worker to nature and to himself.

Private property is thus derived from the analysis of the concept of *alienated labor;* that is, alienated man, alienated labour, alienated life, and estranged man.

We have, of course, derived the concept of *alienated labour* (*alienated life*) from political economy, from the analysis of the *movement of private property*. But the analysis of this concept shows that although private property appears to be the basis and cause of alienated labour, it is rather a consequence of the latter, just as the gods are *fundamentally* not the cause but the product of confusion of human reason. At a later stage, however, there is a reciprocal influence.

Only in the final state of the development of private property is its secret revealed, namely, that it is on one hand the *product* of alienated labour, and on the other hand the *means* by which labour is alienated, *the realization of this alienation.* . . .

Just as *private property* is only the sensuous expression of the fact that man is at the same time an *objective* fact for himself and becomes an alien and non-human object for himself; just as his manifestation of life is also his alienation of life and his self-realization a loss of reality, the emergence of an *alien* reality; so the positive supersession of private property, i.e. the *sensuous* appropriation of the human essence and of human life, of objective man and of human *creations*, by and for man, should not be taken only in the sense of *immediate*, exclusive *enjoyment*, or only in the sense of *possession* or *having*. Man appropriates his manifold being in an all-inclusive way, and thus as a whole man. All his *human* relations to the world—seeing, hearing, smelling, tasting, touching, thinking, observing, feeling, desiring, acting, loving—in short, all the organs of his individuality, like the organs which are directly communal in form, are in their objective action (their *action in relation to the object*) the appropriation of this object, the appropriation of human reality. The way in which they react to the object is the confirmation of *human reality*. It is human effectiveness and human *suffering*, for suffering humanly considered is an enjoyment of the self for man.

Private property has made us so stupid and partial that an object is only *ours* when we have it, when it exists for us as capital or when it is directly eaten, drunk, worn, inhabited, etc., in short, *utilized* in some way. But private property itself only conceives these various forms of possession as *means of life*, and the life for which they serve as means is the life of *private property*—labour and creation of capital.

The supersession of private property is, therefore, the complete *emancipation* of all the human qualities and senses. It is such an emancipation because these qualities and senses have become *human*, from the subjective as well as the objective point of view. The eye has become a *human* eye when its *object* has become a *human*, social object, created by man and destined for him. The senses have, therefore, become directly theoreticians in practice. They relate themselves to the thing for the sake of the thing, but the thing itself is an *objective human* relation to itself and to man, and vice versa. Need and enjoyment have thus lost their *egoistic* character and nature has lost its mere *utility* by the fact that its utilization has become *human* utilization. . . .

NOTE

1. In this passage Marx reproduces Feuerbach's argument in *Das Wesen des Christentums*.

Wealth

ANDREW CARNEGIE

This article is one of the clearest attempts to justify Social Darwinism. Written in 1889, it defends the pursuit of wealth by arguing that society is strengthened and improved through the struggle for survival in the marketplace. Interestingly, it was written by one of the world's wealthiest men, Andrew Carnegie, who came to the United States as a poor immigrant boy and quickly rose to enormous power. He began his career as a minor employee in a telegraph company, but emerged in a few years as a superintendent of the Pennsylvania Railroad. After the Civil War he entered the iron and steel business, and by 1889 he controlled eight companies which he eventually consolidated into the Carnegie Steel Corporation. Shortly before he died, he merged the Carnegie Steel Corporation with the United States Steel Company.

Carnegie took seriously the task of managing his vast fortune, and he made use of many of the ideas which are presented in the following article. He gave generously to many causes, including public libraries, public education, and the development of international peace.

The problem of our age is the proper administration of wealth, so that the ties of brotherhood may still bind together the rich and poor in harmonious relationship. The conditions of human life have not only been changed, but revolutionized, within the past few hundred years. In former days there was little difference between the dwelling, dress, food, and environment of the chief and those of his retainers. The Indians are today where civilized man then was. When visiting the Sioux, I was led to the wigwam of the chief. It was just like the others in external appearance, and even within the difference was trifling between it and those of the poorest of his braves. The contrast between the palace of the millionaire and the cottage of the laborer with us today measures the change which has come into civilization.

This change, however, is not to be deplored, but welcomed as highly beneficial. It is well, nay essential, for the progress of the race, that the houses of some should be homes for all that is highest and best in literature and art, and for all the refinements of civilization, rather than that none should be so. Much better this great irregularity than universal squalor. Without wealth there can be no Maecetions. When these apprentices rose to be masters, there was little or no change in their mode of life, and they, in turn, educated in the same routine succeeding apprentices. There was,

First published in the *North American Review*, June 1889.

substantially, social equality, and even political equality, for those engaged in industrial pursuits had then little or no political voice in the State.

But the inevitable result of such a mode of manufacture was crude articles at high prices. Today the world obtains commodities of excellent quality at prices which even the generation preceding this would have deemed incredible. In the commercial world similar causes have produced similar results, and the race is benefited thereby. The poor enjoy what the rich could not before afford. What were the luxuries have become the necessaries of life. The laborer has now more comforts than the farmer had a few generations ago. The farmer has more luxuries than the landlord had, and is more richly clad and better housed. The landlord has books and picturers rarer, and appointments more artistic, than the King could then obtain.

The price we pay for this salutary change is, no doubt, great. We assemble thousands of operatives in the factory, in the mine, and in the counting-house, of whom the employer can know little or nothing, and to whom the employer is little better than a myth. All intercourse between them is at an end. Rigid Castes are formed, and, as usual, mutual ignorance breeds mutual distrust. Each Caste is without sympathy for the other, and ready to credit anything disparaging in regard to it. Under the law of competition, the employer of thousands is forced into the strictest economies, among which the rates paid to labor figure prominently, and often there is friction between the employer and the employed, between capital and labor, between rich and poor. Human society loses homogeneity.

The price which society pays for the law of competition, like the price it pays for cheap comforts and luxuries, is also great; but the advantages of this law are also greater still, for it is to this law that we owe our wonderful material development, which brings improved conditions in its train. But, whether the law be benign or not, we must say of it, as we say of the change in the conditions of men to which we have referred: It is here; we cannot evade it; no substitutes for it have been found; and while the law may be sometimes hard for the individual, it is best for the race, because it insures the survival of the fittest in every department. We accept and welcome, therefore, as conditions to which we must accomodate ourselves, great inequality of environment, the concentration of business, industrial and commercial, in the hands of a few, and the law of competition between these, as being not only beneficial, but essential for the future progress of the race. Having accepted these, it follows that there must be great scope for the exercise of special ability in the merchant and in the manufacturer who has to conduct affairs upon a great scale. That this talent for organization and management is rare among men is proved by the fact that it invariably secures for its possessor enormous rewards, no matter where or under what laws or conditions. The experienced in affairs always rate the MAN whose services can be obtained as a partner as not only the first consideration, but such as to render the question of his capital scarcely worth considering, for such men soon create capital; while, without the special talent required, capital soon takes wings. Such men become interested in firms or corporations using millions; and estimating only simple interest to be made upon the capital invested, it is inevitable that their income must exceed their expenditures, and that they must accumulate wealth. Nor is there any middle ground which such men can occupy, because the great manufacturing or commercial concern which does not earn at least interest upon its capital soon becomes bankrupt. It must either go forward or fall behind: to stand still is impossible. It is a condition essential for its successful operation that it should be thus far profitable, and even that, in addition to interest on capital, it should make a profit. It is a law, as certain as any of the others named, that men possessed of this peculiar talent for affairs, under the free play of economic forces, must, of necessity, soon be in receipt of more revenue than can be judiciously expended upon themselves, and this law is as beneficial for the race as the others.

Objections to the foundations upon which society is based are not in order, because the condition of the race is better with these than it has been with any others which have been tried. Of the effect of any new substitutes proposed we cannot be sure. The Socialist or Anarchist who seeks to overturn present conditions is to be regarded as attacking the foundation upon which civilization itself rests, for civilization took its start from the day that the capable, industrious workman said to his incompetent and lazy fellow, "If thou dost not sow, thou shalt not reap," and thus ended primitive Communism by separating the drones from the bees. One who studies this subject will soon be brought face to face with the conclusion that upon the sacredness of property civilization itself depends—the right of the laborer to his hundred dollars in the savings bank, and equally the legal right of the millionaire to his millions. To those who propose to substitute Communism for this intense Individualism the answer, therefore, is: The race has tried that. All progress from that barbarous day to the present time has resulted from its displacement. Not evil, but good, has come to the race from the accumulation of wealth by those who have the ability and energy that produce it. But even if we admit for a moment that it might be better for the race to discard its present foundation, Individualism—that it is a nobler ideal that man should labor, not for himself alone, but in and for a brotherhood of his fellows, and share with them all in common, realizing Swedenborg's idea of Heaven, where, as he says, the angels derive their happiness, not from laboring for self, but for each other—even admit all this, and a sufficient answer is, This is not evolution, but revolution. It necessitates the changing of human nature itself—a work of aeons, even if it were good to change it, which we cannot know. It is not practicable in our day or in our age. Even if desirable theoretically, it belongs to another and long-succeeding sociological stratum. Our duty is with what is practicable now; with the next step possible in our day and generation. It is criminal to waste our energies in endeavoring to uproot, when all we can profitably or possibly accomplish is to bend the universal tree of humanity a little in the direction most favorable to the production of good fruit under existing circumstances. We might as well urge the destruction of the highest existing type of man because he failed to reach our ideal as to favor the destruction of Individualism, Private Property, the Law of Accumulation of Wealth, and the Law of Competition; for these are the highest results of human experience, the soil in which society so far has produced the best fruit. Unequally or unjustly, perhaps, as these laws sometimes operate, and imperfect as they appear to the Idealist, they are nevertheless, like the highest type of man, the best and most valuable of all that humanity has yet accomplished.

We start, then, with a condition of affairs under which the best interests of the race are promoted, but which inevitably gives wealth to the few. Thus far, accepting conditions as they exist, the situation can be surveyed and pronounced good. The question then arises—and, if the foregoing be correct, it is the only question with which we have to deal—What is the proper mode of administering wealth after the laws upon which civilization is founded have thrown it into the hands of the few? And it is of this great question that I believe I offer the true solution. It will be understood that *fortunes* are here spoken of, not moderate sums saved by many years of effort, the returns from which are required for the comfortable maintenance and education of families. This is not *wealth*, but only *competence*, which it should be the aim of all to acquire.

. . . Indeed, it is difficult to set bounds to the share of a rich man's estate which should go at his death to the public through the agency of the state, and by all means such taxes should be graduated, beginning at nothing upon moderate sums to dependents, and increasing rapidly as the amounts swell, until of the millionaire's hoard, as of Shylock's at least

"_____ The other half
Comes to the privy coffer of the state."

This policy would work powerfully to induce the rich man to attend to the administration of wealth during his life, which is the end that society should always have in view, as being that by far most fruitful for the people. Nor need it be feared that this policy would sap the root of enterprise and render men less anxious to accumulate, for to the class whose ambition it is to leave great fortunes and be talked about after their death, it will attract more attention, and, indeed, be a somewhat nobler ambition to have enormous sums paid over to the state from their fortunes.

There remains, then, only one mode of using great fortunes; but in this we have the true antidote for the temporary unequal distribution of wealth, the reconciliation of the rich and the poor—a reign of harmony—another ideal, differing, indeed, from that of the Communist in requiring only the further evolution of existing conditions, not the total overthrow of our civilization. It is founded upon the present most intense individualism, and the race is prepared to put it in practice by degrees whenever it pleases. Under its sway we shall have an ideal state, in which the surplus wealth of the few will become, in the best sense, the property of the many, because administered for the common good, and this wealth, passing through the hands of the few, can be made a much more potent force for the elevation of our race than if it had been distributed in small sums to the people themselves. Even the poorest can be made to see this, and to agree that great sums gathered by some of their fellow-citizens and spent for public purposes, from which the masses reap the principal benefit, are more valuable to them than if scattered among them through the course of many years in trifling amounts.

The best uses to which surplus wealth can be put have already been indicated. Those who would administer wisely must, indeed, be wise, for one of the serious obstacles to the improvement of our race is indiscriminate charity. It were better for mankind that the millions of the rich were thrown into the sea than so spent as to encourage the slothful, the drunken, the unworthy. Of every thousand dollars spent in so-called charity today, it is probable that $950 is unwisely spent; so spent, indeed, as to produce the very evils which it proposes to mitigate or cure. A well-known writer or philosophic books admitted the other day that he had given a quarter of a dollar to a man who approached him as he was coming to visit the house of his friend. He knew nothing of the habits of this beggar; knew not the use that would be made of this money, although he had every reason to suspect that it would be spent improperly. This man professed to be a disciple of Herbert Spencer; yet the quarter-dollar given that night will probably work more injury than all the money which its thoughtless donor will ever be able to give in true charity will do good. He only gratified his own feelings, saved himself from annoyance— and this was probably one of the most selfish and very worst actions of his life, for in all respects he is most worthy.

In bestowing charity, the main consideration should be to help those who will help themselves; to provide part of the means by which those who desire to improve may do so; to give those who desire to rise the aids by which they may rise; to assist, but rarely or never to do all. Neither the individual nor the race is improved by alms-giving. Those worthy of assistance, except in rare cases, seldom require assistance. The really valuable men of the race never do, except in cases of accident or sudden change. Every one has, of course, cases of individuals brought to his own knowledge where temporary assistance can do genuine good, and these he will not overlook. But the amount which can be wisely given by the individual for individuals is necessarily limited by his lack of knowledge of the circumstance connected with each. He is the only true reformer who is as careful and as anxious not to aid the unworthy as he is to aid the worthy, and perhaps, even more so, for in alms-giving more injury is probably done by rewarding vice than by relieving virtue.

Thus is the problem of Rich and Poor to be solved. The laws of accumulation will be left free; the laws of distribution free. Individualism will continue, but the millionaire will be but a trustee for the poor; intrusted for a season with a great part of the increased wealth of the community, but administrating it for the community far better than it could or would have done for itself. The best minds will thus have reached a stage in the development of the race in which it is clearly seen that there is no mode of disposing of surplus wealth creditable to thoughtful and earnest men into whose hands it flows save by using it year by year for the general good. This day already dawns. But a little while, and although, without incurring the pity of their fellows, men may die sharers in great business enterprises from which their capital cannot be or has not been withdrawn, and is left chiefly at death for public uses, yet the man who dies leaving behind him millions of available wealth, which was his to administer during life, will pass away "unwept, unhonored, and unsung," no matter to what uses he leaves the dross which he cannot take with him. Of such as these the public verdict will then be: "The man who dies thus rich dies disgraced."

Such, in my opinion, is the true Gospel concerning Wealth, obedience to which is destined some day to solve the problems of the Rich and the Poor, and to bring "Peace on earth, among men Good-Will."

Property and Profit: Modern Discussions

———————————◆◆———————————

Case Study

Dayton Hudson Corporation: Conscience and Control

KENNETH E. GOODPASTER AND ROBERT C. KENNEDY

> *"To those who assert that business should operate only in its own best interests, I contend that corporate social responsibility is in our best interest. It is in the interest of our survival."*

BRUCE B. DAYTON
CHAIRMAN, EXECUTIVE COMMITTEE
DAYTON HUDSON CORPORATION
MAY 20, 1976

Just before lunch, the legal team re-entered the meeting to share what they had been discussing. They said they had a possible "showstopper," an alternative that might permit the company to remain independent in its current form. Kenneth A. Macke, 48, CEO of the Minneapolis-based Dayton Hudson Corporation (DHC), listened intently.

Only a short time before, Macke had made it clear that he was dissatisfied with the strategies that had been discussed during the morning meeting. He had scheduled the meeting for Thursday, June 11, 1987, and opened it as

Assistant professor Robert C. Kennedy, University of St. Thomas (St. Paul, MN), prepared this case under the supervision of Kenneth E. Goodpaster, Koch Professor of Business Ethics at the University of St. Thomas and Visiting Professor, Harvard Business School, as the basis for class discussion rather than to illustrate either effective or ineffective handling of an administrative situation. Assistant professor Randel S. Carlock, also of the University of St. Thomas, contributed to the research and editing process. The writing of this case was sponsored by the Council on Foundations, 1828 L Street NW, Washington, D.C.

a general might convene a council of war. With him were some of the senior managers of the company and a number of outside advisers, assembled to formulate a strategy for defending the company against an emerging hostile takeover threat. These advisers included representatives of Goldman, Sachs (DHC's investment bankers), Kekst and Co., and the New York law firm of Wachtell, Lipton, Rosen and Katz. One discussion focused on the financial options, while in another room DHC's legal staff and their advisers discussed legal defenses. The debate in each group ranged widely, and at one point or another, in the words of one participant, "every imaginable option" was considered.

To the financial team it was clear that every alternative entailed fighting the battle for the company's future in New York. They considered attempts to block the raider's access to needed financial resources as well as various plans to restructure the company and make it unattractive to the raider. Every participant was aware of the need for quick and decisive action.

Eight days earlier, on Wednesday, June 3, 1987, DHC's stock had increased in value by nearly $3 per share in unusually heavy trading, to close at about $50.62. To the casual observer, this increase was puzzling, for the company had, only a few months earlier, reported its first earnings decline in sixteen years. Since then, the stock had traded between about $42 and $45, and volume had been relatively low. Furthermore, nothing obvious had happened to account for the sudden increase in price and volume.

To the professional observer, however, the change was not so surprising. Once a favorite of Wall Street because of its consistently strong earnings, the company had fallen out of favor. In the opinion of many observers, its earnings decline was caused by the poor performance of one of its four operating companies. Furthermore, management had not kept investors and analysts well-informed about efforts to correct the problems. As a result, DHC's stock traded at a price that some analysts felt undervalued the company.

Macke was confident that DHC would rebound and post strong earnings growth within a year or two. In late May and early June, however, he watched his company's stock with growing concern. SEC regulations specified that anyone acquiring 5% or more of a company's stock must file a disclosure. No such disclosure had been filed. However, alerted by the unusual market activity, and by rumors circulating on Wall Street, Macke and his management team feared that the company might become the target of a hostile takeover attempt. By June 3 this appeared highly likely, and shortly afterwards, in response to the probable threat, Macke called together a Task Force of senior managers that had been formed some years earlier to deal with such a situation. Included in this group were Boake Sells (president and COO), Willard Schull (CFO), James Hale (senior vice president and general counsel), Peter Hutchinson (vice president for external affairs and chairman of the Dayton Hudson Foundation), and Ann Berkelew (vice president for corporate public relations).

With the help of their Wall Street advisers the team was able to identify the likely raider as the Dart Group Corporation, a Maryland-based discounter with a recent history of unsuccessful takeover attempts. Though the Dart Group had not made a concrete proposal, nor even publicly acknowledged its interest in the company, Macke and his team were aware that they needed to act quickly if they were to protect the company from being put in play.[1] On Wednesday, June 10, DHC's stock was the second most heavily traded on the New York Stock Exchange. Since June 3 it had risen in value by over $4.50.

THE DAYTON HUDSON CORPORATION

The Dayton Hudson Corporation described itself as "a growth company focusing exclusively on retailing." Headquartered in Minneapolis, the company operated 475 stores in 34 states at the end of 1986, employing some 120,000 people nationwide (full-time and part-time). In that year it had pretax earnings of $494.2 million on sales of $9,259.1 million.

⚓

Operating Structures and Policies

DHC was composed of four operating companies and a corporate headquarters. This structure reflected DHC's fundamental management philosophy which favored decentralization. The operating companies were:

Target: an upscale discount store chain. In 1986 Target produced 47% of DHC's revenues and 47.4% of pretax profits, with earnings of $311 million on sales of $4,355 million.

Mervyn's: a highly promotional, popularly priced, value-oriented department store company. In 1986 Mervyn's produced 31% of DHC's revenues and 24.4% of pretax profits, with earnings of $160 million on sales of $2,862 million.

Dayton Hudson Department Store Company (DHDSC): the largest traditional department store operation in the United States. In 1986 DHDSC produced 17% of DHC's revenues and 25.2% of pretax profits, with earnings of $166 million on sales of $1,566 million.

Lechmere's: a hardgoods retail store company. In 1986 Lechmere's produced 5% of DHC's revenues and 3% of pretax profits, with earnings of $19.5 million on sales of $476 million.

The operating companies made autonomous decisions about merchandising and buying, and had responsibility for profits and return on investment. They were made accountable to corporate headquarters through an annual planning cycle, considered to be crucial to DHC's management process. This annual planning cycle included a strategy and human resources review, an agreement on capital allocation, the setting of financial goals, and a performance appraisal. However, despite the apparent autonomy granted to the operating companies, Macke continued to pay close attention to details and "needle" his executives in an effort to improve performance.

Financial Policies

DHC's stated financial goal was to provide its shareholders with a superior return on their investment while maintaining a conservative financial position. More particularly, the company preferred to own assets where possible, to meet external needs with long-term debt, and to maintain a maximum debt ratio of 45% (including capital and operating leases). The majority of the company's growth was financed through internally generated funds.

In its 1986 Annual Report, DHC stated that its performance objectives were to "earn an after-tax return on beginning shareholders' equity (ROE) of 18%," to "sustain an annual growth in earnings per share (EPS) of 15%," and to "maintain a strong rating of [its] senior debt." The Report also noted that "the incentive compensation of corporate management and the management of each operating company is based on return on investment, as well as growth in earnings."

These goals, however, were not extrapolated from past performance. The ROE had averaged 15.3% in the period 1975–86, and the earnings per share growth had only been above 15% five times in those twelve years.

Though DHC remained a profitable company, 1986 was a disappointing year. Revenues increased by 12% and passed the $9 billion mark, but net earnings per share dropped by 9%. The principal reason appears to have been difficulty with the Mervyn's division, where operating profits fell by more than 34%. DHC's Annual Report for 1986 acknowledged a problem with Mervyn's and attributed the dramatic decline in profits to an organizational restructuring and to a need to reduce margins in order to remain competitive.

More specifically, Mervyn's had expanded significantly in Texas, adding buying and sales offices there in 1984 which duplicated some services performed at its California headquarters. The oil price collapse made these functions redundant and the company was forced to close that office and reorganize at considerable expense. These difficulties distracted management attention and marketing mistakes were made. Coupled with increased competition, these factors, and the efforts made to correct for them, were responsible for poor performance in 1986.

This was the second year of poor performance for Mervyn's (in 1985 operating profits had increased by only 9.7%), a sharp contrast to the previous two years, when profits had increased by 21% each year. Since the decline began when Macke became chairman, some observers raised questions about his ability to manage the corporation.

Customer Service

DHC was strongly customer-oriented. The stated merchandising objective of each of the operating companies was to fulfill the value expectations of customers more effectively than the competition. They consciously aimed to do this by providing superior value in five categories: assortment, quality, fashion, convenience and pricing. One concrete sign of this orientation was the long-standing corporate policy of accepting the return of merchandise for a full refund, no questions asked. Stories abounded, especially in Minnesota, about the lengths to which the company was willing to go to honor this policy.

Corporate Community Involvement

In 1946 the Dayton Company became the first major American corporation to initiate a policy by which it donated 5% of its federal taxable income to non-profit organizations. (It was a charter member of Minnesota's "5% Club," an organization founded in 1976 whose membership consisted of corporations that donated 5% of their annual taxable income.) This policy had continued without interruption, and in 1987 DHC's contributions totaled nearly $20 million (principally to arts and social action organizations). These contributions were distributed throughout the states in which DHC did business. The four states which generated the largest revenues for the company were California, Minnesota, Texas, and Michigan, but contributions were not proportioned to revenues.

Eighty percent of DHC's contributions were made in two areas: the arts and social action,[2] each receiving roughly equal amounts. The remaining community giving funds were contributed to other programs and projects that addressed responsiveness to special community needs and opportunities; and innovative partnerships with other community leaders. The company was Minnesota's largest private donor and a mainstay of many of the arts organizations in the Twin Cities. In the past, it had helped fund such activities as job creation programs, neighborhood renovations, and child care and chemical abuse programs.

Observers considered DHC's community involvement program to be distinctive in several ways. Among these was the company's commitment to maintain a professional staff, "held to standards as rigorous as any profit center within the corporation, with specific goals, objectives and performance review." Another was the decision to commit 6% of their giving budget to emerging issues in social action and the arts. As Peter Hutchinson, chairman of the Dayton Hudson Foundation, commented, "Armed with an integrated view of needs and opportunities, we must . . . adapt our programs to changing circumstances. . . . Regardless of the means, our goal must be to bring programs and constituents together in a common vision and commitment for the future."

DHC's concern for social responsibility extended into other aspects of its business as well. In 1978, for example, Kenneth Dayton (then chairman and CEO of the company) was one of the principal organizers of the Minnesota Project on Corporate Responsibility. This organization sponsored seminars and other programs aimed at encouraging and strengthening a sense of social responsiveness in Minnesota corporations. James Shannon, then executive director of the General Mills Foundation, commented in a guest editorial in the *Minneapolis Star Tribune*, "In a community nationally known for its corporate support of the arts, social services and education, the Dayton Hudson Corp. is the flagship for dozens of other publicly and privately held corporations committed to the proposition that a successful company has an obligation to be a good corporate citizen."

DHC's relations with the public were not always smooth, however. There were times when its concern for communities was questioned. In 1983, for example, Hudson's flagship store in downtown Detroit was closed. From DHC's perspective the store had become old and inefficient, and the business climate in downtown Detroit unsupportive. Mayor Coleman Young's view was different. As he told the *Detroit Free Press*, "I don't think Hudson's demonstrated any sense of responsibility or citizenship after growing in this city and off this city for almost 100 years."

The following year, 1984, Dayton's and Hudson's operations were consolidated into the Dayton Hudson Department Store Company, with a single headquarters in Minneapolis. Once again, Detroit objected since the move resulted in the loss of about 1,000 jobs for the city, many of them well-paid management positions. Ann Barkelew, DHC's vice president for public relations, commented in the *Minneapolis Star Tribune*, "Our decision to bring the headquarters [to Minneapolis] was a business decision. The whole purpose in combining the companies was to do things better."

THE DART GROUP CORPORATION

The Dart Group Corporation's 1987 Annual Report (year ending January 31, 1987) was spartan and no-nonsense. Its only two photographs, which appeared on the first page, were of Herbert Haft, founder and chairman, and Robert Haft, president and Herbert's older son. There were no photographs of the discount retail outlets they operated or of satisfied customers, nor did other members of management or the board of directors appear. Instead, attention was focused exclusively on information about Dart's operations and finances. And not without reason, for Dart's net income more than tripled in fiscal 1987.

According to the Annual Report, Dart operated retail discount auto parts stores through the Trak Auto Corporation, operated retail discount book stores through the Crown Books Corporation, and operated a financial business which dealt in bankers' acceptances. The present company was a successor to Dart Drug, a Washington, D.C. retail drug store chain founded by Herbert Haft. Haft built a chain of stores from one store he opened in 1954 by selling most of his merchandise at discount prices. At the time the minimum price for many brand name products was set by the manufacturer, and Haft was often in violation of fair trade laws in selling at a discount. While the practice provoked a number of supplier suits, it also attracted thousands of customers. As the suburbs of Washington grew, Dart Drug grew with them. In the 1970s, Dart pioneered the concept of a "super" drugstore, that sold not only the traditional drugs and cosmetics, but beer, lawn furniture, lumber, auto parts, and almost anything else the Hafts could find.

While Robert Haft was a student at the Harvard Business School in the mid-70s, he wrote a paper exploring the idea of selling books through discount retail outlets. By some accounts, he was motivated to set the idea in motion after listening to a Dayton Hudson executive who spoke at Harvard. Dayton Hudson operated B. Dalton Booksellers at the time and the executive claimed that a discount book chain could not be successful. Robert earned an MBA in 1977 and later established Crown Books, which sold both hardcover and paperback books at a discount. By 1986 Crown Books operated about 200 stores nationally, with 1986 earnings of $5.5 million on revenues of $154 million.

In 1984, Dart's drug store division was sold to its employees. In the three years prior to the sale the Hafts boosted profitability by sharply cutting costs. They accomplished this in part by dramatic reductions in inventory (e.g., stocking far fewer sizes and varieties of merchandise), and customer services (e.g., declining to give cash refunds). According to a *Fortune* magazine article, they were well known among their suppliers as tough customers. They acquired a reputation of paying late and demanding discounts. Suppliers were frequently reluctant to insist on their terms and risk losing a large customer, so they often made concessions. By 1987, the independent Dart Drug Stores were struggling to survive, burdened with large interest payments and a poor reputation. In an effort to win back customers, the new owners ran ads in the *Washington Post* announcing that the stores were no longer owned or operated by the Hafts.

Attempts to Acquire Other Businesses

DHC was not the first corporation in which the Hafts took an interest. Between 1983 and 1986 they attempted to acquire Supermarkets General Corp., Jack Eckerd Drug Stores, Revco Inc., Federated Department Stores, May Department Stores and the giant supermarket chain, Safeway Stores. In each case they failed, but their failures were spectacularly profitable. They realized a $9 million profit on the sale of their Jack Eckerd stock, $40 million in their unsuccessful attempt to purchase Supermarkets General, and $97 million when they failed to take over Safeway. Not surprisingly, the value of Dart Group stock rose from $10.75 in 1982 to over $150 per share in 1987.

Target companies have seriously questioned, and seriously resisted, the Hafts' attempts to acquire them. Like many other corporate raiders, the Hafts relied on "junk bonds" as part of the financial component of their proposals, and issuers like Drexel Burnham Lambert indicated that they were "highly confident" that financing could be arranged. Yet unlike many other raiders, the Hafts always targeted businesses close to their own experience. They remained in the retail industry and attempted to acquire chains, especially where their low-margin expertise might be valuable. Since they were always unsuccessful in their acquisition attempts, accusations by critics that they intended to sell off the major assets of the target companies were, while speculative, not entirely unreasonable. For their part, the Hafts insisted that they planned to operate, rather than break up, the companies they targeted.

However, even when a takeover attempt failed, the target company could face a difficult time. In 1986, the Dart Group was unsuccessful in an attempt to acquire Safeway Stores. The management of Safeway eluded the Hafts by taking the company private with a leveraged buyout. This involved taking on $4.2 billion in debt in order to purchase outstanding stock. As a result, Safeway, once the largest supermarket chain in the United States, was compelled to sell off profitable British and Australian holdings. In addition, it sold or closed 251 stores in the United States. Many of these stores were in small towns that had complained bitterly about the move. While Safeway's streamlining substantially improved profitability, it was still left with an enormous debt burden to service.

The Events Leading up to Early June 1987

In 1986, DHC offered its B. Dalton division for sale. At that time B. Dalton, founded by one of the Dayton brothers in the 1960s, was one of the two largest and most successful retail bookselling chains in the United States. However, DHC had decided to pursue a strategy focused on the operation of large stores that offered a broad spectrum of merchandise. The typical B. Dalton store was fairly small and specialized in books and computer software. Among those seriously interested in acquiring B. Dalton was the Dart Group. Ultimately they were unsuccessful, and the division was sold to Barnes and Noble. According to one rumor, the negotiations broke down when personal hostilities flared up between senior executives of DHC and the Hafts.

Nevertheless, in their negotiations the Hafts had the opportunity to become familiar with DHC. While they recognized value in the company, they were critical of DHC's management. In a later interview with the *Minneapolis Star Tribune*, Robert Haft criticized DHC's retail strategies. "This thing is slowly going downhill," he said. According to *Business Week*, they felt that their own successful experience in managing discount retail outlets made them well suited to manage DHC properly.

In the spring of 1987, when DHC announced its first decline in earnings in sixteen years, the Hafts saw an opportunity. Though the significant drop in DHC's stock price discouraged some investors, the Hafts felt there was good reason to think that the company still had the potential for solid earnings. The Target division had acquired a number of important leases in California and was poised for expansion. With proper management, Mervyn's could certainly be turned around. Moreover, the board of directors and senior management collectively owned a very small portion of DHC's stock, far less than would be required to exercise a controlling influence.

By that same spring the legal climate was becoming less conducive to hostile takeovers. Provisions of an Indiana law that gave the state considerable power to restrict such takeovers had been upheld by the U.S. Supreme Court in April. Some Minnesota corporations (though not DHC) had lobbied hard for similar legislation in 1984, but it had failed to pass, partly because many legislators felt that it would not be upheld by the courts. The Supreme Court's decision, however, came too late to influence the 1987 session of the Minnesota legislature, which adjourned on May 18.

ANOTHER ALTERNATIVE?

During the week of June 8, the Task Force met frequently and Macke remained in constant communication with the board of directors. As alternatives were generated, however, each one seemed unacceptable to management and the board.

At the meeting on June 11, Macke himself made clear his opposition to a "bust up" takeover, one that would require breaking up the corporation and selling off parts to repay the debts incurred by the takeover. He and his management team were convinced that it was best for all the corporation's constituencies—stockholders, customers, employees, and communities— that the company remain intact. As the possibilities were discussed, some were set aside rather easily. They found greenmail,[3] in the words of one participant, to be a "repugnant" alternative. They were also repelled by various schemes to take on debt or sell off assets, which, as another participant put it, would involve doing to themselves exactly what they feared the Hafts would do. Nor were they convinced that the financial defenses would be successful. They realized that if they chose to fight a financial battle, the action would take place in New York, where they had less influence. On the other hand, they had considerable influence in Minnesota, but it was not clear how to bring that influence to bear.

As Macke listened to the legal team, he anticipated the direction of their proposal. Would this alternative take advantage of DHC's strengths and preserve the integrity of the company? Or would it be flawed like all the others?

On Thursday, June 11, while Macke and his management team were meeting with their advisers, Wendy McDowall was beginning a well-earned fishing vacation. Director of Government Affairs for DHC, she had just finished several grueling months as the company's chief lobbyist at the Minnesota legislature. The 1987 session, which adjourned May 18, had been more difficult than most and everyone involved was relieved to see it end. By this morning Wendy had been at a cabin on the North Shore of Lake Superior for only a day or two. As she sipped a cup of coffee she turned on the radio and was stunned by the news she heard. DHC's stock had been the second most actively traded issue the day before. Although she did not know quite what she could do to help, she quickly decided that she could not continue fishing while her company was in danger. Within the hour she was in her car speeding back to Minneapolis.

That afternoon, after listening to discussion about alternative defenses, Macke had made it clear to his team that the responsibility for the decision would be his. Later that evening, after consulting with the board of directors, he decided to approach the governor regarding a special session of the legislature to strengthen Minnesota's corporate takeover statute. It seemed to be the alternative that took best advantage of the company's strengths, all things considered, and the one most likely to succeed. But many obstacles still lay in the path.

The strategy that DHC laid out with respect to the legislators was simple in theory, but was complicated to execute in such a short time. Their aim was to help legislators understand clearly what was at stake and to help them become comfortable with the idea of a special session *and* with amending the statute. To accomplish this they did five things.

First, they hired some of the most experienced professional lobbyists in the state to ensure that every legislator would be contacted personally. Second, they commissioned an opinion poll to discover the reaction of citizens to DHC's plight and the proposed special session. Third, they prepared an information packet for each legislator. By coincidence, the June 22, 1987 issue of *Fortune* magazine carried an article on the Hafts entitled "The Most Feared Family in Retailing." The article, which was included in an information packet, described the Hafts's businesses and detailed their efforts to acquire a national retailer, with a special sidebar about the damage done to Safeway.

Fourth, they made strenuous efforts to contact newspapers in rural Minnesota and urge them to publish editorials supporting the special session. Fifth, they planned to send DHC executives to every community in the state where DHC had a store and where there was an important media instrument.

Some tactics, however, were rejected. DHC's advertising department had been asked earlier in the week to develop some ideas for advertisements that could be placed in newspapers to inform the public and gather support. On the afternoon of the 20th, management discussed what to do with the proposed ads. A couple of years earlier, Dayton's department stores had offered a small, white stuffed bear as a Christmas premium to customers. The response to "Santabear" had been overwhelming and the company had become closely associated with the toy, especially in Minnesota (see Exhibit 2). Some of the ads attempted to capture attention by suggesting that Santabear was at risk. After considerable debate a decision was made not to use the ads. Management was concerned that they might be perceived as too manipulative.

Sunday, June 21

Lobbying efforts were put on hold for Father's Day. In the afternoon, Commerce Commissioner Hatch drove to Montevideo, a rural town not far from the Twin Cities, to attend a parade. He asked people there what they thought about calling a special session to address DHC's problem. For the most part they were not enthusiastic about the plan.

In the evening, two lawyers from the Attorney General's office completed a memo evaluating DHC's proposed bill. They concluded that it probably did not violate the state constitution.

Monday, June 22

Early in the morning, Steve Watson, president of the Dayton Hudson Department Store Company, and Leary boarded the company plane to fly around the state implementing their plan to make media appearances and meet with legislators. By evening they had visited four different cities.

In the afternoon, Hatch reviewed options with Perpich. They could a) call the special session and try to pass the proposal, b) modify the proposal and recommend only those provisions that had been tested in the courts, c) promote strong provisions restraining greenmail and golden parachutes, or d) do nothing at all. In the evening, Hatch attended a fund raiser in St. Cloud, in the heart of Minnesota's farming community. Once again he asked people about the plan to call a special session. Once again he received a negative response. People in attendance wanted to know when a special session would be called to help farmers in danger of losing their land.

Tuesday, June 23

In the morning, the results of the opinion poll commissioned over the weekend were released. A large majority of citizens, 85%, favored the special session and the proposed toughening of the takeover statute. At the Capitol, a joint meeting of the House Judiciary and Commerce Committees convened. Macke was the first to testify, but, as the *Minneapolis Star-Tribune* reported, his performance was anything but smooth. Out of his element and disconcerted by recent developments, he seemed nervous and abrupt. He told the committees that he not only believed in a free market, but also in a fair market. "During the last three weeks," he said, "30 percent of our stock was traded. This means that 30 percent of our stock is owned by people who have held it for less than three weeks." Later, an attorney representing DHC reported, "In 10 minutes or less, more than 3 percent of the stock changed hands this morning."

But the most startling moment came when Macke announced that another attempt to acquire the company had begun that morning. A $6.8 billion offer had been made by a Cincinnati stock analyst thought to be representing a wealthy Ohio family. In a matter of hours, the paper value of the company increased by nearly a billion dollars. By the afternoon, however, the offer was shown to be bogus and the stock analyst was found to have had a history of mental illness. The incident graphically underscored the volatility of the circumstances in which the company found itself, and drove home the urgency of the situation to the legislators.

Also that morning a variety of demands began to surface for additional agenda items, threatening to force the special session out of control. By afternoon, it became clear that compromises were necessary and that DHC needed to make some concessions in its proposed amendments.

No decision was reached by the Committees that night, except to postpone a recommendation for the governor until the following day. Macke and his team closed the day not knowing what recommendation to expect.

The joint House committees agreed on Wednesday, June 24, to recommend a special session to the governor, and endorsed a bill quite similar to what DHC proposed. But the hearings on the Senate side ran into trouble. Commerce Commissioner Hatch was determined to see that provisions were contained in the bill that made golden parachutes illegal and strongly discouraged greenmail. He threatened to recommend against a special session if he failed to receive support on these issues. "If you don't include them," he told the Senate hearing, "it's just big business crawling into bed with big government." DHC, however, opposed the greenmail provision. After considerable discussion, all sides agreed to language severely restricting both golden parachutes and greenmail. Senate leaders then decided to join the House in recommending a special session.

Legislative leaders met with Perpich in the afternoon and agreed on a very limited agenda for the special session. However, disagreement between the House and Senate versions of the bill surfaced. Perpich refused to call the special session until everyone agreed on one bill, and insisted that agreement be reached in time for an announcement on the 10:00 P.M. news.

Negotiations involving legislators from both houses and DHC lawyers began at 7:30 in the evening, and two hours later the House members left the meeting in frustration when they could not reach agreement over the question of a "sunset" provision. Communication resumed, however, and minutes before the 10:00 P.M. deadline, agreement was reached by phone. Perpich announced the special session on television and ordered the legislature to convene at 2:00 P.M. the following day.

The Provisions of the Bill

In 1986, the Indiana legislature passed the Control Share Acquisitions Act (CSAA). This statute placed restrictions on attempts to acquire a controlling interest in a company without approval of the board of directors, but only applied to those Indiana corporations that elected to be covered. Shortly after it went into effect, a company that was the apparent target of a hostile takeover chose to be protected by the act. The bidder immediately sued and a lower court found in its favor, as did the court of appeals. However, in April 1987, the U.S. Supreme Court reversed the decision and upheld the statute. Indiana's CSAA subsequently became the model for DHC's proposal, as well as for similar legislation in other states.

The bill proposed in the Minnesota legislature aimed to protect companies by addressing the problem of tender offers. It required approval of the majority of disinterested shareholders before a bidder could gain voting rights for a controlling share of the stock. It also required the approval of a majority of the disinterested members of the board of directors (i.e., those who were neither managers nor representatives of bidders) before the bidder could enter any business combination with the target. Furthermore, and perhaps most importantly, it prohibited the sale of a target company's assets to pay debts incurred in financing a hostile takeover for a period of five years.

One of the most controversial provisions of the Minnesota bill, however, was the stipulation that the board of directors of a target company could legitimately take into consideration the interests of a wide range of groups in exercising their "business judgment." In discharging their duties, directors were authorized to consider "the interests of the corporation's employees, customers, suppliers, and creditors, the economy of the state and nation, community and societal considerations, and the long-term as well as short-term interests of the corporation and its shareholders including the possibility that these interests may be best served by the continued independence of the corporation."

Finally, the bill introduced measures which virtually prohibited golden parachutes and the payment of greenmail, but the greenmail provision was not scheduled to become effective until some months afterwards.

Despite the rhetoric of the opposing speeches, the bill passed by an overwhelming margin: 120-5 in the House and 57-0 in the Senate. Perpich made the 10:00 P.M. news as he signed the bill into law.

Macke sent a letter to DHC's employees in Minnesota thanking them for their support. He also urged them to write their legislators once more to express their appreciation, and he invited them to corporate headquarters that day to sign a banner to be given to the governor.

DHC's corporation headquarters occupied several floors of the IDS Center, the tallest building in downtown Minneapolis. On the first floor of that building was a large enclosed courtyard and it was there that DHC held an enormous ice cream social for anyone who cared to come. A life-sized Santabear worked the crowd and hundreds of DHC employees stopped by to sign the giant banner that read simply, "Thanks, Minnesota."

⚜

Macke was angry, and only half-surprised, as he read the letter he just received from Herbert Haft. The raider was back.

The letter, dated July 23, 1987, announced that a new partnership had been formed under Haft's control, the Madison Partnership. The stated intention of this partnership was to purchase in excess of $15 million of outstanding DHC stock over the next twelve months, and perhaps even to acquire a controlling interest in the company. At the time that this letter was written, the Hafts owned a relatively small amount of DHC's stock. On Friday, the day after the letter was made public, DHC's stock rose $4.37, and closed at $52.00 per share.

In the following weeks, the Hafts took no further public action. Secretly, however, the Madison Partnership continued to purchase DHC stock, but stopped short of the 5 percent level which would have required SEC notification. As rumors circulated to the effect that DHC would have to restructure or recapitalize in order to fend off the Hafts, the company's stock price drifted between about $50.00 and $54.00 per share. Though some observers believed that the Hafts merely wanted to make a quick profit by putting the stock into play again, others began to think that they were serious about acquiring the company.

The silence was broken on Wednesday, September 17, 1987, when Macke received another letter from Herbert Haft. That same day the contents of the letter were released by the Hafts to the media. In this letter the Hafts proposed a business combination between DHC and a newly formed affiliate of the Dart Group, New Dayton Hudson. Assuming that DHC's board of directors approved, and that the necessary financing could be arranged, the Hafts proposed to pay DHC stockholders $65 in cash for 95% of their shares and stock in New Dayton Hudson for the balance. (The necessary financing included more than $5 billion in bank loans and $1.7 billion in junk bonds. The Hafts did not have a commitment for the bank loans, and the required bond issue was many times larger than any that their investment banker, Paine Webber, Inc., had handled before.)

The Hafts also made three notable concessions. First, they offered to continue DHC's "current policies regarding employees, management, suppliers, customers, community and corporate responsibilities, and support of charities." Second, they proposed that corporate headquarters would remain in Minneapolis. Third, they promised to donate to Minnesota charities any profits they might realize from their ownership of DHC's stock in the event that the shareholders disapproved of the acquisition agreement.

A variety of reactions followed almost immediately. Nearly 5.5 million shares of DHC stock changed hands the following day, up from 770,000 on the 17th, and the price rose from $52.87 to $58. On September 18, a class action lawsuit was filed by five DHC shareholders against the board of directors, which sought to force the board to negotiate with the Hafts. The suit charged the board with "gross abuse of trust." Though the next scheduled meeting of DHC's board of directors was to take place in October, Macke called an extraordinary meeting for Friday, September 25.

In the meantime, in a sharp departure from an established practice of avoiding publicity, Robert Haft made an unexpected visit to the Twin Cities on Monday, September 21. While there he arranged to give interviews to the local media and emphasized the Dart Group's determination to acquire *and* operate Dayton Hudson's businesses. Critical of DHC's management, he told the *Minneapolis Star Tribune*, "This thing is going downhill. The company has spent $3 billion [in expansion and remodeling funds] since 1982 and they've gotten virtually nothing from it." He also reaffirmed the promise to continue DHC's policy of contributions and community involvement, and emphatically denied that he and his father would accept greenmail.

Two days later, on September 23, Boake Sells, DHC's chief operating officer, announced his resignation. He left to take a management position with the Cleveland-based Revco D.S., Inc., which owned the Revco drug store chain. The company had recently been taken private through a leveraged buy-out and Sells was asked to become the new CEO. He insisted that the negotiations for the position began before the Dart Group's initial effort to acquire DHC, but to some observers the timing of the move indicated instability and internal division in DHC's top management team.

When DHC's board of directors met, it rejected the Haft's offer, saying "We believe that Dayton Hudson's shareholders and other constituencies should continue to have the opportunity to fully realize the benefits of the businesses we are operating." That day the stock price closed at $59.00 per share.

The following Tuesday, September 29, another letter from Herbert Haft was delivered to Macke. This letter, also released to the media, was substantially the same as the letter of September 17. However, the cash portion of the offer was raised to $68 per share. In addition, Haft urged the board of directors to arrange a meeting as soon as possible to discuss the proposal so that it could be placed before the stockholders "for their vote." Rather than call another special meeting, Macke planned to put this offer before the board at its regular October meeting.

That same day, the Hafts filed preliminary proxy materials with the SEC as a first step toward removing DHC's board of directors in favor of a board which would be receptive to their takeover proposal. According to the revised Minnesota takeover legislation, they needed support from shareholders controlling 25% of DHC's stock in order to call a special meeting. Observers noted that, since much of the stock was in the hands of speculators and institutional investors, that hurdle was probably not too difficult to overcome. DHC's stock closed that day at $59.75.

Ten days later, Governor Rudy Perpich of Minnesota entered the arena again. He sent a letter to the governors of seven other states in which DHC did a significant amount of business and in which there was a public pension fund with holdings of the company's stock. While he declined to make concrete suggestions about what the governors could do, he did remind them that DHC paid taxes, employed their citizens and made sizable charitable contributions in their states.

On Wednesday, October 14, DHC's board of directors once again rejected the Hafts' proposal. By then the company's stock price had fallen to $52.87 per share. The following day DHC filed in U.S. District Court against the Dart Group, charging that the Hafts were in violation of securities laws and regulations, and seeking to prevent them from soliciting proxies for an attempt to remove the members of the board. On October 16, calling the DHC suit "frivolous," the Hafts responded with their own suit, demanding current information about the identity of DHC's shareholders.

As each side prepared to do battle, however, events overtook them both. On Friday, October 16, DHC's stock participated in a sharp drop in prices across the board, and fell to $44.75 per share (see Exhibit 2).

The following Monday, October 19, the New York Stock Exchange experienced the single greatest drop in value in its history. The Dow Jones Index plummeted 508 points, and DHC's stock fell to $30.00 per share. Though it received little attention at the time, the SEC disclosed that same day that it was investigating the Dart Group's activities for possible violations of securities laws. The investigation was prompted by allegations that the company was operating as an unregistered investment firm.

On Tuesday, October 20, Robert Haft announced that the Dart Group had sold about a third of its shares in DHC and would not pursue its attempt to acquire the company. In an interview with the *Wall Street Journal*, he said, "The markets have changed so drastically that to continue would not be prudent." He added, however, that they were still determined to acquire a larger retailer and were confident that they would be able to do so in the future. "We're still optimistic people," he said.

A New York consultant specializing in corporate takeovers has commented that one of the most dangerous periods in the defensive process occurs immediately after the original raider is driven off. The surviving company is often weakened by its defensive efforts and its stock price may fall dramatically as the raider pulls out. At precisely this point the company may be especially vulnerable to another raider. In the wake of the stock market's sharp decline of October 19, DHC's management was aware that it needed to give some attention to the problem of the company's future, both immediately and in the long-term.

A strategy emerged that had three dimensions, or goals. According to one of the company's senior executives these three goals were 1) to control more of the stock, 2) to adapt to the changes in the company's environment, and 3) to achieve higher levels of performance.

In early 1987, as the Hafts began to consider their attempt to acquire DHC, there were approximately 97.4 million shares of the company's common stock outstanding. Between October 19, 1987 and January 31, 1988, the company repurchased 11.8 million shares for about $339.6 million (at an average value of $29 per share).

Because of the events of 1987, management realized that both the profile of the company's stockholders and the environment in which the company did business had changed. The stockholders were no longer individuals who shared the values of the company, but were often large institutional investors for whom performance tended to take precedence over good corporate citizenship. Furthermore, it became imperative to recognize where DHC's constituencies really were, and to find ways to serve them more effectively. As one executive put it, "The terms of the debate were changed forever. In June, the geography was Minnesota and New York. By October, the geography included every state in which Dayton Hudson did business."

Despite these events, DHC reaffirmed its commitment to its policy of community involvement even when faced with losses or declining growth in profitability. Nevertheless, changes were made in the company's pattern of corporate contributions. The managers of the Dayton Hudson Foundation were aware that the goal of improved performance had implications for their activities as well as for the profit centers of the company. For example, rather than separately channelling contributions through each of its operating divisions, the company began to process all its contributions through the Foundation. In this way, without retreating from its commitment to a 5% giving level, it sought to make its community involvement more visible and to show more clearly what its contributions were accomplishing.

Efforts were also begun to proportion contributions more closely to the amount of business the company did in each community. The kind of proxy fight threatened by the Hafts made it clear that stockholders, who were distributed throughout the country, and not predominantly in the upper Midwest as they had once been, needed to understand the consequences of their votes. As a result, it was critically important to export the company's long-standing policy of corporate community involvement outside of the headquarters community.

Following the successful defense of the company, Macke focused management's attention on the goal of creating value for stockholders through improved performance that would be at least equal to the value they would have received from the Hafts. According to a member of his management team, he was convinced that controlling more of the outstanding stock and making corporate community involvement more effective, while critically important, were not sufficient by themselves. The third leg of the tripod had to be the kind of performance that would pay off on his promise that it was best for all concerned that DHC remain independent and intact.

EPILOGUE

• DHC announced, in July of 1989, that it planned to create an Employee Stock Ownership Plan (ESOP). At the time of the announcement, approximately 77 million shares of common stock were outstanding, and the plan called for the acquisition of up to 7 milion shares.

• DHC's revenues for 1989 were $13.6 billion, a 47% increase over revenues for 1986. Earnings per share for 1989 were $5.35, a 104% increase. Return on beginning equity rose to 22%, from 14.5% in 1988 and 13.1% in 1986.

• In February, 1990, the Dart Group agreed to settle a complaint filed by the Securities and Exchange Commission which had charged the company with securities law violations. The SEC contended that, over a period of five years, the company had received so much of its income from trading stocks that it should be registered as an investment company, and so be subject to strict disclosure requirements. The settlement, however, did not require the Dart Group to register as an investment company, but did require them to abide by investment company rules and to make their books available for close SEC examination for a period of three years.

• On June 22, 1990, DHC completed the acquisition of the Chicago-based Marshall Field & Company, for just in excess of $1 billion.

• On June 25, 1990, exactly three years after the Minnesota legislature met in special session, DHC's stock closed at $71.38 per share.

NOTES

1. When a company's stockholder base becomes destabilized, i.e., when a large proportion of the stock is in the hands of short-term holders (arbitrageurs, for example), the company's stock is said to be "in play." Up to this point, strictly speaking, DHC's efforts were focused on preventing the stock from being put in play.
2. A very wide variety of social action projects were funded, including literacy programs, job skills training programs, development programs for minority businesses, and neighborhood renewal programs.
3. "Greenmail" is a payment made to a raider, and not to other stockholders, by a target company in exchange for the raider's stock, where the price paid is higher than the market value of the stock.

The Social Responsibility of Business Is to Increase Its Profits

MILTON FRIEDMAN

When I hear businessmen speak eloquently about the "social responsibilities of business in a free-enterprise system," I am reminded of the wonderful line about the Frenchman who discovered at the age of 70 that he had been speaking prose all his life. The businessmen believe that they are defending free enterprise when they declaim that business is not concerned "merely" with profit but also with promoting desirable "social" ends; that business has a "social conscience" and takes seriously its responsibilities for providing employment, eliminating discrimination, avoiding pollution and whatever else may be the catchwords of the contemporary crop of reformers. In fact they are—or would be if they or anyone else took them seriously—preaching pure and unadulterated socialism. Businessmen who talk this way are unwitting puppets of the intellectual forces that have been undermining the basis of a free society these past decades.

The discussions of the "social responsibilities of business" are notable for their analytical looseness and lack of rigor. What does it mean to say that "business" has responsibilities? Only people can have responsibilities. A corporation is an artificial person and in this sense may have artificial responsibilities, but "business" as a whole cannot be said to have responsibilities, even in this vague sense. The first step toward clarity to examining the doctrine of the social responsibility of business is to ask precisely what it implies for whom.

Presumably, the individuals who are to be responsible are businessmen, which means individual proprietors or corporate executives. Most of the discussion of social responsibility is directed at corporations, so in what follows I shall mostly neglect the individual proprietors and speak of corporate executives.

In a free-enterprise, private-property system, a corporate executive is an employee of the owners of the business. He has direct responsibility to his employers. That responsibility is to conduct the business in accordance with their desires, which generally will be to make as much money as possible while conforming to the basic rules of the society, both those embodied in law and those embodied in ethical custom. Of course, in some cases his employers may have a different objective. A group of persons might establish a corporation for an eleemosynary purpose—for example, a hospital or a school. The manager of such a corporation will not have money profit as his objectives but the rendering of certain services.

In either case, the key point is that, in his capacity as a corporate executive, the manager is the agent of the individuals who own the corporation or establish the eleemosynary institution, and his primary responsibility is to them.

Needless to say, this does not mean that it is easy to judge how well he is performing his task. But at least the criterion of performance is straightforward, and the persons among whom a voluntary contractual arrangement exists are clearly defined.

Of course, the corporate executive is also a person in his own right. As a person, he may have many other responsibilities that he recognizes or assumes voluntary—to his family, his conscience, his feelings of charity, his church, his clubs, his city, his country. He may feel impelled by these responsibilities to devote part of his income to causes he regards as worthy, to refuse to work for particular corporations, even to leave his job, for example, to join his country's armed forces. If we wish, we may refer to some of these responsibilities as "social responsibilities." But in these respects he is acting as a principal, not an agent; he is spending his own money or time or energy, not the money of his employers or the time or energy he has contracted to devote to their purposes. If these are "social responsibilities," they are the social responsibilities of individuals, not of business.

What does it mean to say that the corporate executive has a "social responsibility" in his capacity as businessman? If this statement is not pure rhetoric, it must mean that he is to act in some way that is not in the interest of his employers. For example, that he is to refrain from increasing the price of the product in order to contribute to the social objective of preventing inflation, even though a price increase would be in the best interests of the corporation. Or that he is to make expenditures on reducing pollution beyond the amount that is in the best interests of the corporation or that is required by law in order to contribute to the social objective of improving the environment. Or that, at the expense of corporate profits, he is to hire "hardcore" unemployed instead of better qualified available workmen to contribute to the social objective of reducing poverty.

In each of these cases, the corporate executive would be spending someone else's money for a general social interest. Insofar as his actions in accord with his "social responsibility" reduce returns to stockholders, he is spending their money. Insofar as his actions raise the price to customers, he is spending customers' money. Insofar as his actions lower the wages of some employees, he is spending their money.

The stockholders or the customers or the employees could separately spend their own money on the particular action if they wished to do so. The executive is exercising a distinct "social responsibility," rather than serving as an agent of the stockholders or the customers or the employees, only if he spends the money in a different way than they would have spent it.

But if he does this, he is in effect imposing taxes, on the one hand, and deciding how the tax proceeds shall be spent, on the other.

This process raises political questions on two levels: principle and consequences. On the level of political principle, the imposition of taxes and the expenditure of tax proceeds are governmental functions. We have established elaborate constitutional, parliamentary and judicial provisions to control these functions, to assure that taxes are imposed so far as possible in accordance with the preferences and desires of the public—after all, "taxation without representation" was one of the battle cries of the American Revolution. We have a system of checks and balances to separate the legislative function of imposing taxes and enacting expenditures from the executive function of collecting taxes and administering expenditure programs and from the judicial function of mediating disputes and interpreting the law.

Here the businessman—self-selected or appointed directly or indirectly by stockholders—is to be simultaneously legislator, executive and jurist. He is to decide whom to tax by how much and for what purpose, and he is to spend the proceeds—all this guided only by general exhortations from on high to restrain inflation, improve the environment, fight poverty and so on and on.

The whole justification for permitting the corporate executive to be selected by the stockholders is that the executive is an agent serving the interests of his principal. This justification disappears when the corporate executive imposes taxes and spends the proceeds for "social" purposes. He becomes in effect a public employee, a civil servant, even though he remains in name an employee of a private enterprise. On grounds of political principle, it is intolerable that such civil servants—insofar as their actions in the name of social responsibility are real and not just window dressing—should be selected as they are now. If they are to be civil servants, then they must be elected through a political process. If they are to impose taxes and make expenditures to foster "social" objectives, then political machinery must be set up to make the assessment of taxes and to determine through a political process the objectives to be served.

This is the basic reason why the doctrine of "social responsibility" involves the acceptance of the socialist view that political mechanisms, not market mechanisms, are the appropriate way to determine the allocation of scarce resources to alternative uses.

On the grounds of consequences, can the corporate executive in fact discharge his alleged "social responsibilities"? On the one hand, suppose he could get away with spending the stockholders' or customers' or employees' money. How is he to know how to spend it? He is told that he must contribute to fighting inflation. How is he to know what action of his will contribute to that end? He is presumably an expert in running his company—in producing a product or selling it or financing it. But nothing about his selection makes him an expert on inflation. Will his holding down the price of his product reduce inflationary pressure? Or, by leaving more spending power in the hands of his customers, simply divert it elsewhere? Or, by forcing him to produce less because of the lower price, will it simply contribute to shortages? Even if he could answer these questions, how much cost is he justified in imposing on his stockholders, customers, and employees for this social purpose? What is his appropriate share and what is the appropriate share of others?

And, whether he wants to or not, can he get away with spending his stockholders', customers' or employees' money? Will not the stockholders fire him? (Either the present ones or those who take over when his actions in the name of social responsibility have reduced the corporation's profits and the price of its stock.) His customers and his employees can desert him for other producers and employers less scrupulous in exercising their social responsibilities.

This facet of "social responsibility" doctrine is brought into sharp relief when the doctrine is used to justify wage restraint by trade unions. The conflict of interest is naked and clear when union officials are asked to subordinate the interest of their members to some more general purpose. If union officials try to enforce wage restraint, the consequence is likely to be wildcat strikes, rank-and-file revolts and the emergence of strong competitors for their jobs. We thus have the ironic phenomenon that union leaders—at least in the U.S.—have objected to Government interference with the market far more consistently and courageously than have business leaders.

The difficulty of exercising "social responsibility" illustrates, of course, the great virtue of private competitive enterprise—it forces people to be responsible for their own actions and makes it difficult for them to "exploit" other people for either selfish or unselfish purposes. They can do good—but only at their own expense.

Many a reader who has followed the argument this far may be tempted to remonstrate that it is all well and good to speak of Government's having the responsibility to impose taxes and determine expenditures for such "social" purposes as controlling pollution or training the hard-core unemployed, but that the problems are too urgent to wait on the slow course of political processes, that the exercise of social responsibility by businessmen is a quicker and surer way to solve pressing current problems.

Aside from the question of fact—I share Adam Smith's skepticism about the benefits that can be expected from "those who affect to trade for the public good"—this argument must be rejected on grounds of principle. What it amounts to is an assertion that those who favor the taxes and expenditures in question have failed to persuade a majority of their fellow citizens to be of like mind and that they are seeking to attain by undemocratic procedures what they cannot attain by democratic procedures. In a free society it is hard for "evil" people to do "evil," especially since one man's good is another's evil.

I have, for simplicity, concentrated on the special case of the corporate executive, except only for the brief digression on trade unions. But precisely the same argument applies to the newer phenomenon of calling upon stockholders to require corporations to exercise social responsibility (the recent G.M. crusade for example). In most of these cases, what is in effect involved is some stockholders trying to get other stockholders (or customers or employees) to contribute against their will to "social" causes favored by the activists. Insofar as they succeed, they are again imposing taxes and spending the proceeds.

The situation of the individual proprietor is somewhat different. If he acts to reduce the returns of his enterprise in order to exercise his "social responsibility," he is spending his own money, not someone else's. If he wishes to spend his money on such purposes, that is his right, and I cannot see that there is any objection to his doing so. In the process, he, too, may impose costs on employees and customers. However, because he is far less likely than a large corporation or union to have monopolistic power, any such side effects will tend to be minor.

Of course, in practice the doctrine of social responsibility is frequently a cloak for actions that are justified on other grounds rather than a reason for those actions.

To illustrate, it may well be in the long-run interest of a corporation that is a major employer in a small community to devote resources to providing amenities to that community or to improving its government. That may make it easier to attract desirable employees, it may reduce the wage bill or lessen losses from pilferage and sabotage or have other worthwhile effects. Or it may be that, given the laws about the deductibility of corporate charitable contributions, the stockholders can contribute more to charities they favor by having the corporation make the gift than by doing it themselves, since they can in that way contribute an amount that would otherwise have been paid as corporate taxes.

In each of these—and many similar—cases, there is a strong temptation to rationalize these actions as an exercise of "social responsibility." In the present climate of opinion, with its widespread aversion to "capitalism," "profits," and "soulless corporation" and so on, this is one way for a corporation to generate goodwill as a by-product of expenditures that are entirely justified in its own self-interest.

It would be inconsistent of me to call on corporate executives to refrain from this hypocritical window-dressing because it harms the foundations of a free society. That would be to call on them to exercise a "social responsibility"! If our institutions, and the attitudes of the public make it in their self-interest to cloak their actions in this way, I cannot summon much indignation to denounce them. At the same time, I can express admiration for those individual proprietors or owners of closely held corporations or stockholders of more broadly held corporations who disdain such tactics as approaching fraud.

Whether blameworthy or not, the use of the cloak of social responsibility, and the nonsense spoken in its name by influential and prestigious businessmen, does clearly harm the foundations of a free society. I have been impressed time and again by the schizophrenic character of many businessmen. They are capable of being extremely far-sighted and clearheaded in matters that are internal to their businesses. They are incredibly short-sighted and muddle-headed in matters that are outside their businesses but affect the possible survival of business in general. This short-sightedness is strikingly exemplified in the calls from many businessmen for wage and price guidelines or controls or income policies. There is nothing that could do more in a brief period to destroy a market system and replace it by a centrally controlled system than effective governmental control of prices and wages.

The short-sightedness is also exemplified in speeches by businessmen on social responsibility. This may gain them kudos in the short run. But it helps to strengthen the already too prevalent view that the pursuit of profits is wicked and immoral and must be curbed and controlled by external forces. Once this view is adopted, the external forces that curb the market will not be the social consciences, however highly developed, of the pontificating executives; it will be the iron fist of Government bureaucrats. Here, as with price and wage controls, businessmen seem to me to reveal a suicidal impulse.

The political principle that underlies the market mechanism is unanimity. In an ideal free market resting on private property, no individual can coerce any other, all cooperation is voluntary, all parties to such cooperation benefit or they need not participate. There are no values, no "social" responsibilities in any sense other than the shared values and responsibilities of individuals. Society is a collection of individuals and of the various groups they voluntarily form.

The political principle that underlies the political mechanism is conformity. The individual must serve a more general social interest—whether that be determined by a church or a dictator or a majority. The individual may have a vote and say in what is to be done, but if he is overruled, he must conform. It is appropriate for some to require others to contribute to a general social purpose whether they wish to or not.

Unfortunately, unanimity is not always feasible. There are some respects in which conformity appears unavoidable, so I do not see how one can avoid the use of the political mechanism altogether.

But the doctrine of "social responsibility" taken seriously would extend the scope of the political mechanism to every human activity. It does not differ in philosophy from the most explicitly collectivist doctrine. It differs only by professing to believe that collectivist ends can be attained without collectivist means. That is why, in my book *Capitalism and Freedom*, I have called it a "fundamentally subversive doctrine" in a free society, and I have said that in such a society, "there is one and only one social responsibility of business—to use its resources and engage in activities designed to increase its profits so long as it stays within the rules of the game, which is to say, engages in open and free competition without deception or fraud."

Social Responsibility and Economic Efficiency

KENNETH J. ARROW

This paper makes some observations on the widespread notion that the individual has some responsibility to others in the conduct of his economic affairs. It is held that there are a number of circumstances under which the economic agent should forgo profit or other benefits to himself in order to achieve some social goal, especially to avoid a disservice to other individuals. For the purpose of keeping the discussion within bounds, I shall confine my attention to the obligations that might be imposed on business firms. Under what circumstances is it reasonable to expect a business firm to refrain from maximizing its profits because it will hurt others by doing so? What institutions can we expect to serve the function not merely of limiting profits but of limiting them in just those ways that will avoid harm to others? Is it reasonable to expect that ethical codes will arise or be created? My purpose in discussing these questions is not so much to achieve definitive answers as to analyze the kinds of consideration that enter into discussing them.

First of all, it may be well to review what possible ways there are by which the economic activity of one firm may affect other members of the economy. A substantial list comes to mind; a few illustrations will serve. A firm affects others by competing with them in the product markets and in the factor markets, in the buying of labor, buying of other goods for its use, and in the selling of its products. It pays wages to others. It buys goods

This is a revised version of the Carl Synder Memorial Lecture delivered at the University of California, Santa Barbara, April 1972.

Kenneth J. Arrow, Professor of Economics, Harvard University, *Public Policy*, Vol. XXi, No. 3, Summer, 1973. Reprinted by permission.

from others. It sets prices to its customers, and so enters into an economic relation with them. The firm typically sets working conditions, including— of greatest importance—conditions that affect the health and possibility for accident within the plant. We are reminded in recent years that the firm, as well as the private individual, is a contributor to pollution. Pollution has a direct effect on the welfare of other members of the economy. Less mentioned, but of the same type, are the effects of economic activity on congestion. Bringing a new plant into an already crowded area is bound to create costs, disservices, and disutilities to others in the area if by nothing else than by crowding the streets and the sidewalks and imposing additional burdens on the public facilities of the area. Indeed, although congestion has not been discussed as much as has pollution, it may have greater economic impact and probably even greater health costs. Certainly the number of automobile deaths arising from accidents far exceeds the health hazards arising from automobile pollution. The firm affects others through determining the quality of its products, and again, among the many aspects of product quality we may especially single out the qualities of the product with respect to its pollution-creating ability, as in the case of automobiles, and with respect to its safety, the hazards it poses to its user. The question of social responsibility takes very different forms with regard to the different items on this varied list. It is not a uniform characteristic at all.

Let us first consider the case against social responsibility: the assumption that the firms should aim simply to maximize their profits. One strand of that argument is empirical rather than ethical or normative. It simply states that firms *will* maximize their profits. The impulse to gain, it is argued, is very strong and the incentives for selfish behavior are so great that any kind of control is likely to be utterly ineffectual. This argument has some force but is by no means conclusive. Any mechanism for enforcing or urging social responsibility upon firms must of course reckon with a profit motive, with a desire to evade whatever response of controls are imposed. But it does not mean that we cannot expect any degree of responsibility at all.

One finds a rather different argument, frequently stated by some economists. It will probably strike the noneconomist as rather strange, at least at first hearing. The assertion is that firms *ought* to maximize profits; not merely do they like to do so but there is practically a social obligation to do so. Let me briefly sketch the argument:

Firms buy the goods and services they need for production. What they buy they pay for and therefore they are paying for whatever costs they impose upon others. What they receive in payment by selling their goods, they receive because the purchaser considers it worthwhile. This is a world of voluntary contracts; nobody *has* to buy the goods. If he chooses to buy it, it must be that he is getting a benefit measured by the price he pays. Hence, it is argued, profit really represents the net contribution that the firm makes to the social good, and the profits should therefore be made as large as possible. When firms compete with each other, in selling their goods or in buying labor or other services, they may have to lower their selling prices in order to get more of the market for themselves or raise their wages; in either case the benefits which the firm is deriving are in some respects shared with the population at large. The forces of competition prevent the firms from engrossing too large a share of the social benefit. For example, if a firm tries to reduce the quality of its goods, it will sooner or later have to lower the price which it charges because the purchaser will no longer find it worthwhile to pay the high price. Hence, the consumers will gain from price reduction at the same time as they are losing through quality deterioration. On detailed analysis it appears the firm will find it privately profitable to reduce quality under these circumstances only if, in fact, quality reduction is a net social benefit, that is, if the saving in cost is worth more to the consumer than the quality reduction. Now, as far as it goes this argument is sound. The problem is that it may not go far enough.

Under the proper assumptions profit maximization is indeed efficient in the sense that it can achieve as high a level of satisfaction as possible for any one consumer without reducing the levels of satisfaction of other consumers or using more resources than society is endowed with. But the limits of the argument must be stressed. I want to mention two well-known points in passing without making them the principal focus of discussion. First of all, the argument assumes that the forces of competition are sufficiently vigorous. But there is no social justification for profit maximization by monopolies. This is an important and well-known qualification. Second, the distribution of income that results from unrestrained profit maximization is very unequal. The competitive maximizing economy is indeed efficient—this shows up in high average incomes—but the high average is accompanied by widespread poverty on the one hand and vast riches, at least for a few, on the other. To many of us this is a very undesirable consequence.

Profit maximization has yet another effect on society. It tends to point away from the expression of altruistic motives. Altruistic motives are motives whose gratification is just as legitimate as selfish motives, and the expression of those motives is something we probably wish to encourage. A profit-maximizing, self-centered form of economic behavior does not provide any room for the expression of such motives.

If the three problems above were set aside, many of the ways by which firms affect others should not be tampered with. Making profits by competition is, if anything, to be encouraged rather than discouraged. Wage and price bargains between the firm and uncoerced workers and customers represent mutually beneficial exchanges. There is, therefore, no reason within the framework of the discussion to interfere with them. But these examples far from exhaust the list of interactions with which we started. The social desirability of profit maximization does not extend to all the interactions on the list. There are two categories of effects where the arguments for profit maximization break down: The first is illustrated by pollution or congestion. Here it is no longer true (and this is the key to these issues) that the firm in fact does pay for the harm it imposes on others. When it takes a person's time and uses it at work, the firm is paying for this, and therefore the transaction can be regarded as a beneficial exchange from the point of view of both parties. We have no similar mechanism by which the pollution which a firm imposes upon its neighborhood is paid for. Therefore the firm will have a tendency to pollute more than is desirable. That is, the benefit to it or to its customers from the expanded activity is really not as great, or may not be as great, as the cost it is imposing upon the neighborhood. But since it does not pay that cost, there is no profit incentive to refrain.

The same argument applies to traffic congestion when no change is made for the addition of cars or trucks on the highway. It makes everybody less comfortable. It delays others and increases the probability of accidents; in short, it imposes a cost upon a large number of members of the society, a cost which is not paid for by the imposer of the cost, at least not in full. The person congesting is also congested, but the costs he is imposing on others are much greater than those he suffers himself. Therefore there will be a tendency to over-utilize those goods for which no price is charged, particularly scarce highway space.

There are many other examples of this kind, but these two will serve to illustrate the point in question: some effort must be made to alter the profit-maximizing behavior of firms in those cases where it is imposing costs on others which are not easily compensated through an appropriate set of prices.

The second category of effects where profit maximization is not socially desirable is that in which there are quality effects about which the firm knows more than the buyer. In my examples I will cite primarily the case of quality in the product sold, but actually very much the same considerations apply to the quality of working conditions. The firm is frequently in a better position to know the consequences (the health hazards, for example) involved in working conditions than the worker is, and the considerations I am about to discuss in the case of sale of goods have a direct parallel in the analysis of working conditions in the relation of a firm to its workers. Let me illustrate by considering the sale of a used car. (Similar considerations apply to the sale of new cars.) A used car has potential defects and typically the seller knows more about the defects than the buyer. The buyer is not in a position to distinguish among used cars, and therefore he will be willing to pay the same amount for two used cars of differing quality because he cannot tell the difference between them. As a result, there is an inefficiency in the sale of used cars. If somehow or other the cars were distinguished as to their quality, there would be some buyers who would prefer a cheaper car with more defects because they intend to use it very little or they only want it for a short period, while others will want a better car at a higher price. In fact, however, the two kinds of car are sold indiscriminately to the two groups of buyers at the same price, so that we can argue that there is a distinct loss of consumer satisfaction imposed by the failure to convey information that is available to the seller. The buyers are not necessarily being cheated. They may be, but the problem of inefficiency would remain if they weren't. One can imagine a situation where, from past experience, buyers of used cars are aware that cars that look alike may turn out to be quite different. Without knowing whether a particular car is good or bad, they do know that there are good and bad cars, and of course their willingness to pay for the cars is influenced accordingly. The main loser from a monetary viewpoint may not be the customer, but rather the seller of the good car. The buyer will pay a price which is only appropriate to a lottery that gives him a good car or a bad car with varying probabilities, and therefore the seller of the good car gets less than the value of the car. The seller of the bad car is, of course, the beneficiary. Clearly then, if one could arrange to transmit the truth from the sellers to the buyers, the efficiency of the market would be greatly improved. The used-car illustration is an example of a very general phenomenon.

Consider now any newly produced complex product, such as a new automobile. The seller is bound to know considerably more about its properties than all but a very few of its buyers. In order to develop the car, the producer has had to perform tests of one kind or another. He knows the outcome of the tests. Failure to reveal this knowledge works against the efficiency of satisfying consumers' tastes. The argument of course applies to any aspect of the quality of a product, durability or the ability to perform under trying circumstances or differing climatic conditions. Perhaps we are most concerned about the safety features of the automobile. The risks involved in the use of automobiles are not trivial, and the kind of withholding of safety information which has been revealed to exist in a number of cases certainly cannot be defended as a socially useful implication of profit maximization. The classical efficiency arguments for profit maximization do not apply here, and it is wrong to obfuscate the issue by invoking them.

Perhaps even more dramatic, though on a smaller scale, are the repeated examples of misleading information about the risks and use of prescription drugs and other chemicals. These again manifest the same point. Profit maximization can lead to consequences which are clearly socially injurious. This is the case if the buyers are on the average deceived—if, for example, they have higher expectations than are in fact warranted. They are also injured when on the average they are not deceived but merely uncertain, although here the argument is more subtle. One consequence may be the excessively limited use of some new drugs, for example. If the users of the drugs become fully aware of the risks involved but are not able to assess the risk with respect to any particular drug, the result may be an indiscriminate rejection of new treatments which is rational from the point of view of the user; this, in the long run, may be just as serious an error as the opposite.

Defenders of unrestricted profit maximization usually assume that the consumer is well informed or at least that he becomes so by his own experience, in repeated purchases, or by information about what has happened to other people like him. This argument is empirically shaky; even the ability of individuals to analyze the effects of their own past purchases may be limited, particularly with respect to complicated mechanisms. But there are two further defects. The risks, including death, may be so great that even one misleading experience is bad enough, and the opportunity to learn from repeated trials is not of much use. Also, in a world where the products are continually changing, the possibility of learning from experience is greatly reduced. Automobile companies are continually introducing new models which at least purport to differ from what they were in the past, though doubtless the change is more external than internal. New drugs are being introduced all the time; the fact that one has had bad experiences with one drug may provide very little information about the next one.

Thus there are two types of situation in which the simple rule of maximizing profits is socially inefficient: the case in which costs are not paid for, as in pollution, and the case in which the seller has considerably more knowledge about his product than the buyer, particularly with regard to safety. In these situations it is clearly desirable to have some idea of social responsibility, that is, to experience an obligation, whether ethical, moral, or legal. Now we cannot expect such an obligation to be created out of thin air. To be meaningful, any obligation of this kind, any feeling or rule of behavior has to be embodied in some definite social institution. I use that term broadly: a legal code is a social institution in a sense. Exhortation to do good must be made specific in some external form, a steady reminder and perhaps enforcer of desirable values. Part of the need is simply for factual information as a guide to individual behavior. A firm may need to be told what is right and what is wrong when in fact it is polluting, or which safety requirements are reasonable and which are too extreme or too costly to be worth consideration. Institutionalization of the social responsibility of firms also serves another very important function. It provides some assurance to any one firm that the firms with which it is in competition will also accept the same responsibility. If a firm has some code imposed from the outside, there is some expectation that other firms will obey it too and therefore there is some assurance that it need not fear any excessive cost to its good behavior.

Let me then turn to some alternative kinds of institutions that can be considered as embodying the possible social responsibilities of firms. First, we have legal regulation, as in the case of pollution where laws are passed about the kind of burning that may take place, and about setting maximum standards for emissions. A second category is that of taxes. Economists, with good reason, like to preach taxation as opposed to regulation. The movement to tax polluting emissions is getting under way and there is a fairly widely backed proposal in Congress to tax sulfur dioxide emissions from industrial smokestacks. That is an example of the second kind of institutionalization of social responsibility. The responsibility is made very clear: the violator pays for violations.

A third very old remedy or institution is that of legal liability—the liability of the civil law. One can be sued for damages. Such cases apparently go back to the Middle Ages. Regulation also extends back very far. There was an ordinance in London about the year 1300 prohibiting the burning of coal, because of the smoke nuisance.

The fourth class of institutions is represented by ethical codes. Restraint is achieved not by appealing to each individual's conscience but rather by having some generally understood definition of appropriate behavior. Let me discuss the advantages and disadvantages of these four institutions.

In regard to the first two, regulation and taxes, I shall be rather brief because these are the more familiar. We can have regulations governing pollution. We can also regulate product safety. We may even have standards to insure quality in dimensions other than safety. The chief drawback of direct regulation is associated with the fact that it is hard to make regulations flexible enough to meet a wide variety of situations and yet simple enough to be enforceable. In addition, there is a slowness in response to new situations. For example, if a new chemical, such as a pesticide, comes on the market and after a period of time is recognized as a danger, it requires a long and complicated process to get this awareness translated into legal action. One problem is that legislative time is a very scarce factor; a proposal to examine the problems involved in some pesticide may at any given time be competing with totally different considerations for the attention of the legislature or regulatory body. In short, there is considerable rigidity in most regulatory structures. For certain purposes it is clear that regulation is best but it is equally clear that it is not useful as a universal device. In the case of taxes on the effects, rather than on the causes, there is a little more built-in flexibility. To combat pollution, taxation is probably the most appropriate device; a tax is imposed on the emission by the plant, whether in water or in air. Now this means the plant is free to find its own way of minimizing the tax burden. It is not told it must do one thing, such as raising smokestacks to a certain height. It is free to try to find the cheapest way of meeting the pollution problem. It may well decide that the profitability situation is such that it will continue to pollute and sell the product presumably at a somewhat higher price. This decision is not necessarily bad; it implies that the product is in fact much desired and it provides an automatic test of the market to see whether it is worth polluting or not, because in effect the consumer is ultimately paying for the pollution he induces. However, it is difficult to see how this method, useful though it is in the case of pollution, would have any relevance to safety, to see how one could frame a tax which would make very much sense. Taxation appears to be a rather blunt instrument for controlling product safety.

Legal liability can be and has been applied; i.e., courts have allowed damages in cases arising out of pollution or out of injury or death due to unsafe products. The nature of the law in this area is still evolving; under our system this means that it is being developed by a sequence of court decisions. Just exactly what the company or its officers have to know before they can be regarded as liable for damages due to unsafe products is not yet clear. No doubt it would certainly be held even today that if officers of a company were aware that a product had a significant probability of a dangerous defect and they sold it anyway without saying so, and if the defect occurred, legal liability would be clear. But it is frequently hard to establish such knowledge. No doubt if society wants to use the route of legal liability as a way of imposing social responsibility, then it can change the principles on which the decision is based. For example, one might throw the burden of proof on the company, so that in the case of any new product they have to run tests to show positively that it is safe. Their failure to make such tests would be an indication of their liability. One could imagine changes of this kind which would bring the law more into line with what is desirable. But there are some intrinsic defects in the liability route which, in my opinion, make it unsuitable in its present form as a serious method of achieving social control or of imposing responsibility on profit-making firms. First, litigation is costly. In many cases there are social wrongs or social inefficiencies which are quite significant in the aggregate and are perceived by a large number of people, each of whom bears a small part of the cost. This is characteristic of pollution and may be the case with certain kinds of quality standards. It really does not pay any particular person to sue, and if a few people do sue it does not really do the company much harm.

Another problem is that the notion of liability in law is really too simple a concept. Legal liability tends to be an all-or-none proposition. Consider a product such as plastic bags. They are perfectly all right for storing clothes or food but there is a risk that small children will misuse them, with serious consequences. One would hardly want to say that there is any legal liability ascribable to the plastic-bag makers, for even the safest product can be misused. On the other hand, one might argue that a product that can be misused ought to be somewhat discouraged and perhaps some small degree of responsibility should be imposed, particularly if no adequate warning is issued. The law does not permit any such distinctions. Thus, in an automobile case, one party or the other must be found wrong, even though in fact a crash may clearly be due to the fact that both drivers were behaving erratically, and it would be reasonable to have some splitting of responsibility. At present, with some minor exceptions, the law does not permit this, and I suppose it would confuse legal proceedings irreparably to start introducing partial causation. Economists are accustomed to the idea that almost nothing happens without the cooperation of a number of factors, and we have large bodies of doctrine devoted to imputing in some appropriate way the consequences of an action to all of its causes. It is for these reasons that this kind of crude liability doctrine seems to be unsuitable in many cases.

A number of other problems with litigation could be mentioned. Consider very high-risk situations that involve a very low probability of death or other serious adverse consequence, as in the case of drugs, or possible radiation from nuclear power plants. The insurance companies are willing to insure because the probability is low. But once insurance is introduced the incentive to refrain from incurring the risk is dulled. If you are insured against a loss you have less of an incentive to prevent it. In the field of automobile liability, it has become clear that the whole system of liability has to a very great extent broken down. The result is a widespread movement toward no-fault insurance, which in effect means people are compensated for their losses but no attempt is made to charge damages to the persons responsible. Responsibility is left undecided.

Finally, litigation does not seem suitable for continuing problems. Pollution will be reduced but not eliminated; indeed it is essentially impossible to eliminate it. There remain continuous steady damages to individuals. These should still be charged to firms in order to prevent them from polluting more. But enforcement by continuous court action is a very expensive way of handling a repetitive situation. It is silly to keep on going to court to establish the same set of facts over and over again. For these reasons taxes which have the same incentive effects are superior.

Let me turn to the fourth possibility, ethical code. This may seem to be a strange possibility for an economist to raise. But when there is a wide difference in knowledge between the two sides of the market, recognized ethical codes can be, as has already been suggested, a great contribution to economic efficiency. Actually we do have examples of this in our everyday lives, but in very limited areas. The case of medical ethics is the most striking. By its very nature there is a very large difference in knowledge between the buyer and the seller. One is, in fact, buying precisely the service of someone with much more knowledge than you have. To make this relationship a viable one, ethical codes have grown up over the centuries, both to avoid the possibility of exploitation by the physician and to assure the buyer of medical services that he is not being exploited. I am not suggesting that these are universally obeyed, but there is a strong presumption that the doctor is going to perform to a large extent with your welfare in mind. Unnecessary medical expenses or other abuses are perceived as violations of ethics. There is a powerful ethical background against which we make this judgment. Behavior that we would regard as highly reprehensible in a physician is judged less harshly when found among businessmen. The medical profession is typical of professions in general. All professions involve a situation in which knowledge is unequal on two sides of the market by the very definition of the profession, and therefore there have grown up ethical principles that afford some protection to the client. Notice there is a mutual benefit in this. The fact is that if you had sufficient distrust of a doctor's services, you wouldn't buy them. Therefore the physician wants an ethical code to act as assurance to the buyer, and he certainly wants his competitors to obey this same code, partly because any violation may put him at a disadvantage but more especially because the violation will reflect on him, since the buyer of the medical services may not be able to distinguish one doctor from another. A close look reveals that a great deal of economic life depends for its viability on a certain limited degree of ethical commitment. Purely selfish behavior of individuals is really incompatible with any kind of settled economic life. There is almost invariably some element of trust and confidence. Much business is done on the basis of verbal assurance. It would be too elaborate to try to get written commitments on every possible point. Every contract depends for its observance on a mass of unspecified conditions which suggest that the performance will be carried out in good faith without insistence on sticking literally to its wording. To put the matter in its simplest form, in almost every economic transaction, in any exchange of goods for money, somebody gives up his valuable asset before he gets the other's, either the goods are given before the money or the money is given before the goods. Moreover there is a general confidence that there won't be any violation of the implicit agreement. Another example in daily life of this kind of ethics is the observance of queue discipline. People line up; there are people who try to break in ahead of you, but there is an ethic which holds that this is bad. It is clearly an ethic which is in everybody's interest to preserve; one waits at the end of the line this time, and one is protected against somebody's coming in ahead of him.

In the context of product safety, efficiency would be greatly enhanced by accepted ethical rules. Sometimes it may be enough to have an ethical compulsion to reveal all the information available and let the buyer choose. This is not necessarily always the best. It can be argued that under some circumstances setting minimum safety standards and simply not putting out products that do not meet them would be desirable and should be felt by the businessman to be an obligation.

Now I've said that ethical codes are desirable. It doesn't follow from that that they will come about. An ethical code is useful only if it is widely accepted. Its implications for specific behavior must be moderately clear, and above all it must be clearly perceived that the acceptance of these ethical obligations by everybody does involve mutual gain. Ethical codes that lack the latter property are unlikely to be viable. How do such codes develop? They may develop as a consensus out of lengthy public discussion of obligations, discussion which will take place in legislatures, lecture halls, business journals, and other public forums. The codes are communicated by the very process of coming to an agreement. A more formal alternative would be to have some highly prestigious group discuss ethical codes for safety standards. In either case to become and to remain a part of the economic environment, the codes have to be accepted by the significant operating institutions and transmitted from one generation of executives to the next through standard operating procedures, through education in business schools, and through indoctrination of one kind or another. If we seriously expect such codes to develop and to be maintained, we might ask how the agreements develop and above all, how the codes remain stable. After all, an ethical code, however much it may be in the interest of all, is, as we remarked earlier, not in the interest of any one firm. The code may be of value to the running of the system as a whole, it may be of value to all firms if all firms maintain it, and yet it will be to the advantage of any one firm to cheat—in fact the more so, the more other firms are sticking to it. But there are some reasons for thinking that ethical codes can develop and be stable. These codes will not develop completely without institutional support. That is to say, there will be need for focal organizations, such as government agencies, trade associations, and consumer defense groups, or all combined to make the codes explicit, to iterate their doctrine and to make their presence felt. Given that help, I think the emergence of ethical codes on matters such as safety at least, is possible. One positive factor here is something that is a negative factor in other contexts, namely that our economic organization is to such a large extent composed of large firms. The corporation is no longer a single individual; it is a social organization with internal social ties and internal pressures for acceptability and esteem. The individual members of the corporation are not only parts of the corporation but also members of a larger society whose esteem is desired. Power in a large corporation is necessarily diffused; not many individuals in such organizations feel so thoroughly identified with the corporation that other kinds of social pressures become irrelevant. Furthermore, in a large, complex firm where many people have to participate in any decision, there are likely to be some who are motivated to call attention to violations of the code. This kind of check has been conspicuous in government in recent years. The Pentagon Papers are an outstanding illustration of the fact that within the organization there are those who recognize moral guilt and take occasion to blow the whistle. I expect the same sort of behavior to occur in any large organization when there are well-defined ethical rules whose violation can be observed.

One can still ask if the codes are likely to be stable. Since it may well be possible and profitable for a minority to cheat, will it not be true that the whole system may break down? In fact, however, some of the pressures work in the other direction. It is clearly in the interest of those who are obeying the codes to enforce them, to call attention to violations, to use the ethical and social pressures of the society at large against their less scrupulous rivals. At the same time the value of maintaining the system may well be apparent to all, and no doubt ways will be found to use the assurance of quality generated by the system as a positive asset in attracting consumers and workers.

One must not expect miraculous transformations in human behavior. Ethical codes, if they are to be viable, should be limited in their scope. They are not a universal substitute for the weapons mentioned earlier, the institutions, taxes, regulations, and legal remedies. Further, we should expect the codes to apply only in situations where the firm has superior knowledge of the situation. I would not want the firm to act in accordance with some ethical principles in regard to matters of which it has little knowledge. For example, with quality standards which consumers can observe, it may not be desirable that the firm decide for itself, at least on ethical grounds, because it is depriving the consumer of the freedom of choice between high-quality, high-cost and low-quality, low-cost products. It is in areas where someone is typically misinformed or imperfectly informed that ethical codes can contribute to economic efficiency.

Justice

Case Study

International Computer Sales

Laura Nadel and Hesh Wiener

Would you sell a computer to Hitler?

You remember Hitler. He maimed, tortured, and killed millions of people. They were, as far as he was concerned, enemies of the state. That, he felt, was enough.

Some people escaped. But imagine if Hitler had had a computer to keep track of his victims and intended victims. Log in. Type GIVE ME THE NAMES OF 20 JEWS AND 30 CATHOLICS IN BERLIN. And . . . but why go on? Hitler died a long time ago. These things don't happen anymore. Or do they?

There are countries on this earth with governments so cruel that you can't find words to condemn their actions. And these governments carry out their missions, it seems, with the aid of computers. American computers.

In Chile, Uruguay, Argentina, or Brazil, an agent of the secret police can come to your door and ask you detailed questions about one of your friends—or even about someone you hardly know. If you do not answer satisfactorily, you may be threatened or taken away.

If you are taken away by the secret police, you may be tortured. According to the United Nations report, you could be hung upside down in a vat of urine or forced to eat vomit until your memory improves. If it doesn't what follows will make you wish you had drowned in the tank in which you were hanging. You may be told that your loved ones will be treated even more harshly, although you probably can't imagine what more harshly means.

Like all modern police forces, secret police agencies have the latest in crime information systems, as sophisticated as their governments can afford. For example, according to a knowledgeable refugee, the Chilean government's computer systems store complete information about "the opposi-

Laura Nadel and Hesh Wiener, "Would You Sell a Computer to Hitler?" Reprinted from *Computer Decisions*, February 1977, pp. 22–26, © 1977, Hayden Publishing Company.

tion, those considered leftists or suspects. The computer has all the facts." In South America, such systems are running on American computers—the United States is the technological supplier of choice in this hemisphere.

The American computer manufacturers that supply Latin American governments with computers say they are not aware that their machines are used by the secret police. But they do concede that it is not possible for them to control how their machines are used by their customers. Most vendors say that they cannot take responsibility for the ultimate use to which their products are put.

"We are in a position similar to a car manufacturer," says IBM's director of information, Dan Burnham. "If General Motors sells you a car, and you use it to kill someone, that doesn't make General Motors responsible.

"Once the manufacturer sells the automobile, there's no guarantee it won't be used to commit a crime."

Control Data Corp.'s vice president Roger G. Wheeler, speaking for that company, concedes the responsibility of a manufacturer, especially a manufacturer of computers of awesome capacity. CDC, alone among American mainframe vendors, has a corporate policy governing the sale of its machines.

"Our own sense of responsibility," says Wheeler, "would not permit us to provide a computer system for any purpose that abridges human rights and dignity."

Asked whether IBM has a similar policy, Dan Udell, and IBM public relations officer, said that "IBM's official policy is to act in accordance with U.S. national policy in dealing with all countries."

IBM has substantial interests in Latin America. In Brazil, for example, IBM's factory in São Paulo makes System 370s. In Argentina, IBM builds high-speed line printers. In Uruguay, IBM has an enormous service bureau and data center. In Chile, IBM has no plants but does have a data center in Santiago.

It is in Santiago that the DINA, Chile's secret police, is headquartered. In the old offices of the Pan American Bank, an eight-story building, the DINA directors oversee their work. Sources say that there are computers in this building, computers of American manufacture, which may well be linked to other DINA offices and police organizations by Chile's sophisticated telecommunications complex.

Communications links in Chile include a modern ITT telephone system said to be as good as any in the United States, an extensive microwave network for long distance communications, satellite links, and government radio channels. These facilities enable the DINA to keep in touch with its more specialized offices.

On Jose Arietta street, on the outskirts of the Chilean capital, is a building officially known as Villa Grimaldi, commonly called the Palace of Laughter. It is here that victims of the secret police may be taken for torture. Ultimately, victims are sent to concentration camps or prisons, of which there are many in Chile. Villa Grimaldi, according to United Nations sources, has extensive communications equipment.

The use of computers by the secret police in Chile was first brought to public attention by the National Council of Churches. Reports received by the council indicated that an American computer was destined to become a tool of the DINA.

NCC representatives went to an IBM shareholder's meeting on April 28, 1975, with the hope that they could halt IBM's planned installation of a 370/145 at the University of Chile in Santiago. They claimed that the system would be used by the police agencies of that country, not the university.

"The Chileans did purchase a 145," IBM's Burnham explains, "and they told us they weren't doing it for intelligence purposes." IBM decided to trust the Chileans.

"If I was the Chilean military junta, I wouldn't put my computer in the University of Chile," reasons Burnham. However, he says, he does "understand the generals have taken over the university."

The National Council of Churches is more definite on this issue than any IBM spokesman. William Wipfler, the Latin-American director of NCC feels that IBM does indeed have a responsibility in this matter.

"We called the attention of IBM to the repeated violations of human rights in Chile and asked them to reconsider their plans to install the 145."

The National Council of Churches backed their pleas with proxies totaling 200,000 shares of IBM stock.

"The question is not whether they would sell computers to Hitler," says Wipfler, "but whether they would sell gas chambers to Hitler. Either way you're giving him weapons. When you know who Hitler is, you can't pretend you don't know what he's doing with your equipment."

Frank Cary, IBM chairman, spoke at the 1975 meeting in response to the church group's protest.

"We don't think the installation of a computer on the campus of the University of Chile has any sinister implications at all."

Sinister, according to Washington journalist Tom Mechling, is hardly the word. "The University of Chile would be a real Machiavellian place to put the things. On the basis of what I've learned from extremely reliable sources, I'm very much convinced that that computer is being used for name, rank, and serial number. These people who say they can't know what it's being used for suffer from the Eichmann syndrome. They claim they're only carrying out orders."

But IBM did send Dan Udell down to Santiago.

"We checked it out in detail. It's used for payroll, for processing student aptitude tests, for enrollment statistics and applications to college. To the best of our knowledge there are no other applications."

Perhaps the 145 at the University of Chile is not used by the secret police. But there is another, more direct link between the university and the Chilean secret police, a link typical of those that connect various Chilean institutions.

The leading computer service bureau in Chile is ECOM (Empressa Nacional de Computacion), an organization that provides extensive computer support to the government. This relationship is a long-standing one, according to the Chilean refugee now living in England. But, our source indicates, that relationship now includes computer support for DINA operation.

The president of ECOM is Rene Peralta, a former official of the Chilean Navy. He is also the former head of computation at the University of Chile, the very organization now training people in the use of a 370/145. The chairman of ECOM is an active general in the Chilean Army.

Our source claims that the systems at ECOM include modern powerful American computers. The services provided by ECOM include teleprocessing—the software there is capable of running database applications.

On May 20, 1975, General Pinochet, head of Chile's military junta, dedicated a 370/145 at the Technical University. This computer has been linked to other campuses by telex lines, according to Chilean sources.

The Technical University system is one of several shared by the Chilean Association of University Computing Centers. Among the members of this association are the University of Chile, Catholic University, University of Concepción, and ECOM.

Today, the Technical University is headed by Army Colonel Reyes. Commenting on this, an informed exile said "interrelationships between the universities and the military are natural" in Chile.

In addition to Peralta, there is another figure whose name comes up whenever computers and repression in Chile is discussed. He is Patricio Leniz, a former civil engineer who, according to informed sources, was a key software man on the computer projects of the DINA.

Patricio Leniz is the brother of Fernando Leniz, former minister of the military junta ruling Chile. Fernando Leniz is also the former chairman of *El Mercurio*, Chile's right-wing newspaper.

Further substantiation of the DINA's use of computers comes from refugees' accounts of mass arrests in Chile. Those rounded up surrender their identification cards which are quickly processed. Suspects are separated from the detainees and ID cards are soon returned to those free. The rapid checking of names against police files requires an on-line computer facility. Other stories from individuals detained by police corroborate the rapid checking of dossiers.

IBM is not the only American manufacturer that sells computers to Chile. Burroughs also sells machines there. Neil Jackson, Burroughs director of communications, said that the Chileans have one older machine which Burroughs sold them in 1970. This, he points out, was three governments ago.

Jackson's statement conflicts with a report that there are Burroughs maniframes at the Technical University, the Catholic University, and at the government's service bureau, ECOM.

Jackson stated that "Burrough's official policy is that we never comment on the political affairs of any of the 120 countries with which we do business, including our own."

Suppose a B3500 is now used for police purposes? "Obviously we hope it's not," said Jackson. "We're not aware of any use by any of our customers for any purposes that violate human rights."

Refugees from other Latin American police states also tell of the use of computer printouts during interrogations to cross-check data provided by detainees. According to these exiles, dossiers are shared among the police forces of Argentina, Chile, Uruguay, and Brazil.

The most detailed report of the use of computer-generated information during a police interrogation comes from a clergyman. He entered Uruguay and was picked up by the police there for questioning. During the ordeal the police tried to get him to talk about a Catholic priest they were investigating.

When detained for questioning, the clergyman was presented with a computer printout describing the details of the career of his colleague. On the printout were all the addresses at which the sought-after priest had lived, his salary at each point in his career, his telephone numbers and his relations with other Catholics in Uruguay.

The interrogated clergyman said that the most incredible thing about the questioning was that, as far as he could tell, the man the police sought had never been in Uruguay.

This printout, a church spokesman claims, could not have been stolen from the personnel files of the Catholic church; it must have come from some police computer system. Police in Latin America, he said, keep close tabs on many priests.

The idea of using computing equipment to support police activities in Latin America has been promoted by the United States government. During the early years of this decade the Agency for International Development (AID) provided South American police forces with weapons, training, and data processing equipment under its "public safety" programs.

In the AID document describing U.S. assistence to the government of Venezuela, contract 529-11-710-022, U.S. officials report that "the technical groundwork has been laid for the country's public safety agencies, through electronic data processing and related processes, to pool their identification and intelligence data in a central location for more efficient coordination and rapid distribution of relevant facts and leads."

AID's Office of Public Safety, in a report on its assistance to Brazilian authorities, specifically lists IBM systems among police equipment shipped to that country.

Is this practice continuing? An AID official said that that agency no longer provides police equipment to Latin states. But AID does "provide computers to Chile."

The computers are included with moneys earmarked for activities other than "public safety." An AID official said that a recent grant for agriculture included a "computer component." He added that there is no practical way for AID personnel in Washington to check on the ultimate use to which such a computer is put. Informed sources state that the Chilean Institute of Agriculture building in Calle Belgrado, Santiago, is a center of communications for the DINA.

Evidence that Latin American authorities use computers for repression is abundant. Yet there seems to be no way for either computer manufacturers or humane government to halt this activity.

What little hope there is for a change in these practices may lie with the United Nations, a body limited to persuasive power.

The United Nations has been concerned about the possible use of computers as an aid to police in dictatorships. The proposed United Nations code of ethics states:

"It would seem imperative for computer experts to have some training in human rights concepts and in certain aspects of the law.

"In computer based decision-making, the computer user should bear in mind the need to protect and promote the rights of the individual."

Can the United Nations actually halt the use of computers by police states? Can it prevent automation of "the final solution"?

"The U.N. has no methods of enforcing its principles," says Leonore Hooley, a United Nations human rights officer.

"We operate on the principle of nonintervention in the internal affairs of countries."

Case Study ᐟ

The Oil Rig

Joanne B. Ciulla

This description focuses on one of the three exploratory rigs which have been drilling for several years along the coast of Angola, under contract to a major U.S. multinational oil company. All three rigs are owned and operated by a large U.S. drilling company.

A student Case Study from *Business Ethics Module*, 1990, by Dr. Joanne B. Ciulla University of Richmond. Reprinted with permission.

The "Explorer IV" rig is a relatively small jack-up (i.e., with legs) with dimensions of approximately 200 ft. by 100 ft. which houses a crew of 150 men. The crew comprises laborers, roustabouts (unskilled laborers) and maintenance staff, and 30 expatriot workers who work as roughnecks, drillers or in administrative or technical positions. The top administrator on the Explorer IV is the "tool pusher," an American expat, who wields almost absolute authority over matters pertaining to life on the rig.

The crew quarters on the Explorer IV were modified for operations in Angola. A second galley was installed on the lower level and cabins on this level were enlarged to permit a dormitory style arrangement of 16 persons per room. This lower level is the "Angolan section" of the rig, where the 120 local workers eat, sleep, and socialize during their 28 day "hitch."

The upper level houses the 30 expats in an area equal in square footage to that of the Angolan section. The Expat section's quarters are semiprivate with baths and this section boasts its own galley, game room and movie room. Although it is nowhere explicitly written, a tacit regulation exists prohibiting Angolan workers from entering the Expat section of the rig, except in emergencies. The only Angolans exempt from this regulation are those assigned to the highly valued positions of cleaning or galley staff in the Expat section. These few positions are highly valued because of the potential for receiving gifts or recovering discarded razors, etc. from the expats.

The separation of Angolan workers from Expats is reinforced by several other rig policies. Angolan laborers travel to and from the rig by boat (an eighteen hour trip) whereas the expats are transported by helicopter. Also, medical attention is dispensed by the British R.N. throughout the day, but only during shift changes for the Angolans (except in emergencies). When there are serious injuries, the response is different for the two groups. If, for example, a finger is severed, expats are rushed to Luanda for reconstructive surgery, whereas Angolan workers have the amputation operation performed on the rig by a medic.

Angolan workers are issued grey coveralls and expats receive red coveralls. Meals in the two galleys are vastly different; they are virtually gourmet in the Expat galley and somewhat more proletarian in the Angolan section. The caterers informed the author that the two galleys' budgets were nearly equal (despite the gross disparity in numbers served).

Communication between Expats and Angolans is notable by its absence on the Explorer IV. This is principally because none of the expats speaks Portuguese and none of the Angolans speaks more than a few words of English. Only the chef of the Portuguese catering company speaks both English and Portuguese, and consequently, he is required to act as interpreter in all emergency situations. In the working environment, training and coordination of effort is accomplished via sign language or repetition of example.

From time to time an entourage of Angolan government officials visits the Explorer IV. These visits normally last only for an hour or so, but invariably, the officials dine with the expats and take a brief tour of the equipment before returning to shore via helicopter. Never has an entourage expressed concern about the disparity in living conditions on the rig, nor have the officials bothered to speak with the Angolan workers. Observers comment that the officials seem disinterested in the situation of the Angolan workers, most of whom are from outside of the capital city.

The rig's segregated environment is little affected by the presence of an American black. The American black is assigned to the expat section and is, of course, permitted to partake of all expat privileges. Nevertheless, it should be noted that there are few American blacks in the international drilling business and those few are frequently less than completely welcomed into the rig's social activities.

Distributive Justice

John Rawls

We may think of a human society as a more or less self-sufficient association regulated by a common conception of justice and aimed at advancing the good of its members.[1] As a co-operative venture for mutual advantage, it is characterized by a conflict as well as an identity of interests. There is an identity of interests since social co-operation makes possible a better life for all than any would have if everyone were to try to live by his own efforts; yet at the same time men are not indifferent as to how the greater benefits produced by their joint labours are distributed, for in order to further their own aims each prefers a larger to a lesser share. A conception of justice is a set of principles for choosing between the social arrangements which determine this division and for underwriting a consensus as to the proper distributive shares.

Now at first sight the most rational conception of justice would seem to be utilitarian. For consider: each man in realizing his own good can certainly balance his own losses against his own gains. We can impose a sacrifice on ourselves now for the sake of a greater advantage later. A man quite properly acts, as long as others are not affected, to achieve his own greatest good, to advance his ends as far as possible. Now, why should not a

From John Rawls, "Distributive Justice," *Philosophy, Politics, and Society,* 3rd series, ed. by Peter Laslett and W. G. Runciman (Basil Blackwell, Oxford; Barnes & Noble Books, Div. Harper & Row, Publishers, New York, 1967). Reprinted by permission of the author and publisher.

society act on precisely the same principle? Why is not that which is rational in the case of one man right in the case of a group of men? Surely the simplest and most direct conception of the right, and so of justice, is that of maximizing the good. This assumes a prior understanding of what is good, but we can think of the good as already given by the interests of rational individuals. Thus just as the principle of individual choice is to achieve one's greatest good, to advance so far as possible one's own system of rational desires, so the principle of social choice is to realize the greatest good (similarly defined) summed over all the members of society. We arrive at the principle of utility in a natural way: by this principle a society is rightly ordered, and hence just, when its institutions are arranged so as to realize the greatest sum of satisfactions.

The striking feature of the principle of utility is that it does not matter, except indirectly, how this sum of satisfactions is distributed among individuals, any more than it matters, except indirectly, how one man distributes his satisfactions over time. Since certain ways of distributing things affect the total sum of satisfactions, this fact must be taken into account in arranging social institutions; but according to this principle the explanation of common-sense precepts of justice and their seemingly stringent character is that they are those rules which experience shows must be strictly respected and departed from only under exceptional circumstances if the sum of advantages is to be maximized. The precepts of justice are derivative from the one end of attaining the greatest net balance of satisfactions. There is no reason in principle why the greater gains of some should not compensate for the lesser losses of others; or why the violation of the liberty of a few might not be made right by a greater good shared by many. It simply happens, at least under most conditions, that the greatest sum of advantages is not generally achieved in this way. From the standpoint of utility the strictness of common-sense notions of justice has a certain usefulness, but as a philosophical doctrine it is irrational.

If, then, we believe that as a matter of principle each member of society has an inviolability founded on justice which even the welfare of everyone else cannot override, and that a loss of freedom for some is not made right by a greater sum of satisfactions enjoyed by many, we shall have to look for another account of the principles of justice. The principle of utility is incapable of explaining the fact that in a just society the liberties of equal citizenship are taken for granted, and the rights secured by justice are not subject to political bargaining nor to the calculus of social interests. Now, the most natural alternative to the principle of utility is its traditional rival, the theory of the social contract. The aim of the contract doctrine is precisely to account for the strictness of justice by supposing that its principles arise from an agreement among free and independent persons in an original position of equality and hence reflect the integrity and equal sovereignty of the rational persons who are the contractees. Instead of supposing that a conception of right, and so a conception of justice, is simply an extension of the principle of choice for one man to society as a whole, the contract doctrine assumes that the rational individuals who belong to society must choose together, in one joint act, what is to count among them as just and unjust. They are to decide among themselves once and for all what is to be their conception of justice. This decision is thought of as being made in a suitably defined initial situation one of the significant features of which is that no one knows his position in society, nor even his place in the distribution of natural talents and abilities. The principles of justice to which all are forever bound are chosen in the absence of this sort of specific information. A veil of ignorance prevents anyone from being advantaged or disadvantaged by the contingencies of social class and fortune; and hence the bargaining problems which arise in everyday life from the possession of this knowledge do not affect the choice of principles. On the contract doctrine, then, the theory of justice, and indeed ethics itself, is part of the general theory of rational choice, a fact perfectly clear in its Kantian formulation.

Once justice is thought of as arising from an original agreement of this kind, it is evident that the principle of utility is problematical. For why should rational individuals who have a system of ends they wish to advance agree to a violation of their liberty for the sake of a greater balance of satisfactions enjoyed by others? It seems more plausible to suppose that, when situated in an original position of equal right, they would insist upon institutions which returned compensating advantages for any sacrifices required. A rational man would not accept an institution merely because it maximized the sum of advantages irrespective of its effect on his own interests. It appears, then, that the principle of utility would be rejected as a principle of justice, although we shall not try to argue this important question here. Rather, our aim is to give a brief sketch of the conception of distributive shares implicit in the principles of justice which, it seems, would be chosen in the original position. The philosophical appeal of utilitarianism is that it seems to offer a single principle on the basis of which a consistent and complete conception of right can be developed. The problem is to work out a contractarian alternative in such a way that it has comparable if not all the same virtues.

In our discussion we shall make no attempt to derive the two principles of justice which we shall examine; that is, we shall not try to show that they would be chosen in the original position.[2] It must suffice that it is plausible that they would be, at least in preference to the standard forms of traditional theories. Instead we shall be mainly concerned with three questions: first, how to interpret these principles so that they define a consistent and complete conception of justice; second, whether it is possible to arrange the institutions of a constitutional democracy so that these principles are satisfied, at least approximately; and third, whether the conception of distributive shares which they define is compatible with common-sense notions of justice. The significance of these principles is that they allow for the strictness of the claims of justice; and if they can be understood so as to yield a consistent and complete conception, the contractarian alternative would seem all the more attractive.

The two principles of justice which we shall discuss may be formulated as follows: first, each person engaged in an institution or affected by it has an equal right to the most extensive liberty compatible with a like liberty for all; and second, inequalities as defined by the institutional structure or fostered by it are arbitrary unless it is reasonable to expect that they will work out to everyone's advantage and provided that the positions and offices to which they attach or from which they may be gained are open to all. These principles regulate the distributive aspects of institutions by controlling the assignment of rights and duties throughout the whole social structure, beginning with the adoption of a political constitution in accordance with which they are then to be applied to legislation. It is upon a correct choice of a basic structure of society, its fundamental system of rights and duties, that the justice of distributive shares depends.

The two principles of justice apply in the first instance to this basic structure, that is, to the main institutions of the social system and their arrangement, how they are combined together. Thus, this structure includes the political constitution and the principal economic and social institutions which together define a person's liberties and rights and affect his life-prospects, what he may expect to be and how well he may expect to fare. The intuitive idea here is that those born into the social system at different positions, say in different social classes, have varying life-prospects determined, in part, by the system of political liberties and personal rights, and by the economic and social opportunities which are made available to these positions. In this way the basic structure of society favours certain men over others, and these are the basic inequalities, the ones which affect their whole life-prospects. It is inequalities of this kind, presumably inevitable in any society, with which the two principles of justice are primarily designed to deal.

Now the second principle holds that an inequality is allowed only if there is reason to believe that the institution with the inequality, or permitting it, will work out for the advantage of every person engaged in it. In the case of the basic structure this means that all inequalities which affect life-prospects, say the inequalities of income and wealth which exist between social classes, must be to the advantage of everyone. Since the principle applies to institutions, we interpret this to mean that inequalities must be to the advantage of the representative man for each relevant social position; they should improve each such man's expectation. Here we assume that it is possible to attach to each position an expectation, and that this expectation is a function of the whole institutional structure: it can be raised and lowered by reassigning rights and duties throughout the system. Thus the expectation of any position depends upon the expectations of the others, and these in turn depend upon the pattern of rights and duties established by the basic structure. But it is not clear what is meant by saying that inequalities must be to the advantage of every representative man. . . . [One] . . . interpretation [of what is meant by saying that inequalities must be to the advantage of every representative man] . . . is to choose some social position by reference to which the pattern of expectations as a whole is to be judged, and then to maximize with respect to the expectations of this representative man consistent with the demands of equal liberty and equality of opportunity. Now, the one obvious candidate is the representative man of those who are least favoured by the system of institutional inequalities. Thus we arrive at the following idea: the basic structure of the social system affects the life-prospects of typical individuals according to their initial places in society, say the various income classes into which they are born, or depending upon certain natural attributes, as when institutions make discriminations between men and women or allow certain advantages to be gained by those with greater natural abilities. The fundamental problem of distributive justice concerns the differences in life-prospects which come about in this way. We interpret the second principle to hold that these differences are just if and only if the greater expectations of the more advantaged, when playing a part in the working of the whole social system, improve the expectations of the least advantaged. The basic structure is just throughout when the advantages of the more fortunate promote the well-being of the least fortunate, that is, when a decrease in their advantages would make the least fortunate even worse off than they are. The basic structure is perfectly just when the prospects of the least fortunate are as great as they can be.

In interpreting the second principle (or rather the first part of it which we may, for obvious reasons, refer to as the difference principle), we assume that the first principle requires a basic equal liberty for all, and that the resulting political system, when circumstances permit, is that of a constitutional democracy in some form. There must be liberty of the person and political equality as well as liberty of conscience and freedom of thought. There is one class of equal citizens which defines a common status for all. We also assume that there is equality of opportunity and a fair competition for the available positions on the basis of reasonable qualifications. Now, given this background, the differences to be justified are the various economic and social inequalities in the basic structure which must inevitably arise in such a scheme. These are the inequalities in the distribution of income and wealth and the distinctions in social prestige and status which attach to the various positions and classes. The difference principle says that these inequalities are just if and only if they are part of a larger system in which they work out to the advantage of the most unfortunate representative man. The just distributive shares determined by the basic structure are those specified by this constrained maximum principle.

Thus, consider the chief problem of distributive justice, that concerning the distribution of wealth as it affects the life-prospects of those starting out in the various income groups. These income classes define the relevant representative men from which the social system is to be judged. Now, a son of a member of the entrepreneurial class (in a capitalist society) has a better prospect than that of the son of an unskilled labourer. This will be true, it seems, even when the social injustices which presently exist are removed and the two men are of equal talent and ability; the inequality cannot be done away with as long as something like the family is maintained. What, then, can justify this inequality in life-prospects? According to the second principle it is justified only if it is to the advantage of the representative man who is worse off, in this case the representative unskilled labourer. The inequality is permissible because lowering it would, let's suppose, make the working man even worse off than he is. Presumably, given the principle of open offices (the second part of the second principle), the greater expectations allowed to entrepreneurs has the effect in the longer run of raising the life-prospects of the labouring class. The inequality in expectation provides an incentive so that the economy is more efficient, industrial advance proceeds at a quicker pace, and so on, the end result of which is that greater material and other benefits are distributed throughout the system. Of course, all of this is familiar, and whether true or not in particular cases, it is the sort of thing which must be argued if the inequality in income and wealth is to be acceptable by the difference principle.

We should now verify that this interpretation of the second principle gives a natural sense in which everyone may be said to be made better off. Let us suppose that inequalities are chain-connected: that is, if an inequality raises the expectations of the lowest position, it raises the expectations of all positions in between. For example, if the greater expectations of the representative entrepreneur raises that of the unskilled labourer, it also raises that of the semi-skilled. Let us further assume that inequalities are close-knit: that is, it is impossible to raise (or lower) the expectation of any representative man without raising (or lowering) the expectations of every other representative man, and in particular, without affecting one way or the other that of the least fortunate. There is no loose-jointedness, so to speak, in the way in which expectations depend upon one another. Now with these assumptions, everyone does benefit from an inequality which satisfies the difference principle, and the second principle as we have formulated it reads correctly. For the representative man who is better off in any pair-wise comparison gains by being allowed to have his advantage, and the man who is worse off benefits from the contribution which all inequalities make to each position below. Of course, chain-connection and close-knitness may not obtain; but in this case those who are better off should not have a veto over the advantages available for the least advantaged. The stricter interpretation of the difference principle should be followed, and all inequalities should be arranged for the advantage of the most unfortunate even if some inequalities are not to the advantage of those in middle positions. Should these conditions fail, then, the second principle would have to be stated in another way.

It may be observed that the difference principle represents, in effect, an original agreement to share in the benefits of the distribution of natural talents and abilities, whatever this distribution turns out to be, in order to alleviate as far as possible the arbitrary handicaps resulting from our initial starting places in society. Those who have been favoured by nature, whoever they are, may gain from their good fortune only on terms that improve the well-being of those who have lost out. The naturally advantaged are not to gain simply because they are more gifted, but only to cover the costs of training and cultivating their endowments and for putting them to use in a way which improves the position of the less fortunate. We are led to the difference principle if we wish to arrange the basic social structure so that no one gains (or loses) from his luck in the natural lottery of talent and ability, or from his initial place in society, without giving (or receiving) compensating advantages in return. (The parties in the original position are not said to be attracted by this idea and so agree to it; rather, given the symmetries of their situation, and particularly their lack of knowledge, and so on, they will find it to their interest to agree to a principle which can be understood in this way.) And we should note also that when the difference principle is perfectly satisfied, the basic structure is optimal by the efficiency principle. There is no way to make anyone better off without making someone worse off, namely, the least fortunate representative man. Thus the two principles of justice define distributive shares in a way compatible with efficiency, at least as long as we move on this highly abstract level. If we want to say (as we do, although it cannot be argued here) that the demands of justice have an absolute weight with respect to efficiency, this claim may seem less paradoxical when it is kept in mind that perfectly just institutions are also efficient.

Our second question is whether it is possible to arrange the institutions of a constitutional democracy so that the two principles of justice are satisfied, at least approximately. We shall try to show that this can be done provided the government regulates a free economy in a certain way. More fully, if law and government act effectively to keep markets competitive, resources fully employed, property and wealth widely distributed over time, and to maintain the appropriate social minimum, then if there is equality of opportunity underwritten by education for all, the resulting distribution will be just. Of course, all of these arrangements and policies are familiar. The only novelty in the following remarks, if there is any novelty at all, is that this framework of institutions can be made to satisfy the difference principle. To argue this, we must sketch the relations of these institutions and how they work together.

First of all, we assume that the basic social structure is controlled by a just constitution which secures the various liberties of equal citizenship. Thus the legal order is administered in accordance with the principle of legality, and liberty of conscience and freedom of thought are taken for granted. The political process is conducted, so far as possible, as a just procedure for choosing between governments and for enacting just legislation. From the standpoint of distributive justice, it is also essential that there be equality of opportunity in several senses. Thus, we suppose that, in addition to maintaining the usual social overhead capital, government provides for equal educational opportunities for all either by subsidizing private schools or by operating a public school system. It also enforces and underwrites equality of opportunity in commercial ventures and in the free choice of occupation. This result is achieved by policing business behaviour and by preventing the establishment of barriers and restriction to the desirable positions and markets. Lastly, there is a guarantee of a social minimum which the government meets by family allowances and special payments in times of unemployment, or by a negative income tax.

In maintaining this system of institutions the government may be thought of as divided into four branches. Each branch is represented by various agencies (or activities thereof) charged with preserving certain social and economic conditions. These branches do not necessarily overlap with the usual organization of government, but should be understood as purely conceptual. Thus the allocation branch is to keep the economy feasibly competitive, that is, to prevent the formation of unreasonable market power. Markets are competitive in this sense when they cannot be made more so consistent with the requirements of efficiency and the acceptance of the facts of consumer preferences and geography. The allocation branch is also charged with identifying and correcting, say by suitable taxes and subsidies wherever possible, the more obvious departures from efficiency caused by the failure of prices to measure accurately social benefits and costs. The stabilization branch strives to maintain reasonably full employment so that there is no waste through failure to use resources and the free choice of occupation and the deployment of finance is supported by strong effective demand. These two branches together are to preserve the efficiency of the market economy generally.

The social minimum is established through the operations of the transfer branch. Later on we shall consider at what level this minimum should be set, since this is a crucial matter; but for the moment, a few general remarks will suffice. The main idea is that the workings of the transfer branch take into account the precept of need and assign it an appropriate weight with respect to the other common-sense precepts of justice. A market economy ignores the claims of need altogether. Hence there is a division of labour between the parts of the social system as different institutions answer to different common-sense precepts. Competitive markets (properly supplemented by government operations) handle the problem of the efficient allocation of labour and resources and set a weight to the conventional precepts associated with wages and earnings (the precepts of each according to his work and experience, or responsibility and the hazards of the job, and so on), whereas the transfer branch guarantees a certain level of well-being and meets the claims of need. Thus it is obvious that the justice of distributive shares depends upon the whole social system and how it distributes total income, wages plus transfers. There is with reason strong objection to the competitive determination of total income, since this would leave out of account the claims of need and of a decent standard of life. From the standpoint of the original position it is clearly rational to insure oneself against these contingencies. But now, if the appropriate minimum is provided by transfers, it may be perfectly fair that the other part of total income is competitively determined. Moreover, this way of dealing with the claims of need is doubtless more efficient, at least from a theoretical point of view, than trying to regulate prices by minimum wage standards and so on. It is preferable to handle these claims by a separate branch which supports a social minimum. Henceforth, in considering whether the second principle of justice is satisfied, the answer turns on whether the total income of the least advantaged, that is, wages plus transfers, is such as to maximize their long-term expectations consistent with the demands of liberty.

Finally, the distribution branch is to preserve an approximately just distribution of income and wealth over time by affecting the background conditions of the market from period to period. Two aspects of this branch may be distinguished. First of all, it operates a system of inheritance and gift taxes. The aim of these levies is not to raise revenue, but gradually and continually to correct the distribution of wealth and to prevent the concentrations of power to the detriment of liberty and equality of opportunity. It is perfectly true, as some have said,[3] that unequal inheritance of wealth is no more inherently unjust than unequal inheritance of intelligence; as far as possible the inequalities founded on either should satisfy the difference principle. Thus, the inheritance of greater wealth is just as long as it is to the advantage of the worst off and consistent with liberty, including equality of opportunity. Now by the latter we do not mean, of course, the equality of expectations between classes, since differences in life-prospects arising from the basic structure are inevitable, and it is precisely the aim of the second principle to say when these differences are just. Indeed, equality of opportunity is a certain set of institutions which assures equally good education and chances of culture for all and which keeps open the competition for positions on the basis of qualities reasonably related to performance, and so on. It is these institutions which are put in jeopardy when inequalities and concentrations of wealth reach a certain limit; and the taxes imposed by the distribution branch are to prevent this limit from being exceeded. Naturally enough where this limit lies is a matter for political judgment guided by theory, practical experience, and plain hunch; on this question the theory of justice has nothing to say.

The second part of the distribution branch is a scheme of taxation for raising revenue to cover the costs of public goods, to make transfer payments, and the like. This scheme belongs to the distribution branch since the burden of taxation must be justly shared. Although we cannot examine the legal and economic complications involved, there are several points in favour of proportional expenditure taxes as part of an ideally just arrangement. For one thing, they are preferable to income taxes at the level of common-sense precepts of justice, since they impose a levy according to how much a man takes out of the common store of goods and not according to how much he contributes (assuming that income is fairly earned in return for productive efforts). On the other hand, proportional taxes treat everyone in a clearly defined uniform way (again assuming that income is fairly earned) and hence it is preferable to use progressive rates only when they are necessary to preserve the justice of the system as a whole, that is, to prevent large fortunes hazardous to liberty and equality of opportunity, and the like. If proportional expenditure taxes should also prove more efficient, say because they interfere less with incentives, or whatever, this would make the case for them decisive provided a feasible scheme could be worked out.[4] Yet these are questions of political judgment which are not our concern; and, in any case, a proportional expenditure tax is part of an idealized scheme which we are describing. It does not follow that even steeply progressive income taxes, given the injustice of existing systems, do not improve justice and efficiency all things considered. In practice we must usually choose between unjust arrangements and then it is a matter of finding the lesser injustice.

Whatever form the distribution branch assumes, the argument for it is to be based on justice: we must hold that once it is accepted the social system as a whole—the competitive economy surrounded by a just constitutional legal framework—can be made to satisfy the principles of justice with the smallest loss in efficiency. The long-term expectations of the least advantaged are raised to the highest level consistent with the demands of equal liberty. In discussing the choice of a distribution scheme we have made no reference to the traditional criteria of taxation according to ability to pay or benefits received; nor have we mentioned any of the variants of the sacrifice principle. These standards are subordinate to the two principles of justice; once the problem is seen as that of designing a whole social system, they assume the status of secondary precepts with no more independent force than the precepts of common sense in regard to wages. To suppose otherwise is not to take a sufficiently comprehensive point of view. In setting up a just distribution branch these precepts may or may not have a place depending upon the demands of the two principles of justice when applied to the entire system. . . .

The sketch of the system of institutions satisfying the two principles of justice is now complete. . . .

In order . . . to establish just distributive shares a just total system of institutions must be set up and impartially administered. Given a just constitution and the smooth working of the four branches of government, and so on, there exists a procedure such that the actual distribution of wealth, whatever it turns out to be, is just. It will have come about as a consequence of a just system of institutions satisfying the principles to which everyone would agree and against which no one can complain. The situation is one of pure procedural justice, since there is no independent criterion by which the outcome can be judged. Nor can we say that a particular distribution of wealth is just because it is one which could have resulted from just institutions although it has not, as this would be to allow too much. Clearly there are many distributions which may be reached by just institutions, and this is true whether we count patterns of distributions among social classes or whether we count distributions of particular goods and services among particular individuals. There are indefinitely many outcomes and what makes one of these just is that it has been achieved by actually carrying out a just scheme of co-operation as it is publicly understood. It is the result which has arisen when everyone receives that to which he is entitled given his and others' actions guided by their legitimate expectations and their obligations to one another. We can no more arrive at a just distribution of wealth except by working together within the framework of a just system of institutions than we can win or lose fairly without actually betting.

This account of distributive shares is simply an elaboration of the familiar idea that economic rewards will be just once a perfectly competitive price system is organized as a fair game. But in order to do this we have to begin with the choice of a social system as a whole, for the basic structure of the entire arrangement must be just. The economy must be surrounded with the appropriate framework of institutions, since even a perfectly efficient price system has no tendency to determine just distributive shares when left to itself. Not only must economic activity be regulated by a just constitution and controlled by the four branches of government, but a just saving-function must be adopted to estimate the provision to be made for future generations. . . .

NOTES

1. In this essay I try to work out some of the implications of the two principles of justice discussed in "Justice as Fairness," which first appeared in the *Philosophical Review*, 1958, and which is reprinted in *Philosophy, Politics and Society*, Series II, pp. 132–57.
2. This question is discussed very briefly in "Justice as Fairness," see pp. 138–41. The intuitive idea is as follows. Given the circumstances of the original position, it is rational for a man to choose as if he were designing a society in which his enemy is to assign him his place. Thus, in particular, given the complete lack of knowledge (which makes the choice one uncertainty), the fact that the decision involves one's life-prospects as a whole and is constrained by obligations to third parties (e.g., one's descendants) and duties to certain values (e.g., to religious truth), it is rational to be conservative and so to choose in accordance with an analogue of the maximum principle. Viewing the situation in this way, the inter-

pretation given to the principles of justice earlier is perhaps natural enough. Moreover, it seems clear how the principle of utility can be interpreted; it is the analogue of the Laplacean principle for choice uncertainty. (For a discussion of these choice criteria, see R. D. Luce and H. Raiffa, *Games and Decisions* [1957], pp. 275–98.)
3. Example F. von Hayek, *The Constitution of Liberty* (1960), p. 90.
4. See N. Kaldor, *An Expenditure Tax* (1955).

The Entitlement Theory

ROBERT NOZICK

The minimal state is the most extensive state that can be justified. Any state more extensive violates people's rights. Yet many persons have put forth reasons purporting to justify a more extensive state. It is impossible within the compass of this book to examine all the reasons that have been put forth. Therefore, I shall focus upon those generally acknowledged to be most weighty and influential, to see precisely wherein they fail. In this chapter we consider the claim that a more extensive state is justified, because necessary (or the best instrument) to achieve distributive justice; in the next chapter we shall take up diverse other claims.

The term "distributive justice" is not a neutral one. Hearing the term "distribution," most people presume that some thing or mechanism uses some principle or criterion to give out a supply of things. Into this process of distributing shares some error may have crept. So it is an open question, at least, whether *re*distribution should take place; whether we should do again what has already been done once, though poorly. However, we are not in the position of children who have been given portions of pie by someone who now makes last minute adjustments to rectify careless cutting. There is no *central* distribution, no person or group entitled to control all the resources, jointly deciding how they are to be doled out. What each person gets, he gets from others who give to him in exchange for something, or as a gift. In a free society, diverse persons control different resources, and new holdings arise out of the voluntary exchanges and actions of persons. There is no more a distributing or distribution of shares than there is a distributing of mates in a society in which persons choose whom they shall marry. The total result is the product of many individual decisions which the different individuals involved are entitled to make. Some uses of the term "distribution," it is true, do not imply a previous distributing appropriately judged by some criterion (for example, "probability distribution"); nevertheless, despite the title of this chapter, it would be best to use a terminology that clearly is neutral. We shall speak of people's holdings; a principle of justice in holdings describes (part of) what justice tells us (requires) about holdings. I shall state first what I take to be the correct view about justice in holdings, and then turn to the discussion of alternate views.

I

THE ENTITLEMENT THEORY

The subject of justice in holdings consists of three major topics. The first is the *original acquisition of holdings*, the appropriation of unheld things. This includes the issues of how unheld things may come to be held, the process, or processes, by which unheld things may come to be held, the things that may come to be held by these processes, the extent of what comes to be held by a particular process, and so on. We shall refer to the complicated truth about this topic, which we shall not formulate here, as the principle of justice in acquisition. The second topic concerns the *transfer of holdings* from one person to another. By what processes may a person transfer holdings to another? How may a person acquire a holding from another who holds it? Under this topic come general descriptions of voluntary exchange, and gift and (on the other hand) fraud, as well as reference to particular conventional details fixed upon in a given society. The complicated truth about this subject (with placeholders for conventional details) we shall call the principle of justice in transfer. (And we shall suppose it also includes principles governing how a person may divest himself of a holding, passing it into an unheld state.)

If the world were wholly just, the following inductive definition would exhaustively cover the subject of justice in holdings.

1. A person who acquires a holding in accordance with the principle of justice in acquisition is entitled to that holding.
2. A person who acquires a holding in accordance with the principle of justice in transfer, from someone else entitled to the holding, is entitled to the holding.
3. No one is entitled to a holding except by (repeated) applications of 1 and 2.

The complete principle of distributive justice would say simply that a distribution is just if everyone is entitled to the holdings they possess under the distribution.

A distribution is just if it arises from another just distribution by legitimate means. The legitimate means of moving from one distribution to another are specified by the principle of justice in transfer. The legitimate first "moves" are specified by the principle of justice in acquisition.[1] Whatever arises from a just situation by just steps is itself just. The means of change specified by the principle of justice in transfer preserve justice. As correct rules of inference are truth-preserving, and any conclusion deduced via repeated application of such rules from only true premises is itself true, so the means of transition from one situation to another specified by the principle of justice in transfer are justice-preserving, and any situation actually arising from repeated transitions in accordance with the principle from a just situation is itself just. The parallel between justice-preserving transformations and truth-preserving transformations illuminates where it fails as well as where it holds. That a conclusion could have been deduced by truth-preserving means from premises that are true suffices to show its truth. That from a just situation a situation *could* have arisen via justice-preserving means does *not* suffice to show its justice. The fact that a thief's victims voluntarily *could* have presented him with gifts does not entitle the thief to his ill-gotten gains. Justice in holdings is historical; it depends upon what actually has happened. We shall return to this point later.

Not all actual situations are generated in accordance with the two principles of justice in holdings: the principle of justice in acquisition and the principle of justice in transfer. Some people steal from others, or defraud them, or enslave them, seizing their product and preventing them from living as they choose, or forcibly exclude others from competing in exchanges. None of these are permissible modes of transition from one situation to another. And some persons acquire holdings by means not sanctioned by the principle of justice in acquisition. The existence of past injustice (previous violations of the first two principles of justice in holdings) raises the third major topic under justice in holdings: the rectification of injustice in holdings. If past injustice has shaped present holdings in various ways, some identifiable and some not, what now, if anything, ought to be done to rectify these injustices? What obligations do the performers of injustice have toward those whose position is worse than it would have been had the injustice not been done? Or, than it would have been had compensation been paid promptly? How, if at all, do things change if the beneficiaries and those made worse off are not the direct parties in the act of injustice, but, for example, their descendants? Is an injustice done to someone whose holding was itself based upon an unrectified injustice? How far back must one go in wiping clean the historical slate of injustices? What may victims of injustice permissibly do in order to rectify the injustices being done to them, including the many injustices done by persons acting through their government? I do not know of a thorough or theoretically sophisticated treatment of such issues. Idealizing greatly, let us suppose theoretical investigation will produce a principle of rectification. This principle uses historical infomation about previous situations and injustices done in them (as defined by the first two principles of justice and rights against interference), and information about the actual course of events that flowed from these injustices, until the present, and it yields a description (or descriptions) of holdings in the society. The principle of rectification presumably will make use of its best estimate of subjunctive information about what would have occurred (or a probability distribution over what might have occurred, using the expected value) if the injustice had not taken place. If the actual description of holdings turns out not to be one of the descriptions yielded by the principle, then one of the descriptions yielded must be realized.

The general outlines of the theory of justice in holdings are that the holdings of a person are just if he is entitled to them by the principles of justice in acquisition and transfer, or by the principle of rectification of injustice (as specified by the first two principles). If each person's holdings are just, then the total set (distribution) of holdings is just. To turn these general outlines into a specific theory we would have to specify the details of each of the three principles of justice in holdings: the principle of acquisition of holdings, the principle of transfer of holdings, and the principle of rectification of violations of the first two principles. I shall not attempt that task here. (Locke's principle of justice in acquisition is discussed below.)

HISTORICAL PRINCIPLES
AND END-RESULT PRINCIPLES

The general outlines of the entitlement theory illuminate the nature and defects of other conceptions of distributive justice. The entitlement theory of justice in distribution is *historical*; whether a distribution is just depends upon how it came about. In contrast, *current time-slice principles* of justice hold that the justice of a distribution is determined by how things are distributed (who has what) as judged by some *structural* principle(s) of just distribution. A utilitarian who judges between any two distributions by seeing which has the greater sum of utility and, if the sums tie, applies some fixed equality criterion to choose the more equal distribution, would hold a current time-slice principle of justice. As would someone who had a fixed schedule of trade-offs between the sum of happiness and equality. According to a current time-slice principle, all that needs to be looked at, in judging the justice of a distribution, is who ends up with what; in comparing any two distributions one need look only at the matrix presenting the distributions. No further information need be fed into a principle of justice. It is a consequence of such principles of justice that any two structurally identical distributions are equally just. (Two distributions are structurally identical if they present the same profile, but perhaps have different persons occupying the particular slots. My having ten and your having five, and my having five and your having ten are structurally identical distributions.) Welfare economics is the theory of current time-slice principles of justice.

The subject is conceived as operating on matrices representing only current information about distribution. This, as well as some of the usual conditions (for example, the choice of distribution is invariant under re-labeling of columns), guarantees that welfare economics will be a current time-slice theory, with all of its inadequacies.

Most persons do not accept current time-slice principles as constituting the whole story about distributive shares. They think it relevant in assessing the justice of a situation to consider not only the distribution it embodies, but also how that distribution came about. If some persons are in prison for murder or war crimes, we do not say that to assess the justice of the distribution in the society we must look only at what this person has, and that person has, and that person has, . . . at the current time. We think it relevant to ask whether someone did something so that he *deserved* to be punished, deserved to have a lower share. Most will agree to the relevance of further information with regard to punishments and penalties. Consider also desired things. One traditional socialist view is that workers are entitled to the product and full fruits of their labor; they have earned it; a distribution is unjust if it does not give the workers what they are entitled to. Such entitlements are based upon some past history. No socialist holding this view would find it comforting to be told that because the actual distribution A happens to coincide structurally with the one he desires D, A therefore is no less just than D; it differs only in that the "parasitic" owners of capital receive under A what the workers are entitled to under D, and the workers receive under A what the owners are entitled to under D, namely very little. This socialist rightly, in my view, holds onto the notions of earning, producing, entitlement, desert, and so forth, and he rejects current time-slice principles that look only to the structure of the resulting set of holdings. (The set of holdings resulting from what? Isn't it implausible that how holdings are produced and come to exist has no effect at all on who should hold what?) His mistake lies in his view of what entitlements arise out of what sorts of productive processes.

We construe the position we discuss too narrowly by speaking of *current* time-slice principles. Nothing is changed if structural principles operate upon a time sequence of current time-slice profiles and, for example, give someone more now to counterbalance the less he has had earlier. A utilitarian or an egalitarian or any mixture of the two over time will inherit the difficulties of his more myopic comrades. He is not helped by the fact that *some* of the information others consider relevant in assessing a distribution is reflected, unrecoverably, in past matrices. Henceforth, we shall refer to such unhistorical principles of distributive justice, including the current time-slice principles, as *end-result principles* or *end-state principles*.

In contrast to end-result principles of justice, *historical principles* of justice hold that past circumstances or actions of people can create differential entitlements or differential deserts to things. An injustice can be worked by moving from one distribution to another structurally identical one, for the second, in profile the same, may violate people's entitlements or deserts; it may not fit the actual history.

🌿

HOW LIBERTY UPSETS PATTERNS

It is not clear how those holding alternative conceptions of distributive justice can reject the entitlement conception of justice in holdings. For suppose a distribution favored by one of these nonentitlement conceptions is realized. Let us suppose it is your favorite one and let us call this distribution D_1; perhaps everyone has an equal share, perhaps shares vary in accordance with some dimension you treasure. Now suppose that Wilt Chamberlain is greatly in demand by basketball teams, being a great gate attraction. (Also suppose contracts run only for a year, with players being free agents.) He signs the following sort of contract with a team: In each home game, twenty-five cents from the price of each ticket of admission goes to him. (We ignore the question of whether he is "gouging" the owners, letting them look out for themselves.) The season starts, and people cheerfully attend his team's games; they buy their tickets, each time dropping a separate twenty-five cents of their admission price into a special box with Chamberlain's name on it. They are excited about seeing him play; it is worth the total admission price to them. Let us suppose that in one season one million persons attend his home games, and Wilt Chamberlain winds up with $250,000, a much larger sum than the average income and larger even than anyone else has. Is he entitled to this income? Is this new distribution D_2, unjust? If so, why? There is *no* question about whether each of the people was entitled to the control over the resources they held in D_1; because that was the distribution (your favorite) that (for the purposes of argument) we assumed was acceptable. Each of these persons *chose* to give twenty-five cents of their money to Chamberlain. They could have spent it on going to the movies, or on candy bars, or on copies of *Dissent* magazine, or of *Monthly Review*. But they all, at least one million of them, converged on giving it to Wilt Chamberlain in exchange for watching him play basketball. If D_1 was a just distribution, and people voluntarily moved from it to D_2, transferring parts of their shares they were given under D_1 (what was it for if not to do something with?), isn't D_2 also just? If the people were entitled to dispose of the resources to which they were entitled (under D_1), didn't this include their being entitled to give it to, or exchange it with, Wilt Chamberlain? Can anyone else complain on grounds of justice? Each other person already has his legitimate share under D_1. Under D_1, there is nothing that anyone has that anyone else has a claim of justice against. After someone transfers something to Wilt Chamberlain, third parties *still* have their legitimate shares; *their* shares are not changed. By what process could such a transfer among two persons give rise to a legitimate claim of distributive justice on a portion of what was transferred, by a third party who had no claim of justice on any holding of the others *before* the transfer? To cut off objections irrelevant here, we might imagine the exchanges occurring in a socialist society, after hours. After playing whatever basketball he does in his daily work, or doing whatever other daily work he does, Wilt Chamberlain decides to put in *overtime* to earn additional money. (First his work quota is set; he works time over that.) Or imagine it is a skilled juggler people like to see, who puts on shows after hours.

Why might someone work overtime in a society in which it is assumed their needs are satisfied? Perhaps because they care about things other than needs. I like to write in books that I read, and to have easy access to books for browsing at odd hours. It would be very pleasant and convenient to have the resources of Widener Library in my back yard. No society, I assume, will provide such resources close to each person who would like them as part of his regular allotment (under D_1). Thus, persons either must do without some extra things that they want, or be allowed to do something extra to get some of these things. On what basis could the inequalities that would eventuate be forbidden? Notice also that small factories would spring up in a socialist society, unless forbidden. I melt down some of my personal possessions (under D_1) and build a machine out of the material. I offer you, and others, a philosophy lecture once a week in exchange for your cranking the handle on my machine, whose products I exchange for yet other things, and so on. (The raw materials used by the machine are given to me by others who possess them under D_1, in exchange for hearing lectures.) Each person might participate to gain things over and above their allotment under D_1. Some persons even might want to leave their job in socialist industry and work full time in this private sector. I shall say something more about these issues in the next chapter. Here I wish merely to note how private property even in means of production would occur in a socialist society that did not forbid people to use as they wished some of the resources they are given under the socialist distribution D_1. The socialist society would have to forbid capitalist acts between consenting adults.

The general point illustrated by the Wilt Chamberlain example and the example of the entrepreneur in a socialist society is that no end-state principle or distributional patterned principle of justice can be continuously realized without continuous interference with people's lives. Any favored pattern would be transformed into one unfavored by the principle, by people choosing to act in various ways; for example, by people exchanging goods and services with other people, or giving things to other people, things the transferrers are entitled to under the favored distributional pattern. To maintain a pattern one must either continually interfere to stop people from transferring resources as they wish to, or continually (or periodically) interfere to take from some persons resources that others for some reason chose to transfer to them. (But if some time limit is to be set on how long people may keep resources others voluntarily transfer to them, why let them keep these resources for *any* period of time? Why not have immediate confiscation?) It might be objected that all persons voluntarily will choose to refrain from actions which would upset the pattern. This presupposes unrealistically (1) that all will most want to maintain the pattern (are those who don't, to be "reeducated" or forced to undergo "self-criticism"?), (2) that each can gather enough information about his own actions and the ongoing activities of others to discover which of his actions will upset the pattern, and (3) that diverse and far-flung persons can coordinate their actions to dove-tail into the pattern. Compare the manner in which the market is neutral among persons' desires, as it reflects and transmits widely scattered information via prices, and coordinates persons' activities.

It puts things perhaps a bit too strongly to say that every patterned (or end-state) principle is liable to be thwarted by the voluntary actions of the individual parties transferring some of their shares they receive under the principle. For perhaps some *very* weak patterns are not so thwarted. Any distributional pattern with any egalitarian component is overturnable by the voluntary actions of individual persons over time; as is every patterned condition with sufficient content so as actually to have been proposed as presenting the central core of distributive justice. Still, given the possibility that some weak conditions or patterns may not be unstable in this way, it would be better to formulate an explicit description of the kind of interesting and contentful patterns under discussion, and to prove a theorem about their instability. Since the weaker the patterning, the more likely it is that the entitlement system itself satisfies it, a plausible conjecture is that any patterning either is unstable or is satisfied by the entitlement system.

⬇

NOTE

1. Applications of the principle of justice in acquisition may also occur as part of the move from one distribution to another. You may find an unheld thing now and appropriate it. Acquisitions also are to be understood as included when, to simplify, I speak only of transitions by transfers.

•Part Four•

EMPLOYER-EMPLOYEE RELATIONSHIPS
Introduction

———————•———————

EMPLOYEE RIGHTS

A number of years ago the B. F. Goodrich Corporation became involved in serious ethical problems over the testing procedures it used in the fulfillment of a government contract for jet aircraft brakes. According to an account written by one of the company's employees, the pressures in this incident upon corporate employees, including those of job security and advancement were so strong that they resulted in the falsifying of engineering specifications so that Goodrich could market dangerous and defective aircraft brakes. The dilemma of Kermit Vandivier, who finally "blew the whistle" on Goodrich, is a revealing illustration of some of the conflicts that can occur between self-interest, job responsibility, and one's sense of right and wrong.

This case illustrates a pressing contemporary concern: the relationship between employers and employees, especially in the area of employee rights. Do employees have rights in the workplace despite having voluntarily entered into a formal employee-employer relationship? For example, does a worker have the right to blow the whistle on a dangerous product without reprisal from management? Does he or she have a right to refuse a lie detector or polygraph test without being fired? Does he or she have the right to participate, directly or indirectly, in the management of the organization for which he or she works? And what are the concomitant rights of employers vis-à-vis their employees? What might an employer justifiably and reasonably expect in terms of loyalty and trust from his or her employees? These questions are among those falling under the heading of "employee rights," and their discussion has become one of the most heated and controversial in the field of business ethics.

When talking about employee rights, a few philosophical distinctions about the concept of rights are in order. We take the term "right" for granted, often forgetting that only a few centuries ago, the term was unknown. The first instance of the word in English appeared during the sixteenth century in the phrase "the rights of Englishmen." But the "rights of Englishmen" referred literally to Englishmen, not Englishwomen, and included only those who owned property. History waited for the English philosopher John Locke to provide the word "right" with its present, far-reaching significance. In Locke's writings the word came to refer to something which, by definition, is possessed unconditionally by all rational adult human beings. The talk of rights in our own Declaration of Independence and Constitution owes much to Locke's early doctrine of rights.

Philosophers disagree about the precise definition of a right. Three of the most widely used definitions are (1) a right is a justified claim (for example, the right to freedom); (2) a right is an entitlement to something, held against someone else (for example, the right to equal protection is an entitlement which requires positive action on the part of others, including the government); and (3) a right is a "trump" over a collective goal. The right to worship as one pleases, for example, overrides or "trumps" the collective goal of ideological unity within our society, and thus overrides any claims by certain groups or by a government that certain religions must be suppressed for the sake of the common good.

Rights may be divided into legal rights and moral rights. The former are rights that are either specified formally by law or protected by it. In the United States, the right to sue, to have a jury trial, to own property, and to have a free public education are legal rights. Not all such rights were included in the founding documents of the U.S. government: The right to free publication, the right of women and blacks to vote, and the right of workers to form unions were historical additions made in the nineteenth and twentieth centuries. Moral rights, on the other hand, are rights that are not necessarily protected and specified by the laws. Moral rights are rights everyone has or should have—that is, they are normative claims about what people are entitled to—but they may not be universally recognized or incorporated into law. They would include, for example, the right to be treated with equal respect, the right to equal freedom, and the right not to be systematically deceived or harmed. The law might stop short of preventing private clubs, for instance, from excluding Jews and blacks, yet most of us would agree that Jews and blacks have a moral right in such situations not to be excluded. Similarly, South African law protects the apartheid system, yet few of us feel that those laws are morally correct.

Turning to employee rights, although the Constitution and Bill of Rights protect the political rights of citizens, as late as 1946 the Supreme Court argued that the protection of the right to due process under the Fourteenth Amendment does not extend to private industry unless particular business is performing a public function.[1] It is not that some rights are denied to employees in private industry, but rather that they are not always explicitly protected nor are employers always restrained when rights are abrogated.

One of the most controversial issues in the area of employee rights, then, is whether, given that employees have some moral rights, those rights should remain only as *moral* rights or also be protected as *legal* rights. Until recently, the lack of protection of employee rights has been rationalized by appealing to the common-law doctrine, the principle of Employment at Will (EAW), a principle that states that in the absence of law or a specific contract an employer may hire, fire, demote, or promote an employee whenever the employer wishes without having to justify that action. In criticizing Employment at Will in the article "Reciprocity and Role Responsibilities," Patricia Werhane asserts that the three grounds upon which Employment at Will are typically defended are also grounds on which it can be attacked. Considerations of equal freedom, efficiency, and freedom of contract are often introduced in support of the prerogative of employers to fire at will. But the doctrine of Employment at Will, Werhane asserts, can reflect inequality of freedom between employee and employer, can produce inefficient outcomes, and can be inconsistent with the employee's freedom of contract. The exercise of freedom, in particular, requires a respect for the equal exercise of freedom by others—a respect that the Employment at Will doctrine fails to reflect.

A related reason that the Employment at Will doctrine is flawed, says Werhane, stems from the fact that employment relationships are reciprocal. In particular, the duties of employees to employers are only meaningful in a context where employers have duties to employees, and the existence of such employer duties can be shown to be inconsistent with Employment at Will—at least as the doctrine is usually interpreted. At a minimum, Werhane argues, the free exercise of management requires that employees be given reasons, publicly stated and verifiable, for firing decisions.

Sissela Bok takes a hard look at one of the most difficult issues affecting Employment and Will and workplace freedom: whistleblowing. While she notes that the topic is rife with moral conflicts, she concludes that whistleblowing is often the only course available to a concerned employee. It is important, in turn, for any potential whistleblower to understand the broader panorama of issues against which whistleblowing occurs, for example, of group loyalty, openness, authority, and the public interest. Equally important is the need for the employee to first exhaust less dramatic remedies before crying "foul" to the world. Only with such understanding, and by exploring alternative remedies, can an employee make an informed and correct decision about whether or not to blow the whistle.

EQUAL OPPORTUNITY AND AFFIRMATIVE ACTION

One important moral right that directly concerns business is the right of everyone to be treated equally in matters of hiring, pay, and promotion. If a person may be said to have such rights, business managers presumably have a corresponding obligation not to pursue discriminatory policies. For example, business organizations should be obliged to hire on the basis of applicant competence without being swayed by irrelevant factors such as sex, race, or ethnic origin. Most business people today recognize this obligation, one which is enforced fully in the law. A more controversial issue is whether business has an obligation to go beyond the point of merely not discriminating, to pursue what is called affirmative action. Affirmative action programs are of at least three sorts:

1. those which pursue a policy of deliberately hiring and promoting equally qualified minorities and women when considering candidates for a position;
2. those which pursue a policy of deliberately favoring qualified, but not necessarily equally qualified, minorities and women when hiring or promoting; and
3. those which establish quota systems to regulate the percentage of minority members hired or promoted in accordance with an ideal distribution of race, sex, creed, or ethnicity.

Perhaps the most common objection to affirmative action programs is that they are inconsistent, that is, that they make the same mistakes they hope to remedy. If discrimination entails using a morally irrelevant characteristic, such as a person's skin color, as a factor in hiring, is affirmative action itself perpetuating unjust discrimination? In giving preference to, say, blacks over whites, are such programs using the same morally irrelevant characteristic previously used in discriminatory practices, thus themselves committing discrimination? This and other criticisms of affirmative action programs are offered by Barry Gross in his article "Is Turn About Fair Play?"

Defenders of affirmative action argue that these programs are, all things considered, fair and consistent. They are not merely necessary to compensate past injustices in employment practices, injustices which clearly damaged the well-being and prospects of many members of society. Rather, they are also necessary to guarantee fairness in hiring and promotion for future generations. How will minority applicants ever seriously compete for positions in, say, medical school unless the educational and economic opportunities for minorities and non-minorities are equalized? And how will educational and economic opportunities be equalized unless minorities are able to attain a fair share of society's highest level of jobs?

In an article reprinted in this section, Richard Wasserstrom defends the legitimacy of claims against society by minorities. Some philosophers defend affirmative action as a form of compensation because what is being compensated in affirmative action programs is not racial (or sexual) discrimination, as Gross alleges, but rather the wrongs suffered by those qualified persons not originally hired because of their race or sex.

Wasserstrom argues that although affirmative action programs may be discriminatory, they are not as discriminatory as the original discrimination which was part of a whole social structure relegating women and minorities to second-class citizenship. Although affirmative action programs in employment *do* take into account race and sex, this is no less fair than other common employment practices which do not always hire or promote the most qualified either. Wasserstrom suggests that since we do not live in a perfect meritocracy, those who are minimally qualified deserve an equal opportunity with those who are more able. Furthermore, this seems a small price to pay for the resulting improvement in the racial-sexual mix in society.

While extremely important, affirmative action is only one of the issues at the center of the constellation of issues involving race and sex. Another concerns the problems of parenting in modern industrialized society, especially in the U.S. where a high percentage of both parents in two parent families, and of single parents in single parent families, work outside the home. Earlier, in section II, James Coleman asserted that the modern corporation is ill-equipped to accommodate the needs of children in society. For many parents, and perhaps especially for women accustomed to societal pressures to be active in the rearing of children, the problem is all too real: the balancing of career and family can create enormous psychological stress. The article "Management Women and the New Facts of Life" by Felice N. Schwartz reprinted in this section discusses an aspect of this problem. It is one of the most-discussed and controversial pieces to appear in the *Harvard Business Review*. It quickly became known as the "mommytrack" article for its recommendation that women managers should be identified early by upper management as falling into one of two tracks: "career primary" and "career and family." This way, argues Schwartz, everyone gets what she wants. Career-primary women are not blamed for the fact that some women have more family-oriented commitments; career and family women are not blamed for not putting in lots of overtime hours; and corporate managers are able effectively to tap the full talent of the labor pool. In the often critical responses to this view (also reprinted in this section) we learn how many people, including active feminists, regard Schwartz's view as reactionary and wrong-headed. Not the least of their concerns is that such a view mistakenly turns an issue that is properly a *parenting* issue, into something that is only a *women*'s issue.

Issues of discrimination and affirmative action are connected to, but distinct from, another important issue, namely, the question of comparable worth. Comparable worth entails the notion of fair treatment in job classification and compensation. It includes the idea of equal pay for equal work in similar jobs, a notion of particular importance for women, whose average wage, according to recent surveys, is still at least 30% lower than those of men in similar positions. Most important, the principle of comparable worth tries to establish guidelines for fairness in job measurement for jobs of comparable value—even when those jobs are radically different. Although equal pay for similar jobs is achievable, as John Boatright points out, it is difficult to determine and compare the worth of jobs that are dissimilar. One has to take into account such subjective factors as skill level, effort, responsibility, and working conditions to ascertain whether job segregation, as well as wage discrimination, has occurred. Comparable worth, then, is a concept which must be carefully defined and clarified.

NOTE

1. *Marsh v. State of Alabama*, 66 S. Ct. 276 (1946).

Employee Rights

Case Study

The Aircraft Brake Scandal

KERMIT VANDIVIER

The B. F. Goodrich Company is what business magazines like to refer to as "a major American corporation." It has operations in a dozen states and as many foreign countries; and of these far-flung facilities, the Goodrich plant at Troy, Ohio, is not the most imposing. It is a small, one-story building, once used to manufacture airplanes. Set in the grassy flatlands of west-central Ohio, it employs only about six hundred people. Nevertheless, it is one of the three largest manufacturers of aircraft wheels and brakes, a leader in a most profitable industry. Goodrich wheels and brakes support such well-known planes as the F111, the C5A, the Boeing 727, the XB70, and many others.

Contracts for aircraft wheels and brakes often run into millions of dollars, and ordinarily a contract with a total value of less than $70,000, though welcome, would not create any special stir of joy in the hearts of Goodrich sales personnel. But purchase order P-237138—issued on June 18, 1967, by the LTV Aerospace Corporation, ordering 202 brake assemblies for a new Air Force plane at a total price of $69,417—was received by Goodrich with considerable glee. And there was good reason. Some ten years previously, Goodrich had built a brake for LTV that was, to say the least, considerably less than a rousing success. The brake had not lived up to Goodrich's promises, and after experiencing considerable difficulty, LTV had written off Goodrich as a source of brakes. Since that time, Goodrich salesmen had been unable to sell so much as a shot of brake fluid to LTV. So in 1967, when LTV requested bids on wheels and brakes for the new A7D light attack aircraft it proposed to build for the Air Force, Goodrich submitted a bid that was absurdly low, so low that LTV could not, in all prudence, turn it down.

Goodrich had, in industry parlance, "bought into the business." The company did not expect to make a profit on the initial deal; it was prepared, if necessary, to lose money. But aircraft brakes are not something that can be ordered off the shelf. They are designed for a particular aircraft, and once an aircraft manufacturer buys a brake, he is forced to purchase all replacement parts from the brake manufacturer. The $70,000 that Goodrich would get for making the brake would be a drop in the bucket when compared with the cost of the linings and other parts the Air Force would have to buy from Goodrich during the lifetime of the aircraft.

There was another factor, besides the low bid, that had undoubtedly influenced LTV. All aircraft brakes made today are of the disk type, and the bid submitted by Goodrich called for a relatively small brake, one containing four disks and weighing only 106 pounds. The weight of any aircraft is extremely important: the lighter a part is, the heavier the plane's payload can be.

The brake was designed by one of Goodrich's most capable engineers, John Warren. A tall, lanky, blond graduate of Purdue, Warren had come from the Chrysler Corporation seven years before and had become adept at aircraft brake design. The happy-go-lucky manner he usually maintained belied a temper that exploded whenever anyone ventured to offer criticism of his work, no matter how small. On these occasions, Warren would turn red in the face, often throwing or slamming something and then stalking from the scene. As his co-workers learned the consequences of criticizing him, they did so less and less readily, and when he submitted his preliminary design for the A7D brake, it was accepted without question.

Warren was named project engineer for the A7D, and he, in turn, assigned the task of producing the final production design to a newcomer to the Goodrich engineering stable, Searle Lawson. Just turned twenty-six, Lawson had been out of the Northrop Institute of Technology only one year when he came to Goodrich in January 1967. He had been assigned to various "paper projects" to break him in, and after several months spent reviewing statistics and old brake designs, he was beginning to fret at the lack of challenge. When told he was being assigned to his first "real" project, he was elated and immediately plunged into his work.

The major portion of the design had already been completed by Warren, and major subassemblies for the brake had already been ordered from Goodrich suppliers. Naturally, however, before Goodrich could start making the brakes on a production basis, much testing would have to be done. Lawson would have to determine the best materials to use for the linings and discover what minor adjustments in the design would have to be made.

Then, after the preliminary testing and after the brake was judged ready for production, one whole brake assembly would undergo a series of grueling, simulated braking stops and other severe trials called qualification tests. These tests are required by the military, which gives very detailed specifications on how they are to be conducted, the criteria for failure, and so on. They are performed in the Goodrich plant's test laboratory, where huge machines called dynamometers can simulate the weight and speed of almost any aircraft.

Searle Lawson was well aware that much work had to be done before the A7D brake could go into production, and he knew that LTV had set the last two weeks in June 1968 as the starting dates for flight tests. So he decided to begin testing immediately. Goodrich's suppliers had not yet delivered the brake housing and other parts, but the brake disks had arrived, and using the housing from a brake similar in size and weight to the A7D brake, Lawson built a prototype. The prototype was installed in a test wheel and placed on one of the big dynamometers in the plant's test laboratory. Lawson began a series of tests, "landing" the wheel and brake at the A7D's landing speed and braking it to a stop. The main purpose of these preliminary tests was to learn what temperatures would develop within the brake during the simulated stops and to evaluate lining materials tentatively selected for use.

During a normal aircraft landing the temperatures inside the brake may reach 1,000 degrees, and occasionally a bit higher. During Lawson's first simulated landings, the temperature of his prototype brake reached 1,500 degrees. The brake glowed a bright cherry-red and threw off incandescent particles of metal and lining material as the temperature reached its peak. After a few such stops, the brake was dismantled and the linings were found to be almost completely disintegrated. Lawson chalked this first failure up to chance, and ordering new lining materials, tried again.

The second attempt was a repeat of the first. The brake became extremely hot, causing the lining materials to crumble into dust.

After the third such failure, Lawson, inexperienced though he was, knew that the fault lay not in defective parts or unsuitable lining material but in the basic design of the brake itself. Ignoring Warren's original computations, Lawson made his own, and it didn't take him long to discover where the trouble lay—the brake was too small. There simply was not enough surface area on the disks to stop the aircraft without generating the excessive heat that caused the linings to fail.

The answer to the problem was obvious, but far from simple—the four-disk brake would have to be scrapped, and a new design, using five disks, would have to be developed. The implications were not lost on Lawson. Such a step would require junking the four-disk-brake subassemblies, many of which had now begun to arrive from the various suppliers. It would also mean several weeks of preliminary design and testing and many more weeks of waiting while the suppliers made and delivered the new subassemblies.

Yet, several weeks had already gone by since LTV's order had arrived, and the date for delivery of the first production brakes for flight testing was only a few months away.

Although John Warren had more or less turned the A7D over to Lawson, he knew of the difficulties Lawson had been experiencing. He had assured the younger engineer that the problem resolved around getting the right kind of lining material. Once that was found, he said, the difficulties would end.

Despite the evidence of the abortive tests and Lawson's careful computations, Warren rejected the suggestion that the four-disk brake was too light for the job. He knew that his superior had already told LTV, in rather glowing terms, that the preliminary tests on the A7D brake were very successful. Indeed, Warren's superiors weren't aware at this time of the troubles on the brake. It would have been difficult for Warren to admit not only that he had made a serious error in his calculations and original design but that his mistakes had been caught by a green kid, barely out of college.

Warren's reaction to a five-disk brake was not unexpected by Lawson, and seeing that the four-disk brake was not to be abandoned so easily, he took his calculations and dismal test results one step up the corporate ladder.

At Goodrich, the man who supervises the engineers working on projects slated for production is called, predictably, the projects manager. The job was held by a short, chubby, bald man named Robert Sink. Some fifteen years before, Sink had begun working at Goodrich as a lowly draftsman. Slowly, he worked his way up. Despite his geniality, Sink was neither respected nor liked by the majority of the engineers, and his appointment as their supervisor did not improve their feelings toward him. He possessed only a high-school diploma, and it quite naturally rankled those who had gone through years of college to be commanded by a man whom they considered their intellectual inferior. But, though Sink had no college training, he had something even more useful: a fine working knowledge of company politics.

Puffing on a meerschaum pipe, Sink listened gravely as young Lawson confided his fears about the four-disk brake. Then he examined Lawson's calculations and the results of the abortive tests. Despite the fact that he was not a qualified engineer, in the strictest sense of the word, it must certainly have been obvious to Sink that Lawson's calculations were correct and that a four-disk brake would never work on the A7D.

But other things of equal importance were also obvious. First, to concede that Lawson's calculations were correct would also mean conceding that Warren's calculations were incorrect. As projects manager, not only was he responsible for Warren's activities, but in admitting that Warren had erred he would also have to admit that he had erred in trusting Warren's judgment. It also meant that, as projects manager, it would be he who would have to explain the whole messy situation to the Goodrich hierarchy, not only at Troy but possibly on the corporate level at Goodrich's Akron offices. And having taken Warren's judgment of the four-disk brake at face value, he had assured LTV, not once but several times, that about all there was left to do on the brake was pack it in a crate and ship it out the door.

There's really no problem at all, he told Lawson. After all, Warren was an experienced engineer, and if he said the brake would work, it would work. Just keep on testing and probably, maybe even on the very next try, it'll work out just fine.

Lawson was far from convinced, but without the support of his superiors there was little he could do except keep on testing. By now, housings for the four-disk brake had begun to arrive at the plant, and Lawson was able to build a production model of the brake and begin the formal qualification tests demanded by the military.

The first qualification attempts went exactly as the tests on the prototype had. Terrific heat developed within the brakes, and after a few short, simulated stops the linings crumbled. A new type of lining material was ordered and once again an attempt to qualify the brake was made. Again, failure.

Experts were called in from lining manufacturers, and new lining "mixes" were tried, always with the same result. Failure.

It was now the last week in March 1968, and flight tests were scheduled to begin in seventy days. Twelve separate attempts had been made to qualify the brake, and all had failed. It was no longer possible for anyone to ignore the glaring truth that the brake was a dismal failure and that nothing short of a major design change could ever make it work.

On April 4, the thirteenth attempt at qualification was begun. This time no attempt was made to conduct the tests by the methods and techniques spelled out in the military specifications. Regardless of how it had to be done, the brake was to be "nursed" through the required fifty simulated stops.

Fans were set up to provide special cooling. Instead of maintaining pressure on the brake until the test wheel had come to a complete stop, the pressure was reduced when the wheel had decelerated to around 15 mph, allowing it to "coast" to a stop. After each stop, the brake was disassembled and carefully cleaned, and after some of the stops, internal brake parts were machined in order to remove warp and other disfigurations caused by the high heat.

By these and other methods, all clearly contrary to the techniques established by the military specifications, the brake was coaxed through the fifty stops. But even using these methods, the brake could not meet all the requirements. On one stop the wheel rolled for a distance of 16,000 feet, or over three miles, before the brake could bring it to a stop. The normal distance required for such a stop was around 3,500 feet.

On April 11, the day the thirteenth test was completed, I became personally involved in the A7D situation.

I had worked in the Goodrich test laboratory for five years, starting first as an instrumentation engineer, then later becoming a data analyst and technical writer. As part of my duties, I analyzed the reams and reams of instrumentation data that came from the many testing machines in the lab, then transcribed all of it to a more usable form for the engineering department. When a new-type brake had successfully completed the required qualification tests, I would issue a formal qualification report.

Qualification reports are an accumulation of all the data and test logs compiled during the qualification tests and are documentary proof that a brake has met all the requirements established by the military specifications and is therefore presumed safe for flight testing. Before actual flight tests are conducted on a brake, qualification reports have to be delivered to the customer and to various government officials.

On April 11, I was looking over the data from the latest A7D test, and I noticed that many irregularities in testing had been noted on the test logs.

Technically, of course, there was nothing wrong with conducting tests in any manner desired, so long as the test was for research purposes only. But qualification test methods are clearly delineated by the military, and I knew that this test had been a formal qualification attempt. One particular notation on the test logs caught my eye. For some of the stops, the instrument that recorded the brake pressure had been deliberately miscalibrated so that, while the brake pressure used during the stops was recorded as 1,000 psi (pounds per square inch)—the maximum pressure that would be available on the A7D aircraft—the pressure had actually been 1,100 psi.

I showed the test logs to the test lab supervisor, Ralph Gretzinger, who said he had learned from the technician who had miscalibrated the instrument that he had been asked to do so by Lawson. Lawson, said Gretzinger, readily admitted asking for the miscalibration, saying he had been told to do so by Sink.

I asked Gretzinger why anyone would want to miscalibrate the data-recording instruments.

"Why? I'll tell you why," he snorted. "That brake is a failure. It's way too small for the job, and they're not ever going to get it to work. They're getting desperate, and instead of scrapping the damned thing and starting over, they figure they can horse around down here in the lab and qualify it that way."

An expert engineer, Gretzinger had been responsible for several innovations in brake design. It was he who had invented the unique brake system used on the famous XB70. "If you want to find out what's going on," said Gretzinger, "ask Lawson; he'll tell you."

Curious, I did ask Lawson the next time he came into the lab. He seemed eager to discuss the A7D and gave me the history of his months of frustrating efforts to get Warren and Sink to change the brake design. "I just can't believe this is really happening," said Lawson, shaking his head slowly. "This isn't engineering, at least not what I thought it would be.

Back in school, I thought that when you were an engineer, you tried to do your best, no matter what it cost. But this is something else."

He sat across the desk from me, his chin propped in his hand. "Just wait," he warned. "You'll get a chance to see what I'm talking about. You're going to get in the act too, because I've already had the word that we're going to make one more attempt to qualify the brake, and that's it. Win or lose, we're going to issue a qualification report!"

I reminded him that a qualification report could be issued only after a brake had successfully met all military requirements, and therefore, unless the next qualification attempt was a success, no report would be issued.

"You'll find out," retorted Lawson. "I was already told that regardless of what the brake does on test, it's going to be qualified." He said he had been told in those exact words at a conference with Sink and Russell Van Horn.

This was the first indication that Sink had brought his boss, Van Horn, into the mess. Although Van Horn, as manager of the design engineering section, was responsible for the entire department, he was not necessarily familiar with all phases of every project, and it was not uncommon for those under him to exercise the what-he-doesn't-know-won't-hurt-him philosophy. If he was aware of the full extent of the A7D situation, it meant that Sink had decided not only to call for help but to look toward that moment when blame must be borne and, if possible, shared.

Also, if Van Horn had said, "Regardless of what the brake does on test, it's going to be qualified," then it could only mean that, if necessary, a false qualification report would be issued. I discussed this possibility with Gretzinger, and he assured me that under no circumstances would such a report ever be issued.

"If they want a qualification report, we'll write them one, but we'll tell it just like it is," he declared emphatically. "No false data or false reports are going to come out of this lab."

On May 2, 1968, the fourteenth and final attempt to qualify the brake was begun. Although the same improper methods used to nurse the brake through the previous tests were employed, it soon became obvious that this too would end in failure.

When the tests were about half completed, Lawson asked if I would start preparing the various engineering curves and graphic displays that were normally incorporated in a qualification report. I flatly refused to have anything to do with the matter and immediately told Gretzinger what I had been asked to do. He was furious and repeated his previous declaration that under no circumstances would any false data or other matter be issued from the lab.

"I'm going to get this settled right now, once and for all," he declared. "I'm going to see Line [Russell Line, manager of the Goodrich Technical Services Section, of which the test lab was a part] and find out just how far this thing is going to go!" He stormed out of the room.

In about an hour, he returned and called me to his desk. He sat silently for a few moments, then muttered, half to himself, "I wonder what the hell they'd do if I just quit?" I didn't answer and I didn't ask him what he meant. I knew. He had been beaten down. He had reached the point when the decision had to be made. Defy them now while there was still time—or knuckle under, sell out.

"You know," he went on uncertainly, looking down at his desk, "I've been an engineer for a long time, and I've always believed that ethics and integrity were every bit as important as theorems and formulas, and never once has anything happened to change my beliefs. Now this . . . Hell, I've got two sons I've got to put through school and I just . . ." His voice trailed off.

He sat for a few more minutes, then, looking over the top of his glasses, said hoarsely, "Well, it looks like we're licked. The way it stands now, we're to go ahead and prepare the data and other things for the graphic presentation in the report, and when we're finished, someone up-stairs will actually write the report.

"After all," he continued, "we're just drawing some curves, and what happens to them after they leave here—well, we're not responsible for that."

I wasn't at all satisfied with the situation and decided that I too would discuss the matter with Russell Line, the senior executive in our section.

Tall, powerfully built, his teeth flashing white, his face tanned to a coffee-brown by a daily stint with a sunlamp, Line looked and acted every inch the executive. He had been transferred from the Akron offices some two years previously, and he commanded great respect and had come to be well liked by those of us who worked under him.

He listened sympathetically while I explained how I felt about the A7D situation, and when I had finished, he asked me what I wanted him to do about it. I said that as employees of the Goodrich Company we had a responsibility to protect the company and its reputation if at all possible. I said I was certain that officers on the corporate level would never know-ingly allow such tactics as had been employed on the A7D.

"I agree with you," he remarked, "but I still want to know what you want me to do about it."

I suggested that in all probability the chief engineer at the Troy plant, H. C. "Bud" Sunderman, was unaware of the A7D problem and that he, Line, could tell him what was going on.

Line laughed, good-humoredly. "Sure, I could, but I'm not going to. Bud probably already knows about this thing anyway, and if he doesn't, I'm sure not going to be the one to tell him."

"But why?"

"Because it's none of my business, and it's none of yours. I learned a long time ago not to worry about things over which I had no control. I have no control over this."

I wasn't satisfied with this answer, and I asked him if his conscience wouldn't bother him if, say, during flight tests on the brake, something should happen resulting in death or injury to the test pilot.

"Look," he said, becoming somewhat exasperated, "I just told you I have no control over this. Why should my conscience bother me?"

His voice took on a quiet, soothing tone as he continued. "You're just getting all upset over this thing for nothing. I just do as I'm told, and I'd advise you to do the same."

I made no attempt to rationalize what I had been asked to do. It made no difference who would falsify which part of the report or whether the actual falsification would be by misleading numbers or misleading words. Whether by acts of commission or omission, all of us who contributed to the fraud would be guilty. The only question left for me to decide was whether or not I would become a party to the fraud.

Before coming to Goodrich in 1963, I had held a variety of jobs, each a little more pleasant, a little more rewarding than the last. At forty-two, with seven children, I had decided that the Goodrich Company would probably be my "home" for the rest of my working life. The job paid well, it was pleasant and challenging, and the future looked reasonably bright. My wife and I had bought a home and we were ready to settle down into a comfortable, middle-age, middle-class rut. If I refused to take part in the A7D fraud, I would have either to resign or be fired. The report would be written by someone anyway, but I would have the satisfaction of knowing I had no part in the matter. But bills aren't paid with personal satisfaction, nor house payments with ethical principles. I made my decision. The next morning, I telephoned Lawson and told him I was ready to begin on the qualification report.

I had written dozens of qualification reports, and I knew what a "good" one looked like. Resorting to the actual test data only on occasion, Lawson and I proceeded to prepare page after page of elaborate, detailed engineering curves, charts, and test logs, which purported to show what had happened during the formal qualification tests. Where temperatures were too high, we deliberately chopped them down a few hundred degrees, and where they were too low, we raised them to a value that would appear reasonable to the LTV and military engineers. Brake pressure, torque values, distances, times—everything of consequence was tailored to fit.

Occasionally, we would find that some test either hadn't been performed at all or had been conducted improperly. On those occasions, we "conducted" the test—successfully, of course—on paper.

For nearly a month we worked on the graphic presentation that would be a part of the report. Meanwhile, the final qualification attempt had been completed, and the brake, not unexpectedly, had failed again.

We finished our work on the graphic portion of the report around the first of June. Altogether, we had prepared nearly two hundred pages of data, containing dozens of deliberate falsifications and misrepresentations.

I delivered the data to Gretzinger, who said that he had been instructed to deliver it personally to the chief engineer, Bud Sunderman, who in turn would assign someone in the engineering department to complete the written portion of the report. He gathered the bundle of data and left the office. Within minutes, he was back with the data, his face white with anger.

"That damned Sink's beat me to it," he said furiously. "He's already talked to Bud about this, and now Sunderman says no one in the engineering department has time to write the report. He wants us to do it, and I told him we couldn't."

The words had barely left his mouth when Russell Line burst in the door. "What the hell's all the fuss about this damned report?" he demanded.

Patiently, Gretzinger explained. "There's no fuss. Sunderman just told me that we'd have to write the report down here, and I said we couldn't. Russ," he went on, "I've told you before that we weren't going to write the report. I made my position clear on that a long time ago."

Line shut him up with a wave of his hand and, turning to me, bellowed, "I'm getting sick and tired of hearing about this damned report. Now, write the goddamn thing and shut up about it!" He slammed out of the office.

Gretzinger and I just sat for a few seconds looking at each other. Then he spoke.

"Well, I guess he's made it pretty clear, hasn't he? We can either write the thing or quit. You know, what we should have done was quit a long time ago. Now, it's too late."

Somehow I wasn't at all surprised at the turn of events, and it didn't really make that much difference. As far as I was concerned, we were all up to our necks in the thing anyway, and writing the narrative portion of the report couldn't make me more guilty than I already felt myself to be.

Within two days, I had completed the narrative, or written portion, of the report. As a final sop to my own self-respect, in the conclusion of the report I wrote, "The B. F. Goodrich P/N 2–1162–3 brake assembly does not meet the intent or the requirements of the applicable specification documents and therefore is not qualified."

This was a meaningless gesture, since I knew that this would certainly be changed when the report went through the final typing process. Sure enough, when the report was published, the negative conclusion had been made positive.

One final and significant incident occurred just before publication.

Qualification reports always bear the signature of the person who has prepared them. I refused to sign the report, as did Lawson. Warren was later asked to sign the report. He replied that he would "when I receive a signed statement from Bob Sink ordering me to sign it."

The engineering secretary who was delegated the responsibility of "dogging" the report through publication told me later that after I, Lawson, and Warren had all refused to sign the report, she had asked Sink if he would sign. He replied, "On something of this nature, I don't think a signature is really needed."

On June 5, 1968, the report was officially published and copies were delivered by hand to the Air Force and LTV. Within a week flight tests were begun at Edwards Air Force Base in California. Searle Lawson was sent to California as Goodrich's representative. Within approximately two weeks, he returned because some rather unusual incidents during the tests had caused them to be canceled.

His face was grim as he related stories of several near crashes during landings—caused by brake troubles. He told me about one incident in which, upon landing, one brake was literally welded together by the intense heat developed during the test stop. The wheel locked, and the plane skidded for nearly 1,500 feet before coming to a halt. The plane was jacked up and the wheel removed. The fused parts within the brake had to be pried apart.

That evening I left work early and went to see my attorney. After I told him the story, he advised that, while I was probably not actually guilty of fraud, I was certainly part of a conspiracy to defraud. He advised me to go to the Federal Bureau of Investigation and offered to arrange an appointment. The following week he took me to the Dayton office of the FBI and after I had been warned that I would not be immune from prosecution, I disclosed the A7D matter to one of the agents. The agent told me to say nothing about the episode to anyone and to report any further incidents to him. He said he would forward the story to his superiors in Washington.

A few days later, Lawson returned from a conference with LTV in Dallas and said that the Air Force, which had previously approved the qualification report, had suddenly rescinded that approval and was demanding to see some of the raw test data. I gathered that the FBI had passed the word.

Omitting any reference to the FBI, I told Lawson I had been to an attorney and that we were probably guilty of conspiracy.

"Can you get me an appointment with your attorney?" he asked. Within a week, he had been to the FBI and told them of his part in the mess. He too was advised to say nothing but to keep on the job reporting any new development.

Naturally, with the rescinding of Air Force approval and the demand to see raw test data, Goodrich officials were in a panic. A conference was called for July 27, a Saturday morning affair at which Lawson, Sink, Warren, and I were present. We met in a tiny conference room in the deserted engineering department. Lawson and I, by now openly hostile to Warren and Sink, ranged ourselves on one side of the conference table while Warren sat on the other side. Sink, chairing the meeting, paced slowly in front of a blackboard, puffing furiously on a pipe.

The meeting was called, Sink began, "to see where we stand on the A7D." What we were going to do, he said, was to "level" with LTV and tell them the "whole truth" about the A7D. "After all," he said, "they're in this thing with us, and they have the right to know how matters stand."

"In other words," I asked, "we're going to tell them the truth?"

"That's right," he replied. "We're going to level with them and let them handle the ball from there."

"There's one thing I don't quite understand," I interjected. "Isn't it going to be pretty hard for us to admit to them that we've lied?"

"Now, wait a minute," he said angrily. "Let's don't go off half-cocked on this thing. It's not a matter of lying. We've just interpreted the information the way we felt it should be."

"I don't know what you call it," I replied, "but to me it's lying, and it's going to be damned hard to confess to them that we've been lying all along."

He became very agitated at this and repeated, "We're not lying," adding, "I don't like this sort of talk."

I dropped the matter at this point, and he began discussing the various discrepancies in the report.

We broke for lunch, and afterward, I came back to the plant to find Sink sitting alone at his desk, waiting to resume the meeting. He called me over and said he wanted to apologize for his outburst that morning. "This thing has kind of gotten me down," he confessed, "and I think you've got the wrong picture. I don't think you really understand everything about this."

Perhaps so, I conceded, but it seemed to me that if we had already told LTV one thing and then had to tell them another, changing our story completely, we would have to admit we were lying.

"No," he explained patiently, "we're not really lying. All we were doing was interpreting the figures the way we knew they should be. We were just exercising engineering license."

During the afternoon session, we marked some forty-three discrepant points in the report; forty-three points that LTV would surely spot as occasions where we had exercised "engineering license."

After Sink listed those points on the blackboard, we discussed each one individually. As each point came up, Sink would explain that it was probably "too minor to bother about," or that perhaps it "wouldn't be wise to open that can of worms," or that maybe this was a point that "LTV just wouldn't understand." When the meeting was over, it had been decided that only three points were "worth mentioning."

Similar conferences were held during August and September, and the summer was punctuated with frequent treks between Dallas and Troy and demands by the Air Force to see the raw test data. Tempers were short, and matters seemed to grow worse.

Finally, early in October 1968, Lawson submitted his resignation, to take effect on October 25. On October 18, I submitted my own resignation, to take effect on November 1. In my resignation, addressed to Russell Line, I cited the A7D report and stated: "As you are aware, this report contains numerous deliberate and willfull misrepresentations which, according to legal counsel, constitute fraud and expose both myself and others to criminal charges of conspiracy to defraud. . . . The events of the past seven months have created an atmosphere of deceit and distrust in which it is impossible to work. . . ."

On October 25, I received a sharp summons to the office of Bud Sunderman. Tall and graying, impeccably dressed at all times, he was capable of producing a dazzling smile or a hearty chuckle or immobilizing his face into marble hardness, as the occasion required.

I faced the marble hardness when I reached his office. He motioned me to a chair. "I have your resignation here," he snapped, "and I must say you have made some rather shocking, I might even say irresponsible, charges. This is very serious."

Before I could reply, he was demanding an explanation. "I want to know exactly what the fraud is in connection with the A7D and how you can dare accuse this company of such a thing!"

I started to tell some of the things that had happened during the testing, but he shut me off saying, "There's nothing wrong with anything we've done here. You aren't aware of all the things that have been going on behind the scenes. If you had known the true situation, you would never have made these charges." He said that in view of my apparent "disloyalty" he had decided to accept my resignation "right now," and said it would be better for all concerned if I left the plant immediately. As I got up to leave he asked me if I intended to "carry this thing further."

I answered simply, "Yes," to which he replied, "Suit yourself." Within twenty minutes, I had cleaned out my desk and left. Forty-eight hours later, the B. F. Goodrich Company recalled the qualification report and the four-disk brake, announcing that it would replace the brake with a new, improved, five-disk brake at no cost to LTV.

Ten months later, on August 13, 1969, I was the chief government witness at a hearing conducted before Senator William Proxmire's Economy in Government Subcommittee. I related the A7D story to the committee, and my testimony was supported by Searle Lawson, who followed me to the witness stand. Air Force officers also testified, as well as a four-man team from the General Accounting Office, which had conducted an investigation of the A7D brake at the request of Senator Proxmire. Both Air Force and GAO investigators declared that the brake was dangerous and had not been tested properly.

Testifying for Goodrich was R. G. Jeter, vice-president and general counsel of the company, from the Akron headquarters. Representing the Troy plant was Robert Sink. These two denied any wrongdoing on the part of the Goodrich Company, despite expert testimony to the contrary by Air

Force and GAO officials. Sink was quick to deny any connection with the writing of the report or directing of any falsifications, claiming to have been on the West Coast at the time. John Warren was the man who had supervised its writing, said Sink.

As for me, I was dismissed as a high-school graduate with no technical training, while Sink testified that Lawson was a young, inexperienced engineer. "We tried to give him guidance," Sink testified, "but he preferred to have his own convictions."

About changing the data to figures in the report, Sink said: "When you take data from several different sources, you have to rationalize among those data what is the true story. This is part of your engineering know-how." He admitted that changes had been made in the data, "but only to make them more consistent with the overall picture of the data that is available."

Jeter pooh-poohed the suggestion that anything improper occurred, saying: "We have thirty-odd engineers at this plant . . . and I say to you that it is incredible that these men would stand idly by and see reports changed or falsified. . . . I mean you just do not have to do that working for anybody . . . Just nobody does that."

The four-hour hearing adjourned with no real conclusion reached by the subcommittee. But the following day the Department of Defense made sweeping changes in its inspection, testing, and reporting procedures. A spokesman for the DOD said the changes were a result of the Goodrich episode.

The A7D is now in service, sporting a Goodrich-made five-disk brake, a brake that works very well, I'm told. Business at the Goodrich plant is good. Lawson is now an engineer for LTV and has been assigned to the A7D project, possibly explaining why the A7D's new brakes work so well. And I am now a newspaper reporter.

At this writing, those remaining at Goodrich—including Warren—are still secure in the same positions, all except Russell Line and Robert Sink.

Line has been rewarded with a promotion to production superintendent, a large step upward on the corporate ladder. As for Sink, he moved up into Line's old job.

Case Study

The Copper "O" Company ⁽⁴⁻²⁾

Thomas F. McMahon, C.S.V.

The XYZ Company is a multinational electronics corporation. It is listed in *Forbes* as one of the top fifty companies in total assets. XYZ has a plant on Chicago's near northwest side, which manufactures printed circuit boards. High concentrations of copper are flushed down the sewer. The Metropolitan Sanitary District allows 3 milligrams per litre; any amount above 3 milligrams per litre is in violation of the city's Pure Air and Water Ordinance. XYZ has been flushing 5 to 6 milligrams per litre of copper—both particulate and solution—into the city sewerage system. Copper is toxic to water creatures but has little effect on humans (unless it becomes copper sulfate). The sanitary district is much more concerned with cadmium and cyanide than with copper contamination. When the engineers of the sanitary district observe excessive chemical discharge, they generally provide a "reasonable" time (six months) to correct the infringement through systems of filters, settling tanks, or other equipment.

On a number of occasions during the past three years, Bill Jones, plant manager, has confronted his immediate superiors about the existing violation. They keep postponing any definite answer about installing antipollution equipment. During Bill's most recent confrontation six months ago, they told Bill (1) that the present plant has been sold to another company; (2) that XYZ is building a new plant installed with the most advanced antipollution equipment in the suburbs within two years; (3) that no city inspector has ever tested this particular discharge since the inception of the printed circuit boards about four years ago.

Bill frequently wonders about his responsibility to the firm, his superiors, his workers, and his own family, as well as his obligation to his profession, local community, and a healthy environmental "quality-of-life." During the last few months, he found out that XYZ hired a public relations firm to promote the "concerned citizen about the environment" stance which XYZ is taking on its new plant. He wondered whether he should "blow the whistle" on the XYZ Company. He also mused over the role of the public relations firm: one black shoe from the sludge in Chicago; one white shoe from the clean environment in the suburbs.

Reprinted by permission of the author.

Employee and Employer Rights in an Institutional Context ய-۱۲

Patricia H. Werhane

The common law principle of Employment at Will (EAW) states that in the absence of a specific contract or law, an employer may hire, fire, demote, or promote any employee (not covered by contract or law) when that employer wishes. The theory is that employers have rights—rights to control what happens in the workplace. These include decisions concerning all business operations, extending of course to the hiring and placement of employees. Although EAW is a common-law doctrine, until recently it virtually dictated employment relationships.

What are the justifications for EAW? How would one defend this idea? EAW is sometimes justified on the basis of property rights. It is contended that the rights to freedom and to property ownership are valid rights and that they include the right to use freely and to improve what one owns. According to this view, an employer has the right to dispose of her business and those who work for that business (and thus affect it) as she sees fit. Instituting employee rights such as due process or the protection of whistle blowers, for example, would restrict an employer's freedom to do what she wishes with her business, thus violating property rights.

In the twentieth century, employer property rights have changed. Businesses are mainly corporations owned by a large number of changing shareholders and managed by employees who usually own little or no stock in the company. The board of directors represents the owner-shareholder interests, but most business decisions are in the hands of managers. Despite this division of ownership from management, however, proprietory ownership rights of employers have translated themselves into management rights. Contemporary management sees itself as having the rights to control business and therefore to control employment. From a utilitarian perspective, control of a company by its managers is thought of as essential for maximum efficiency and productivity. To disrupt this would defeat the primary purpose of free enterprise organizations. Moreover, according to its proponents, EAW preserves the notion of "freedom of contract," the right of persons and organizations to enter freely into binding voluntary agreements (e.g., employment agreements) of their choice.

That managers see themselves in the role of proprietors is, of course, too simple a description. In complex organizations there is a hierarchy of *at-will* relationships. Each manager is an at-will employee, but sees himself

Used by permission of the author.

as proprietor of certain responsibilities to the organization and as being in control of certain other employees whom the manager can dismiss at will, albeit within certain guidelines of legal restraint. That manager, in turn, reports to someone else who is herself an at-will employee responsible to another segment of the organization. These at-will relationships are thought to preserve equal employee and employer freedoms because, just as a manager can demote or fire an at-will employee at any time, so too an employee, any employee, can quit whenever he or she pleases for any reason whatsoever. Notice a strange anomaly here. Employees have responsibilities to their managers and are not free to make their own choices in the workplace. At the same time, employees are conceived of as autonomous persons who are at liberty to quit at any time.

Notice, too, that there is sometimes a sort of Social Darwinist theory of management functioning in many of these relationships. Managers are so-titled because it is felt that they are the most capable. By reason of education and experience and from the perspective of their position, they allegedly know what is best for the organization or the part of the organization they manage. This gives them the right to manage other employees. The employees they manage (who themselves may be managers of yet other employees) have roles within the organization to carry out the directives of their managers, and so on.

The employee-manager hierarchy of at-will employment relationships is both more complex and more simple in union-management relationships. It is more complex because often the relationship is specified or restricted by a number of well-defined rules for seniority, layoffs, dismissals, and so on. It is more simple because by and large union employees are *employees*, not managers. Their role responsibilities defined by hierarchical relationships are clear-cut, and those wishing to change or move up to management usually must give up union membership.

This oversimplified, crude, overstated, overview of hierarchical employment relationships in business may not currently exist in the ways I have described in any business. Yet such relationships are at least *implicit* in many businesses and perpetuated in the law by a continued management or employer-biased interpretation of the principle of EAW.

Despite the fact that the principle of EAW is defended on a number of grounds—including that it allegedly protects equal employee and manager freedoms, that it promotes efficiency, and that it preserves the notion of freedom of contract—EAW violates all of these for the following reasons. EAW does not preserve equal freedoms because in most employment relationships employer-managers are in positions of greater power than employees. This in itself does not undermine EAW, but the potential abuse of this power is what is at issue. Employees and managers allegedly have equal rights—rights to be fired or to quit at any time for any reason. But an at-will employee is seldom in a position within the law to inflict harm on an employer. Legally sanctioned at-will treatment by employers of employees can, however, harm employees. This is because when an employee is fired arbitrarily without some sort of grievance procedure, a hearing or an appeal, he cannot demonstrate that he was fired without good reason. Employees who have been fired have much more difficulty getting new jobs than those who have not been fired, even when that treatment was unjustified. Because arbitrarily fired employees are treated like those who deserved to lose their jobs, EAW puts such employees at an unfair disadvantage compared with other workers. The principle of EAW, then, does not preserve equal freedoms because it is to the advantage of the employer or manager and to the unfair disadvantage of the fired employee.

Worse, at-will practices violate the very right upon which EAW is allegedly based. Part of the appeal of EAW is that it protects the freedom of contract—the right to make employment agreements of one's choice. Abolishing EAW is coercive, according to its proponents, because this forces employers involuntarily to change their employment practices. But at-will employment practices too are or can be coercive. This is because when an employee is fired without sufficient reasons employers or managers place this person involuntarily in a personally harmful position unjustified by her behavior, a position that an employee would never choose. Thus the voluntary employment agreement according to which such practices are allowed is violated.

It is argued that EAW maximizes efficiency. But what is to prevent a manager from hiring a mentally retarded son-in-law or firing a good employee on personal grounds, actions that themselves damage efficiency? On a more serious level, if managers have prerogatives, these are based on a claim to the right to freedom—the freedom to conduct business as one pleases. But if this is a valid claim, then one must grant equal freedoms to everyone, including employees. Otherwise managers are saying that *they* have greater rights than other persons. This latter claim brings into question a crucial basis of democratic capitalism, namely that every person has *equal* rights, the most important of which is the equal right to freedom. The notion of equal rights does not necessarily imply that employees and managers have equal or identical prerogatives in business decision making or in managing a company. But what is implied is that the exercise of freedom requires a respect for the equal exercise of freedom by others, although the *kind* of exercises in each case may be different. EAW practices, then, are inconsistent practices because they do not preserve equal freedoms, they do not protect freedom of contract for both parties, and they do not guarantee efficiencies in the workplace. A number of thinkers contend that the principle should be abolished or disregarded in the law.

Interestingly, however, one can *defend* at least some employee rights from a consistent interpretation of the principle of EAW. This is because to be consistent the demands of EAW, principally the demand of management for the freedom to control business, require an equal respect for employee freedoms. In other words, if EAW is to be justified on the basis of the right to freedom, it can only be justified for that reason if it respects everyone's freedoms equally. Otherwise, managers' alleged freedoms are merely unwarranted licenses to do anything they please, even abridging employee rights, and thus have no moral or constitutional basis. Such equal respect for employee rights cannot always be interpreted as equal participation in management decisions. Extending and respecting employee freedoms requires balancing equal but not necessarily identical liberties. The free exercise of management employment decisions, however, does seem to require that employees be given reasons, publicly stated and verfiable, for management decisions that affect employees, including hiring and firing. In this way voluntary choices in the job market are truly equal to management employment choices. Moreover, freedom of choice in management decision making requires allowing legitimate whistle blowing, conscientious objection, and even striking without employer retaliation when an employee is asked to perform illegal, immoral, and/or socially dangerous jobs, or when such practices occur in the workplace. I am suggesting that a proper interpretation of EAW is not inconsistent with granting some employee rights. It is the misinterpretation of EAW that has served as a basis for the exercise of management prerogatives at the expense of employee rights.

Employers and managers, of course, will not always be happy to grant these freedoms to employees, because such freedoms are often seen as giving employees too many rights. Other managers identify extending employee freedoms with participatory management programs that, they argue, would abridge management responsibilities. Neither of these consequences, however, necessarily follows from extending employee rights. On the other hand, continuing the present imbalance of freedoms in the workplace perpetuates injustices. Worse, from the perspective of management this is a highly risky policy in an age of employee enlightenment and a concern for employee rights. Many managers are sympathetic to arguments defending employee rights. However, they fear that instituting employee rights in the workplace entails government regulation of and intervention in the affairs of business, all of which is intrusive, expensive, and time-consuming. But there is no reason why businesses cannot voluntarily institute employment reforms, and in the climate of a surging interest in employee rights, such voluntary actions would help prevent government intervention and regulation.

Turning to a second moral justification for employee rights, balancing employee and employer freedoms in the workplace is also justified because of what I shall call the reciprocal nature of employment relationships. Employment relationships, which are by and large hierarchical role relationships, tend to be destructive of employee rights, yet this need not be so, and in fact quite the contrary is required. The reasons for this are the following. In the workplace both management and employees have role responsibilities that are a source of job accountability. A person holding a job is held accountable for a certain performance; it is sometimes not considered unjust to dismiss someone for failure to perform his or her job even if the employer pays poorly and sometimes even if the employer does not respect other employee rights. Employee job accountability in this context is usually described as first-party duties of the employee to a manager or to the organization for whom one works. However, this description is incomplete. There are, in addition, duties on the part of the manager or the institution to the employee who is held accountable. These obligations arise in part from the role responsibilities of the party to whom an employee is answerable and in part because of the nature of the relationship. These obligations, which are often neglected in an analysis of accountability, are reciprocal or correlative obligations implied by role responsibility to the employee in question. This notion of reciprocity, I shall argue, is crucial in employment relationships.

The notion of reciprocity in any social relationship is grounded on the basic fact that each party is a person or a group of persons. As the philosopher Carol Gould puts it,

> Reciprocity may be defined as a social relation among agents in which each recognizes the other as an agent, that is, as equally free, and each acts with respect to the other on the basis of a shared understanding and a free agreement to the effect that the actions of each with respect to the other are equivalent.[1]

This does not mean that each party must treat the other in the same way in every respect, but rather that each treats the other with equal respect and as equal possessors of rights and benefits. Because they are social relationships between persons or between persons and institutions developed by persons, accountability relationships entail this notion of reciprocity.

Reciprocity in accountability relationships operates in part, as follows. If I am accountable for my actions to a certain group or institution because of my role in that group or institution, this accountability implicitly assumes a reciprocal accountability to me on the part of the institution to whom I am answerable. The obligations in each relationship are not necessarily contractual, but the strength of my role obligations depends at least in part on equally forceful, though obviously not identical, role obligations of the second party to me. And if no such reciprocal obligations exist, or if they are not respected, my accountability to that individual, group, or institution weakens.

What this brief analysis of role accountability suggests in the workplace is that when taking a job an employee has responsibilities connected with that job, responsibilities that are often only implicitly stated. At the same time, accountability does not consist merely of first-party duties of employees to employers or managers; it is also defined in reciprocal relationships with the party to whom one is accountable. The reason for this is that employee-employer relationships are both social and contractual arrangements. They are social because they are relationships entered into between persons or between persons and organizations created and run by persons. They are at least implicitly contractual ones voluntarily entered into and freely dissolvable by both parties. Therefore, if employees are accountable to managers or employers, managers or employers are also accountable for upholding their part of the agreement by being reciprocally accountable, albeit in different ways, to their employees.

The reciprocal nature of employee-employer relationships entails some important employee rights, in particular the rights to fair treatment and respect. What might constitute such fair treatment and respect? Obviously, fair pay or a living wage in exchange for work is an essential part of just treatment in the workplace. But if, in addition to working, employees are expected to respect and be fair to their employers, then employers have reciprocal obligations that go beyond merely offering fair pay. Employee respect demands from a manager a correlative respect for employee privacy, employee information, and for due process in the workplace, even for at-will employees.

Due process demands not that employees not be dismissed, but rather that any employer action meet impartial standards of reasonableness, the same sort of reasonableness expected of employees. Similarly, if an employee is to respect his or her employer and the decisions of that employer, the employer needs to honor the privacy of the employee as a human being, including protecting with confidentiality personnel information and respecting the privacy of employee activities outside the workplace. Respect for the employee also involves keeping the employee well-informed about his or her job, the quality of his or her work, and the stability of the company. This is a two-pronged responsibility. It entails not only the requirement that all employees are equally entitled to information, but the recognition that all employees actually in fact *have* such information. Employees have rights not merely to be informed but also to be communicated with in ways they understand.

The employee rights just enumerated—the rights to privacy, to employee information, and the right to due process—are moral rights that result from the nature of role accountability in the workplace. Like the right to freedom that is implied by a consistent interpretation of EAW, these rights are moral rather than legal rights, so employers need not respect them. But if the reciprocal requirements of employment accountability relationships are not met by employers or managers, those employers or managers undermine the basis for employee accountability in the workplace.

NOTE

1. Carol Gould, "Economic Justice, Self-Management and the Principle of Reciprocity," in *Economic Justice*, ed. Kenneth Kipnis and Diana T. Meyers (Totowa, N.J.: Rowman and Allanheld, 1985), pp. 213–214.

Whistleblowing and Professional Responsibility

SISSELA BOK

"Whistleblowing" is a new label generated by our increased awareness of the ethical conflicts encountered at work. Whistleblowers sound an alarm from within the very organization in which they work, aiming to spotlight neglect or abuses that threaten the public interest.

The stakes in whistleblowing are high. Take the nurse who alleges that physicians enrich themselves in her hospital through unnecessary surgery; the engineer who discloses safety defects in the braking systems of a fleet of new rapid-transit vehicles; the Defense Department official who alerts Congress to military graft and overspending: all know that they pose a threat to those whom they denounce and that their own careers may be at risk.

MORAL CONFLICTS

Moral conflicts on several levels confront anyone who is wondering whether to speak out about abuses or risks or serious neglect. In the first place, he must try to decide whether, other things being equal, speaking out is in fact in the public interest. This choice is often made more complicated by factual uncertainties: Who is responsible for the abuse or neglect? How great is the threat? And how likely is it that speaking out will precipitate changes for the better?

In the second place, a would-be whistleblower must weigh his responsibility to serve the public interest against the responsibility he owes to his colleagues and the institution in which he works. While the professional ethic requires collegial loyalty, the codes of ethics often stress responsibility to the public over and above duties to colleagues and clients. Thus the

From Sissela Bok, "Whistleblowing and Professional Responsibility," *New York University Education Quarterly*, 11 (Summer 1980): 2–7. Reprinted with permission.

United States Code of Ethics for Government Servants asks them to "expose corruption wherever uncovered" and to "put loyalty to the highest moral principles and to country above loyalty to persons, party, or government."[1] Similarly, the largest professional engineering association requires members to speak out against abuses threatening the safety, health, and welfare of the public.[2]

A third conflict for would-be whistleblowers is personal in nature and cuts across the first two: even in cases where they have concluded that the facts warrant speaking out, and that their duty to do so overrides loyalties to colleagues and institutions, they often have reason to fear the results of carrying out such a duty. However strong this duty may seem in theory, they know that, in practice, retaliation is likely. As a result, their careers and their ability to support themselves and their families may be unjustly impaired.[3] A government handbook issued during the Nixon era recommends reassigning "undesirables" to places so remote that they would prefer to resign. Whistleblowers may also be downgraded or given work without responsibility or work for which they are not qualified; or else they may be given many more tasks than they can possibly perform. Another risk is that an outspoken civil servant may be ordered to undergo a psychiatric fitness-for-duty examination,[4] declared unfit for service, and "separated" as well as discredited from the point of view of any allegations he may be making. Outright firing, finally, is the most direct institutional response to whistleblowers.

Add to the conflicts confronting individual whistleblowers the claim to self-policing that many professions make, and professional responsibility is at issue in still another way. For an appeal to the public goes against everything that "self-policing" stands for. The question for the different professions, then, is how to resolve, insofar as it is possible, the conflict between professional loyalty and professional responsibility toward the outside world. The same conflicts arise to some extent in all groups, but professional groups often have special cohesion and claim special dignity and privileges.

The plight of whistleblowers has come to be documented by the press and described in a number of books. Evidence of the hardships imposed on those who chose to act in the public interest has combined with a heightened awareness of professional malfeasance and corruption to produce a shift toward greater public support of whistleblowers. Public service law firms and consumer groups have taken up their cause; institutional reforms and legislation have been proposed to combat illegitimate reprisals.[5]

Given the indispensable services performed by so many whistleblowers, strong public support is often merited. But the new climate of acceptance makes it easy to overlook the dangers of whistleblowing: of uses in error or in malice; of work and reputations unjustly lost for those falsely accused; of privacy invaded and trust undermined. There comes a level of internal prying and mutual suspicion at which no institution can function.

And it is a fact that the disappointed, the incompetent, the malicious, and the paranoid all too often leap to accusations in public. Worst of all, ideological persecution throughout the world traditionally relies on insiders willing to inform on their colleagues or even on their family members, often through staged public denunciations or press campaigns.

No society can count itself immune from such dangers. But neither can it risk silencing those with a legitimate reason to blow the whistle. How then can we distinguish between different instances of whistleblowing? A society that fails to protect the right to speak out even on the part of those whose warnings turn out to be spurious obviously opens the door to political repression. But from the moral point of view there are important differences between the aims, messages, and methods of dissenters from within.

NATURE OF WHISTLEBLOWING

Three elements, each jarring, and triply jarring when conjoined, lend acts of whistleblowing special urgency and bitterness: dissent, breach of loyalty, and accusation.

Like all dissent, whistleblowing makes public a disagreement with an authority or a majority view. But whereas dissent can concern all forms of disagreement with, for instance, religious dogma or government policy or court decisions, whistleblowing has the narrower aim of shedding light on negligence or abuse, or alerting to a risk, and of assigning responsibility for this risk.

Would-be whistleblowers confront the conflict inherent in all dissent: between conforming and sticking their necks out. The more repressive the authority they challenge, the greater the personal risk they take in speaking out. At exceptional times, as in times of war, even ordinarily tolerant authorities may come to regard dissent as unacceptable and even disloyal.[6]

Furthermore, the whistleblower hopes to stop the game; but since he is neither referee nor coach, and since he blows the whistle on his own team, his act is seen as a violation of loyalty. In holding his position, he has assumed certain obligations to his colleagues and clients. He may even have subscribed to a loyalty oath or a promise of confidentiality. Loyalty to colleagues and to clients comes to be pitted against loyalty to the public interest, to those who may be injured unless the revelation is made.

Not only is loyalty violated in whistleblowing, hierarchy as well is often opposed, since the whistleblower is not only a colleague but a subordinate. Though aware of the risks inherent in such disobedience, he often hopes to keep his job.[7] At times, however, he plans his alarm to coincide with leaving the institution. If he is highly placed, or joined by others, resigning in protest may effectively direct public attention to the wrongdoing at issue.[8] Still another alternative, often chosen by those who wish to be safe from retaliation, is to leave the institution quietly, to secure another post, and then to blow the whistle. In this way, it is possible to speak with the authority and knowledge of an insider without having the vulnerability of that position.

It is the element of accusation, of calling a "foul," that arouses the strongest reactions on the part of the hierarchy. The accusation may be of neglect, of willfully concealed dangers, or of outright abuse on the part of colleagues or superiors. It singles out specific persons or groups as responsible for threats to the public interest. If no one could be held responsible—as in the case of an impending avalanche—the warning would not constitute whistleblowing.

The accusation of the whistleblower, moreover, concerns a present or an imminent threat. Past errors or misdeeds occasion such an alarm only if they still affect current practices. And risks far in the future lack the immediacy needed to make the alarm a compelling one, as well as the close connection to particular individuals that would justify actual accusations. Thus an alarm can be sounded about safety defects in a rapid-transit system that threaten or will shortly threaten passengers, but the revelation of safety defects in a system no longer in use, while of historical interest, would not constitute whistleblowing. Nor would the revelation of potential problems in a system not yet fully designed and far from implemented.[9]

Not only immediacy, but also specificity, is needed for there to be an alarm capable of pinpointing responsibility. A concrete risk must be at issue rather than a vague foreboding or a somber prediction. The act of whistleblowing differs in this respect from the lamentation or the dire prophecy. An immediate and specific threat would normally be acted upon by those at risk. The whistleblower assumes that his message will alert listeners to something they do not know, or whose significance they have not grasped because it has been kept secret.

The desire for openness inheres in the temptation to reveal any secret, sometimes joined to an urge for self-aggrandizement and publicity and the hope for revenge for past slights or injustices. There can be pleasure, too—righteous or malicious—in laying bare the secrets of co-workers and in setting the record straight at last. Colleagues of the whistleblower often suspect his motives: they may regard him as a crank, as publicity-hungry, wrong about the facts, eager for scandal and discord, and driven to indiscretion by his personal biases and shortcomings.

For whistleblowing to be effective, it must arouse its audience. Inarticulate whistleblowers are likely to fail from the outset. When they are greeted by apathy, their message dissipates. When they are greeted by disbelief, they elicit no response at all. And when the audience is not free to receive or to act on the information—when censorship or fear of retribution stifles response—then the message rebounds to injure the whistleblower. Whistleblowing also requires the possibility of concerted public response: the idea of whistleblowing in an anarchy is therefore merely quixotic.

Such characteristics of whistleblowing and strategic considerations for achieving an impact are common to the noblest warnings, the most vicious personal attacks, and the delusions of the paranoid. How can one distinguish the many acts of sounding an alarm that are genuinely in the public interest from all the petty, biased, or lurid revelations that pervade our querulous and gossip-ridden society? Can we draw distinctions between different whistleblowers, different messages, different methods?

We clearly can, in a number of cases. Whistleblowing may be starkly inappropriate when in malice or error, or when it lays bare legitimately private matters having to do, for instance, with political belief or sexual life. It can, just as clearly, be the only way to shed light on an ongoing unjust practice such as drugging political prisoners or subjecting them to electroshock treatment. It can be the last resort for alerting the public to an impending disaster. Taking such clear-cut cases as benchmarks, and reflecting on what it is about them that weighs so heavily for or against speaking out, we can work our way toward the admittedly more complex cases in which whistleblowing is not so clearly the right or wrong choice, or where different points of view exist regarding its legitimacy—cases where there are moral reasons both for concealment and for disclosure and where judgments conflict. Consider the following cases[10]:

A. As a construction inspector for a federal agency, John Samuels (not his real name) had personal knowledge of shoddy and deficient construction practices by private contractors. He knew his superiors received free vacations and entertainment, had their homes remodeled and found jobs for their relatives—all courtesy of a private contractor. These superiors later approved a multimillion no-bid contract with the same "generous" firm.

Samuels also had evidence that other firms were hiring nonunion laborers at a low wage while receiving substantially higher payments from the government for labor costs. A former superior, unaware of an office dictaphone, had incautiously instructed Samuels on how to accept bribes for overlooking sub-par performance.

As he prepared to volunteer this information to various members of Congress, he became tense and uneasy. His family was scared and the fears were valid. It might cost Samuels thousands of dollars to protect his job. Those who had freely provided Samuels with information would probably recant or withdraw their friendship. A number of people might object to his using a dictaphone to gather information. His agency would start covering up and vent its collective wrath upon him. As for reporters and writers, they would gather for a few days, then move on to the next story. He would be left without a job, with fewer friends, with massive battles looming, and without the financial means of fighting them. Samuels decided to remain silent.

B. Engineers of Company "A" prepared plans and specifications for machinery to be used in a manufacturing process and Company "A" turned them over to Company "B" for production. The engineers of Company "B," in reviewing the plans and specifications, came to the conclusion that they included certain miscalculations and technical deficiencies of a nature that the final product might be unsuitable for the purposes of the ultimate users, and that the equipment, if built according to the original plans and specifications, might endanger the lives of persons in proximity to it. The engineers of Company "B" called the matter to the attention of appropriate officials of their employer who, in turn, advised Company "A." Company "A" replied that its engineers felt that the design and specifications for the equipment were adequate and safe and that Company "B" should proceed to build the equipment as designed and specified. The officials of Company "B" instructed its engineers to proceed with the work.

C. A recently hired assistant director of admissions in a state university begins to wonder whether transcripts of some applicants accurately reflect their accomplishments. He knows that it matters to many in the university community, including alumni, that the football team continue its winning tradition. He has heard rumors that surrogates may be available to take tests for a fee, signing the names of designated applicants for admission, and that some of the transcripts may have been altered. But he has no hard facts. When he brings the question up with the director of admissions, he is told that the rumors are unfounded and asked not to inquire further into the matter.

INDIVIDUAL MORAL CHOICE

What questions might those who consider sounding an alarm in public ask themselves? How might they articulate the problem they see and weigh its injustice before deciding whether or not to reveal it? How can they best try to make sure their choice is the right one? In thinking about these questions it helps to keep in mind the three elements mentioned earlier: dissent, breach of loyalty, and accusation. They impose certain requirements—of accuracy and judgment in dissent; of exploring alternative ways to cope with improprieties that minimize the breach of loyalty; and of fairness in accusation. For each, careful articulation and testing of arguments are needed to limit error and bias.

Dissent by whistleblowers, first of all, is expressly claimed to be intended to benefit the public. It carries with it, as a result, an obligation to consider the nature of this benefit and to consider also the possible harm that may come from speaking out: harm to persons or institutions and, ultimately, to the public interest itself. Whistleblowers must, therefore, begin by making every effort to consider the effects of speaking out versus those of remaining silent. They must assure themselves of the accuracy of their reports, checking and rechecking the facts before speaking out; specify the degree to which there is genuine impropriety; consider how imminent is the threat they see, how serious, and how closely linked to those accused of neglect and abuse.

If the facts warrant whistleblowing, how can the second element— breach of loyalty—be minimized? The most important question here is whether the existing avenues for change within the organization have been explored. It is a waste of time for the public as well as harmful to the institution to sound the loudest alarm first. Whistleblowing has to remain a last alternative because of its destructive side effects: it must be chosen only when other alternatives have been considered and rejected. They may be rejected if they simply do not apply to the problem at hand, or when there is not time to go through routine channels or when the institution is so corrupt or coercive that steps will be taken to silence the whistleblower should he try the regular channels first.

What weight should an oath or a promise of silence have in the conflict of loyalties? One sworn to silence is doubtless under a stronger obligation because of the oath he has taken. He has bound himself, assumed specific obligations beyond those assumed in merely taking a new position. But even such promises can be overridden when the public interest at issue is strong enough. They can be overridden if they were obtained under duress or through deceit. They can be overridden, too, if they promise something that is in itself wrong or unlawful. The fact that one has promised silence is no excuse for complicity in covering up a crime or a violation of the public's trust.

The third element in whistleblowing—accusation—raises equally serious ethical concerns. They are concerns of fairness to the persons accused of impropriety. Is the message one to which the public is entitled in the first place? Or does it infringe on personal and private matters that one has no right to invade? Here, the very notion of what is in the public's best "interest" is at issue: "accusations" regarding an official's unusual sexual or religious experiences may well appeal to the public's interest without being information relevant to "the public interest."

Great conflicts arise here. We have witnessed excessive claims to executive privilege and to secrecy by government officials during the Watergate scandal in order to cover up for abuses the public had every right to discover. Conversely, those hoping to profit from prying into private matters have become adept at invoking "the public's right to know." Some even regard such private matters as threats to the public: they voice their own religious and political prejudices in the language of accusation. Such a danger is never stronger than when the accusation is delivered surreptitiously. The anonymous accusations made during the McCarthy period regarding political beliefs and associations often injured persons who did not even know their accusers or the exact nature of the accusations.

From the public's point of view, accusations that are openly made by identifiable individuals are more likely to be taken seriously. And in fairness to those criticized, openly accepted responsibility for blowing the whistle should be preferred to the denunciation or the leaked rumor. What is openly stated can more easily be checked, its source's motives challenged, and the underlying information examined. Those under attack may otherwise be hard put to defend themselves against nameless adversaries. Often they do not even know that they are threatened until it is too late to respond. The anonymous denunciation, moreover, common to so many regimes, places the burden of investigation on government agencies that may thereby gain the power of a secret police.

From the point of view of the whistleblower, on the other hand, the anonymous message is safer in situations where retaliation is likely. But it is also often less likely to be taken seriously. Unless the message is accompanied by indications of how the evidence can be checked, its anonymity, however safe for the source, speaks against it.

During the process of weighing the legitimacy of speaking out, the method used, and the degree of fairness needed, whistleblowers must try to compensate for the strong possibility of bias on their part. They should be scrupulously aware of any motive that might skew their message: a desire for self-defense in a difficult bureaucratic situation, perhaps, or the urge to seek revenge, or inflated expectations regarding the effect their message will have on the situation. (Needless to say, bias affects the silent as well as the outspoken. The motive for holding back important information about abuses and injustice ought to give similar cause for soul-searching.)

Likewise, the possibility of personal gain from sounding the alarm ought to give pause. Once again there is then greater risk of a biased message. Even if the whistleblower regards himself as incorruptible, his profiting from revelations of neglect or abuse will lead others to question his motives and to put less credence in his charges. If, for example, a government employee stands to make large profits from a book exposing the iniquities in his agency, there is danger that he will, perhaps even unconsciously, slant his report in order to cause more of a sensation.

A special problem arises when there is a high risk that the civil servant who speaks out will have to go through costly litigation. Might he not justifiably try to make enough money on his public revelations—say, through books or public speaking—to offset his losses? In so doing he will not strictly speaking have *profited* from his revelations: he merely avoids being financially crushed by their sequels. He will nevertheless still be suspected at the time of revelation, and his message will therefore seem more questionable.

Reducing bias and error in moral choice often requires consultation, even open debate[11]: methods that force articulation of the moral arguments at stake and challenge privately held assumptions. But acts of whistleblowing present special problems when it comes to open consultation. On the one hand, once the whistleblower sounds his alarm publicly, his arguments will be subjected to open scrutiny; he will have to articulate his reasons for speaking out and substantiate his charges. On the other hand, it will then be too late to retract the alarm or to combat its harmful effects, should his choice to speak out have been ill-advised.

For this reason, the whistleblower owes it to all involved to make sure of two things: that he has sought as much and as objective advice regarding his choice as he can *before* going public; and that he is aware of the arguments for and against the practice of whistleblowing in general, so that he can see his own choice against as richly detailed and coherently structured a background as possible. Satisfying these two requirements once again has special problems because of the very nature of whistleblowing: the more corrupt the circumstances, the more dangerous it may be to seek consultation before speaking out. And yet, since the whistleblower himself may have a biased view of the state of affairs, he may choose not to consult others when in fact it would be not only safe but advantageous to do so; he may see corruption and conspiracy where none exists.

NOTES

1. Code of Ethics for Government Service passed by the U.S. House of Representatives in the 85th Congress (1958) and applying to all government employees and office holders.
2. Code of Ethics of the Institute of Electrical and Electronics Engineers, Article IV.
3. For case histories and descriptions of what befalls whistleblowers, see Rosemary Chalk and Frank von Hippel, "Due Process for Dissenting Whistle-Blowers," *Technology Review* 81 (June–July 1979): 48–55; Alan S. Westin and Stephen Salisbury, eds., *Individual Rights in the Corporation* (New York: Pantheon, 1980); Helen Dudar, "The Price of Blowing the Whistle," *New York Times Magazine*, 30 October 1979, pp. 41–54; John Edsall, *Scientific Freedom and Responsibility* (Washington, D.C.: American Association for the Advancement of Science, 1975), p. 5; David Ewing, *Freedom Inside the Organization* (New York: Dutton, 1977); Ralph Nader, Peter Petkas, and Kate Blackwell, *Whistle Blowing* (New York: Grossman, 1972); Charles Peter and Taylor Branch, *Blowing the Whistle* (New York: Praeger, 1972).
4. Congressional hearings uncovered a growing resort to mandatory psychiatric examinations.
5. For an account of strategies and proposals to support government whistleblowers, see Government Accountability Project, *A Whistleblower's Guide to the Federal Bureaucracy* (Washington, D.C.: Institute for Policy Studies, 1977).
6. See, e.g., Samuel Eliot Morison, Frederick Merk, and Frank Friedel, *Dissent in Three American Wars* (Cambridge: Harvard University Press, 1970).
7. In the scheme worked out by Albert Hirschman in *Exit, Voice and Loyalty* (Cambridge: Harvard University Press, 1970), whistleblowing represents "voice" accompanied by a preference not to "exit," though forced "exit" is clearly a possibility and "voice" after or during "exit" may be chosen for strategic reasons.
8. Edward Weisband and Thomas N. Franck, *Resignation in Protest* (New York: Grossman, 1975).
9. Future developments can, however, be the cause for whistleblowing if they are seen as resulting from steps being taken or about to be taken that render them inevitable.
10. Case A is adapted from Louis Clark, "The Sound of Professional Suicide," *Barrister*, Summer 1978, p. 10; Case B is Case 5 in Robert J. Baum and Albert Flores, eds., *Ethical Problems of Engineering* (Troy, N.Y.: Rensselaer Polytechnic Institute, 1978), p. 186.
11. I discuss these questions of consultation and publicity with respect to moral choice in chapter 7 of Sissela Bok, *Lying* (New York: Pantheon, 1978); and in *Secrets* (New York: Pantheon Books, 1982), Ch. IX and XV.

Equal Opportunity and Affirmative Action

Case Study

Foreign Assignment

THOMAS DUNFEE AND DIANA ROBERTSON

Sara Strong graduated with an MBA from UCLA four years ago. She immediately took a job in the correspondent bank section of the Security Bank of the American Continent. Sara was assigned to work on issues pertaining to relationships with correspondent banks in Latin America. She rose rapidly in the section and received three good promotions in three years. She consistently got high ratings from her superiors, and she received particularly high marks for her professional demeanor.

In her initial position with the bank, Sara was required to travel to Mexico on several occasions. She was always accompanied by a male colleague even though she generally handled similar business by herself on trips within the United States. During her trips to Mexico she observed that Mexican bankers seemed more aware of her being a woman and were personally solicitous to her, but she didn't discern any major problems. The final decisions on the work that she did were handled by male representatives of the bank stationed in Mexico.

A successful foreign assignment was an important step for those on the "fast track" at the bank. Sara applied for a position in Central or South America and was delighted when she was assigned to the bank's office in Mexico City. The office had about twenty bank employees and was headed by William Vitam. The Mexico City office was seen as a preferred assignment by young executives at the bank.

After a month, Sara began to encounter problems. She found it difficult to be effective in dealing with Mexican bankers—the clients. They appeared reluctant to accept her authority and they would often bypass her in important matters. The problem was exacerbated by Vitam's compliance

CASE STUDY by Thomas Dunfee and Diana Robertson, "Foreign Assignment," the Wharton School of Business, The University of Pennsylvania. Reprinted by permission of the authors.

in her being bypassed. When she asked that the clients be referred back to her, Vitam replied, "Of course that isn't really practical." Vitam made matters worse by patronizing her in front of clients and by referring to her as "my cute assistant" and "our lady banker." Vitam never did this when only Americans were present, and in fact treated her professionally and with respect in internal situations.

Sara finally complained to Vitam that he was undermining her authority and effectiveness; she asked him in as positive a manner as possible to help her. Vitam listened carefully to Sara's complaints, then replied: "I'm glad that you brought this up, because I've been meaning to sit down and talk to you about my little game-playing in front of the clients. Let me be frank with you. Our clients think you're great, but they just don't understand a woman in authority, and you and I aren't going to be able to change their attitudes overnight. As long as the clients see you as my assistant and deferring to me, they can do business with you. I'm willing to give you as much responsibility as they can handle your having. I *know* you can handle it. But we just have to tread carefully. You and I know that my remarks in front of clients don't mean anything. They're just a way of playing the game Latin style. I know it's frustrating for you, but I really need you to support me on this. It's not going to affect your promotions, and for the most part you really will have responsibility for these clients' accounts. You just have to act like it's my responsibility." Sara replied that she would try to cooperate, but that basically she found her role demeaning.

As time went on, Sara found that the patronizing actions in front of clients bothered her more and more. She spoke to Vitam again, but he was firm in his position, and urged her to try to be a little more flexible, even a little more "feminine."

Sara also had a problem with Vitam over policy. The Mexico City office had five younger women who worked as receptionists and secretaries. They were all situated at work stations at the entrance to the office. They were required to wear standard uniforms that were colorful and slightly sexy. Sara protested the requirement that uniforms be worn because (1) they were inconsistent to the image of the banking business and (2) they were demeaning to the women who had to wear them. Vitam just curtly replied that he had received a lot of favorable comments about the uniforms from clients of the bank.

Several months later, Sara had what she thought would be a good opportunity to deal with the problem. Tom Fried, an executive vice present who had been a mentor for her since she arrived at the bank, was coming to Mexico City; she arranged a private conference with him. She described her problems and explained that she was not able to be effective in this environment and that she worried that it would have a negative effect on her chance of promotion within the bank. Fried was very careful in his response. He spoke of certain "realities" that the bank had to respect and he urged her to "see it through" even though he could understand how she would feel that things weren't fair.

Sara found herself becoming more aggressive and defensive in her meetings with Vitam and her clients. Several clients asked that other bank personnel handle their transactions. Sara has just received an Average rating, which noted "the beginnings of a negative attitude about the bank and its policies."

Propmore Corporation

PETER MADSEN AND JOHN FLEMING

SITUATION I

A Luncheon Harassment

After a two hour purchasing meeting in the morning, Bill Smith, an Airgoods Corporation Sales Representative, had invited Jane Thompson to lunch. They left at noon. An hour and a half later, Jane stormed into Don Bradford's office, obviously upset. When Don asked what was wrong, Jane told him in very strong terms that Bill Smith had sexually harassed her during and after the luncheon.

According to Jane, Bill made some sexual comments and suggestions toward the end of the meal. She considered this to be offensive and unwelcome. Jane, however, told Bill to take her back to the office. He attempted to make light of the situation and said he was only joking, but on the way back he made some further comments and several casual physical contacts to which she objected. When they arrived at the company, Bill was embarrassed and tried to apologize. But Jane entered the office before he could finish.

Jane demanded that the Airgoods Corporation be taken off the bidder list for the raw material contract and that Airgoods' President be informed of the unseemly and illegal behavior of one of his salesmen. She would also consider taking legal action against Bill Smith through the Equal Employment Opportunity Commission for sexual harassment. Also, Jane stated she would investigate suing the Propmore Corporation for failure to protect her from this form of discrimination while she was performing her duties as

This case was developed by Peter Madsen and John Fleming for the Arthur Andersen & Co. SC Business Ethics Program. Reprinted by permission of Arthur Andersen and the authors.

an employee of the company. At the end of this outburst, Jane abruptly left Don's office.

Don was significantly troubled. Jane played a critical role in getting bids for the raw material contract. He needed her. Yet he knew that if he kept Airgoods on the bidder list, it might be difficult for her to view this vendor objectively.

Don was somewhat concerned about Jane's threat to sue Propmore but doubted that she had a very good case. Still, such an action would be costly in legal fees, management time, and damage to the company's image.

Don wasn't sure what to do about the bidder list. Airgoods had an excellent record as a reliable vendor for similar contracts. Propmore might be at a disadvantage if Airgoods was eliminated. On the other hand, Don firmly believed in standing behind his subordinates.

At this point, he needed more information on what constitutes sexual harassment and what policy guidelines his company had established. He examined two documents: the EEOC Definition of Sexual Harassment (Appendix 1) and the Propmore Corporation's Policy HR-13, on Sexual Harassment (Appendix 2).

SITUATION II

Gathering More Information

Don Bradford had met Bill Smith, the Airgoods Corporation Salesman, on several occasions but did not feel he really knew him. To learn more about Bill, Don talked with his other key buyer, Bob Peters. Bob had dealt with Bill on many contracts in the past. After Don finished recounting the incident concerning Jane, Bob smiled. In his opinion, it was just a "boys will be boys" situation that got blown out of proportion. It may have been more than a joke, but Bob did not think Bill would do something "too far out." He pointed out that Bill had been selling for ten years and knew how to treat a customer.

Don's next step was a visit to the division personnel office. In addition to going through Jane's file, he wanted to discuss the matter with Ann Perkins, the division's Human Resource Manager. Fortunately, Ann was in her office and had time to see him immediately.

Don went over the whole situation with Ann. When he had finished his account, Ann was silent for a minute. Then she pointed out that this was a strange sexual harassment situation: it did not happen at the company, and the alleged harasser was not a member of the Propmore organization. The extent of the company's responsibility was not clear.

She had heard of cases where employees held their companies responsible for protecting them from sexual harassment by employees of other organizations. But the harassment had taken place on company premises, where some degree of direct supervision and protection could have been expected.

Ann filled out a slip authorizing Don to see Jane's personnel file. He took the file to an empty office and went through its contents.

There were the expected hiring and annual evaluation forms, which revealed nothing unusual and only confirmed his own high opinion of Jane.

Then Don came to an informal note at the back of the file. It summarized a telephone reference check with the personnel manager of Jane's former employer. The note indicated that Jane had complained of being sexually harassed by her supervisor. The personnel manager had "checked it out" with the supervisor, who claimed "there was nothing to it." The note also indicated that Jane was terminated two months after this incident for "unsatisfactory work."

Don returned to his office and called his functional superior, Mr. Stewart, to inform him of the situation. Mr. Stewart was the Corporate Vice-President of Procurement. He had known Bill Smith personally for a number of years. He told Don that Bill's wife had abandoned him and their three children several years ago. Although Bill had a reputation for occasional odd behavior, he was known in the industry as a hard-working salesperson who provided excellent service and follow-through on his accounts.

SITUATION III

A Telephone Call

Don felt he needed even more information to make a thorough investigation. He contemplated calling Bill Smith. In fairness to Bill, he should hear his version of what happened during the luncheon. But he knew he was not responsible for the actions of a non-employee. Furthermore, he wondered if talking to Bill would upset Jane even more if she found out. And would it be a proper part of an investigation mandated by company policy?

As Don considered his options, the phone rang. It was Bill Smith's boss, Joe Maxwell. He and Bill had talked about the luncheon, he said, and wanted to know if Jane had reported anything.

"Don, I don't know what you know about that meeting," said Joe, "but Bill has told me all the facts, and I thought we could put our heads together and nip this thing in the bud."

Don wasn't sure if this call was going to help or hinder him in his decision making. At first, he felt Joe was trying to unduly influence him. Also, he wasn't sure if the call was a violation of Jane's right to confidentiality. "Joe, I'm not sure we should be discussing this matter at all," said Don. "We might be jumping the gun. And what if Jane—"

"Wait, wait," Joe interrupted. "This thing can be put to rest if you just hear what really happened. We've been a good supplier for some time now. Give us the benefit of the doubt. We can talk 'off the record' if you want. But don't close the door on us."

"Okay," said Don, "let's talk off the record. I'll hear Bill's version, but I won't reach a conclusion over the phone. Our policy requires an investigation, and when that's complete, I'll let you know our position."

"Gee, Don," said Joe, "I don't think you even need an investigation. Bill says the only thing that went on at lunch was some innocent flirtation. Jane was giving him the old 'come on,' you know. She was more than friendly to him, smiling a lot and laughing at his jokes. Bill saw all the signals and just responded like a full-blooded male."

"You mean Jane was the cause of his harassing her?" Don asked.

"No, he didn't harass her," Joe said with urgency in his voice. "He only flirted with her because he thought she was flirting with him. It was all very innocent. These things happen every day. He didn't mean any harm. Just the opposite. He thought there was a chance for a nice relationship. He likes her very much and thought the feeling was mutual. No need to make a federal case out of it. These things happen—that's all. Remember when you asked out one of my saleswomen, Don? She said 'no,' but she didn't suggest sexual harassment. Isn't this the same thing?"

"I don't know. Jane was really upset when she came to me. She didn't see it as just flirting that went on," said Don.

"Come on, Don," insisted Joe. "Give her some time to calm down. You know how women can be sometimes. Maybe she has PMS. Why don't you let things just settle down before you do anything rash and start that unnecessary investigation? I bet in a couple days, you can talk to Jane and convince her it was just a misunderstanding. I'll put someone else on this contract, and we'll forget the whole thing ever happened. We've got to think about business first, right?"

Joe Maxwell's phone call put things in a new light for Don. if it was only innocent flirtation, why should good relations between Propmore and Airgoods be damaged? Yet he knew he had an obligation to Jane. He just wasn't sure how far that obligation went.

APPENDIX 1

Equal Employment Opportunity Commission Definition of Sexual Harassment

"Unwelcome sexual advances, requests for sexual favors and other verbal or physical contact of a sexual nature constitute sexual harassment when (1) submission to such conduct is made either explicitly or implicitly a term or condition of an individual's employment, (2) submission to or rejection of such conduct by an individual is used as the basis for employment decisions affecting such individual, or (3) such conduct has the purpose or effect of unreasonably interfering with an individual's work performance or creating an intimidating, hostile or offensive working environment."

"Applying general Title VII principles, an employer, employment agency, joint apprenticeship committee or labor organization (hereinafter collectively referred to as 'employer') is responsible for its acts and those of its agents and supervisory employees with respect to sexual harassment regardless of whether the employer knew or should have known of their occurrence."

—*EEOC guideline based on the Civil Rights Act of 1964, Title VII*

APPENDIX 2

The Propmore Corporation Policy HR-13

Policy area: Sexual Harassment

Purpose: The purpose of Policy HR-13 is to inform employees of the company that The Propmore Corporation forbids practices of sexual harassment on the job and that disciplinary action may be taken against those who violate this policy.

Policy statement: In keeping with its long-standing tradition of abiding by pertinent laws and regulations, The Propmore Corporation forbids practices of sexual harassment on the job which violate Title VII of the Civil Rights Act of 1964. Sexual harassment on the job, regardless of its intent, is against the law. Employees who nevertheless engage in sexual harassment practices face possible disciplinary action which includes dismissal from the company.

Policy implementation: Those who wish to report violations of Policy HR-13 shall file a written grievance with their immediate supervisors within two weeks of the alleged violation. In conjunction with the Legal Department, the supervisor will investigate the alleged violation and issue his or her decision based upon the findings of this investigation within 30 days of receiving the written grievance.

Is Turn About Fair Play?

BARRY R. GROSS

. . . The balance of argument weighs against reverse discrimination for four interrelated sets of reasons. First, the procedures designed to isolate the discriminated are flawed. Second, the practice has undesirable and dangerous consequences. Third, it fails to fit any of the models of compensation or reparations. Fourth, it falls unjustly upon both those it favors and those it disfavors. I conclude that if to eliminate discrimination against the members of one group we find ourselves discriminating against another, we have gone too far.

Sociologically, groups are simply not represented in various jobs and at various levels in percentages closely approximating their percentage of the population. When universities in general and medical schools in particular discriminated heavily against them, Jews were represented in the medical profession in far greater percentages than their percentage of the population. At the same time, they were represented in far lower percentages in banking, finance, construction, and engineering than their percentage in the population, especially the population of New York City. A similar analysis by crudely drawn group traits—Jew, Roman Catholic, WASP, Irish, and so forth—of almost any trade, business or profession would yield similar results.

But the argument from population percentages may be meant not as an analysis of what is the case, but as an analysis of what ought to be the case. A proponent might put it this way: It is true that groups are not usually represented in the work force by their percentage in the population at large, but minority C has been systematically excluded from the good places. Therefore, in order to make sure that they get some of them, we should systematically include them in the good places, and a clear way of doing it is by their percentage in the population. Or we might conclude instead: therefore, in order to make up for past exclusion, they should be included in the good places as reparation, and an easy way to do it is by their percentage in the population.

If the definition of a minority discriminated against is *ipso facto* their representation in certain jobs in percentages less than their percentage in the general population, then one has to remark that the reasoning is circular. For we are trying to prove: (1) that minority C is discriminated against.

We use a premise (3) that minority C is underrepresented in good jobs. Since (1) does not follow from (3) (mere underrepresentation not be-

From *Reverse Discrimination*, ed. Barry R. Gross (Buffalo, N.Y.: Prometheus Books, 1977). Reprinted from the *Journal of Critical Analysis*, Vol. 5 (Jan.–Apr. 1975).

ing even *prima facie* evidence of discrimination), it is necessary to insert (2) that their underrepresentation is due to discrimination. But this completes the circle.

A critic might reply that we know perfectly well what is meant. The groups discriminated against are blacks, Puerto Ricans, Mexican-Americans, American Indians, and women. He is correct, though his answer does not tell us *how to find out* who is discriminated against. This critic, for example, left out Jews and Orientals. If he should reply that Jews and Orientals do well enough, we point out that the question was not "Who fails to do well?" but rather, "Who is discriminated against?" This argument shows that the mechanisms for identifying the victims of discrimination and for remedying it are seriously deficient.

Even if we allow that the percentage of the group in the work force versus its percentage in the population is the criterion of discrimination, who is discriminated against will vary depending upon how we divide the groups. We may discover that Republicans are discriminated against by our literary or intellectual journals—*New York Review, Dissent, Commentary.* We may also discover that wealthy Boston residents are discriminated against by the Los Angeles Dodgers, that women are discriminated against by the Army, and that idiots (we hope) are discriminated against by universities.

What employment or profession a person chooses depends upon a number of variables—background, wealth, parents' employment, schooling, intelligence, drive, ambition, skill, and not least, luck. Moreover, the analysis will differ depending upon what group identification or stratification you choose. None seems to have priority over the others. Every person can be typed according to many of these classifications. It seems, therefore, that the relevant analysis cannot even be made, much less justified.

In addition, some proponents of the population-percentage argument seem to hold: (4) From the contingent fact that members of the group C were discriminated against, it follows necessarily that they are underrepresented in the good positions. They then go on to assert (5) if members of group C were not discriminated against they would not be underrepresented, or (6) if they are underrepresented, then they are discriminated against.

But clearly (4) is itself a contingent, not a necessary truth. Clearly also neither (5) nor (6) follows from it, (5) being the fallacy of denying the antecedent and (6) the fallacy of affirming the consequent. Lastly, neither (5) nor (6) is necessarily true. The members of a group might simply lack interest in certain jobs (for example, Italians in the public-school system are in short supply). Could one argue that, even though neither (4), (5), nor (6) is *necessarily* true, the mere fact of underrepresentation in certain occupations does provide evidence of discrimination? The answer is no—no more than the fact of "overrepresentation" in certain occupations is evidence of favoritism.

At most, underrepresentation can be used to support the contention of discrimination when there is *other* evidence as well.

FAIR PLAY: OUGHT WE TO DISCRIMINATE IN REVERSE?

There are at least three difficulties with reverse discrimination: first, it is inconsistent; second, it licenses discrimination; third, it is unfair.

If we believe the principle that equal opportunity is a right of everyone, then if members of group C are excluded from enjoying certain opportunities merely because they are members of group C, their right is being abrogated. They are entitled to this right, but so is everybody else, even those persons who presently deny it to them. If both are made to enjoy equal opportunity, then both are enjoying their right. To give either oppressors or oppressed more than equal opportunity is equally to deny the rights of one or the other in violation of the principle of equal opportunity.

Proponents of reverse discrimination seem to be caught on the horns of a dilemma: either discrimination is illegitimate or it is not. If it is illegitimate, then it ought not to be practiced against anyone. If it is not, then there exists no reason for *now* favoring blacks, Puerto Ricans, Chicanos, Indians, women, and so forth over whites.

Two strategies present themselves. Either we can analyze one disjunct with a view to showing that distinctions can be made which require compensation or reparations in the form of reverse discrimination to be made to wronged individuals or groups; or we can try to soften one of the disjuncts so as to make a case for exceptions in favor of the wronged. The first appeals both to our reason and our sense of justice. The second appeals to our emotions. I shall argue that neither strategy works.[1]

Now reverse discrimination can take several forms, but I think that what many of its proponents have in mind is a strong form of compensation—a form which requires us to discriminate against non-C members and favor C members even if less qualified. One may well wonder whether there is not a little retribution hidden in this form of compensation.

THE "SOFTENED" GENERAL PRINCIPLE

The argument for construing reverse discrimination as compensation or reparation has a great appeal which can be brought out by contrasting it with another approach. One might agree that as a general rule reverse discrimination is illegitimate but that it need not be seen as universally illegitimate. In particular, in the case where people have been so heavily discriminated against as to make it impossible for them now to gain a good life, there is no possibility of their having a fair chance, no possibility of their starting out on anything like equal terms, then and only then is it legitimate to discriminate in their favor and hence against anyone else.

Against this "softened" general principle I shall urge two sorts of objections which I call respectively "practical" and "pragmatic." Against the reparations type of argument, I shall urge first that there is some reason to think the conditions for exacting and accepting them are lacking, and second that, owing to the peculiar nature of their reparations to be exacted (reverse discrimination), the very exaction of them is unreasonable and unfair to both parties—exactors and exactees.

I mention briefly two sorts of practical objections to the "softened" general principle. First, it is simply the case that when discrimination is made in favor of someone regardless of his qualifications, there is the greatest possible danger that the person getting the position will not be competent to fill it. Second, when a person is placed in a position because of discrimination in his favor, he may come to feel himself inferior.[2] This may easily lead to the permanent conferral of inferior status on the group, an inferiority which is all the stronger because self-induced. Its psychological effects should not be underestimated.

The pragmatic objection to the "softened" general principle is much stronger. Discrimination in any form is invidious. Once licensed, its licenses rebound upon its perpetrators as well as others. Principles tend to be generalized without consideration of restrictions or the circumstances to which they were intended to apply. Students of the Nazi movement will have noticed that in licensing the discrimination, isolation, persecution, and "final solution" of the Jews, the Nazis (foreign and German) licensed their own. (Hitler's plans for extermination included political groups, for example, the Rohm faction of the SA, as well as other racial groups, for example, Slavs and Balts who fought on the German side.) It is necessary to be quite careful what principles one adopts. In view of the long and bloody history of discrimination, one ought to be very chary of sanctioning it.

COMPENSATIONS, REPARATIONS, AND RESTITUTION

Because it escapes most of these objections, the reparations argument becomes very attractive. What is more obvious than the principle that people ought to be compensated for monetary loss, pain and suffering inflicted by others acting either as agents of government or as individuals? From the negligence suit to reparations for war damage, the principle is comfortable, familiar, and best of all, legal. For victims of broken sidewalks, open wells, ignored stop signs, the conditions under which damages are awarded are quite clear. (1) There is specific injury, specific victim, specific time and place. (2) A specific individual or set of individuals must be found responsible either (a) by actually having done the injury, or (b) by failing to act in such a way (for example, repairing the sidewalk, sealing the well) so as to remove a particular potential source of injury on their property. (3) A reasonable assessment of the monetary value of the claim can be made. In such cases no moral blame is attached to the person forced to pay compensation.

But reparations are somewhat less clear. How much does Germany owe France for causing (losing?) World War I? Can we say that *Germany* caused the war? Germany did pay, at least in part, based upon rough calculations of the cost of the Allied armies, including pensions, the loss of allied GNP, indemnities for death and for the destruction of property. . . .

INAPPLICABILITY OF THESE PARADIGMS

Can reverse discrimination be construed to fit any of these paradigms? Can favoring blacks, Chicanos, Indians, women, and so forth over whites or males be seen as compensation, reparations, or restitution? The answer is no for two general reasons and for several which are specific to the various paradigms. The general reasons are, first, that responsibility for discrimination past and present and for its deleterious consequences is neither clearly assigned nor accepted. Some seem to think that the mere fact of its existence makes all whites (or males in the case of antifeminism) responsible.[3] But I do not know an analysis of responsibility which bears out this claim. Second, there is a great difficulty, if not an impossibility, in assigning a monetary value to the damage done and compensation allegedly owed— that is to say, reverse discrimination.

If we turn to the negligence paradigm, all the conditions seem to fail. *Specific* injury is lacking, *specific* individual responsibility is lacking, and there is no way to assess the monetary value of the "loss." Indeed, in the case of reverse discrimination it is not monetary value which is claimed but preferential treatment. Under the large-scale reparations paradigm two conditions beyond responsibility are lacking. There are no governments or government-like agencies between which the transfer could take place, and there is no *modus agendi* for the transfer to take place.

Where the transfer is to be of preferential treatment, it is unclear how it is even to be begun. So we come to the third paradigm: individual restitution. This is much closer, for it deals with compensating individual victims of persecution. Again, however, it fails to provide a model, first, because reverse discrimination cannot be looked at in monetary terms, and second, even if it could, the restitution is designed to bring a person back to where he was before deprivation. In the case of the minorities in question, there can be no question of restoring them to former positions or property. Precisely, the point of the reparation is to pay them for what they, because of immoral social practices, never had in the first place. . . .

JUSTICE

Finally, if we ignore all that has been said and simply go ahead and discriminate in reverse, calling it reparation, it remains to ask whether it would be either reasonable or just? I think the answer is no. It is possible to hold that in some set of cases, other things being equal, compensation is required and yet to argue either that since other things are not equal compensation is not required, or that even if some compensation is required it ought not to take the form of reverse discrimination. Certainly, from the fact that some form of compensation or reparation must be made it does not follow that any *specific* form of compensation is in order. If X is discriminated against in awarding professorships because he is a member of C group, it scarcely follows that if compensation is in order it *must* take the form of his being discriminated in favor of for another professorship, at least not without adopting the principle of "an eye for an eye" (and only an *eye* for an eye?). Consider X being turned down for an apartment because he is a C member. Must compensation consist just in his being offered another ahead of anybody else? Even if he has one already? To go from the relatively innocuous principle that where *possible* we ought to compensate for damages, to sanction reverse discrimination as the proper or preferred form of redress, requires us to go beyond mere compensation to some principle very much like "let the punishment mirror the crime." But here the person "punished," the person from which the compensation is exacted, is often not the "criminal." Nor will it help to say that the person deprived of a job or advancement by reverse discrimination is not really being punished or deprived, since the job did not belong to him in the first place. Of course it didn't; nor did it belong to the successful candidate. What belonged to both is equal consideration, and that is what one of them is being deprived of.[4]

There is an element of injustice or unfairness in all reparations. The money derived from taxes paid by all citizens is used for reparations regardless of whether they were responsible for, did nothing about, opposed, or actually fought the policies or government in question. Yet we say that this is the only way it can be done, that the element of unfairness is not great, and that on the whole it is better that this relatively painless way of appropriating money from Jones, who is innocent, be used than that the victims of persecution or crime go uncompensated. But the consequences of reverse discrimination are quite different, especially when it is based upon group membership rather than individual desert. It is possible and is sometimes the case that though most C members are discriminated against, Y is a C member who had met with no discrimination at all. Under the principle that all C members should be discriminated in favor of, we would offer "compensation" to Y. But what are we compensating him *for*? By hypothesis he was no victim of discrimination. Do we compensate him for what happened to others? Do we pay Jones for what we buy from Smith? We seem to be compensating him for being a C member, but why? Do we secretly hold C members inferior? Some claim that society as a whole must bear the burden of reparation. But then reverse discrimination will hardly do the trick. It does not exact redress from the government, or even from all white (responsible?) citizens equally, but falls solely against those who apply for admissions, or jobs *for which blacks or other minorities are applying at the same time.* By the same token, it does not compensate or "reparate" all minority persons equally but merely those applying for admission, jobs, promotions, and so forth. Those whose positions are secure would not be paid. A white person who fought for civil rights for blacks may be passed over for promotion or displaced, a victim of reverse discrimination, while a Ku Klux Klan man at the top of the job ladder pays nothing. This would be a laughably flawed system if it were not seriously advocated by responsible people, and partly implemented by the government. Surely, it violates the principles of both compensatory and distributive justice.

NOTES

1. For examples of these strategies, see the article by J. W. Nickel . . . herein.
2. *Contra* this objection see Irving Thalberg, "Justifications of Institutional Racism," *The Philosophical Forum*, Winter 1972.
3. See Thalberg. For an interesting catalogue of "irresponsible use of 'responsibility,'" see Robert Stover, "Responsibility for the Cold War—A Case Study in Historical Responsibility," *History and Theory*, 1972. For a clear-cut analysis that more than mere presence on the scene is required to show responsibility, see S. Levinson, "Responsibility for Crimes of War," *Philosophy and Public Affairs*, Spring 1973.
4. See Gertrude Ezorsky, "It's Mine," *Philosophy and Public Affairs*, Spring 1974.

A Defense of Programs
of Preferential Treatment

RICHARD WASSERSTROM

Many justifications of programs of preferential treatment depend upon the claim that in one respect or another such programs have good consequences or that they are effective means by which to bring about some desirable end, e.g., an integrated, equalitarian society. I mean by "programs of preferential treatment" to refer to programs such as those at issue in the *Bakke* case—programs which set aside a certain number of places

Richard Wasserstrom, "A Defense of Programs of Preferential Treatment," *National Forum: The Phi Kappa Phi Journal*, LVIII, No. 1 (Winter 1978). Reprinted with permission.

(for example, in a law school) as to which memb€
example, persons who are non-white or female)
mum qualifications (in terms of grades and test
admission to those places over some member
possess higher qualifications (in terms of grad'

Many criticisms of programs of prefere·
programs, even if effective, are unjustifiable bੁ
portant sense unfair or unjust. In this paper I presenь ᴗ
such programs by showing that two of the chief arguments oı.
unfairness or injustice of these programs do not work in the way oɾ ᴗ
degree supposed by critics of these programs.

The first argument is this. Opponents of preferential treatment programs sometimes assert that proponents of these programs are guilty of
intellectual inconsistency, if not racism or sexism. For, as is now readily
acknowledged, at times past employers, universities, and many other social
institutions did have racial or sexual quotas (when they did not practice
overt racial or sexual exclusion), and many of those who were most concerned to bring about the eradication of those racial quotas are now un-
troubled by the new programs which reinstitute them. And this, it is
claimed, is inconsistent. If it was wrong to take race or sex into account
when blacks and women were the objects of racial and sexual policies and
practices of exclusion, then it is wrong to take race or sex into account
when the objects of the policies have their race or sex reversed. Simple
considerations of intellectual consistency—of what it means to give racism
or sexism as a reason for condemning these social policies and practices—
require that what was a good reason then is still a good reason now.

The problem with this argument is that despite appearances, there is
no inconsistency involved in holding both views. Even if contemporary
preferential treatment programs which contain quotas are wrong, they are
not wrong for the reasons that made quotas against blacks and women
pernicious. The reason why is that the social realities do make an enormous difference. The fundamental evil of programs that discriminated
against blacks or women was that these programs were a part of a larger
social universe which systematically maintained a network of institutions
that unjustifiably concentrated power, authority, and goods in the hands of
white male individuals, and which systematically consigned blacks and
women to subordinate positions in the society.

Whatever may be wrong with today's affirmative action programs and
quota systems, it should be clear that the evil, if any, is just not the same.
Racial and sexual minorities do not constitute the dominant social group.
Nor is the conception of who is a fully developed member of the moral and
social community one of an individual who is either female or black. Quotas that prefer women or blacks do not add to an already relatively overabundant supply of resources and opportunities at the disposal of members
of these groups in the way in which the quotas of the past did maintain and

the overabundant supply of resources and opportunities already to white males.

The same point can be made in a somewhat different way. Sometimes ple say that what was wrong, for example, with the system of racial scrimination in the South was that it took an irrelevant characteristic, namely race, and used it systematically to allocate social benefits and burdens of various sorts. The defect was the irrelevance of the characteristic used—race—for that meant that individuals ended up being treated in a manner that was arbitrary and capricious.

I do not think that was the central flaw at all. Take, for instance, the most hideous of the practices, human slavery. The primary thing that was wrong with the institution was not that the particular individuals who were assigned the place of slaves were assigned there arbitrarily because the assignment was made in virtue of an irrelevant characteristic, their race. Rather, it seems to me that the primary thing that was and is wrong with slavery is the practice itself—the fact of some individuals being able to own other individuals and all that goes with that practice. It would not matter by what criterion individuals were assigned; human slavery would still be wrong. And the same can be said for most if not all of the other discrete practices and institutions which comprised the system of racial discrimination even after human slavery was abolished. The practices were unjustifiable—they were oppressive—and they would have been so no matter how the assignment of victims had been made. What made it worse, still, was that the institutions and the supporting ideology all interlocked to create a system of human oppression whose effects on those living under it were as devastating as they were unjustifiable.

Again, if there is anything wrong with the programs of preferential treatment that have begun to flourish within the past ten years, it should be evident that the social realities in respect to the distribution of resources and opportunities make the difference. Apart from everything else, there is simply no way in which all of these programs taken together could plausibly be viewed as capable of relegating white males to the kind of genuinely oppressive status characteristically bestowed upon women and blacks by the dominant social institutions and ideology.

The second objection is that preferential treatment programs are wrong because they take race or sex into account rather than the only thing that does matter—that is, an individual's qualifications. What all such programs have in common and what makes them all objectionable, so this argument goes, is that they ignore the persons who are more qualified by bestowing a preference on those who are less qualified in virtue of their being either black or female.

There are, I think, a number of things wrong with this objection based on qualifications, and not the least of them is that we do not live in a society in which there is even the serious pretense of a qualification requirement for many jobs of substantial power and authority. Would anyone claim, for example, that the persons who comprise the judiciary are there because they are the most qualified lawyers or the most qualified persons to be judges? Would anyone claim that Henry Ford II is the head of the Ford Motor Company because he is the most qualified person for the job? Part of what is wrong with even talking about qualifications and merit is that the argument derives some of its force from the erroneous notion that we would have a meritocracy were it not for programs of preferential treatment. In fact, the higher one goes in terms of prestige, power and the like, the less qualifications seem ever to be decisive. It is only for certain jobs and certain places that qualifications are used to do more than establish the possession of certain minimum competencies.

But difficulties such as these to one side, there are theoretical difficulties as well which cut much more deeply into the argument about qualifications. To begin with, it is important to see that there is a serious inconsistency present if the person who favors "pure qualifications" does so on the ground that the most qualified ought to be selected because this promotes maximum efficiency. Let us suppose that the argument is that if we have the most qualified performing the relevant tasks we will get those tasks done in the most economical and efficient manner. There is nothing wrong in principle with arguments based upon the good consequences that will flow from maintaining a social practice in a certain way. But it is inconsistent for the opponent of preferential treatment to attach much weight to qualifications on this ground, because it was an analogous appeal to the good consequences that the opponent of preferential treatment thought was wrong in the first place. That is to say, if the chief thing to be said in favor of strict qualifications and preferring the most qualified is that it is the most efficient way of getting things done, then we are right back to an assessment of the different consequences that will flow from different programs, and we are far removed from the considerations of justice or fairness that were thought to weigh so heavily against these programs.

It is important to note, too, that qualifications—at least in the educational context—are often not connected at all closely with any plausible conception of social effectiveness. To admit the most qualified students to law school, for example—given the way qualifications are now determined—is primarily to admit those who have the greatest chance of scoring the highest grades at law school. This says little about efficiency except perhaps that these students are the easiest for the faculty to teach. However, since we know so little about what constitutes being a good, or even successful lawyer, and even less about the correlation between being a very good law student and being a very good lawyer, we can hardly claim very confidently that the legal system will operate most effectively if we admit only the most qualified students to law school.

To be at all decisive, the argument for qualifications must be that those who are the most qualified deserve to receive the benefits (the job, the place in law school, etc.) because they are the most qualified. The introduction of the concept of desert now makes it an objection as to justice or fairness of the sort promised by the original criticism of the programs. But now the problem is that there is no reason to think that there is any strong sense of "desert" in which it is correct that the most qualified deserve anything.

Let us consider more closely one case, that of preferential treatment in respect to admission to college or graduate school. There is a logical gap in the inference from the claim that a person is most qualified to perform a task, e.g., to be a good student, to the conclusion that he or she deserves to be admitted as a student. Of course, those who deserve to be admitted should be admitted. But why do the most qualified deserve anything? There is simply no necessary connection between academic merit (in the sense of being most qualified) and deserving to be a member of a student body. Suppose, for instance, that there is only one tennis court in the community. Is it clear that the two best tennis players ought to be the ones permitted to use it? Why not those who were there first? Or those who will enjoy playing the most? Or those who are the worst and, therefore, need the greatest opportunity to practice? Or those who have the chance to play least frequently?

We might, of course, have a rule that says that the best tennis players get to use the court before the others. Under such a rule the best players would deserve the court more than the poorer ones. But that is just to push the inquiry back one stage. Is there any reason to think that we ought to have a rule giving good tennis players such a preference? Indeed, the arguments that might be given for or against such a rule are many and varied. And few if any of the arguments that might support the rule would depend upon a connection between ability and desert.

Someone might reply, however, that the most able students deserve to be admitted to the university because all of their earlier schooling was a kind of competition, with university admission being the prize awarded to the winners. They deserve to be admitted because that is what the rule of the competition provides. In addition, it might be argued, it would be unfair now to exclude them in favor of others, given the reasonable expectations they developed about the way in which their industry and performance would be rewarded. Minority-admission programs, which inevitably prefer some who are less qualified over some who are more qualified, all possess this flaw.

There are several problems with this argument. The most substantial of them is that it is an empirically implausible picture of our social world. Most of what are regarded as the decisive characteristics for higher education have a great deal to do with things over which the individual has neither control nor responsibility: such things as home environment, socioeconomic class of parents, and, of course, the quality of the primary and secondary schools attended. Since individuals do not deserve having had any of these things vis-à-vis other individuals, they do not, for the most part, deserve their qualifications. And since they do not deserve their abilities they do not in any strong sense deserve to be admitted because of their abilities.

To be sure, if there has been a rule which connects say, performance at high school with admission to college, then there is a weak sense in which those who do well at high school deserve, for that reason alone, to be admitted to college. In addition, if persons have built up or relied upon their reasonable expectations concerning performance and admission, they have a claim to be admitted on this ground as well. But it is certainly not obvious that these claims of desert are any stronger or more compelling than the competing claims based upon the needs of or advantages to women or blacks from programs of preferential treatment. And as I have indicated, all rule-based claims of desert are very weak unless and until the rule which creates the claim is itself shown to be a justified one. Unless one has a strong preference for the status quo, and unless one can defend that preference, the practice within a system of allocating places in a certain way does not go very far at all in showing that that is the right or the just way to allocate those places in the future.

A proponent of programs of preferential treatment is not at all committed to the view that qualifications ought to be wholly irrelevant. He or she can agree that, given the existing structure of any institution, there is probably some minimal set of qualifications without which one cannot participate meaningfully within the institution. In addition, it can be granted that the qualifications of those involved will affect the way the institution works and the way it affects others in the society. And the consequences will vary depending upon the particular institution. But all of this only establishes that qualifications, in this sense, are relevant, not that they are decisive. This is wholly consistent with the claim that race or sex should today also be relevant when it comes to matters such as admission to college or law school. And that is all that any preferential treatment program—even one with the kind of quota used in the *Bakke* case—has ever tried to do.

I have not attempted to establish that programs of preferential treatment are right and desirable. There are empirical issues concerning the consequences of these programs that I have not discussed, and certainly not settled. Nor, for that matter, have I considered the argument that justice may permit, if not require, these programs as a way to provide compensation or reparation for injuries suffered in the recent as well as distant past, or as a way to remove benefits that are undeservedly enjoyed by those of the dominant group. What I have tried to do is show that it is wrong to think that programs of preferential treatment are objectionable in the centrally important sense in which many past and present discriminatory features of our society have been and are racist and sexist. The social realities as to power and opportunity do make a fundamental difference. It is also wrong to think that programs of preferential treatment are in any strong sense either unjust or unprincipled. The case for programs of preferential treatment could, therefore, plausibly rest both on the view that such programs are not unfair to white males (except in the weak, rule-dependent sense described above) and on the view that it is unfair to continue the present set of unjust—often racist and sexist—institutions that comprise the social reality. And the case for these programs could rest as well on the proposition that, given the distribution of power and influence in the United States today, such programs may reasonably be viewed as potentially valuable, effective means by which to achieve admirable and significant social ideals of equality and integration.

Management Women
and the New Facts of Life

Felice N. Schwartz

The cost of employing women in management is greater than the cost of employing men. This is a jarring statement, partly because it is true, but mostly because it is something people are reluctant to talk about. A new study by one multinational corporation shows that the rate of turnover in management positions is 2½ times higher among top-performing women than it is among men. A large producer of consumer goods reports that one half of the women who take maternity leave return to their jobs late or not at all. And we know that women also have a greater tendency to plateau or to interrupt their careers in ways that limit their growth and development. But we have become so sensitive to charges of sexism and so afraid of confrontation, even litigation, that we rarely say what we know to be true. Unfortunately, our bottled-up awareness leaks out in misleading metaphors ("glass ceiling" is one notable example), veiled hostility, lowered expectations, distrust, and reluctant adherence to Equal Employment Opportunity requirements.

Career interruptions, plateauing, and turnover are expensive. The money corporations invest in recruitment, training, and development is less likely to produce top executives among women than among men, and the invaluable company experience that developing executives acquire at every level as they move up through management ranks is more often lost.

The studies just mentioned are only the first of many, I'm quite sure.

Reprinted by permission of the *Harvard Business Review* January–February 1989. Copyright © 1989 by the President and Fellows of Harvard College. All rights reserved.

Demographic realities are going to force corporations all across the country to analyze the cost of employing women in managerial positions, and what they will discover is that women cost more.

But here is another startling truth: The greater cost of employing women is not a function of inescapable gender differences. Women *are* different from men, but what increases their cost to the corporation is principally the clash of their perceptions, attitudes, and behavior with those of men, which is to say, with the policies and practices of male-led corporations.

It is terribly important that employers draw the right conclusions from the studies now being done. The studies will be useless—or worse, harmful—if all they teach us is that women are expensive to employ. What we need to learn is how to reduce that expense, how to stop throwing away the investments we make in talented women, how to become more responsive to the needs of the women that corporations *must* employ if they are to have the best and the brightest of all those now entering the work force.

The gender differences relevant to business fall into two categories: those related to maternity and those related to the differing traditions and expectations of the sexes. Maternity is biological rather than cultural. We can't alter it, but we can dramatically reduce its impact on the workplace and in many cases eliminate its negative effect on employee development. We can accomplish this by addressing the second set of differences, those between male and female socialization. Today, these differences exaggerate the real costs of maternity and can turn a relatively slight disruption in work schedule into a serious business problem and a career derailment for individual women. If we are to overcome the cost differential between male and female employees, we need to address the issues that arise when female socialization meets the male corporate culture and masculine rules of career development—issues of behavior and style, of expectation, of stereotypes and preconceptions, of sexual tension and harassment, of female mentoring, lateral mobility, relocation, compensation, and early identification of top performers.

🌵

The one immutable, enduring difference between men and women is maternity. Maternity is not simply childbirth but a continuum that begins with an awareness of the ticking of the biological clock, proceeds to the anticipation of motherhood, includes pregnancy, childbirth, physical recuperation, psychological adjustment, and continues on to nursing, bonding, and child rearing. Not all women choose to become mothers, of course, and among those who do, the process varies from case to case depending on the health of the mother and baby, the values of the parents, and the availability, cost, and quality of child care.

In past centuries, the biological fact of maternity shaped the traditional roles of the sexes. Women performed the home-centered functions that related to the bearing and nurturing of children. Men did the work that required great physical strength. Over time, however, family size contracted, the community assumed greater responsibility for the care and education of children, packaged foods and household technology reduced the work load in the home, and technology eliminated much of the need for muscle power at the workplace. Today, in the developed world, the only role still uniquely gender related is childbearing. Yet men and women are still socialized to perform their traditional roles.

Men and women may or may not have some innate psychological disposition toward these traditional roles—men to be aggressive, competitive, self-reliant, risk taking; women to be supportive, nurturing, intuitive, sensitive, communicative—but certainly both men and women are capable of the full range of behavior. Indeed, the male and female roles have already begun to expand and merge. In the decades ahead, as the socialization of boys and girls and the experience and expectations of young men and women grow steadily more androgynous, the differences in workplace behavior will continue to fade. At the moment, however, we are still plagued by disparities in perception and behavior that make the integration of men and women in the workplace unnecessarily difficult and expensive.

Let me illustrate with a few broadbrush generalizations. Of course, these are only stereotypes, but I think they help to exemplify the kinds of preconceptions that can muddy the corporate waters.

Men continue to perceive women as the rearers of their children, so they find it understandable, indeed appropriate, that women should renounce their careers to raise families. Edmund Pratt, CEO of Pfizer, once asked me in all sincerity, "Why would any woman choose to be a chief financial officer rather than a full-time mother?" By condoning and taking pleasure in women's traditional behavior, men reinforce it. Not only do they see parenting as fundamentally female, they see a career as fundamentally male—either an unbroken series of promotions and advancements toward CEOdom or stagnation and disappointment. This attitude serves to legitimize a woman's choice to extend maternity leave and even, for those who can afford it, to leave employment altogether for several years. By the same token, men who might want to take a leave after the birth of a child know that management will see such behavior as a lack of career commitment, even when company policy permits parental leave for men.

Women also bring counterproductive expectations and perceptions to the workplace. Ironically, although the feminist movement was an expression of women's quest for freedom from their home-based lives, most women were remarkably free already. They had many responsibilities, but they were autonomous and could be entrepreneurial in how and when they carried them out. And once their children grew up and left home, they were essentially free to do what they wanted with their lives. Women's traditional role also included freedom from responsibility for the financial support of their families. Many of us were socialized from girlhood to expect our husbands to take care of us, while our brothers were socialized from an equally early age to complete their educations, pursue careers, climb the ladder of success, and provide dependable financial support for their families. To the extent that this tradition of freedom lingers subliminally, women tend to bring to their employment a sense that they can choose to change jobs or careers at will, take time off, or reduce their hours.

Finally, women's traditional role encouraged particular attention to the quality and substance of what they did, specifically to the physical, psychological, and intellectual development of their children. This traditional focus may explain women's continuing tendency to search for more than monetary reward—intrinsic significance, social importance, meaning—in what they do. This too makes them more likely than men to leave the corporation in search of other values.

The misleading metaphor of the glass ceiling suggests an invisible barrier constructed by corporate leaders to impede the upward mobility of women beyond the middle levels. A more appropriate metaphor, I believe, is the kind of cross-sectional diagram used in geology. The barriers to women's leadership occur when potentially counterproductive layers of influence on women—maternity, tradition, socialization—meet management strata pervaded by the largely unconscious preconceptions, stereotypes, and expectations of men. Such interfaces do not exist for men and tend to be impermeable for women.

One result of these gender differences has been to convince some executives that women are simply not suited to top management. Other executives feel helpless. If they see even a few of their valued female employees fail to return to work from maternity leave on schedule or see one of their most promising women plateau in her career after the birth of a child, they begin to fear there is nothing they can do to infuse women with new energy and enthusiasm and persuade them to stay. At the same time, they know there is nothing they can do to stem the tide of women into management ranks.

Another result is to place every working woman on a continuum that runs from total dedication to career at one end to a balance between career and family at the other. What women discover is that the male corporate culture sees both extremes as unacceptable. Women who want the flexibility to balance their families and their careers are not adequately committed to the organization. Women who perform as aggressively and competitively as men are abrasive and unfeminine. But the fact is, business needs all the talented women it can get. Moreover, as I will explain, the women I call career-primary and those I call career-and-family each have particular value to the corporation.

Women in the corporation are about to move from a buyer's to a seller's market. The sudden, startling recognition that 80 percent of new entrants in the work force over the next decade will be women, minorities, and immigrants has stimulated a mushrooming incentive to "value diversity."

Women are no longer simply an enticing pool of occasional creative talent, a thorn in the side of the EEO officer, or a source of frustration to corporate leaders truly puzzled by the slowness of their upward trickle into executive positions. A real demographic change is taking place. The era of sudden population growth of the 1950s and 1960s is over. The birth rate has dropped about 40%, from a high of 25.3 live births per 1,000 population in 1957, at the peak of the baby boom, to a stable low of a little more than 15 per 1,000 over the last 16 years, and there is no indication of a return to a higher rate. The tidal wave of baby boomers that swelled the recruitment pool to overflowing seems to have been a one-time phenomenon. For 20 years, employers had the pick of a very large crop and were able to choose males almost exclusively for the executive track. But if future population remains fairly stable while the economy continues to expand, and if the new information society simultaneously creates a greater need for creative, educated managers, then the gap between supply and demand will grow dramatically and, with it, the competition for managerial talent.

The decrease in numbers has even greater implications if we look at the traditional source of corporate recruitment for leadership positions—white males from the top 10% of the country's best universities. Over the past decade, the increase in the number of women graduating from leading universities has been much greater than the increase in the total number of graduates, and these women are well represented in the top 10% of their classes.

The trend extends into business and professional programs as well. In the old days, virtually all MBAs were male. I remember addressing a meeting at the Harvard Business School as recently as the mid-1970s and looking out at a sea of exclusively male faces. Today, about 25% of that audience would be women. The pool of male MBAs from which corporations have traditionally drawn their leaders has shrunk significantly.

Of course, this reduction does not have to mean a shortage of talent. The top 10% is at least as smart as it always was—smarter, probably, since it's now drawn from a broader segment of the population. But it now consists increasingly of women. Companies that are determined to recruit the same number of men as before will have to dig much deeper into the male pool, while their competitors will have the opportunity to pick the best people from both the male and female graduates.

Under these circumstances, there is no question that the management ranks of business will include increasing numbers of women. There remains, however, the question of how these women will succeed—how long they will stay, how high they will climb, how completely they will fulfill their promise and potential, and what kind of return the corporation will realize on its investment in their training and development.

There is ample business reason for finding ways to make sure that as many of these women as possible will succeed. The first step in this process is to recognize that women are not all alike. Like men, they are individuals with differing talents, priorities, and motivations. For the sake of simplicity, let me focus on the two women I referred to earlier, on what I call the career-primary woman and the career-and-family woman.

Like many men, some women put their careers first. They are ready to make the same trade-offs traditionally made by the men who seek leadership positions. They make a career decision to put in extra hours, to make sacrifices in their personal lives, to make the most of every opportunity for professional development. For women, of course, this decision also requires that they remain single or at least childless or, if they do have children, that they be satisfied to have others raise them. Some 90% of executive men but only 35% of executive women have children by the age of 40. The *automatic* association of all women with babies is clearly unjustified.

The secret to dealing with such women is to recognize them early, accept them, and clear artificial barriers from their path to the top. After all, the best of these women are among the best managerial talent you will ever see. And career-primary women have another important value to the company that men and other women lack. They can act as role models and mentors to younger women who put their careers first. Since upwardly mobile career-primary women still have few role models to motivate and inspire them, a company with women in its top echelon has a significant advantage in the competition for executive talent.

Men at the top of the organization—most of them over 55, with wives who tend to be traditional—often find career women "masculine" and difficult to accept as colleagues. Such men miss the point, which is not that these women are just like men but that they are just like the *best* men in the organization. And there is such a shortage of the best people that gender cannot be allowed to matter. It is clearly counterproductive to disparage in a woman with executive talent the very qualities that are most critical to the business and that might carry a man to the CEO's office.

Clearing a path to the top for career-primary women has four requirements:

1. Identify them early.
2. Give them the same opportunity you give to talented men to grow and develop and contribute to company profitability. Give them client and

customer responsibility. Expect them to travel and relocate, to make the same commitment to the company as men aspiring to leadership positions.

3. Accept them as valued members of your management team. Include them in every kind of communication. Listen to them.

4. Recognize that the business environment is more difficult and stressful for them than for their male peers. They are always a minority, often the only woman. The male perception of talented, ambitious women is at best ambivalent, a mixture of admiration, resentment, confusion, competitiveness, attraction, skepticism, anxiety, pride, and animosity. Women can never feel secure about how they should dress and act, whether they should speak out or grin and bear it when they encounter discrimination, stereotyping, sexual harassment, and paternalism. Social interaction and travel with male colleagues and with male clients can be charged. As they move up, the normal increase in pressure and responsibility is compounded for women because they are women.

Stereotypical language and sexist day-to-day behavior do take their toll on women's career development. Few male executives realize how common it is to call women by their first names while men in the same group are greeted with surnames, how frequently female executives are assumed by men to be secretaries, how often women are excluded from all-male social events where business is being transacted. With notable exceptions, men are still generally more comfortable with other men, and as a result women miss many of the career and business opportunities that arise over lunch, on the golf course, or in the locker room.

☙

The majority of women, however, are what I call career-and-family women, women who want to pursue serious careers while participating actively in the rearing of children. These women are a precious resource that has yet to be mined. Many of them are talented and creative. Most of them are willing to trade some career growth and compensation for freedom from the constant pressure to work long hours and weekends.

Most companies today are ambivalent at best about the career-and-family women in their management ranks. They would prefer that all employees were willing to give their all to the company. They believe it is in their best interests for all managers to compete for the top positions so the company will have the largest possible pool from which to draw its leaders.

"If you have both talent and motivation," many employers seem to say, "we want to move you up. If you haven't got that motivation, if you want less pressure and greater flexibility, then you can leave and make room for a new generation." These companies lose on two counts. First, they fail to amortize the investment they made in the early training and experience of management women who find themselves committed to family as well as to career. Second, they fail to recognize what these women could do for their middle management.

The ranks of middle managers are filled with people on their way up and people who have stalled. Many of them have simply reached their limits, achieved career growth commensurate with or exceeding their capabilities, and they cause problems because their performance is mediocre but they still want to move ahead. The career-and-family woman is willing to trade off the pressures and demands that go with promotion for the freedom to spend more time with her children. She's very smart, she's talented, she's committed to her career, and she's satisfied to stay at the middle level, at least during the early child-rearing years. Compare her with some of the people you have there now.

Consider a typical example, a woman who decides in college on a business career and enters management at age 22. For nine years, the company invests in her career as she gains experience and skills and steadily improves her performance. But at 31, just as the investment begins to pay off in earnest, she decides to have a baby. Can the company afford to let her go home, take another job, or go into business for herself? The common perception now is yes, the corporation can afford to lose her unless, after six or eight weeks or even three months of disability and maternity leave, she returns to work on a full-time schedule with the same vigor, commitment, and ambition that she showed before.

But what if she doesn't? What if she wants or needs to go on leave for six months or a year or, heaven forbid, five years? In this worst-case scenario, she works full-time from age 22 to 31 and from 36 to 65—a total of 38 years as opposed to the typical male's 43 years. That's not a huge difference. Moreover, my typical example is willing to work part-time while her children are young, if only her employer will give her the opportunity. There are two rewards for companies responsive to this need: higher retention of their best people and greatly improved performance and satisfaction in their middle management.

The high-performing career-and-family woman can be a major player in your company. She can give you a significant business advantage as the competition for able people escalates. Sometimes too, if you can hold on to her, she will switch gears in mid-life and reenter the competition for the top. The price you must pay to retain these women is threefold: you must plan for and manage maternity, you must provide the flexibility that will allow them to be maximally productive, and you must take an active role in helping to make family supports and high-quality, affordable child care available to all women.

🌱

The key to managing maternity is to recognize the value of high-performing women and the urgent need to retain them and keep them productive. The first step must be a genuine partnership between the woman and her boss. I know this partnership can seem difficult to forge. One of my own senior executives came to me recently to discuss plans for her maternity leave and subsequent return to work. She knew she wanted to come back. I wanted to make certain that she would. Still, we had a somewhat awkward conversation, because I knew that no woman can predict with certainty when she will be able to return to work or under what conditions. Physical problems can lengthen her leave. So can a demanding infant, a difficult family or personal adjustment, or problems with child care.

I still don't know when this valuable executive will be back on the job full-time, and her absence creates some genuine problems for our organization. But I do know that I can't simply replace her years of experience with a new recruit. Since our conversation, I also know that she wants to come back, and that she *will* come back—part-time at first—unless I make it impossible for her by, for example, setting an arbitrary date for her full-time return or resignation. In turn, she knows that the organization wants and needs her and, more to the point, that it will be responsive to her needs in terms of working hours and child-care arrangements.

In having this kind of conversation it's important to ask concrete questions that will help to move the discussion from uncertainty and anxiety to some level of predictability. Questions can touch on everything from family income and energy level to child care arrangements and career commitment. Of course you want your star manager to return to work as soon as possible, but you want her to return permanently and productively. Her downtime on the job is a drain on her energies and a waste of your money.

🌱

For all the women who want to combine career and family—the women who want to participate actively in the rearing of their children and who also want to pursue their careers seriously—the key to retention is to provide the flexibility and family supports they need in order to function effectively.

Time spent in the office increases productivity if it is time well spent, but the fact that most women continue to take the primary responsibility for child care is a cause of distraction, diversion, anxiety, and absenteeism—to say nothing of the persistent guilt experienced by all working mothers. A great many women, perhaps most of all women who have always performed at the highest levels, are also frustrated by a sense that while their children are babies they cannot function at their best either at home or at work.

In its simplest form, flexibility is the freedom to take time off—a couple of hours, a day, a week—or to do some work at home and some at the office, an arrangement that communication technology makes increasingly feasible. At the complex end of the spectrum are alternative work schedules that permit the woman to work less than full-time and her employer to reap the benefits of her experience and, with careful planning, the top level of her abilities.

Part-time employment is the single greatest inducement to getting women back on the job expeditiously and the provision women themselves most desire. A part-time return to work enables them to maintain responsibility for critical aspects of their jobs, keeps them in touch with the changes constantly occurring at the workplace and in the job itself, reduces stress and fatigue, often eliminates the need for paid maternity leave by permitting a return to the office as soon as disability leave is over, and, not least, can greatly enhance company loyalty. The part-time solution works particularly well when a work load can be reduced for one individual in a department or when a full-time job can be broken down by skill levels and apportioned to two individuals at different levels of skill and pay.

I believe, however, that shared employment is the most promising and will be the most widespread form of flexible scheduling in the future. It is feasible at every level of the corporation except at the pinnacle, for both the short and the long term. It involves two people taking responsibility for one job.

Two red lights flash on as soon as most executives hear the words "job sharing": continuity and client-customer contact. The answer to the continuity question is to place responsibility entirely on the two individuals sharing the job to discuss everything that transpires—thoroughly, daily, and on their own time. The answer to the problem of client-customer contact is yes, job sharing requires reeducation and a period of adjustment. But as both client and supervisor will quickly come to appreciate, two contacts means that the customer has continuous access to the company's representative, without interruptions for vacation, travel, or sick leave. The two people holding the job can simply cover for each other, and the uninterrupted, full-time coverage they provide together can be a stipulation of their arrangement.

Flexibility is costly in numerous ways. It requires more supervisory time to coordinate and manage, more office space, and somewhat greater benefits costs (though these can be contained with flexible benefits plans, prorated benefits, and, in two-paycheck families, elimination of duplicate benefits). But the advantages of reduced turnover and the greater productivity that results from higher energy levels and greater focus can outweigh the costs.

A few hints:

- Provide flexibility selectively. I'm not suggesting private arrangements subject to the suspicion of favoritism but rather a policy that makes flexible work schedules available only to high performers.
- Make it clear that in most instances (but not all) the rates of advancement and pay will be appropriately lower for those who take time off or who work part-time than for those who work full-time. Most career-and-family women are entirely willing to make that trade-off.
- Discuss costs as well as benefits. Be willing to risk accusations of bias. Insist, for example, that half time is half of whatever time it takes to do the job, not merely half of 35 or 40 hours.

The woman who is eager to get home to her child has a powerful incentive to use her time effectively at the office and to carry with her reading and other work that can be done at home. The talented professional who wants to have it all can be a high performer by carefully ordering her priorities and by focusing on objectives rather than on the legendary 15-hour day. By the time professional women have their first babies—at an average age of 31—they have already had nine years to work long hours at a desk, to travel, and to relocate. In the case of high performers, the need for flexibility coincides with what has gradually become the goal-oriented nature of responsibility.

⚜

Family supports—in addition to maternity leave and flexibility—include the provision of parental leave for men, support for two-career and single-parent families during relocation, and flexible benefits. But the primary ingredient is child care. The capacity of working mothers to function effectively and without interruption depends on the availability of good, affordable child care. Now that women make up almost half the work force and the growing percentage of managers, the decision to become involved in the personal lives of employees is no longer a philosophical question but a practical one. To make matters worse, the quality of child care has almost no relation to technology, inventiveness, or profitability but is more or less a pure function of the quality of child care personnel and the ratio of adults to children. These costs are irreducible. Only by joining hands with government and the public sector can corporations hope to create the vast quantity and variety of child care that their employees need.

Until quite recently, the response of corporations to women has been largely symbolic and cosmetic, motivated in large part by the will to avoid litigation and legal penalties. In some cases, companies were also moved by a genuine sense of fairness and a vague discomfort and frustration at the absence of women above the middle of the corporate pyramid. The actions they took were mostly quick, easy, and highly visible—child care information services, a three-month parental leave available to men as well as women, a woman appointed to the board of directors.

When I first began to discuss these issues 26 years ago, I was sometimes able to get an appointment with the assistant to the assistant in personnel, but it was only a courtesy. Over the past decade, I have met with the CEOs of many large corporations, and I've watched them become involved with ideas they had never previously thought much about. Until recently, however, the shelf life of that enhanced awareness was always short. Given pressing, short-term concerns, women were not a front-burner issue. In the past few months, I have seen yet another change. Some CEOs and top management groups now take the initiative. They call and ask us to show them how to shift gears from a responsive to a proactive approach to recruiting, developing, and retaining women.

I think this change is more probably a response to business needs—to concern for the quality of future profits and managerial talent—than to uneasiness about legal requirements, sympathy with the demands of women and minorities, or the desire to do what is right and fair. The nature of such business motivation varies. Some companies want to move women to higher positions as role models for those below them and as beacons for talented young recruits. Some want to achieve a favorable image with employees, customers, clients, and stockholders. These are all legitimate motives. But I think the companies that stand to gain most are motivated as well by a desire to capture competitive advantage in an era when talent and competence will be in increasingly short supply. These companies are now ready to stop being defensive about their experience with women and to ask incisive questions without preconceptions.

Even so, incredibly, I don't know of more than one or two companies that have looked into their own records to study the absolutely critical issue of maternity leave—how many women took it, when and whether they returned, and how this behavior correlated with their rank, tenure, age, and performance. The unique drawback to the employment of women is the physical reality of maternity and the particular socializing influence maternity has had. Yet to make women equal to men in the workplace we have chosen on the whole not to discuss this single most significant difference between them. Unless we do, we cannot evaluate the cost of recruiting, developing, and moving women up.

Now that interest is replacing indifference, there are four steps every company can take to examine its own experience with women:

1. Gather quantitative data on the company's experience with management-level women regarding turnover rates, occurrence of and return from maternity leave, and organizational level attained in relation to tenure and performance.
2. Correlate this data with factors such as age, marital status, and presence and age of children, and attempt to identify and analyze why women respond the way they do.
3. Gather qualitative data on the experience of women in your company and on how women are perceived by both sexes.
4. Conduct a cost-benefit analysis of the return on your investment in high-performing women. Factor in the cost to the company of women's negative reactions to negative experience, as well as the probable cost of corrective measures and policies. If women's value to your company is greater than the cost to recruit, train, and develop them—and of course I believe it will be—then you will want to do everything you can to retain them.

We have come a tremendous distance since the days when the prevailing male wisdom saw women as lacking the kind of intelligence that would allow them to succeed in business. For decades, even women themselves have harbored an unspoken belief that they couldn't make it because they couldn't be just like men, and nothing else would do. But now that women have shown themselves the equal of men in every area of organizational activity, now that they have demonstrated that they can be stars in every field of endeavor, now we can all venture to examine the fact that women and men are different.

On balance, employing women is more costly than employing men. Women can acknowledge this fact today because they know that their value to employers exceeds the additional cost and because they know that changing attitudes can reduce the additional cost dramatically. Women in management are no longer an idiosyncrasy of the arts and education. They have always matched men in natural ability. Within a very few years, they will equal men in numbers as well in every area of economic activity.

The demographic motivation to recruit and develop women is compelling. But an older question remains: Is society better for the change? Women's exit from the home and entry into the work force has certainly created problems—an urgent need for good, affordable child care; troubling questions about the kind of parenting children need; the costs and difficulties of diversity in the workplace; the stress and fatigue of combining work and family responsibilities. Wouldn't we all be happier if we could turn back the clock to an age when men were in the workplace and women in the home, when male and female roles were clearly differentiated and complementary?

Nostalgia, anxiety, and discouragement will urge many to say yes, but my answer is emphatically no. Two fundamental benefits that were unattainable in the past are now within our reach. For the individual, freedom of choice—in this case the freedom to choose career, family, or a combination of the two. For the corporation, access to the most gifted individuals in the country. These benefits are neither self-indulgent nor insubstantial. Freedom of choice and self-realization are too deeply American to be cast aside for some wistful vision of the past. And access to our most talented human resources is not a luxury in this age of explosive international competition but rather the barest minimum that prudence and national self-preservation require.

Comments on Felice N. Schwartz' "Management Women and the New Facts of Life"

Nancy Evans
President and Publisher
Doubleday & Company, Inc.
New York, New York

The future of women in management is not as dire as Felice N. Schwartz paints it to be in "Management Women and the New Facts of Life" (January–February 1989). When I was starting out in publishing, older women used to say to me, "Well, you're never going to have a child are you? That'll wreck your career." I finally did choose to have a child—and I still have my career. I'm not saying I do it all; I do get tired. But to say that women have to choose between having a child and having a career is no longer true. Many women perform magnificently in their jobs *and* raise children. Unfortunately, there isn't much press on these women.

In fact, the popular media misrepresent what is really going on with women in the workplace, tending to see things in black and white. But it is more complex than that.

Child care is one reason that many women with families are making it. Women in upper management usually can afford at-home child care, which enables them to go full speed ahead with their careers. But women in middle management may find the cost of good child care crippling. Government and corporations don't offer enough solutions yet.

Support at home also helps women succeed. I often notice to whom successful women are married and what their relationships are like. Usually, these women marry men who are secure and decent, and each partner takes part in raising the children and helping with household responsibilities. Who does what doesn't become an issue, so the women don't end up working two jobs.

Schwartz says that "women tend to bring to their employment a sense that they can choose to change jobs or careers at will, take time off, or reduce their hours." That is nonsense. Most women can't afford to change jobs or take time off. But women are working four days a week—and still getting their jobs done.

With so much technology available, women can now work at home one day a week—as many do. During the last few weeks of my pregnancy, we set up a fax machine at my house, brought in an assistant, and held meetings at my home. There are ways of doing things so that business doesn't stop and women don't become exhausted. The key is integrating and organizing.

Regarding the author's point that "women's continuing tendency to search for more than monetary reward . . . makes them more likely than men to leave the corporation in search of other values," I believe everyone—women and men—wants his or her work to have meaning. Both men and women are reevaluating how much to put into their work and how much to put into their families. They are earnest about wanting to be involved with their children and with each other.

I see a positive swing in our culture today. People in positions of power are acting on their good impulses. Gannet Company managers take their families with them when they attend weekend meetings, for example. Integrating family life and work isn't just good for people; it makes good business sense.

Deborah Biondolillo
Vice President
Human Resources
Apple Computer, Inc.
Cupertino, California

The scenarios described by Ms. Schwartz indicate that she based her conclusions on traditional companies where lifetime employment and linear career paths are the norm and where value to the company is measured by the management level achieved. But with the information age, a new kind of corporate environment is emerging, replacing the traditional industrial-age organization. These "third wave" companies are based on flexible structures that support a changing work force, market, and economy.

My company is an example of this new type of organization. We don't expect a lifetime commitment from our employees, but we have created an exciting, flexible environment that allows us to attract and retain the most talented individuals in the technology industry. We've done this by providing options—from job sharing to day care to sabbaticals. There are no "tracks" at Apple, only individual paths based on the choices our employees make in balancing career and personal needs. Some choose to emphasize their careers first, others, their families. But many choose *both*—and are successful in doing so.

Individuals at all levels in today's work force change jobs, and often careers, several times in their working lives. Many leave the work force part time or temporarily to pursue educational and training opportunities, to raise a child, or for any number of reasons. In this environment, Schwartz's recommended early identification of an individual's career path becomes not only impossible but also undesirable. It establishes barriers instead of providing the options people need.

The two-track approach does a disservice to all employees and forces both men and women into predefined roles that are inappropriate today. It is time for corporate America to respond to individual issues, not gender issues, and foster the kind of environment that leads to satisfying careers *and* personal lives.

Faith A. Wohl
Director
Work Force Partnering Division
E.I. du Pont de Nemours and Company, Inc.
Wilmington, Delaware

Felice Schwartz proposes a new form of corporate triage. Separate the women, she urges corporations, into those with a primary interest in career and those who want both a career and a family. Propel the former into the high-potential, executive-suite orbit. The latter can follow a different track on a lower curve.

Even if I could climb the intellectual and emotional hurdles this concept presents, I would still see at least two negative outcomes. First, we would perpetuate the present situation in which most women at upper levels don't have families, while the majority of their male peers do. We might end up with more women at the table, but the level of common ground and shared experiences would be no greater.

Second, and far more important, what are we to say to men? The most startling result of a new study here at Du Pont is that the attitudes of men concerning work and family issues are rapidly approaching those of women, a significant change over what we saw in a similar study just four years ago.

The workplace must be flexible enough to allow both men and women to balance work and family commitments as they choose, without artificial assumptions by employers. Men—at least Du Pont's—are saying loud and clear: "We're part of this too. The care of children is affecting our careers as well as those of our wives." That's the real "new fact of life" on the table.

John H. Bryan, Jr.
Chairman and CEO
Sara Lee Corporation
Chicago, Illinois

Felice Schwartz's provocative opening sentence has stirred much unwarranted criticism of an article that, if closely read, can do much for the advancement of women in business. It is grossly unfair to accuse her of setting back working women; indeed, she has made the advancement of women managers a key business issue. The fact is, some working women do take time off for maternity leave, and this does add some cost to companies that invest time and money in their training and development. The flap over her article does not change that truth.

What her article has done is to encourage my company to look more closely at policies to advance the development of women's careers. In the corporate world, there are people who are committed to paying the price for career advancement, and there are those who are not. It's important for companies to recognize that both men and women exhibit varying degrees of career commitment.

In our company there are many women employees who have small children at home, and these women are as willing as many men to make the same trade-offs to pursue rapid career advancement. But there are also women for whom family is such a strong priority that they cannot give the same amount of time and energy to career advancement. Thus their comfort and advancement in the workplace can be hindered.

Schwartz's commonsense ideas encourage corporations to provide a work environment that allows all employees, especially working parents, to contribute their talents and skills to the corporation without sacrificing family life.

In her nearly three decades at Catalyst, Schwartz has earned the confidence and respect of business executives everywhere. She has worked with them to advance the visibility of women's issues. Her article continues that important work. We in corporate management must make our environment more compatible for all parents—men and women alike.

Anne Stevens
Engineering Department Head
Linden Technology Center
Exxon Chemical Company
Linden, New Jersey

The article by Felice Schwartz describes roles for today's corporate women both narrowly and restrictively. The article presents executive woman as similar to the "traditional" model of the executive man who would give up almost anything to get ahead. There are women and men succeeding in corporations today who would argue that this is not what contemporary proponents of cultural change are striving for.

I am a "career-primary woman" who heads an engineering department for Exxon Chemicals. I am married and have two children. When my children were small, I very carefully planned child care to accommodate my work and travel schedules and my children's social and educational growth. My children know who their parents are and who raises them.

During the nine years that I have been with Exxon, I have enjoyed good progress in both position and responsibility. Based on my progress and that of other women at Exxon, I would not attribute advancement to family status.

The "barriers" to advancement for women are more complex than maternity. Focusing heavily on maternity as a chief criterion in identifying women with executive potential does not represent accurately what we have experienced. The significant barriers are created from biases, subjective versus objective opinions of performance, and lack of a clear, consistent statement of the requirements for being a successful managerial woman. The corporate environment needs to change to support further advancement and retention of women. Simply learning how to cope better with one aspect of our biological differences will not ensure progress if the environment remains nonsupportive. Long before women held executive positions, companies dealt adequately with problems created by transfers, resignations, and illness among managers.

Schwartz did not amplify some of the real financial and productivity benefits women contribute to organizations. As she stated, women pay particular attention to the quality and substance of what they do. In an era of intense global competition and widespread corporate change, these strengths and women's more participative leadership style align with necessary changes in culture.

Several of us women in management and professional positions at Exxon cannot identify with management women as the author characterizes them. We are women of differing talents, working long, hard hours and making the personal sacrifices required to succeed, while maintaining a family life. We are not trying to get ahead by imitating male behavior. We want to be recognized and rewarded for the contributions we make as individuals. We view the demographic changes taking place in the United States as adding value to a renewed competitive edge. The technical and business innovations achievable from women's perspectives will generate increased corporate profits and help to maintain the United States's position in worldwide economic and humanistic leadership.

The Debate
over Comparable Worth

JOHN R. BOATRIGHT

In 1981, a strike was called by a union representing about half of the 4,000 municipal workers in San Jose, California. One issue in the strike was the union's insistence that the city spend $3.2 million over four years to upgrade the salaries of non-management employees in female dominated jobs. A study recently conducted by the city with the aid of a national consulting firm revealed considerable differences in salary between men and women in comparable positions. Using a point-factor evaluation system, with points being assigned for knowledge, problem solving, accountability, and working conditions, the study showed that Senior Chemists, for example, (501 points) received $29,094 annually, while the salary for the comparable female dominated job of Senior Librarian (496 points) was $23,348. The male dominated job category of Painter (173 points) was held by the study to be comparable to that of Secretary (177 points), but the pay for painters and secretaries was $24,518 and $17,784 respectively. The nine day strike ended after the city council pledged to spend $1.45 million over two years to upgrade salaries in the lowest paid female dominated positions and to bargain in good faith in subsequent years to close the wage gap further. Mayor Janet Gray Hayes hailed the settlement as "the first giant step toward fairness in the workplace for women."

The situation in San Jose is remarkable only for the response of the city to the problem of the undervaluing of jobs held predominantly by women. It is well documented that women earn less than men. The figure at the end of 1989 was that the median income for women was 68 percent of the earnings for men. This earnings gap has been relatively constant over the past fifty years with the difference in pay between men and women dipping in recent years before rising again. In 1939, women who were employed full time, year-round earned 63.6 percent of the wages of men who were similarly employed, and this figure remained above 63 percent during the middle of the 1950s. In 1972, the earnings of women as a percentage of men's fell to a record low of 56.6, and by 1981 the figure had risen only to 59.2 percent.

Women are not the only group with lower earnings. The income of racial minorities is also substantially less than that of whites. With increasing access to education and the elimination of discrimination in hiring and promotion, though, black men have made significant economic gains. In 1959, the mean salary of black men was 71 percent of the earnings of the average white man. Ten years later the figure had risen to 75 percent, and

Reprinted by permission of the author.

by 1975 the percentage had increased to 85. Conventional remedies for discrimination have thus proven effective in reducing wage differences between blacks and whites but not those between men and women. As a result, advocates of women's rights have sought out new means of attacking this form of discrimination.

THE PRINCIPLE OF COMPARABLE WORTH

The means chosen is the principle of *comparable worth*. This principle holds that dissimilar jobs can still be compared with respect to certain features and that jobs which are similar with respect to these features ought to be paid the same. The job of a secretary, for example, is quite different from that of a painter, but if it can be shown that the two jobs require a similar degree of skill and effort, then secretaries and painters should be paid at the same rate. Expressed in this way, the principle of comparable worth provides a method for setting wages that is an alternative to market forces operating according to the laws of supply and demand.

On the standard economic view, wages are determined largely by the contribution workers make to *productivity*. More technically, the pay of any given worker is a function of the net addition that worker makes to the revenues of the employer. The value of a job, then, on the economic view, is what the work of an employee is worth to an employer, and this value is measured largely by the price a worker can command in the marketplace. In a competitive labor market in which workers are free to move from one job to another and employers are forced to compete for their services, the laws of supply and demand will result in a state of equilibrium in which the wages of workers match their productivity.

Advocates of the principle of comparable worth hold the view that compensation ought to be based on *job content*. This is typically done by a process known as job evaluation, which measures and compares the features of a job for which a worker ought to be compensated. The general features considered in most job evaluation systems are skill, effort, responsibility, and working conditions. Each job is assigned a certain number of points from a range for each feature; these points are added together to arrive at a total; different jobs are then ranked according to their total number of points. Compensation is based on these rankings so that jobs with the same number of points are paid the same and jobs with more points carry higher rates of pay.

The use of job evaluations to set wages is a familiar practice in American business. Since the 1920s, companies have employed methods for measuring the content of jobs in order to provide a rational means for setting wages where market forces alone are inadequate for the task. While the laws of supply and demand determine the overall level of wages for different kinds of work, they are not suited for making fine distinctions between the multitude of jobs in large organizations, especially where the productivity of individual workers is difficult to measure. This method also gives managers a great deal of control over decisions about wages and the deployment of labor, which is especially valuable in dealing with a unionized workforce.

Job evaluation studies are used extensively in the public sector, since governments are largely insulated from market forces. In order to attract and retain competent personnel and to maintain equity among different jobs, civil service systems on the local, state, and federal levels evaluate the content of jobs and set wages according to the value of comparable jobs in the private sector. Prior to the study of nonmanagement workers in San Jose, for example, the city conducted a job evaluation of salaried managers in the municipal government. The purpose was merely to ensure that all salaries were competitive in order to prevent other cities in the area from luring managers away with offers of higher pay. Washington, which was the first state to conduct a comparable worth study to determine the extent of discrimination against women, had been required since 1960 to pay workers the prevailing "market rate," which was determined by an elaborate salary survey of state jobs and jobs in business and industry. No attempt was made to compare every state job with jobs in the private sector. Rather, the compensation for a few "benchmark" jobs was set by determining the wages which work of that kind would command in a competitive market, and the pay for other state jobs was set by comparing them with the "benchmark" jobs.

Two Versions of the Principle

There are two different versions of the principle of comparable worth. In one version, the value of a job is determined by features of the work performed—by the content of the job, in other words, as opposed to supply and demand. Unlike the value of other goods, then, the value of labor is not the same as the market price, and the possibility exists that the wages resulting from market forces undervalue (or in some cases overvalue) the work performed. The principle of comparable worth, in this version, is offered as a morally preferable alternative to the market, especially when the market price does not accurately reflect the value of the work performed.

A second version of the principle of comparable worth does not maintain that there is a concept of value other than the price that a worker can command in a competitive market. Because of discrimination, however, the wages that are actually paid to some workers are not the same as what they would be paid if there were no discrimination. Since the skill and effort required to perform a job are largely the features that enable workers to command a certain price for their labor in a free market, a comparison of jobs according to their content provides a means for determining whether discrimination exists and what wages would be without the presence of discrimination. In this version, comparable worth is a method for detecting discrimination in the labor market and correcting it. It is not an alternative to the market but an adjunct which frees the market from the distorting force of discrimination.

The difference between the two versions of the principle of comparable worth can be expressed in the language of rights. The first version claims that each worker has a right to be paid according to the content of the job performed and that this right is violated when one worker is paid less than another for performing comparable work, whatever the reason for the difference in pay. The right involved in the second version is simply the right not to be discriminated against in the setting of wages, that is, the right not to be paid lower wages simply because the work is performed predominantly by persons of a certain sex or race. The principle "equal pay for comparable work," in this version, is thus a means for protecting an already existing right rather than the creation of a new right.

In order to justify the principle of comparable worth in the first version, it is necessary to demonstrate that the only morally relevant features for setting wages are those which concern the character of the work performed and that all other differences, such as those resulting from the forces of supply and demand, are morally irrelevant. This is by no means an easy task. The justification of the second version of the principle is much easier. A defender need only show that the market has operated in a discriminatory manner and that setting wages on the basis of job content is better suited than any other means for a nondiscriminatory labor market. Since the second version is what most advocates intend, it is the one considered in the remainder of this discussion.

THE EQUAL PAY ACT AND TITLE VII

The principle of comparable worth ("equal pay for comparable work") is not the same as the principle embodied in the Equal Pay Act of 1963 (EPA). Passed by Congress as an amendment to the Fair Labor Standards Act, the EPA prohibits an employer from paying men and women in the same establishment different wages for jobs which require "equal skill, effort, and responsibility," and which are performed under the same conditions. Exceptions are allowed by the act for differences due to any factor other than sex, such as seniority, a merit system, and compensation based on productivity. As interpreted by the courts, the EPA applies to employees who perform substantially the same but not necessarily identical work.[1] The principle embodied in the EPA can be expressed, therefore, as "equal pay for the *same* work" rather than "equal pay for *comparable* work."

While Title VII of the 1964 Civil Rights Act provides more extensive protection against wage discrimination than the EPA, the courts have not ruled that the failure of employers to pay equal wages for work of comparable worth is a violation of Title VII. The issue was raised in a suit filed by a woman, Alberta Gunther, and three coworkers who were employed as jail matrons in Washington County, Oregon. Since the matrons were responsible for fewer inmates than males guards and performed some clerical duties which were not shared by their male counterparts, the jobs were held by the courts to be dissimilar. Consequently, there was no violation of the EPA. Still, the women argued that the difference in pay was the result of intentional discrimination on the basis of sex. In support of their argument they cited a county commissioned study that evaluated the job of jail matron at 95 percent of the market value of the guards' job. While the male guards received the full recommended wages, the women were paid only 70 percent of theirs. As a result, the women earned one-third less than the men. In a 5-4 decision, the Supreme Court ruled that Alberta Gunther and her co-workers could sue under Title VII for equal pay for work that is comparable to but not substantially the same as that performed by men. The decision emphasized, however, that the matrons' suit was "not based on the controversial concept of 'comparable worth'," but that they "seek to prove by direct evidence, that their wages were depressed because of *intentional sex discrimination*."[2]

ARE WAGE DIFFERENCES DUE TO DISCRIMINATION?

One important issue in the debate over comparable worth is whether the difference in earnings between men and women is due to discrimination or whether it results from the impersonal workings of the labor market. If discrimination is not the cause of the earnings gap, then there is no substance to the claim that women are being unfairly compensated for the work they do and hence there is no need to adopt remedial measures, such as a system of compensation based on the principle of comparable worth. Of course, a comparable worth system could still be advanced as a morally preferable method of setting wages (the first version of the principle) or as a pragmatic step toward reducing the disparity in earnings between the sexes as a socially desirable goal.

The main evidence for discrimination in compensation is statistical. Unfortunately, the statistical evidence—which indisputably documents the existence of an earnings gap between men and women—is explainable in a variety of ways, not all of which point to discrimination as the culprit. One reason why men earn more is that they work more hours, and so a distinction has to be made between income (the amount actually received in a paycheck) and wages (the amount earned for each hour worked). Earnings also increase with experience, and women, who voluntarily leave the work force more often to raise a family and pursue other interests, have a shorter work history on the average than men. When comparisons are made between male and female workers with the same number of years of experience or between never married women and men, the wage gap narrows, though not by much. By 1980, women who had never married, for example, still earned only 65 percent as much as men their own age.

Success also depends on a willingness to acquire an education and specialized training, to accept positions of greater responsibility, to relocate when necessary, and to make other sacrifices. These are examples of what economists call *human capital,* which is the amount of resources invested in order to increase the productivity of individual workers. If men "invest" more in themselves and thereby increase their value to employers, then they can rightly expect to be paid more. It can be objected, however, that insofar as women leave the work force more often and are less willing to do what is necessary to build a career, their choices simply reflect the lower return which their investment in human capital brings in a job market which discriminates against them. The result is a "chicken-and-egg" question: Do women earn less because they have less human capital, or do women rationally choose to invest less in themselves because of low pay?

By far the most significant factor in explaining the lower wages of women is the segregation of jobs according to sex. Women are crowded into traditionally female occupations that are not highly valued by the market in the first place, and the large number of women competing for jobs further depresses wages. Of the 553 occupations listed in the 1970 census, 310 were 80 percent or more male dominated, while women held 80 percent or more of the jobs in 50 of the occupations. Further, 70 percent of men and 54 percent of women were in occupations where workers of their own sex held more than 70 percent of the jobs. And 25 percent of women workers were employed in occupations which were 95 percent female.

Experts are sharply divided on whether women are forced into traditionally female occupations because they are the only jobs available or whether they freely choose them because of a preference for certain kinds of work. Advocates of the latter view cite gender differences in the factors that contribute to job satisfaction. According to some studies, women are willing to sacrifice some income for clean, safe, comfortable work, and they place more value than men on interpersonal relations, the opportunity to serve others, and the intrinsic interest of a job.[3] As a result, some of the gap between the earnings of men and women may be due to the higher wages employers must offer to induce workers (who are predominantly men) to perform less desirable work, while women compete among themselves for more attractive jobs.

If the explanation of the pay gap is that women are confined by discrimination to female dominated jobs, then one solution is to remove the barriers to the advancement of women into traditionally male lines of work by more rigorous enforcement of Title VII. This is an alternative to comparable worth known as *realignment,* which involves reducing the extent of job segregation according to sex. In the view of many experts, however, realignment does not address the source of the problem, which can be succinctly stated as follows:

> Women are paid less because they are in women's jobs, and women's jobs are paid less because they are done by women. The reason is that women's work—in fact, virtually anything done by women—is characterized as less valuable.[4]

As an illustration: the formerly male dominated job of bank teller has been largely taken over by women. The result has not been an increase in the opportunities of women for higher pay but a decrease in the relative earning power (as well as the prestige) of this kind of work. If the undervaluing of work done by women is a significant factor in explaining why men earn more, then comparable worth is likely to be a more effective strategy than realignment.

To summarize this portion of the discussion, some of the differences in male and female earnings are due to the choices women make. These are (perhaps) the result of inherent differences between men and women, and certainly they result from social forces which operate outside the job market. There are also many structural features of the job market which play a role. Among these are differences between industries and firms within an industry, regional differences, age distribution in the work force, unionization, and a host of other variables that have not been adequately studied. Whatever residual amount is left unaccounted for by these factors is due to discrimination against women. The only conclusion to emerge consistently from the many studies on the question, though, is that we do not know how much that residual amount is.

MEASURING JOB CONTENT

A second issue in the comparable worth debate is whether it is possible to measure job content in such a way that the resulting comparisons are meaningful and reliable. Some critics use the analogy of comparing apples and oranges to support their contention that no significant comparison can be made between extremely dissimilar jobs. Other opponents of comparable worth argue that job evaluations are not wholly objective and are potentially discriminatory. The evaluator must use judgment, first, in determining the features to be taken into account and their relative weight and, second, in deciding the number of points to assign for each feature in evaluating a job. And studies have shown that there is considerable variation in the results obtained by different evaluators. There is a tendency, for example, for the judgment of an evaluator to reflect the prevailing status and pay of the jobs being evaluated, with the result that the evaluation simply ratifies the existing practices of an employer. This is a problem known as "policy capturing."

A study of comparable worth conducted by the National Academy of Sciences for the Equal Employment Opportunity Commission also cites the problem that the judgment of evaluators may also introduce a systematic bias against women.[5] The potential for introducing bias is vividly illustrated by an evaluation of the job of bindery workers in the U.S. Government Printing Office.[6] Not only did the evaluator assign women fewer points for performing work with the same features (lifting heavy objects and handling confidential material, for example), but the skill and effort required for the work done by women was consistently underestimated. The evaluator gave no points to the women for stitching bindings, for example, since sewing is a skill possessed by most women!

The response of supporters of comparable worth is that there are carefully designed, generally reliable techniques for conducting job evaluations which are not open to the critics' charge. The reasons why some workers deserve to be paid more than others refer to factors that are inherent in all jobs. The high pay of truck drivers is deserved because of the long grueling hours and the heavy responsibility of hauling valuable cargo. But nursing is also exhausting work on which the lives of patients often depend. So these two jobs have much in common despite the obvious differences.

The reliability of a comparable worth study depends on how it is conducted. Experts in the field recommend that a committee of employees be formed, so that the choice of factors and the assignment of weights are done by people who are thoroughly familiar with the jobs being evaluated. In the San Jose study, the city's personnel department distributed questionnaires to employees in order to gather firsthand information on each job. After interviews with approximately 20 percent of the respondents, detailed job descriptions were written, and a committee was formed to study and evaluate every job. This committee consisted of an equal number of men and women, and before a decision was made, seven of the ten members had to agree on the number of points to be assigned for each factor. Furthermore, the factors used and their weight can be validated by applying a job evaluation system only to white males, where discrimination is not present, and comparing actual earnings with those predicted by system.

THE EFFECT ON THE LABOR MARKET

A third issue in the debate is the charge of many opponents of comparable worth that ignoring market forces will undermine the ability of the market to price and allocate labor in an efficient manner, with a resultant lowering of productivity. One beneficial effect of market forces, for example, is to provide incentives for workers to leave crowded areas with low productivity jobs for which there is a declining demand and to prepare themselves for more productive work in newer areas where the demand is greater. Paying workers on the basis of job content will remove this valuable incentive. The introduction of comparable worth, moreover, is likely to be accompanied by a complex administrative structure that will increase the hand of government in business decision making and further impair productivity.

A major difficulty with arguments based on the virtues of a free market is that they assume that wages are now set in an efficient manner by the workings of an impersonal economy, when in fact the actual wage setting practices of employers are highly arbitrary and discriminatory. The issues in this dispute are highly complex and form the basis for competing theories in labor economics. In opposition to mainline economists who hold that wages are determined largely by human capital in a competitive market, a growing number of economists, commonly known as "institutionalists," stress the importance of structural features of labor markets and features that are peculiar to specific industries.[7]

One of these structural features is the existence of *internal* labor markets. Most jobs are filled by the transfer or promotion of workers already employed, so that the practices and relationships within a firm, including collective bargaining agreements, play a much more important role than the supply of labor on the outside. In addition, some jobs involve unique firm-specific tasks for which employees receive extensive on-the-job training. In the absence of an external market for these jobs, wages cannot be set by the laws of supply and demand, and other means must be used. Institutionalists further cite the existence of *dual* labor markets. Alongside a primary market consisting of "good" jobs, with high status and pay, fringe benefits, and advancement opportunities, there exists a secondary market of low-paying dead end "bad" jobs. The primary market is largely the preserve of white males, while women and minorities are heavily represented in the secondary market.

Institutionalist theories of labor markets suggest strategies for reducing discrimination which are quite different from those of the standard economic view. Instead of encouraging women to prepare themselves for entering male dominated lines of work (the market solution), it may be more effective to scrutinize the personnel practices of firms and especially the way in which employees are selected in the internal market for on-the-job training and other opportunities. If the dual market theory is correct, then discrimination is likely to persist unless more "good" jobs are created and upward mobility from "bad" jobs is increased. Compensation systems based on the principle of comparable worth can serve to enhance both of these strategies.

THE ISSUE OF COST

A fourth and final issue in the debate is the cost of implementing a system of compensation based on comparable worth. In addition to the indirect cost of reduced efficiency, there is also the direct cost of raising the wages of women (and some men) in undervalued jobs. Faced with the need to meet the increased payroll cost, employers may be led to increase prices, thus producing inflation, or to lower the wages of the men (and a few women) in predominantly male lines of work. The $1.45 million committed by the city of San Jose to implement comparable worth over two years was still considerably short of the union's estimate $5.4 million over four years. The Minnesota legislature set aside $21.8 million to be spent in 1983–84 to eliminate about half of the wage gap that was estimated to be due to discrimination against women among the 9,000 state employees. In 1984, Iowa began the first phase of a comparable worth plan at a cost of $10 million. Estimates of the cost, both direct and indirect, of eliminating wage discrimination nationwide range between $2 billion and $150 billion.

The National Academy of Sciences report concludes that "because of the complexity of market processes, actions intended to have one result may well turn out to have other, even perverse, consequences."[8] One of these unintended consequences might be to harm the women who are supposed to be the beneficiaries. This is because another way for employers to reduce their payroll costs is by increasing capital investment so as to cut down on the number of workers in less productive jobs. And the workers thrown out of jobs will tend to be women with less training and experience. According to one writer, "Nine secretaries working at word processors might become more cost-effective than twelve secretaries working at typewriters."[9] The nine secretaries who are still employed will benefit by higher wages, but the other three will lose.

Advocates of comparable worth respond that the estimates of cost and predictions of unintended consequences are overstated. Helen Remick and Ronnie J. Steinberg point out that

> . . . the assumption underlying these estimates is that *all* wage discrimination in *all* work organizations is going to be rectified all at once and tomorrow. . . . Most legal reforms that impact upon the labor market have been implemented in stages: either the scope of coverage is initially restricted and gradually expanded to cover a larger proportion of employees over time, or the legal standard is introduced in steps.[10]

Furthermore, if increased pay is owed to women in undervalued jobs as a matter of right, then justice requires that society be willing to bear the burden, no matter what the cost.

With regard to the impact on the employment of women, evidence one way or the other is scarce, since comparable worth has not been extensively implemented in the United States. The only available evidence comes from the experience of Australia. Between 1969 and 1975, a system of comparable worth was adopted in stages. In the decade of the 1970s, the ratio of women's earnings to those of men rose from 65 percent to 86 percent. Experts who have studied the Australian experience agree that the economic impact has been slight. One study reports that while the number of women employed continued to rise, due to an expanding economy, the rate was one-third less than it would have been otherwise, and the unemployment among women increased by 0.5 percent.[11] These consequences, while not insignificant, fall short of the dire predictions made before Australia adopted a comparable worth system.

CONCLUSION

The comparable worth debate teaches many valuable lessons. It shows us, first, the importance of an accurate understanding of the problem at hand. The existence of a wage gap is a fact, but a great deal of careful analysis is necessary to determine whether the differences in pay are due to discrimination or other causes. Second, the debate forces us to address a fundamental issue in any economic system, namely how should wages be determined? What is a just wage? One version of the comparable worth principle challenges the basis tenet of our economic system, that our labor is worth what it can command in the marketplace. The content of a job and not supply and demand, its advocates say, should determine what we receive. Even if we accept the version of the principle that seeks to use comparable worth as a remedy for discrimination in the market, we still have to ask, is this the best solution to the problem? Insofar as the wage gap is due to discrimination, it ought to be eliminated. About this there can be no dispute. But many strategies have been proposed for dealing with the problem, and more, perhaps, will be developed. Each solution involves a host of factors that need to be considered before we settle on any one.

NOTES

1. The landmark case is *Schultz v. Wheaton Glass Company*, 21 F.2d 259 (3d Cir. 1970), *cert. denied* 398 U.S. 905 (1970).
2. *Gunther v. County of Washington*, 452 U.S. 967 (1981).
3. See, for example, Guiseppi A. Forgionne and Vivian E. Peters, "Differences in Job Motivation and Satisfaction among Male and Female Managers," *Human Relations*, 35 (1982), pp. 101–118.
4. Sharon Toffey Shepela and Ann T. Viviano, "Some Psychological Factors Affecting Job Segregation and Wages," in Helen Remick, ed., *Comparable Worth and Wage Discrimination* (Philadelphia: Temple University Press, 1984), p. 47.
5. Donald J. Treiman and Heidi I. Hartmann, eds., *Women, Work, and Wages: Equal Pay for Jobs of Equal Value* (Washington, D.C.: National Academy Press, 1981).

6. *Thompson v. Boyle*, 499 F. Supp. 1147 (D.D.C. 1980).
7. See P. B. Doeringer and M. J. Piore, *Internal Labor Markets and Manpower Analysis* (Lexington, MA: D. C. Heath, 1971); and Francine Blau, *Equal Pay in the Office* (Lexington, MA: Lexington Press, 1978).
8. Treiman and Hartmann, *Women, Work, and Wages*, pp. 65–66.
9. Michael Evan Gold, *A Dialogue on Comparable Worth* (Ithaca, NY: ILR Press, 1983), p. 55.
10. Helen Remick and Ronnie J. Steinberg, "Technical Possibilities and Political Realities: Concluding Remarks," in Remick, *Comparable Worth and Wage Discrimination*, p. 290.
11. Robert G. Gregory and Robert C. Duncan, "Segmented Labor Market Theories and the Australian Experience of Equal Pay for Women," *Journal of Post Keynesian Economics*, 3 (1981), pp. 403–428.

•Part Five•

CONTEMPORARY BUSINESS ISSUES
Introduction

Modern business is undergoing dramatic changes. Smaller companies find it harder to compete as large corporations take bigger and bigger pieces of the economic pie. Today the 1,000 largest U.S. firms account for 72 percent of the sales, 86 percent of the employees, and 85 percent of the profits of all U.S. industrial corporations. Fewer than 150 corporations now hold the same share of manufacturing assets as did the 1,000 largest corporations in 1941. Other changes include alterations in corporate organizational structure, expansion into multinational markets, consumer unrest over advertising, and fears about pollution and the loss of natural resources. While these changes have been taking place, business has become more aware of itself not only as an economic institution but as an active participant in the surrounding community.

From an ethical standpoint, the transformation of business is significant. Changes in the goals and structure of the corporation have caused changes in the expectations of employees and consumers. For example, the shift away from the domination of the corporation by a single person has prompted greater participation by employees in corporate decisions. Professional managers, many of whom do not even own stock in the companies they manage, now control most of the largest and most influential corporations in the world. Technological changes, too, have played their role, generating a wider array of products and vastly more efficient means, such as television, for advertising them. With these advances have come moral doubts about the content of advertisements and the psychological impact of advertising on society.

Society has also changed its views about economic growth. It was once routinely assumed that economic growth should be pursued at every turn: greater production, higher incomes, and larger gross national products. Now critics complain that clean air, abundant wildlife, and adequate energy sources will vanish if we persist unreflectively in our search for greater economic prosperity. We seem to be driven to the point of asking whether an ever-increasing standard of living is possible without endangering the ecological systems that support technology and human life. And more and more people are also asking whether the unabated quest for economic prosperity doesn't erode human values such as freedom and creativity.

THE ENVIRONMENT

In recent years attention has been drawn to the fact that we live on a planet which, despite its apparent abundance, possesses finite natural resources. Never-ending economic growth involves either a never-ending consumption of these resources or discovery of substitutes. Is it wise, then, to persist in our goal of technological and economic expansion when our stocks of natural resources are continually dwindling? Critics of economic growth argue that we may soon approach the limits of those natural resources, and human needs may outstrip the technological know-how required to develop substitutes. To avoid this disaster such critics propose a radical reordering of the economy so that we actively control growth and work to replace lost resources. In contrast, a number of other economists argue that economic growth is both necessary and valuable. It enhances human life, it is necessary to provide for the development of the Third World economies, and it allows us to develop the technologies necessary to repair our previous ecological errors.

In "Ethics and Ecology," the philosopher William Blackstone questions economic optimism. Rights, Blackstone asserts, flow from the capacities that make us uniquely human, and these capacities require a liveable environment for their proper development. Whatever the future holds, we must recognize that human beings have a *right* to a livable environment. Thus we need to manage the environment for our own long-term survival and future well-being.

Bracketing questions of scarcity, Mark Sagoff and Tom Regan examine deeper environmental issues. Sagoff, in his article, "Why Political Questions Are Not All Economic," questions the claim that environmental problems are merely economic problems concerning distribution of costs and benefits. The identification of environmental problems as economic ones contends that if consumers prefer and are willing to pay for a clean environment, for recycled products, and national parks, then it is efficient to develop these assets. It follows that if consumers find it more efficient and less costly to pollute or waste, then one should not interfere with their market preferences. The difficulty with this thesis, Sagoff argues, is that many of our preferences are not market preferences. Sagoff questions economic preferences as the ultimate judge of worthiness, he challenges the neutrality of economic claims, and cogently defends the importance of noneconomic value. Sagoff points out that we find value in clean air, the preservation of the spotted owl, and virgin national forests despite their costs. Sagoff challenges us to take into account these nonmarket values which, more than market values, play a central role in human choice.

Taking a radically different approach, Tom Regan argues that we need no less than an "ethic of the environment." The environment itself has inherent value as part of the natural order, independent of its relationship to, and its utilitarian value for, human beings. So a valid environmental ethic treats nonsentient as well as sentient beings as having moral standing. Only by adopting such a view can the natural order be preserved.

The *Exxon Valdez* case raises a number of environmental issues. While Exxon will probably not suffer major economic losses as a result of the clean-up costs from the spill, the long-term damage to the environment cannot yet be calculated. Moreover, as the case illustrates, more is at issue than economic costs. The oil spill violated the ecology of the region. It violated environmental rights of human and nonhuman Valdez inhabitants, and, Regan would argue, it violated rights of the natural order itself. The harms of those violations as well as economic costs must be taken into account in judging the disaster.

ADVERTISING

Advertising is big business. It accounts for one fifth of the total selling costs of American industry, lagging behind only sales promotion and direct salesmanship in its total cost.[1] In 1982, U.S. ad agencies grossed $6.51 billion, and their customers paid $44.2 billion for space and time in the mass media. Increasingly, however, critics are raising the question: "Is society getting what it pays for?"

Until the latter part of the nineteenth century, many of the commonest articles of consumption, such as soap and clothing, were made at home. Products were in short supply, and religious leaders habitually preached against the vanity of materialism. But following 1875 most consumer industries were fully mechanized, an event which resulted in an explosion of items for daily use and led to an obvious task: someone had to persuade the public that all the new consumer products were worth having. A significant portion of that burden fell to the growing industry of advertising. Once complete, the transformation that advertising helped create ushered in a dramatic new age.

A standard criticism of advertising is that it deceives. At least two major theories of advertising can be appealed to in making this criticism, the first relying on a conception of advertising as "persuasion," the second as "information." If, as John Kenneth Galbraith argues in "The Dependence Effect," the principal function of advertising is to establish the consumer's desire for a product (and hence his willingness to pay), advertising may be equated with persuasion. Just as Tom Sawyer encouraged his friends to help him whitewash his famous fence, so modern advertisers encourage consumers to buy their toothpaste, chewing gum, and deodorants. In both cases, clever salesmanship makes an item more attractive than it would be otherwise; but in both cases there is no guarantee that the listeners are better off with their new desires than they were without them.

A second theory sees advertising not as persuasion, but as information. How, its defenders ask, can you persuade people without telling them something? Furthermore, since a market economy relies on information to help consumers make choices that maximize their welfare, advertising's service to society is to provide consumers with two essential kinds of information about products: their characteristics (including quality) and their price. Yet insofar as advertising is seen as information, one can easily doubt the information values of many television and magazine advertisements. Advertisements frequently rely on mere association; for example, an advertisement for whiskey reads: "Increase the value of your holdings. Old Charter Bourbon Whiskey—The Final Step Up." This, and many advertisements like it, seem to provide little or no hard information about price or quality. Furthermore, the source of an advertisement is said to be "tainted," since the persons responsible for generating it have a vested interest in persuading consumers; they have a vested interest, in short, in making profits, not in being objective.

Yet another view, sometimes called the competitive efficiency view, defends the social importance of advertising. This view affirms the information value of advertising while granting that advertisements frequently contain little specific information about price or quality and, moreover, often "puff" or exaggerate the worth of products. But puffery, notes the theory, is an accepted part of salesmanship, and it would be a mistake to view the public as a collection of gullible fools. No one really believes an advertisement that suggests drinking Old Charter Bourbon will increase one's stock-market holdings. Specific product information, furthermore, is only one kind of information important for market efficiency: another is information about the existence or availability of the product, and advertising supplies this kind of information in abundance. Competition in the marketplace is efficient only when consumers are able to compare rival products; and this is possible only if they know what products are available.

In his article "Advertising and Behavior Control," Robert Arrington defends the information value of advertising and denies that in most instances it controls behavior or threatens autonomy. Advertising does not so much create desires, he argues, as redirect them. Hence, if we are to accept this account, our desires for Grecian Formula 16, Mazda Rx-7s, and Pongo Peach lipstick depend ultimately upon our prior hopes for youth, power, adventure, or ravishing beauty, not upon desires that Madison Avenue creates.

Whatever one thinks about the information value of advertising, the issue of children's advertising poses special problems. How, if at all, should advertisers shift their approach in light of the fact that children lack the judgment and experience required to even understand, much less, evaluate information? Also, are there limits to the amount of puffery or violence that should appear in children's advertising? These questions, along with the more standard ones about advertising, are raised in the case study "Toy Wars."

CORPORATE GOVERNANCE

In the case study "A. H. Robins: The Dalkon Shield," we read about a well-publicized incident involving corporate governance, or the lack of it. For years, A. H. Robins Company manufactured and sold an IUD known as the Dalkon Shield. But despite claims by the company that its product was the best on the market, thousands of suits were brought against A. H. Robins for illness and death caused, according to the suits, by the Dalkon Shield. In 1985, in response to the suits, A. H. Robins declared bankruptcy. What brings about problems like those at Robins? What motives distinguish, and what systems separate, good from bad management? In this last section of the book, we take up the pressing issues of corporate governance.

In a provocative article, "Who Rules the Corporation," corporate critics Ralph Nader, Joel Seligman, and Mark Green assert that the legal image of the corporation, in which the board of directors controls the corporation from the vantage point of final power, is a myth. Managers rule the corporation, not directors, and what is more, the chief executive officer chooses the board members, not *vice versa*. The problem is that upper management's privileged position insulates it from moral criticism and allows serious breaches of morality and legality. In effect, business executives are unaccountable, and the only solution is a restructuring of the system of corporate governance that reestablishes their accountability. Thus restructuring, it is argued, will involve, among other things, the placing of professional full-time directors-persons who represent more than the narrow interests of stockholders—on corporate boards.

In a far more optimistic appraisal of the current state of corporate governance, the respected business executive Irving Shapiro (formerly board chairman of E. I du Pont de Nemours & Company) argues that the present system of corporate governance is sound and its methods morally defensible. Changes are needed, but they should be gradual, not sudden, and of a kind that extends the successful reforms of the past decades, for example, the placing of more "outside directors" on the board (outside directors are persons who are not employed by the corporation they direct). A fundamental mistake would be made by adopting the "Noah's Ark" approach to board composition, in which board members would represent the many interest groups affected by the corporation: employees, suppliers, local communities, and shareholders. The mistake would lie in creating a board that lacked the managerial expertise and cohesiveness necessary to govern corporate affairs effectively.

NOTE
1. Roger Draper, "The Truth About Advertising," *New York Review of Books*, XXX-III, no. 7 (1986), p. 14.

The Environment

Case Study

Exxon's Knee-Deep in the Big Muddy

MICHAEL G. BOWEN AND F. CLARK POWER

THE PRE-ACCIDENT PERIOD

On Friday, March 13, 1968, a field containing an estimated 10 billion barrels of oil was discovered under the North Slope of Alaska at Prudhoe Bay. One year later, a consortium of seven oil companies, now named the Alyeska Pipeline Service Company, announced plans to construct an 800 mile long underground pipeline to some point in southern Alaska where the crude oil could be transferred to tankers and shipped to refineries in the lower 48 states. The eventual choice for the oil terminal was an ice-free port, tucked away in the Chugach Mountains on the northern banks of Prince William Sound, that provided easy access to the Gulf of Alaska and shipping lanes to California: the town of Valdez.

The oil companies' original plans called for construction to begin on the trans-Alaskan pipeline in the following year (1970). They projected that the pipeline would be completed two years later. Approximately two million barrels of oil per day would be pumped from stations on the North Slope to Valdez Harbor, where tankers would carry the oil south. The companies, however, had not counted on the powerful reaction of environmental interest groups to their plans. Those groups forced Alyeska into protracted legislative and court battles.

Over the next four years the environmental and economic effects of the proposed pipeline were subject to intense scrutiny. There was little substantive disagreement on the purely economic issues: the oil companies, the state of Alaska, and many Alaskans would make a great deal of money if the pipeline were built. Many other benefits would directly result from the pipeline project. Of these, perhaps the most important was the development of a major new domestic source of oil reserves which would reduce the United States' dependency on foreign energy sources. There was also surprisingly little disagreement on the environmental issues. The oil companies admitted that there was the possibility of accidents and spills, perhaps major ones. There was agreement that the permafrost along the pipeline would melt, that wildlife would be adversely affected, and that portions of Alaska's wilderness and extraordinary scenery would be either defaced or destroyed.

There was substantial disagreement, however, on how to estimate the benefits and costs that would accrue from shipping oil across Alaska. How should the tangible benefit of economic development in the region be weighed against the intangible costs of defacing Alaska's pristine scenery; of disturbing the habitat of the vanishing bald eagles, bears, and caribou; of poisoning fish and damaging the food chain?

The trans-Alaskan pipeline was approved, however, in 1973 when the U.S. Congress, reacting to the possibility of fuel shortages in this country and to the repeated assurances of oil industry and government experts that policies and procedures would be put in place to meet environmental contingencies, cut off the court challenges that had delayed construction. At a U.S. Department of the Interior hearing held in Anchorage in 1971, for example, Alyeska representatives pledged that the environmental effects of the pipeline operations would be minimal, promising prompt and effective handling of any land or sea spill. They announced that an oil response plan would be prepared so that operations at the Port of Valdez and in Prince William Sound would be the safest in the world. While the Alyeska consortium would shoulder responsibility to clean up any spills, the task of monitoring Alyeska's preparedness would be handled by the Coast Guard and the state of Alaska. Behind the scenes, Alyeska officials recognized (as can be documented in their actual cleanup plan) that it would be impossible for them to clean up a major spill.

Only Once in 241 Years

For the first couple of years after oil began flowing through the pipeline in 1977, Alyeska's performance at responding to oil spills, as reported by state of Alaska officials, was excellent. Detailed records were kept on the cleanup of even very minor spills, such as crankcase oil dripping underneath a parked automobile. No doubt part of this vigilance was due to the public uproar over the 1978 sinking of the supertanker *Amoco Cadiz* off the coast of France, which resulted in a spill six times larger than that of the *Exxon Valdez*.

Alyeska's safety record for the first decade of the pipeline's operation appeared remarkably strong. Although 25 percent of the oil pumped from the ground in the United States passes through the Port of Valdez, by the end of 1988, 400 reported spills had leaked only about 200 barrels into the

Alaskan waters. In the three month period from November, 1988 through January, 1989, however, forty-three spills were reported in Alaskan waters—ranging in size from 10,000 to 2 million gallons—including a 1,700 barrel leak (efficiently contained and cleaned up) from a tanker docked at the Valdez terminal. In spite of this increase in accidents, Alyeska officials still seemed content that a major spill was not a realistic possibility.

Their confidence was based on an independent consulting report conducted for the oil company consortium and approved by the state, which concluded that a spill of between 1,000–2,000 barrels (46,000–92,000 gallons) was the most likely disaster that would occur in the projected 30 year lifetime of the Valdez terminal. Because the route from Valdez Harbor to the Gulf of Alaska was relatively easy to navigate, and because of the safeguards to be put in place before shipping began, a catastrophic spill like that of the *Exxon Valdez* was thought to be extremely unlikely—only once in 241 years. Nevertheless, when it was time for Alyeska and the state to negotiate a new three-year contingency plan, the state requested that Alyeska develop a scenario for dealing with a major spill. Alyeska balked, as they had whenever regulatory demands had been made. The compromise left Alyeska geared up to contain and clean up spills almost 175 times smaller than the one that occurred.

Why did the state of Alaska ever agree to such a plan? What had happened to the oversight that the state and the Coast Guard had promised? From the moment the pipeline opened, the people of Alaska had benefitted from the approximately $400,000 per hour in state revenues that have accrued. In the ensuing years, as the state became more and more financially dependent on oil monies and as no major spill had occurred, vigilance over the pipeline operation slowly began to relax.

Warnings?

The first warnings concerning the deterioration of state monitoring and Alyeska's ill-preparedness came from Dan Lawn, Alaska's Department of Environmental Conservation (DEC) Inspector in 1983, who detailed his charges in a 1984 memo. For all practical purposes they were ignored. In 1984, Alyeska failed to contain a relatively small (60 barrel) simulated loading spill in a state administered test of their response capability. In a 1986 test, Lawn judged that Alyeska failed again, although other judges rated Alyeska's performance as marginally passable. As Lawn became more critical, Alyeska officials resorted to calling him a "jerk and a trouble maker," and George Nelson, the President, admits trying to get Lawn fired. Lawn persisted in his warnings, predicting only three months before the Valdez incident that the odds favored a major spill and that no one would be prepared.

Why wasn't anyone listening, especially at the state and federal levels? Three reasons appear obvious. First, the collapse of oil prices that occurred in between 1984 and 1985 dropped the state's oil income from over $4 billion per year to under $2 billion per year. Alaska, which generated over 80 percent of its revenues from oil, was forced to cut services. Subsequently, the agency charged with monitoring Alyeska and the operations at the Valdez terminal, the DEC, cut staff to the point where there was no full-time state monitor of the oil terminal operations.

Second, the relative absence of serious trouble seemed to justify reductions in preparedness. With the safe passage of so many vessels through the Sound, the Coast Guard came to believe that it could responsibly reduce its inspections of tankers coming into and leaving Valdez Harbor. Over time, staffing of the Coast Guard monitoring station was cut back; around-the-clock supervision at the radar console was eliminated; and to reduce paperwork, the Coast Guard stopped manual plotting of ships' courses in and out of the channel in 1987. Further, the Coast Guard also judged proposals for an advanced radar system and an additional navigation monitoring system that would have tracked tanker traffic through the channel more effectively (and would have included a radar site on Bligh Island) to be too costly for the added safety.

Third, as public attention shifted to other environmental concerns, pressure to develop technology to prevent and clean up low-probability spills eased. For example, the Federal Government decided in 1987 to shut down the Oil and Hazardous Material Simulated Environmental Test Tank (OHMSETT) research facility in New Jersey.

Exxon

The relatively sudden, drastic drop in oil prices hit oil companies hard. In contrast to foreign competitors, the domestic companies in the industry had added pressure on them to become more productive and efficient in order to meet heavy short-term financial performance requirements coming from the U.S. investment community. What this meant in general was that companies had to curtail what could be identified as "unnecessary" expenditures within their organizations so that profitability would be stabilized at an acceptable level. Precautionary measures, such as putting double hulls around tankers—effectively reducing cargo area by 25% and dramatically increasing the cost of oil vessels—were simply ruled out as not cost-effective.

Unlike many of its competitors in the oil industry that had resorted to heavy cost cutting and organizational restructuring in the early to mid-1980s, the Exxon Corporation initially turned to a diversification strategy to bolster sagging performance. During this time, Exxon invested heavily in non-oil ventures such as office automation and electrical equipment, both later proving to be costly failures. More drastic internal changes began at Exxon in late 1986 only a few months before Lawrence Rawl, a long-time Exxon employee who was described by co-workers as blunt and arrogant, became chairman. Armed with a reputation as a heavy handed "cost-cutter," Rawl directed Exxon's downsizing. Within two years, he had cut employment 30 percent to around 100,000, slashing away at layers of bureaucracy, consolidating operations, and selling off unprofitable businesses.

Efforts to become more productive at Exxon during this time often meant large changes in the way the company did business and worked with employees. In addition to layoffs, reassignments, and job restructuring, Exxon looked to implement any technological improvements which would lower its costs of doing business. This led to, among other things, taking the industry lead in constructing new more highly automated oil tankers (such as the *Exxon Valdez*), which functioned with smaller crews.

To implement plans for higher efficiency within the company, managers were given some latitude in devising the desired productivity improvements. Some embraced the ideas of noted management expert W. Edwards Deming. The chief importer of modern Japanese management techniques, Deming stressed commitment to change, continuous innovation and quality improvement, and removal of communication barriers between workers and supervisors. Other managers subscribed to the Japanese practice of finding and achieving maximum productivity through pushing work systems to their productive limits, i.e., to the point where they start to crack and workers can no longer handle the load. While implementing these changes, management discovered, as have many companies that have been put through similar restructuring, that predictable problems arose: serious complaints of overwork, an erosion of management confidence, and sagging morale. "The problem with restructuring," Rawl later said, "is the human factor: Can people perform the job they're given? You can't test a person like a computer chip."

The changes that were made at the Exxon Corporation in those days did, however, seem to "work" for the company's shareholders. In 1987, for example, a leaner and meaner Exxon netted $375 million more than it had the previous year. In total, Exxon earned a net profit of $48,400 per employee that year: more than double the profit of key competitor Amoco and five times more than Mobil in the same period.

March 23, 1989

On Thursday night, March 23, 1989, no one was particularly worried about the *Exxon Valdez* or any of the other tankers taking on crude oil in Valdez Harbor. The Alaskan economy although still depressed, was recovering from its deepest financial woes. Its officials, nevertheless, had not deemed it necessary to enhance vigilance of oil operations there. Perhaps no one from the DEC knew about or was concerned with the fact that Alyeska's single oil spill emergency barge was in dry dock for repairs.

For the leaders of the Exxon Corporation, this also seemed like just another quiet night. Exxon Chairman Lawrence Rawl spent the evening at home. For Captain Hazelwood, his officers, and the crew, it had been another exhausting day. Having put in long hours, the usual double duty, as the ship was loading, all were very tired. Even so, Hazelwood and two of his mates stopped by a local tavern for a few drinks. At 9:25 P.M. the supertanker left the terminal at Valdez Harbor loaded with 1,250,000 barrels of crude oil.

There was nothing out of the ordinary going on in Prince William Sound that evening, not even the free floating icebergs drifting through the waters of the Sound. As had become the routine timesaving practice, Captain Hazelwood steered around them, rather than following the safer procedure of slowing down and staying in his traffic lane. For members of the U.S. Coast Guard on duty in Valdez, this seemed to be an uneventful night just like all of the other nights since the port was opened to oil traffic twelve years earlier.

AT THE TIME OF THE ACCIDENT

Four minutes after midnight on March 24, 1989, about two and one-half hours into their journey south, with an inexperienced third mate in command, the crew of the *Exxon Valdez* felt a sudden jolt and the ship begin to shudder, a sickening ten-second shudder. Eventually more than 240,000 barrels, or about 11 million gallons, of crude oil would gush into the surrounding waters. Captain Hazelwood later said:

> I knew we'd struck something; something major had happened to the vessel. I didn't know, but over the years you feel different things. I'd had engines blow up, other groundings, but it's an unhealthy feeling.

Afterward, Captain Hazelwood recalled his feelings, "You don't know if you want to cry, throw up, or scream all at the same time; knowing at the same time you've got a job to do." Despite these mixed feelings, or perhaps because of them, the captain rushed to the ship's bridge from his quarters below, and went to work. With the supertanker listing on its right side—oil gushing from a 600 foot tear in its hull—and apparently balancing precariously on a narrow ledge, the *Exxon Valdez's* chief mate James Kunkel told the captain that he feared for all of their lives, and that he thought the supertanker would capsize if it came off the reef.

At 12:26 A.M., 22 minutes after striking the reef, Captain Hazelwood (as he tells it: "trying not to cry, and [trying to] be reasonably businesslike") matter-of-factly radioed the Coast Guard station at Valdez. He was later to be criticized by the state of Alaska for being so calm in his radio transmissions. In Valdez, the Coast Guard watchperson who took the call put down the paperwork he had been busy with, adjusted the radar so that the Exxon Valdez came into view, and confirmed that the supertanker was indeed aground on Bligh Reef. Several minutes later, the superintendent of operations at Alyeska's Valdez terminal was awakened with news of the accident. Following the "book" on such incidents, he told a subordinate to take charge and went back to sleep. When Coast Guard Vice Admiral Clyde Robbins was informed about the grounding, he responded: "That's impossible. We have the perfect system." As he watched the oil from his ship pouring into the water, Joseph Hazelwood thought: "My world as I had known it had come to an end."

At approximately 12:49 A.M., Captain Hazelwood radioed the Coast Guard that despite having a little trouble with the third mate, and the fact that the ship had been "holed," he was trying to get the ship off the reef and would get back in touch as soon as he could.

Exxon's Response

At 8:30 A.M. that morning (4:30 A.M. Valdez time), the kitchen phone rang as Rawl was having breakfast in his Westchester County, N.Y., home. He remembered asking the caller what had happened, if a rudder had broken, and if the ship had lost its engine.

> At that point I didn't even know what it hit. All I knew was that it hit something and it was holed pretty badly. . . . When you have a large ship on the rocks, and they tell you it's leaking oil, you know it is going to be bad, bad, bad.

To deal with the unfolding crisis situation, Rawl, deciding not to waste time driving to his New York City office, began setting up conference calls from his home while his wife canceled Easter plans with the family.

Right from the start, Rawl says he "knew" that human error was to blame for the accident. Later, hearing that blood alcohol tests on the ship's captain, administered more than 10 hours after the grounding, showed that the captain was legally drunk under Alaska law, Rawl said that he was not surprised. As events that day unfolded, he quickly began to deal with the corporate-level issues related to the growing disaster. Three critical policy questions had to be answered:

1. What should Exxon's official stance be on the grounding? Should the company assume responsibility for the accident?
2. Should he, as chief executive of the company that employed the tanker's crew and owned the ship and the oil pouring into Prince William Sound, immediately go to Alaska to take charge of the situation and demonstrate Exxon's concern for what was happening?
3. How should information about the spill and subsequent containment and cleanup efforts be disseminated?

Rawl and Exxon's other top managers decided that the company would immediately accept responsibility for the grounding and for cleaning up the damage. With regard to the second question, Rawl's initial instinct was to go to Alaska, but fellow managers later talked him out of the notion. They argued that if he went, he would probably just be in the way, and that he could better serve the company's interests from his office in New York. It was a decision that, in light of subsequent intense criticism, he would later regret: "I wake up in the night questioning the decision to stay home."

His—Exxon's—decision to inform news organizations of events in Valdez on a "real time" basis was also a decision that he came to regret. Only Exxon employees in Valdez were to provide information as that information became available. Reacting to charges that Exxon had manipulated and suppressed information back in the oil shortage days after the Arab embargo in the mid-1970s, Rawl said that he just wanted to get the information out: "At least you can't be accused of distorting data or slicking it up before it's presented to the press." But his new strategy still left the media frustrated and suspicious. Phone lines to Alaska were constantly jammed, Exxon officials there were often unavailable for comment, and the news conferences that took place in the "real time" off-hours made it next to impossible for the media networks and newspapers to present timely reports. "It just didn't work" Rawl said in retrospect.

CONTAINMENT AND CLEANUP

From the beginning, attempts to contain and clean the oil slick from the waters and beaches of Prince William Sound were beset by many of the problems that often curse hastily put together crisis organizations. There was even some confusion about who was in charge: Eighteen hours after the spill, Exxon took over control from Alyeska.

Technical, Legal, and Moral Issues

Alyeska's lack of preparedness and inability to cope with such a large spill almost immediately became the subjects of verbal sparring over technicalities in and interpretations of the clean up contingency plan. When the *Exxon Valdez* ran aground, the oil spill emergency barge was unloaded and in dry dock; it took 12 hours (the plan called for 5) to mobilize and travel the 28 miles from port in Valdez Harbor to the site of the accident. Further complicating things, barges and pumps, which could have limited the spill by offloading the remaining oil from the stricken ship, were not immediately available. Because of these problems, Dennis Kelso, Commissioner of the Alaska Department of Environmental Conservation, called Alyeska's emergency plan "the biggest piece of maritime fiction since *Moby Dick.*" An Alyeska official replied to this charge, "This was a joint plan. We did exactly what the state [and federal governments] wanted. We did not deceive anyone, and we responded very well."

As the spill spread, eventually fouling 1,200 miles of shoreline in the

Sound, technological problems and questions plagued decision makers. Fears of legal liability also seem to have played a major role in hindering early cleanup efforts. Lawyers representing Exxon, Alyeska, the state of Alaska, and the Coast Guard, for example, all urged their clients not to risk taking the initiative in cleanup efforts because of potential for later liability claims. "The legal system crippled our ability to make decisions," Alaska's Governor Steve Cowper said at the time. "Protecting themselves [Exxon] from a lawsuit was more important than cleaning up oil." Exxon President Lee Raymond countered that the state had deliberately held-up cleanup efforts to bolster its own legal case. "They have been preparing for litigation from day one," he charged.

Soon after the accident, in an apparent move to shift blame for the accident, Exxon released to the press private information regarding Captain Joseph Hazelwood's history of drinking problems, and then fired him. Rawl denied, however, that Hazelwood was fired for being drunk: "A lot of the public and press think we fired him because we thought he was drunk on the ship; but we never said that, and we have cautioned people not to assume it." Rawl clarified: "Hazelwood was terminated because he had violated company policies, such as not being on the bridge and for having consumed alcohol within four hours of boarding the ship." Hazelwood saw the situation differently; he asserted that it was a commonly accepted practice for a ship's captain to issue simple instructions to the crew and then leave the bridge. When asked why Exxon and the state of Alaska both attempted to focus the blame for the incident on him, he replied that he didn't know, but then said:

> I could be a lightning rod, easy target, scapegoat to take the heat. I would say the same for the state of Alaska. They came after me, hammer and tong, figuring I'd fold like a cheap suit. I imagine they're a bit surprised I didn't.

The outcome of all of this sparring and legal wrangling was an expensive public relations war involving Exxon, the state of Alaska, and to some extent the former captain of the *Exxon Valdez*. More important perhaps than these, however, was the withholding of important scientific data about the effects of the spill, collected by the many scientists on the scene, which could not be shared until later used in court.

Problems With Cleaning Up the Oil

From the first day, Exxon argued that but for Alaska's bureaucratic fumbling it could have sprayed chemical dispersants (which reduce the surface tension of oil and allow it to break up into small droplets and scatter more easily into the water) on the spill that would have reduced subsequent damage. Not so, answers the state of Alaska, explaining that in the first few days after the spill when dispersants might have helped somewhat, Exxon had far too little chemicals available to do any good and the calm seas would have prevented the chemicals from mixing thoroughly enough to make them effective. There were also scientific questions raised about the toxicity of the dispersants and about their efficacy even under ideal conditions. The evidence shows that such chemically treated oil first scatters, then comes back together, sinks, resurfaces, and eventually washes ashore as tar balls: even though the oil seems to disappear, it simply does not go away.

Another severe problem for those trying to contain the spill was that the physical properties of an oil slick change over time. While the most toxic parts of the oil evaporate within about 20 hours, the remainder mixes with the salt water and sea debris creating after about 14 days a heavy, thick, reddish-brown mousse. As the mousse collects even more debris, however, that which doesn't amass on the beaches eventually can turn into an even thicker muck that will sink to the bottom. The thickening of the oil made it very difficult for the 60 skimmer vessels to vacuum the mess from the surface of the water and pump it into barges. Exxon's water clean up coordinator Jim O'Brien indicated that the cleanup operation was doomed from the start:

> There's an important thing people must realize in planning for a spill of this size: No amount of equipment will clean it all up, even if they give you a month's notice to get ready. Look at the expanse of water involved, and figure the time it takes to deploy boats and skimmers and support vessels at 12 knots. Skimmers need barges to collect their oil. Crews need food, ships need fuel, and somebody has to collect the garbage. And nothing works if the weather's bad.

The sticky mousse that ended up on the shores of Prince William Sound filled the nooks and crannies along the jagged coastal areas, saturating the surface and subsurfaces of the beaches, and pooling in some places to depths of over four feet. The strategy for cleaning these from the rocky beaches quickly focused on removing the gross oil and then letting the residue biodegrade over time. On the beaches of Prince William Sound, where 90 percent of the oil went ashore, this meant that the mousse had to be first scooped up, mopped, or blotted up before the rocks could be scrubbed semi-clean. Once this was done, the scrubbing was often done by hand but more generally by high pressure hoses. The hoses would shoot scalding water to loosen and then flush the oil that had by now weathered to a substance somewhat like asphalt back into the water where cold water hoses would direct it to off-shore skimmers. Another technique called bioremediation, used experimentally in places, involved spraying a special nitrogen-phosphorus fertilizer mix onto the shore in an attempt to stimulate oil eating bacteria. It was hoped that this would double the pace of nature's self-cleanup efforts.

Controversy raged over every step of the cleanup effort, with critics finding fault in every technique. Some believed that the hot water scrubbing by killing fish and surviving micro-organisms wreaked greater environmental havoc than the oil. Others complained that bio-remediation, although it seemed to work in the few areas in which it was tried, would leave unsightly, non-toxic asphalt hydrocarbons to stain the beaches, and would induce undesirable plankton growth in the Sound. Still others protested that the debris and garbage created by the cleanup crews were in themselves ecological disasters. Health experts voiced concerns that the cleanup workers were poorly trained, ill-equipped (many did not have breathing masks), and exposed to oil for long periods of time. They warned that exposure to oil and its vapors can lead to nausea, breathing difficulties, rashes, kidney and nervous system damage, as well as cancer.

For many critics, the clean-up efforts served no other purpose than the public relations interests of the principals (Exxon, the state of Alaska, and the Coast Guard) responsible for the mess in the first place. Many experts believe that, beyond the initial wildlife kills and the temporary (an estimated 3 to 6 years) destruction of the scenery, the lasting effects of the spill on the environment will be minimal. The cleanup had little beneficial effect on the environment, possibly added to the adverse consequences, and as a practical matter amounted to nothing more than a (multi) billion dollar public relations campaign to assuage the anger of the people of Alaska, environmentalists, the larger general public, and Congress. The oil industry, in particular, had a lot at stake in public opinion. They greatly feared the potential political damage that any adverse publicity would have on requests for future off-shore drilling rights and for permission to explore for gas and oil in other environmentally sensitive areas in Alaska and elsewhere in the U.S. One of the great ironies of the cleanup effort is perhaps best expressed on the most popular t-shirt sold in Valdez during the summer of 1989: "Cleanup '89. It's not just a job, it's a ----ing waste of time."

In all, Exxon paid out anywhere from $1 to $3 billion (there have been several different numbers reported), while employing approximately 11,500 people in the cleanup effort. In addition, Exxon compensated Alaskan fishermen some $200,000 for lost income due to the spill. There was no compensation for the 980 otters, 138 eagles, and 33,126 other birds killed, nor even a reliable way of estimating the value of loss.

As the cleanup operation shut down on September 15, 1989, in advance of the harsh Alaskan winter, Exxon publicized its accomplishments: 60,000 barrels of recovered oil, and 1087 miles of oiled beach now environmentally stable. The state of Alaska countered that the cleanup had actually recovered less that 30,000 barrels of oil and that only about 118 miles of beaches were safe for wildlife and new vegetation growth. Despite their release of an ambiguously worded memo on July 19, 1989 that seemed to state that, the job being finished, the company would not return again in the Spring to resume cleanup efforts—a memo that had generated enormous public outrage—Exxon returned to Prince William Sound on May 1,

1990 to do what was necessary, as established by Coast Guard recommendations, to make things right.

SOURCES

Behar, R. "Exxon Strikes Back: Interview with Lawrence Rawl," *Time*, March 26, 1990, pp. 62–63.

Byrne, J. A. "The Rebel Shaking Up Exxon," *Business Week*, July 18, 1988, pp. 104–111.

"Conoco alters stand on tankers," Associated Press report appearing in the *South Bend Tribune*, April 11, 1990.

DiIanni, D. "The Big Spill," for NOVA. PBS air-date: February 27, 1990. 1990 WGBH Educational Foundation. Transcript by Journal Graphics, 267 Broadway, New York, NY 10007.

Hodgson, B. "Alaska's Big Spill: Can the Wilderness Heal?" *National Geographic*, January, 1990, pp. 2–43.

Interview with Joseph Hazelwood conducted by Connie Chung, telecast on *Saturday Night With Connie Chung*, March 31, 1990.

Satchell, M. & Carpenter, B. "A Disaster That Wasn't," *U.S. News & World Report*, September 18, 1989, pp. 60–69.

Solomon, J. "Strategies for Handling The Arrest of an Employee," *Wall Street Journal*, March 29, 1990.

Stigler, G. "What an Oil Spill Is Worth," *Wall Street Journal*, April 17, 1990.

Sullivan, A. "Exxon's Restructuring In the Past Is Blamed For Recent Accidents: Cost cuts in '86 helped profit, but did they make spills, refinery fire more likely?" *Wall Street Journal*, March 16, 1990.

Sullivan, A. "Rawl Wishes He'd Visited Valdez Sooner: Exxon Chief Regrets Actions Right After Oil Spill," *Wall Street Journal*, June 6, 1989.

Tobias, M. "Black Tide," for the *Discovery Channel*, air-date: March 18, 1990.

Tuttle, J. "Anatomy of an Oil Spill," for FRONTLINE. PBS air-date: March 20, 1990. 1990 WGBH Educational Foundation. Transcript by Journal Graphics, 267 Broadway, New York, NY 10007.

Wall Street Journal, "Oil spill cleanup's still protect workers poorly, unions say," April 10, 1990.

Wall Street Journal, "Review and Outlook: Cleaning Up Oil," March 30, 1990.

Ethics and Ecology

WILLIAM T. BLACKSTONE

THE RIGHT TO A LIVABLE ENVIRONMENT AS A HUMAN RIGHT

. . . Let us first ask whether the right to a livable environment can properly be considered to be a human right. For the purposes of this paper, however, I want to avoid raising the more general question of whether there are any human rights at all. Some philosophers do deny that any human rights exist.[1] In two recent papers I have argued that human rights do exist (even though such rights may properly be overridden on occasion by other morally relevant reasons) and that they are universal and inalienable (although the actual exercise of such rights on a given occasion is alienable).[2] My argument for the existence of universal human rights rests, in the final analysis, on a theory of what it means to be human, which specifies the capacities for rationality and freedom as essential, and on the fact that there are no relevant grounds for excluding any human from the opportunity to develop and fulfill his capacities (rationality and freedom) as a human. This is not to deny that there are criteria which justify according human rights in quite different ways or with quite different modes of treatment for different persons, depending upon the nature and degree of such capacities and the existing historical and environmental circumstances.

If the right to a livable environment were seen as a basic and inalienable human right, this could be a valuable tool (both inside and outside of legalistic frameworks) for solving some of our environmental problems, both on a national and on an international basis. Are there any philosophical and conceptual difficulties in treating this right as an inalienable human right? Traditionally we have not looked upon the right to a decent environment as a human right or as an inalienable right. Rather, inalienable human or natural rights have been conceived in somewhat different terms; equality, liberty, happiness, life, and property. However, might it not be possible to view the right to a livable environment as being entailed by, or as constitutive of, these basic human or natural rights recognized in our political tradition? If human rights, in other words, are those rights which each human possesses in virtue of the fact that he is human and in virtue of the fact that those rights are essential in permitting him to live a human life (that is, in permitting him to fulfill his capacities as a rational and free being), then might not the right to a decent environment be properly categorized as such a human right? Might it not be conceived as a right which has emerged as a result of changing environmental conditions and the impact of those conditions on the very possibility of the realization of other rights such as liberty and equality?[3] Let us explore how this might be the case.

Given man's great and increasing ability to manipulate the environment, and the devastating effect this is having, it is plain that new social institutions and new regulative agencies and procedures must be initiated on both national and international levels to make sure that the manipulation is in the public interest. It will be necessary, in other words, to restrict or stop some practices and the freedom to engage in those practices. Some look upon such additional state planning, whether national or international, as unnecessary further intrusion on man's freedom. Freedom is, of course, one of our basic values, and few would deny that excessive state control of human action is to be avoided. But such restrictions on individual freedom now appear to be necessary in the interest of overall human welfare and the rights and freedoms of *all* men. Even John Locke with his stress on freedom as an inalienable right recognized that this right must be construed so that it is consistent with the equal right to freedom of others. The whole point of the state is to restrict unlicensed freedom and to provide the conditions for equality of rights for all. Thus it seems to be perfectly consistent with Locke's view and, in general, with the views of the founding fathers of this country to restrict certain rights or freedoms when it can be shown that such restriction is necessary to insure the equal rights of others. If this is so, it has very important implications for the rights to freedom and to property. These rights, perhaps properly seen as inalienable (though this is a controversial philosophical question), are not properly seen as unlimited or unrestricted. When values which we hold dear conflict (for example, individual or group freedom and the freedom of all, individual or group rights and the rights of all, and individual or group welfare and the welfare of the general public) something has to give; some priority must be established. In the case of the abuse and waste of environmental resources, less individual freedom and fewer individual rights for the sake of greater public welfare and equality of rights seem justified. What in the past had been properly regarded as freedoms and rights (given what seemed to be unlimited natural resources and no serious pollution problems) can no longer be so construed, at least not without additional restrictions. We must recognize both the need for such restrictions and the fact that none of our rights can be realized without a livable environment. Both public welfare and equality of rights now require that natural resources not be used simply according to the whim and caprice of individuals or simply for personal profit. This is not to say that all property rights must be denied and that the state must own all productive property, as the Marxist argues. It is to insist that those rights be qualified or restricted in the light of new ecological data and in the interest of the freedom, rights, and welfare of all.

The answer then to the question, Is the right to a livable environment a human right? is yes. Each person has this right qua being human and because a livable environment is essential for one to fulfill his human capacities. And given the danger to our environment today and hence the danger to the very possibility of human existence, access to a livable environment must be conceived as a right which imposes upon everyone a correlative moral obligation to respect.[4] . . .

ECOLOGY AND ECONOMIC RIGHTS

We suggested above that it is necessary to qualify or restrict economic or property rights in the light of new ecological data and in the interest of the freedom, rights, and welfare of all. In part, this suggested restriction is predicated on the assumption that we cannot expect private business to provide solutions to the multiple pollution problems for which they themselves are responsible. Some companies have taken measures to limit the polluting effect of their operations, and this is an important move. But we are deluding ourselves if we think that private business can function as its own pollution police. This is so for several reasons: the primary objective of private business is economic profit. Stockholders do not ask of a company, "Have you polluted the environment and lowered the quality of the environment for the general public and for future generations?" Rather they ask, "How high is the annual dividend and how much higher is it than the year before?" One can hardly expect organizations whose basic norm is economic profit to be concerned in any great depth with the long-range effects of their operations upon society and future generations or concerned with the hidden cost of their operations in terms of environmental quality to society as a whole. Second, within a free enterprise system companies compete to produce what the public wants at the lowest possible cost. Such competition would preclude the spending of adequate funds to prevent environmental pollution, since this would add tremendously to the cost of the product—unless all other companies would also conform to such antipollution policies. But in a free enterprise economy such policies are not likely to be self-imposed by businessmen. Third, the basic response of the free enterprise system to our economic problems is that we must have greater economic growth or an increase in gross national product. But such growth many ecologists look upon with great alarm, for it can have devastating long-range effects upon our environment. Many of the products of uncontrolled growth are based on artificial needs and actually detract from, rather than contribute to, the quality of our lives. A stationary economy, some economists and ecologists suggest, may well be best for the quality of man's environment and of his life in the long run. Higher GNP does not automatically result in an increase in social well-being, and it should not be used as a measuring rod for assessing economic welfare. This becomes clear when one realizes that the GNP aggregates the dollar value of all goods and services produced—the cigarettes as well as the medical treatment of lung cancer, the petroleum from offshore wells as well as the detergents required to clean up after oil spills, the electrical energy produced and the medical and cleaning bills resulting from the air-pollution that is caused by fuel used for generating the electricity. The GNP allows no deduction for negative production, such as lives lost from unsafe cars or environmental destruction perpetrated by telephone, electric and gas utilities, lumber companies, and speculative builders.[5]

To many persons, of course, this kind of talk is not only blasphemy but subversive. This is especially true when it is extended in the direction of additional controls over corporate capitalism. (Some ecologists and economists go further and challenge whether corporate capitalism can accommodate a stationary state and still retain its major features.[6]) The fact of the matter is that the ecological attitude forces one to reconsider a host of values which have been held dear in the past, and it forces one to reconsider the appropriateness of the social and economic systems which embodied and implemented those values. Given the crisis of our environment, there must be certain fundamental changes in attitudes toward nature, man's use of nature, and man himself. Such changes in attitudes undoubtedly will have far-reaching implications for the institutions of private property and private enterprise and the values embodied in these institutions. Given that crisis we can no longer look upon water and air as free commodities to be exploited at will. Nor can the private ownership of land be seen as a lease to use that land in any way which conforms merely to the personal desires of the owner. In other words, the environmental crisis is forcing us to challenge what had in the past been taken to be certain basic rights of man or at least to restrict those rights. And it is forcing us to challenge institutions which embodied those rights.

Much has been said . . . about the conflict between these kinds of rights, and the possible conflict between them is itself a topic for an extensive paper. Depending upon how property rights are formulated, the substantive content of those rights, it seems plain to me, can directly conflict with what we characterize as human rights. In fact our moral and legal history demonstrate exactly that kind of conflict. There was a time in the recent past when property rights embodied the right to hold human beings in slavery. This has now been rejected, almost universally. Under nearly any interpretation of the substantive content of human rights, slavery is incompatible with those rights.

The analogous question about rights which is now being raised by the data uncovered by the ecologist and by the gradual advancement of the ecological attitude is whether the notion of property rights should be even further restricted to preclude the destruction and pollution of our environmental resources upon which the welfare and the very lives of all of us and of future generations depend. Should our social and legal system embrace property rights or other rights which permit the kind of environmental exploitation which operates to the detriment of the majority of mankind? I do not think so. The fact that a certain right exists in a social or legal system does not mean that it ought to exist. I would not go so far as to suggest that all rights are merely rule-utilitarian devices to be adopted or discarded whenever it can be shown that the best consequences thereby follow.[7] But if a right or set of rights systematically violates the public welfare, this is prima facie evidence that it ought not to exist. And this certainly seems to be the case with the exercise of certain property rights today.

In response to this problem, there is today at least talk of "a new economy of resources," one in which new considerations and values play an important role along with property rights and the interplay of market forces. Economist Nathaniel Wollman argues that "the economic past of 'optimizing' resource use consists of bringing into an appropriate relationship the ordering of preferences for various experiences and the costs of acquiring those experiences. Preferences reflect physiological-psychological responses to experience or anticipated experience, individually or collectively revealed, and are accepted as data by the economist. A broad range of noneconomic investigations is called for to supply the necessary information."[8]

Note that Wollman says that noneconomic investigations are called for. In other words the price system does not adequately account for a number of value factors which should be included in an assessment. "It does not account for benefits or costs that are enjoyed or suffered by people who were not parties to the transaction."[9] In a system which emphasizes simply the interplay of market forces as a criterion, these factors (such as sights, smells and other aesthetic factors, justice, and human rights—factors which are important to the well-being of humans) are not even considered. Since they have no direct monetary value, the market places no value whatsoever on them. Can we assume, then, that purely economic or market evaluations provide us with data which will permit us to maximize welfare, if the very process of evaluation and the normative criteria employed exclude a host of values and considerations upon which human welfare depend? The answer to this question is plain. We cannot make this assumption. We cannot rely merely upon the interplay of market forces or upon the sovereignty of the consumer. The concept of human welfare and consequently the notion of maximizing that welfare requires a much broader perspective than the norms offered by the traditional economic perspective. A great many things have value and use which have no economic value and use. Consequently we must broaden our evaluational perspective to include the entire range of values which are essential not only to the welfare of man but also to the welfare of other living things and to the environment which sustains all of life. And this must include a reassessment of rights.

ETHICS AND TECHNOLOGY

I have been discussing the relationship of ecology to ethics and to a theory of rights. Up to this point I have not specifically discussed the relation of technology to ethics, although it is plain that technology and its development is responsible for most of our pollution problems. This topic deserves separate treatment, but I do want to briefly relate it to the thesis of this work.

It is well known that new technology sometimes complicates our ethical lives and our ethical decisions. Whether the invention is the wheel or a contraceptive pill, new technology always opens up new possibilities for human relationships and for society, for good and ill. The pill, for example, is revolutionizing sexual morality, for its use can preclude many of the bad consequences normally attendant upon premarital intercourse. *Some* of the strongest arguments against premarital sex have been shot down by this bit of technology (though certainly not all of them). The fact that the use of the pill can prevent unwanted pregnancy does not make premarital sexual intercourse morally right, nor does it make it wrong. The pill is morally neutral, but its existence does change in part the moral base of the decision to engage in premarital sex. In the same way, technology at least in principle can be neutral—neither necessarily good nor bad in its impact on other aspects of the environment. Unfortunately, much of it is bad—very bad. But technology can be meshed with an ecological attitude to the benefit of man and his environment.

I am not suggesting that the answer to technology which has bad environmental effects is necessarily more technology. We tend too readily to assume that new technological developments will always solve man's problems. But this is simply not the case. One technological innovation often seems to breed a half-dozen additional ones which themselves create more environmental problems. We certainly do not solve pollution problems, for example, by changing from power plants fueled by coal to power plants fueled by nuclear energy, if radioactive waste from the latter is worse than pollution from the former. Perhaps part of the answer to pollution problems is less technology. There is surely no real hope of returning to nature (whatever that means) or of stopping *all* technological and scientific development, as some advocate. Even if it could be done, this would be too extreme a move. The answer is not to stop technology, but to guide it toward proper ends, and to set up standards of antipollution to which all technological devices must conform. Technology has been and can be used to destroy and pollute an environment, but it can also be used to save and beautify it. What is called for is purposeful environmental engineering, and this engineering calls for a mass of information about our environment, about the needs of persons, and about basic norms and values which are acceptable to civilized men. It also calls for priorities on goals and for compromise where there are competing and conflicting values and objectives. Human rights and their fulfillment should constitute at least some of those basic norms, and technology can be used to implement those rights and the public welfare.

NOTES

1. See Kai Nielsen's "Scepticism and Human Rights," *Monist*, 52, no. 4 (1968):571–94.
2. See my "Equality and Human Rights," *Monist*, 52, no. 4 (1968):616–39 and my "Human Rights and Human Dignity," in Laszlo and Gotesky, eds., *Human Dignity*.
3. Almost forty years ago Aldo Leopold stated that "there is as yet no ethic dealing with man's relationship to land and to the nonhuman animals and plants which grow upon it. Land, like Odysseus' slave girls, is still property. The land relation is still strictly economic entailing privileges but not obligations." (See Leopold's "The Conservation Ethic," *Journal of Forestry*, 32, no. 6 [October 1933]:634–43.) Although some important changes have occurred since he wrote this, no systematic ethic or legal structure has been developed to socialize or institutionalize the obligations to use land properly.
4. The right to a livable environment might itself entail other rights, for example, the right to population control. Population control is obviously essential for quality human existence. This issue is complex and deserves a separate essay, but I believe that the moral framework explicated above provides the grounds for treating population control both as beneficial and as moral.
5. See Melville J. Ulmer, "More Than Marxist," *New Republic*, 26 December 1970, p. 14.
6. See Murdock and Connell, "All about Ecology," *Center Magazine*, 3, no. 1 (January–February 1970), p. 63.
7. Some rights, I would argue, are inalienable, and are not based merely on a contract (implicit or explicit) or merely upon the norm of maximizing good consequences. (See David Braybrooke's *Three Tests for Democracy: Personal Rights, Human Welfare, Collective Preference* [New York: Random House, 1968], which holds such a rule-utilitarian theory of rights, and my "Human Rights and Human Dignity," for a rebuttal.)
8. Nathaniel Wollman, "The New Economics of Resources," *Daedalus* 96, pt. 2, (Fall 1967):1100.
9. Ibid.

At the Shrine of Our Lady of Fatima *or* Why Political Questions Are Not All Economic

MARK SAGOFF

Lewiston, New York, a well-to-do community near Buffalo, is the site of the Lake Ontario Ordinance Works, where years ago the federal government disposed of the residues of the Manhattan Project. These radioactive wastes are buried but are not forgotten by the residents who say that when the wind is southerly, radon gas blows through the town. Several parents at a recent Lewiston conference I attended described their terror on learning that cases of leukemia had been found among area children. They feared for their own lives as well. On the other side of the table, officials from New York State and from local corporations replied that these fears were ungrounded. People who smoke, they said, take greater risks than people who live close to waste disposal sites. One speaker talked in terms of "rational methodologies of decisionmaking." This aggravated the parents' rage and frustration.

The speaker suggested that the townspeople, were they to make their decision in a free market and if they knew the scientific facts, would choose to live near the hazardous waste facility. He told me later they were irrational—"neurotic"—because they refused to recognize or to act upon their own interests. The residents of Lewiston were unimpressed with his analysis of their "willingness to pay" to avoid this risk or that. They did not see what risk-benefit analysis had to do with the issues they raised.

If you take the Military Highway (as I did) from Buffalo to Lewiston, you will pass through a formidable wasteland. Landfills stretch in all directions and enormous trucks—tiny in that landscape—incessantly deposit sludge which great bulldozers then push into the ground. These machines are the only signs of life, for in the miasma that hangs in the air, no birds, not even scavengers, are seen. Along colossal power lines which criss-cross this dismal land, the dynamos at Niagra send electric power south, where factories have fled, leaving their remains to decay. To drive along this road is to feel, oddly, the mystery and awe one experiences in the presence of so much power and decadence.

⚜

From *Arizona Law Review*, Vol. 23 (Pt. 1 of 2), 1981, pp. 1283–98. Copyright © 1982 by the Arizona Board of Regents. Reprinted by permission.

POLITICAL AND ECONOMIC DECISIONMAKING

This essay concerns the economic decisions we make about the environment. It also concerns our political decisions about the environment. Some people have suggested that ideally these should be the same, that all environmental problems are problems in distribution. According to this view, there is an environmental problem only when some resource is not allocated in equitable and efficient ways.[1]

This approach to environmental policy is pitched entirely at the level of the consumer. It is his or her values that count, and the measure of these values is the individual's willingness to pay. The problem of justice or fairness in society becomes, then, the problem of distributing goods and services so that more people get more of what they want to buy: a condo on the beach, a snowmobile for the mountains, a tank full of gas, a day of labor. The only values we have, according to this view, are those that a market can price.[2]

How much do you value open space, a stand of trees, an "unspoiled" landscape? Fifty dollars? A hundred? A thousand? This is one way to measure value. You could compare the amount consumers would pay for a townhouse or coal or a landfill to the amount they would pay to preserve an area in its "natural" state. If users would pay more for the land with the house, the coal mine, or the landfill, then without—less construction and other costs of development—than the efficient thing to do is to improve the land and thus increase its value. This is why we have so many tract developments, pizza stands, and gas stations. How much did you spend last year to preserve open space? How much for pizza and gas? "In principle, the ultimate measure of environmental quality," as one basic text assures us, "is the value people place on these . . . services or their *willingness to pay*."[3]

Willingness to pay: what is wrong with that? The rub is this: not all of us think of ourselves simply as *consumers*. Many of us regard ourselves *as citizens* as well. We act as consumers to get what we want *for ourselves*. We act as citizens to achieve what we think is right or best *for the community*. The question arises, then, whether what we want for ourselves individually as consumers is consistent with the goals we would set for ourselves collectively as citizens. Would I vote for the sort of things I shop for? Are my preferences as a consumer consistent with my judgments as a citizen?

They are not. I am schizophrenic. Last year, I fixed a couple of tickets and was happy to do so since I saved fifty dollars. Yet, at election time, I helped to vote the corrupt judge out of office. I speed on the highway; yet I want the police to enforce laws against speeding. I used to buy mixers in returnable bottles—but who can bother to return them? I buy only disposables now, but to soothe my conscience, I urge my state senator to outlaw one-way containers. I love my car; I hate the bus. Yet I vote for candidates who promise to tax gasoline to pay for public transportation. And of course

I applaud the Endangered Species Act, although I have no earthly use for the Colorado squawfish or the Indiana bat. I support almost any political cause that I think will defeat my consumer interests. This is because I have contempt for—although I act upon—those interests. I have an "Ecology Now" sticker on a car that leaks oil everywhere it's parked.

The distinction between consumer and citizen preferences has long vexed the theory of public finance. Should the public economy serve the same goals as the household economy? May it serve, instead, goals emerging from our association as citizens? The question asks if we may collectively strive for and achieve only those items we individually compete for and consume. Should we aspire, instead, to public goals we may legislate as a nation?

The problem, insofar as it concerns public finance, is stated as follows by R. A. Musgrave, who reports a conversation he had with Gerhard Colm:

> He [Colm] holds that the individual voter dealing with political issues has a frame of reference quite distinct from that which underlies his allocation of income as a consumer. In the latter situation the voter acts as a private individual determined by self-interest and deals with his personal wants; in the former, he acts as a political being guided by his image of a good society. The two, Colm holds, are different things.[4]

Are these two different things? Stephen Marglin suggests that they are. He writes:

> the preferences that govern one's unilateral market actions no longer govern his actions when the form of reference is shifted from the market to the political arena. The Economic Man and the Citizen are for all intents and purposes two different individuals. It is not a question, therefore, of rejecting individual . . . preference maps; it is, rather, that market and political preference maps are inconsistent.[5]

Marglin observes that if this were true, social choices optimal under one set of preferences would not be optimal under another. What, then, is the meaning of "optimality?" He notices that if we take a person's true preferences to be those expressed in the market, we may neglect or reject the preferences that person reveals in advocating a political cause or position. "One might argue on welfare grounds," Marglin speculates, "for authoritarian rejection of individuals' politically revealed preferences in favor of their market revealed preferences!"[6]

COST-BENEFIT ANALYSIS VS. REGULATION

On February 19, 1981, President Reagan published Executive Order 12,291[7] requiring all administrative agencies and departments to support every new major regulation with a cost-benefit analysis establishing that the benefits of the regulation to society outweigh its costs. The order directs the Office of Management and Budget (OMB) to review every such regulation on the basis of the adequacy of the cost-benefit analysis supporting it. This is a departure from tradition. Historically, regulations have been reviewed not by OMB but by the courts on the basis of the relation of the regulation to authorizing legislation, not to cost-benefit analysis.

A month earlier, in January, 1981, the Supreme Court heard lawyers for the American Textile Manufacturers Institute argue against a proposed Occupational Safety and Health Administration (OSHA) regulation which would have severely restricted the acceptable levels of cotton dust in textile plants.[8] The lawyers for industry argued that the benefits of the regulation would not equal the costs.[9] The lawyers for the government contended that the law required the tough standard.[10] OSHA, acting consistently with Executive Order 12,291, asked the Court not to decide the cotton dust case in order to give the agency time to complete the cost-benefit analysis required by the textile industry.[11] The Court declined to accept OSHA's request and handed down its opinion in *American Textile Manufacturers v. Donovan* on June 17, 1981.[12]

The Supreme Court, in a 5-3 decision, found that the actions of regulatory agencies which conform to the OSHA law need not be supported by cost-benefit analysis.[13] In addition, the Court asserted that Congress, in writing a statute, rather than the agencies in applying it, has the primary responsibility for balancing benefits and costs.[14] The Court said:

> When Congress passed the Occupational Health and Safety Act in 1970, it chose to place pre-eminent value on assuring employees a safe and healthful working environment, limited only by the feasibility of achieving such an environment. We must measure the validity of the Secretary's actions against the requirements of that Act.[15]

The opinion upheld the finding of the District of Columbia Court of Appeals that "Congress itself struck the balance between costs and benefits in the mandate to the agency."[16]

The Appeals Court opinion in *American Textile Manufacturers v. Donovan* supports the principle that legislatures are not necessarily bound to a particular conception of regulatory policy. Agencies that apply the law therefore may not need to justify on cost-benefit grounds the standards they set. These standards may conflict with the goal of efficiency and still express our political will as a nation. That is, they may reflect not the personal choices of self-interested individuals, but the collective judgments we make on historical, cultural, aesthetic, moral, and ideological grounds.[17]

The appeal of the Reagan Administration to cost-benefit analysis, however, may arise more from political than economic considerations. The intention, seen in the most favorable light, may not be to replace political or ideological goals with economic ones, but to make economic goals more apparent in regulation. This is not to say that Congress should function to reveal a collective willingness-to-pay just as markets reveal an individual willingness-to-pay. It is to suggest that Congress should do more to balance economic with ideological, aesthetic, and moral goals. To think that environmental or worker safety policy can be based exclusively on aspiration for a "natural" and "safe" world is as foolish as to hold that environmental law can be reduced to cost-benefit accounting. The more we move to one extreme, as I found in Lewiston, the more likely we are to hear from the other.

SUBSTITUTING EFFICIENCY FOR SAFETY

The labor unions won an important political victory when Congress passed the Occupational Safety and Health Act of 1970.[18] That Act, among other things, severely restricts worker exposure to toxic substances. It instructs the Secretary of Labor to set "the standard which most adequately assures, to the extent feasible . . . that no employee will suffer material impairment of health or functional capacity even if such employee has regular exposure to the hazard . . . for the period of his working life."[19]

Pursuant to this law, the Secretary of Labor in 1977 reduced from ten to one part per million (ppm) the permissable ambient exposure level for benzene, a carcinongen for which no safe threshold is known. The American Petroleum Institute thereupon challenged the new standard in court.[20] It argued, with much evidence in its favor, that the benefits (to workers) of the one ppm standard did not equal the costs (to industry).[21] The standard therefore did not appear to be a rational response to a market failure in that it did not strike an efficient balance between the interests of workers in safety and the interests of industry and consumers in keeping prices down.

The Secretary of Labor defended the tough safety standard on the ground that the law demanded it.[22] An efficient standard might have required safety until it cost industry more to prevent a risk than it cost workers to accept it. Had Congress adopted this vision of public policy— one which can be found in many economics texts[23]—it would have treated workers not as ends-in-themselves but as means for the production of overall utility. This, as the Secretary saw it, was what Congress refused to do.[24]

The United States Court of Appeals for the Fifth Circuit agreed with the American Petroleum Institute and invalidated the one ppm benzene standard.[25] On July 2, 1980, the Supreme Court affirmed the decision in *American Petroleum Institute v. Marshall*[26] and remanded the benzene standard back to OSHA for revision. The narrowly based Supreme Court decision was divided over the role economic considerations should play in judicial review. Justice Marshall, joined in dissent by three other justices, argued that the Court had undone on the basis of its own theory of regulatory policy an act of Congress inconsistent with that theory.[27] He concluded that the plurality decision of the Court "requires the American worker to return to the political arena to win a victory that he won before in 1970."[28]

The decision of the Supreme Court is important not because of its consequences, which are likely to be minimal, but because of the fascinating questions it raises. Shall the courts uphold only those political decisions that can be defended on economic grounds? Shall we allow democracy only to the extent that it can be construed either as a rational response to a market failure or as an attempt to redistribute wealth? Should the courts say that a regulation is not "feasible" or "reasonable"—terms that occur in the OSHA law[29]—unless it is supported by a cost-benefit analysis?

The problem is this: An efficiency criterion, as it is used to evaluate public policy, assumes that the goals of our society are contained in the preferences individuals reveal or would reveal in markets. Such an approach may appear attractive, even just, because it treats everyone as equal, at least theoretically, by according to each person's preferences the same respect and concern. To treat a person with respect, however, is also to listen and to respond intelligently to his or her views and opinions. This is not the same thing as to ask how much he or she is willing to pay for them. The cost-benefit analyst does not ask economists how much they are willing to pay for what they believe, that is, that the workplace and the environment should be made efficient. Why, then, does the analyst ask workers, environmentalists, and others how much they are willing to pay for what they believe is right? Are economists the only ones who can back their ideas with reasons while the rest of us can only pay a price? The cost-benefit approach treats people as of equal worth because it treats them as of no worth, but only as places or channels at which willingness to pay is found.[30]

LIBERTY: ANCIENT AND MODERN

When efficiency is the criterion of public safety and health, one tends to conceive of social relations on the model of a market, ignoring competing visions of what we as a society should be like. Yet it is obvious that there are competing conceptions of what we should be as a society. There are some who believe on principle that worker safety and environmental quality ought to be protected only insofar as the benefits of protection balance the costs. On the other hand, people argue—also on principle—that neither worker safety nor environmental quality should be treated merely as a commodity to be traded at the margin for other commodities, but rather each should be valued for its own sake. The conflict between these two principles is logical or moral, to be resolved by argument or debate. The question whether cost-benefit analysis should play a decisive role in policymaking is not to be decided by cost-benefit analysis. A contradiction between principles—between contending visions of the good society—cannot be settled by asking how much partisans are willing to pay for their beliefs.

The role of the *legislator*, the political role, may be more important to the individual than the role of *consumer*. The person, in other words, is not to be treated merely as a bundle of preferences to be juggled in cost-benefit analyses. The individual is to be respected as an advocate of ideas which are to be judged according to the reasons for them. If health and environmental statutes reflect a vision of society as something other than a market by requiring protections beyond what are efficient, then this may express not legislative ineptitude but legislative responsiveness to public values. To deny this vision because it is economically inefficient is simply to replace it with another vision. It is to insist that the ideas of the citizen be sacrificed to the psychology of the consumer.

We hear on all sides that government is routinized, mechanical, entrenched, and bureaucratized; the jargon alone is enough to dissuade the most mettlesome meddler. Who can make a difference? It is plain that for many of us the idea of a national political community has an abstract and suppositious quality. We have only our private conceptions of the good, if no way exists to arrive at a public one. This is only to note the continuation, in our time, of the trend Benjamin Constant described in the essay *De La Liberte des Anciens Comparee a Celle des Modernes*.[31] Constant observes that the modern world, as opposed to the ancient, emphasizes civil over political liberties, the rights of privacy and property over those of community and participation. "Lost in the multitude," Constant writes, "the individual rarely perceives the influence that he exercises," and, therefore, must be content with "the peaceful enjoyment of private independence."[32] The individual asks only to be protected by laws common to all in his pursuit of his own self-interest. The citizen has been replaced by the consumer; the tradition of Rousseau has been supplanted by that of Locke and Mill.

Nowhere are the rights of the moderns, particularly the rights of privacy and property, less helpful than in the area of the natural environment. Here the values we wish to protect—cultural, historical, aesthetic, and moral—are public values. They depend not so much upon what each person wants individually as upon what he or she thinks is right for the community. We refuse to regard worker health and safety as commodities; we regulate hazards as a matter of right. Likewise, we refuse to treat environmental resources simply as public goods in the economist's sense. Instead, we prevent significant deterioration of air quality not only as a matter of individual self-interest but also as a matter of collective self-respect. How shall we balance efficiency against moral, cultural, and aesthetic values in policy for the workplace and the environment? No better way has been devised to do this than by legislative debate ending in a vote. This is very different from a cost-benefit analysis terminating in a bottom line.

VALUES ARE NOT SUBJECTIVE

It is the characteristic of cost-benefit analysis that it treats all value judgments other than those made on its behalf as nothing but statements of preference, attitude, or emotion, insofar as they are value judgments. The cost-benefit analyst regards as true the judgment that we should maximize efficiency or wealth. The analyst believes that this view can be backed by reasons,[33] but does not regard it as a preference or want for which he or she must be willing to pay. The cost-benefit analyst tends to treat all other normative views and recommendations as if they were nothing but subjective reports of mental states. The analyst supposes in all such cases that "this is right" and "this is what we ought to do" are equivalent to "I want this" and "this is what I prefer." Value judgments are beyond criticism if, indeed, they are nothing but expressions of personal preference; they are incorrigible since every person is in the best position to know what he or she wants. All valuation, according to this approach, happens *in foro interno*; debate *in foro publico* has no point. With this approach, the reasons that people give for their views do not count; what does count is how much they are willing to pay to satisfy their wants. Those who are willing to pay the most, for all intents and purposes, have the right view; theirs is the more informed opinion, the better aesthetic judgment, and the deeper moral insight.

The assumption that valuation is subjective, that judgments of good and evil are nothing but expressions of desire and aversion, is not unique to economic theory.[34] There are psychotherapists—Carl Rogers is an example—who likewise deny the objectivity or cognitivity of valuation.[35] For Rogers, there is only one criterion of worth: it lies in "the subjective world of the individual. Only he knows it fully."[36] The therapist shows his or her client that a "value system is not necessarily something imposed from without, but is something experienced."[37] Therapy succeeds when the client "perceives himself in such a way that no self-experience can be discriminated as more or less worthy of positive self-regard than any other. . . ."[38] The client then "tends to place the basis of standards within himself, recognizing that the 'goodness' or 'badness' of any experience or perceptual object is not something inherent in that object, but is a value placed in it by himself."[39]

Rogers points out that "some clients make strenuous efforts to have the therapist exercise the valuing function, so as to provide them with guides for action."[40] The therapist, however, "consistently keeps the locus of evaluation with the client."[41] As long as the therapist refuses to "exercise the valuing function" and as long as he or she practices an "unconditional positive regard"[42] for all the affective states of the client, then the therapist remains neutral among the client's values or "sensory and visceral experiences."[43] The role of the therapist is legitimate, Rogers suggests, because of this value neutrality. The therapist accepts all felt preferences as valid and imposes none on the client.

Economists likewise argue that their role as policy-makers is legitimate because they are neutral among competing values in the client society. The political economist, according to James Buchanan, "is or should be ethically neutral: the indicated results are influenced by his own value scale only insofar as this reflects his membership in a larger group."[44] The economist might be most confident of the impartiality of his or her policy recommendations if he or she could derive them formally or mathematically from individual preferences. If theoretical difficulties make such a social welfare function impossible,[45] however, the next best thing, to preserve neutrality, is to let markets function to transform individual preference orderings into a collective ordering of social states. The analyst is able then to base policy on preferences that exist in society and are not necessarily his own.

Economists have used this impartial approach to offer solutions to many significant social problems, for example, the controversy over abortion. An economist argues that "there is an optimal number of abortions, just as there is an optimal level of pollution, or purity . . . . Those who oppose abortion could eliminate it entirely, if their intensity of feeling were so strong as to lead to payments that were greater at the margin than the price anyone would pay to have an abortion."[46] Likewise, economists, in order to determine whether the war in Vietnam was justified, have estimated the willingness to pay of those who demonstrated against it.[47] Following the same line of reasoning, it should be possible to decide whether Creationism should be taught in the public schools, whether black and white people should be segregated, whether the death penalty should be enforced, and whether the square root of six is three. All of these questions arguably depend upon how much people are willing to pay for their subjective preferences or wants. This is the beauty of cost-benefit analysis: no matter how relevant or irrelevant, wise or stupid, informed or uninformed, responsible or silly, defensible or indefensible wants may be, the analyst is able to derive a policy from them—a policy which is legitimate because, in theory, it treats all of these preferences as equally valid and good.

PREFERENCE OR PRINCIPLE?

In contrast, consider a Kantian conception of value.[48] The individual, for Kant, is a judge of values, not a mere haver of wants, and the individual judges not for himself or herself merely, but as a member of a relevant community or group. The central idea in a Kantian approach to ethics is that some values are more reasonable than others and therefore have a better claim upon the assent of members of the community as such.[49] The world of obligation, like the world of mathematics or the world of empirical fact, is public not private, and objective standards of argument and criticism apply. Kant recognized that values, like beliefs, are subjective states of mind which have an objective content as well. Therefore, both values and beliefs are either correct or mistaken. A value judgment is like an empirical or theoretical judgment in that it claims to be *true* not merely to be *felt*.

We have, then, two approaches to public policy before us. The first, the approach associated with normative versions of welfare economics, asserts that the only policy recommendation that can or need be defended on objective grounds is efficiency or wealth-maximization. The Kantian approach, on the other hand, assumes that many policy recommendations may be justified or refuted on objective grounds. It would concede that the approach of welfare economics applies adequately to some questions, for example, those which ordinary consumer markets typically settle. How many yo-yos should be produced as compared to how may frisbees? Shall pens have black ink or blue? Matters such as these are so trivial it is plain that markets should handle them. It does not follow, however, that we should adopt a market or quasi-market approach to every public question.

A market or quasi-market approach to arithmetic, for example, is plainly inadequate. No matter how much people are willing to pay, three will never be the square root of six. Similarly, segregation is a national curse and the fact that we are willing to pay for it does not make it better, but only us worse. The case for abortion must stand on the merits; it cannot be priced at the margin. Our failures to make the right decisions in these matters are failures in arithmetic, failures in wisdom, failures in taste, failures in morality—but not market failures. There are no relevant markets which have failed.

What separates these questions from those for which markets are appropriate is that they involve matters of knowledge, wisdom, morality, and taste that admit of better or worse, right or wrong, true or false, and not mere economic optimality. Surely environmental questions—the protection of wilderness, habitats, water, land, and air as well as policy toward environmental safety and health—involve moral and aesthetic principles and not just economic ones. This is consistent, of course, with cost-effectiveness and with a sensible recognition of economic constraints.

The neutrality of the economist is legitimate if private preferences or subjective wants are the only values in question. A person should be left free to choose the color of his or her necktie or necklace, but we cannot justify a theory of public policy or private therapy on that basis. If the patient seeks moral advice or tries to find reasons to justify a choice, the therapist, according to Rogers' model, would remind him or her to trust his visceral and sensory experiences. The result of this is to deny the individual status as a cognitive being capable of responding intelligently to reasons; it reduces him or her to a bundle of affective states. What Rogers' therapist does to the patient the cost-benefit analyst does to society as a whole. The analyst is neutral among our "values"—having first imposed a theory of what value is. This is a theory that is impartial among values and for that reason fails to treat the persons who have them with respect or concern. It does not treat them even as persons but only as locations at which wants may be found. The neutrality of economics is not a basis for its legitimacy. We recognize it as an indifference toward value—an indifference so deep, so studied, and so assured that at first one hesitates to call it by its right name.

THE CITIZEN AS JOSEPH K.

The residents of Lewiston at the conference I attended demanded to know the truth about the dangers that confronted them and the reasons for those dangers. They wanted to be convinced that the sacrifice asked of them was legitimate even if it served interests other than their own. One official from a large chemical company dumping wastes in the area told them in reply that corporations were people and that people could talk to people about their feelings, interests, and needs. This sent a shiver through the audience. Like Joseph K. in *The Trial*,[50] the residents of Lewiston asked for an explanation, justice, and truth, and they were told that their wants would be taken care of. They demanded to know the reasons for what was continually happening to them. They were given a personalized response instead.

This response, that corporations are "just people serving people," is consistent with a particular view of power. This is the view that identifies power with the ability to get what one wants as an individual, that is, to satisfy one's personal preferences. When people in official positions in corporations or in the government put aside their personal interests, it would follow that they put aside their power as well. Their neutrality then justifies them in directing the resources of society in ways they determine to be best. This managerial role serves not their own interests but those of their clients. Cost-benefit analysis may be seen as a pervasive form of this paternalism. Behind this paternalism, as William Simon observes of the lawyer-client relationship, lies a theory of value that tends to personalize power. "It resists understanding power as a product of class, property, or institutions and collapses power into the personal needs and dispositions of the individuals who command and obey."[51] Once the economist, the therapist, the lawyer, or the manager abjures his own interests and acts wholly on behalf of client individuals, he appears to have no power of his own and thus justifiably manipulates and controls everything. "From this perspective it becomes difficult to distinguish the powerful from the powerless. In every case, both the exercise of power and submission to it are portrayed as a matter of personal accommodation and adjustment."[52]

The key to the personal interest or emotive theory of value, as one commentator has rightly said, "is the fact that emotivism entails the obliteration of any genuine distinction between manipulative and nonmanipulative social relations."[53] The reason is that once the affective self is made the source of all value, the public self cannot participate in the exercise of power. As Philip Reiff remarks, "the public world is constituted as one vast stranger who appears at inconvenient times and makes demands viewed as purely external and therefore with no power to elicit a moral response."[54] There is no way to distinguish the legitimate authority that public values and public law create from tyranny.[55]

"At the rate of progress since 1900," Henry Adams speculates in his *Education*, "every American who lived into the year 2000 would know how to control unlimited power."[56] . . . Yet in the 1980s, the citizens of Lewiston, surrounded by dynamos, high tension lines, and nuclear wastes, are powerless. They do not know how to criticize power, resist power, or justify power—for to do so depends on making distinctions between good and evil, right and wrong, innocence and guilt, justice and injustice, truth and lies. These distinctions cannot be made out and have no significance within an emotive or psychological theory of value. To adopt this theory is to imagine society as a market in which individuals trade voluntarily and without coercion. No individual, no belief, no faith has authority over them. To have power to act as a nation we must be able to act, at least at times, on a public philosophy, conviction, or faith. We cannot abandon the moral function of public law. The antinomianism of cost-benefit analysis is not enough.

NOTES

1. *See, e.g.*, W. BAXTER, PEOPLE OR PENGUINS: THE CASE FOR OPTIMAL POLLUTION ch. 1 (1974). *See generally* A. FREEMAN, R. HAVEMAN, A. KNEESE, THE ECONOMICS OF ENVIRONMENTAL POLICY (1973) [hereinafter A. FREEMAN].
2. Posner makes this point well in discussing wealth maximization as an ethical concept. "The only kind of preference that counts in a system of wealth-maximization," he writes, "is . . . one that is backed up by money—in other words, that is registered in a market." Posner, *Utilitarianism, Economics, and Legal Theory*, 8 J. LEGAL STUD. 103, 119 (1979).
3. A. FREEMAN, *supra* note 6, at 23.
4. R. MUSGRAVE, THE THEORY OF PUBLIC FINANCE 87-88 (1959).
5. Marglin, *The Social Rate of Discount and the Optimal Rate of Investment*, 77 Q.J. ECON. 95, 98 (1963).
6. *Id.*
7. 46 Fed. Reg. 13,193 (1981). The order specifies that the cost-benefit requirement shall apply "to the extent permitted by law."
8. American Fed'n of Labor, etc. v. Marshall, 617 F.2d 636 (D.C. Cir. 1979), *cert. granted sub nom.* American Textile Mfrs. Inst., Inc. v. Marshall, 49 U.S.L.W. 3208 (1981).
9. 49 U.S.L.W. 3523-24.
10. *Id.*
11. *Id.*
12. American Textile Mfrs. Inst., Inc. v. Donovan, 49 U.S.L.W. 4720 (1981).

13. *Id.* at 4724-29.
14. *Id.* at 4726-29.
15. *Id.* at 4733-34.
16. *Id.* at 4726-29.
17. To reject cost-benefit analysis as a basis for policymaking is not necessarily to reject cost-effectiveness analysis which is an altogether different thing. For this difference, *see* Baram, *Cost-Benefit Analysis: An Inadequate Basis for Health, Safety, and Environmental Regulatory Decisionmaking*, 8 Ecology L. Q. 473 (1980). "*Cost-benefit analysis* . . . is used by the decisionmaker to establish societal goals as well as the means for achieving these goals, whereas *cost-effectiveness analysis* only compares alternative means for achieving 'given' goals." *Id.* at 478 (footnote omitted). In practice, regulatory uses of cost-benefit analysis stifle and obstruct the achievement of legislated health, safety, and environmental goals. *Id.* at 473. Further, to the extent that economic factors are permissible considerations under enabling statutes, agencies should engage in cost-effectiveness analysis, which aids in determining the least costly means to designated goals, rather than cost-benefit analysis, which improperly determines regulatory ends as well as means. *Id.* at 474.
18. Pub. L. No. 91-596, 84 Stat. 1596 (1970) (codified at 29 U.S.C. §§ 651-678 (1970)).
19. 29 U.S.C. § 655(b)(5) (1970).
20. American Petroleum Inst. v. Marshall, 581 F.2d 493 (5th Cir. 1978), *aff'd*, 448 U.S. 607 (1980).
21. 581 F.2d at 501-05.
22. *Id.* at 501.
23. *See, e.g.*, R. Posner, Economic Analysis of Law I & II (1973). In G. Calabresi, The Costs of Accidents *passim* (1970), the author argues that accident law balances two goals, "efficiency" and "equality" or "justice."
24. American Petroleum Inst. v. Marshall, 581 F.2d 493, 503-05 (5th Cir. 1978).
25. *Id.* at 505.
26. 448 U.S. 607 (1980).
27. *Id.* at 719.
28. *Id.*
29. 29 U.S.C. §§ 655(b)(5) & 652(8) (1975).
30. For a similar argument against utilitarianism, *see* Hart, *Between Utility and Rights*, 79 Colum. L. Rev. 828, 829-31 (1979).
31. B. Constant, De La Liberte des Anciens Comparee a Celle des Modernes (1819)
32. *Oeuvres Politiques de Benjamin Constant*, 269 (C. Louandre, ed. 1874), *quoted in* S. Wolin, Politics and Vision 281 (1960).
33. There are arguments that whatever reasons may be given are not good. *See generally* Dworkin, *Why Efficiency?* 8 Hofstra L. Rev. 563 (1980); Dworkin, *Is Wealth a Value?* 9 J. Legal Stud. 191 (1980); Kennedy, *Cost-Benefit Analysis of Entitlement Problems: A Critique*, 33 Stan. L. Rev. 387 (1980); Rizzo, *The Mirage of Efficiency*, 8 Hofstra L. Rev. 641 (1980); Sagoff, *Economic Theory and Environmental Law*, 79 Mich. L. Rev. 1393 (1981).
34. This is the emotive theory of value. For the classic statement, *see* C. Stevenson, Ethics and Language chs. 1 & 2 (144). For criticism, *see* Blanshard, *The New Subjectivism in Ethics*, 9 Philosophy & Phenomenological Research 504 (1949). For a statement of the related interest theory of value, *see generally* R. Perry, General Theory of Value (1926); E. Westermarck, Ethical Relativity chs. 3–5 (1932). For criticisms of subjectivism in ethics and a case for the objective theory presupposed here, *see generally* P. Edwards, The Logic of Moral Discourse (1955) and W. Ross, The Right and the Good (1930).

35. My account is based on C. Rogers, On Becoming a Person (1961); C. Rogers, Client Centered Therapy (1965); and Rogers, A *Theory of Therapy, Personality, and Interpersonal Relationships, as Developed in the Client Centered Framework*, 3 Psychology: A Study of a Science 184 (1959). For a similar account used as a critique of the lawyer-client relation, *see* Simon, *Homo Psychologicus: Notes on a New Legal Formalism*, 32 Stan. L. Rev. 487 (1980).
36. Rogers, *supra* note 40, at 210.
37. C. Rogers, Client Centered Therapy 150 (1965).
38. Rogers, *supra* note 40, at 208.
39. C. Rogers, *supra* note 42, at 139.
40. *Id.* at 150.
41. *Id.*
42. Rogers, *supra* note 40, at 208.
43. *Id.* at 523-24.
44. Buchanan, *Positive Economics, Welfare Economics, and Political Economy* 2 J.L. & Econ. 124, 127 (1959).
45. K. Arrow, Social Choice and Individual Values I-V (2d ed. 1963).
46. H. Macaulay & B. Yandle, Environmental Use and the Market 120-21 (1978).
47. *See generally* Cicchetti, Freeman, Haveman, & Knetsch, *On the Economics of Mass Demonstrations: A Case Study of the November 1969 March on Washington*, 61 Am. Econ. Rev. 719 (1971).
48. I. Kant, Foundations of the Metaphysics of Morals (1969). I follow the interpretation of Kantian ethics of W. Sellars, Science and Metaphysics ch. vii (1968) and Sellars, *On Reasoning About Values*, 17 Am. Phil. Q. 81 (1980).
49. *See* A. Macintyre, After Virtue 22 (1981).
50. F. Kafka, The Trial (rev. ed. trans. 1957). Simon applies this anology to the lawyer-client relationship. Simon, *supra* note 40, at 524.
51. Simon, *supra* note 40, at 495.
52. *Id.*
53. A. Macintyre, *supra* note 54, at 22.
54. P. Reiff, The Triumph of the Therapeutic: Uses of Faith After Freud 52 (1966).
55. That public law regimes inevitably lead to tyranny seems to be the conclusion of H. Arendt, The Human Condition (1958); K. Popper, The Open Society and Its Enemies (1966); L. Strauss, Natural Right and History (1953). For an important criticism of this conclusion in these authors, *see generally* Holmes, *Aristippus In and Out of Athens*, 73 Am. Pol. Sci. Rev. 113 (1979).
56. H. Adams, *supra* note 1, at 476.

The Nature and Possibility of an Environmental Ethic

Tom Regan

A conception of an environmental ethic is set forth which involves postulating that nonconscious natural objects can have value in their own right, independently of human interests. Two kinds of objection are considered: (1) those that deny the possibility (the intelligibility) of developing an ethic of the environment that accepts this postulate, and (2) those that deny the necessity of constructing such an ethic. Both types of objection are found wanting. The essay concludes with some tentative remarks regarding the notion of inherent value.

I. INTRODUCTION

Is an environmental ethic possible? Answers to this question presuppose that we have an agreed upon understanding of the nature of an environmental ethic. Evidently we do not, and one fundamental problem for this burgeoning area of ethics is to say what such an ethic must be like. In the present essay, I characterize and defend, although incompletely, a particular conception of an environmental ethic. My modest objective is to show that there is something worth thinking about completing.

II. TWO CONDITIONS OF AN ENVIRONMENTAL ETHIC

The conception I favor accepts the following two conditions:

(1) An environmental ethic must hold that there are nonhuman beings which have moral standing.[1]

(2) An environmental ethic must hold that the class of those beings which have moral standing includes but is larger than the class of conscious beings—that is, all conscious beings and some nonconscious beings must be held to have moral standing.

If both conditions are accepted, then a theory that satisfies neither of them is not a false environmental ethic; it is not an environmental ethic at all. Any theory that satisfies (1), but does not satisfy (2) might be regarded as a

Originally published in *Environmental Ethics* 3, 1 (Spring 1981): pp. 19–34. Reprinted by permission.

theory "on the way to becoming" such an ethic, in that it satisfies a necessary condition, but, since it fails to satisfy condition (2), it fails to qualify as a genuine environmental ethic. Only theories that satisfy (2), on the conception advanced here, can properly be regarded as environmental ethics, whether true, reasonable, or otherwise.

Though only a necessary condition, (1) assists us in distinguishing between (a) an ethic *of* the environment, and (b) an ethic *for the use* of the environment. Suppose we think that only the interests of human beings matter morally. Then it certainly would be possible to develop a homocentric ethic for the use of the environment. Roughly speaking, such an ethic would declare that the environment ought to be used so that the quality of human life, including possibly that of future generations, ought to be enhanced. I do not say developing such an ethic (what I shall call "a management ethic") would be simple or unimportant, but a management ethic falls short of an ethic of the environment, given the conditions stated earlier. It restricts the loci of value to the lives and interests of *human* beings, whereas an environmental ethic requires that we recognize the moral standing of nonhumans.

L. W. Sumner advances considerations which, if accepted, would lead us to an ethical theory that satisfies condition (1) and thereby takes us beyond a management ethic.[2] Sumner argues that the lives and interests of nonhuman animals, not just those of human beings, ought to be taken into account in their own right. Recognition of this fact, he states, marks "the beginning of a genuine environmental consciousness."[3] Other thinkers have advanced similar arguments.[4] Despite many differences, these thinkers share the belief that only *conscious* beings can have moral standing. I shall refer to theories that embody this belief as *kinship theories* because they grow out of the idea that beings resembling humans in the quite fundamental way of being conscious, and thus to this extent kin to us, have moral standing. I shall have more to say about kinship theories below (section 4).

Management and kinship theories are clearly distinct. Management theories direct us, for example, to preserve wildlife if this is in the interest of human beings, including (possibly) the interest of generations yet unborn. Animals in the wild are not themselves recognized as having interests or value that ought to be taken into account. Given a kinship ethic, however, wild animals, in their own right, figure in the moral arithmetic, though precisely how we are to carry out the required computations is unclear. When, for example, there is a clash between the preservation of wild animals and the economic development of the wilderness, it is unclear how conflicting interests are to be weighed. The value of survival of how many caribou, for example, equals the disvalue of how much financial loss to oil investors in Northern Canada?

Whatever difficulties may exist for management or kinship theories in weighing conflicting claims, however, these difficulties seem to be compounded if we move beyond these theories to ones that meet condition (2), for then we are required, it appears, to deal with the possibility that human and animal interests might come into conflict with the survival or flourishing of nonconscious beings, and it is extremely doubtful whether such conflicts can *in principle* admit of rational adjudication.

I do not wish to minimize the difficulties that attend the development of an environmental ethic which is consequentialist in nature (e.g., some form of utilitarianism). There are difficulties of comparison, perhaps themselves great enough to foreclose the possibility of developing a consequentialist environmental ethic. I shall have more to say on this matter as we proceed. First, though, a more fundamental problem requires our attention. Is it even logically possible for a theory to meet both the conditions I have recommended for an environmental ethic? The answer clearly is no if compelling reasons can be given for limiting moral standing *only* to conscious beings. In the following section I reject three arguments that attempt to establish this restriction.

III. ARGUMENTS AGAINST THE POSSIBILITY OF AN ENVIRONMENTAL ETHIC

The first argument to be considered I call the "interest argument":

(1) The only beings which can have moral standing are those beings which can have interests.

(2) The only beings which can have interests are those which have the capacity for consciousness.

(3) Therefore, the only beings which can have moral standing are beings having the capacity for consciousness.

Now, this argument, as I have argued elsewhere against a similar argument,[5] has apparent plausibility because it exploits an ambiguity in the concept of something having interests. To speak of A's interests in X might mean either (a) that A is interested in (wants, desires, hopes for, cares about, etc.) X, or (b) that X is in A's interest (that X will contribute to A's good, or well-being, or welfare). Clearly *if* the only beings which can have moral standing are those which can be interested in things (have desires, wants, etc.), then only conscious beings can have moral standing. The idea of nonconscious beings having desires, wants, etc., at least in any literal sense, seems plainly unintelligible. If, on the other hand, we mean beings which can be benefited or harmed by what is given or denied them, then it is an open question whether the class of beings which can have moral standing is coextensive with the class of beings having the capacity for consciousness. Perhaps other beings can have a good or value that can be advanced or retarded depending on what is done to them. The interest argument provides us with no resolution of this question, and so fails to demonstrate the impossibility of an environmental ethic.

A second argument, which I shall call the "sentience argument," closely resembles the interest argument and is vulnerable to the same type of objection:[6]

(1) The only beings which can have moral standing are those which are sentient.

(2) The only beings which are sentient are those which have the capacity for consciousness.

(3) Therefore, the only beings which can have moral standing are those which have the capacity for consciousness.

I shall limit my critical remarks to step (1). How might it be supported? First, one might argue that only sentient beings have interests; that is, one might seek to support the sentience argument by invoking the interest argument, but since we have shown this latter argument is incomplete, at best, this defense of the sentience argument must bear the same diagnosis. A second defense consists in claiming that it is "meaningless"[7] to think that nonconscious beings possibly have moral standing. This is unconvincing. *If* it is meaningless, there ought to be some way of illuminating why this is so, and this illumination is not provided by the mere charge of meaninglessness itself. Such a defense has more the aura of rhetoric than of philosophy.

A third defense consists in arguing that the only beings having moral standing are those having value in their own right, *and* that only sentient beings have value of this kind. This defense, as I argue in a moment, is a token of the argument type I call the "goodness argument." Its major liability is that by itself it provides no justification for its two central claims— namely, (a) that only beings which can have value in their own right can have moral standing, and (b) that only sentient beings have value in their own right. For reasons to which I come below, I believe (b) is false while (a) is true. Meanwhile, neither is self-evident and so each stands in need of rational defense, something not provided by the sentience argument itself.

The final argument to be considered is the goodness argument:

(1) The only beings which can have moral standing are those which can have a good of their own.

(2) The only beings which can have a good of their own are those capable of consciousness.

(3) Therefore, the only beings which can have moral standing are those capable of consciousness.

Premise (1) of the goodness argument seems to identify a fundamental presupposition of an environmental ethic. The importance of this premise is brought out when we ask for the grounds on which we might rest the obligation to preserve any existing X. Fundamentally, two types of answer are possible. First, preserving X is necessary to bring about future good or prevent future evil for beings other than X; on this account X's existence has instrumental value. Second, the obligation we have might be to X itself, independently of X's instrumental value, because X has a good or value in its own right. Given our conditions for an environmental ethic, not all of the values recognized in nonconscious nature can be instrumental. Only if we agree with premise (1) of the goodness argument, therefore, can we have a necessary presupposition of an environmental ethic. How inherent goodness or value can be intelligibly ascribed to nonconscious beings is a difficult question, one we shall return to later (section 5). At present, we must consider the remainder of the goodness argument, since if sound, it rules out the logical possibility of nonconscious beings having a good or value of their own.

"The only beings which have a good of their own," premise (2) states, "are those capable of consciousness." What arguments can be given to support this view? I have examined suggested answers elsewhere at length.[8] What these arguments come to in the end, if I am right, is the thesis that consciousness is a logically necessary condition of having only *a certain kind* of good of one's own, happiness. Thus, though we may speak, metaphorically of a "happy azalea" or a "contented brocoli," the only sorts of beings which literally can have happiness are conscious beings. There is no disputing this. What is disputable is the tacit assumption that this is the *only* kind of good or value a given X can have in its own right. Unless or until a compelling supporting argument is supplied, for limiting inherent goodness to happiness, the goodness argument falls short of limiting moral standing to just those beings capable of consciousness.

Four truths result if the argument of the present section is sound. First, an environmental ethic must recognize that the class of beings having moral standing is larger than the class of conscious beings. Second, the basis on which an environmental ethic must pin this enlargement is the idea that nonconscious beings can have a good or value in their own right. Third, though it remains to be ascertained what this goodness or value is, it is not happiness; and fourth, efforts to show that nonconscious beings cannot have moral standing fail to show this. The conclusion we guardedly reach, then, is that the impossibility of an environmental ethic has not been shown.

IV. ARGUMENTS AGAINST THE NECESSITY OF AN ENVIRONMENTAL ETHIC

We turn now to a second series of objections against an environmental ethic, all of which concede that it is *possible* that nonconscious beings may have value in themselves, and thus that it is *possible* to develop an environmental ethic, but which all deny, nonetheless, that there are good enough reasons for holding that nonconscious beings *do* have a good or value in their own right. There are, these objections hold in common, alternative ways of accounting for the moral dimensions of our relationship to the environmental which are rationally preferable to postulating inherent value in it. Thus, while granting the possibility of an environmental ethic, the four views about to be considered deny its necessity.

The Corruption of Character Argument

Advocates of this argument insist that it is wrong to treat nonconscious nature in certain ways—e.g., unchecked strip mining—but account for this by urging that people who engage in such activities tend to become similarly ruthless in their dealings with people. Just as Kant speculated that those who act cruelly to animals develop the habit of cruelty, and so are likely to be cruel to their fellow man,[9] so similarly those who indiscriminately destroy the natural environment will develop destructive habits that will in time wreak havoc on their neighbor. Our duties to act toward the environment in certain ways are thus explained without our having to postulate value *in* the environment.

This argument cannot be any stronger than its central empirical thesis that those who treat the environment in certain ways will be inclined to treat their fellow humans in analogous ways. I do not believe there is any hard empirical evidence at hand which supports this hypothesis. Comparing the crime rates of strip miners and accountants would probably provide a good deal of hard empirical data against it. Indeed, one cannot help wondering if the very reverse habits might not be fostered by instructing persons to do anything they want to the environment, if no person is harmed, while insisting on strict prohibitions in our dealings with persons. There would appear to be just as much (or just as little) empirical data to support this hypothesis as there is to support the hypothesis central to the corruption of character argument. On empirical grounds, the argument lacks credibility.

The Offense Against an Ideal Argument

This argument differs from the corruption of character argument in that it does not rest its case on an unsupported empirical claim. The argument alleges, quite apart from how those who treat nature end up treating other humans, that those persons who plunder the environment violate an ideal of human conduct, that ideal being not to destroy anything unthinkingly or gratuitously. This argument is open to a fatal objection. It would be an eccentric ideal which, on the one hand, enjoined those who would fulfill it to act in a certain way or to become a certain kind of person, and, on the other hand, held that there was no value in acting in those ways or in being that kind of person. For example, acting with integrity or becoming a compassionate person are intelligible human ideals, but part at least of what makes them intelligible is the implicit judgment that integrity and compassion are fitting ways to behave. However, the fitting way to act in regard to X clearly involves a commitment to regarding X as having value. Honesty is an ideal, not simply because I am a good person if honest, but also because honesty is a fitting way *to act toward* beings possessed of a certain kind of value—e.g., autonomy. An ideal which enjoins us not to act toward X in a certain way but which denies that X has any value is either unintelligible or pointless. Ideals, in short, involve the recognition of the value of *that toward which* one acts. If we are told that treating the environment in certain ways offends against an ideal of human conduct we are not being given a position that is an alternative to, or inconsistent with, the view that nonconscious objects have a value of their own. The fatal objection which the offense against an ideal argument encounters, is that, rather than offering an alternative to the view that some nonconscious objects have inherent value, it presupposes that they do.

The Utilitarian Argument

To speak of *the* utilitarian argument is misleading. A wide variety of utilitarian argument is possible, even including positions which hold that some nonconscious beings do have value in their own right.[10] I shall restrict my attention to forms of utilitarianism that deny this, focusing mainly on hedonistic utilitarianism.[11]

Abstractly and roughly, hedonistic utilitarianism holds that an action is right if no alternative action produces a better balance of pleasure over pain for all those affected. A theory of this type is "on the way to becoming" an environmental ethic if, as utilitarians since Bentham have argued, animals are sentient, and thus, given the utilitarian criteria, have moral standing. But hedonistic utilitarianism fails to satisfy the second condition of an environmental ethic and thus fails to qualify as an ethic of the environment. Its shortcomings are highlighted by asking, "Why not plastic trees? Why not lawns of astro-turf, or mountains of papier-maché suitably coated with vinyl to withstand harsh weather?" Stories find their way almost daily into the popular press which illustrate that a plastic environment is increasingly within the reach of modern technology. If, as Martin Krieger argues, "the demand for rare environments is a learned one," then "conscious public choice can manipulate this learning so that the environments which people learn to use and want reflect environments which are likely to be available at low cost."[12] Thus, as Mark Sagoff sees it, "This is the reason that the redwoods are (given Krieger's position) replaceable by plastic trees."[13] "The advertising that created rare environments," Krieger writes, "can create plentiful (e.g., plastic) substitutes."[14]

A hedonistic utilitarianism cannot quarrel over the *source* of environmentally based pleasures, whether they arise from real stands of redwoods or plastic replicas. Provided only that the pleasures are equal in the relevant respects (e.g., of equal duration and intensity), both are of equal value. To the suggestion that pleasures rooted in real redwoods are "higher" or "nobler" than those rooted in plastic ones, the reply must be that there is a long, untold story surrounding the idea of "higher" and "lower" pleasures, that no hedonistic utilitarian has yet succeeded in telling this story, and, indeed, that it may be inconsistent for a hedonistic utilitarian to believe this. Other things being equal, if a plastic environment can give rise to pleasures equal in value to those arising out of a natural environment, we will have just as much or as little reason to preserve the latter as to manufacture the former. Moreover, if the pleasures flowing from the manufactured environment should happen to outweigh those accompanying the natural environment, we would then have greater reason to enlarge the world of plastic trees and reduce that of living ones.

It is open to utilitarians to argue in response that theirs is a theory designed for living in the world as it is, not in the world as it might be, a theory to be used in actual, not wildly hypothetical situations. While it might conceivably be the case that more pleasure would result from plastic than from real environments, this simply is not the way things are.[15] Unfortunately for this type of reply, things seem to be otherwise. As Krieger notes, "Federal environmental policy is such that the rich get richer and the poor get poorer."[16] Commenting on this, Sagoff writes that

> rich people, for example, have the background and leisure to cultivate a taste in beautiful environments and only they have the money to live in or near them. Rising property values in protected areas drive the poor out. If the pleasures of the poor were measured equally with those of the rich, then quicker than you can say "cost-benefit analysis," there would be parking lots, condominiums and plastic trees.[17]

The empirical point is that, in the world as it actually is, there are grounds for thinking that environmental protection efforts favor the interests of a powerful elite rather than maximizing the pleasures of all, as hedonistic utilitarianism requires. Thus, if protectionist policies do not serve the cause of utility as much as would a plastic takeover, then hedonistic utilitarianism obliges us to move in the direction of a world of plastic trees, even in the world as it actually is. If a *reductio* is possible in assessing theories relating to our duties regarding the environment, hedonistic utilitarianism falls victim to this form of refutation.

The Embodiment of Cultural Values Argument

According to this argument, the natural environment, or certain parts of it, symbolize or express certain of our culture's values. In Sagoff's words, "Our rivers, forests, and wildlife . . . serve our society as paradigms of concepts we cherish," for example, freedom, integrity, power.[18] "A wild area may be powerful, majestic, free; an animal may express courage, innocence, purpose, and strength. As a nation we value these qualities: the obligation toward nature is an obligation toward them."[19] Thus, we are to preserve the environment because in doing so we preserve these natural expressions of the values of our culture.

This argument is not intended to be utilitarian. The claim is not made that the consequences of natural preservation will be better, all considered, if we preserve wilderness areas, for example, than if we allow their development for commercial purposes. Whether we ought to preserve wilderness is not to be settled by cost-benefit analysis. Rather, since our obligation is to the cultural values themselves embodied in nature, our obligation to preserve the natural environment cannot be overridden by or, for that matter, based upon calculations about the comparative value of the consequences of respecting them. The propriety of respect for cultural values is not a consequence of its being useful to respect them.

Because this argument is avowedly nonconsequentialist and not just nonutilitarian, it is reasonably clear that it must stand independently of the corruption of character argument. Moreover, though in some ways similar to the offense against an ideal argument, the two are distinct, for the offense argument involves the principle that certain ways of acting run counter to an ideal of human nature, whereas the embodiment of cultural values argument involves the principle that certain ways of acting violate an ideal of how a member of a particular culture ought to behave. Since it is conceivable that persons might act in accordance with their culture's ideals and yet violate a proposed ideal of human nature (e.g., if one's culture values militancy, while pacifism is an ideal of human nature), and vice versa, there is reason not to conflate the embodiment and the offense arguments.

What the embodiment argument has in common with the other arguments considered here is the view that environmental objects have no value in their own right. This is perhaps not so clear in the present case because the embodiment argument carries with it "objectivitist" presuppositions. Advocates of this argument do hold that the environment itself has certain objective qualities—e.g., majesty, power, freedom. These *qualities* are *in* nature no less than are, say, chromosomes. But the *value* these qualities have is not something else that is *in them* independently of the dominant interest of a given culture ("our cultural heritage"). On the contrary, what qualities in nature are valuable is a consequence of what qualities are essential in one's cultural heritage. For example, if freedom is a dominant cultural value, then, since animals or rivers in the wild embody this quality, they have value and ought to be preserved. What *qualities* a natural object expresses is an objective question, but the *value* a natural object has is not something it has objectively in its own right, but only as it happens to embody those qualities valued by one's culture.

The embodiment argument provides an enormously important and potentially powerful basis for a political-legal argument on behalf of the preservation of American wilderness. It is easy to see how one may use it to argue for "what is best" in American society: freedom, integrity, independence, loyalty, etc. It is the speculative developer rather than the conservationist who seems to be running roughshod over our nation's values. On this view, Disneyland, not Yosemite, seems un-American. Moreover, by insisting that such values as freedom and integrity cannot be trumped even if the consequences of doing so are utilitarian, advocates of the embodiment argument strike a blow which helps to counter the developer's argument that the commercial development of the wilderness will bring about better consequences, more pleasure to more people, than leaving it undeveloped. The embodiment argument replies that, though this may be true, it just so happens to be irrelevant. Given the nature of values such as freedom, integrity, etc., it is inappropriate to destroy their expression in nature in the name of utilitarian consequences. The rhetorical force of such arguments can be great, and can be a powerful practical weapon in the war for the preservation of nature.

But the embodiment argument does not have comparable philosophical strength. Two problems in particular haunt it. First, how are we to establish what our culture's values are? Sagoff states that we are to do this by consulting our artistic (cultural) history. However, if we do this we do not hear a chorus singing the same tune; on the contrary, there is much dissonance, some of which Sagoff himself mentions (e.g., the view of wilderness as an adversary to be tamed versus the view that it is to be cherished). Moreover, even if we were to arrive at a cultural consensus, the basis which Sagoff recommends is suspiciously elitist, reminding one of Ross' reference to "the judgment of the best people" in the determination of what is valuable.[20] Implicit in Sagoff's way of establishing what our cultural values are is an evaluative estimate of whose judgment to trust. The cards are stacked against the developer from the outset, since developers normally do not have the time or inclination to dabble in arts, history, and letters. It is not surprising, therefore, that developers take a back seat to the values of freedom, integrity, etc. The argument is indeed potentially a powerful political weapon, but fundamental questions go begging.

A second problem is no less severe. Cultural values can be relative, both between different cultures and within the same culture at different times. Thus, even were we to concede that *our* cultural values up to now call for the preservation of nature, that would entail nothing whatever about what environmental policies ought to be pushed in *other* countries (e.g., in Kenya or India, where many species of wild animals are endangered). Nor would it guarantee even in our own country that future environmental policy should continue to be protectionist. If plastic trees are possible, our culture might evolve to prefer them over real ones, in which case the embodiment of cultural values argument would sanction replacing natural with plastic flora.

Sagoff recognizes the possibility of significant changes in a culture's dominant values. He observes that we might "change the nature of our cultural heritage"[21] and then goes on to imagine what a changed cultural heritage might be like—e.g., imagining a four-lane highway painted through *Christina's World*. However, I do not believe he realizes the full significance of the issues at hand. If, as he supposes, hedonistic utilitarianism falls victim to a *reductio* by allowing that a plastic environment might be just as good or better than a living one, consistency requires that we reach the same judgment *re* the embodiment of cultural values argument. That argument, too, allows that a plastic environment might be just as good or better than a natural one, *if* the dominant value of our culture were to become plasticized.

I conclude this section, therefore, not by claiming to have shown that nonconscious natural objects do have a good or value of their own, independent of human interests. I only conclude that the principal arguments that might be advanced for thinking that we can reasonably account for our duties regarding the environment short of postulating such value in nature fail to do so. Thus, neither the possibility of, nor the need for, postulating that nonconscious natural objects have a value that is independent of human interests, has been rationally undermined.

V. INHERENT GOODNESS?

In this final section, I offer some tentative remarks about the nature of inherent goodness, emphasizing their tentativeness and incompleteness. I comment first on five different but related ideas.

(1) *The presence of inherent value in a natural object is independent of any awareness, interest, or appreciation of it by any conscious being.* This does not tell us what objects are inherently good or why, only that *if* an object is inherently good its value must *inhere in (be in)* the object itself. Inherent value is not conferred upon objects in the manner of an honorary degree. Like other properties in nature, it must be discovered. Contrary to the *Tractatus*, there *is* value *in* the world, if natural objects are inherently valuable.

(2) *The presence of inherent value in a natural object is a consequence of its possessing those other properties which it happens to possess.* This follows from (1), given the further assumption that inherent goodness is a consequential or supervenient property. By insisting that inherent goodness depends on an object's *own* properties, the point made in (1) that inherent goodness is a value possessed by the object independently of any awareness is reemphasized. *Its* goodness depends on *its* properties.

(3) *The inherent value of a natural object is an objective property of that object.* This differs from but is related to Sagoff's objectivity of the freedom and majesty of natural objects. Certain stretches of the Colorado River, for example, are free, not subjectively, but objectively. The freedom expressed by (or in) the river is an objective fact. But this goes beyond Sagoff's position by insisting that *the value of the river's being free* also is an objective property of the river. If the river is inherently good, in the sense explained in (1), then it is *a fact about the river* that it is good inherently.

(4) *The inherent value of a natural object is such that toward it the fitting attitude is one of admiring respect.* This brings out the appropriateness of regarding what is inherently valuable in a certain way and thus provides a way of connecting what is inherently valuable in the environment with an ideal of human nature. In part, the ideal in question bids us be appreciative of the values nature holds, not merely as a resource to be used in the name of human interests, but inherently. The ideal bids us, further, to regard what is inherently valuable with both admiration and respect. Admiration is fitting because not everything in nature is inherently valuable (what is is to be admired both because of its value *and* because of its comparative uniqueness). Respect is appropriate because this is a fitting attitude to have toward that which has value in its own right. One must realize that its being valuable is not contingent on one's happening to value it, so that to treat it *merely* as a means to human ends is to mistreat it. Such treatment shows a lack of respect for its being something which has value independently of these ends. Thus, I fall short of the ideal if I gratuitously destroy what has inherent value, or even if I regard it merely as having value only relative to human desires. But half the story about ideals of human nature remains untold if we leave out the part about the value inherent in those things toward which we can act in the ideal way. So it is vital to insist that our having ideals is neither to deny nor diminish the further point that this ideal requires postulating inherent value in nature, independently of these ideals.

(5) *The admiring respect of what is inherently valuable in nature gives rise to the preservation principle.* By the "preservation principle" I mean a principle of nondestruction, noninterference, and, generally, nonmeddling. By characterizing this in terms of a principle, moreover, I am emphasizing that preservation (letting be) be regarded as a moral imperative. Thus, if I regard wild stretches of the Colorado River as inherently valuable and regard these sections with admiring respect, I also think it wrong to destroy these sections of the river; I think one ought not to meddle in the river's affairs, as it were.

A difficult question to answer is whether the preservation principle gives us a principle of absolute or of prima facie duty. It is unclear how it can be absolute, for it appears conceivable that in some cases letting be what is at present inherently good in nature may lead to value diminution or loss in the future. For example, because of various sedimentary changes, a river which is now wild and free might in time be transformed into a small, muddy creek; thus, it might be necessary to override the preservation principle in order to preserve or increase what is inherently valuable in nature. However, even if the preservation principle is regarded as being only prima facie, it is still possible to agree on at least one point with those who regard it as absolute, i.e., the common rejection of the "human interests principle," which says:

> Whenever human beings can benefit more from overriding the preservation principle than if they observe it, the preservation principle ought to be overridden.

This principle *must* be rejected by anyone who accepts the preservation principle because it distorts the very conception of goodness underlying that principle. If the sort of value natural objects possess is inherent, then one fails to show a proper respect for these objects if one is willing to destroy them merely on the grounds that this would benefit human beings. Since such destruction is precisely what the human interests principle commits one to, one cannot *both* accept the preservation principle, absolute or prima facie, *and* also accept the human interests principle. The common enemy of all preservationists are those who accept the human interests principle.

This brief discussion of the preservation principle may also cast some light on the problem of making intelligible cross species value comparisons, e.g., in the case of the survival of caribou versus the economic development of wilderness. The point preservationists must keep in mind is that to ask how many caribou lives equals in value the disvalue of how much economic loss is unanswerable because it is an improper question. It confounds two incommensurable kinds of good, the inherent good of the caribou with the noninherent good of economic benefits. Indeed, because these kinds of good are incommensurable, a utilitarian or consequentialist environmental ethic, which endeavors to accommodate both kinds of goodness, is doomed to fail. The inherent value of the caribou cannot be cashed in in terms of human economic benefit, and such a theory ends up providing us with no clear moral direction. For the preservationist, the proper philosophical response to those who would uproot the environment in the name of human benefit is to say that they fail to understand the very notion of something being inherently good.

Two questions which I have not endeavored to answer are: (a) what, if anything in general, makes something inherently good, and (b) how can we know, if we can, what things are inherently good? The two questions are not unrelated. If we could establish that there is something (X) such that, whenever any object (Y) has X it is inherently good, we could then go on to try to establish how we can know that any object has X. Unfortunately, I now have very little to say about these questions, and what little I do have to say concerns only how not to answer them.

Two possible answers to question (a) merit mention. The first is that an object (X) is inherently good if it is good of its kind. This is a view I have assumed and argued for elsewhere,[22] but it now appears to me to be completely muddled. The concept of inherent goodness cannot be reduced to the notion of something being good of its kind, for though I believe that we can conceive of the goodness any X has, if X is good of its kind, as a value it has in its own right, there is no reason to believe that we ought to have the attitude of admiring respect toward what is (merely) good of its kind. A good murderer is good-of-his-kind, but is not thereby a proper object of admiring respect, and similarly in the case of natural objects. The type of inherent goodness required by an environmental ethic is conceptually distinct from being good of its kind.[23]

The second possible answer to (a) is that life makes something inherently good. To what extent this view is connected with Schweitzer's famous ethic of reverence for life, or with Kenneth Goodpaster's recent argument[24] for considering life as a necessary and sufficient condition of something being "morally considerable." I do not know, and I cannot here explore these matters in detail. But limiting the class of beings which have inherent value to the class of living beings seems to be an arbitrary decision and one that does not serve well as a basis for an environmental ethic. That it appears arbitrary is perhaps best seen by considering the case of beauty, since in nature, as in art, it is not essential to the beauty of an object to insist that something living be involved.

As for question (b), I have even less to say and that is negative also. My one point is that we cannot find out what is inherently good merely by finding out what those things are toward which we have admiring respect. All that this tells us is facts about the people who have this attitude. It does not tell us whether it is the fitting attitude to have. To put the point differently, we can be as mistaken in our judgment that something is inherently good as we can be in our judgment about how old or how heavy it is. Our feeling one way or another does not settle matters one way or the other.

How, then, are we to settle these matters? I wish I knew. I am not even certain that they can be settled in a rationally coherent way, and hence the tentativeness of my closing remarks. But more fundamentally, there is the earlier question about the very possibility of an environmental ethic. If I am right, the development of what can properly be called an environmental ethic requires that we postulate inherent value in nature. I have tried to say something about this variety of goodness as well as something about its role in an ethic of the environment. If my remarks have been intelligible and my arguments persuasive, then, though the project is far from complete, we at least know the direction in which we must move to make headway in environmental ethics, and that is no small advantage.

NOTES

1. By the expression *moral standing* I mean the following: X has moral standing if and only if X is a being such that we morally ought to determine how X will be affected in the course of determining whether we ought to perform a given act or adopt a given policy. In the present essay the question of whether beings having moral standing have rights can be regarded as an open question, though in my view they do. See my "An Examination and Defense of One Argument Concerning Animal Rights," *Inquiry* 22(1979): 189–219. See also in this regard Kenneth Goodpaster, "On Being Morally Considerable," *Journal of Philosophy* 75(1978): 308–325. Though the class of nonconscious beings includes artifacts and works of art, I normally have natural objects or collections of such objects in mind. For stylistic reasons I sometimes use the more general expression, *nonconscious objects*, and sometimes the more specific, *natural objects* or "collections of natural objects." Also for stylistic reasons I speak interchangeably of "our duties in regard to nature," "in regard to the environment," or "in regard to natural objects or collections of natural objects." I trust that no grievous conceptual errors or partisan causes will be found lodged in my taking this liberty with language.
2. L. S. Sumner, "A Matter of Life and Death," *Nous* 10 (1976):145–71.
3. Ibid., p. 164.
4. See in particular Peter Singer, *Animal Liberation* (New York: Random House, 1975) and Andrew Linzey, *Animal Rights* (London: SCM Press, 1976). For a critical assessment of this position as it is related to the topic of animal rights, see my essay "Examination and Defense," noted above.
5. See my article "Feinberg on What Sorts of Beings Can Have Rights," *Southern Journal of Philosophy* 14 (1976): 485–98, and "McCloskey on Why Animals Cannot Have Rights," *Philosophical Quarterly* 27 (1976): 251–57. For a defense of McCloskey's position, see R. G. Frey, "Interests and Animal Rights," *Philosophical Quarterly* 27 (1977): 254–59. But see also my reply to Frey, "Frey On Interests and Animal Rights," *Philosophical Quarterly* 27 (1977): 355–37. The occasion for this exchange is McCloskey's important essay, "Rights," *Philosophical Quarterly* 15 (1965): 115–27.
6. Singer in *Animal Liberation* would seem to be committed to this position. See especially pp. 8–9.
7. Singer, p. 8.
8. See my critical essay on Feinberg, footnote 9. But see also my discussion of inherent goodness in section 3 above.
9. Kant, *Lectures on Ethics*, "Duties to Animals and Spirits." Relevant portions are reprinted in *Animal Rights and Human Obligations*, ed. Tom Regan and Peter Singer (Englewood Cliffs: Prentice-Hall, 1976), pp. 122–23.
10. See G. E. Moore, *Principia Ethica* (Cambridge: University Press, 1903), p. 28.
11. My discussion of the utilitarian argument owes a good deal to Mark Sagoff's important essay, "On Preserving the Natural Environment," *Yale Law Journal* 84 (197): 205–67. I discuss Sagoff's own views below.
12. Martin Krieger, "What's Wrong with Plastic Trees?" *Science*, 179 (1973): 446–55, quotations on pp. 451 and 453; quoted by Sagoff, p. 206.
13. Sagoff, p. 206–7.
14. Krieger, p. 451; quoted by Sagoff, p. 207.
15. R. M. Hare, for example, defends utilitarianism in this manner. See his "Ethical Theory and Utilitarianism" in *Contemporary British Philosophy* 4, ed. H. D. Lewis (London, 1976).
16. Martin Krieger, "Six Propositions on the Poor and Pollution" *Policy Sciences* 1 (1970): 311–24; quotation on p. 318; quoted by Sagoff, p. 210.
17. Sagoff, p. 210.

18. Ibid., p. 229.
19. Ibid., p. 245.
20. W. D. Ross, *The Right and the Good* (Oxford: Clarendon Press, 1963), p. 41.
21. Sagoff, p. 259.
22. See my essay on Feinberg, footnote 9.
23. Thus, I do not retract my arguments against Feinberg as they relate to the idea of something's being good of its kind. What I do retract is the misidentification, on my part, of inherent goodness with this type of goodness. Recognizing that something is good of its kind does not call forth my admiring respect; recognizing its being inherently good does.
24. Goodpaster, "On Being Morally Considerable."

Advertising

Case Study

Toy Wars

MANUEL G. VELASQUEZ

Early in 1986, Tom Daner, president of the advertising company of Daner
Associates, was contacted by the sales manager of Crako Industries, Mike
Teal.[1] Crako Industries is a family-owned company that manufactures children's toys and had long been a favorite and important client of Daner
Associates. The sales manager of Crako Industries explained that the company had just developed a new toy helicopter. The toy was modeled on the
military helicopters that had been used in Vietnam and that had appeared
in the "Rambo" movies. Mike Teal explained that the toy was developed in
response to the craze for military toys that had been sweeping the nation in
the wake of the Rambo movies. The family-owned toy company had initially resisted moving into military toys, since members of the family objected to the violence associated with such toys. But as segments of the toy
market were increasingly taken over by military toys, the family came to
feel that entry into the military toy market was crucial for their business.
Consequently, they approved development of a line of military toys, hoping
that they were not entering the market too late. Mike Teal now wanted
Daner Associates to develop a television advertising campaign for the toy.

The toy helicopter Crako designers had developed was about one
and one-half feet long, battery-operated, and made of plastic and steel.
Mounted to the sides were detachable replicas of machine guns and a detachable stretcher modeled on the stretchers used to lift wounded soldiers
from a battlefield. Mike Teal of Crako explained that they were trying to
develop a toy that had to be perceived as "more macho" than the top-
selling "G. I. Joe" line of toys. If the company was to compete successfully
in today's toy market, according to the sales manager, it would have to
adopt an advertising approach that was even "meaner and tougher" than
what other companies were doing. Consequently, he continued, the advertising clips developed by Daner Associates would have to be "mean and
macho." Television advertisements for the toy, he suggested, might show

the helicopter swooping over buildings and blowing them up. The more violence and mayhem the ads suggested, the better. Crako Industries was relying heavily on sales from the new toy, and some Crako managers felt that the company's future might depend on the success of this toy.

Tom Daner was unwilling to have his company develop television advertisements that would increase what he already felt was too much violence in television aimed at children. In particular, he recalled a television ad for a tricycle with a replica machine gun mounted on the handlebars. The commercial showed the tricycle being pedaled through the woods by a small boy as he chased several other boys fleeing before him over a dirt path. At one point the camera closed in over the shoulder of the boy, focused through the gun sight, and showed the gun sight apparently trying to aim at the backs of the boys as they fled before the tricycle's machine gun. Ads of that sort had disturbed Tom Daner and had led him to think that advertisers should find other ways of promoting these toys. He suggested, therefore, that instead of promoting the Crako helicopter through violence, it should be presented in some other manner. When Teal asked what he had in mind, Tom was forced to reply that he didn't know. But at any rate, Tom pointed out, the three television networks would not accept a violent commercial aimed at children. All three networks adhered to an advertising code that prohibited violent, intense, or unrealistic advertisements aimed at children.

This seemed no real obstacle to Teal, however. Although the networks might turn down children's ads when they were too violent, local television stations were not as squeamish. Local television stations around the country regularly accepted ads aimed at children that the networks had rejected as too violent. The local stations inserted the ads as spots on their non-network programming, thereby circumventing the Advertising Codes of the three national networks. Daner Associates would simply have to place the ads they developed for the Crako helicopter through local television stations around the country. Mike Teal was firm: if Daner Associates would not or could not develop a "mean and tough" ad campaign, the toy company would move their account to an advertiser who would. Reluctantly, Tom Daner agreed to develop the advertising campaign. Crako Industries accounted for $1 million of Daner's total revenues.

Like Crako Industries, Daner Associates is also a family-owned business. Started by his father almost fifty years ago, the advertising firm that Tom Daner now ran had grown dramatically under his leadership. In 1975 the business had grossed $3 million; ten years later it had revenues of $25 million and provided a full line of advertising services. The company was divided into three departments (Creative, Media, and Account Executive), each of which had about 12 employees. Tom Daner credited much of the company's success to the many new people he had hired, especially a group with M.B.A.s who had developed new marketing strategies based on more thorough market and consumer analyses. Most decisions, however, were made by a five-person executive committee consisting of Tom Daner, the Senior Account Manager, and the three department heads. As owner-president, Tom's view tended to color most decisions, producing what one of the members called a "benevolent dictatorship." Tom himself was an enthusiastic, congenial, intelligent, and widely read person. During college he had considered becoming a missionary priest but had changed his mind and was now married and the father of three daughters. His personal heros included Thomas Merton, Albert Schweitzer, and Tom Dooley.

When Tom Daner presented the Crako deal to his Executive Committee, he found they did not share his misgivings. The other Committee members felt that Daner Associates should give Crako exactly the kind of ad Crako wanted: one with a heavy content of violence. Moreover, the writers and artists in the Creative Department were enthused with the prospect of letting their imaginations loose on the project, several feeling that they could easily produce an attention-grabbing ad by "out-violencing" current television programming. The Creative Department, in fact, quickly produced a copy-script that called for videos showing the helicopter "flying out of the sky with machine guns blazing" at a jungle village below. This kind of ad, they felt, was exactly what they were being asked to produce by their client, Crako Industries.

But after viewing the copy, Tom Daner refused to use it. They should produce an ad, he insisted, that would meet their client's needs but that would also meet the guidelines of the national networks. The ad should not glorify violence and war but should somehow support cooperation and family values. Disappointed and somewhat frustrated, the Creative Department went back to work. A few days later they presented a second proposal: an ad that would show the toy helicopter flying through the family room of a home as a little boy plays with it; then the scene shifts to show the boy on a rock rising from the floor of the family room; the helicopter swoops down and picks up the boy as though rescuing him from the rock where he had been stranded. Although the Creative Department was mildly pleased with their attempt, they felt it was too "tame." Tom liked it, however, and a version of the ad was filmed.

A few weeks later Tom Daner met with Mike Teal and his team and showed them the film. The viewing was not a success. Teal turned down the ad. Referring to the network regulations, which other toy advertisements were breaking as frequently as motorists broke the 55 mile per hour speed law, he said, "That commercial is going only 55 miles an hour when I want one that goes 75." If the next version was not "tougher and meaner," Crako Industries would be forced to look elsewhere.

Disappointed, Tom Daner returned to the people in his Creative Department and told them to go ahead with designing the kind of ad they had originally wanted: "I don't have any idea what else to do." In a short time the Creative Department had an ad proposal on his desk that called for scenes showing the helicopter blowing up villages. Shortly afterwards a small set was constructed depicting a jungle village sitting next to a bridge stretching over a river. The ad was filmed using the jungle set as a background.

When Tom saw the result he was not happy. He decided to meet with his Creative Department and air his feelings. "The issue here," he said, "is basically the issue of violence. Do we really want to present toys as instruments for beating up people? This ad is going to promote aggression and violence. It will glorify dominance and do it with kids who are terrifically impressionable. Do we really want to do this?" The members of the Creative Department, however, responded that they were merely giving their client what the client wanted. That client, moreover, was an important account. The client wanted an aggressive "macho" ad, and that was what they were providing. The ad might violate the regulations of the television networks, but there were ways to get around the networks. Moreover, they said, every other advertising firm in the business was breaking the limits against violence set by the networks. Tom made one last try: why not market the toy as an adventure and fantasy toy? Film the ad again, he suggested, using the same jungle backdrop. But instead of showing the helicopter shooting at a burning village, show it flying in to rescue people from the burning village. Create an ad that shows excitement, adventure, and fantasy, but no aggression. "I was trying," he said later, "to figure out a new way of approaching this kind of advertising. We have to follow the market or we can go out of business trying to moralize to the market. But why not try a new approach? Why not promote toys as instruments that expand the child's imagination in a way that is positive and that promotes cooperative values instead of violence and aggression?"

A new film version of the ad was made, now showing the helicopter flying over the jungle set. Quick shots and heightened background music give the impression of excitement and danger. The helicopter flies dramatically through the jungle and over a river and bridge to rescue a boy from a flaming village. As lights flash and shoot haphazardly through the scene the helicopter rises and escapes into the sky. The final ad was clearly exciting and intense. And it promoted saving of life instead of violence against life.

It was clear when the final version was shot, however, that it would not clear the network censors. Network guidelines require that sets in children's ads must depict things that are within the reach of most children so that they do not create unrealistic expectations. Clearly the elaborate jungle set (which cost $25,000 to construct) was not within the reach of most children, and consequently most children would not be able to recreate the scene of the ad by buying the toy. Moreover, network regulations stipulate that in children's ads scenes must be filmed with normal lighting that does not create undue intensity. Again clearly the helicopter ad, which created excitement by using quick changes of light and fast cuts, did not fall within these guidelines.

After reviewing the film Tom Daner reflected on some last-minute instructions Crako's sales manager had given him when he had been shown the first version of the ad: The television ad should show things being blown up by the guns of the little helicopter and perhaps even some blood on the fuselage of the toy; the ad had to be violent. Now Tom had to make a decision. Should he risk the account by submitting only the rescue mission ad? Or should he let Teal also see the ad that showed the helicopter shooting up the village, knowing that he would probably prefer that version if he saw it? And was the rescue mission ad really that much different from the ad that showed the shooting of the village? Did it matter that the rescue mission ad still violated some of the network regulations? What if he offered Teal only the rescue mission ad and Teal accepted the "rescue approach" but demanded he make it more violent; should he give in? And should Tom risk launching an ad campaign that was based on this new untested approach? What if the ad failed to sell the Crako toy? Was it right to experiment with a client's product, especially a product that was so important to the future of the client's business? Tom was unsure what he should do. He wanted to show Teal only the rescue mission commercial, but he felt he first had to resolve these questions in his own mind.

NOTE

1. Although the events described in this case are real, all names of the individuals and the companies involved are fictitious; in addition, several details have been altered to disguise the identity of participants.

The Dependence Effect

JOHN KENNETH GALBRAITH

The theory of consumer demand, as it is now widely accepted, is based on two broad propositions, neither of them quite explicit but both extremely important for the present value system of economists. The first is that the urgency of wants does not diminish appreciably as more of them are satisfied or, to put the matter more precisely, to the extent that this happens it is not demonstrable and not a matter of any interest to economists or for economic policy. When man has satisfied his physical needs, then psychologically grounded desires take over. These can never be satisfied or, in any case, no progress can be proved. The concept of satiation has very little standing in economics. It is neither useful nor scientific to speculate on the comparative cravings of the stomach and the mind.

The second proposition is that wants originate in the personality of the consumer or, in any case, that they are given data for the economist. The latter's task is merely to seek their satisfaction. He has no need to inquire how these wants are formed. His function is sufficiently fulfilled by maximizing the goods that supply the wants.

The notion that wants do not become less urgent the more amply the individual is supplied is broadly repugnant to common sense. It is something to be believed only by those who wish to believe. Yet the conventional wisdom must be tackled on its own terrain. Intertemporal comparisons of an individual's state of mind do rest on doubtful grounds. Who can say for sure that the deprivation which afflicts him with hunger is more painful than the deprivation which afflicts him with envy of his neighbour's new car? In the time that has passed since he was poor his soul may have become subject to a new and deeper searing. And where a society is concerned, comparisons between marginal satisfactions when it is poor and those when it is affluent will involve not only the same individual at different times but different individuals at different times. The scholar who wishes to believe that with increasing affluence there is no reduction in the urgency of desires and goods is not without points for debate. However plausible the case against him, it cannot be proved. In the defence of the conventional wisdom this amounts almost to invulnerability.

However, there is a flaw in the case. If the individual's wants are to be urgent they must be original with oneself. They cannot be urgent if they must be contrived for him. And above all they must not be contrived by the process of production by which they are satisfied. For this means that the whole case for the urgency of production, based on the urgency of wants, falls to the ground. One cannot defend production as satisfying wants if that production creates the wants.

Were it so that man on arising each morning was assailed by demons which instilled in him a passion sometimes for silk shirts, sometimes for kitchenware, sometimes for chamber-pots, and sometimes for orange squash, there would be every reason to applaud the effort to find the goods, however odd, that quenched this flame. But should it be that his passion was the result of his first having cultivated the demons, and should it also be that his passion was the result of his first having cultivated the demons, and should it also be that his effort to allay it stirred the demons to ever greater and greater effort, there would be question as to how rational was his solution. Unless restrained by conventional attitudes, he might wonder if the solution lay with more goods or fewer demons.

So it is that if production creates the wants it seeks to satisfy, or if the wants emerge *pari passu* with the production, then the urgency of the wants can no longer be used to defend the urgency of the production. Production only fills a void that it has itself created.

The even more direct link between production and wants is provided by the institutions of modern advertising and salesmanship. These cannot be reconciled with the notion of independently determined devices, for their central function is to create desires—to bring into being wants that previously did not exist.[1] This is accomplished by the producer of the goods or at his behest. A broad empirical relationship exists between what is spent on production of consumers' goods and what is spent in synthesizing the desires for that production. A new consumer product must be introduced with a suitable advertising campaign to arouse an interest in it. The path for an expansion of output must be paved by a suitable expansion in the advertising budget. Outlays for the manufacturing of a product are not more important in the strategy of modern business enterprise than outlays for the manufacturing of demand for the product. None of this is novel. All would be regarded as elementary by the most retarded student in the nation's most primitive school of business administration. The cost of this want formation is formidable. In 1956 total advertising expenditure—though, as noted, not all of it may be assigned to the synthesis of wants—amounted to about ten thousand million dollars. For some years it had been increasing at a rate in excess of a thousand million dollars a year. Obviously, such outlays must be integrated with the theory of consumer demand. They are too big to be ignored.

But such integration means recognizing that wants are dependent on production. It accords to the producer the function both of making the goods and of making the desires for them. It recognizes that production, not only passively through emulation, but actively through advertising and related activities, creates the wants it seeks to satisfy.

The businessman and the lay reader will be puzzled over the emphasis which I give to a seemingly obvious point. The point is indeed obvious. But it is one which, to a singular degree, economists have resisted. They have sensed, as the layman does not, the damage to established ideas which lurks in these relationships. As a result, incredibly, they have closed their eyes (and ears) to the most obtrusive of all economic phenomena, namely modern want creation.

This is not to say that the evidence affirming the dependence of wants on advertising has been entirely ignored. It is one reason why advertising has so long been regarded with such uneasiness by economists. Here is something which cannot be accommodated easily to existing theory. More pervious scholars have speculated on the urgency of desires which are so obviously the fruit of such expensively contrived campaigns for popular attention. Is a new breakfast cereal or detergent so much wanted if so much must be spent to compel in the consumer the sense of want? But there has been little tendency to go on to examine the implications of this for the theory of consumer demand and even less for the importance of production and productive efficiency. These have remained sacrosanct. More often the uneasiness has been manifested in a general disapproval of advertising and advertising men, leading to the occasional suggestion that they shouldn't exist. Such suggestions have usually been ill received.

And so the notion of independently determined wants still survives. In the face of all the forces of modern salesmanship it still rules, almost undefiled, in the textbooks. And it still remains the economist's mission— and on few matters is the pedagogy so firm—to seek unquestioningly the means for filling these wants. This being so, production remains of prime urgency. We have here, perhaps, the ultimate triumph of the conventional wisdom in its resistance to the evidence of the eyes. To equal it one must imagine a humanitarian who was long ago persuaded of the grievous shortage of hospital facilities in the town. He continues to importune the passers-by for money for more beds and refuses to notice that the town doctor is deftly knocking over pedestrians with his car to keep up the occupancy.

And in unravelling the complex we should always be careful not to overlook the obvious. The fact that wants can be synthesized by advertising, catalysed by salesmanship, and shaped by the discreet manipulations of the persuaders shows that they are not very urgent. A man who is hungry need never be told of his need for food. If he is inspired by his appetite, he is immune to the influence of Messrs. Batten, Barton, Durstine and Osborn. The latter are effective only with those who are so far removed from physical want that they do not already know what they want. In this state alone men are open to persuasion.

The general conclusion of these pages is of such importance for this essay that it had perhaps best be put with some formality. As a society becomes increasingly affluent, wants are increasingly created by the process by which they are satisfied. This may operate passively. Increases in consumption, the counterpart of increases in production, act by suggestion or emulation to create wants. Or producers may proceed actively to create wants through advertising and salesmanship. Wants thus come to depend on output. In technical terms it can no longer be assumed that welfare is greater at an all-around higher level of production than at a lower one. It may be the same. The higher level of production has, merely, a higher level of want creation necessitating a higher level of want satisfaction. There will be frequent occasion to refer to the way wants depend on the process by which they are satisfied. It will be convenient to call it the Dependence Effect.

The final problem of the productive society is what it produces. This manifests itself in an implacable tendency to provide an opulent supply of some things and a niggardly yield of others. This disparity carries to the point where it is a cause of social discomfort and social unhealth. The line which divides our area of wealth from our area of poverty is roughly that which divides privately produced and marketed goods and services from publicly rendered services. Our wealth in the first is not only in startling contrast with the meagreness of the latter, but our wealth in privately produced goods is, to a marked degree, the cause of crisis in the supply of public services. For we have failed to see the importance, indeed the urgent need, of maintaining a balance between the two.

This disparity between our flow of private and public goods and services is no matter of subjective judgment. On the contrary, it is the source of the most extensive comment which only stops short of the direct contrast being made here. In the years following World War II, the papers of any major city—those of New York were an excellent example—told daily of the shortages and shortcomings in the elementary municipal and metropolitan services. The schools were old and overcrowded. The police force was under strength and underpaid. The parks and playgrounds were insufficient. Streets and empty lots were filthy, and the sanitation staff was underequipped and in need of men. Access to the city by those who work there was uncertain and painful and becoming more so. Internal transportation was overcrowded, unhealthful, and dirty. So was the air. Parking on the streets had to be prohibited, and there was no space elsewhere. These deficiencies were not in new and novel services but in old and established ones. Cities have long swept their streets, helped their people move around, educated them, kept order, and provided horse rails for vehicles which sought to pause. That their residents should have a non-toxic supply of air suggests no revolutionary dalliance with socialism.

The contrast was and remains evident not alone to those who read. The family which takes its mauve and cerise, air-conditioned, power-steered, and power-braked car out for a tour passes through cities that are badly paved, made hideous by litter, blighted buildings, billboards, and posts for wires that should long since have been put underground. They pass on into a countryside that has been rendered largely invisible by commercial art. (The goods which the latter advertise have an absolute priority in our value system. Such aesthetic considerations as a view of the countryside accordingly come second. On such matters we are consistent.) They picnic on exquisitely packaged food from a portable icebox by a polluted stream and go on to spend the night at a park which is a menace to public health and morals. Just before dozing off on an air-mattress, beneath a nylon tent, amid the stench of decaying refuse, they may reflect vaguely on the curious unevenness of their blessings. Is this, indeed, the American genius?

The case for social balance has, so far, been put negatively. Failure to keep public services in minimal relation to private production and use of goods is a cause of social disorder or impairs economic performance. The matter may now be put affirmatively. By failing to exploit the opportunity to expand public production we are missing opportunities for enjoyment which otherwise we might have had. Presumably a community can be as well rewarded by buying better schools or better parks as by buying bigger cars. By concentrating on the latter rather than the former it is failing to maximize its satisfactions. As with schools in the community, so with public services over the country at large. It is scarcely sensible that we sould satisfy our wants in private goods with reckless abundance, while in the case of public goods, on the evidence of the eye, we practice extreme self-denial. So, far from systematically exploiting the opportunities to derive use and pleasure from these services, we do not supply what would keep us out of trouble.

The conventional wisdom holds that the community, large or small, makes a decision as to how much it will devote to its public services. This decision is arrived at by democratic process. Subject to the imperfections and uncertainties of democracy, people decide how much of their private income and goods they will surrender in order to have public services of which they are in greater need. Thus there is a balance, however rough, in the enjoyments to be had from private goods and services and those rendered by public authority.

It will be obvious, however, that this view depends on the notion of independently determined consumer wants. In such a world one could with some reason defend the doctrine that the consumer, as a voter, makes an independent choice between public and private goods. But given the dependence effect—given that consumer wants are created by the process by which they are satisfied—the consumer makes no such choice. He is subject to the forces of advertising and emulation by which production creates its own demand. Advertising operates exclusively, and emulation mainly, on behalf of privately produced goods and services.[2] Since management and emulative effects operate on behalf of private production, public services will have an inherent tendency to lag behind. Car demand which is expensively synthesized will inevitably have a much larger claim on income than parks or public health or even roads where no such influence operates. The engines of mass communication, in their highest state of development, assail the eyes and ears of the community on behalf of more beer but not of more schools. Even in the conventional wisdom it will scarcely be contended that this leads to an equal choice between the two.

The competition is especially unequal for new products and services. Every corner of the public psyche is canvassed by some of the nation's most talented citizens to see if the desire for some merchantable product can be cultivated. No similar process operates on behalf of the nonmerchantable services of the state. Indeed, while we take the cultivation of new private wants for granted we would be measurably shocked to see it applied to public services. The scientist or engineer or advertising man who devotes himself to developing a new carburetor, cleanser, or depilatory for which the public recognizes no need and will feel none until an advertising campaign arouses it, is one of the valued members of our society. A politician or a public servant who dreams up a new public service is a wastrel. Few public offences are more reprehensible.

So much for the influences which operate on the decision between public and private production. The calm decision between public and private consumption pictured by the conventional wisdom is, in fact, a remarkable example of the error which arises from viewing social behaviour out of context. The inherent tendency will always be for public services to fall behind private production. We have here the first of the causes of social imbalance.

NOTES

1. Advertising is not a simple phenomenon. It is also important in competitive strategy and what creation is, ordinarily, a complementary result of efforts to shift the demand curve of the individual firm at the expense of others or (less importantly, I think) to change its shape by increasing the degree of product differentiation. Some of the failure of economists to identify advertising with want creation may be attributed to the undue attention that its use in purely competitive strategy has attracted. It should be noted, however, that the competitive manipulation of consumer desire is only possible, at least on any appreciable scale, when such need is not strongly felt.
2. Emulation does operate between communities. A new school or a new highway in one community does exert pressure on others to remain abreast. However, as compared with the pervasive effects of emulation in extending the demand for privately produced consumers' goods there will be agreement, I think, that this intercommunity effect is probably small.

Advertising and Behavior Control

ROBERT L. ARRINGTON

Consider the following advertisements:

1. "A woman in *Distinction Foundations* is so beautiful that all other women want to kill her."
2. Pongo Peach color from Revlon comes "from east of the sun . . . west of the moon, where each tomorrow dawns." It is "succulent on your lips" and

Robert L. Arrington, "Advertising and Behavior Control," *Journal of Business Ethics*, Vol. 1, No. 1, February 1982, pp. 3–12. Copyright © 1982 by D. Reidel Publishing Company. Reprinted by permission of Kluwer Academic Publishers.

"sizzling on your finger tips (And on your toes, goodness knows)." Let it be your "adventure in paradise."

3. "Musk by English Leather—The Civilized Way to Roar."

4. "Increase the value of your holdings. Old Charter Bourbon Whiskey—The Final Step Up."

5. Last Call Smirnoff Style: "They'd never really miss us, and it's kind of late already, and its quite a long way, and I could build a fire, and you're looking very beautiful, and we could have another martini, and its awfully nice just being home . . . you think?"

6. A Christmas Prayer. "Let us pray that the blessings of peace be ours—the peace to build and grow, to live in harmony and sympathy with others, and to plan for the future with confidence." New York Life Insurance Company.

These are instances of what is called puffery—the practice by a seller of making exaggerated, highly fanciful, or suggestive claims about a product or service. Puffery, within ill-defined limits, is legal. It is considered a legitimate, necessary, and very successful tool of the advertising industry. Puffery is not just bragging; it is bragging carefully designed to achieve a very definite effect. Using the techniques of so-called motivational research, advertising firms first identify our often hidden needs (for security, conformity, oral stimulation) and our desires (for power, sexual dominance and dalliance, adventure) and then they design ads which respond to these needs and desires. By associating a product, for which we may have little or no direct need or desire, with symbols reflecting the fulfillment of these other, often subterranean interests, the advertisement can quickly generate large numbers of consumers eager to purchase the product advertised. What woman in the sexual race of life could resist a foundation which would turn other women envious to the point of homicide? Who can turn down an adventure in paradise, east of the sun where tomorrow dawns? Who doesn't want to be civilized and thoroughly libidinous at the same time? Be at the pinnacle of success—drink Old Charter. Or stay at home and dally a bit—with Smirnoff. And let us pray for a secure and predictable future, provided for by New York Life, God willing. It doesn't take very much motivational research to see the point of these sales pitches. Others are perhaps a little less obvious. The need to feel secure in one's home at night can be used to sell window air conditioners, which drown out small noises and provide a friendly, dependable companion. The fact that baking a cake is symbolic of giving birth to a baby used to prompt advertisements for cake mixes which glamorized the "creative" housewife. And other strategies, for example involving cigar symbolism, are a bit too crude to mention, but are nevertheless very effective.

Don't such uses of puffery amount to manipulation, exploitation, or downright control? In his very popular book *The Hidden Persuaders*, Vance Packard points out that a number of people in the advertising world have frankly admitted as much:

As early as 1941 Dr. Dichter (an influential advertising consultant) was exhorting ad agencies to recognize themselves for what they actually were—"one of the most advanced laboratories in psychology." He said the successful ad agency "manipulates human motivations and desires and develops a need for goods with which the public has at one time been unfamiliar—perhaps even undesirous of purchasing." The following year *Advertising Agency* carried an ad man's statement that psychology not only holds a promise for understanding people but "ultimately for controlling their behavior."[1]

Such statements lead Packard to remark: "With all this interest in manipulating the customer's subconscious, the old slogan 'let the buyer beware' began taking on a new and more profound meaning."[2]

B. F. Skinner, the high priest of behaviorism, has expressed a similar assessment of advertising and related marketing techniques. Why, he asks, do we buy a certain kind of car?

> Perhaps our favorite TV program is sponsored by the manufacturer of that car. Perhaps we have seen pictures of many beautiful or prestigeful persons driving it—in pleasant or glamorous places. Perhaps the car has been designed with respect to our motivational patterns: the device on the hood is a phallic symbol; or the horsepower has been stepped up to please our competitive spirit in enabling us to pass other cars swiftly (or, as the advertisements say, 'safely'). The concept of freedom that has emerged as part of the cultural practice of our group makes little or no provision for recognizing or dealing with these kinds of control.[3]

In purchasing a car we may think we are free, Skinner is claiming, when in fact our act is completely controlled by factors in our environment and in our history of reinforcement. Advertising is one such factor.

A look at some other advertising techniques may reinforce the suspicion that Madison Avenue controls us like so many puppets. T.V. watchers surely have noticed that some of the more repugnant ads are shown over and over again, *ad nauseam*. My favorite, or most hated, is the one about A-1 Steak Sauce which goes something like this: Now, ladies and gentlemen, what *is* hamburger? It has succeeded in destroying my taste for hamburger, but it has surely drilled the name of A-1 Sauce into my head. And that is the point of it. Its very repetitiousness has generated what ad theorists call *information*. In this case it is indirect information, information derived not from the content of what is said but from the fact that it is said so often and so vividly that it sticks in one's mind—i.e., the information yield has increased. And not only do I always remember A-1 Sauce when I go to the grocers, I tend to assume that any product advertised so often has to be good—and so I usually buy a bottle of the stuff.

Still another technique: On a recent show of the television program "Hard Choices" it was demonstrated how subliminal suggestion can be used to control customers. In a New Orleans department store, messages to the effect that shoplifting is wrong, illegal, and subject to punishment were blended into the Muzak background music and masked so as not to be consciously audible. The store reported a dramatic drop in shoplifting. The program host conjectured whether a logical extension of this technique would be to broadcast subliminal advertising messages to the effect that the store's $15.99 sweater special is the "bargain of a lifetime." Actually, this application of subliminal suggestion to advertising has already taken place. Years ago in New Jersey a cinema was reported to have flashed subthreshold ice cream ads onto the screen during regular showings of the film—and, yes, the concession stand did a landslide business.

Puffery, indirect information transfer, subliminal advertising—are these techniques of manipulation and control whose success shows that many of us have forfeited our autonomy and become a community, or herd, of packaged souls?[4] The business world and the advertising industry certainly reject this interpretation of their efforts. *Business Week*, for example, dismissed the charge that the science of behavior, as utilized by advertising, is engaged in human engineering and manipulation. It editorialized to the effect that "it is hard to find anything very sinister about a science whose principle conclusion is that you get along with people by giving them what they want."[5] The theme is familiar: businesses just give the consumer what he/she wants; if they didn't they wouldn't stay in business very long. Proof that the consumer wants the products advertised is given by the fact that he buys them, and indeed often returns to buy them again and again.

The techniques of advertising we are discussing have had their more intellectual defenders as well. For example, Theodore Levitt, Professor of Business Administration at the Harvard Business School, has defended the practice of puffery and the use of techniques depending on motivational research.[6] What would be the consequences, he asks us, of deleting all exaggerated claims and fanciful associations from advertisements? We would be left with literal descriptions of the empirical characteristics of products and their functions. Cosmetics would be presented as facial and bodily lotions and powders which produce certain odor and color changes; they would no longer offer hope or adventure. In addition to the fact that these products would not then sell as well, they would not, according to Levitt, please us as much either. For it is hope and adventure we want when we buy them. We want automobiles not just for transportation, but for the feelings of power and status they give us. Quoting T. S. Eliot to the effect that "Human kind cannot bear very much reality," Levitt argues that advertising is an effort to "transcend nature in the raw," to "augment what nature has so crudely fashioned." He maintains that "everybody everywhere wants to modify, transform, embellish, enrich and reconstruct the world around him." Commerce takes the same liberty with reality as the artist and the priest—in all three instances the purpose is "to influence the audience by creating illusions, symbols, and implications that promise more than pure functionality." For example, "to amplify the temple in men's eyes, (men of cloth) have, very realistically, systematically sanctioned the embellishment of the houses of the gods with the same kind of luxurious design and expensive decoration that Detroit puts into a Cadillac." A poem, a temple, a Cadillac—they all elevate our spirits, offering imaginative promises and symbolic interpretations of our mundane activities. Seen in this light, Levitt claims, "Embellishment and distortion are among advertising's legitimate and socially desirable purposes." To reject these techniques of advertising would be "to deny man's honest needs and values."

Phillip Nelson, a Professor of Economics at SUNY-Binghamton, has developed an interesting defense of indirect information advertising.[7] He argues that even when the message (the direct information) is not credible, the fact that the brand is advertised, and advertised frequently, is valuable indirect information for the consumer. The reason for this is that the brands advertised most are more likely to be better buys—losers won't be advertised a lot, for it simply wouldn't pay to do so. Thus even if the advertising claims made for a widely advertised product are empty, the consumer reaps the benefit of the indirect information which shows the product to be a good buy. Nelson goes so far as to say that advertising, seen as information and especially as indirect information, does not require an intelligent human response. If the indirect information has been received and has had its impact, the consumer will purchase the better buy even if his explicit reason for doing so is silly, e.g., he naively believes an endorsement of the product by a celebrity. Even though his behavior is overtly irrational, by acting on the indirect information he is nevertheless doing what he ought to do, i.e., getting his money's worth. "'Irrationality' is rational," Nelson writes, "if it is cost-free."

I don't know of any attempt to defend the use of subliminal suggestion in advertising, but I can imagine one form such an attempt might take. Advertising information, even if perceived below the level of conscious awareness, must appeal to some desire on the part of the audience if it is to trigger a purchasing response. Just as the admonition not to shoplift speaks directly to the superego, the sexual virtues of TR-7's, Pongo Peach, and Betty Crocker cake mix present themselves directly to the id, bypassing the pesky reality principle of the ego. With a little help from our advertising friends, we may remove a few of the discontents of civilization and perhaps even enter into the paradise of polymorphous perversity.

The defense of advertising which suggests that advertising simply is information which allows us to purchase what we want, has in turn been challenged. Does business, largely through its advertising efforts, really make available to the consumer what he/she desires and demands? John Kenneth Galbraith has denied that the matter is as straightforward as this.[8] In his opinion the desires to which business is supposed to respond, far from being original to the consumer, are often themselves created by business. The producers make both the product and the desire for it, and the "central function" of advertising is "to create desires." Galbraith coins the term "The Dependence Effect" to designate the way wants depend on the same process by which they are satisfied.

David Braybrooke has argued in similar and related ways.[9] Even though the consumer is, in a sense, the final authority concerning what he wants, he may come to see, according to Braybrooke, that he was mistaken in wanting what he did. The statement "I want x," he tells us, is not incorrigible but is "ripe for revision." If the consumer had more objective information than he is provided by product puffing, if his values had not been mixed up by motivational research strategies (e.g., the confusion of sexual and automotive values), and if he had an expanded set of choices instead of the limited set offered by profit-hungry corporations, then he might want something quite different from what he presently wants. This shows, Braybrooke thinks, the extent to which the consumer's wants are a function of advertising and not necessarily representative of his real or true wants.

The central issue which emerges between the above critics and defenders of advertising is this: do the advertising techniques we have discussed involve a violation of human autonomy and a manipulation and control of consumer behavior, *or* do they simply provide an efficient and cost-effective means of giving the consumer information on the basis of which he or she makes a free choice? Is advertising information, or creation of desire?

To answer this question we need a better conceptual grasp of what is involved in the notion of autonomy. This is a complex, multifaceted concept, and we need to approach it through the more determinate notions of (a) autonomous desire, (b) rational desire and choice, (c) free choice, and (d) control or manipulation. In what follows I shall offer some tentative and very incomplete analyses of these concepts and apply the results to the case of advertising.

(a) AUTONOMOUS DESIRE

Imagine that I am watching T.V. and see an ad for Grecian Formula 16. The thought occurs to me that if I purchase some and apply it to my beard, I will soon look younger—in fact I might even be myself again. Suddenly I want to be myself! I want to be young again! So I rush out and buy a bottle. This is our question: was the desire to be younger manufactured by the commercial, or was it 'original to me' and truly mine? Was it autonomous or not?

F. A. von Hayek has argued plausibly that we should not equate nonautonomous desires, desires which are not original to me or truly mine, with those which are culturally induced.[10] If we did equate the two, he points out, then the desires for music, art, and knowledge could not properly be attributed to a person as original to him, for these are surely induced culturally. The only desires a person would really have as his own in this case would be the purely physical ones for food, shelter, sex, etc. But if we reject the equation of the nonautonomous and the culturally induced, as von Hayek would have us do, then the mere fact that my desire to be young again is caused by the T.V. commercial—surely an instrument of popular culture transmission—does not in and of itself show that this is not my own, autonomous desire. Moreover, even if I never before felt the need to look young, it doesn't follow that this new desire is any less mine. I haven't always liked 1969 Aloxe Corton Burgundy or the music of Satie, but when the desires for these things first hit me, they were truly mine.

This shows that there is something wrong in setting up the issue over advertising and behavior control as a question whether our desires are truly ours *or* are created in us by advertisements. Induced and autonomous desires do not separate into two mutually exclusive classes. To obtain a better understanding of autonomous and nonautonomous desires, let us consider some cases of a desire which a person does not *acknowledge* to be his own even though he *feels* it. The kleptomaniac has a desire to steal which in many instances he repudiates, seeking by treatment to rid himself of it. And if I were suddenly overtaken by a desire to attend an REO concert, I would immediately disown this desire, claiming possession or momentary madness. These are examples of desires which one might have but with which one would not identify. They are experienced as foreign to one's character or personality. Often a person will have what Harry Frankfurt calls a second-order desire, that is to say, a desire *not* to have another desire.[11] In such cases, the first-order desire is thought of as being nonautonomous, imposed on one. When on the contrary a person has a second-order desire to maintain and fulfill a first-order desire, then the first-order desire is truly his own, autonomous, original to him. So there is in fact a distinction between desires which are the agent's own and those which are not, but this is not the same as the distinction between desires which are innate to the agent and those which are externally induced.

If we apply the autonomous/nonautonomous distinction derived from Frankfurt to the desires brought about by advertising, does this show that advertising is responsible for creating desires which are not truly the agent's own? Not necessarily, and indeed not often. There may be some desires I feel which I have picked up from advertising and which I disown—for instance, my desire for A-1 Steak Sauce. If I act on these desires it can be said that I have been led by advertising to act in a way foreign to my nature. In these cases my autonomy has been violated. But most of the desires induced by advertising I fully accept, and hence most of these desires are autonomous. The most vivid demonstration of this is that I often return to purchase the same product over and over again, without regret or remorse. And when I don't, it is more likely that the desire has just faded than that I have repudiated it. Hence, while advertising may violate my autonomy by leading me to act on desires which are not truly mine, this seems to be the exceptional case.

Note that this conclusion applies equally well to the case of subliminal advertising. This may generate subconscious desires which lead to purchases, and the act of purchasing these goods may be inconsistent with other conscious desires I have, in which case I might repudiate my behavior and by implication the subconscious cause of it. But my subconscious desires may not be inconsistent in this way with my conscious ones; my id may be cooperative and benign rather than hostile and malign. Here again, then, advertising may or may not produce desires which are 'not truly mine'.

What are we to say in response to Braybrooke's argument that insofar as we might choose differently if advertisers gave us better information and more options, it follows that the desires we have are to be attributed more to advertising than to our own real inclinations? This claim seems empty. It amounts to saying that if the world we lived in, and we ourselves, were different, then we would want different things. This is surely true, but it is equally true of our desire for shelter as of our desire for Grecian Formula 16. If we lived in a tropical paradise, we would not need or desire shelter. If we were immortal, we would not desire youth. What is true of all desires can hardly be used as a basis for criticizing some desires by claiming that they are nonautonomous.

(b) RATIONAL DESIRE AND CHOICE

Braybrooke might be interpreted as claiming that the desires induced by advertising are often irrational ones in the sense that they are not expressed by an agent who is in full possession of the facts about the products advertised or about the alternative products which might be offered him. Following this line of thought, a possible criticism of advertising is that it leads us to act on irrational desires or to make irrational choices. It might be said that our autonomy has been violated by the fact that we are prevented from following our rational wills or that we have been denied the 'positive freedom' to develop our true, rational selves. It might be claimed that the desires induced in us by advertising are false desires in that they do not reflect our essential, i.e., rational essence.

The problem faced by this line of criticism is that of determining what is to count as rational desire or rational choice. If we require that the desire or choice be the product of an awareness of *all* the facts about the product, then surely every one of us is always moved by irrational desires and makes nothing but irrational choices. How could we know all the facts about a product? If it be required only that we possess all of the *available* knowledge about the product advertised, then we still have to face the problem that not all available knowledge is *relevant* to a rational choice. If I am purchasing a car, certain engineering features will be, and others won't be, relevant, *given what I want in a car.* My prior desires determine the relevance of information. Normally a rational desire or choice is thought to be one based upon relevant information, and information is relevant if it shows how other, prior desires may be satisfied. It can plausibly be claimed that it is such prior desires that advertising agencies acknowledge, and that the agencies often provide the type of information that is relevant in light of these desires. To the extent that this is true, advertising does not inhibit our rational wills or our autonomy as rational creatures.

It may be urged that much of the puffery engaged in by advertising does not provide relevant information at all but rather makes claims which are not factually true. If someone buys Pongo Peach in anticipation of an adventure in paradise, or Old Charter in expectation of increasing the value of his holdings, then he/she is expecting purely imaginary benefits. In no literal sense will the one product provide adventure and the other increased capital. A purchasing decision based on anticipation of imaginary benefits is not, it might be said, a rational decision, and a desire for imaginary benefits is not a rational desire.

In rejoinder it needs to be pointed out that we often wish to purchase subjective effects which in being subjective are nevertheless real enough. The feeling of adventure or of enhanced social prestige and value are examples of subjective effects promised by advertising. Surely many (most?) advertisements directly promise subjective effects which their patrons actually desire (and obtain when they purchase the product), and thus the ads provide relevant information for rational choice. Moreover, advertisements often provide accurate indirect information on the basis of which a person who wants a certain subjective effect rationally chooses a product. The mechanism involved here is as follows.

To the extent that a consumer takes an advertised product to offer a subjective effect and the product does not, it is unlikely that it will be purchased again. If this happens in a number of cases, the product will be taken off the market. So here the market regulates itself, providing the mechanism whereby misleading advertisements are withdrawn and misled customers are no longer misled. At the same time, a successful bit of puffery, being one which leads to large and repeated sales, produces satisfied customers and more advertising of the product. The indirect information provided by such large-scale advertising efforts provides a measure of verification to the consumer who is looking for certain kinds of subjective effect. For example, if I want to feel well dressed and in fashion, and I consider buying an Izod Alligator shirt which is advertised in all of the magazines and newspapers, then the fact that other people buy it and that this leads to repeated advertisements shows me that the desired subjective effect is real enough and that I indeed will be well dressed and in fashion if I purchase the shirt. The indirect information may lead to a rational decision to purchase a product because the information testifies to the subjective effect that the product brings about.

Some philosophers will be unhappy with the conclusion of this section, largely because they have a concept of true, rational, or ideal desire which is not the same as the one used here. A Marxist, for instance, may urge that any desire felt by alienated man in a capitalistic society is foreign to his true nature. Or an existentialist may claim that the desires of inauthentic men are themselves inauthentic. Such concepts are based upon general theories of human nature which are unsubstantiated and perhaps incapable of substantiation. Moreover, each of these theories is committed to a concept of an ideal desire which is normatively debatable and which is distinct from the ordinary concept of a rational desire as one based upon relevant information. But it is in the terms of the ordinary concept that we express our concern that advertising may limit our autonomy in the sense of leading us to act on irrational desires, and if we operate with this concept we are driven again to the conclusion that advertising may lead, but probably most often does not lead, to an infringement of autonomy.

(c) FREE CHOICE

It might be said that some desires are so strong or so covert that a person cannot resist them, and that when he acts on such desires he is not acting freely or voluntarily but is rather the victim of irresistible impulse or an unconscious drive. Perhaps those who condemn advertising feel that it produces this kind of desire in us and consequently reduces our autonomy.

This raises a very difficult issue. How do we distinguish between an impulse we *do* not resist and one we *could* not resist, between freely giving in to a desire and succumbing to one? I have argued elsewhere that the way to get at this issue is in terms of the notion of acting for a reason.[12] A person acts or chooses freely if he does so for a reason, that is, if he can adduce considerations which justify in his mind the act in question. Many of our actions are in fact free because this condition frequently holds. Often, however, a person will act from habit, or whim, or impulse, and on these occasions he does not have a reason in mind. Nevertheless he often acts voluntarily in these instances, i.e., he could have acted otherwise. And this is because if there *had been* a reason for acting otherwise of which he was aware, he would in fact have done so. Thus acting from habit or impulse is not necessarily to act in an involuntary manner. If, however, a person is aware of a good reason to do x and still follows his impulse to do y, then he can be said to be impelled by irresistable impulse and hence to act involuntarily. Many kleptomaniacs can be said to act involuntarily, for in spite of their knowledge that they likely will be caught and their awareness that the goods they steal have little utilitarian value to them, they nevertheless steal. Here their 'out of character' desires have the upper hand, and we have a case of compulsive behavior.

Applying these notions of voluntary and compulsive behavior to the case of behavior prompted by advertising, can we say that consumers influenced by advertising act compulsively? The unexciting answer is: sometimes they do, sometimes not. I may have an overwhelming, T.V. induced urge to own a Mazda Rx-7 and all the while realize that I can't afford one without severely reducing my family's caloric intake to a dangerous level. If, aware of this good reason not to purchase the car, I nevertheless do so, this shows that I have been the victim of T.V. compulsion. But if I have the urge, as I assure you I do, and don't act on it, or if in some other possible world I could afford an Rx-7, then I have not been the subject of undue influence by Mazda advertising. Some Mazda Rx-7 purchasers act compulsively; others do not. The Mazda advertising effort *in general* cannot be condemned, then, for impairing its customers' autonomy in the sense of limiting free or voluntary choice. Of course the question remains what should be done about the fact that advertising may and does *occasionally* limit free choice.

In the case of subliminal advertising we may find an individual whose subconscious desires are activated by advertising into doing something his calculating, reasoning ego does not approve. This would be a case of compulsion. But most of us have a benevolent subconsciousness which does not overwhelm our ego and its reasons for action. And therefore most of us can respond to subliminal advertising without thereby risking our autonomy. To be sure, if some advertising firm developed a subliminal technique which drove all of us to purchase Lear jets, thereby reducing our caloric intake to the zero point, then we would have a case of advertising which could properly be censured for infringing our right to autonomy. We should acknowledge that this is possible, but at the same time we should recognize that it is not an inherent result of subliminal advertising.

(d) CONTROL OR MANIPULATION

Briefly let us consider the matter of control and manipulation. Under what conditions do these activities occur? In a recent paper on "Forms and Limits of Control" I suggested the following criteria.[13]

A person C controls the behavior of another person P *if*

1. C intends P to act in a certain way A;
2. C's intention is causally effective in bringing about A; and
3. C intends to ensure that all of the necessary conditions of A are satisfied.

These criteria may be elaborated as follows. To control another person it is not enough that one's actions produce certain behavior on the part of that person; additionally one must intend that this happen. Hence control is the intentional production of behavior. Moreover, it is not enough just to have the intention; the intention must give rise to the conditions which bring about the intended effect. Finally, the controller must intend to establish by his actions any otherwise unsatisfied necessary conditions for the production of the intended effect. The controller is not just influencing the outcome, not just having input; he is as it were guaranteeing that the sufficient conditions for the intended effect are satisfied.

Let us apply these criteria of control to the case of advertising and see what happens. Conditions (1) and (3) are crucial. Does the Mazda manufacturing company or its advertising agency intend that I buy an Rx-7? Do they intend that a certain number of people buy the car? *Prima facie* it seems more appropriate to say that they *hope* a certain number of people will buy it, and hoping and intending are not the same. But the difficult term here is 'intend'. Some philosophers have argued that to intend A it is necessary only to desire that A happen and to believe that it will. If this is correct, and if marketing analysis gives the Mazda agency a reasonable belief that a certain segment of the population will buy its product, then, assuming on its part the desire that this happen, we have the conditions necessary for saying that the agency intends that a certain segment purchase the car. If I am a member of this segment of the population, would it then follow that the agency intends that I purchase an Rx-7? Or is control referentially opaque? Obviously we have some questions here which need further exploration.

Let us turn to the third condition of control, the requirement that the controller intend to activate or bring about any otherwise unsatisfied necessary conditions for the production of the intended effect. It is in terms of this condition that we are able to distinguish brainwashing from liberal education. The brainwasher arranges all of the necessary conditions for belief. On the other hand, teachers (at least those of liberal persuasion) seek only to influence their students—to provide them with information and enlightenment which they may absorb *if they wish*. We do not normally think of teachers as controlling their students, for the students' performances depend as well on their own interests and inclinations.

Now the advertiser—does he control, or merely influence, his audience? Does he intend to ensure that all of the necessary conditions for purchasing behavior are met, or does he offer information and symbols which are intended to have an effect only *if* the potential purchaser has certain desires? Undeniably advertising induces some desires, and it does this intentionally, but more often than not it intends to induce a desire for a particular object, *given* that the purchaser already has other desires. Given a desire for youth, or power, or adventure, or ravishing beauty, we are led to desire Grecian Formula 16, Mazda Rx-7s, Pongo Peach, and Distinctive Foundations. In this light, the advertiser is influencing us by appealing to independent desires we already have. He is not creating those basic desires. Hence it seems appropriate to deny that he intends to produce all of the necessary conditions for our purchases, and appropriate to deny that he controls us.

Let me summarize my argument. The critics of advertising see it as having a pernicious effect on the autonomy of consumers, as controlling their lives and manufacturing their very souls. The defense claims that advertising only offers information and in effect allows industry to provide consumers with what they want. After developing some of the philosophical dimensions of this dispute, I have come down tentatively in favor of the advertisers. Advertising may, but certainly does not always or even frequently, control behavior, produce compulsive behavior, or create wants which are not rational or are not truly those of the consumer. Admittedly it may in individual cases do all of these things, but it is innocent of the charge of intrinsically or necessarily doing them or even, I think, of often doing so. This limited potentiality, to be sure, leads to the question whether advertising should be abolished or severely curtailed or regulated because of its potential to harm a few poor souls in the above ways. This is a very difficult question, and I do not pretend to have the answer. I only hope that the above discussion, in showing some of the kinds of harm that can be done by advertising and by indicating the likely limits of this harm, will put us in a better position to grapple with the question.

NOTES

1. Vance Packard, *The Hidden Persuaders* (Pocket Books, New York, 1958), pp. 20–21.
2. *Ibid.*, p. 21.
3. B. F. Skinner, "Some Issues Concerning the Control of Human Behavior: A Symposium," in Karlins and Andrews (eds.), *Man Controlled* (The Free Press, New York, 1972).
4. I would like to emphasize that in what follows I am discussing these techniques of advertising from the standpoint of the issue of control and not from that of deception.
5. Quoted by Packard, *op. cit.*, p. 220.
6. Theodore Levitt, "The Morality (?) of Advertising," *Harvard Business Review* **48** (1970), 84–92.
7. Phillip Nelson, "Advertising and Ethics," in Richard T. De George and Joseph A. Pichler (eds.), *Ethics, Free Enterprise, and Public Policy* (Oxford University Press, New York, 1978), pp. 187–98.
8. John Kenneth Galbraith, "The Dependence Effect," *The Affluent Society;* reprinted in this volume, pp. 437–443.
9. David Braybrooke, "Skepticism of Wants, and Certain Subversive Effects of Corporations on American Values," in Sidney Hook (ed.), *Human Values and Economic Policy* (New York University Press, New York, 1967); reprinted in Beauchamp and Bowie (eds.), *op. cit.*, pp. 502–8.

10. F. A. von Hayek, "The Non Sequitur of the 'Dependence Effect,'" Southern Economic Journal (1961).
11. Harry Frankfurt, "Freedom of the Will and the Concept of a Person," Journal of Philosophy LXVIII (1971), 5–20.
12. Robert L. Arrington, "Practical Reason, Responsibility and the Psychopath," Journal for the Theory of Social Behavior 9 (1979), 71–89.
13. Robert L. Arrington, "Forms and Limits of Control," delivered at the annual meeting of the Southern Society for Philosophy and Psychology, Birmingham, Alabama, 1980.

Corporate Governance

A. H. Robins:
The Dalkon Shield

A. R. GINI AND TERRY SULLIVAN

On August 21, 1985, A. R. Robins of Richmond, Virginia—the seventeenth largest pharmaceutical house in America and corporately rated as number 392 in the Fortune 500—filed for reorganization under Chapter 11 of the 1978 Federal Bankruptcy Code. On the surface, Robins seemed to be a thriving company. Its popular products, including Robitussin cough syrup, Chap Stick lip balm, and Sergeant's flea and tick collars for cats and dogs, generated record sales in 1985 of $706 million with a net income in excess of $75 million. Robins' petition for protection under Chapter 11 stems directly from the "blitz of litigation" over a product it has not produced since 1974, the Dalkon Shield intrauterine birth control device. At the time it filed for bankruptcy Robins had been deluged with more than 12,000 personal injury lawsuits charging that the Dalkon Shield was responsible for countless serious illnesses and at least 20 deaths among the women who used it.

In many ways this bankruptcy petition mimes and mirrors (Johns-) Manville's unprecedented request for reorganization in 1982. Manville, the nation's, if not the world's, largest producer of asbestos, claimed that it was succumbing to a "blitz of toxic torts" and therefore could not carry on with business as usual. In August 1982 Manville was facing 16,500 suits on behalf of people who claimed to have contracted cancer and other diseases caused by asbestos and the asbestos-related products that the company produced.

Like Manville, A. H. Robins is defending and explaining its actions by claiming that it simply cannot go on and fulfill its immediate and potential obligations to its stockholders, customers, employees, and litigants (claimants) unless it takes dramatic financial action. In filing for Chapter 11

Robins has won at least temporary respite from its legal woes. Although the company will continue operating during the reorganization, all suits now pending are frozen and no new suits can be filed. While the company develops a plan to handle its liabilities, it is up to the bankruptcy courts to deal with all present claims as well as to establish guidelines for the handling of any future claims.[1] Whatever the final results, the Dalkon Shield case may well turn out to be the worst product liability nightmare that a U.S. drugmaker or major corporation has ever suffered.[2]

⚜

The A. H. Robins Company is essentially a family owned and operated organization. The original company was founded by Albert Hartley Robins, a registered pharmacist, in 1866 in Richmond, Virginia. His grandson, E. Claiborne Robins, built and directed the company into a multinational conglomerate which was able to obtain Fortune 500 status by the middle of the twentieth century. While E. Claiborne Robins remains Chairman of the Board, E. Claiborne Junior is now the firm's president and CEO. Both the family and the company are much liked and respected in their home state. Generations of employees have repeatedly claimed that E. Claiborne Senior was at his worst a "benevolent despot" and at his best a kind and gentle man sincerely interested in quality control as well as his employees' well being. By all reports E. Claiborne Junior seems to be following in his father's footsteps. Moreover, the family's kindness has not been limited to its employees. In 1969 E. Claiborne Senior personally donated over $50 million to the University of Richmond. Since then the Robins family has given at least $50 million more to the university, and additional millions to other universities and to diverse other causes. In December 1983 *Town and Country* magazine listed Claiborne Senior among the top five of "The Most Generous Americans."

Both the family and the company take pride in having "always gone by the book" and always giving their customers a good product at a fair price. In its 120 years of operation the company had done business without having a single product-liability lawsuit filed against it. Critics now claim that Robins has been involved in a directly ordered, prolonged institutional cover-up of the short- and long-term effects of the use of the Dalkon Shield. Moreover, many critics claim that, more than just stonewalling the possible side effects of the Shield, Robins is guilty of marketing a product they knew to be relatively untested, undependable, and therefore potentially dangerous. Robins is accused of having deceived doctors, lied to women, perjured itself to federal judges, and falsified documentation to the FDA. According to Morton Mintz, Robins' most outspoken critic, thousands, probably tens of thousands, of women who trusted the doctors who trusted A. H. Robins paid a ghastly price for the use of the Dalkon Shield: chronic pelvic infections, impairment or loss of childbearing capacity, children with multiple birth defects, unwanted abortions, recurring health problems, and chronic pain.

IUDs are among the most ancient forms of contraception, known for more than two thousand years. Exactly how an IUD prevents conception is not known. It may interfere with the fertilization of the eggs, but most experts believe that when inserted into the uterus it prevents pregnancy by making it difficult for a fertilized egg to attach itself to the wall of the uterus. Over the centuries the materials used in the fabrication of IUDs include ebony, glass, gold, ivory, pewter, wood, wool, diamond-studded platinum, copper, and plastic.[3] The Dalkon Shield was developed by Dr. Hugh J. Davis, a former professor of obstetrics and gynecology at the Johns Hopkins University, and Irwin Lerner, an electrical engineer. In 1970 they sold their rights to the Shield to Robins, who agreed to pay royalties on future sales and $750,000 in cash. Between 1971 and 1974 Robins sold 4.5 million Dalkon Shields around the world, including 2.85 million in the United States.

By the late 1960s large numbers of women had become concerned about the safety of the Pill. These women formed an ever-growing potential market for an alternative means of birth control. Many of these women switched to "barrier" methods of birth control, particularly the diaphragm, which, when used with spermicidal creams or jellies, can be highly effective, though inconvenient. Others turned to IUDs, which, although convenient, previously had been considered unsafe—causing pelvic infections, irregular bleeding, uterine cramps, and accidental expulsion. Robins leapt at an opportunity to develop a new market with their product. The company's task was to convince physicians that the Shield was as effective as oral contraceptives in preventing pregnancies and that it was safer, better designed, and afforded greater resistance to inadvertent expulsion from the uterus than other IUDs.[4]

In January 1971 Robins began to sell the Dalkon Shield, promoting it as the "modern, superior," "second generation" and—most importantly—"safe" intrauterine device for birth control. The Shield itself is a nickel-sized plastic device that literally looks like a badge or a shield with spikes around the edges and a thread-sized "nylon tail string," which allowed both the wearer and the physician a means to guarantee that the device had not been expelled. The Shield was relatively inexpensive. The device itself sold for between $3.00 and $4.50 (its production costs were an incredibly low figure of $.25 a Shield). The only other cost associated with the Shield was the doctor's office fee for insertion and a recommended yearly pelvic examination. Dr. Hugh Davis claimed that the Dalkon Shield was the safest and most effective IUD because it is "the only IUD which is truly anatomically engineered for optimum uterine placement, fit, tolerance, and retention."[5] Davis was able to persuade a large number of physicians of the effectiveness of the Shield in an article he published in the "Current Investigation" section of the *American Journal of Obstetrics and Gynecology* in February

1970. The article described a study conducted at the Johns Hopkins Family Planning Clinic involving 640 women who had worn the Shield for one year. His analysis was based on 3,549 women-months of experience. Davis cited five pregnancies, ten expulsions, nine removals for medical reasons, and three removals for personal reasons. His startling results: tolerance rate (nonexpulsion), 96 percent; pregnancy rate, 1.1 percent. The A. H. Robins Company reprinted no fewer than 199,000 copies of the Davis article for distribution to physicians.[6]

While various executives strongly recommended that other studies be commissioned to validate Davis's results, in January 1971 Robins began to market and sell the Shield on the basis of Davis's limited analysis. Robins' decision to produce and sell the Shield based on Davis's statistics may not coincide with the highest standards of scientific research, but it did not violate any FDA statutes and was therefore perfectly legal. At the time Robins produced the Shield, FDA had no regulatory policies in force regarding IUDs of any kind. While FDA had the authority to regulate the production, testing, and sales of all new prescriptions, it could only *recommend* testing on new medical devices. It could not monitor, investigate, or police a device unless charges of lack of effectiveness, injury, or abuse were formally leveled against the device or the producer.

In December 1970 Robins commissioned a major long-term study to reinforce Davis's results. The study concentrated on ten clinics, seven in the United States and one each in Canada, Nova Scotia, and British Columbia. Between December 1970 and December 1974 (six months after Robins suspended domestic sales) 2,391 women were fitted with the Shield. The first results came out in November 1972, with only about half of the women enrolled in the study. The statistics showed a sixteen month pregnancy rate of 1.6 percent. The Robins home office was more than pleased and immediately communicated this information to its sales staff. Thirteen months later, with all the women now participating in the program, less happy figures began to show up. The pregnancy rate after six months was 2.1 percent; after twelve months, 3.2 percent; after eighteen months, 3.5 percent; and after twenty-three months, 4.1 percent. In a final report published as a confidential internal document in August 1975 the final figures and results were even more devastating. The pregnancy rate after six months was 2.6 percent; after twelve months, 4.2 percent; after eighteen months, 4.9 percent; and after twenty-four months, 5.7 percent. Two of the scientists involved in this project submitted a minority report claiming that the Shield was even less effective than these already damaging figures indicated. They claimed that the pregnancy rate during the first year was much higher: after six months, 3.3 percent; and after twelve months, 5.5 percent. This twelve-month pregnancy rate is exactly five times *higher than* the rate Robins advertised and promoted—1.1 percent—to catapult the Shield to leadership in the IUD business.[7] This minority report was never disclosed to the medical community by Robins. Nor did Robins communicate these results to its own sales force. It did report some of these findings to FDA in July 1974, but only after the company had suspended domestic sales earlier that June.

Soon after the Shield entered the marketplace, independent research results began to appear in both national and foreign journals of medicine. In 1970 and 1971 Dr. Mary O. Gabrielson, working out of clinics in San Francisco and Oakland, did an eighteen-month study on 937 women with results that Robins would not want to advertise. The rate of medical removals was 26.4 percent; the pregnancy rate, 5.1 percent. In 1973 the *British Medical Journal* published a study showing a 4.7 percent pregnancy rate in Shield users.[8] Again because there was no law requiring disclosure of this new research information, Robins did not rush to inform the general public, the medical community, or the FDA.

At the same time that the Robins Company was receiving research results pointing to poor statistical effectiveness of the Shield, they also began to receive more and more "single physician experience" reports warning and complaining about some of the medical consequences from using the Shield. These physician's reports plus the statistics generated from controlled clinical reports began to portray the Shield as neither effective nor safe.

The primary cause of concern for Shield users proved to be a much higher incidence of uterine/pelvic bacterial infections. PID (pelvic inflammatory disease) is a highly virulent and very painful, difficult to cure, life threatening infection, which more often than not impairs or destroys a woman's ability to bear children. Of those women who conceived with the Shield in place (approximately 110,000 in the United States), an estimated 60 percent of them miscarried after suffering severe bacterial infections (PID). In 1974 FDA reported that over 245 women in their fourth to sixth month of pregnancy suffered the relatively rare bacterially-induced miscarriage called septic spontaneous abortions. For fifteen women, these septic abortions were fatal.[9] Moreover, hundreds of women throughout the world who had conceived while wearing the Shield gave birth prematurely to children with grave congenital defects, including blindness, cerebral palsy, and mental retardation.[10]

Scientists now believe that the systemic cause for these virulent forms of bacterial infection is the nylon tail of the Shield itself. The Dalkon Shield tail string runs between the vagina, where bacteria are always present, and the uterus, which is germ free. It then passes through the cervix, where cervical mucus is the body's natural defense against bacterial invasion of the uterus. Robins claimed that cervical mucus would stop all germs from entering and infecting the uterus. To the naked eye, the Dalkon Shield tail string is an impervious monofilament, meaning that bacteria on it could not get into it. Actually, however, it is a cylindrical sheath encasing 200 to 450 round monofilaments separated by spaces. While the string was knotted at both ends, neither end was actually sealed. Therefore, any bacteria that got into the spaces between the filaments would be insulated from the body's natural antibacterial action while being drawn into the uterus by "wicking," a phenomenon similar to that by which a string draws the melting wax of a candle to the flame. Scientists believe that the longer the Shield and its string/tail is in place, the greater the chances for its deterioration and infiltration, thereby inducing infection in the uterus. Scientists now also contend that the "syndrome of spontaneous septic abortions" that occurred to women who had the Shield in place in the early second trimester of their pregnancy was caused by the tail string. That is, radical and sudden infection occurred when the uterus expanded to the point where it tended to pull the tail string into itself, thereby bringing on instant, often lethal, contamination.[11]

In the summer of 1983 the Centers for Disease Control in Atlanta and the FDA recommended that all women still using the Shield should contact their physicians and have it immediately removed. The Agencies found that women using the Shield had a fivefold increase in risk for contracting PID as compared to women using other types of IUDs. No change in contraceptive practice was recommended for women using any other type of IUD.[12] In April 1985 two studies funded by the National Institute of Health announced yet another dire warning. These studies showed that childless IUD wearers who have had PID run a higher risk of infertility if their devices were Shields than if they were other makes.[13]

Throughout all of this, A. H. Robins officials appeared to be unaware of, or at best indifferent to, the issues, facts, and effects of their product. The company assumed the position of complete denial of any intentional wrongdoing or any malicious intent to evade full public disclosure of pertinent medical information about the safety and effectiveness of the Shield. On numerous separate occasions both in public forums and under oath, E. Claiborne Robins, Senior, has claimed near ignorance of Robins' sixteen-year involvement with the Dalkon Shield. At a series of depositions taken in 1984 Robins Senior swore that he was unable to recall ever having discussed the Shield with his son, the company's chief executive officer and president. When asked, "You certainly knew, when you started marketing this device, that PID was a life-threatening disease, did you not?" Robins testified: "I don't know that. I never thought of it as life-threatening." Did he know it could destroy fertility? "Maybe I should, but I don't know that. I have heard that, but I am not sure where." Carl Lunsford, senior vice-president for research and development, swore he could recall no "expression of concern" by any company official about PID, and he didn't remember having "personally wondered" about the toll it was taking. He had not tried to find out how many users had died. He had not "personally reviewed" *any* studies on the Shield's safety or effectiveness. When asked if he had "any curiosity" regarding the millions of dollars the company had been paying out in punitive damages to settle lawsuits, his answer was, "No."[14] The case of William Forrest, vice-president and general counsel of

A. H. Robins, further strains belief. He has been described by E. Claiborne Junior as one of the company's "two most instrumental" persons in the Dalkon Shield situation. He was in effect in charge of all Shield matters and related legal issues for over a decade. In a trial proceeding, Forrest testified that his wife had worn a Shield until it was surgically removed. She had also had a hysterectomy. Although IUD removals and hysterectomies were frequently connected and simultaneous events for many infected Shield wearers, Forrest steadfastly denied any connection in his wife's case and gave vague and widely differing dates for the two events. He and his wife, he explained, did not discuss such matters in detail. Indeed, Forrest gave a series of confusing accounts of his wife's hysterectomy and its possible relationship to the Shield she had worn.

> Q: Did her doctor advise her that her hysterectomy was in any way related to the Dalkon Shield?
> A: Not that I know of, no, sir.
> Q: Did you ever ask her that?
> A: I don't recall. I may have asked her that. I don't recall the doctor telling her that. . . .
> Q: . . . Are you telling the ladies and gentlemen of the jury that you and your wife have never had a discussion concerning whether or not the Dalkon Shield played a part in her hysterectomy?
> A: Well, certainly, as I indicated to you, we had very general discussions. Now, if I asked her whether that played a part, I don't recall specifically if I did. If I did, to my knowledge, there was no indication that it did.[15]

The company's response to all claims of faulty product design and limited testing procedures has been counter assertions or counter claims regarding the faulty or improper use of the product by the user or the physician. The company has steadfastly maintained that there were no special dangers inherent in the device. In a report to FDA they stated: "Robins believes that serious scientific questions exist about whether the Dalkon Shield poses a significantly different risk of infection than other IUDs." Their continuous theme has been that doctors, not the device, have caused any infections associated with the Shield. The company was committed to the notion that pregnancy and removal rates could be kept extremely low by proper placement of the Shield. They also contended that user abuse played a part in the Shield's supposed malfunctioning. They defined user abuse as poor personal hygiene habits, sexual promiscuity or excessive sexual activity, or physical tampering with the device itself.

According to three different independent investigative reports,[16] the company's public face of calm denial and counterargument masked an internal conspiring to conceal information from the public, the court system, and the FDA. These reports (books) claim documented evidence of the multilevel cover-up. They claim that Robins quashed all documentation debating and contesting Dr. Hugh Davis's celebrated pregnancy rate of only 1.1 percent, and that Robins knew of the real significance and traumatic effect of the wicking process of the tail string but did nothing about it. Not only did the company know that the nylon cord used on the tail could degenerate and cause infection, but as early as the summer of 1972 the company was warned in writing by one of its chief consultants, Dr. Thad Earl, that pregnant women should have the Shield immediately removed to avoid "abortion and septic infection." These reports also contend that on at least three separate occasions executives and officials of Robins lost or destroyed company files and records specifically requested by the Federal Appellate Courts and the FDA.

By May 1974 Robins could no longer avoid the evidence presented to it by FDA implicating the Shield in numerous cases of spontaneous septic abortions and in the death of at least four women as a result. These findings were disclosed in a letter sent by the company to 120,000 doctors. In June 1974 Robins suspended the U.S. distribution and sale of the Shield. In January 1975 Robins called back and completely removed the Shield from the market. The company termed the action a "market withdrawal," not a recall, because it was undertaken voluntarily and not at the direct order of FDA. In September 1980 Robins again wrote the medical community suggesting as a purely precautionary measure that doctors remove the Shield from their patients. In October 1984 Robins initiated a $4 million television, newspaper, and magazine advertising campaign warning and recommending that all women still wearing the device have it removed at Robins's expense. In April 1985 Robins publicly set aside $615 million to settle legal claims from women who had used the Shield. This reserve is the largest provision of its kind to date in a product liability case. In May 1985 a jury in Wichita, Kansas, awarded nearly $9 million to a woman who had charged that the use of the Shield caused her to undergo a hysterectomy. The award was the largest ever made in the history of litigation involving the Shield. Officials of the Robins Company felt that adverse decisions of this magnitude could mean that their $615 million fund would prove to be inadequate. On August 21, 1985, Robins filed for Chapter 11 protection, citing litigation relating to the Shield as the main cause for its actions. Company spokesmen said that it hoped that the Federal Bankruptcy Court in Richmond would set up a payment schedule that would enable it to survive while insuring that victims "would be treated fairly." E. Claiborne Robins, Jr., called it "essential that we move to protect the company's economic viability against those who would destroy it for the benefit of a few."[17] The intriguing financial irony in all of this is that when Robins filed for Chapter 11 it had already spent, at a conservative estimate, $500 million in settlements, litigation losses, and legal fees for a product it had only manufactured for three years and from which it had only realized $500,000 in real profits![18]

The central issues in this case revolve around the answers to four critical questions:

1. Is A. H. Robins telling the truth about its knowledge of the health factors involved in the use of the Dalkon Shield? Is it true that they had no awareness of the connection between PID and spontaneous septic abortions and the nylon tail of the Shield? Or is it the case, as many of their critics contend, that they have conspired for over sixteen years to both deny and cover up any knowledge of the short- and long-term effects of wearing the Shield?

2. Even if Robins is not guilty of conspiring to misinform its customers, why didn't simple "prudence" lead the company to go public immediately when "single physician experience" and the results of their own and outside testing procedures indicated from the beginning that there were serious drawbacks, limitations, and dangers inherent in the product? Moreover, after suspending production in 1974 because of FDA findings, why did Robins wait until 1984 to recommend that all women still wearing the Shield have it removed?

3. Is the 1978 Federal Bankruptcy Code a proper and valid means of seeking relief from immediate and possible future liability?

4. Is it simply the case, as Morton Mintz—Dalkon critic and corporate watchdog—has stated, that Robins knowingly and willfully placed greed before human welfare because the corporate structure itself is oriented toward profit and away from liability?

Robins claims that it produced a well-conceived, well-researched, and perfectly acceptable product well within the standards of the industry. They contend that any and all ill effects arising from the use of the Shield are the results of unexpected and unforeseeable technical or material breakdowns. At no time did they conspire to defraud the public. They maintain that family honor and the general reputation of the company simply would not allow for such behavior. Officials of the company further claim that just because their actions are unusual and unorthodox, it does not mean that they are acting in an immoral or illegal fashion. They insist that filing for bankruptcy was unavoidable and in the best interest of its stockholders and creditors. Moreover, they feel that in the long run their decision will better benefit those who have suffered from medical complications arising from the use of the Shield. Robins perceives the filing for Chapter 11 as the only orderly way possible for the company to treat everyone fairly.

In all candor it must be remembered that Robins's actions are not without danger. To the extent that Robins is using Chapter 11 as a shelter against the rush of product-liability litigation, the company is nevertheless taking a gamble. Robins must now operate under the eye of a federal bankruptcy judge, and as Lawrence King, Professor of Law at NYU, has said in regard to the Manville case, "Once you file, there is always a risk of liquidation."[19] For example, as part of their reorganization arrangement with the court, Robins agreed to a class action procedure in which they would begin a 91 nation advertisement campaign to announce to all former users their right to file a claim for compensation for any health problems that may have been caused by the Shield. All potential claimants are given a case number and sent a questionnaire to determine if they qualify for a financial settlement. As of June 1986 more than 300,000 claims have been filed against Robins![20] Numbers such as these may completely overwhelm the bankruptcy court's ability to reorganize and reestablish the company on a sound financial basis.

There are several lessons lurking in this case. The first of them has to do with the dangers held by the combination of a legalistic society and a highly technological one—or, perhaps more clearly, in a society based upon notions of individual freedom suddenly caught up in rapid innovation. Generally speaking, we hold, in America, that that which is not specifically prohibited is permitted. The danger comes when technology continually creates inventions for which there are no categories and hence no rules. FDA clearly is charged with safeguarding health and monitoring the pharmaceutical industry, among others. The Dalkon Shield is clearly a contraceptive capable of creating physical good or ill, and yet because it is a device, neither a food nor drug, and because neither FDA nor A. H. Robins would act at the outset on anything other than the exact literal definition of the rules, no real consideration was given to the medical consequences of the Shield. FDA felt it lacked the authority and A. H. Robins felt no moral imperative that was not specifically imposed upon them. We have left all interpretations of intention, all exercise of reasonableness, to the court systems—expert and de facto agents. The second lesson can be found in that the Dalkon Shield itself may have been a genuinely safe, useful product, even a breakthrough, as the first effective IUD. The danger was ancillary to the device—the "wicking" action of the tail string—and had Robins followed the usual FDA approval guidelines for drugs, this flaw might have been discovered, and perhaps eliminated. It was in adhering only to the letter of the regulations and in using this exclusion of devices to rush into production and quicker profits that the company began a course which may end in its own demise.

Given all of this conflicting data, perhaps there is only one thing we can say with certainty in regard to Robins's production of the Dalkon Shield: "In the pharmaceutical world, products that fail can cripple companies as well as people."[21]

NOTES
1. A. R. Gini, "Manville: The Ethics of Economic Efficiency?" *Journal of Business Ethics*, 3 (1984), p. 66.

2. *Time*, September 2, 1985, p. 32.
3. Morton Mintz, *At Any Cost* (New York: Pantheon Books, 1985), p. 25.
4. Ibid., p. 29.
5. Ibid., p. 82.
6. Ibid., pp. 29–31.
7. Ibid., pp. 86–88.
8. Ibid., pp. 81, 82.
9. *FDA Consumer*, May 1981, p. 32.
10. Morton Mintz, "At Any Cost," *The Progressive*, November 1985, p. 21.
11. *At Any Cost*, pp. 131–48 and 149–72.
12. *FDA Consumer*, July–August 1983, p. 2.
13. *Wall Street Journal*, April 11, 1985, p. 1.
14. Mintz, "At Any Cost," *The Progressive*, p. 24.
15. Mintz, *At Any Cost*, p. 111.
16. Mintz, *At Any Cost* (New York: Pantheon Books, 1985). Sheldon Engelmayer
    and Robert Wagman, *Lord's Justice* (New York: Anchor Press/Doubleday,
    1985). Susan Perry and Jim Dawson, *Nightmare: Women and the Dalkon Shield*
    (New York: Macmillan Publishing, 1985).
17. *New York Times*, August 22, 1985, pp. 1, 6.
18. *Time*, November 26, 1984, p. 86.
19. Gini, "Manville: The Ethics of Economic Efficiency?" p. 68.
20. *Wall Street Journal*, June 26, 1986, p. 10.
21. *U.S. News and World Report*, September 2, 1985, p. 12.

Who Rules the Corporation?

RALPH NADER, MARK GREEN, AND JOEL SELIGMAN

All modern state corporation statutes describe a common image of corporate governance, an image pyramidal in form. At the base of the pyramid
are the shareholders or owners of the corporation. Their ownership gives
them the right to elect representatives to direct the corporation and to
approve fundamental corporate actions such as mergers or bylaw amendments. The intermediate level is held by the board of directors, who are
required by a provision common to nearly every state corporation law "to
manage the business and affairs of the corporation." On behalf of the
shareholders, the directors are expected to select and dismiss corporate
officers; to approve important financial decisions; to distribute profits; and
to see that accurate periodic reports are forwarded to the shareholders.
Finally, at the apex of the pyramid are the corporate officers. In the eyes of
the law, the officers are the employees of the shareholder owners. Their

authority is limited to those responsibilities which the directors delegate to them.

In reality, this legal image is virtually a myth. In nearly every large American business corporation, there exists a management autocracy. One man—variously titled the President, or the Chairman of the Board, or the Chief Executive Officer—or a small coterie of men rule the corporation. Far from being chosen by the directors to run the corporation, this chief executive or executive clique chooses the board of directors and, with the acquiescence of the board, controls the corporation

The common theme of many instances of mismanagement is a failure to restrain the power of these senior executives. A corporate chief executive's decisions to expand, merge, or even violate the law can often be made without accountability to outside scrutiny. There is, for example, the detailed disclosures of the recent bribery cases. Not only do these reports suggest how widespread corporate foreign and domestic criminality has become; they also provide a unique study in the pathology of American corporate management.

At Gulf Corporation, three successive chief executive officers were able to pay out over $12.6 million in foreign and domestic bribes over a 15-year period without the knowledge of "outside" or nonemployee directors on the board. At Northrop, chairman Thomas V. Jones and vice president James Allen were able to create and fund the Economic and Development Corporation, a separate Swiss company, and pay $750,000 to Dr. Hubert Weisbrod, a Swiss attorney, to stimulate West German jet sales without the knowledge of the board or, apparently, other senior executives. At 3M, chairman Bert Cross and finances vice president Irwin Hansen ordered the company insurance department to pay out $509,000 for imaginary insurance and the bookkeeper to fraudulently record the payments as a "necessary and proper" business expense for tax purposes. Ashland Oil Corporation's chief executive officer, Orwin E. Atkins, involved at least eight executives in illegally generating and distributing $801,165 in domestic political contributions, also without question. . . .

The legal basis for such a consolidation of power in the hands of the corporation's chief executive is the proxy election. Annually the shareholders of each publicly held corporation are given the opportunity of either attending a meeting to nominate and elect directors or returning proxy cards to management or its challengers signing over their right to vote. Few shareholders personally attend meetings. Sylvan Silver, a Reuters correspondent who covers over 100 Wilmington annual meetings each year, described representative 1974 meetings in an interview: At Cities Service Company, the 77th largest industrial corporation with some 135,000 shareholders, 25 shareholders actually attended the meeting; El Paso Natural Gas with 125,000 shareholders had 50 shareholders; at Coca Cola, the 69th largest corporation with 70,000 shareholders, 25 shareholders attended the annual meeting; at Bristol Meyers with 60,000 shareholders a like 25 shareholders appeared. Even "Campaign GM," the most publicized shareholder challenge of the past two decades, attracted no more than 3,000 of General Motors' 1,400,000 shareholders, or roughly two-tenths of one percent.

Thus corporate directors are almost invariably chosen by written proxies. Yet management so totally dominates the proxy machinery that corporate elections have come to resemble the Soviet Union's euphemistic "Communist ballot"—that is, a ballot which lists only one slate of candidates. Although federal and state laws require the annual performance of an elaborate series of rituals pretending there is "corporate democracy," in 1973, 99.7 percent of the directorial elections in our largest corporations were uncontested. . . .

THE BEST DEMOCRACY MONEY CAN BUY

The key to management's hegemony is money. Effectively, only incumbent management can nominate directors—because it has a nearly unlimited power to use corporate funds to win board elections while opponents must prepare separate proxies and campaign literature entirely at their own expense.

There is first management's power to print and post written communications to shareholders. In a typical proxy contest, management will "follow up" its initial proxy solicitation with a bombardment of five to ten subsequent mailings. As attorneys Edward Aranow and Herb Einhorn explain in their treatise, *Proxy Contests for Corporate Control:*

> Perhaps the most important aspect of the follow-up letter is its role in the all-important efforts of a soliciting group to secure the *latest-dated* proxy from a stockholder. It is characteristic of every proxy contest that a large number of stockholders will sign and return proxies to one faction and then change their minds and want to have their stock used for the opposing faction.

The techniques of the Northern States Power Company in 1973 are illustrative. At that time, Northern States Power Company voluntarily employed cumulative voting, which meant that only 7.2 percent of outstanding shares was necessary to elect one director to Northern's 14-person board. Troubled by Northern's record on environmental and consumer issues, a broadly based coalition of public interest groups called the Citizens' Advocate for Public Utility Responsibility (CAPUR) nominated Ms. Alpha Snaby, a former Minnesota state legislator, to run for director. These groups then successfully solicited the votes of over 14 percent of all shareholders, or more than twice the votes necessary to elect her to the board.

Northern States then bought back the election. By soliciting proxies a second, and then a third time, the Power Company was able to persuade (or confuse) the shareholders of 71 percent of the 2.8 million shares cast for Ms. Snaby to change their votes.

Larger, more experienced corporations are usually less heavy-handed. Typically, they will begin a proxy campaign with a series of "build-up" letters preliminary to the first proxy solicitation. In Campaign GM, General Motors elevated this strategy to a new plateau by encasing the Project on Corporate Responsibility's single 100-word proxy solicitation within a 21-page booklet specifically rebutting each of the Project's charges. The Project, of course, could never afford to respond to GM's campaign. The postage costs of soliciting GM's 1,400,000 shareholders alone would have exceeded $100,000. The cost of printing a document comparable to GM's 21-page booklet, mailing it out, accompanied by a proxy statement, a proxy card, and a stamped return envelope to each shareholder might have run as high as $500,000.

Nor is it likely that the Project or any other outside shareholder could match GM's ability to hire "professional" proxy solicitors such as Georgeson & Company, which can deploy up to 100 solicitors throughout the country to personally contact shareholders, give them a campaign speech, and urge them to return their proxies. By daily tabulation of returned proxies, professional solicitors are able to identify on a day-to-day basis the largest blocks of stock outstanding which have yet to return a favorable vote. . . .

THE STATE OF THE BOARD

But does not the board of directors with its sweeping statutory mandate "to manage the business and affairs of every corporation" provide an internal check on the power of corporate executives? No. Long ago the grandiloquent words of the statutes ceased to have any operative meaning. "Directors," William O. Douglas complained in 1934, "do not direct." "[T]here is one thing all boards have in common, regardless of their legal position," Peter Drucker has written. *"They do not function."* In Robert Townsend's tart analysis, "[M]ost big companies have turned their boards of directors into nonboards. . . . In the years that I've spent on various boards I've never heard a single suggestion from a director (made as a director *at* a board meeting) that produced any result at all."

Recently these views are corroborated by Professor Myles Mace of the Harvard Business School, the nation's leading authority on the performance of boards of directors. In *Directors—Myth and Reality*, Mace summarized the results of hundreds of interviews with corporate officers and directors.

Directors do not establish the basic objectives, corporate strategies or broad policies of large and medium-size corporations, Mace found. Management creates the policies. The board has a right of veto but rarely exercises it. As one executive said, "Nine hundred and ninety-nine times out of a thousand, the board goes along with management. . . ." Or another, "I can't think of a single time when the board has failed to support a proposed policy of management or failed to endorse the recommendation of management."

The board does not select the president or other chief executive officers. "What is perhaps the most common definition of a function of the board of directors—namely, to select the president—was found to be the greatest myth," reported Mace. "The board of directors in most companies, except in a crisis, does not select the president. The president usually chooses the man who succeeds him to that position, and the board complies with the legal amenities in endorsing and voting his election." A corporate president agreed: "The former company president tapped me to be president, and I assure you that I will select my successor when the time comes." Even seeming exceptions such as RCA's 1975 ouster of Robert Sarnoff frequently turn out to be at the instigation of senior operating executives rather than an aroused board.

The board's role as disciplinarian of the corporation is more apparent than real. As the business-supported Conference Board conceded, "One of the most glaring deficiencies attributed to the corporate board . . . is its failure to monitor and evaluate the performance of the chief executive in a concrete way." To cite a specific example, decisions on executive compensation are made by the president—with perfunctory board approval in most situations. In the vast majority of corporations, Professor Mace found, the compensation committee, and the board which approves the recommendations of the compensation committee, "are not decision-making bodies.". . .

Exceptions to this pattern become news events. In reporting on General Motors' 1971 annual shareholders' meeting, the *Wall Street Journal* noted that "The meeting's dramatic highlight was an impassioned and unprecedented speech by the Rev. Leon Sullivan, GM's recently appointed Negro director, supporting the Episcopal Church's efforts to get the company out of South Africa. It was the first time that a GM director had ever spoken against management at an annual meeting." Now Reverend Sullivan is an unusual outside director, being General Motor's first black director and only "public interest" director. But what makes Leon Sullivan most extraordinary is that he was the first director in *any* major American corporation to come out publicly against his own corporation when its operations tended to support apartheid. . . .

REVAMPING THE BOARD

The modern corporation is akin to a political state in which all powers are held by a single clique. The senior executives of a large firm are essentially not accountable to any other officials within the firm. These are precisely the circumstances that, in a democratic political state, require a separation of powers into different branches of authority. As James Madison explained in the *Federalist* No. 47:

> The accumulation of all powers, legislative, executive, and judiciary, in the same hands, whether of one, a few or many, and whether hereditary, self-appointed, or elective, may justly be pronounced the very definition of tyranny. Were the federal constitution, therefore, really chargeable with this accumulation of power, or with a mixture of powers, having a dangerous tendency to such an accumulation, no further arguments would be necessary to inspire a universal reprobation of the system.

A similar concern over the unaccountability of business executives historically led to the elevation of a board of directors to review and check the actions of operating management. As a practical matter, if corporate governance is to be reformed, it must begin by returning the board to this historical role. The board should serve as an internal auditor of the corporations, responsible for constraining executive management from violations of law and breach of trust. Like a rival branch of government, the board's function must be defined as separate from operating management. Rather than pretending directors can "manage" the corporation, the board's role as disciplinarian should be clearly described. Specifically, the board of directors should:

- establish and monitor procedures that assure that operating executives are informed of and obey applicable federal, state, and local laws;
- approve or veto all important executive management business proposals such as corporate bylaws, mergers, or dividend decisions;
- hire and dismiss the chief executive officer and be able to disapprove the hiring and firing of the principal executives of the corporation; and
- report to the public and the shareholders how well the corporation has obeyed the law and protected the shareholders' investment.

It is not enough, however, to specify what the board should do. State corporations statutes have long provided that "the business and affairs of a corporation shall be managed by a board of directors," yet it has been over a century since the boards of the largest corporations have actually performed this role. To reform the corporation, a federal chartering law must also specify the manner in which the board performs its primary duties.

First, to insure that the corporation obeys federal and state laws, the board should designate executives responsible for compliance with these laws and require periodic signed reports describing the effectiveness of compliance procedures. Mechanisms to administer spot checks on compliance with the principal statutes should be created. Similar mechanisms can insure that corporate "whistle blowers" and nonemployee sources may communicate to the board—in private and without fear of retaliation—knowledge of violations of law.

Second, the board should actively review important executive business proposals to determine their full compliance with law, to preclude conflicts of interest, and to assure that executive decisions are rational and informed of all foreseeable risks and costs. But even though the board's responsibility here is limited to approval or veto of executive initiatives, it should proceed in as well-informed a manner as practicable. To demonstrate rational business judgment, the directorate should require management "to prove its case." It should review the studies upon which management relied to make a decision, require management to justify its decision in terms of costs or rebutting dissenting views, and, when necessary, request that outside experts provide an independent business analysis.

Only with respect to two types of business decisions should the board exceed this limited review role. The determination of salary, expense, and benefit schedules inherently possesses such obvious conflicts of interest for executives that only the board should make these decisions. And since the relocation of principal manufacturing facilities tends to have a greater effect on local communities than any other type of business decision, the board should require management to prepare a "community impact statement." This public report would be similar to the environmental impact statements presently required by the National Environmental Policy Act. It would require the corporation to state the purpose of a relocation decision; to compare feasible alternative means; to quantify the costs to the local community; and to consider methods to mitigate these costs. Although it would not prevent a corporation from making a profit-maximizing decision, it would require the corporation to minimize the costs of relocation decisions to local communities.

To accomplish this restructuring of the board requires the institutionalization of a new profession: the full-time "professional" director. Corporate scholars frequently identify William O. Douglas' 1940 proposal for "salaried, professional experts [who] would bring a new responsibility and authority to directorates and a new safety to stockholders" as the origin of the professional director idea. More recently, corporations including Westinghouse and Texas Instruments have established slots on their boards to be filled by full-time directors. Individuals such as Harvard Business School's Myles Mace and former Federal Reserve Board chairman William McChesney Martin consider their own thoroughgoing approach to boardroom responsibilities to be that of a "professional" director.

To succeed, professional directors must put in the substantial time necessary to get the job done. One cannot monitor the performance of Chrysler's or Gulf's management at a once-a-month meeting; those firms' activities are too sweeping and complicated for such ritual oversight. The obvious minimum here is an adequate salary to attract competent persons to work as full-time directors and to maintain the independence of the board from executive management.

The board must also be sufficiently staffed. A few board members alone cannot oversee the activities of thousands of executives. To be able to appraise operating management, the board needs a trim group of attorneys, economists, and labor and consumer advisors who can analyze complex business proposals, investigate complaints, spot-check accountability, and frame pertinent inquiries.

The board also needs timely access to relevant corporate data. To insure this, the board should be empowered to nominate the corporate financial auditor, select the corporation's counsel, compel the forwarding and preservation of corporate records, require all corporate executives or representatives to answer fully all board questions respecting corporate operations, and dismiss any executive or representative who fails to do so.

This proposed redesign for corporate democracy attempts to make executive management accountable to the law and shareholders without diminishing its operating efficiency. Like a judiciary within the corporation, the board has ultimate powers to judge and sanction. Like a legislature, it oversees executive activity. Yet executive management substantially retains its powers to initiate and administer business operations. The chief executive officer retains control over the organization of the executive hierarchy and the allocation of the corporate budget. The directors are given ultimate control over a narrow jurisdiction: Does the corporation obey the law, avoid exploiting consumers or communities, and protect the shareholders' investment? The executive contingent retains general authority for all corporate operations.

No doubt there will be objections that this structure is too expensive or that it will disturb the "harmony" of executive management. But it is unclear that there would be any increased cost in adopting an effective board. The true cost to the corporation could only be determined by comparing the expense of a fully paid and staffed board with the savings resulting from the elimination of conflicts of interest and corporate waste. In addition, if this should result in a slightly increased corporate expense, the appropriateness must be assessed within a broader social context: should federal and state governments or the corporations themselves bear the primary expense of keeping corporations honest? In our view, this cost should be placed on the corporations as far as reasonably possible.

It is true that an effective board will reduce the "harmony" of executive management in the sense that the power of the chief executive or senior executives will be subject to knowledgeable review. But a board which monitors rather than rubber-stamps management is exactly what is necessary to diminish the unfettered authority of the corporate chief executive or ruling clique. The autocratic power these individuals presently possess has proven unacceptably dangerous: it has led to recurring violations of law, conflicts of interest, productive inefficiency, and pervasive harm to consumers, workers, and the community environment. Under normal circumstances there should be a healthy friction between operating executives and the board to assure that the wisest possible use is made of corporate resources. When corporate executives are breaking the law, there should be no "harmony" whatsoever.

ELECTION OF THE BOARD

Restructuring the board is hardly likely to succeed if boards remain as homogeneously white, male, and narrowly oriented as they are today. Dissatisfaction with current selection of directors is so intense that analysts of corporate governance, including Harvard Law School's Abram Chayes, Yale political scientist Robert Dahl, and University of Southern California Law School Professor Christopher Stone, have each separately urged that the starting point of corporate reform should be to change the way in which the board is elected.

Professor Chayes, echoing John Locke's principle that no authority is legitimate except that granted by "the consent of the governed," argues that employees and other groups substantially affected by corporate operations should have a say in its governance:

> Shareholder democracy, so-called, is misconceived because the shareholders are not the governed of the corporations whose consent must be sought. . . . Their interests are protected if financial information is made available, fraud and overreaching are prevented, and a market is maintained in which their shares may be sold. A priori, there is no reason for them to have any voice, direct or representational, in [corporate decision making]. They are no more affected than nonshareholding neighbors by these decisions. . . .
>
> A more spacious conception of "membership," and one closer to the facts of corporate life, would include all those having a relation of sufficient intimacy with the corporation or subject to its powers in a sufficiently specialized way. Their rightful share in decisions and the exercise of corporate power would be exercised through an institutional arrangement appropriately designed to represent the interests of a constituency of members having a significant common relation to the corporation and its power.

Professor Dahl holds a similar view: "[W]hy should people who own shares be given the privileges of citizenship in the government of the firm when citizenship is denied to other people who also make vital contributions to the firm?" he asks rhetorically. "The people I have in mind are, of course, employees and customers, without whom the firm could not exist, and the general public, without whose support for (or acquiescence in) the myriad protections and services of the state the firm would instantly disappear. . . ." Yet Dahl finds proposals for interest group representation less desirable than those for worker self-management. He also suggests consideration of codetermination statutes such as those enacted by West Germany and ten other European and South American countries under which shareholders and employees separately elect designated portions of the board.

From a different perspective, Professor Stone has recommended that a federal agency appoint "general public directors" to serve on the boards of all the largest industrial and financial firms. In certain extreme cases such as where a corporation repeatedly violates the law, Stone recommends that the federal courts appoint "special public directors" to prevent further delinquency.

There are substantial problems with each of those proposals. It seems impossible to design a general "interest group" formula which will assure that all affected constituencies of large industrial corporations will be represented and that all constituencies will be given appropriate weight. Even if such a formula could be designed, however, there is the danger that consumer or community or minority or franchisee representatives would become only special pleaders for their constituents and otherwise lack the loyalty or interest to direct generally. This defect has emerged in West Germany under codetermination. Labor representatives apparently are indifferent to most problems of corporate management that do not directly affect labor. They seem as deferential to operating executive management as present American directors are. Alternatively, federally appointed public directors might be frozen out of critical decision-making by a majority of "privately" elected directors, or the appointing agency itself might be biased.

Nonetheless, the essence of the Chayes-Dahl-Stone argument is well taken. The boards of directors of most major corporations are, as CBS's Dan Rather criticized the original Nixon cabinet, too much like "twelve grey-haired guys named George." The quiescence of the board has resulted in important public and, for that matter, shareholder concerns being ignored.

An important answer is structural. The homogeneity of the board can only be ended by giving to each director, in addition to a general duty to see that the corporation is profitably administered, a separate oversight responsibility, a separate expertise, and a separate constituency so each important public concern would be guaranteed at least one informed representative on the board. There might be nine corporate directors, each of whom is elected to a board position with one of the following oversight responsibilities:

1. Employee welfare
2. Consumer protection
3. Environmental protection and community relations
4. Shareholder rights
5. Compliance with law
6. Finances

7. Purchasing and marketing
8. Management efficiency
9. Planning and research

By requiring each director to balance responsibility for representing a particular social concern against responsibility for the overall health of the enterprise, the problem of isolated "public" directors would be avoided. No individual director is likely to be "frozen out" of collegial decision-making because all directors would be of the same character. Each director would spend the greater part of his or her time developing expertise in a different area; each director would have a motivation to insist that a different aspect of a business decision be considered. Yet each would simultaneously be responsible for participating in all board decisions, as directors now are. So the specialized area of each director would supplement but not supplant the director's general duties. . . .

To maintain the independence of the board from the operating management it reviews also requires that each federally chartered corporation shall be directed by a purely "outside" board. No executive, attorney, representative, or agent of a corporation should be allowed to serve simultaneously as a director of that same corporation. Directorial and executive loyalty should be furthered by an absolute prohibition of interlocks. No director, executive, general counsel, or company agent should be allowed to serve more than one corporation subject to the Federal Corporate Chartering Act.

Several objections may be raised. First, how can we be sure that completely outside boards will be competent? Corporate campaign rules should be redesigned to emphasize qualifications. This will allow shareholder voters to make rational decisions based on information clearly presented to them. It is also a fair assumption that shareholders, given an actual choice and role in corporate governance, will want to elect the men and women most likely to safeguard their investments.

A second objection is that once all interlocks are proscribed and a full-time outside board required, there will not be enough qualified directors to staff all major firms. This complaint springs from that corporate mentality which, accustomed to 60-year-old white male bankers and businessmen as directors, makes the norm a virtue. In fact, if we loosen the reins on our imagination, America has a large, rich, and diverse pool of possible directorial talent from academics and public administrators and community leaders to corporate and public interest lawyers.

But directors should be limited to four two-year terms so that boards do not become stale. And no director should be allowed to serve on more than one board at any one time. Although simultaneous service on two or three boards might allow key directors to "pollinize" directorates by comparing their different experiences, this would reduce their loyalty to any one board, jeopardize their ability to fully perform their new directorial responsibilities, and undermine the goal of opening up major boardrooms to as varied a new membership as is reasonable.

The shareholder electoral process should be made more democratic as well. Any shareholder or allied shareholder group which owns .1 percent of the common voting stock in the corporation or comprises 100 or more individuals and does not include a present executive of the corporation, nor act for a present executive, may nominate up to three persons to serve as directors. This will exclude executive management from the nomination process. It also increases the likelihood of a diverse board by preventing any one or two sources from proposing all nominees. To prevent frivolous use of the nominating power, this proposal establishes a minimum shareownership condition.

Six weeks prior to the shareholders' meeting to elect directors, each shareholder should receive a ballot and a written statement on which each candidate for the board sets forth his or her qualifications to hold office and purposes for seeking office. All campaign costs would be borne by the corporation. These strict campaign and funding rules will assure that all nominees will have an equal opportunity to be judged by the shareholders. By preventing directorates from being bought, these provisions will require board elections to be conducted solely on the merit of the candidates. . . .

Finally, additional provisions will require cumulative voting and forbid "staggered" board elections. Thus any shareholder faction capable of jointly voting approximately 10 percent of the total number of shares cast may elect a director.

A NEW ROLE FOR SHAREHOLDERS

The difficulty with this proposal is the one that troubled Juvenal two millenia ago: *Quis custodiet ipsos custodes*, or Who shall watch the watchmen? Without a full-time body to discipline the board, it would be so easy for the board of directors and executive management to become friends. Active vigilance could become routinized into an uncritical partnership. The same board theoretically elected to protect shareholder equity and internalize law might instead become management's lobbyist.

Relying on shareholders to discipline directors may strike many as a dubious approach. Historically, the record of shareholder participation in corporate governance has been an abysmal one. The monumental indifference of most shareholders is worse than that of sheep; sheep at least have some sense of what manner of ram they follow. But taken together, the earlier proposals—an outside, full-time board, nominated by rival shareholder groups and voted on by beneficial owners—will increase involvement by shareholders. And cumulative voting insures that an aroused minority of shareholders—even one as small as 9 or 10 percent of all share-holders—shall have the opportunity to elect at least one member of the board.

But that alone is hardly sufficient. At a corporation the size of General Motors, an aggregation of 10 percent of all voting stock might require the allied action of over 200,000 individuals—which probably could occur no more than once in a generation. To keep directors responsive to law and legitimate public concerns requires surer and more immediate mechanisms. In a word, it requires arming the victims of corporate abuses with the powers to swiftly respond to them. For only those employees, consumers, racial or sex minorities, and local communities harmed by corporate depredations can be depended upon to speedily complain. By allowing any victim to become a shareholder and by permitting any shareholder to have an effective voice, there will be the greatest likelihood of continuing scrutiny of the corporation's directorate. . . .

Shareholders are not the only ones with an incentive to review decisions of corporate management; nor, as Professors Chayes and Dahl argue, are shareholders the only persons who should be accorded corporate voting rights. The increasing use by American corporations of technologies and materials that pose direct and serious threats to the health of communities surrounding their plants requires the creation of a new form of corporate voting right. When a federally chartered corporation engages, for example, in production or distribution of nuclear fuels or the emission of toxic air, water, or solid waste pollutants, citizens whose health is endangered should not be left, at best, with receiving money damages after a time-consuming trial to compensate them for damaged property, impaired health, or even death.

Instead, upon finding a public health hazard by three members of the board of directors or 3 percent of the shareholders, a corporate referendum should be held in the political jurisdiction affected by the health hazard. The referendum would be drafted by the unit triggering it—either the three board members or a designate of the shareholders. The affected citizens by majority vote will then decide whether the hazardous practice shall be allowed to continue. This form of direct democracy has obvious parallels to the intiative and referendum procedures familiar to many states—except that the election will be paid for by a business corporation and will not necessarily occur at a regular election. . . .

This type of election procedure is necessary to give enduring meaning to the democratic concept of "consent of the governed." To be sure, this proposal goes beyond the traditional assumption that the only affected or relevant constituents of the corporation are the shareholders. But no longer can we accept the Faustian bargain that the continued toleration of corporate destruction of local health and property is the cost to the public of doing business. In an equitable system of governance, the perpetrators should answer to their victims.

Power and Accountability: The Changing Role of the Corporate Board of Directors

IRVING S. SHAPIRO

The proper direction of business corporations in a free society is a topic of intense and often heated discussion. Under the flag of corporate governance there has been a running debate about the performance of business organizations, together with a flood of proposals for changes in the way corporate organizations are controlled.

It has been variously suggested that corporate charters be dispensed by the Federal Government as distinct from those of the states (to tighten the grip on corporate actions); that only outsiders unconnected to an enterprise be allowed to sit on its board of directors or that, as a minimum, most of the directors should qualify as "independent"; that seats be apportioned to constituent groups (employees, women, consumers and minorities, along with stockholders); that boards be equipped with private staffs, beyond the management's control (to smoke out facts that hired executives might prefer to hide or decorate); and that new disclosure requirements be added to existing ones (to provide additional tools for outside oversight of behavior and performance).

Such proposals have come from the Senate Judiciary Committee's antitrust arm; from regulatory agency spokesmen, most notably the current head of the Securities and Exchange Commission, Harold Williams, and a predecessor there, William Cary; from the professoriat in schools of law and business; from the bench and bar; and from such observers of the American scene as Ralph Nader and Mark Green.[1]

Suggestions for change have sometimes been offered in sympathy and sometimes in anger. They have ranged from general pleas for corporations to behave better, to meticulously detailed reorganization charts. The span in itself suggests part of the problem: "Corporate Governance" (like Social Responsibility before it) is not a subject with a single meaning, but is a shorthand label for an array of social and political as well as economic concerns. One is obliged to look for a way to keep discussion within a reasonable perimeter.

There appears to be one common thread. All of the analyses, premises, and prescriptions seem to derive in one way or another from the question of accountability: Are corporations suitably controlled, and to whom

Excerpted from a paper presented in the Fairless Lecture Series, Carnegie-Mellon University, October, 24, 1979. Reprinted by permission.

or what are they responsible? This is the central public issue, and the focal point of this paper.

One school of opinion holds that corporations cannot be adequately called to account because there are systemic economic and political failings. In this view, nothing short of a major overhaul will serve. What is envisioned, at least by many in this camp, are new kinds of corporate organizations constructed along the lines of democratic political institutions. The guiding ideology would be communitarian, with the needs and rights of the community emphasized in preference to profit-seeking goals now pursued by corporate leaders (presumably with Darwinian abandon, with natural selection weeding out the weak, and with society left to pick up the external costs).

BOARDS CHANGING FOR BETTER

Other critics take a more temperate view. They regard the present system as sound and its methods of governance as morally defensible. They concede, though, that changes are needed to reflect new conditions. Whether the changes are to be brought about by gentle persuasion, or require the use of a two-by-four to get the mule's attention, is part of the debate.

This paper sides with the gradualists. My position, based on a career in industry and personal observation of corporate boards at work, is that significant improvements have been made in recent years in corporate governance, and that more changes are coming in an orderly way; that with these amendments, corporations are accountable and better monitored than ever before; and that pat formulas or proposals for massive "restructuring" should be suspect. The formula approach often is based on ignorance of what it takes to run a large enterprise, on false premises as to the corporate role in society, or on a philosophy that misreads the American tradition and leaves no room for large enterprises that are both free and efficient.

The draconian proposals would almost certainly yield the worst of all possibilities, a double-negative trade-off. They would sacrifice the most valuable qualities of the enterprise system to gain the least attractive features of the governmental system. Privately owned enterprises are geared to a primary economic task, that of joining human talents and natural resources in the production and distribution of goods and services. That task is essential, and two centuries of national experience suggest these conclusions: The United States has been uncommonly successful at meeting economic needs through reliance on private initiative; and the competitive marketplace is a better course-correction device than governmental fiat. The enterprise system would have had to have failed miserably before the case could be made for replacing it with governmental dictum.

Why should the public have any interest in the internal affairs of corporations? Who cares who decides? Part of the answer comes from recent news stories noting such special problems as illegal corporate contributions to political campaigns, and tracking the decline and fall of once-stout companies such as Penn Central. Revelations of that kind raise questions about the probity and competence of the people minding the largest stores. There is more to it than this, though. There have always been cases of corporate failures. Small companies have gone under too, at a rate far higher than their larger brethren.[2] Instances of corruption have occurred in institutions of all sizes, whether they be commercial enterprises or some other kind.

Corporate behavior and performance are points of attention, and the issue attaches to size, precisely because people do not see the large private corporation as entirely private. People care about what goes on in the corporate interior because they see themselves as affected parties whether they work in such companies or not.

There is no great mystery as to the source of this challenge to the private character of governance. Three trends account for it. First is the growth of very large corporations. They have come to employ a large portion of the work force, and have become key factors in the nation's technology, wealth and security. They have generated admiration for their prowess, but also fear of their imputed power.

The second contributing trend is the decline of owner-management. Over time, corporate shares have been dispersed. The owners have hired managers, entrusted them with the power to make decisions, and drifted away from involvement in corporate affairs except to meet statutory requirements (as, for example, to approve a stock split or elect a slate of directors).

That raises obvious practical questions. If the owners are on the sidelines, what is to stop the managers from remaining in power indefinitely, using an inside position to control the selection of their own bosses, the directors? Who is looking over management's shoulder to monitor performance?

The third element here is the rise in social expectations regarding corporations. It is no longer considered enough for a company to make products and provide commercial services. The larger it is, the more it is expected to assume various obligations that once were met by individuals or communities, or were not met at all.

With public expectations ratcheting upward, corporations are under pressure to behave more like governments and embrace a universe of problems. That would mean, of necessity, that private institutions would focus less on problems of their own choice.

If corporations succumbed to that pressure, and in effect declared the public's work to be their own, the next step would be to turn them into institutions accountable to the public in the same way that units of government are accountable.

But the corporation does not parallel the government. The assets in corporate hands are more limited and the constituents have options. There are levels of appeal. While the only accountability in government lies within government itself—the celebrated system of checks and balances among the executive, legislative, and judicial branches—the corporation is in a different situation: It has external and plural accountability, codified in the law and reinforced by social pressure. It must "answer" in one way or another to all levels of government, to competitors in the marketplace who would be happy to have the chance to increase their own market share, to employees who can strike or quit, and to consumers who can keep their wallets in their pockets. The checks are formidable even if one excludes for purposes of argument the corporation's initial point of accountability, its stockholders (many of whom do in fact vote their shares, and do not just use their feet).

The case for major reforms in corporate governance rests heavily on the argument that past governmental regulation of large enterprises has been impotent or ineffectual. This is an altogether remarkable assertion, given the fact that the nation has come through a period in which large corporations have been subjected to an unprecedented flood of new legislation and rule making. Regulation now reaches into every corporate nook and cranny—including what some people suppose (erroneously) to be the sanctuary of the boardroom.

Market competition, so lightly dismissed by some critics as fiction or artifact, is in fact a vigorous force in the affairs of almost all corporations. Size lends no immunity to its relentless pressures. The claim that the largest corporations somehow have set themselves above the play of market forces or, more likely, make those forces play for themselves, is widely believed. Public opinion surveys show that. What is lacking is any evidence that this is so. Here too, the evidence goes the other way. Objective studies of concentrated industries (the auto industry, for instance) show that corporate size does not mean declining competitiveness, nor does it give assurance that the products will sell.

Everyday experience confirms this. Consider the hard times of the Chrysler Corporation today, the disappearance of many once-large companies from the American scene, and the constant rollover in the membership list of the "100 Largest," a churning process that has been going on for years and shows no signs of abating.[3]

If indeed the two most prominent overseers of corporate behavior, government and competition, have failed to provide appropriate checks and balances, and if that is to be cited as evidence that corporations lack accountability, the burden of proof should rest with those who so state.

The basics apply to Sears, Roebuck as much as to Sam's appliance shop. Wherever you buy the new toaster, it should work when it is plugged in. Whoever services the washing machine, the repairman should arrive at the appointed time, with tools and parts.

Special expectations are added for the largest firms, however. One is that they apply their resources to tasks that invite economies of scale, providing goods and services that would not otherwise be available, or that could be delivered by smaller units only at considerable loss of efficiency. Another is that, like the elephant, they watch where they put their feet and not stamp on smaller creatures through clumsiness or otherwise.

A second set of requirements can be added, related not to the markets selected by corporations individually, but to the larger economic tasks that must be accomplished in the name of the national interest and security. In concert with others in society, including big government, big corporations are expected to husband scarce resources and develop new ones, and to foster strong and diverse programs of research and development, to the end that practical technological improvements will emerge and the nation will be competitive in the international setting.

Beyond this there are softer but nonetheless important obligations: To operate with respect for the environment and with careful attention to the health and safety of people; to honor and give room to the personal qualities employees bring to their jobs, including their need to make an identifiable mark and to realize as much of their potential as possible; to lend assistance in filling community needs in which corporations have some stake; and to help offset community problems which in some measure corporations have helped to create.

This is not an impossible job, only a difficult one. Admitting that the assignment probably is not going to be carried out perfectly by any organization, the task is unlikely to be done even half well unless some boundary conditions are met. Large corporations cannot fulfill their duties unless they remain both profitable and flexible. They must be able to attract and hold those volunteer owners; which is to say, there must be the promise of present or future gain. Companies must have the wherewithal to reinvest significant amounts to revitalize their own capital plants, year after year in unending fashion. Otherwise, it is inevitable that they will go into decline versus competitors elsewhere, as will the nation.

Flexibility is no less important. The fields of endeavor engaging large business units today are dynamic in nature. Without an in-and-out flow of products and services, without the mobility to adapt to shifts in opportunities and public preferences, corporations would face the fate of the buggy-whip makers.

Profitability and flexibility are easy words to say, but in practice they make for hard decisions. A company that would close a plant with no more than a passing thought for those left unemployed would and should be charged with irresponsibility; but a firm that vowed never to close any of its plants would be equally irresponsible, for it might be consigning itself to a pattern of stagnation that could ultimately cost the jobs of the people in all of its plants.

The central requirement is not that large corporations take the pledge and bind themselves to stated actions covering all circumstances, but that they do a thoughtful and informed job of balancing competing (and ever changing) claims on corporate resources, mediating among the conflicting (also changing) desires of various constituencies, and not giving in to any one-dimensional perspective however sincerely felt. It is this that describes responsible corporate governance.

Certainly, corporations do not have the public mandate or the resources to be what Professor George Lodge of the Harvard Business School would have them be, which is nationally chartered community-oriented collectives.[4] Such a mission for corporations would be tolerable to society only if corporations were turned into minigovernments—but that takes us back to the inefficiency problem noted earlier. The one task governments have proven they almost always do badly is to run production and distribution organizations. The only models there are to follow are not attractive. Would anyone seriously argue that the public would be ahead if General Motors were run along the lines of Amtrak, or Du Pont were managed in the manner of the U.S. Postal System?

Once the roles are defined, the key to success in running a large corporation is to lay out a suitable division of labor between the board and the management, make that division crystal clear on both sides, and staff the offices with the right people. Perhaps the best way to make that split is to follow the pattern used in the U.S. Constitution, which stipulates the powers of the Federal Government and specifies that everything not covered there is reserved to the states or the people thereof. The board of directors should lay claim to five basic jobs, and leave the rest to the paid managers.

The duties the board should not delegate are these:

1. The determination of the broad policies and the general direction the efforts of the enterprise should take.
2. The establishment of performance standards—ethical as well as commercial—against which the management will be judged, and the communication of these standards to the management in unambiguous terms.
3. The selection of company officers, and attention to the question of succession.
4. The review of top management's performance in following the overall strategy and meeting the board's standards as well as legal requirements.
5. The communication of the organization's goals and standards to those who have a significant stake in its activities (insiders and outsiders both) and of the steps being taken to keep the organization responsive to the needs of those people.

The establishment of corporate strategy and performance standards denotes a philosophy of active stewardship, rather than passive trusteeship. It is the mission of directors to see that corporate resources are put to creative use, and in the bargain subjected to calculated risks rather than simply being tucked into the countinghouse for safekeeping.

That in turn implies certain prerequisites for board members of large corporations which go beyond those required of a school board member, a trustee of a charitable organization, or a director of a small, local business firm. In any such assignments one would look for personal integrity, interest and intelligence, but beyond these there is a dividing line that marks capability and training.

The stakes are likely to be high in the large corporation, and the factors confronting the board and management usually are complex. The elements weighing heavily in decisions are not those with which people become familiar in the ordinary course of day-to-day life, as might be the case with a school board.

Ordinarily the management of a corporation attends to such matters as product introductions, capital expansions, and supply problems. This in no way reduces the need for directors with extensive business background, though. With few exceptions, corporate boards involve themselves in strategic decisions and those involving large capital commitments. Directors thus need at least as much breadth and perspective as the management, if not as much detailed knowledge.

If the directors are to help provide informed and principled oversight of corporate affairs, a good number of them must provide windows to the outside world. That is at least part of the rationale for outside directors, and especially for directors who can bring unique perspective to the group. There is an equally strong case, though, for directors with an intimate knowledge of the company's business, and insiders may be the best qualified to deliver that. What is important is not that a ratio be established, but that the group contain a full range of the competences needed to set courses of action that will largely determine the long-range success of the enterprise.

BOARDS NEED WINDOWS

The directors also have to be able and willing to invest considerable time in their work. In this day and age, with major resources on the line and tens of thousands of employees affected by each large corporation, there should be no seat in the boardroom for people willing only to show up once a month to pour holy water over decisions already made. Corporate boards need windows, not window dressing!

There are two other qualities that may be self-evident from what has been said, but are mentioned for emphasis. Directors must be interested in the job and committed to the overall purpose of the organization. However much they may differ on details of accomplishment, they must be willing to work at the task of working with others on the board. They ought to be able to speak freely in a climate that encourages open discussion, but to recognize the difference between attacking an idea and attacking the person who presents it. No less must they see the difference between compromising tactics to reach consensus and compromising principles.

Structures and procedures, which so often are pushed to the fore in discussions of corporate governance, actually belong last. They are not unimportant, but they are subordinate.

Structure follows purpose, or should, and that is a useful principle for testing some of the proposals for future changes in corporate boards. Today, two-thirds to three-quarters of the directors of most large corporations are outsiders, and it is being proposed that this trend be pushed still further, with the only insider being the chief executive officer, and with a further stipulation that he not be board chairman. This idea has surfaced from Harold Williams, and variations on it have come from other sources.

The idea bumps into immediate difficulties. High-quality candidates for boards are not in large supply as it is. Conflicts of interest would prohibit selection of many individuals close enough to an industry to be familiar with its problems. The disqualification of insiders would reduce the selection pool to a still smaller number, and the net result could well be corporate boards whose members were less competent and effective than those now sitting.

Experience would also suggest that such a board would be the most easily manipulated of all. That should be no trick at all for a skillful CEO, for he would be the only person in the room with a close, personal knowledge of the business.

The objective is unassailable: Corporate boards need directors with independence of judgment; but in today's business world, independence is not enough. In coping with such problems as those confronting the electronics corporations beset by heavy foreign competition, or those encountered by international banks which have loans outstanding in countries with shaky governments, boards made up almost entirely of outsiders would not just have trouble evaluating nuances of the management's performance; they might not even be able to read the radar and tell whether the helmsman was steering straight for the rocks.

If inadequately prepared individuals are placed on corporate boards, no amount of sincerity on their part can offset the shortcoming. It is pure illusion to suppose that complex business issues and organizational problems can be overseen by people with little or no experience in dealing with such problems. However intelligent such people might be, the effect of their governance would be to expose the people most affected by the organization—employees, owners, customers, suppliers—to leadership that would be (using the word precisely) incompetent.

It is sometimes suggested that the members of corporate boards ought to come from the constituencies—an employee-director, a consumer-director, an environmentalist-director, etc. This Noah's Ark proposal, which is probably not to be taken seriously, is an extension of the false parallel between corporations and elected governments. The flaw in the idea is all but self-evident: People representing specific interest groups would by definition be committed to the goals of their groups rather than any others; but it is the responsibility of directors (not simply by tradition but as a matter of law as well) to serve the organization as a whole. The two goals are incompatible.

If there were such boards they would move at glacial speed. The internal political maneuvering would be Byzantine, and it is difficult to see how the directors could avoid an obvious challenge of accountability. Stockholder suits would pop up like dandelions in the spring.

One may also question how many people of ability would stand for election under this arrangement. Quotas are an anathema in a free society, and their indulgence here would insult the constituencies themselves—a woman on the board not because she is competent but only because she is female; a black for black's sake; and so on ad nauseam.

A certain amount of constituency pleading is not all bad, as long as it is part of a corporate commitment. There is something to be said for what Harold Williams labels "tension," referring to the divergence in perspective of those concerned primarily with internal matters and those looking more at the broader questions. However, as has been suggested by James Shepley, the president of Time, Inc., "tension" can lead to paralysis, and is likely to do so if boards are packed with groups known to be unsympathetic to the management's problems and business realities.

As Shepley commented, "The chief executive would be out of his mind who would take a risk-laden business proposition to a group of directors who, whatever their other merits, do not really understand the fine points of the business at hand, and whose official purpose is to create 'tension.' "[5]

Students of corporate affairs have an abundance of suggestions for organizing the work of boards, with detailed structures in mind for committees on audit, finance, and other areas; plus prescriptions for membership. The danger here is not that boards will pick the wrong formula—many organization charts could be made to work—but that boards will put too much emphasis on the wrong details.

The idea of utilizing a committee system in which sub-groups have designated duties is far more important than the particulars of their arrangement. When such committees exist, and they are given known and specific oversight duties, it is a signal to the outside world (and to the management) that performance is being monitored in a no-nonsense fashion.

It is this argument that has produced the rule changes covering companies listed on the New York Stock Exchange, calling for audit committees chaired by outside directors, and including no one currently active in management. Most large firms have moved in that direction, and the move makes sense, for an independently minded audit committee is a potent instrument of corporate oversight. Even a rule of that kind, though, has the potential of backfiring.

Suppose some of the directors best qualified to perform the audit function are not outsiders? Are the analytical skills and knowledge of career employees therefore to be bypassed? Are the corporate constituencies well served by such an exclusionary rule, keeping in mind that all directors, insiders or outsiders, are bound by the same legal codes and corporate books are still subject to independent, outside audit? It is scarcely a case of the corporate purse being placed in the hands of the unwatched.

Repeatedly, the question of structure turns on the basics: If corporations have people with competence and commitment on their boards, structure and process fall into line easily; if people with the needed qualities are missing or the performance standards are unclear, corporations are in trouble no matter whose guidebook they follow. Equally, the question drives to alternatives: The present system is surely not perfect, but what is better?

By the analysis presented here the old fundamentals are still sound, no alternative for radical change has been defended with successful argument, and the best course appears to be to stay within the historical and philosophical traditions of American enterprise, working out the remaining problems one by one.

NOTES

1. U.S. Senate, Committee on the Judiciary Subcommittee on Antitrust, Monopoly and Business Rights; Address by Harold M. Williams, *Corporate Accountability*, Fifth Annual Securities Regulation Institute, San Diego, California (January 18, 1978); W. Cary, *A Proposed Federal Corporate Minimum Standards Act*, 29 Bus. Law. 1101 (1974) and W. Cary, *Federalism and Corporate Law: Reflections Upon Delaware*, 83 Yale L. J. 663 (1974); D. E. Schwartz, *A Case for Federal Chartering of Corporations*, 31 Bus. Law. 1125 (1976); M. A. Eisenberg, *Legal Modes of Management Structure in the Modern Corporation; Officers, Directors and Accountants*, 63 Calif. L. Rev. 375 (1975); A. J. Goldberg, *Debate on Outside Directors*, New York Times, October 29, 1972 (§ 3, p. 1); Ralph Nader and Mark Green, *Constitutionalizing the Corporation: The Case for Federal Chartering of Giant Corporations* (1976).
2. See "Sixty Years of Corporate Ups, Downs and Outs," *Forbes*, September 15, 1977, p. 127 et seq.
3. See Dr. Betty Bock's Statement before Hearings on S. 600, Small and Independent Business Protection Act of 1979, April 25, 1979.
4. G. Lodge, *The New American Ideology* (1975).
5. Shepley, *The CEO Goes to Washington*, Remarks to Fortune Corporation Communications Seminar, March 28, 1979.

Biographical Information

KENNETH ALPERN
Kenneth D. Alpern is a member of the Philosophy Department at DePaul University. He works in ethical theory and the history of ethics as well as in applied ethics. His anthology on moral and legal issues of new reproductive technologies, tentatively entitled *Reproductive Technology and Human Values*, is forthcoming from Oxford University Press.

ROBERT L. ARRINGTON
Robert L. Arrington is Professor of Philosophy and Interim Dean of the College of Arts and Sciences at Georgia State University. He received his undergraduate degree from Vanderbilt University and did his graduate work at Tulane University. He was an Honorary Woodrow Wilson Fellow, and he held an ACLS Fellowship in 1974–75. His areas of specialization include ethics and the philosophy of Wittgenstein. He is author of *Rationalism, Realism, and Relativism: Perspectives in Contemporary Moral Epistemology* (Cornell, 1989) and co-editor of Wittgenstein's *Philosophical Investigations: Text and Context* (Routledge, forthcoming).

KENNETH J. ARROW
Dr. Arrow was born in 1921 and educated at The City College and Columbia University. After military service in World War II, he received his Ph.D. from Columbia in 1951 and was Research Associate at the Cowles Commission for Research in Economics 1947–1949. He subsequently held faculty positions at the University of Chicago, Harvard University, Stanford University, the last from 1949 to 1968 and again from 1979 to date. Among other current positions, he is also External Professor at the Santa Fe Institute and Senior Fellow by Courtesy of the Hoover Institution. He has received a number of honors, including honorary degrees, the John Bates Clark Medal of the American Economic Association, the Nobel Memorial Prize in Economic Science, and the von Neumann Prize of The Institute of Management Sciences and the Operations Research Society of America. He has authored or co-authored seven books and about 170 papers.

WILLIAM BLACKSTONE
William Blackstone received his B.A. from Elan College and his M.A. and Ph.D. from Duke University. He was professor of philosophy and religion at the University of Georgia, where he was also chairman of the Division of Social Sciences. A member of the American Philosophical Associa-

490

tion and numerous other philosophical societies, William Blackstone authored *Philosophy and the Human Conditions, Religious Knowledge and Religion*, and many other books and articles on ethical and environmental issues.

JOHN R. BOATRIGHT

John R. Boatright is Professor of Philosophy at John Carroll University. A specialist in business ethics, he is author of *Ethics and the Conduct of Business*, published by Prentice-Hall, and serves on the Ethical Review Board of *Business Ethics Quarterly*.

SISSELA BOK

Sissela Bok was born in Sweden and educated in Switzerland, France, and the United States. She received a Ph.D. in philosophy from Harvard University in 1970. She has taught philosophy at Brandeis University since 1985 and earlier taught courses in ethics and decision making at Harvard Medical School and the John F. Kennedy School of Government. She is the author of numerous articles on ethics, literature, and biography, and of: *Lying: Moral Choice in Public and Private Life* (1978); *Secrets: On the Ethics of Concealment and Revelation* (1982); *A Strategy for Peace* (1989); as well as *Alva Myrdel: A Daughter's Memoir* (1991).

MICHAEL G. BOWEN

Michael G. Bowen is an Assistant Professor of Management in the College of Business Administration at the University of Notre Dame. He has published and lectured on topics relating to sensemaking and learning issues as they apply to the recommitment of resources to questionable courses of action. His publications include "The Escalation Phenomenon Reconsidered: Decision Dilemmas or Decision Errors?" in the *Academy of Management Review* (1987).

NORMAN E. BOWIE

Norman E. Bowie is the Elmer L. Andersen Chair of Corporate Responsibility and holds a joint appointment in the Departments of Strategic Management and Organization and Philosophy at the University of Minnesota. Professor Bowie is co-author of *Business Ethics* (second edition) and the co-editor of *Ethical Theory and Business* (third edition). He is the author or co-editor of nine other books on professional ethics and political philosophy and is a frequent contributor to scholarly journals and conferences.

ROGENE BUCHHOLZ

Dr. Rogene A. Buchholz is the Legendre-Soule Professor of Business Ethics at Loyola University, New Orleans. He previously taught at the University of Texas at Dallas, Washington University at St. Louis, and the University of Minnesota. He is the author of nine books in the areas of business and public policy, business ethics, and environment. Articles by Dr. Buchholz have appeared in *Human Relations, Journal of Management Studies, Personnel Psychology, Journal of Applied Psychology, Industrial and Labor Relations Review, Academy of Management Journal, Harvard Business Review,* and *Journal of Business Ethics.*

ANDREW CARNEGIE

Andrew Carnegie was born in Scotland in 1835 and emigrated to the United States with his family in 1848. He worked in a cotton factory and as a telegraph operator and introduced sleeping cars for the Pennsylvania Railroad. Foreseeing the future demand for iron and steel, he left the railroad and founded the Keystone Bridge Company and began to amass his fortune. The Carnegie companies was incorporated into USS in 1901, when Carnegie retired and devoted himself to philanthropy, for which he is deservedly famous today.

ALBERT CARR

Albert Carr was born in 1902 and educated at the University of Chicago, Columbia University, and the London School of Economics. He was active in business and politics, serving as economic advisor to President Truman. He wrote numerous books and articles, among them *Truman, Stalin, and Peace,* and *Business as a Game.* In addition, he authored several films and television plays. He died in 1971.

JOANNE B. CIULLA

Joanne Ciulla is the Coston Family Chair in Leadership and Ethics at the Jepson School of the University of Richmond. A Ph.D. in philosophy, she has also held academic posts at LaSalle University, the Harvard Business School, the Wharton School and Oxford University. Ciulla has published a number of articles on business ethics. Her book *Honest Work* will appear in 1993.

JAMES S. COLEMAN

James S. Coleman is University Professor, Department of Sociology, University of Chicago. He is a member of the National Academy of Sciences, the American Philosophical Society, the American Academy of Arts and Sciences and the Royal Swedish Academy of Sciences. His publications include *The Asymmetric Society, Individual Interest,* and *Collective Action.* He was the principal author of *Equality of Educational Opportunity.*

THOMAS J. DONALDSON

Thomas Donaldson is the John Carroll Professor of Business Ethics at Georgetown University. Books he has authored or edited include *The Ethics of International Business* (1989); *Corporations and Morality* (1982); *Issues in Moral Philosophy* (1986) and *Case Studies in Business Ethics* (1984).

He is a founding member and past president of the Society for Business Ethics and a member of the editorial boards of the *Journal of Business Ethics, Business Ethics Quarterly*, and the *Employee Responsibilities and Rights Journal*. He is general editor of the book series *Soundings*, which publishes books dealing with ethics, economics, and business, for Notre Dame University Press.

THOMAS DUNFEE

Thomas W. Dunfee is the Kolodny Professor of Social Responsibility at the Wharton School, University of Pennsylvania. He has published articles on business law and business ethics in numerous journals, including the *Northwestern University Law Review, American Business Law Journal, Journal of Business Ethics, Business and Professional Ethics Journal* and *Business Ethics Quarterly*. He was president of the American Business Law Association, 1989-1990, and is a former editor-in-chief of the *American Business Law Journal*.

WILLIAM M. EVAN

William M. Evan is Professor of Management and Sociology at the Wharton School, University of Pennsylvania. He is best known for his contributions to organization theory and the sociology of law. Evan's work on "the organization set" laid the groundwork for much of interorganizational theory, especially stakeholder theory.

DAVID EWING

David Walkley Ewing attended Amherst College and received an LL.B. from Harvard in 1949. Until recently he was the managing editor of the *Harvard Business Review* and a consultant on editorial problems to business and industrial firms. His works include *Long Range Planning for Management, Effective Marketing Action, The Managerial Mind*, and *Writing for Results*.

JOHN FLEMING

John Fleming is professor emeritus of management at the University of Southern California and a member of the Arthur Andersen Ethics Advisory Council. His research is in business ethics, corporate social responsibility, and strategy.

R. EDWARD FREEMAN

Dr. Freeman joined the Darden Graduate School of Business Administration in 1987 as Elis and Signe Olsson Professor of Business Administration and Director of the Olsson Center for Applied Ethics. Prior to coming to the Darden School, Dr. Freeman taught at University of Minnesota, and the Wharton School, University of Pennsylvania. Freeman's areas of interest are business ethics, business policy and strategy, and organizational behavior. His most recent books are *Ethica and Agency Theory* (with

N. Bowie), *Business Ethics: The State of the Art, The Logic of Strategy* (with D. Gilbert, Jr., E. Hartman & J. Mauries), *Management*, 5th Edition (with J. Stoner), and *Corporate Strategy and the Search for Ethics* (with D. Gilbert, Jr.). He published *Strategic Management: A Stakeholder Approach* with Pitman Publishing in 1984.

PETER A. FRENCH

Peter French is Lennox Distinguished Professor and Professor of Philosophy at Trinity University. He received a B.A. from Gettysburg College, an M.A. from the University of Southern California, and a Ph.D. from the University of Miami. He is the editor of *Midwestern Studies in Philosophy* and the *Journal of Social Philosophy*. He has taught at the University of Delaware, the University of Minnesota, and Dalhousie University. His published works include *The Scope of Morality, Collective and Corporate Responsibility*, and *The Spectrum of Responsibility*.

MILTON FRIEDMAN

Milton Friedman, U.S. laissez-faire economist, Emeritus Professor at the University of Chicago, and Senior Research Fellow at the Hoover Institution, is one of the leading modern exponents of liberalism in the 19th-century European sense. He is the author of *Capitalism and Freedom* and co-author of *A Monetary History of the United States*, and *Free to Choose*. He was awarded the Nobel Prize for Economics in 1976.

JOHN KENNETH GALBRAITH

John Kenneth Galbraith, perhaps best known for having served as a key advisor to John F. Kennedy, was educated at the University of Guelph and the University of California at Berkeley. He taught at Harvard and Princeton until 1942, when he was called to serve in a variety of government positions. He later returned to Harvard but remained active in public affairs and specifically as Kennedy's Ambassador to India. A prolific writer, he is the author of *American Capitalism: the Concept of Countervailing Power, The Affluent Society, The New Industrial State Economics, The Public Purpose, The Age of Uncertainty* and many many others.

A. R. GINI

A. R. Gini is Associate Professor of Philosophy and Adjunct Professor in the Institute of Industrial Relations at Loyola University Chicago. Besides lecturing to community and professional organizations, he consults on corporate ethics and employee relations and is regularly heard on National Public Radio's Chicago affiliate, WBEZ-FM. His published work includes essays, articles and case studies on a variety of problems in American philosophy, philosophical anthropology and business ethics. He has also published *Philosophical Issues in Human Rights*, (Werhane, Gini, Ozar) Random House, 1986; *It Comes With the Territory: An Inquiry Into the Nature of Work,* (Gini, Sullivan) Random House, January 1989; and *Case Studies in Business Ethics* (Donaldson, Gini) Prentice-Hall, Fall 1989. He is the Managing Editor of *Business Ethics Quarterly,* a journal of the Society for Business Ethics.

KENNETH GOODPASTER

Kenneth Goodpaster received his A.B. in mathematics from the University of Notre Dame and his M.A. and Ph.D. in philosophy from the University of Michigan. He has published widely on moral philosophy and applied ethics. His publications include *Perspectives on Morality: Essays of William K. Frankena, Ethics and Problems of the 21st Century, Regulation, Values and the Public Interest, Ethics in Management,* and *Policies and Persons: A Casebook in Business Ethics* (2nd Edition 1991). In 1980, Goodpaster joined the faculty of the Harvard University Graduate School of Business Administration, where he developed and taught a course entitled "Ethical Aspects of Corporate Policy" and led the design of the required ethics module, "Decision Making and Ethical Values." In 1989, Goodpaster accepted the David and Barbara Koch Chair in Business Ethics at the University of St. Thomas, St. Paul, Minnesota.

EDMUND R. GRAY

Dr. Gray is Professor of Management, Loyola Marymount University and formerly, Chair of the Department of Management at Loyola Marymount University and also Louisiana State University. He is the author and editor of five books and author of numerous articles in journals such as *Sloan Management Review, Academy of Management Journal* and *Business Horizons.*

MARK GREEN

Mark Green is currently the Director of the Corporate Accountability Research Group. He is a well-known and respected critic of the American business system and U.S. government policy, and has often co-authored articles and shared projects with Ralph Nader.

BARRY GROSS

Barry Gross is Professor of Philosophy at York College, City University of New York and a visiting scholar of law at Columbia University. He received his B.A. from New York University, his M.A. from the University of Colorado, and his Ph.D. from the University of Toronto. He has previously taught at Northern Illinois University and DePaul University, and is a member of the Mind Association, the American Philosophical Association, and AAAS. He is the editor of *Reverse Discrimination* as well as the author of *Discrimination in Reverse: Is Turn About Fair Play?* and numerous articles.

R. M. HARE

Professor Hare, one of the leading moral philosophers of the twentieth century, was educated at Balliol College, Oxford and was a Fellow and Tutor at Balliol from 1947 to 1966, and Professor of Moral Philosophy at Corpus Christi College Oxford until 1983. He is the author of 12 books including *The Language of Morals* and *Freedom and Reason*. Professor Hare currently has an appointment at the University of Florida.

ROBERT D. HAY

Robert Hay is University Professor of Management at the University of Arkansas. He retired in 1990 after 41 years of teaching, research and service. He is the author of 11 books and numerous articles and cases.

MICHAEL HOOKER

Michael Hooker is President of the University of Maryland Baltimore County. From 1982 to 1986 he was President of Bennington College in Vermont. Before that Dr. Hooker was Dean of Graduate and Undergraduate Studies at John Hopkins, where he also taught philosophy. Prior to going to Hopkins, he was Assistant Professor of Philosophy at Harvard. Dr. Hooker received his B.A., with highest honors, from the University of North Carolina at Chapel Hill. His M.A. and Ph.D. are from the Five College Consortium (University of Massachusetts, Amherst, Smith, Mount Holyoke, and Hampshire College).

IMMANUEL KANT

Immanuel Kant was born in 1724 in East Prussia where he took his master's degree at Konigsberg in 1755 and began teaching at the University as a *Privatdozent*, teaching a wide variety of subjects including mathematics, physics, and geography in addition to philosophy. Kant's publications during this period, primarily concerning the natural sciences, won him considerable acclaim in Germany, but he is best known today for his three critiques—the *Critique of Pure Reason*, the *Critique of Practical Reason*, and the *Critique of Judgement*—written and published after he obtained his professorship. Kant died in 1804.

ARTHUR L. KELLY

Arthur Kelly is a graduate of Yale University with a M.B.A. from the University of Chicago. He was formerly a management consultant with A. T. Kearney, Inc., and later served as president and chief executive officer of LaSalle Steel Company. Currently Mr. Kelly is president of KEL Industries, a Chicago holding and investment company, and serves on a number of boards of directors.

JOHN LADD

John Ladd is Professor of Philosophy at Brown University, having received an A.B., A.M., and Ph.D. from Harvard University, and an M.A. from the University of Virginia. He is a member of numerous societies and associations, among them the American Philosophical Association and the New York Academy of Sciences. He authored *The Structure of a Moral Code* and *Ethical Issues Relating to Life and Death*.

STEFANIE ANN LENWAY

Stephanie Lenway is Associate Professor in the Department of Strategic Management at the Carlson School of Management, University of Minnesota. Professor Lenway received her Ph.D. from the University of California at Berkeley in Business and Public Policy in 1982. Her past research has concentrated on the political role of business in U.S. international trade policy and the impact of trade protection on corporate competitive strategy. She has also written a book on business involvement in the Tokyo Round negotiations of the General Agreement on Tariffs and Trade.

JOHN LOCKE

John Locke was born in 1632, and educated in classics, near-eastern languages, scholastic philosophy, and later in medicine. Active and influential in political affairs of his time, Locke was forced to flee England and his position at Oxford after his close friend, the Earl of Shaftesbury, was tried for treason in 1681. After events turned to his advantage he returned to England from exile in Holland and subsequently published his two most famous works, the *Essay Concerning Human Understanding* and *Two Treaties of Government*. Following years of bad health, England's famous empiricist and political philosopher died in 1704.

PETER MADSEN

Peter Madsen is Executive Director of the Center for the Advancement of Applied Ethics, Carnegie Mellon University, and Adjunct Associate Professor in Public Policy and Ethics at CMU's Heinz School. He has conducted ethics training for such organizations as Alcoa, Westinghouse, PPG Industries, and Phillips Petroleum. He is co-editor of *The Essentials of Business Ethics* and *The Essentials of Government Ethics* and is the author of various articles on ethics.

KARL MARX

Karl Marx, the famous German political philosopher and revolutionary socialist, was born in 1818. His radical Hegelianism and militant atheism precluded an academic career in Prussia, and he subsequently lived the life of an exile in Paris and London. Financially supported by Friedrich Engels, he devoted himself to research and the development of his theory of socialism, and to agitation for social reforms. The *Communist*

Manifesto was written in collaboration with Engels in 1847. His greatest work, *Das Kapital*, remained unfinished at the time of his death in 1883 and was carried to completion by Engels from posthumous papers.

BOWEN McCOY

Bowen McCoy was a managing director of Morgan Stanley and President of Morgan Stanley Realty Inc. He is also an elder of the United Presbyterian Church.

THOMAS F. McMAHON, C.S.V.

Professor of Socio-Legal Studies at Loyola University Chicago and Director of the Loyola Center for Values in Business, McMahon received his S.T.D. from the University of St. Thomas Aquinas "Angelicum," and an M.B.A. from George Washington University. Author of over fifty articles on business ethics, he is currently researching the role of religion in business. He was ordained in 1954 as a member of the Viatorians.

RALPH NADER

Lawyer and famous consumer advocate, Ralph Nader received an A.B. from Princeton and an LL.B. from Harvard. He received national attention in 1965 when he published *Unsafe at Any Speed*, critical of General Motors, and was subsequently investigated by General Motors, who, according to a congressional decision, violated his rights of privacy. He is the author of *Taming the Giant Corporation*, *The Menace of Atomic Energy*, *The Big Boys: Power and Position in American Business*, and *Winning the Insurance Game*, among many other publications.

ROBERT NOZICK

Arthur Kingsley Professor of Philosophy at Harvard University, Robert Nozick is the author of *Anarchy, State, and Utopia* (National Book Award 1975), *Philosophical Explanations* (Ralph Waldo Emerson Award of Phi Beta Kappa, 1982), and most recently, *The Examined Life*.

MARK PASTIN

Mark Pastin, Professor of Management and Director for the Center for Ethics at Arizona State University, received his B.A. from the University of Pittsburgh and his A.M. and Ph.D. from Harvard University. He has been a National Endowment for the Humanities Research Fellow and visiting Professor of Philosophy at the University of Michigan, Ann Arbor, and at the University of Maryland. He has published widely in journals on ethics and epistemology.

F. CLARK POWER

F. Clark Power is Association Professor in the Program of Liberal Studies at the University of Notre Dame and former President of the Association for Moral Education. He did his doctoral studies in human development at Harvard's Graduate School of Education. His research focuses on moral development and education. He is the principal author of *Lawrence Kohlberg's Approach to Moral Education* and co-author of *The Measurement of Moral Judgement* and *The Challenge of Pluralism: Education, Politics, and Values.*

PAUL PRESTON

Paul Preston is Associate Professor of Management at the University of Texas at San Antonio. Professor Preston's Ph.D. in Organizational Development is from the University of Colorado and he has had over twenty years experience working in and with health care managers and organizations. Professor Preston has written over 200 articles, cases, films, and videocassettes on a wide range of topics, and is the author of fourteen books on communication, management, and administration including *Management for Supervisors* (Prentice-Hall, 1983) and more recently, *Leadership Strategies for Health Care Managers.*

JOHN RAWLS

John Rawls is Professor of Philosophy at Harvard University and is among the leading moral and political theorists of this century. His book *A Theory of Justice* is a contemporary classic; it has prompted wide-ranging comment and discussion, not only by philosophers but by economists, sociologists, political and legal theorists, and others. He is the author of numerous articles as well.

TOM REGAN

Tom Regan received his undergraduate education at Thiel College and was awarded the M.A. and Ph.D. degrees by the University of Virginia. Since 1967 he has taught philosophy at North Carolina State University, where he has twice been elected Outstanding Teacher and, in 1977, was named Alumni Distinguished Professor. He was Distinguished Visiting Scholar at the University of Calgary, and has served as Visiting Distinguished Professor of Philosophy at Brooklyn College. His books include *The Case for Animal Rights* (1983), *Bloomsbury's Prophet: G. E. Moore and the Development of His Moral Philosophy* (1986), and *The Thee Generation: Reflections on the Coming Revolution* (1991).

DIANA C. ROBERTSON

Diana C. Robertson is Senior Fellow in Business Ethics in the Legal Studies Department of the Wharton School, University of Pennsylvania. Robertson has been Visiting Lecturer at the London Business School, and she has received the University of Pennsylvania Provost's Award for Distinguished Teaching. Dr. Robertson received a B.A. degree from Northwestern University and an M.A. and Ph.D. in sociology from U.C.L.A. In addition, she studied sociology of organizations at Harvard University.

MARK SAGOFF

Mark Sagoff, Director of the Institute for Philosophy and Public Policy at the University of Maryland, holds an A.B. from Harvard and a Ph.D. in philosophy from the University of Rochester. He has taught at Princeton, the University of Pennsylvania, the University of Wisconsin (Madison), and Cornell. Dr. Sagoff has published widely in journals of philosophy, law, and public policy. His book, *The Economy of the Earth: Philosophy, Law and the Environment*, was published by Cambridge University Press in 1988.

FELICE N. SCHWARTZ

Felice Schwartz is president and founder of Catalyst, the national not-for-profit organization that works with business to effect change for women. Schwartz consults with corporate leaders about women and workplace issues. She is the author of the McKinsey-Award-winning *Harvard Business Review* article which sparked the heated "Mommy Track" debate. Extensively quoted in numerous publications, she has appeared on the *Today Show, Nightline* and the *MacNeil/Lehrer Newshour*. Schwartz serves on the board of directors of the Business Council of New York State and the Advisory Board of the National Women's Political Caucus.

JOEL SELIGMAN

Joel Seligman is Professor in the University of Michigan Law School.

IRVING S. SHAPIRO

Irving Shapiro is retired chairman of the finance committee and former chairman of the board with E.I. du Pont Nemours & Co.

ADAM SMITH

Adam Smith, first known as a moral philosopher, is now famous as a political economist. He was born in 1723 in Scotland and was later elected Professor of Logic at the University of Glasgow. He published *Theory of Moral Sentiments* in 1759 to great acclaim. He resigned his professorship at Glasgow and after ten years of work published *The Wealth of Nations*, for which his fame has endured. In 1778 he was appointed a commissioner of customs for Scotland. He died in 1790.

TERRY J. SULLIVAN

Terry Sullivan is a former university administrator with over eighteen years of experience. He is currently a free-lance writer and consultant to a number of colleges, universities and associations. His work, including essays on popular culture, have appeared in *Planning for Higher Education*, the *Chicago Tribune, GO Magazine, Washington Magazine* and elsewhere. He is regularly heard on WBEZ-FM, National Public Radio's Chicago affiliate.

KERMIT VANDIVIER

Kermit Vandivier was formerly a data analyst and technical writer at the B. F. Goodrich plant in Troy, Ohio, where he blew the whistle in 1967. Since 1968 he has been a journalist at the *Troy Daily News*. He has served in several capacities at the newspaper, including a tour of duty as a correspondent in Vietnam in 1970, as Sunday Editor and as Cable News Director. He is currently a columnist-staff writer and is writing a book, *Twentieth Century Troy*, scheduled for publication in 1992.

MANUEL G. VELASQUEZ

Manuel Velasquez is Charles J. Dirksen Professor of Business Ethics at Santa Clara University. He received his B.A. from Gonzaga University and his M.A. and Ph.D. from the University of California at Berkeley. He is a member of the American Philosophical Association and the Academy of Management. He is the author of *Business Ethics*, co-editor with Cynthia Rostankowski of *Ethical Theory*, and author of *Philosophy: A Text With Readings*.

RICHARD WASSERSTROM

Richard Wasserstrom is Presidential Professor in Moral Philosophy at the University of California, Santa Cruz. He received a Ph.D. in philosophy from the University of Michigan, an LL.B. from Stanford University, and an LL.D. from Amherst College. He is the author of *Philosophy and Social Issues: Five Studies*, and *The Judicial Decision*, the editor of *Today's Moral Problems*, and the author of numerous articles in ethics and social and legal philosophy.

CARL PIERCE WELLMAN

Professor Wellman is the Hortense and Tobias Lewin Distinguished Professor in the Humanities at Washington University where he has taught since 1966. He is the author of six books and has written widely on ethics and theories of rights. He has served on the editorial board of *Ethics* and as a founder and an officer of both the American and International Societies of Law and Social Philosophy.

PATRICIA H. WERHANE

Patricia Werhane is the Henry J. Wirtenberger Professor of Business Ethics at Loyola University Chicago. She is the editor or author of several books and articles on business ethics, including *Adam Smith and His Legacy for Modern Capitalism*; *Persons, Rights, and Corporations*; and *Profit and Responsibility*. She serves on the editorial board of a number of journals and is the Editor-in-chief of *Business Ethics Quarterly*.

THOMAS W. ZIMMER

Thomas W. Zimmer is presently Professor of Management at Clemson University where he teaches and studies strategic management and organizational theory. In addition, he is Associate Director of Clemson University's Emerging Technology Development and Marketing Center. Dr. Zimmer is the author of six books and over sixty-five articles in such prestigious journals as: *The Academy of Management Journal, Research Management, Human Resources Management, Advanced Management Journal, Management Review, Nation's Business, IEEE Transactions in Engineering Management, Journal of Operations Management, Journal of Business Ethics, Personnel Administrator,* and the *Management of Personnel Quarterly.* Dr. Zimmer was formerly employed by the McDonnell Douglas Corporation.

Biographical information for Robert C. Kennedy, David L. Kirp, Laura Nadel, and Hesh Wiener was unavailable at the time of publication.